COMPETITIVE ANAGEMENT

ONE WE

THE IRWIN/MCGRAW-HILL SERIES

COMPETITIVE MANUFACTURING MANAGEMENT

Continuous Improvement
Lean Production
Customer-Focused Quality

John M. Nicholas
Loyola University Chicago

**Irwin
McGraw-Hill**

Boston   Burr Ridge, IL   Dubuque, IA   Madison, WI   New York   San Francisco   St. Louis
Bangkok   Bogotá   Caracas   Lisbon   London   Madrid
Mexico City   Milan   New Delhi   Seoul   Singapore   Sydney   Taipei   Toronto

McGraw-Hill

A Division of *The McGraw-Hill Companies*

COMPETITIVE MANUFACTURING MANAGEMENT
International Editions 1998

8 9 10 MPM FC 20 9 8 7

Library of Congress Cataloging-in-Publication Data

Nicholas, John M. (date)
    Competitive manufacturing management: continuous improvement,
lean production, customer-focused quality / John M. Nicholas.
        p.   cm.
    ISBN 0-256-21727-0
    1. Production management.   2. Costs, Industrial.   3. Quality
control.   I. Title.
    TS155.N43   1998
    658.5–dc21   97-27344

http://www.mhhe.com

When ordering this title, use ISBN 0-07-115820-0

Printed in Singapore

To Frank and Emily,
Elmer and Dolores

PREFACE

Around 1989, after having talked to some former students who had become practitioners and consultants in manufacturing and having read Richard Schonberger's *World-Class Manufacturing: The Lessons of Simplicity Applied* (The Free Press, 1986), Robert Hall's *Zero Inventories* (Dow Jones-Irwin, 1983), and Kiyoshi Suzaki's *The New Manufacturing Challenge* (The Free Press, 1987), I decided to offer a course for operations management majors focused exclusively on just-in-time (JIT) and total quality management (TQM). While developing the curriculum, I encountered what seemed to be three difficulties: JIT and TQM are two very broad topics, they are highly interrelated, and there was no textbook.

Some people equate JIT and TQM with production and quality control techniques. In fact each is a complete management philosophy that encompasses not only techniques but also convictions about the role of workers and how to treat employees and suppliers. The volume of journal literature about JIT and TQM was enormous.

Having grasped the expanse of the subject areas, I decided to focus only on JIT. I soon learned, however, that JIT and TQM are highly related and that (as explained in Chapter 4) you cannot completely understand JIT without also somewhat understanding TQM. To cover JIT, I would also have to cover aspects of TQM.

I then set out to find a textbook. At the time there were a few textbooks on TQM and some trade books on JIT, but the TQM books were not about JIT, and the JIT books were written for practicing managers in a style and at a level inappropriate for college students. Hence, to the chagrin of my class, the required material for the course came to consist of a TQM textbook, a JIT trade book, and a packet of journal articles. Trade books do not include homework questions and problems, so I had to prepare them on my own. Over the years I supplemented more and more of this material with my own writings. About the time that these writings covered half the topics in the course, I decided to write a book and put everything in one place.

At times it did seem as if, indeed, I was writing about *everything,* since JIT and TQM touch on virtually every aspect of management. To contain the size of the book and make sure I could finish it, I had to restrict the coverage of many topics. (After all, I kept reminding myself, this is an *introductory* book on JIT and TQM, albeit an in-depth one.) There is much to know about these subjects, and I have included references in the endnotes for interested readers. You can also learn about manufacturing JIT and TQM from *Production and Inventory Management* and *Target,* the journals of the American Production and Inventory Control Society and the Association for Manufacturing Excellence, respectively.

Not long ago a friend, Avi Soni, asked me whether JIT is dead. This was based on his observation that the appearance of the term JIT in articles and seminars is declining. In the ensuing conversation we agreed that the reason for the decline is probably because concepts associated with JIT have been absorbed into mainstream production management and into what is now termed manufacturing excellence or competitive manufacturing. Management concepts seem to come and go with the seasons, but the important ones remain active, even though the terminology changes. Although Richard Schonberger, still among the most prolific and best writers in the field, seldom uses the term in his recent book *World-Class Manufacturing: The Next Decade* (The Free Press, 1996), familiar JIT concepts run throughout the book. JIT is alive and well. Avi Soni could question the status of JIT because the company where he is employed as a manager began the transition to JIT/TQM more than a decade ago and now has a JIT/TQM modus operandi. Folks at his plant do not think of what they are doing as innovative or different and probably not as JIT/TQM, per se.

In and around my city, Chicago, there are enough factories that one has ample opportunity to see both the best and the worst in manufacturing management. I have been excited and encouraged in visiting plants that have embraced continuous improvement, lean production, and customer-focused quality. Managers and workers in these plants display high enthu-

siasm in talking about what they are doing. Students of mine often express the same level of enthusiasm. Yes, they discover, JIT/TQM is cool—in a way. Some students (sometimes the same ones) also express frustration because of problems in their workplace and management's ignorance about JIT/TQM or unwillingness to change. I can relate to that, having visited plants that seem like throwbacks to 50 years ago and talked to workers who dislike their jobs and managers who are out of touch with the workforce and customers.

The management concepts and principles described in this book will guide manufacturing practice for the next few decades, at least. They have become very much a part of today's business, mostly because they work. Beyond that, I personally find some of the principles satisfying because of the somewhat high level of responsibility and dignity they attach to the jobs of workers on the shop floor. I was raised in a working-class family and always felt that my parents' abilities far exceeded what they could exercise in the workplace. My dad was one of the smartest and all-around most capable men I have ever known and I always thought he could build or fix anything requiring mechanical, electrical, or carpentry skill. When I think about teams of workers in JIT/TQM organizations, I envision people like my parents, for certainly they are representative of many millions of workers. That is not to say that JIT/TQM organizations are a kind of utopia, but that, on balance, workers in JIT/TQM factories have more opportunity to find meaning in their jobs and to get more earned respect from management than workers in other factories.

Einstein said, "I know why there are so many people who love chopping wood. In this activity one immediately sees the results." JIT and TQM practices are that way too. Both represent pragmatic approaches to chopping away at waste and problems in organizations. In many factories you can start to see results on the shop floor not too long after putting aspects of JIT and TQM into practice (improvements on the balance sheet happen too, but they take a little longer).

AUDIENCE AND USE OF THIS BOOK

Competitive Manufacturing Management was written for three audiences:

1. Bachelor of business and MBA students *majoring* in production and operations management.
2. Industrial and manufacturing engineering students.
3. Practicing manufacturing managers and engineers seeking an understanding of JIT/TQM.

It is intended for a second-level course in production and operations management. Students who have already taken an introductory course should be readily able to understand the material.

It will be difficult to cover all of this book in depth in a typical one-term college course, and the instructor must decide on which topics to focus. The book is divided into an introductory chapter and five main parts. Chapter 1 and Part I provide foundation concepts for everything that follows. Part II covers lean production and core concepts of JIT manufacturing. I believe that everything in this part should be covered in some depth. Part III is about design quality and manufacturing quality control. In schools that offer courses in TQM and SPC, portions of this part may be scanned or deleted. Chapters 12 and 15, however, should be read since they describe concepts used in later chapters. Part IV covers integrated planning and control in pull production—another key aspect of JIT. Depending on students' prior exposure to planning and control, however, portions of this part may also be scanned or deleted. Part V covers topics important to the success of JIT/TQM but not usually included in a manufacturing book. At minimum, Chapter 19 should be read in full. My suggestion is to not completely skip any chapter. Most of the topics in this book are interrelated: to gain a full understanding of JIT/TQM, it is necessary to know about all of them.

John M. Nicholas

ACKNOWLEDGMENTS

In writing *Competitive Manufacturing Management* I have been fortunate to have had the assistance of many bright and capable people. Two are my friends and colleagues at Loyola University Chicago, Drs. James Zydiak and Enrique Venta who read many parts of this book and provided useful suggestions. Others who helped the most were my research assistants during the last 3 years, Sosamma Mammen, Marco Menaguale, Marlene Abeysinghe, and Omar Saner. In case you find the going difficult with some of what you will read, you can only imagine what it was like for them many drafts earlier. On the other hand, if perchance the material reads with exceptional clarity, it is no doubt partly due to their exceptional efforts. I also wish to credit Leslie Bailyn and Diane Petrozzo for their editing and gopher support, and Dr. Larry Metzger for reviewing and critiquing Chapter 20.

Thanks also to Mr. Avi Soni and Mr. Al Brouilette, two enthusiastic managers on the front lines and at the leading edge of manufacturing. I learned a great deal about JIT/TQM from frequent visits to their plants and discussions with them and their co-workers.

I also want to acknowledge the reviewers of this book whose comments and suggestions greatly improved the end product: Mary Jo Maffei, formerly University of Cincinnati; Behnam Malakooti, Case Western Reserve University; Unny Menon, California Polytechnic State University; George Schneller, Baruch College—CUNY; Kenneth Ramsing, University of Oregon; Joe Biggs, California Polytechnic State University; Karen Donohue, University of Pennsylvania; Vaidyanathan Jayaraman, University of Southern Mississippi; Pitu Mirchandani, University of Arizona; Byron Finch, Miami University; and George Petrakis, University of Missouri.

Thanks also to the folks at Irwin/McGraw-Hill, especially to Dick Hercher for encouraging me from the beginning, Carol Rose for reviewing and improving the entire manuscript, and Maggie Rathke for attending to myriad details and bringing them all together between two covers.

xi

Finally there is my wife Sharry, who has my deepest appreciation for patiently assuming responsibility for managing virtually every aspect of our home life so I could work undistracted.

The assistance of so many people made writing this book not only doable but enjoyable. Most of them share with me an excitement about modern methods of manufacturing management. My one wish is that you, after having read this book, come away with that same sense of excitement.

My apologies in advance for any typos and mistakes. I had final say over everything, so I accept responsibility for these as well as for any other source of anguish this book might cause. For your sake I hope there aren't too many, but I do appreciate hearing from you about them.

John M. Nicholas

BRIEF CONTENTS

CONTENTS

COMPETITIVE MANUFACTURING MANAGEMENT

1 RACE WITHOUT A FINISH LINE

In 1982 David Kearns became CEO of Xerox Corporation.[1] At the time, Xerox was one of America's premier companies, a household name, the company that invented the paper copier, and an employer of 100,000 people. But Kearns knew that if something radical wasn't done, Xerox would probably be out of business before the end of the decade. He had learned that the Japanese were selling products for what it was costing Xerox to make them and that Japanese companies had targeted Xerox's market share for takeover. Already Xerox's market share was less than 15%, down precipitously from more than 90% a decade earlier. But the Japanese alone were not the cause. There was no quality control to speak of at Xerox. Overhead and inventory costs were excessive, and the company was overloaded with managers. Further, Xerox had lost touch with its customers. In the beginning Xerox had had few competitors but now it had many, and customers were flocking to them.

Kearns and a core group of unconventional corporate thinkers mapped out a strategy and successfully remade the company. By the late 1980s Xerox had doubled its production output, cut its costs by nearly 50%, reduced its product development cycle time by nearly a year, and improved the performance of its copiers by 45% during the first 30 days after installation. By 1990 Xerox had become the producer of the highest quality office products in the world and had gained back market share from the Japanese. Xerox accomplished this not with government subsidies, trade barriers, or import quotas but rather by adopting a new management approach that included the tenets of total quality management and just-in-time production.

Successful recovery is, of course, not the fate of every company that has faced tough competition from overseas. It took Xerox 7 years to reinvent itself, but many companies cannot afford such time. Global competition makes everyone vulnerable. The major players are now in the United States, Japan, and Europe, but the number of qualifiers there and elsewhere is increasing every day. Companies in Pacific rim countries like China, Korea, Taiwan, and Indonesia have also become formidable global players, as have many companies throughout Europe. Considered the sick man of industry since the end of World War II, European industry is mobilizing. Aeronautics is a case in point. Up until the late 1960s, the US was the world leader in the commercial aircraft business, holding nearly 100% of the free-world share of large transports. However, in 1969 a consortium of companies from France, Germany, the UK, and Spain began to pursue that market, and the US share has since steadily declined. The European share is now over 30% and is growing. This is not an insignificant fact given that the aeronautics industry is the single biggest manufacturing contributor to the US balance of trade.

As the number of skilled contenders in a given market increases, so increases the intensity of competition. Initially, in new and growing markets many players can survive by absorbing a portion of the growth in market size. In the global economy the market size is large, but so is the number of players. Eventually, as market size levels out or as players differentiate themselves by ability to compete, the more skilled players drive out the less skilled players.

COMPETITIVE ADVANTAGE: BETTER, CHEAPER, FASTER, MORE AGILE

In no small part what differentiates competitiveness in industrial companies is the way that each designs and builds its products. Paying attention to customers and knowing what they want is a fundamental and important beginning. However, given that several competing companies pay attention to what customers want, the key to competitiveness then becomes production capability. What differentiates winners from losers is that winners are better able to consistently provide products and services that are competitive with regard to quality (better), price (cheaper), time (faster), and agility (more agile).

To this end, companies use different manufacturing strategies and action programs. Following is a comparison of the programs US companies and Japanese companies use to pursue the same goals.[2]

Making Things Better.   US manufacturers rely on CAD/CAM to enhance product design and manufacturability. In contrast, Japanese firms rely on group technology, good condition and proper placement of equipment, smaller manufacturing units, and quality circles. Manufacturers in both countries also rely on statistical control of processes, zero-defects programs, and vendor quality programs.

Making Things Cheaper.   US manufacturers traditionally rely on job enlargement programs and automation and robotics to reduce direct labor content. In contrast, Japanese firms focus on improving products and processes by using value analysis, standardizing products, and reducing lead and cycle times.

Making Things Faster.   US companies rely on robotics and flexible manufacturing systems (FMS), relocation of facilities, and improved labor–management relations to maintain or reduce delivery times. Japanese companies emphasize the continuous reduction of lead and setup times, equipment maintenance, supervisory training, and broadening of workers' jobs.

Being More Agile.   The ability to introduce new products and designs and to respond quickly to changing customer demands is an area of strong interest to the Japanese, and the area in which they maintain the largest competitive lead over US and European firms.[3] While US manufacturers emphasize technology, process flow improvement, quality management, and cross-functional communication improvements, the Japanese believe that agility is an integral part of quality and delivery capability. As such, it is a by-product of action programs to improve these areas. Thus, those programs utilized by the Japanese to produce things better and faster are also aimed at achieving manufacturing agility.

These nations also utilize different approaches for product development. In the US product ideas tend to move sequentially through functional areas (from marketing to engineering to production, and so on), whereas in Japan they are honed in product development *teams*. The latter allows integration of all ideas in the early design stages, takes less time, and results in a better product at lower cost.

JUST-IN-TIME AND TOTAL QUALITY MANAGEMENT

In the past a major difference between competitive strategies in the US and Japan was that the former sought improvement at discrete times through capital intensive means such as automation and new technology, whereas the latter sought improvement through small but continuous refinements in processes and procedures and investment in human capital. **Just-in-time (JIT)** and **total quality management (TQM)**[4] are two management philosophies that, though not disputing the need for high technology or capital-intensive efforts, emphasize continuous attention to fundamentals and to the crucial role of the workers in improvement efforts. Briefly;

· JIT is management that focuses the organization on continuously identifying and removing sources of waste so that processes are continuously improved. JIT is also called *lean production*.

· TQM is management that focuses the organization on knowing the needs and wants of customers and on being capable of fulfilling those needs and wants.

The two philosophies are somewhat mutually dependent, and in certain respects, they are the same. Schonberger says:

JIT itself is a quality improvement tool, mainly because it cuts time delays between process stages so that the trail of causal evidence [to quality problems] does not get cluttered and cold . . . [But] JIT is only one quality aid. Other TQC [total quality control] tools are needed as well, or the rate of quality improvement will not be fast enough. To oversimplify, an end result of JIT without TQC might be fast response to a dwindling number of customers. [However, focusing on TQM without JIT] is fraught with risk [because] companies that are not active in JIT tend to sink capital into plant and equipment by the old wrong rules.[5]

JIT, TQM, AND THE PRODUCTION PIPELINE

Think of a company as a pipeline with raw materials entering at one end and products emerging at the other.[6] (The pipe can be extended conceptually with customer needs or orders going in at one end and products arriving to customers at the other.) The goal is to minimize throughput time, that is, to move materials (or ideas, orders, whatever) through the pipeline as quickly as possible. Shorter throughput time is better because, assuming price and quality remain constant, the company can respond more quickly to changes in customer needs. The customer gets the product sooner, and the company gets the payment sooner.

But the pipeline is seldom uniform or without obstacles; it varies in size and has obstructions throughout. What flows out of the pipeline is limited by the narrowest part of the pipe and the biggest obstruction. Portions of the pipeline that are narrow or obstructed are in reality equivalent to stages of the production process that take more time or where stoppages/slowdowns occur. Obstructions to smooth flow and rapid throughput are commonplace problems, particularly in plants that produce a variety of products with different, fluctuating demands.

To speed up the flow of material through the pipeline, the obstructions must be identified and then eliminated. As each obstruction is eliminated, the flow speeds up, but only by as much as allowed by obstructions *elsewhere* in the pipeline. Identifying the location of obstructions, understanding them, and finding ways to eliminate them are the purposes of JIT and TQM.

The pipeline analogy may give the impression that barriers to production, once identified, can be removed once and for all. In reality that is impossible. First, there is often a large number of phases, stages, or steps, and it is difficult to identify the precise location of all obstructions. Also, the sources of obstruction keep changing— machines deteriorate, workers are replaced, and so on. As some obstructions are removed, new ones appear. Further, the pipeline *itself* and the things that flow *through* it are always changing. Customers' orders change, so the flow rate must be adjusted to accommodate the right kind and quantity of materials. In the analogy, the pipeline diameter might have to be widened. But a pipe that is wider than necessary is wasteful, and so is a flow rate that exceeds demand.

Some managers think that the way to increase output is to increase the *input* flow. This is not true! Once the pipe is full, any increased input simply backs up and overflows (in a manufacturing process, the equivalent is inventory).

The best input flow rate is one that matches the desired output flow rate, and the best pipe diameter is one that allows flow through the pipe to match demand. The products are changing too, so the process must be adapted (the pipeline itself must be modified or replaced) and that introduces a whole new set of obstructions. In short, work on the pipeline is continuous.

JIT and TQM are ways of continuously tinkering so that the pipeline and the material coming out of it are the best possible. JIT continuously seeks ways to make the pipeline more easily adaptable to whatever materials or flow rates are desired and to match the flow of materials as closely as possible to the customer demand. TQM continuously seeks to make the material coming out of the pipeline ever more acceptable to the customer.

THE JIT/TQM DIFFERENCE IN ORGANIZATIONS

Most organizations seek to identify and eliminate obstructions in the pipeline, but two features distinguish JIT/TQM organizations.

First, JIT and TQM greatly increase the number of people who are involved in identifying and eliminating obstructions. Whereas most companies assign professional staff people to diagnose and solve problems, in JIT/TQM organizations, *everyone* does it. People at all levels are trained in analysis and problem-solving techniques and are given some level of responsibility to implement improvements. The general level of authority of workers to make and carry out decisions is much higher in JIT/TQM organizations than elsewhere. Likewise, while all organizations collect data to see what is happening, seldom do they involve workers in collecting the data as is the case in JIT organizations. The major emphasis of JIT/TQM is not simply to measure what is happening, but to measure, diagnose, and *improve* it.

A second difference is in the process employed to identify and prioritize problems and sources of waste. In JIT, the primary process is reduction of inventory. Returning to the pipeline analogy, inventory is like cholesterol buildup inside the pipe: it narrows the pipe's inside diameter and reduces the rate of flow. When the rate of flow is slow enough, other obstructions in the pipeline become comparatively insignificant and are hidden from view. JIT organizations reduce the size of inventory to reveal the obstructions and prioritize them. As inventory is reduced, the flow speeds up, but only by as much as other obstructions in the pipeline allow. With less inventory, the obstructions become visible, which means they can be identified and removed. With each small reduction in inventory, additional obstructions appear, and these become the new priority for removal.

It is important to note, however, that inventory reduction per se is *not* the objective of JIT. Inventory reduction by itself yields a one-time benefit of freed-up capital. Unless problems in the production system, problems previously hidden or ameliorated by the inventory, are resolved, the process will not be improved and might be worsened. This is why companies that try to reduce inventory as a solution rather than as a *tool* to identify, prioritize, and make process improvements usually fail.

The following two sections are abridged histories of the evolution of philosophies and methods in manufacturing and quality. The histories are intended to provide background about the two principal topics of this book, JIT and TQM, and they focus primarily on industries and events that contributed most to modern JIT, TQM, and related manufacturing topics. Words or terms **highlighted** throughout these sections are topics that will be discussed later in the book.

EVOLUTION OF MANUFACTURING

THE MACHINE THAT CHANGED THE WORLD[7]

Probably one of the most informative and interesting introductions to JIT published in the US is *The Machine that Changed the World*. The machine in the title is the automobile. Although the book is about the auto industry, it is equally about production methods and world competition. This section draws on the findings and conclusions of that book.

How and why we arrived at today's quest for better, cheaper, faster, more agile production is in many ways a result of what happened in the auto industry. The automobile is truly the machine that changed the world because twice in this century the auto industry has changed the way all products are made. The first change came after WWI when Henry Ford and Alfred Sloan advanced manufacturing from *craft production* to *mass production*. Whereas for centuries Europe had led the world with the former, America swiftly became the dominant global economy with the latter. The second change came after WWII when Eiji Toyoda and Taiichi Ohno at Toyota Motor Company pioneered JIT. The economic rise of Toyota, as well as other companies and industries in Japan and elsewhere that adopted JIT, was a consequence. A list of notable events in the history of manufacturing is given in Table 1.1.

CRAFTSMANSHIP YIELDS TO INDUSTRIALIZATION

Prior to the beginning of the Industrial Revolution, usually associated with James Watt's development of the steam engine in 1769, the emphasis in production was on skilled craftsmanship. Craft guilds promoted workmanship and manual skills using

TABLE 1.1   Some Notable Events in a Brief History of Manufacturing

Era	Concepts/Events	Dates	Key Figures
Craft production	Craft guilds; manual skills and workmanship	prior to 1900s	
Industrial revolution	Steam engine	1769	James Watt
	Division of labor	1776	Adam Smith
	Interchangeable parts	1780	Eli Whitney
Mass production and scientific management	Principles of scientific management	1911	Frederick Taylor
	Time and motion studies	1911	Frank and Lillian Gilbreth
	Work scheduling; Work incentives	1912	Henry Gantt
	Moving assembly line	1913	Henry Ford
	Functional, divisional organization	1920	Alfred Sloan
	Complete vertical integration	1930s	Henry Ford
	Toyota begins making cars	1935	
Lean production systems	Principles of JIT and lean production	1950s	Taiichi Ohno, Eiji Toyoda
Global competition and flexible manufacturing	FMS	1965	Molin Ltd. (UK)
	CAD/CAM	1965–1970s	
	Material requirements planning	1975	Joseph Orlicky
Mass customization	CIM, EDS	1980s–1990s	

hand tools. Apprentices learned the trade while performing preliminary tasks for a master craftsman, who performed the tasks demanding high-level skill. Almost everything was produced by craftsmen and their apprentices. Not until 1776 when Adam Smith wrote *The Wealth of Nations* did the notion become prominent that dividing tasks among more than one specialist could increase productivity in large-volume production.

Around 1780, Eli Whitney in the US and Nicolas LeBlance in France independently developed the concept of the interchangeable part, which is to make parts in batches such that any one part would meet design tolerances and fit into an assembled product. With the implementation of the interchangeable part in the production of rifles, clocks, wagons, and other products, the slow transformation began that would replace skilled craftsmanship and hand labor with mechanization and a division of labor.

Around the turn of the century Frederick Taylor introduced the idea of improving operations by studying and simplifying them. Always looking for the **best way** to do something, he developed techniques to systemize and improve economies of work motion. He also established a complete management philosophy that included time analysis, wage incentives, infrastructure to separate the responsibilities of management (planning) and workers (doing), an accounting system, and principles for running business on a scientific basis. Taylor inspired legions of contemporaries, including Frank and Lillian Gilbreth, Henry Gantt, and Henri Fayol. The Gilbreths extended Taylor's time study to detailed analysis of motion, and Gantt advocated efficiency and argued for bonuses to ensure that workers completed jobs on time. Their ideas about work measurement, analysis, and management all contributed to a theory of *scientific management*.

One consequence of this theory was to take skills and most thinking from the shop floor (de-skill jobs) and give them to legions of managers and specialists. As this happened, of course, work on the shop floor began to lose its appeal. The advocates of de-skilling factory work by dividing it into narrow, repetitive tasks and taking all control away from workers failed to see the long-term consequences of these practices on worker motivation and organizational flexibility.

It is significant to note that the Japanese never felt comfortable with Taylor's system of specialization and its rigid rules separating responsibilities among workers and between workers and managers. In Japan, workers in factories continued to develop broad-based skills that would allow them to rotate freely among a variety of tasks. This continuing emphasis on skill development, as well as on delegation of authority and the expectation that workers would both plan and do work tasks, resulted in a level of worker commitment virtually unseen in Western manufacturing.[8] The consequence of this would not be recognized until half a century later.

CRAFT PRODUCTION OF AUTOMOBILES

Cars were a luxury that only the rich could afford. They were initially hand-built by skilled craftsmen. Among auto-assembly workers who were the most knowledgeable in design principles, materials, and machine operation, many went on to form their own machine shops and become contractors to the auto-assembly companies.

Few cars were actually identical since every shop that made parts used its own gauging system. Lack of product uniformity did not matter much, however, since most cars were built for individual buyers. Minor design features, location of controls, and some materials were changed to meet buyer preferences.

By the turn of the century, hundreds of companies in Western Europe and North America were producing autos. Fifty companies a year were entering the business, though most lasted less than a year. Each made about 1000 or fewer cars a year and rarely were more than 50 cars made from a single design. Because the small shops that supplied parts lacked resources, there was very little product or process innovation. As a result, cars were poor in terms of consistency, reliability, and driveability.

FORD'S MASS PRODUCTION SYSTEM

As a young machine-shop apprentice, Henry Ford envisioned producing an inexpensive auto. In 1903, at the age of 40, he started the Ford Motor Company and began producing the Model A. Each car was produced on a fixed assembly stand, and a single craftsman assembled all or a major part of it. The worker got his own parts; if a part didn't fit, he filed it until it did. Ford recognized the limitations imposed by parts being inconsistent and introduced to the auto industry Whitney's idea of standardized, interchangeable parts.[9] With interchangeable parts, *any* worker could be trained to assemble a car and all cars would be virtually the same, so anyone could drive and repair one. Thus, Ford began to insist that all parts be produced by using the same gauging system. He also had the parts delivered to the work stands so assemblers could work uninterrupted at one place all day.

By 1908 when the Model T was introduced, Ford had modified the process so that each assembler moved from car to car and did only one task on each car. Though, presumably, such task specialization would increase efficiency, the problem was that faster workers caught up with and had to wait behind slower workers. As a solution, Ford introduced in 1913 the next major innovation in production: a *moving assembly line.* He got the idea at a slaughterhouse watching carcasses on hooks move from workstation to workstation by an overhead bicycle-chain mechanism. The line, which brought the cars past stationary workers, eliminated time wasted by workers walking, and forced slower workers to keep up with the pace of the line. Whereas before it had taken 13 hours to make a car, it now took just $1\frac{1}{2}$. Ford's competition realized the productivity advantage of the combination of interchangeable parts and the moving production line—what became known as Ford's *mass production system*—and eventually that system was adopted by mass-producing industries around the world.

While perfecting the interchangeable part, Ford was also perfecting the "interchangeable worker" by obsessively applying the teachings of Frederick Taylor. Whereas the Ford worker of 1908 gathered parts and tools, repaired tools, fitted parts together, assembled an entire car, and checked everything, the Ford worker of 1915 stood at the moving line and did one simple task.

Eventually, Ford seemed to care more about his process and machines than about the workers. Workers caught slacking off or performing inadequately were quickly replaced. The atmosphere did not inspire workers to volunteer information about problems (much less offer suggestions), so problem solving was assigned to foremen, engineers, and battalions of functionally specialized workers. With time, these specialties all became narrowly subspecialized, eventually so much so that staff in one subspecialty would have difficulty communicating with staff in other subspecialties.

By 1931 Ford had brought every function necessary to car production in-house, the concept of vertical integration taken to the extreme. Not only did the company make all of its own parts, it also controled procurement and processing of basic materials such as steel, glass, and rubber. Ford did this partly because he could produce parts to closer tolerances and tighter schedules than his suppliers and partly because he distrusted his suppliers.

To make parts inexpensively, machines were needed that could produce high volume with little downtime for changeovers. Ford eliminated this downtime by using machines dedicated to one task. Because it is difficult and costly to changeover products using dedicated machines, new products were avoided. But the rigidity of this system did not matter since from 1908 through 1927 Ford produced only the Model T. Throughout this period Ford's goal was to keep increasing Model-T volume so that the cost would continuously decrease. Ford believed that mass production precedes mass consumption because high volume results in lower unit costs and allows prices to be reduced. He hoped eventually the Model T would be everyman's car. (It did, it seemed, become so. By 1926 Ford was the world's leading manufacturer, producing half of all cars. Not until the 1950s did a car outsell the Model T in numbers; that car was the Volkswagen Beetle.)

Quality control was lax. Finished cars were rarely inspected, but they were durable and could be repaired by the average user. This concept was a major selling point.

Even though Ford was able to keep reducing the Model T's production cost and price, in 1926 sales began to slip. Because so little about the car had been changed in 10 years, price had become its sole selling point.

EMERGENCE OF MODERN MASS PRODUCTION

General Motors (GM) was created when William Durant acquired several car companies. Early on this enterprise fared poorly because the companies had separate management and overlapping products. Upon becoming GM's president in 1920, Alfred Sloan instituted a new management philosophy that would complement the mass-production system introduced by Ford. He reorganized GM into five car divisions covering the market continuum, low-end to high-end, and into parts-specialty divisions.[10] He also divided management into functional areas and originated the new functions of financial management and marketing. By 1924 GM had become a serious challenger to Ford.

The production system at Ford put workers under increasing pressure, sometimes pushing them to the extremes of endurance. By 1913, when most jobs at Ford had become menial and relentless, turnover reached 380%. To stem the flow and attract better workers, in 1914 Ford doubled the daily wage to the then-phenomenal amount of $5. The pay hike worked, and most workers came to view Ford as a place of permanent employment, despite unbearable work conditions. But the workers learned they were expendable; in a market turndown, Ford would lay them off in a moment. Not only at Ford, but also at GM and other automakers, workers were considered little more than pieces to manipulate as needed. As a result, the workers organized and formed a union, the United Auto Workers (UAW). By the late 1930s, the UAW had gained enough strength to force the automakers into an agreement whereby seniority, not job competency, would determine which laborers were laid off. Seniority also dictated who got certain job assignments. Management in all major industries, not just automobiles, fought labor unions long and hard, and by the time the unions finally gained power, hate and distrust had swelled. Labor and management had become adversaries and would remain so for the decades ahead.

The system of mass production today is largely a result of the combined influence of Ford, Sloan, and organized labor. Starting in the 1930s, that system served as a means of increasing economic gains for both employers and workers in the US. By 1955 the Big Three US automakers' sales accounted for 95% of the more than 7 million autos sold in the US that year. That was their peak year. Afterward, their share began to dwindle as the share from imports steadily grew.

MASS PRODUCTION AROUND THE WORLD

Economic chaos, nationalism, WWII, and strong attachment to craft production prevented European automakers from widely adopting mass production until the 1950s. When the Europeans did adopt mass production techniques, low wage costs and innovative features gave them a burst of success in world markets. That success was dampened, however, during the 1970s, by which time wages had increased and work hours had decreased to the point where European cars were no longer price competitive. In 1973 the Oil Embargo hit; gasoline prices worldwide soared. Even though the typical US car was a gas-guzzler and the average European car was smaller and more fuel-efficient, the latter was also higher priced and posed no real competitive challenge to US automakers. Elsewhere, however, the real challenge was forming, though it was totally unperceived. It was in Japan.

TOYODA AND OHNO

The Toyoda[11] family had been in the textile business since the 1800s. It began producing cars in 1935, but they were crude and poorly made. In 1950 young Eiji Toyoda visited the Ford River Rouge plant to learn the methods of mass production. The Rouge plant seemed to him a miracle of modern manufacturing. Almost everything that went into an automobile—parts, components, and assemblies—were processed in this one monstrous plant. In one end went raw materials like iron ore and out the other end rolled cars, 7000 a day. Toyoda wanted to learn how the Americans did that. (At this time, the Toyota Motor Company over its entire history had produced fewer than 2700 cars.)

After months of studying the plant, however, Toyoda concluded that Ford's production system was unworkable in Japan. Since Japan had few auto manufacturers at the time, Toyoda wanted to make a variety of cars in just one plant. In the US, only one type of car could be produced in a plant. Because of strong Japanese company unions, he knew he could not readily hire and fire workers as was common in American firms. Also, because of the short supply of capital, he could not invest heavily in modern equipment and technology.

Returning home he called on Taiichi Ohno, his production engineer, to help him develop a workable system. Ohno was no stranger to the ways of mass production, but he had no allegiance to them either. Because of the constraints, Ohno had to design a system that would be less wasteful, more efficient, less costly, and more flexible than traditional mass production methods. The system he and Toyoda developed, called the **Toyota production system,** is the prototype **just-in-time** production system. Though developed for automobile production, the ideas behind the system have since been applied in all kinds of industries.

CASE IN POINT: Toyota Production System — Lean Production and JIT Prototype

Following is a description of the principles of the Toyota production system and of differences between it and traditional mass production. The weaknesses of mass production that Toyoda observed at Ford still exist today in factories everywhere (Ford, however, has since adopted its own version of a JIT production system).

Reduced Setup Times. The American practice was to have hundreds of stamping presses, each for making only one or a few kinds of parts for each kind of car. These huge presses required months to set up. Since Toyota's budget limited procurement to only a few stamping presses, each press would of necessity have to stamp out a variety of parts. To make this practical, the setup times for switching over from stamping one kind of part to another would have to be drastically reduced.

By carefully analyzing existing procedures, Ohno came up with methods that slashed setup times from months to just hours. By organizing procedures, using carts, and training workers to do their own setups, he was eventually able to get the time down on some presses to an amazing *3 minutes,* without die-change specialists.[12] The procedures Ohno developed can be applied to any setup in almost any workplace.

All setup practices are wasteful because they add no value to a product and they tie up labor and equipment. Despite this, the tradition, before Ohno, was to take any setup practice as a given; if the setup took a long time, so be it. In fact (so goes traditional thinking), if a setup took a long time, it would then be necessary to produce things in large batches to justify the setup time. Since setup times were usually long, large-batch production became the norm in manufacturing.

Small-Lot Production. The traditional practice of producing things in large lots (or batches) was justified not only by the high setup cost of semiversatile machinery, but also by the high capital cost of high-speed dedicated machinery.

Dedicated machinery is very efficient, but it is also expensive, and somehow managers feel the expense can be justified if they can keep the machinery running to produce things in massive quantities, regardless of demand.

But producing things in large batches results, on average, in larger inventories because it takes longer to use up the batch, and that, in turn, results in higher holding costs. Plantwide, larger batches also extend lead times because they tie up machines longer and reduce scheduling flexibility. Although the effect on lead time is negligible when demand is constant, it becomes pronounced as demand variability increases.

Large batch sizes also tend to have larger defect costs. Production problems and product defects often happen as a result of setup mistakes or errors that affect only one batch at a time. The larger the batch, the more items affected.

The usual way to determine batch size, the so-called economic order quantity (EOQ), is based roughly on the square root of the ratio of setup costs to holding costs:

$$EOQ = \sqrt{2DS/H},$$

where

    D is demand,
    S is setup cost, and
    H is holding cost.

The formula gives the order quantity that balances total holding cost and total setup costs. Since, traditionally, holding cost has been underestimated because it ignores the effects of batch size on quality and lead times, and since setup cost, a direct function of setup time, is usually large, the formula (and managers' thinking) has been biased toward large batch sizes.

Because Ohno had found ways to make setups short and inexpensive, it became possible for Toyota to economically produce a variety of things in small quantities.

Employee Involvement and Empowerment. US plants employed specialists for doing just about every-

thing. Other than machinists and assembly workers, though, few specialists directly added value to a product. Ohno reasoned that most tasks done by specialists could be done by assembly workers and probably be done better because the assemblers were more familiar with the workplace. To this end he organized his workers by forming teams, and gave them responsibility and training to do many specialized tasks. Each team had a leader who also worked as one of them on the line.

In addition to their assigned work tasks, teams were given responsibility for housekeeping and minor equipment repair. They were also allowed time to meet to discuss problems and find ways to improve the process. Further, they would collect data to help diagnose problems, develop plans to solve the problems, and use suggestions from the specialists who were still on hand but in relatively few numbers compared to those in Detroit. The notion of workers **asking "why" five times** to get to problem root-causes was first introduced at Toyota. Eventually, worker responsibility was expanded to include many areas usually held by specialists, including quality inspection and rework.

Quality at the Source. Ohno saw that the traditional manufacturing process of stationing inspectors at locations throughout and at the end of the line did little to promote product quality. Defects missed by inspectors were passed from one worker to the next. As a product was assembled, defects became progressively more embedded inside and, thus, more difficult to detect. If detected, defective products were scrapped or sent to rework areas; otherwise, they were erroneously passed on to the customer. Thus, relying solely on inspectors was not a practical means by which to eliminate defects and the costs associated with making and reworking them.

Ohno reasoned that to eliminate product defects, they must be discovered and corrected as soon as possible. That meant going to the source of defects and stopping them there. Since workers are in the best position to discover a defect and to immediately fix it, Ohno assigned each worker that responsibility. If the defect could not be readily fixed, any worker could halt the entire line by pulling a cord (called **jidoka,** or line-stop). (At Detroit plants, only supervisors had such authority.) At first the Toyota line was frequently stopped and output was low, but over months and years of refinement the process began to pay off. As the worker teams diagnosed and solved problems, the number of defects began to drop, sources of errors were eliminated, and the quality of parts and assembled products got better. Eventually, the quality of finished goods was so high that the need for rework specialists was practically eliminated.

Equipment Maintenance. Manufacturing organizations laden with work-in-process (WIP) inventory are not much concerned about equipment maintenance because the inventory is a buffer that allows work to continue (for awhile) even when equipment breaks down. Further, many organizations actually bank on key equipment breaking down and carry enough inventory between operations to cover for that eventuality. Some managers are of the belief that the most productive way to run a machine is to run it constantly (three shifts if possible) until it breaks and then to fix it.

This philosophy runs square in the face of waste reduction because, accordingly, inventory is held, operations are idled during equipment repair, and repair costs are often higher.

Organizations that use pull production (described next) or have minimized WIP inventory have little buffer stock, and equipment breakdowns have potential to stop the entire process. Thus, organizations trying to reduce inventories must also reduce equipment breakdowns. Regularly scheduled preventive maintenance can help to curtail such breakdowns.

Consistent with the philosophy of worker empowerment at Toyota, operators are assigned primary responsibility for basic maintenance since they are in the best position to detect signs of malfunction. Maintenance specialists now

diagnose and fix only complex problems, train workers in maintenance, and improve the performance of equipment.

Pull Production. In traditional manufacturing plants, products are fashioned by moving batches of materials from one stage of the process to the next. At each stage an operation is performed on an entire batch. Because batch sizes and processing times vary from stage to stage and because there are usually several jobs that need work at each operation, it is difficult to synchronize the flow of material from one stage to the next. As a result, materials wait at each operation before they are processed, and typically the wait time far exceeds the time to process the batch. Plantwide the result is large amounts of WIP waiting at various stages of completion. In terms of inventory holding costs and lead times, the waste can be staggering.

To reduce these wastes Ohno developed the **pull production** method wherein the quantity of work performed at each stage of the process is dictated solely by the demand for materials from the immediate *next* stage. Ohno also developed a scheme called **Kanban** to coordinate the flow of small containers of materials between stages so that just as a container was used up at one stage, a full container from the previous stage would arrive to replenish it. This is actually where the term **just-in-time** originated. Production batches are kept small by using only small containers to hold materials.

Although pull production reduces waste, it is, in truth, not always an easy system to implement. Toyota took 20 years to work out the process.

Supplier Involvement. Ohno also recognized problems with traditional customer–supplier relationships in the US. Typically the manufacturer would develop detailed specifications for each product part and then contract with suppliers to make the parts through a competitive process that, usually, awarded the lowest bidder. Multiple suppliers for each part were retained, and these suppliers were routinely played one against another to keep prices down. Costly delays and poor quality products often resulted.

Ohno saw the need for a different kind of relationship wherein the manufacturer treats its suppliers as **partners** and, as such, as integral elements of the Toyota production system.

Essentially, suppliers are trained in ways to reduce setup times, inventories, defects, machine breakdowns, etc., and in return they take responsibility for delivering the best possible parts/services to the manufacturer in a timely manner. With this arrangement, the manufacturer, the supplier, and the customer benefit.

By the early 1960s Toyota Motor Company had worked out most of the major principles of JIT production. Eventually all other major Japanese auto firms adopted their own versions of JIT. In 1968 Japan passed West Germany as the number-two producer of vehicles in the world. In 1980 Japan passed the US to become number one.

AMERICA'S FALL FROM MANUFACTURING GRACE[13]

It would be a mistake to assume that Japan's economic success resulted solely from JIT. Japan is a very communal society, and following WWII the ministries of government decided where to concentrate the nation's limited resources to best serve the country The nation's educational system put emphasis on turning out engineers. By creating an excess of engineers, it was felt, more of them could be put on the shop floor where they could tinker with improvement. The cumulative effort of so many talented people working on so many things was incalculable. It was also the case that, deprived of opportunities in aerospace, nuclear, and other cutting-edge technologies with military potential, the cream of Japan's technical brainpower was funneled into more prosaic industries such as autos, steel, and machine tools; in the US such industries were having trouble attracting the best people.

While the Japanese were developing improved methods of production, American manufacturers were being distracted. Beginning in the 1950s a new breed of executives came to power. Here again the change was first seen at Ford, starting with the hiring of a group of young men known as the Whiz Kids, men who during the war had gained a reputation in the Air Corp for prowess in applying analytical techniques to managerial problems.[14] But the Whiz Kids were not car men, nor even product men. Lacking product know-how, they minimized its importance and played up their so-called management systems. Their systems put exclusive emphasis on financial criteria that, (presumably) told management what to do, regardless of market, product, or industry. The group was at first a welcome relief at Ford. Henry Ford had distrusted accountants and fired most of them, so company records and procedures after the war were in total disarray. The Whiz Kids reorganized everything and imposed tight financial and accounting controls. They cleansed the system, though decades later people would question whether their *kind* of cleansing had been best. The issue is not the efficacy of financial management systems; such systems are an important component of modern management. What is wrong is that in the Whiz Kids' brand of management, financial controls are allowed to dominate and smother every other component of business—marketing, engineering, and manufacturing.

At Ford and at most other corporations in the US, a powerful new bureaucracy was installed. As it assumed power it displaced the manufacturing people who had customarily dominated. A class chasm grew: the manufacturing people were blue-collar men who had risen from the factory by energy and zeal; the finance people were professionals who had been to college. Given that one of the easiest ways to bolster profit performance is to curtail capital expenditure and implement cost-cuts, top management, in their zest to improve financial performance, pared back on capital investment and product innovation, made cuts in facilities and labor, closed plants, and moved manufacturing overseas.

Over the next several decades, graduates of America's business schools swelled the ranks of the new elite. The best students went into finance and systems analysis, which had become the fast tracks to senior management. Rarely did good students go into manufacturing, which was viewed as a dead end. It was just as rare in big companies to find a manufacturing person on the board or as president. (Manufacturing in Japan carried higher prestige, and boards there had many men with factory experience.)

As US managers changed their style, they also changed their business agenda. Driving up the price of shares on the stock market became more important than making a good product with a profit.

Japanese producers slowly began to take away market share in autos, steel, and electronics. Rather than learn from them, American managers used the challenge of Japan as a threat to keep wages down. They told workers, "You better take the contract we are offering you or see your jobs moved to another country."

CLIMBING BACK

The Whiz Kids approach to management is still taught in business schools and practiced in corporations, but signs indicate the mistakes of recent decades are being recognized and corrected. There are also signs that US manufacturing is on the road to becoming competitive once more. This is not to say that all is well in US manufacturing or that America will regain its former position of dominance in world production. Many executives still view manufacturing as an expense that must be pared back or fully outsourced. The US is still the most innovative country in the world, but its innovators often have a hard time getting financial backing at home and must look overseas where investors and manufacturers seem more eager to snap up promising new ideas. These manufacturers, of course, become the long-term beneficiaries of American innovativeness.

In US industry more money *is* flowing back into plant improvement, manufacturing, and new products and processes. The function of manufacturing has regained status; it is again becoming common to see manufacturing people in high company positions (the current presidents of the US Big Three Automakers have marketing or engineering backgrounds). But it is too early for US manufacturers to celebrate success. America's rivals are not sitting still. Corporate investment in fundamental scientific research and development in 1996 was the lowest in over a decade, and industry observers say this will surely have a negative effect on America's ability to retain a technological edge in the next century. Since technology is applied science, disinvestment in basic scientific research is a recipe for technological stagnation. The problem is that too many US managers still take the short view in seeking return on investments. Others, meanwhile, like the Japanese, are taking the long view, confident that investments in scientific research and technological innovation will pay off big in the coming decades.

MODERN DEVELOPMENTS

To round out this brief history we note some other manufacturing developments in the last three decades of the twentieth century. These developments can be summarized in two words: computer technology. Since the 1970s, probably the single greatest use of computers in manufacturing has been for **material requirements planning (MRP)** systems. MRP system software links together all information about the parts and components that go into a finished product. Without the computer's capability to manipulate large quantities of data, coordinated scheduling and rescheduling of thousands of parts for producing hundreds of products would be impossible. Seeing the need to integrate production activities with marketing and financial planning, developers later introduced **manufacturing resource planning (MRP II),** which is a much expanded version of MRP that allows companywide input for production planning.

Other noteworthy developments are **computer-aided design, computer-aided manufacturing, flexible manufacturing systems, computer-integrated manufacturing,** and **electronic data interchange.**

Computer-aided design (CAD) enables designers to design a part or product and test its features and compatibility with other parts and products, all with a computer. Computer-aided manufacturing (CAM) refers to software that translates design requirements (communicated from CAD) into instructions for controlling production machinery. Given CAM's dependence on CAD for input, CAD/CAM is often applied as a single, integrated technology.

Flexible manufacturing systems (FMS) aim to achieve high-variety output at low cost. Although a FMS can be manual, the usual notion of FMS is a computer-controlled, automated system. With a computer regulating changes in machine settings, parts, and tools, one machine can perform numerous functions and require very little time for changeover between parts. A large FMS consists of many machines or processes, each with varying degrees of mechanization linked by automatic transfer systems, guided vehicles, or robots, all controlled by a central computer.

The next step beyond FMS is computer-integrated manufacturing (CIM). CIM links CAD/CAM, automated material handling, robotics, and automated manufacturing planning, control, and execution into a single, integrated system. CAD is linked to CAM for instructing and controlling machines, and planning and control is linked to material handling systems so material is on-hand as required by the machines.

Electronic data interchange (EDI) refers to computer-to-computer exchange of information, usually meaning between multiple companies. Translating software converts data from the sending company's computer files to the receiving company's computer files. EDI enables quick, accurate sharing of production schedules and placing of orders between companies that are customers/suppliers to each other.

Computer technology is also responsible for the newest phase of mass manufacturing: **mass customization.** In one scenario, a sales clerk at a clothing store enters into a computer a customer's vital statistics to create a digital blueprint of a pattern, which is transmitted to the factory and instructs a robot to cut the fabric to precise measurements.[15] In another scenario, customers phone an engineer to discuss the kind of part they need, and the engineer enters the specifications into a CAD/CAM system to design a one-of-a-kind part. Overnight, automated machines grind out the custom parts.

In many industries, technologies such as these have cut labor, material, transportation, and inventory costs and have improved manufacturing cycle times, flexibility, product quality, and customer satisfaction. In other cases, however, because the technologies were too costly, poorly implemented, prematurely made obsolete, or ill-suited for the operation, they helped little or made things worse. In a study of FMSs used by companies in Japan and the US it was revealed that while the average US FMS was used to produce 10 types of parts the Japanese FMS produced 93. Said the Harvard professor who did the study, "With few exceptions, the flexible manufacturing systems installed in the United States showed an outstanding lack of flexibility."[16]

THE QUALITY MOVEMENT[17]

Methods for attaining quality were probably first applied by prehistoric humans crafting pottery, clothing, tools, and weapons. Since then methods of quality have evolved along a path that roughly parallels the evolution of methods of production. But methods of production have only been a part of the quality story. Increasingly complex products, more demanding customers, and the growing ferocity of competition have also spurred growing attention toward quality. With these factors as background, the evolution of quality can be traced through four distinct phases: inspection, statistical quality control, quality assurance, and modern total quality management.[18] These phases and related events are shown in Table 1.2.

INSPECTION

In the craft production era, people who formed and fit together parts also inspected the parts and the final assembly. Craftsmen working as individuals set their own quality standards and performed informal inspection by eyeball. Around the seventh century, craftsmen in England began to form associations called guilds, and in time these guilds set standards for work procedures and work conditions.

The earliest kind of industry was domestic, a small group of workers, often a family, who worked independently under the direction of one person, usually the father. With the rise of industrialism in the nineteenth century, domestic shops were supplanted by a growing number of capitalist-owned workshops that *employed* laborers for wages. By the end of the nineteenth century virtually all industrial manufacturing in America and Europe was performed in small shops. In both domestic and capitalist shops, owners set the quality standards, but workers checked the work. As the size of companies grew and greater numbers of noncraftsmen were employed,

TABLE 1.2   Some Notable Events in a Brief History of Manufacturing Quality

Era	Concepts/Events	Dates	Key Figures
Inspection	Craftsmen responsible for both production and quality	Prior to 1900s	
	Role of inspector becomes common	1900s	
	Standardized parts and gauging systems	1900s	
	Control charts and acceptance sampling	1920s	Walter Shewhart, Harold Dodge, Harry Romig
Statistical process control	Theory of SPC published	1931	Walter Shewhart
	US consultants advise Japanese industry	1946– early 1950s	W. Edwards Deming, Joseph Juran, Arnold Feigenbaum
Quality assurance	Cost of quality; total quality control	1950s	Joseph Juran, Arnold Feigenbaum
	Quality control circles (in Japan)	1950s	Kaoru Ishikawa, Taiichi Ohno
	Reliability engineering, zero-defects programs	1960s	
Total quality management	Robust design (in Japan)	1960s	Genichi Taguchi
	Quality function deployment	1972	Kobe Shipyards
	Design for manufacture/ assembly	1980s	Geoffrey Boothroyd, Peter Dewhurst
	Concurrent engineering in US; recognition of TQM by US businesses	1980s– present	

more of the quality checking was done by the owner or supervisor. Eventually, as the number of employees grew to exceed the checking capability of a supervisor, the special position of inspector came into being.

Most early machine shops used gauges to check product dimensions and tolerances, but the gauges were often imprecise and every shop used its own kind of gauges. When Ford and other manufacturers started to demand that the shops produce interchangeable parts, both the system of setting parts standards and inspecting the parts had to be formalized. The same kind of gauges had to be used everywhere, and parts specifications had to be set so that parts made in different places would fit together and defective parts could be identified and sorted out. With the addition of quality inspectors using gauges at places in the moving assembly lines, quality control became an integral part of mass production.

In 1924 Bell Telephone Laboratories formed an inspection engineering department to investigate quality problems and find more rigorous methods for quality control. **Walter Shewhart,** a member of the department, focused on the problem of variation in processes and devised a method, the **control chart,** as a tool to monitor the variation. Two other scientists at Bell, Harold Dodge and Harry Romig, developed **acceptance sampling** as a method of checking a limited number of units in a batch to determine whether the entire batch is acceptable. The contributions of these men helped to improve the quality of Bell's telephone products and services. Development of sampling techniques continued throughout the 1920s and 1930s, but the emphasis remained solely on inspection for defects, not on prevention of defects.

STATISTICAL PROCESS CONTROL

Shewhart realized that problems stemming from random variation in processes were statistical in nature, and he advocated the use of control charts as a way to distinguish natural from unnatural variations in a process. With the 1931 publication of a text explaining the philosophy and applications of a theory he called **statistical process control (SPC),** Shewhart's ideas began to attract attention around the world, especially in England.

Shewhart viewed quality in terms of three categories: manufacturing based, product-based, and user-based. To improve manufacturing-based quality, Shewhart suggested that SPC be used as a way to reduce process variation so that a larger percentage of items produced would conform to requirements. He also suggested drawing samples throughout the process rather than waiting until the end.

During WWII, factories producing at high rates for the war effort and suffering the loss of experienced workers to the military services had to rapidly increase the number of unskilled workers in their employ. Concerned about the resulting decline in product quality, the War Department established a quality control section to refine methods of acceptance sampling. The group developed new sampling techniques to enable producers to meet established **acceptable quality levels,** that is, the maximum percent of defects allowed for a supplier to be considered satisfactory. The section also offered courses nationwide on statistical quality control and acceptance sampling and, as a result, inspectors became more productive and product quality levels improved. The application of methods of quality control, however, remained narrowly confined to companies working in the war effort. After the war the methods would continue to be ignored by the majority of US industry.

Meanwhile postwar Japan was struggling to rebuild its economy. Its early efforts to re-enter world markets were directed at production of inexpensive, easy-to-make products for low-end markets. The products were often poorly designed and poorly manufactured, and the "Made in Japan" label became synonymous with "junk." Knowing such a reputation would be hard to escape or reverse, leaders of government and industry set about to change the image. Rather than deal with innovative product design, they chose manufacturing capability as their quality improvement strategy.

Postwar Japan was occupied by US armed forces under the command of General Douglas MacArthur. Anxious to help Japanese industry get back on its feet, the US government offered its assistance, including advice from American consultants such as **W. Edwards Deming, Joseph Juran,** and **Arnold Feigenbaum.** Deming in particular had an enormous influence on the Japanese because his lectures were attended by CEOs from Japan's largest corporations, including Toyota and Nissan.[19] A disciple of Shewhart, Deming emphasized the principles of SPC and **plan-do-check-act (PDCA).** The philosophy of Deming is summarized in his 14 points for management and serves as a framework for quality and productivity improvement.[20] Deming argued that the process of using acceptable quality levels for quality standards was unacceptable and that companies must engage in **continuous improvement.** Among his 14 points are "constantly try to improve product design and performance through research, development, and innovation" and "constantly try to improve the production and service system." He also argued that quality is not some minor function to be handled by inspectors, but that it has to be a company's central purpose and a priority of top management. Juran, too, argued the key role of top management in quality, a role that by the mid-1950s Japanese executives had come to accept.

Deming taught that it is less costly in the long run to get things right the first time rather than to fix them later. Toyota took that message to the shop floor by teaching its workers to inspect continuously for defects (and if necessary to interrupt production), trace problems to the source, and fix them. Workers were told not to allow a car to pass unless it was perfect; this is the original concept of **quality-at-the-source.** By the late 1950s Deming had become something of a god in Japan. It would be still another 30 years before his own countrymen would accord him recognition.

At a time when Japan was embracing Deming's management philosophy, American industry was embracing the Whiz Kids'.

QUALITY ASSURANCE

Following WWII the US, the only world power not to have had its production capability weakened or destroyed, became the sole worldwide supplier for many kinds of goods. Demand, pent-up by years of war, was enormous, and US manufacturers worked overtime just to keep up. Because customers had few choices, quality was less an issue, so US manufacturers could keep it on the back burner behind volume and profits. Nonetheless, some new developments were requiring greater attention to quality, and these mandated an increase in the scope of quality beyond simple inspection and sampling. This broader scope of activities was termed quality assurance.

The first development in quality assurance came in the early 1950s. Advances in defense, electronics, and aerospace systems required new techniques for assuring adequate system performance, and the discipline of reliability engineering evolved. The reliability of a system depends on product design, materials, manufacture, and product upkeep. In reliability engineering, the functions of engineering, manufacturing, procurement, and maintenance are all recognized as important to assure quality in complex systems.

Also in the early 1950s, Juran initiated the concept of the cost of quality, which reemphasized management's responsibility for quality. According to the concept, quality-related costs lie in two categories: unavoidable and avoidable. Part of Juran's argument was that early decisions about a product, such as its design, have a major influence on avoidable costs incurred on the factory floor or with the customer. By investing more in improvement in design and manufacturing (unavoidable costs), the costs from scrap, rework, warranty payments, and loss of unhappy customers (avoidable costs) are reduced. Since increases in the former are more than offset by decreases in the latter, the total cost is reduced.

Feigenbaum reinforced Juran's argument with his concept of **total quality control**, where total implies that quality control is **everyone's job.** Prior to this, quality control was still viewed as largely the charge of shop-floor inspectors and the quality control (QC) department. Feigenbaum argued that since product development, product manufacturability, and vendor selection were also important elements of quality control, total quality control had to be implemented using **cross-functional teams.** But Feigenbaum's break with tradition was not complete. In his conception of these teams, primary responsibility for quality control was not distributed uniformly among all departments but remained within the QC department.

In the early 1960s the Martin Company, an aerospace firm, initiated the first "zero-defects" (ZD) program whereby workers were offered incentives to reduce defects. Many companies followed with their own ZD programs and succeeded in lowering defect rates. As Deming had 10 years earlier, ZD programs challenged the concept of acceptable quality level and the assumption that a certain level of defects is inevitable. However, the drawback of all ZD programs was an overemphasis on the importance of worker attention to perfection and a complete neglect of quality issues beyond the workers' control.

Although quality assurance programs raised the level of involvement of top management, designers, and shop-floor employees in improving quality, for the most part the emphasis remained on *reducing* product defects. Further, given that quality responsibility still resided mostly within manufacturing, and given the low-level status of manufacturing in the 1960s, 1970s, and 1980s, most companies' attention to quality remained limited. Production managers could not *prove* that greater attention to quality would increase profits, so their requests for additional people, money, or equipment to improve quality were usually denied.

Meanwhile, in Japan, small-group employee-participation programs called **quality-control circles** were forming. In these circles, shop-floor supervisors and workers meet in teams to discuss quality issues. Workers train themselves in quality control techniques and practice the concept of continuous improvement. This allows them to address quality issues that go far beyond reducing product defects. In the late 1970s and early 1980s many US companies, thinking by then that QC circles were the major reason for Japan's growing competitive strength, began to implement their own QC circle programs. In the US, however, QC circles were largely a management fad, and within a few years most of the programs faded away.

TOTAL QUALITY MANAGEMENT

Not until the 1980s did US managers start to recognize that quality could be used as a *strategy* for competitive advantage. They saw the connection between poor quality and loss of profit, a connection strengthened by an increase in consumer activism and liability suits for product defects starting in the 1970s. Also at that time, the US government began to mandate stricter safety regulations and closer policing of the manufacturing, packaging, and holding of products.

The real wake-up call, though, was the incursion of foreign producers, principally Japanese, into prime US markets. The onslaught from Japan seemed almost sudden, but in fact it had been coming for decades. By the early 1980s, the Japanese advantage in quality had become obvious. Though many American managers chose to attribute it to Japan's lead in robotics, in truth the lead had come from slow and systematic refinement of Japan's manufacturing skills. The Japanese had achieved it by *being there* on the factory floor, which was the one place where US managers and engineers had not been.[21] Superior skills and processes had come by way of thousands of incremental improvements, the Japanese concept of **kaizen.**

Though most early advances in quality had principally come from the US, Japan was now initiating its own advances. In the 1970s **Kaoru Ishikawa** and **Genichi Taguchi** gained world recognition for quality achievements. Ishikawa, who was strongly influenced by Deming, became known primarily for his **cause-and-effect diagram** as well as his conception and application of QC circles. Cause-effect is a formal technique for listing factors that could have direct bearing on a quality problem. It is one of the **seven problem-analysis/solving tools** he instituted for use by workers in QC circles. Ishikawa felt that problem-solving skills like these were essential for moving responsibility of quality beyond specialists to the workers, a concept he called companywide quality control.

Taguchi is known for his argument that simply conforming to some tolerance limit is not good enough; that is, quality is the ability to come as close as possible to the target specification. Thus, said Taguchi, the goal should be to **continuously reduce process variation,** or the amount by which output varies from the target (an aspect of continuous improvement). Taguchi felt that products should be designed so performance is insensitive to variations in production factors and operational usage (the concept of **robust design**), and he made contributions to the **design of experiments** for investigating and setting design parameters toward achieving that end.

One problem that always plagued quality-conscious companies was translating what the customer wants into actual products and services without distorting or losing it in product design and manufacture. **Quality function deployment** (QFD), a methodology for determining customer requirements and translating them into specifications that each functional area of the organization can understand and act upon, was first used at Kobe Shipyards in the 1970s and then at Toyota. With QFD the final product or service can usually be developed faster, at lower cost, and better meet customer requirements than with traditional product development methods.

The most recent decade has been called the era of quality slogans and jargon because of the proliferation of slogans and phraseology used by US producers to try to hold on to market share.[22] The value of quality as a competitive tool is now widely accepted, but the problem remains of ensuring that the many principles and prescriptions for quality are adhered to by managers and workers. As a result, much of the emphasis about quality has shifted to include the human aspect of quality and the entire organization. In the current era of quality, the catchword is **total quality management** (TQM).

In the US, TQM refers to a new paradigm, one in which quality is much more than a program and applies to much more than just product defects. As Bounds, et al., say, TQM "is as much about the quality process as it is about quality results or quality products."[23]

Modern TQM programs focus on assuring that the **product design** satisfies both customer requirements and manufacturability requirements and that procured **raw materials** also satisfy these requirements. They also focus on assuring that the **production activities** necessary to produce a product or service achieve the quality requirements and that the **overall quality program** is effective in terms of meeting or exceeding customers' expectations.

THE IMPERATIVE

JIT systems and TQM programs have been adopted by organizations everywhere. Despite variations in the ways JIT/TQM programs are implemented, the fundamental ingredients of these programs remain largely the same. In manufacturing, many of these elements represent a departure from traditional ways, though many of them also conform to principles of good operations and manufacturing management that have been in the books for decades. Some are technically or culturally difficult to implement; some provoke resistance from managers and workers. As a result, JIT/TQM programs require long-term commitment to implement, and few of them will show positive results in the first several months or even years of effort. The alternative of not adopting these programs, however, is potentially disastrous. Players who have successfully adopted the methods of JIT and TQM and who faithfully apply these methods to improve their products and processes have gained a substantial competitive advantage over others within the same market who continue to operate by the old rules of mass production and quality control.

The proof is in the record. It is not an overstatement to say that companies that have been challenged by producers committed to the principles of JIT and TQM have been able to meet or beat those challengers only by committing to the same principles. Companies that were challenged but that did not become JIT/TQM producers, either because they ignored the challenge or did not have time to make the transition, lost; either they chose to drop out of the market, or they were forced to drop out.[24]

ORGANIZATION OF THE BOOK

This book is first and foremost about principles and applications of JIT and TQM. However, it is also about other topics that are important to modern competitive manufacturing and to implementing JIT/TQM philosophies. Two such topics, for example, are cellular manufacturing and activity-based costing. While neither is considered a principle tool or element of JIT or TQM, both are commonly found in JIT/TQM organizations.

The rest of this book is divided into five main parts. Part I is an overview of three concepts fundamental to JIT/TQM philosophies and practices: **continuous improvement, elimination of waste,** and **focus on the customer.** Survival and competitiveness in manufacturing mandate continuous improvement of products and processes— forever striving to be better, faster, cheaper, more agile. Any attempt to improve a process implies the process contains waste, so part of the continuous improvement crusade is to identify waste and eliminate it.

Chapters 2 and 3 examine the strategic importance of improvement in competitive environments, two kinds of improvement **(incremental** and **innovation), sources of waste** in manufacturing, and **basic JIT principles** for waste reduction and process improvement in manufacturing.

In the pursuit of competitive advantage, a company must target its improvement efforts, and that is where the concept of quality comes in. The focus on customer-defined quality is what sets priorities for improvement and waste-reduction efforts. Chapter 4 discusses quality in general and **customer-focused quality** in particular. It introduces the concept of TQM, the role of TQM in continuous improvement, the tasks and responsibilities of functional areas in TQM organizations, and the concepts of quality **benchmarking** and **certification.**

Part II discusses the elements of lean production. JIT has been referred to as *lean production* because it uses less of everything by eliminating sources of waste found in traditional mass production. In a typical manufacturing plant it is easy to find waste in the form of product defects, inventory, overproduced items, idle workers and machines, and unnecessary motion. It is also relatively easy to identify the sources of these wastes and eliminate them through different management and shop-floor practices. This part of the book presents in some depth the core elements of JIT, JIT improvement strategies, JIT methodologies, and a few closely related topics.

Particular methodologies covered include producing **small lot sizes,** reducing process and equipment **setup times, maintaining** an l **improving equipment,** using the **pull system** (Kanban) for production control, organizing facilities into **focused factories** and **workcells,** and **standardizing shop-floor operations.** In combination the topics in this part of the book represent a set of methodologies, all implemented on the shop floor and all interrelated in the sense that effective implementation of one requires substantial implementation of many or all of the others. In every case, the methodologies are aimed not only at improvement, but at institutionalizing the process of continuous improvement. In every case also, shop-floor workers play a central role; that role and the real-life programmatic issues about JIT implementation are also addressed.

Part III of the book deals with issues and tools for improving the quality of manufactured items. A quality product begins with product specifications based on what customers say they want and need. Capturing what customers really want and translating it into a design that is faithful to those wants and that can be produced at low cost and high quality are two necessary aspects of building quality into a product.

Chapter 12 is about **quality of design,** which is the process of designing a product that will both satisfy customer requirements and meet the capability of the manufacturing process. The chapter covers tools for managing the design process, setting design parameters, and integrating customer-engineering-manufacturing requirements. Four topics, **concurrent engineering, quality function deployment, design for manufacture and assembly,** and **robust design/design of experiments** are covered in some depth.

Besides quality of design there must be **quality of conformance:** that is, there must be a process to ensure that manufactured products continuously conform with design requirements. In Chapter 13 the basic concepts of **inspection, fitness-for-use,** and **acceptance sampling** are discussed. Chapter 14 describes concepts of **statistical process control,** including sources of **process variation, process control charts,** and the concept of **process capability.** Reliance on statistical methods can greatly improve a process, but it can never eliminate defects. Chapter 15 discusses systems for eliminating manufacturing defects and the Japanese notion of **pokayoke,** or foolproofing.

Part IV of the book reconsiders many of the lean production and total quality concepts from earlier chapters, but in the context of a working manufacturing system. Assuming the elements of lean production and total quality are well along into implementation, the question then is, "How is production planned and scheduled to take the fullest advantage of these changes?" This part of the book takes a big step back to look at JIT techniques and pull production methods as elements of a total production system, a system that scans the environment, forecasts demand, accumulates orders, translates forecasts and orders into plans and schedules, authorizes material procurement, and executes work tasks to ultimately yield a finished product.

In general, the smoother materials flow through the production system, the better the product quality and the faster and cheaper the production process. Chapter 16 addresses the concept of **production leveling** as a way to smooth fluctuations in production plans and schedules. Chapter 17 addresses two additional prerequisites for smooth flow, **balanced capacity** between operations and **synchronized operations.** Chapter 18 describes a **framework of overall planning and control** to tie together many of the topics from elsewhere in the book. It also addresses the relative roles of centralized systems and decentralized (shop-floor) systems in JIT planning and control and the subject of adapting MRP or push-type systems to pull production. Plants adopting JIT that have extant MRP-based planning and control systems can still use them, but for more limited purposes or in parts of the plant where the product-demand mix is better suited to the MRP approach. The Appendix at the end of the book is provided as a reference for MRP-based planning and control concepts and methods.

The final part of the book deals with the impact of JIT/TQM philosophy on three areas outside the immediate production system: supplier relations, cost accounting, and company goal-setting and measurement. The quality, cost, and delivery performance of every manufacturer depends in large part on the performance of its suppliers. Without agreement between a customer and its suppliers about the quality, cost, delivery, and service expected on materials received, a company will be hard pressed to achieve JIT/TQM ideals. Chapter 19 deals with the concept of **supply chain**

management, the changing role of the purchasing function, and the application of JIT concepts to improve performance and reduce waste throughout the supply chain.

Also important to organizations involved in JIT/TQM is the ability to account for the impact of waste-reduction and improvement efforts on direct operations, overhead, and product costs. Whereas traditional accounting practices tend to overlook or incorrectly assess the contribution of these efforts, **activity-based costing** methods, the subject of Chapter 20, not only more accurately account for improvements in product costing, but are also useful for determining future targets of improvement and waste-reduction efforts.

Management decision making is directed by company goals, which are supported by measures of performance at all levels and functions of the organization. It is fruitless for a company to try to move toward JIT/TQM ideals without first having performance measures compatible with those ideals. The final chapter of the book contrasts **traditional measures** with new, **enlightened measures** of performance, which are measures compatible with JIT/TQM philosophy. The enlightened measures described touch on virtually every major concept and methodology in JIT/TQM manufacturing, so the chapter also serves as a useful summary of the entire book.

Questions

1. Explain how each of the following is a basis for competitive advantage in manufacturing: cost, quality, time, agility.
2. Distinguish between delivery time and time to market.
3. In 10 words or less, what is the primary focus of just-in-time?
4. In 10 words or less, what is the primary focus of total quality management?
5. Discuss the similarities, differences, and interdependencies between JIT and TQM.
6. What is meant by the term *production pipeline?* What does the production pipeline have to do with JIT and TQM?
7. What features differentiate JIT/TQM organizations from other organizations?
8. What is craft production?
9. What is mass production?
10. What were Henry Ford's most significant contributions to mass production?
11. Why did Eiji Toyoda and Taiichi Ohno decide against copying Detroit's system of mass production? How did that lead to the Toyota Production system?
12. Describe the principles of the Toyota production system and how it is a departure from traditional production systems.
13. Explain some of the reasons why America's position as the world's supreme industrial power started to decline in the 1960s and 1970s.
14. What is the relationship between quality and production in craft production?
15. What effect did interchangeability of parts have on product quality?
16. Discuss Walter Shewhart's contributions to quality.

17. What did the phrase "Made in Japan" connote in the decade following the end of World War II? What actions did Japanese government and industry take to change the connotation?
18. What is meant by quality assurance and by total quality control? How is each different from the modern concept of TQM?
19. Why have overseas corporations been successful at capturing large share in US markets? What is the role of manufacturing?
20. What are some potential barriers against adopting industrial policies and manufacturing practices in the US that would help make American industry more competitive?
21. A principle feature of JIT and TQM is large-scale employee involvement and employee empowerment. What do these concepts mean? Why in practice are they considered somewhat radical in US organizations when they are accepted as commonplace in Japanese organizations?

Research Questions

To answer these questions, you should do a literature search and include material beyond this chapter.

1. What are the contributions to quality of W. Edwards Deming? Joseph Juran? Arnold Feigenbaum?
2. What are the contributions to quality of Kaoru Ishikawa? Genichi Taguchi?
3. Name some newsworthy, contemporary companies that are successful (high market share, high profits, leading-edge products, and so on). Which of them are turnaround companies (rebounded after hard times)? Which of them are JIT/TQM companies?
4. What are some big-name companies that during recent decades stopped producing certain products after Asian or European producers aggressively entered the market?

Endnotes

1. D. Kearns and D. Nadler, *Prophets in the Dark: How Xerox Reinvented Itself and Beat Back the Japanese* (New York: HarperBusiness, 1992).
2. A. Roth, A. DeMeyer, and A. Amano, "International Manufacturing Strategies: A Competitive Analysis," *Managing International Manufacturing* (Amsterdam: Elsevier Science, 1989), pp. 187–211.
3. National Center for Manufacturing Sciences, *Competing in World-Class Manufacturing* (Homewood, IL: Business One Irwin, 1990), p. 118.
4. A related philosophy is **time-based competition** (TBC), which, obviously, puts more emphasis on the time criterion. Much of the practice of TBC overlaps with TQM and JIT practices, although an express goal of TBC, one which is not necessarily a goal of JIT or TQM, is to shorten product development times, that is, to improve agility in terms of product redesign and innovation. *See* P. Smith and D. Reinertsen, *Developing Products in Half the Time* (New York: Van Nostrand

Reinhold, 1991); and J. Blackburn, *Time-Based Competition* (Homewood, IL: Business One Irwin), 1991.

5. R. Schonberger, *World Class Manufacturing: The Lessons of Simplicity Applied* (New York: The Free Press, 1986), p. 137.

6. The analogy has been used before. *See* H. Mather, *Competitive Manufacturing* (Englewood Cliffs, NJ: Prentice-Hall, 1988, pp. 12–20; W. Sandras, *Just-in-Time: Making It Happen* (Essex Junction, VT: Oliver Wight, 1992), pp. 7–8.

7. Material in this section is derived from two principal sources: J. Womack, D. Jones, and R. Roos, *The Machine That Changed the World* (New York: Rawson, 1990); and D. Halberstam, *The Reckoning* (New York: Avon Books, 1986).

8. *See* W. Lazonic, *Competitive Advantage on the Shop Floor* (Cambridge, MA: Harvard University, 1990).

9. Ford's innovative contribution to the interchangeable part was in its application and execution: he imposed on all suppliers of each part a single standard to which they were all expected to conform.

10. DuPont and Carnegie Steel also developed new forms of organization. DuPont was the first to establish corporate divisions, and Carnegie was the first to vertically integrate an industry—raw materials to finished product. It was *US* companies that were making the innovations. Nothing like it was happening in Europe.

11. The family name Toyoda means *rice field* in Japanese; the word Toyota, which they chose to call the corporation, has no meaning.

12. J. Womack, D. Jones and R. Roos, *The Machine that Changed the World*, p. 53.

13. Much of this subsection is derived from D. Halberstam, *The Recknoning.* (See note 7).

14. *See* J. Byrne, *The Whiz Kids,* (New York: Currency Doubleday, 1993).

15. G. Rifkin, "Digital Blue Jeans Pour Data and Legs Into Customized Fit," *The New York Times,* Nov. 8, 1994, p. A1.

16. R. Jalkumar, "Postindustrial Manufacturing," *Harvard Business Review,* (Nov–Dec 1986), pp. 69–76.

17. Material in this section is adapted from J. Banks, *Principles of Quality Control* (New York: John Wiley, 1989), pp. 3–26; G. Bounds, L. Yorks, M. Adams, G. Ranney, *Beyond Total Quality Management* (New York: McGraw-Hill, 1994), pp. 46–62.

18. G. Bounds, et al., *ibid.,* p. 47.

19. For Deming's first quality lecture, Japan's top 45 industrialists were invited. All 45 came.

20. M. Walton, *The Deming Management Method* (New York: Perigee, 1986).

21. D. Halberstam, *The Reckoning,* p. 710.

22. J. Banks, *Principles of Quality Control,* p. 17.

23. G. Bounds, et al., *Beyond Total Quality Management,* p. 61.

24. Xerox and Ford are examples of come-back US companies mentioned in this chapter. Chrysler, GM, and Harley-Davidson are also well-known examples that attribute comeback in large part to JIT/TQM. Electronics manufacturers such as Intel, Motorola, Hewlett-Packard, and IBM avoided major market losses by adopting JIT/TQM early (starting in the 1970s). Other examples of companies that have successfully met the competitive challenge with JIT/TQM are General Electric, John Deere, Allen-Bradley, Control Data, Texas Instruments, Honeywell, Black & Decker, Omark, and 3M. There are many hundreds, probably thousands, more.

CONTINUOUS IMPROVEMENT, WASTE ELIMINATION, CUSTOMER FOCUS

The term improvement implies that something about a process has changed for the better. In business operations, improvement is often expressed in terms of changes in the process output or input. For example, increasing the process output–input ratio (O/I) is considered improvement, achieved by either an increased level of output for a fixed level of input or by a reduced level of input for a fixed level of output.

Though more output for the same input or the same output for less input are common ways to measure improvement, too often the view of what constitutes input and output (and, hence, improvement) is narrow and simplistic. Real improvement represents an attempt to make something better while trying to minimize costs and adverse consequences. For example, if a manufacturing process is changed to increase the rate of output, the change is an overall improvement only as long as other aspects of the output or process have not been degraded. If the change results in diminished product quality, increased production cost, worsened working conditions, or increased toxic wastes, the increased output may not be an improvement at all.

In the global marketplace the concept of improvement is synonymous with "never stop trying." External factors (technology, resource availability and costs, and competitors' capabilities) over which an organization has little control but which influence competitiveness and profitability are constantly changing. Inside the organization, factors like work conditions, employee motivations and skills, and processes are changing too. As a result, whatever was good enough yesterday will probably not be good enough tomorrow.

There is also no logical end to customers changing their expectations, either in level or direction, nor to what competing organizations will do to try to meet those expectations. Thus, there can be no such thing as ultimate improvement. Organizations that try to achieve ultimate improvement or are content with staying in one place will be surpassed by others keeping pace with changes. In short, survival and success mandate **continuous improvement.**

Paralleling the idea of continuous improvement is the concept of **elimination of waste.** To use a metaphor, the road to improvement is potholed with waste. Like potholes, sources of waste are everywhere and no matter what you do, they keep coming back. Any attempt to improve a process by increasing output with a fixed level of input or by maintaining the same output from reduced input implies that the process contains waste. Part of continuous improvement is the crusade to identify waste and eliminate it.

In the pursuit of competitive advantage, an organization must be able to *target* its improvement and waste-elimination efforts. There must be some scheme for putting priorities on where to expend time, effort, and resources in improvement and waste-reduction efforts. Here is where the concept of **quality** comes in. In seeking competitive advantage, **customer-focused quality** is the criterion an organization uses for prioritizing improvement and waste-reduction alternatives. Quality has a price, however, so the concept of **value** is important too. To retain or increase a product's value, efforts devoted to increasing product quality must be accompanied by efforts to hold or reduce costs. Lower cost can result from improvement efforts directed solely at costs, though lower cost is also one of the many byproducts of eliminating waste in a process.

To avoid getting into a semantical debate about distinctions between the three concepts of improvement, elimination of waste, and customer-focused quality, let us just say they are all related, which is why they are discussed together here. The concepts and their relation to each other, to JIT and TQM, and to competitive manufacturing are topics of the chapters in Part I:

Chapter 2 : Fundamentals of Continuous Improvement
Chapter 3 : JIT: Value Added and Waste Elimination
Chapter 4 : TQM: Customer-Focused Quality

An organization's ability to survive depends on how well the organization adapts to demands imposed by a changing environment. In modern history, organizations have come and gone, and relatively few have outlived the people who worked in them. Organizations that survive for a century are rare. As global competition intensifies, big companies whose names once meant power and prosperity are being eclipsed and are dying off at an accelerated rate. In many cases, demise is the result of an inability to adapt.

The challenge of change in a business environment comes along many fronts: competitors introduce new products; industries develop new processes and technologies; and the scope of what constitutes the business environment keeps expanding. One time, not so long ago, a US business could feel safe if it had captured most of the market from its domestic competitors. Today no organization anywhere can feel safe just by beating domestic rivals. The business environment has expanded to put US, Asian, and European organizations in direct competition. In many instances US companies have not fared well because what they have been accustomed to giving customers is no longer adequate. This is not necessarily because they are doing a poorer job than before, but rather because new competitors in the global market have changed the definition of what constitutes a good job.

In many cases the new competitors have been able to offer customers something different in terms of products and services that are more innovative, of higher quality, more tailored to their preferences, and less costly. Customer expectations are always expanding, and satisfaction tends to be a fleeting phenomenon. A company's survival and success now depend on its ability to **continuously improve** products and services to meet and exceed customer expectations. The ability of a company to meet new challenges posed by customers in world competitive markets is the qualifying criterion for being a **world-class organization.**

Continuous improvement is measured in terms of producing things better, faster, and cheaper and being more agile. If you run a successful hamburger establishment, you can be assured that someone is trying to produce a hamburger that is better than yours in terms of taste, price, speed and courtesy of delivery, and any other way that will draw customers.

To improve products and services it is necessary to go far beyond the products and services themselves; it is necessary to examine and improve the materials and basic processes intrinsic to them. Continuous improvement is thus synonymous with **continuous process improvement.**

This entire book is, effectively, about improvement, and this chapter sets the stage for everything to follow. We start with a discussion of continuous improvement and, in particular, with what it means to be continuous. Two kinds of improvement, incremental and innovation, are examined, as is the role both play in competitive operations strategy. The importance of actively involving employees in improvement efforts as well as the parts played by particular improvement approaches such as PDCA, value analysis, and reengineering, are also discussed. A supplement to the chapter reviews seven basic problem-solving tools as applied to an example improvement project.

CONTINUOUS IMPROVEMENT AS TACTICS AND STRATEGY[1]

A premise of continuous improvement is that processes and products can be improved without limit. Yet we know intuitively there must be limits, if only because improvements require resources and resources are limited. Part of the continuous improvement process involves knowing where to direct improvement efforts so they contribute the greatest good. This means being able to identify the parts of the system that contribute most to increasing product quality and meeting customer requirements, as well as the ability to recognize when a product, component, or process is already at the level where it is as good as it can get.

INCREMENTAL IMPROVEMENT: KAIZEN

The concept of limits to economical improvement can be described in terms of the S-curve shown in Figure 2.1. The curve shows the relationship between the effort or resources to improve something and the incremental result of that effort. The kind of improvement represented by the S-curve is called **incremental improvement,** which is the process of making something better through the accumulation of small, piecemeal improvements, one at a time.

FIGURE 2.1

The S-curve of incremental improvement.

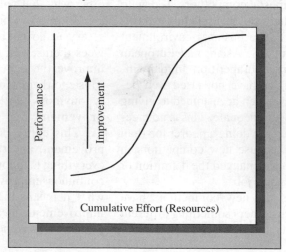

At first progress is slow, hence, the early part of the improvement curve is nearly flat. As the object under scrutiny is better understood, however, learning accelerates and improvement consequently occurs at an accelerated rate. This idea that great improvement eventually comes from a series of small, incremental gains is the Japanese concept of **kaizen.** Accordingly, employees throughout the organization patiently work to continually improve processes in which they are engaged. In contrast, people in US organizations and especially top managers are less patient and quickly abandon improvement opportunities when the return seems less immediate.

Incremental improvement can, over time, lead to substantial improvement, although, as the S-curve illustrates, at some point that improvement will slow. Regardless of the magnitude of effort, the gain in improvement will get smaller and smaller. Only so much can be done economically to improve something, and after that any

---

CASE IN POINT: LCD Technology at RCA and Sharp

A good example of kaizen and of US and Japanese approaches to improvement is Hedrick Smith's discussion of the history of the liquid crystal display (LCD).[2] In 1968 RCA unveiled a new technological discovery, the LCD, a flat display screen that promised to replace cumbersome cathode-ray tubes in TV sets. To transform the new technology into useful products, however, would take years of patient developmental work and considerable financial investment, neither of which RCA's corporate culture supported. In fact, RCA at the time was diversifying into areas like car rental, carpeting, and TV dinners because these provided quick returns, despite taking away funds from RCA's core business, electronics. Unlike founder David Sarnoff, who appreciated technology and pushed for innovation, RCA was at this time run by marketing and financial people who cared more about corporate stability and short-term financial success than industry leadership. After a half-hearted effort at producing LCD wristwatches and calculators, RCA sold its LCD patents to the Japanese in 1973.

Contrast this with what happened at Sharp in Japan. Sharp, a modest-sized radio and TV producer dwarfed by RCA, saw a market niche in lightweight, energy-efficient LCD pocket calculators. It put $200 million into development, and the calculators became a market success. Profits from the calculators provided Sharp a springboard into other LCD and flat-panel display applications. Ultimately Sharp invested $1 billion in developing LCD technology and building plants to manufacture flat-panel displays.

Today LCD technology is everywhere, not only in calculators but also in watches, industrial gauges, clocks, portable color TVs, computers, medical imaging systems, automobile dashboards, and aircraft cockpit controls, to mention a few applications. By the 1990s, Sharp and 18 other Japanese firms controlled 95% of the world market for flat-panel displays. IBM, Apple, and other US manufacturers have become so dependent on LCDs that the Japanese have opened assembly plants in the US to avoid tariffs. In 1994 flat-panel displays and associated electronics drove a $4–$5 billion-a-year industry, projected to rise to *$15–$20 billion a year* by the year 2000.

As for RCA? All it got from the LCD was what it sold the patents for—$2 million.

improvement comes at great expense. The S-curve concept of improvement has universal applicability, regardless of the product or process.

In the past many organizations tended to ignore the notion of improvement. Today, driven by global competition, the significance of improvement is generally recognized. For many companies, process improvement efforts have put them in the mid-range of the S-curve, meaning great gains are being achieved with only moderate effort. Changes to improve work setup are an example. Until the last decade, most companies gave little attention to the time required to changeover and set up equipment and processes. Now many firms are engaged in setup reduction projects and are experiencing dramatic results in terms of improved setup methods and reduced setup times. But as they continue to try to improve the setup for a given operation or process, eventually they will reach a threshold—a point at which it becomes very hard to achieve further time reduction.

IMPROVEMENT THRESHOLD

What happens when the improvement threshold is reached? Does improvement cease? For an existing technology, product, or process, the answer is yes, at least for now, because the cost of further gains becomes just too great.

There is a limit to the amount of incremental improvement possible at practical expense. This is important to note because it means that if further improvement is necessary for the organization to survive, then something new and perhaps radically different is necessary.

INNOVATION IMPROVEMENT

Once the limit is reached, higher performance is achieved only by adopting a new technology or new way (something fundamentally different and innovative, something which does not have that performance limit). This new way appears as a separate, new S-curve, shown as the curve on the right in Figure 2.2. Figure 2.2 illustrates the difference between two approaches to improvement. The continuous, incremental approach is represented by a single S-curve; the **innovative** approach is represented by the jump from one S-curve to the next. For example, vacuum tubes, propeller-driven airplanes, and the open-hearth method of making steel represent three technologies that over decades were incrementally improved. Eventually each technology reached its limit, and little could be gained through additional improvement efforts. The big leap in performance came when these technologies were eclipsed by the introduction of three entirely new technologies: semiconductors, jet engines, and continuous steel casting, respectively. In terms of performance these new technologies far surpassed the old ones. Each became the focus of incremental improvement, and each is now well along its own S-curve, someday to be eclipsed by still newer technologies.

Figure 2.2 also suggests that although the initial change from the old to the new might require substantial initial effort (remember Sharp's investment in flat-panel

FIGURE 2.2

Incremental improvement, each curve; innovation improvement, jump from lower curve to higher curve.

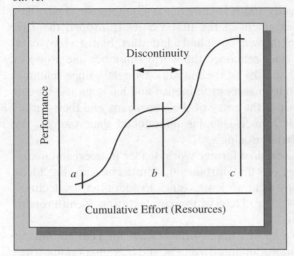

FIGURE 2.3

Systemwide improvement through improvements in components.

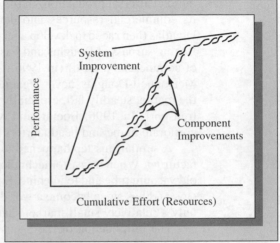

development), once the new way has been adopted, incremental improvements thereafter might be achieved for about the same amount of effort as was needed for the old way ($c - b = b - a$).

The leap from one curve to the next is also the way improvements happen within a given *system*. Figure 2.3 shows how a system—product or process—is moved along its S-curve by virtue of aggregate improvements among its components. Each component is incrementally improved and may even be replaced by new, better ways. Eventually, however, simply improving components is not enough to elevate the performance of the system so the entire system must be replaced. A form of innovation improvement called **process reengineering** will be discussed later.

MAKING THE LEAP

Between the S-curves of two succeeding technologies there is a *discontinuity*. This is the time between crossing over from the old way to the new way. Referring back to Figure 2.2, during the discontinuity the performance of the new technology is less than the old one. Any technology will be at its lowest performance level at the time it is first introduced; the trick is to resist ignoring it because of the initial poor showing.

Many businesses fail to appreciate a new technology's potential for making the current technology obsolete, and at the same time are so caught up with current products or processes that they fail to know that the limit to incremental improvement has been reached. LCDs are one example, commercial jets are another. Early jet aircraft were inefficient and did not perform as well as the best propeller-driven airplanes, so some engine and airframe manufacturers tended to ignore jets in favor of further development of propeller technology. It took only a few years, however, for jet technology to move far ahead of propeller technology, and companies not already involved in the transition were put at a serious competitive disadvantage. Boeing, for example, had always trailed far behind Douglas, until then the world leader in commercial aircraft production. In the early 1950s Boeing made a bold move: it put all of its commercial resources into development of the first US jet transport, the 707. Douglas then raced to develop a jet of its own, but it had a late start. In just a few years, Boeing surpassed Douglas and has since remained the world's number one producer of commercial aircraft (in 1996 it had 70% of the market). Douglas, since renamed McDonnell-Douglas, never regained its market prominence and has seen its share of the market steadily fall, especially since the entry of the Europeans and their Airbus transport. In 1996, Boeing and McDonnell-Douglas announced their merger, the corporate name and headquarters being Boeing's.

A similar misstep happened to Zenith, a former world leader in television manufacturing. When transistor technology was first introduced, Zenith chose to cling to the old vacuum tube and fell behind. Sony meanwhile was quick to adopt the new technology, and has since become a world leader in television manufacturing. Zenith retains only a relatively small market share.

The ramification of the S-curve and its upper limit is that for **real** continuous improvement, there must be both innovation improvement and incremental improvement. At the corporate level, this means strong, continued commitment to research and development for new products, processes, and their components; at the middle management and shop-floor worker levels, it means an openness to new and bold ideas and a willingness to try new ways of doing things. That an organization is comfortably ensconced in a continuous improvement effort does not mean it will excel or even survive, particularly if its efforts involve only incremental improvement of existing products and processes. When the S-curve begins to flatten out, the technology of the particular product or process is ripe for innovation. Whoever takes first advantage of that opportunity will gain the competitive lead.

Of course, knowing which innovations to pursue and which to ignore is not an easy decision, and even large investment in promising technology is no assurance a new technology will meet expectations. For example, in the 1970s the Japanese auto manufacturer Mazda began production of the Wankel engine, which functioned on the rotary principle and was a marked change from the traditional, reciprocating engine. After only a few years Mazda had to cease production because of poor market response, problems with excess pollution, and major difficulties with the engine's rotary seals.

While it is not necessary to draw an actual S-curve for a given product or process, it is important to be aware of the product's or process's approximate position on the curve. For each improvement effort, the degree of improvement achieved for the effort expended should be estimated. As marginal improvements get harder to achieve, that might suggest that the technology is moving into the latter flat portion of the S-curve, in which case it could be time to cut back on incremental efforts and seriously concentrate on finding a whole new approach. Knowing where competitors stand on the S-curve is important too, because the farther along they are on the S-curve, the more likely they are working to make the technological leap. There is little sense in trying to incrementally improve an existing way when the competition is well along in developing a new way that will make it obsolete.

Even after making the technological leap, it is essential to immediately begin incremental improvement to remain competitive. This is necessary because today the process called **reverse engineering** whereby one company takes apart another's invention, analyzes it, copies it, and improves it has become a high art. Though inventions and intellectual property are protected through laws and the efforts of groups such as the World Intellectual Property Organization (a United Nations agency), reverse engineering often gets around such protection. Personal computers are an example. Most components are off-the-shelf, and only the central processing unit (CPU) is patented. By studying the CPU, a competitor can learn its functions and design one that functions virtually the same without violating laws. The point is that simply being the originator of an idea or the first to introduce it does not guarantee that the inventing company will retain any advantage. The leader will be the company that successfully improves and commercializes the invention.

Manufacturing **process improvement** is likewise important because it is not enough to originate an idea for a product, you have to be able to control the manufacture of a product to be able to control the market for it. For example, the US firm Ampex invented the VCR but never developed the manufacturing and marketing means to support it. It sold the technology to Sony, which, of course, became a major manufacturer in a current multibillion-dollar-a-year industry.

The improvement S-curve has relevance to processes at every level of the organization—individual tasks, manufacturing subprocesses and technology, and service processes. No matter what the nature of the task or process (assembling a product, responding to a customer complaint, maintaining a piece of machinery, arranging the layout of a plant or office, or switching over equipment), the dynamics of the S-curve apply. That means virtually everything about an organization's operations can be improved through either incremental or innovative means.

IMPROVEMENT AS STRATEGY

Hayes and Pisano[3] define **manufacturing strategy** as creating the operating capabilities a company will need for the future. Given that improvement alternatives are the stepping stones to achieving long-term organizational goals, then the continuous improvement process should be considered as a strategic tool. Every technology possesses capabilities, though only certain capabilities are essential or relevant to an organization's competitive success. Thus, any decisions about whether to continue improving an existing technology or to work on new ones (and if so, which ones) should be based on assessment of the capabilities each will provide and the importance of those capabilities to competitiveness.

As an illustration, consider a company that is pondering ways to achieve the long-term goals of reduced production lead times and inventories. One way is to work with the existing production process while continuously striving to reduce batch sizes. Another is to adopt a computerized MRP system to improve production scheduling

FIGURE 2.4

Performance improvement opportunities of alternative manufacturing strategies.

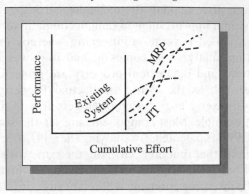

and ordering. A third way is to convert to a JIT pull production system. All three options will impact lead times and inventories, although the similarity stops there. The first option can be started immediately and will cost little. The other two will be very costly, and actual improvements will not be seen until much later. Without fundamental changes to the production planning and control system, improvements in inventory and lead-time reduction will likely soon hit the limit, whereas for the latter two options the opportunity for incremental improvement will likely continue for some time. This concept is shown in Figure 2.4 (the curves are only illustrative; actual shapes and relative positions depend on the nature of the business, product, and manufacturing processes).

The opportunities and capabilities afforded by each alternative must be assessed in terms beyond immediate criteria. Reduced lead times and inventories are one set of goals, but certainly there are others, and the assessment should point out the alternative that best provides capabilities necessary to reach most or all of those goals. Incremental improvement in MRP happens through improvements in data accuracy, shop-floor organization and control procedures, and computer software. Incremental improvement in JIT happens through continuous improvements in setup times, machine maintenance, quality checking, and problem solving and participation by workers on the shop floor. Each option builds different capabilities, and the best option is the one that develops capabilities that the firm will need to capture and maintain a unique position among competitors.

Consider a final example, the decision about whether to try to reduce costs and improve product quality from an existing manufacturing process or to cease producing the product and outsource it to a supplier. Although a reputable supplier could provide immediate improvement in terms of reduced costs and increased quality, by ceasing production the company will relinquish certain skills and capabilities associated with both product design and manufacturing. It will be difficult or impossible to later

FIGURE 2.5

Transfer of technology from outsourcing of production.

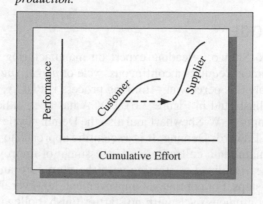

recapture and improve upon these capabilities. If those capabilities represent a core technology of the company, that is, something unique about the company and fundamental to its competitive position, or are something that customers identify with the company, then outsourcing can pose a threat to the company's very survival.

Just as outsourcing diminishes the capabilities of the company to improve upon the outsourced product, it increases the capabilities of the supplier to improve both the product design and its manufacture. These days, product quality and customer service dictate close customer–supplier relations, and through such relations some or much knowledge associated with the product gets transferred to the supplier. Since the supplier already has the capability to make the product, the supplier will be the one to improve upon that capability, and potentially, also to develop a design capability as well. With both design and manufacturing capability, a determined supplier can eventually move out on its own and become a new, formidable competitor in the marketplace. This transfer of technology is illustrated in Figure 2.5. Such a transfer is what happened in television manufacturing where, at one time, Asian firms such as Toshiba served solely as suppliers to US manufacturers. Today Asian firms not only make just about all US-brand TVs, but they also make their own brand and, of course, they are no longer simply suppliers. Outsourcing, like other ways to achieve improvement, must be viewed for the long-term improvement opportunities it affords or precludes.

FINDING AND IMPLEMENTING IMPROVEMENTS

Several methodologies have been developed as guides to the continuous improvement process. This section begins by addressing the PDCA cycle, a somewhat generic methodology for identifying and diagnosing problems. The section also considers two other examples of improvement approaches; *value analysis* (for incremental improvement) and *process reengineering* (for innovation improvement). Later chapters will consider other improvement methodologies such as quality function deployment, and other practices for improvement such as JIT methods for eliminating waste.

PDCA CYCLE

Shigeo Shingo, a leading expert on manufacturing improvement, has said that improvement requires a continuous cycle of *perceiving* and *thinking*.[4] A structured way to apply this perceiving–thinking process is **PDCA,** which stands for plan-do-check-act (illustrated in Figure 2.6). PDCA has been called the **Shewhart cycle,** after its developer A. W. Shewhart and also the Deming cycle after the person who popularized it, W. Edwards Deming. It is a scientific approach to improvement because it employs systematic data collection and assessment of improvement alternatives. The process can be visualized as starting with the **plan step** and moving clockwise through the other steps. For continuous improvement, however, it is better to visualize the process as a continuous cycle with no start or finish. Following is a description of the steps in PDCA.

Plan Step

This step results in a strategy or plan to accomplish improvement. It has four substeps:

1. *Collecting data.* Improvement is always instigated by dissatisfaction, the perception that a problem exists or that things are not as good as they might be. Before seeking a solution, the existence of the problem should be substantiated and its root causes should be identified. Data collection involves systematic observation, documentation, and analysis of data for purposes of verifying, understanding, and getting to the root cause of a problem.

2. *Defining the problem.* Once the source of dissatisfaction is understood and its causes are known, the problem can be defined unambiguously. Clear problem definition is a necessary precursor to solving the problem.

FIGURE 2.6

PDCA problem-solving cycle.

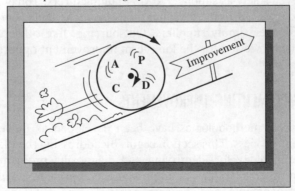

3. *Stating the goal.* A goal is specified as the desired target of the improvement. For example, the goal might be elimination of a particular waste, a more efficient way of doing a task, a more pleasurable environment, etc. The goal should contain acceptable upper and lower limits (levels of improvement), the criticality of achieving the limits (nice to have versus necessary at all costs), and a deadline. The goal must be clear, well defined, and agreed upon by everyone working toward it. In keeping with the philosophy of continuous improvement, the goal is only provisional. Once it is close at hand, the goal may be redefined to be at a higher level or have a different focus or scope. Incremental improvement of a product or process is achieved through this stepwise approach of ever-more ambitious goals.

4. *Solving the problem.* Almost any improvement can be reached by various means. In solving the problem, multiple ways of achieving the goal should be considered as well as the costs and benefits of each.

The end of the plan stage is a strategy or plan to accomplish improvement. The plan includes a clear definition of the problem, the goal, the solution, and the method of implementing the solution. The final method of implementation chosen should describe the specific steps to be taken, people responsible, a schedule, deadlines, and sometimes a budget.

Do Step

This is the implementation of the plan. Plans that call for wide-ranging changes are typically implemented on a piecemeal or trial basis. The implementation and resulting changes are closely monitored and the plan is modified according to circumstances. Weak or ineffective portions of the plan are sifted out and only beneficial parts are retained.

Check Step

Data are collected following implementation and are analyzed to assess resulting changes and to see to what extent improvement goals are being accomplished. Side effects or adverse consequences of changes are noted.

Act Step

In the final step, actions are taken based upon results from the check step. If the changes as planned were successful, they are retained (at least provisionally, until different improvement goals or better procedures are called for). If the changes were successful but were implemented in only a limited way, then they are expanded. If the changes failed, they are scrutinized to see why and to determine what else can be done instead. Changes that caused adverse consequences are revised to reduce the consequences (the idea of total improvement) and are retried. Of course, even when changes as planned appear completely successful, continuous improvement mandates that eventually the action be reviewed again and replaced in favor of something better.

The PDCA process can be used by anyone. It offers the greatest benefit when applied by teams (e.g., shop workers, specialists from cross-functional areas, and managers) because that broadens the inputs to analysis and builds organizational commitment to results. Like most things about continuous improvement, PDCA should be an ongoing process, so therefore its success depends on organizational acceptance and integration.

FIVE-WHY PROCESS

Whenever confronted with a problem, employees at Toyota are conditioned to ask the question "why" five times. The intent of this procedure is to assure that the root causes and not merely superficial symptoms are corrected.

For example, suppose the observed problem is defective parts:

1. *Why* are the parts defective?

Answer: The machines on which they are produced do not maintain the proper tolerance.

2. *Why* do the machines not maintain the proper tolerance?

Answer: The operators of the machines are not properly trained.

3. *Why* are the operators not properly trained?

Answer: The operators keep quitting and have to be replaced with new ones, so the operators are always novices.

4. *Why* do operators keep quitting?

Answer: Working at the machines is repetitive, uncomfortable, and boring.

5. *Why* is the work at the machines repetitive, uncomfortable, and boring?

Answer: The tasks in the operator's job were designed without considering their effect on human beings.

Now, given that answer 5 is taken as the root cause of the problem, a solution can be suggested: Redesign the job so that it is less uncomfortable and more fulfilling for the operator.

In most situations, real problems and root causes are obscured by apparent problems. Notice in the above example how different the solution might have been if the cause had been taken to be the answer to question 2, 3, or 4 instead of 5. Asking "*why*" repeatedly, possibly more than five times, directs the focus toward real causes so problems can be resolved permanently.

The five-why process is not necessarily as simple or straightforward as the example suggests. The real problem is often far afield from the problem as initially perceived, and answering each *why* requires considerable, thoughtful analysis.

VALUE ANALYSIS/VALUE ENGINEERING

Value analysis/value engineering are techniques for assessing the *value* content of the elements of a product or process. Value is what people are willing to pay for something. Since the price customers are willing to pay for something cannot exceed (by much) the value they perceive in it, the cost of the elements involved in the product's components and its manufacture cannot exceed the value contributed by those elements.

The terms value analysis (VA) and value engineering (VE) are sometimes used interchangeably, but the former usually refers to ongoing improvements, especially of processes, while the latter usually refers to first-time design and engineering of a product or process. Both VE and VA emphasize value added by focusing on the ability of product elements (product components) or process elements (steps and procedures) to add to a product's worth in terms of customer expectations. All production and support activities add to a product's cost, but not all add to its value. In similar fashion, all components add to the cost of a product, but they do not all effectively contribute to its functional value. VA and VE look at how much value something adds compared to the cost it adds.

For example, Canon, manufacturer of cameras, copiers, optics, and computers, uses a VE approach to improvement throughout the entire product development and manufacturing life cycle:[5]

> *0 (zero) look VE.* Functional analysis of product components is performed in the early stages of product development. Functional analysis involves setting product objectives and requirements as well as defining the functions each component in the product must serve to achieve the objectives. Cost targets for components are established.
> *First look VE.* Functional analyses are performed during the product design, planning, and trial product stages. The design of the product and its constituent components are improved to narrow the differences between cost targets and present conditions.
> *Second look VE.* Ongoing cost-reduction analyses are performed during manufacturing for the remainder of the product life cycle.

Though our discussion will emphasize VA, the concepts and process for VE are much the same.

Value analysis often focuses on those activities that **transform** materials from one form to another. More generally, VA seeks to define those activities wherein ineffectiveness or failure could jeopardize the company's existence. Rather than simply minimizing the labor content in a product, VA seeks to maximize the contributions (value-added effort) of people in an organization.

A Value Analysis Procedure

The VA approach typically involves a sequence of five phases: **information gathering**, **analysis**, **creation**, **evaluation**, and **implementation**.[6] (Notice the overlap between this approach and the PDCA cycle.) Ideally, this sequence is carried out by a cross-functional team with representatives from marketing, product design, manufacturing engineering, procurement, production planning, and finance.

First, in the **information-gathering** phase, data are collected about the components or elements of the system being scrutinized (a product, process, or some aspect thereof). Information about the cost of the elements, their requirements, and features (functions, attributes, why they are included, etc.) is collected. The worth of each component is estimated based upon the least expensive known alternative to it. Given the worth and cost of each component, the components having the highest cost-to-worth ratio are identified. (As an alternative, components can be rank-ordered in descending cost, and the highest-cost components become the focus of analysis.) These are the components wherein the most could be gained through elimination or substitution with other, lower-cost components. The main emphasis of value analysis is not simply to cut cost but to find alternatives that add the same value for lower cost or that increase the value added for about the same cost.

Next, during the **analysis** phase, the chosen element (component in a product, step in a process, or the product itself) is studied for the function it serves. Whether a step, component, or product, the question is "What does it do?" If the element is a step in a process, the answer should explain why the step is there. If it is a component in a product, the answer should explain what function the component serves in the product. If it is a product, the answer should explain why the product works and why the customer buys it. Another question, "What *should* it do?" may also be asked. Answers to these questions lead to ideas about ways to improve processes/products or suggest the need for entirely new processes/products. Other questions include "Do we need it? Can something else do it better? What are alternatives to doing the same function? Can we make it better (or faster, or cheaper)? Can someone else make it better (or faster, etc.)?"

In the third or **creation** phase, ideas are generated for alternative, possibly better ways of serving the same function as the element under scrutiny. Examples include simplifying the design, replacing nonstandard with standard parts, and using less-expensive materials.

Then, costs and the ability of alternatives to fulfill the required functions are analyzed in the **evaluation phase.** The alternative which seems to have the best chance of fulfilling the function, but at lower cost, is chosen as the replacement. In some cases it is discovered that the element can be eliminated because the function it serves can be served as well by other, existing elements, or that the function it serves is not necessary for fulfilling the purpose of the process or product.

In the final phase, **implementation,** the selected alternative is adopted. The results are monitored for costs and to ensure that the function is being well served by the new element. Data are retained for later analysis and repetition of the process.

The following examples illustrate this approach.

Example   1:   VA for Improvement of an Existing Product

A team of engineers devotes 80 labor hours studying a product and finds the following:

1. Among all components of the product, one, a metal part, can readily be substituted by a plastic part. The substitution will save $0.15 per unit.

2. One of the drilled holes in the frame is a holdover from an earlier model and is unnecessary. Removing the hole saves one step and $1.10 in labor and overhead cost for each unit.

The team then spends 20 more labor hours making changes and performing tests on one unit to ensure that its functioning, reliability, and quality have not been reduced. They discover that by eliminating the hole, the product is somewhat strengthened; this is an important marketing feature that will enable the company to increase the unit sales price by $1.00.

Suppose also that currently the product sells for $45 per unit, costs $22 per unit to manufacture, and sells at a rate of 50,000 units per month. The per-unit cost savings and value-added improvement will be $0.15 + $1.10 + $1.00 = $2.25. Without the change, monthly profit is ($45 − $22) × 50,000 = $1,150,000; with the change, monthly profit is ($45 − $22 + $2.25) × 50,000 = $1,212,500.

If the total salary for the team is $60/hr and if the cost of the VA process is primarily the team's salary, then the VA cost is 100 hrs × $60 = $6000. In summary, for a *one-time* cost of $6000, the *monthly* improvement will be $62,500.

Example   2:   VA for Improvement of an Existing Process

Two engineers each devote 40 hours to studying the parts on a product. For two of the parts shown in Figure 2.7 they discover the following:

FIGURE 2.7

Two parts used in the same product.

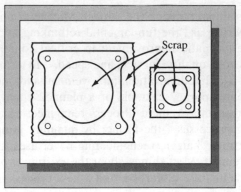

1. Both parts are punched out one at a time on a punch press from the identical kind and gauge of sheet metal.

2. The cost of the sheet metal is $0.23 per large part and $0.14 per small part. Metal left over from the process is sold as scrap; $0.05 is recovered per large part and $0.03 is recovered per small part.

3. The outside dimensions of the small part indicate that it could be produced from scrap punched from the center of the large part.

The engineers each spend another 40 hours investigating how scrap from the large part can be used for the small part. Since the center piece of the large part is shaped differently from the piece of metal from which each small part is currently formed, a new die set must be designed and that will cost $4000. However, in using scrap from the large part, the step of cutting sheet metal into right-size pieces for the small part can be eliminated. That step is estimated to cost about $0.30 per part. Recovery on scrap from both the large and small parts produced from a single piece of metal is estimated at $0.04 per unit. The material cost savings per unit will thus be

$$(0.23 - 0.05) + (0.14 - 0.03) - (0.23 - .04) = 0.29 - 0.19 = 0.10.$$

Suppose current demand for the product which uses one each of these parts is 50,000 per year. On an annual basis, the savings from material and the eliminated step will be $50,000(0.10 + 0.30) = $20,000$. If the engineering charge is $30 per hour per engineer, then the cost of the VA study and the die-set redesign will be $80(2 \times $30) + $4000 = $8,800$. Thus, for a *one time* cost of $8,800, the *annual* savings will be $20,000.

The second example illustrated analysis of an existing process. When the same kind of VA/VE analysis is performed for a proposed process and is in conjunction with a new product design, it is a step in **concurrent engineering** and part of a methodology known as **design for manufacture/assembly;** these two topics are covered in Chapter 12.

Though the potential for improvement in products and processes is often subtle and difficult to identify, the message of VA/VE is this: the reward for inquisitiveness in general and the investigation of existing practices in particular is improvement.

PROCESS REENGINEERING

In the seminal book on the subject, Michael Hammer and James Champy define **reengineering** as "the fundamental rethinking and redesign of business processes to achieve dramatic improvement in critical contemporary measures of performance such as cost, quality, service, and speed."[7] In terms of the improvement S-curve, that sounds a lot like innovation improvement, and, indeed, reengineering is probably the best contemporary example of a planned change process for achieving sweeping, innovative improvement. Process reengineering and kaizen are counterparts in improving processes—the former by quantum jumps, the latter by small, methodical steps. Unlike kaizen, reengineering never uses the existing process as the basis for improvement. Most things about the existing process (rules, procedures, structures, and systems) are discarded, and a new process is invented from scratch to replace them.[8]

Hammer and Champy argue that information technology is the *essential enabler* in reengineering; that is, it permits companies to reengineer processes in ways that otherwise would likely be impossible. For instance, because of information technology

- Field representatives can send and receive information wherever they are (with wireless data and computer systems).
- People and things can be located (with automatic identification and tracking systems).
- Plans can be revised instantaneously (with high-power computing capabilities).
- Information can be displayed everywhere needed (with shared databases).

- Centralized data can be decentralized (with telecommunication networks).
- Decision making can become part of everyone's job (with databases and decision support software).

While technology is decidedly not the source or focus of reengineering change, it is a primary means for breaking rules that govern old processes. For competitive advantage, information technology applications are not something a company can simply purchase from others, because by the time an application becomes commercially available it no longer offers competitive advantage. Companies must closely follow emergent information technology to determine how they can use it in the future to reengineer processes.

REENGINEERING FUNDAMENTALS

Reengineering emphasizes process simplification and elimination of non-value-added steps. The following results of *reengineered* business processes are common:

- Several jobs are combined into one.
- Steps in the process are performed in natural, linear sequence.
- Workers in the process make decisions as part of their job.
- Work is performed where it makes the most sense in order to reduce overall process cost and time and to improve overall performance.
- Processes have multiple versions and applications.
- Checks and controls are reduced by examining aggregate patterns rather than individual instances.
- Hybrid centralized/decentralized operations are common.
- Reconciliation is minimized (see the case in point below).

ROLE OF SYSTEMS ANALYSIS

While reengineering projects are usually performed by cross-functional teams, there is argument that reengineering could be more effective and innovative if the teams included systems analysts and operations researchers, that is, people familiar with the tools and philosophy of systems design, quantification, and assessment.[9] Greg Hansen[10] makes the case with an example from Hammer and Champy's book of IBM's credit-approval process. The process took an average of 6 days and sometimes as long as 20 days per approval, though only 90 minutes of it was value added and the rest was time wasted in hand offs and transactions between departments. An IBM team reengineered the process to use a computerized assistance system to eliminate most hand-off time and reduced the average to 4 hours per approval. Though the new system is a large improvement, as Hansen points out, the question remains, "Why 4 hours if the value-added time in the process is only 90 minutes?" Hansen shows that through system modeling and simulation it is easy to consider ways to reduce steps and get the time down to about 1 hour.

CASE IN POINT: Reengineering Accounts Payable at Ford[11]

The accounts payable department at Ford, which processes bills and pays suppliers, had over 500 employees. Executives visited the Japanese auto manufacturer Mazda (in which Ford owns a 25% interest) and found only five people in its accounts payable department. (Mazda is a smaller company, but no way could that alone account for the hundredfold difference in personnel.) The reality was that Ford's procurement process was bloated and wasteful. Specifically, whenever a purchase order went out, a copy went to accounts payable; when the supplier sent a shipment, the invoice went to accounts payable; and when the shipment arrived at Ford, a copy of the receiving papers also went to accounts payable. The receiving papers had to be matched against the invoice and purchase order. If everything matched, the supplier was sent a check; if not, the source of the mismatch had to be determined, which took a lot of time, held up payment to suppliers, and generated much paperwork.

The new, reengineered procurement process eliminates invoices and mismatched documentation. When a purchase order is being completed, information is simultaneously entered into a database. Upon shipment arrival at the receiving dock, a clerk retrieves the purchase order on a computer terminal. If the shipment and purchase order match, the clerk enters acceptance into the system, which automatically issues a payment check to the vendor. If the shipment and purchase order do not match, the shipment is sent back to the vendor. The accounts payable department now has 125 people.

→ Part of Hansen's point is that a truly innovative system should do *better* than merely mimic the best-possible case for the existing system. The other part is that reengineering requires a systems perspective. That makes sense, for unlike small changes in an existing process where results can readily be understood piecemeal, a process that starts from scratch with a radical new design cannot be understood without a broader, systems perspective. Kaizen relies heavily (often entirely) on people within the process to make suggestions and implement improvements. For reengineering that involvement remains important, but as a source of input data and ideas, and for gaining commitment to the new process. It is not a substitute, however, for modeling and experimentation to optimize the new process design.

EMPLOYEE INVOLVEMENT

TRADITIONAL, EXPERTS-ONLY APPROACH

Opportunity for improvement is everywhere, and you do not have to be a genius to find it. Still, many organizations operate as if improvement is solely the business of managers, consultants, analysts and engineers. The effect of this kind of behavior is to all but quash improvement. When employees learn that seeking out and suggesting improvements is the sole responsibility of specialists, they will stop looking for places needing improvement. If they see a problem, they won't look for a solution, and if they have a solution, they won't tell anyone. Even if they do tell someone, few will listen because "that's not their job." Organization wide, the "experts-only" approach to improvement preconditions everyone except the experts **not** to think about improvement. Since experts make up only a tiny percentage of all employees (near zero in some cases), the realizable potential for improvement becomes minuscule.

IMPROVEMENT: EVERYONE'S JOB

Rather than being complicated or sophisticated, improvement is often the result of doing something very simple. Afterward, people ask, "Why didn't we do this before?" As methods and examples in this book will show, many improvements are derived from logical analysis and common sense; once the problem has been diagnosed, a solution is easy to find. Contrary to what experts might have us believe, improvement does not always involve advanced technical thinking. In fact, such thinking might actually handicap improvement because it leads to overly complex and elegant solutions instead of simple, mundane solutions that might work better and be more cost-effective.

The most expeditious way to find improvement opportunities is to make improvement seeking part of everyone's job. No matter what the task or situation, the people doing the same tasks day-in and day-out often see improvement opportunities or alternatives that the experts overlook. Only when the alternatives require special in-depth analysis or technical expertise to implement should the experts be called in.

OPPORTUNITY, AUTHORITY, SKILLS, RECOGNITION, RESPECT

One reason that Japan was able to make such significant manufacturing gains post-WWII was because Japanese workers had responsibility for improvement and were trained and coaxed to seek out problems and resolve them. While Japanese managers and engineers were making fundamental changes to production systems (innovative improvement), factory workers were making small, continuous changes to better fit these systems to individual processes and day-to-day operations (incremental improvement).

In general, workers must be given the opportunity and skills to make improvements. If they appear uncaring, disinterested, or unmotivated in searching for improvement, it is because they never were given the opportunity or the organization did something to turn them off. Much like the natural curiosity of children that is often stifled by society and educational systems, workers' natural attitudes about improvement are often repressed by management policies, politics, functional and status barriers, and organizational culture. Once workers' attitudes have been soured by a poorly conceived or misdirected improvement effort, nothing short of a reorganization (if that) will be able to restore their motivation.

Schonberger argues that frontline employees and teams should also be involved, at minimum, in planning improvements for their own jobs, and, ideally, even assist in implementing larger-scale changes and strategic planning. He cites Zytec

Corporation, where one-fifth of the workforce from every area of the company critiques the 5-year strategic plans and translates them into measurable monthly goals for themselves.[12]

Beyond responsibility for improvement, workers must be trained in problem-solving and process improvement analysis tools, such as described in the supplement to this chapter. They must master multiple skills and be able to use all of them. The training must be just-in-time, which means train a little, use the training, train a little more, and so on (this is described in Chapter 4).

A few other principles for involving employees in improvement are giving them ownership over process data (data they record and use themselves to monitor and improve the workplace) and rewarding them in ways commensurate with their contributions (pay, prizes, stocks, job opportunities, public recognition, or a simple thank you). To erase the old distinction between white-collar and blue-collar workers, some companies have abolished the word *worker* or even *employee*. Frontline employees are called associates, and managers and staff are called facilitators. At Electronics Controls Company, anyone caught uttering "employee" is fined $1.[13]

With the entire workforce looking for improvement opportunities, one might think that after a while, regardless of motivation, improvement ideas will be exhausted (the upper right of the S-curve). In all companies, however, products keep changing, and the manufacturing processes too, even if in subtle ways; with each change, new opportunities arise for improvement. Thus, whether instigated on the shopfloor or in the boardroom, improvement opportunities will never cease.

Summary

Kaizen is the Japanese concept of long-term, continual improvement through small, incremental changes made one at a time. Incremental improvement takes patience and the foresight that through dedicated effort, small improvements will accumulate and ultimately result in big gains. The improvement potential of every process and technology is limited either by resources or by physical, natural laws. To continue improvement beyond these limits, it is necessary to innovate, to find a new way of doing things that is not subject to the same physical laws or resource constraints. Continuous improvement of products and processes requires both kinds of improvement—incremental and innovation. That point applies to decisions and actions at *all* levels and processes of an organization.

Because different kinds of processes and technologies offer different capabilities and opportunities for improvement, the continuous improvement concept has strategic implications. Some decisions must be considered in light of their effect on precluding or enhancing a company's ability to improve capabilities important to its long-term competitiveness and survival. In choosing among product and process alternatives, managers must take the long view and think about the opportunities for improvement these alternatives offer.

Finding areas needing improvement takes diligent, systematic effort. The Shewhart cycle, PDCA, is a pragmatic, step-by-step approach for collecting and analyzing data, solving problems, and implementing and following up on solutions. The five-why process is a way to get beyond symptoms and to the root causes of problems. Value analysis and value engineering are approaches to improving a system (product and process) through questioning the value of every component or step in the system. Components or steps with no or questionable value are eliminated, and for the remainder, value-enhancing alternatives are sought.

Process reengineering is a form of innovation improvement wherein the old process is replaced by an entirely different one. The emphasis is on determining the most fundamental, stripped down way for a process to effectively accomplish its purpose. Reengineering often relies on modern information technology to do things truly innovative and uniquely suited to the process at hand.

Potential for improvement is everywhere: the more eyes looking for it, the more likely that that potential will be realized. Improvement in manufacturing processes requires involvement from everyone, particularly shop-floor workers.

Chapter Supplement:

BASIC PROBLEM-SOLVING AND IMPROVEMENT TOOLS

Throughout this book, frequent reference is made to improvement and waste-reduction projects conducted by teams of workers, supervisors, and engineers. These teams rely on systematic data collection and analysis techniques and follow the PDCA procedure. This section outlines these techniques, the so-called **seven basic problem-solving (or improvement) tools,** a set of methods for diagnosing problems, uncovering root causes, and solving problems as the way to improvement. The techniques can be applied universally to any type or level of problem and can be used by shop-floor workers, supervisors, staff members, as well as top executives. Sometimes referred to as the *magnificent seven,* they have been described in detail in numerous books on TQM, quality analysis, and methods improvement.[14] The tools are the check sheet, the histogram, Pareto analysis, the scatter diagram, the process flowchart, cause-and-effect analysis, and the run diagram. The following gives a brief description of each tool by way of an example.

CHECK SHEET

The improvement process begins by collecting data to confirm initial perceptions or to suggest a course of action. The check sheet (also called tally sheet) is where data from observations are recorded and tallied. A check sheet is usually designed to suit a particular purpose, so its content and format will vary depending on the type of data being collected. For example, Figure 2.8 shows a check sheet for keeping track of nine possible types of defects observed during the final inspection of a product: rough edges on the body, loose rivets on the frame, paint problems, distorted handle, misalignment of wheels, missing wheel pin, cracked wheel cap, cracked handle, and miscellaneous.

Care must be taken in designing the check sheet, its categories, terminology, and layout. Terms on the check sheet must have clear meaning; those that are somewhat ambiguous or could be construed in different ways (such as "paint problems") must be operationally defined. What constitutes a defect (e.g., the degree of paint problem) must also be defined (e.g., *any*

Figure 2.8

Check sheet.

| Date | Jan. 27 | | Product | R2-D2 |
| Shift | 1 | | Operator/Inspector | Himmelman |

Defect	Tally	Total
Rough edges on body	II	2
Loose rivets on frame	II	2
Paint problems	IIII I	6
Distorted handle	II	2
Misalignment of wheels	IIII II	7
Missing wheel pin	I	1
Cracked wheel cap	II	2
Cracked handle	I	1
Miscellaneous (specify): Chipped trundle	I	1

Total items inspected _____60_____   Total defects | 24

Total items rejected _____9_____

Special data (specify)
    Special instructions: _____

_____

Observations

perceptible amount of paint smudging or only smudging that shows up, say, from a distance of 12 or more inches).

The check sheet and its method of usage should be designed to minimize interobserver subjectivity. Observational results recorded on the check sheet should be the same, no matter who is filling in the sheet. To this end, the observers should be given detailed instructions about how to interpret what they see and how to mark results on the sheet.

HISTOGRAM

The histogram graphically shows the frequency distribution of a variable. Figure 2.9, for example, shows the distribution of total daily defects taken from tally sheets during 31 days of observations. Here, the horizontal scale is divided into intervals that represent the number of defects observed in 1 day; the vertical scale represents the number of days. Each vertical bar

FIGURE 2.9

Histogram with numerical intervals.

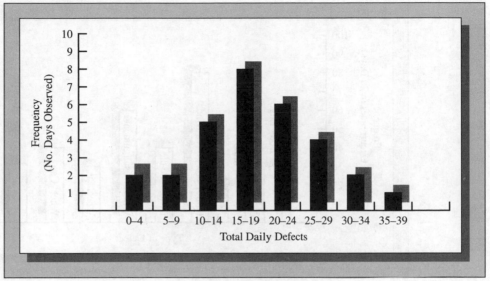

represents the number of days in which a given range of defects was observed. In the figure, the range of each interval is five. For example, the first bar means that for 2 of the 31 days observed, defects numbered from 0 to 4. Histograms such as Figure 2.9 show overall spread or variability of the observations, as well as the mode or the place where observations occur most frequently (15–19 defects per day).

There are a few rules governing the construction of a histogram like Figure 2.9. First, the range of the horizontal scale should extend over the full range of actual, observed values (in the example, number of daily defects observed falls between 0 and 39, the range of the scale). Also, the intervals must be of equal width (in Figure 2.9 the interval is five defects). Finally, there must not be too many or too few intervals (the data should be aggregated within intervals of size that allow the distribution of the data to be clearly shown).

Though the horizontal scale on the histogram typically utilizes numerical intervals, it can also represent nonnumerical classes or categories. For example, the histogram in Figure 2.10 shows the distribution of types of defects observed over four 5-day workweeks. There is no particular arrangement to the classes shown on the horizontal scale; in Figure 2.10 they appear in the same order as they are listed in the check sheet in Figure 2.8. But one thing Figure 2.10 does reveal is that over the 20-day period the prevailing type of defect is paint-related problems.

Figure 2.11 is another type of histogram; it shows the distribution of paint defects aggregated for each month over the last 6 months. On the horizontal scale the monthly intervals have been time-ordered. The increasing frequency indicates that the number of paint defects is on the increase.

Histograms usually do not suggest causes of variation, nor do they show data variation over time (Figure 2.11 does show variation over time, but only because the horizontal scale uses time-dependent data and happens to be time-sequenced). To better understand relationships among different types of data collected and to find causes of problems, other basic problem-solving tools are needed.

Figure 2.10

Histogram with nonnumerical intervals (classes).

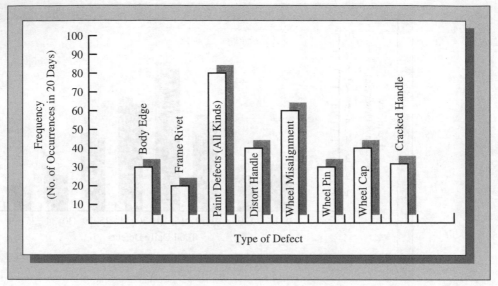

Figure 2.11

Histogram with nonnumerical, time-sequenced intervals.

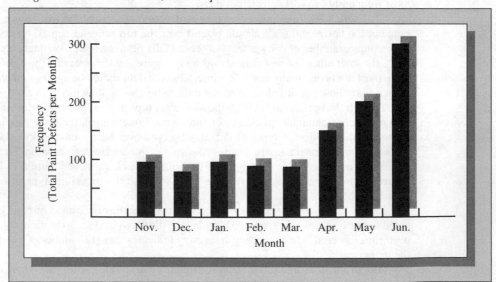

PARETO ANALYSIS

Pareto analysis is a tool for separating the vital few from the trivial many. It is useful for deciding which of several problems to attack first. The kinds of problems that Pareto analysis seeks to identify are those relatively few problems that occur with the greatest frequency (or account for the biggest dollar loss, result in the greatest number of defects, cause the biggest headaches, etc.). A visual tool used to assist in Pareto analysis is the Pareto chart. The Pareto chart looks like a histogram, except the bars are rank-ordered starting on the left with the bar representing the greatest frequency.

In the example, suppose that to better understand the paint-defect problem, data are collected over several weeks to keep track of the various kinds of paint defects that occur. Figure 2.12 shows the Pareto chart for types of paint defects occurring over 20 consecutive shifts. The figure clearly indicates that the major type of paint defect is paint blurring around

FIGURE 2.12

Pareto diagram with cumulative line.

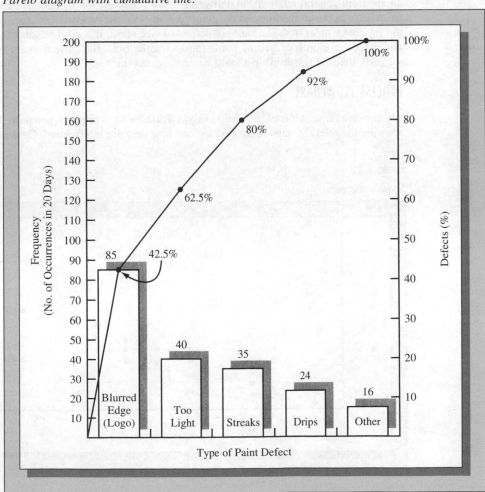

the edges of the product logo. Management considers this a serious problem because the logo is one of the first things that customers notice. If the logo looks sloppy, what must customers think about how the rest of the product is made?

Other information can also be shown on the Pareto chart. The scale on the right of Figure 2.12 shows percentages of total defects; for example, of 200 paint defects, 42.5% are blurred edges, and 20% are too-light paint. The line moving diagonally across the chart shows the cumulative contribution to total paint defects by each category of defects. For example, the first two categories account for 62.5% of all paint defects, the first three categories account for 80%, and so on.

SCATTER DIAGRAM

The scatter diagram is used to expose possible relationships between variables. Suppose in the example that, along with defects, plant temperature at the end of each shift was noted and recorded on the tally sheet. The scatter diagram in Figure 2.13 shows both plant temperature and number of blurry-edge defects occurring in a 40-day observation period. The plot reveals an apparent general relationship between the two variables: the number of paint defects tends to increase as the temperature of the plant goes up. That the two variables seem correlated does not say that temperature is a cause of defects or vice versa. It is even possible that temperature and defects are both caused by some third variable. Still, the pattern in the scatter diagram suggests that the relationship should be investigated further.

PROCESS FLOWCHART

The process flowchart is used to help analyze a process or to pinpoint problems by sequentially showing the relevant steps in the process and how they are interrelated. Care must be taken to

FIGURE 2.13

Scatter diagram.

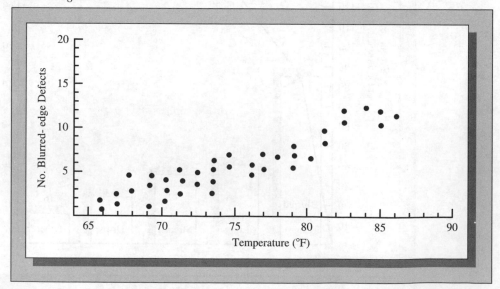

include both value-added and non-value-added activities (work operations, transportation, storage, etc.). Figure 2.14 shows the portion of the paint process that seems relevant to the blurry-edge problem. All of the steps wherein the cause of the problem might exist are shown on the flowchart.

Figure 2.14 is a rather generic type of flowchart, the kind that anyone without specialized technical training might create. Several standardized conventions exist for flowcharting that each result in a different-looking kind of chart. A chart created by, for example, an industrial engineer would look different from one created by a systems analyst. Given the widespread availability of these different standardized charting techniques (format and symbolism used), the problem-solving team should decide in advance which technique would best suit their

FIGURE 2.14

Process flowchart.

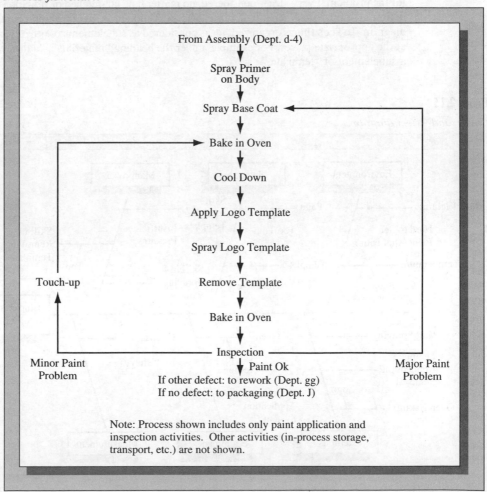

Note: Process shown includes only paint application and inspection activities. Other activities (in-process storage, transport, etc.) are not shown.

needs. Also, the amount of information and detail shown on the chart should depend on the level and depth of information necessary to understand the process.

CAUSE-AND-EFFECT ANALYSIS

Cause-and-effect analysis is used to identify all of the possible contributors (causes) to a given outcome (effect). A diagram called the cause-and-effect diagram (or Ishikawa diagram, after its originator; or fish-bone diagram, because of its appearance) is used in the analysis.[15] Figure 2.15 is such a diagram showing possible causes for blurred edges around the product logo. Causes are typically divided into the categories of manpower, materials, methods, equipment, and environment, though others can be used depending on the problem being studied.

Cause-and-effect analysis for a given problem is usually conducted by a small cross-functional team. The team brainstorms to come up with as many ideas as possible about causes for the problem. Every idea is considered, no matter how far-fetched or ridiculous it might seem at first. As each idea is generated, it is categorized and recorded at the appropriate place on the diagram. To keep things organized, ideas considered as subelements of other ideas are attached at the appropriate places. For example, under the heading "materials", "adhesive" is shown as a subelement of "template."

FIGURE 2.15

Cause-and-effect diagram.

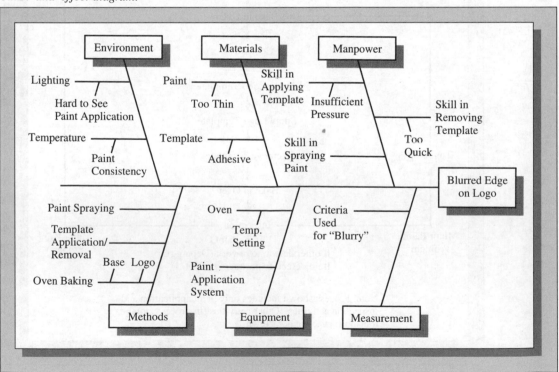

All ideas listed on the diagram are considered as possible root causes of the problem or as candidates for more detailed investigation. The most feasible candidates are identified and scrutinized more closely by using check sheets, Pareto analysis, histograms, process flowcharts, etc.

In the blurry-edge problem, the team was perplexed by the fact that the number of defects seemed to be increasing (Figure 2.11) and that the defects also seemed to increase with temperature (Figure 2.13). They knew that the workers who apply the paint and inspect the product had been doing the same job for years, which would appear to rule out manpower or methods as potential causes. Since the team was unsure about what to do next, they decided to collect more data, but in a different way by using a run diagram.

RUN DIAGRAM[16]

A run diagram shows the results of inspection taken at some prescribed interval (for example, every unit or every tenth unit, or one unit every 10 minutes, etc.). Results are plotted versus time to see if excessive (out-of-ordinary) results or patterns exist. In the example, suppose the attribute being inspected is paint around the edge of the logo and results are classified "0" for no blurring, "1" for some blurring, and "2" for blurring all around. Figure 2.16 shows the results of 100% inspection for two shifts on a given day where each shift produces 60 units. The diagram indicates no clear pattern, which is often the case when the run period is short. Suppose run diagrams with 100% inspection were compiled over a 10-day period and aggregated to give average classification ratings over time. The result, shown in Figure 2.17, suggests a general increase in severity of blurred edges during the day shift and a general decrease during the night shift.

FIGURE 2.16

Run diagram, two shifts.

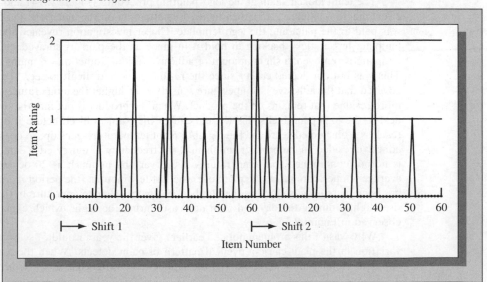

FIGURE 2.17

Ten-day average of run diagrams.

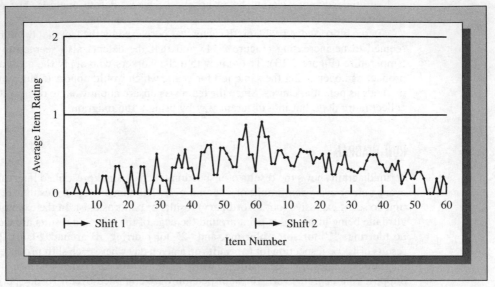

In the example, the problem-solving team took the peculiar pattern in Figure 2.17 as further evidence that neither manpower nor methods were causes of the blurred-edge problem. That left equipment, environment, and materials as likely causes. Environment, in particular, stood out since the scatter diagram (Figure 2.13) had shown a relationship between the number of defects and the temperature.

The team looked again at the logo-painting procedure (Figure 2.14) and the cause-and-effect diagram (Figure 2.15), then focused its attention on the materials. Particular attention was paid to the paint and the logo template. Closer investigation revealed the following: the template has a sticky backing to hold it in place as the paint is sprayed on, and when the template is removed, a slight amount of adhesive residue sometimes remains on the product. This was not considered earlier since the residue is very difficult to see. The team also discovered that the adhesive is temperature sensitive; the higher the temperature of the plant, the more residue that remains on the product. When the product is put into the oven, the residue next to the logo paint melts slightly and causes the paint to bleed before it dries. The visual result is a blurred edge around the logo. As plant temperature goes up, so does the amount of adhesive residue on the product and, hence, the frequency of blurry-edge defects. The factory is not air conditioned and temperatures inside vary by as much as 20 degrees F. Since the average temperature inside the plant over the last few months (the period April through June) has been increasing, so too has the number of defects. Also, temperature in the plant tends to rise slightly during the day and then decrease during the night, which explains the pattern observed in Figure 2.17.

Why wasn't this problem noticed earlier? Over the years wouldn't seasonal temperature variation in the plant cause a cyclical pattern of paint defects? When the team notified the template supplier, they were told that the supplier had switched to a new adhesive in January.

The temperature in the plant at that time was apparently just low enough to cause negligible adhesive residue, and it was not until warmer weather that the problem began to show up. The supplier readily offered to switch to a different adhesive, one that would leave no residue, regardless of the temperature.

As the example suggests, finding the root cause of a problem and solving it can be *sticky!* Still, regardless of the difficulty of the problem, the basic problem-solving tools can be of great aid in collecting and analyzing data, determining root causes, and helping to find solutions.

Questions

1. Explain why change is an essential process for businesses to be competitive. In what ways must businesses keep changing?
2. Compare and contrast incremental improvement with innovation improvement.
3. Explain the concept of the S-curve as it relates to continuous improvement.
4. Give examples of product and process technologies, not mentioned in the chapter, where kaizen led to competitive advantage.
5. Give examples of new product and process technologies not mentioned in the chapter that made older technologies they replaced obsolete, and that led to competitive advantage.
6. Explain the role workers play in continuous improvement.
7. Describe the steps in the Shewhart (or Deming) Cycle.
8. What is the meaning of "Ask why five times"?
9. What are value analysis and value engineering? How are they related to continuous improvement?
10. What is reengineering? Where is reengineering in the context of the S-curve?
11. What are the seven basic problem-solving tools? Describe each.

Problems

1. Analysis of the cost of a product reveals the following sources:

Materials	40%
Direct labor	10%
Overhead and administration	50%
	100%

You are considering ways to reduce the cost of this product. Where should you begin?

2. Below is the number of seconds customers have to wait for a service representative. Create a histogram of the data using 4 seconds as the range of each interval (0-3, 4-7, etc.). What do the data indicate?

   7 8 2 8 4 10 5 7 7 15 21 8 18 14 5 15 22 10 6 10

3. A tally of customer complaints shows the following:

Shipping errors	966
Billing errors	2070
Delivery errors	540
Ambiguous charges	9880
Delivery delays	7430

   Construct a Pareto diagram. What do you conclude?

4. A group of machine operators suspect that the machine speed affects the defect rate. To test this they keep track of the number of defects in same-sized batches produced at different machine speeds. The results are as follows:

Machine Speed (rpm)	Number of Defects	Machine Speed (rpm)	Number of Defects
1900	10	2300	9
2450	17	2550	16
1800	12	2150	6
1850	14	1950	7
2000	6	2100	6
2350	15	2400	12
2200	7	2250	7

   Plot a scatter diagram. What does the diagram indicate?

5. The following numbers are from a tally sheet:

   Total deliveries observed: 1860
   Total deliveries with problems: 204

Delivery Problems	Number
1. Late delivery	120
2. Early delivery	12
3. Shipment batch too large	57
4. Shipment batch too small	56
5. Excessive defects in shipment	13
6. Wrong items delivered	4
	262

    a. Create a histogram showing the frequency of problems.

    b. Modify the histogram into a Pareto diagram.

    c. Why is the sum of the delivery problems, 262, greater than the number of deliveries with problems, 204? In addition to the listing of problems shown, what other information about the problems listed should have been gathered? Design a tally sheet to collect information about the delivery problems that would be more useful than the simple listing shown above.

    d. If you wanted to find solutions to delivery problems, where would you begin? What additional data would you collect?

6. Draw a flow diagram for each of the following processes:

    a. Withdrawing money from an ATM machine.

    b. Programming a VCR to record a one-time broadcast.

    c. An entire day spent downhill skiing (include subprocesses like buying lift tickets, renting equipment, going uphill/downhill, returning equipment, etc.).

    d. Any process with which you are familiar.

7. In each of the processes in problem 6, which steps would you concentrate on to improve the overall process. Explain your criteria for improvement, and suggest what you would do to the steps.

8. Consider the following situations:

    i. You are late to work (or school, a meeting, etc.).

    ii. You are painting a ceiling, and paint is dripping on your face.

    iii. Your average grocery bill is twice your neighbor's.

    iv. You make coffee every morning, but it tastes lousy.

    v. A person who doesn't know you, but who's an important business contact, does not return your phone calls.

    vi. You buy a new appliance, and it won't work.

    a. Draw a cause-and-effect (fishbone) diagram.

    b. To solve the problem, explain which of the causes from the diagram in (*a*) you would look at first.

9. Select a simple product (for example a pen, corkscrew, tape dispenser, etc.). Analyze its components and consider for each what it does (function), what it should do, and how it might be modified or replaced to do the same thing for less cost.

10. In a customer service department, the process for handling complaints is as follows: Representatives take complaints over a 12-hour period. The complaints are collected from each phone representative at the end of the day, and the total list is reviewed by the manager early the next morning. The manager sorts the complaint by severity. Severity is determined by the customer's demand for service (immediate or not), and by the nature of the complaint, that is, whether it is (1) a problem that requires an immediate solution and follow-up call, (2) a problem that requires solution and a follow-up call (though delayed is okay), or (3) a situation that can be handled with a letter.

    If the call regards a technical problem, the manager decides which technical specialist is best qualified to handle it, then forwards the complaint to that person. If the complaint is informational and does not involve a problem requiring a technical solution, the manager directs the complaint to a person who prepares a letter thanking the caller for the complaint. In all cases, if the caller *demands* an immediate response (whether the complaint is technical or informational), a copy of the complaint is made and sent to a person who calls back the complainer that day, or as soon as possible. Before she calls back the complainer, if the complaint is about a technical problem, she calls the technical person assigned the problem to determine if a solution is close at hand, and if not, how long it will take. She then calls the customer.

After a technical specialist solves the problem, he phones the customer. For serious problems that require replacement parts, before calling the customer, the specialist contacts the company warranty specialist to determine whether parts should be sent to the customer free or for a charge, and how much the charge would be. For all complaints that involve a technical problem, a letter is sent 2 weeks later asking the customer about whether the problem was solved, and the customer's satisfaction with follow-up calls and service.

a. Develop the flowchart for this process.

b. Suggest opportunities to improve the quality of service.

11. The president of Zemco Plastics Company sees in the newspaper that his company's closest competitor is spending about three times as much as his company is on R&D for a plastic that both companies currently produce. From information in the article, he concludes that, despite this, the competitor apparently has not gained any discernable technological or profit advantage over his company in that particular plastic. What might Zemco's president conclude about the plastic?

12. Cylo Electronics has two production divisions. In terms of sales volume, cost, and profitability, the two are currently about equal, though the product lines and production processes of each are very different, and Division A has been operating for about 10 years, whereas Division B, only about 4 years. The CEO of Cylo notices that over the last few years, productivity improvement at Division A has been poor, and several product development projects came in very much over budget and over schedule. Division B, in contrast, has been able to continuously reduce its production costs and has been successful in all of its developmental projects. In hopes of improving the situation at Division A, the CEO is considering transferring several product and process designers and engineers from Division B to Division A. Comment.

Endnotes

1. For a look at these concepts as applied to product innovation, *see* R. Foster, *Innovation: The Attacker's Advantage* (New York: Summit Books, 1986).

2. H. Smith, *Rethinking America* (New York: Random House, 1995), pp. 6–27.

3. R. Hayes and G. Pisano, "Beyond World Class: The New Manufacturing Strategy," *Harvard Business Review* (Jan–Feb 1994), pp. 77–86.

4. A. Robinson, *Modern Approaches to Manufacturing Improvement: The Shingo System* (Cambridge, MA: Productivity Press, 1990). Though the concept of thinking and perceiving is discussed on p. 88, virtually the entire first half of this book is about topics related to methods of perceiving, thinking, and PDCA as applied to manufacturing.

5. Japan Management Association, *Canon Production System* (Cambridge, MA: Productivity Press, 1987), Chapter 10.

6. C. Fallon, *Value Analysis to Improve Productivity* (New York: Wiley Interscience, 1971), Chapters 5–9.

7. M. Hammer and J. Champy, *Reengineering the Corporation* (New York, HaperBusiness, 1993); *see also* M. Hammer and S. Stanton, *The Reengineering Revolution* (New York, HarperBusiness, 1995).

8. The term reengineering as applied to business processes is a misnomer since most business processes were never engineered (designed) to start with; they got to where they are in an evolutionary, sometimes arbitrary fashion. Reengineering for most business processes really means engineering the first time.

9. H. Cypress, "Re-engineering," *OR/MS Today,* (February 1994), pp. 18–29.

10. G. Hanson, "A Complex Process: The Case for Automated Assistance in Business Process Re-engineering," *OR/MS Today,* (August 1994), pp. 34–41.

11. Hammer and Champy, *Reengineering the Corporation,* pp. 39–44.

12. R. Schonberger, *World Class Manufacturing: The Next Decade* (New York: The Free Press, 1997), p. 33.

13. *Ibid.,* p. 181.

14. One of the first references to describe all seven in one source is K. Ishikawa, *Guide to Quality Control* (Tokyo: Asia Productivity Organization, 1976).

15. *Ibid.; see also* K. Ishikawa, *What is Total Quality Control?* (Translated by D. Lu) (Englewood Cliffs, NJ: Prentice Hall, 1985), pp. 63–4.

16. Sometimes instead of the run diagram, the control chart is considered the seventh basic problem-solving tool. The subject of control charts, which requires considerable discussion, is covered in Chapter 14.

JIT: VALUE ADDED AND WASTE ELIMINATION

Continuous improvement is an important element of modern manufacturing philosophy and a cornerstone to both JIT and TQM. Another cornerstone mentioned is the concept of **value added.** If something in an organization or process does not add value, it is considered **waste.** A goal of the improvement process is to purge from the organization all things considered wasteful. In a way, the concepts of value added and elimination of waste are two sides of the same coin.

This chapter covers these concepts as well as common sources of waste in organizations. In JIT organizations, sources of waste are identified and eliminated through adherence to a number of **JIT principles.**

The first two JIT principles, **simplification** and **cleanliness and organization,** are the most rudimentary of improvement approaches. Simplification implies elimination of nonessentials, cleanliness and organization imply thoroughness and attention to detail. **Visibility** the third JIT principle, is an aspect of simplification that focuses on data gathering, analysis, and reporting to ensure that shop-floor people get the right information at the right time.

The fourth principle, **cycle timing,** is the idea that production output should be somewhat uniform and yet closely coincide with demand. Through JIT, it is often possible to achieve the seemingly inconsistent goals of meeting fluctuating demand while maintaining uniform production output. **Agility,** the fifth principle, is a manufacturer's ability to switch over products and processes as customers and markets dictate. The techniques for agile manufacturing introduced here are elaborated throughout the book. The sixth principle, **variability reduction,** refers to continuing efforts to reduce process variation. Process variability is a prime source of waste and a contributor to poor quality, cost, and time performance. The final principle, **measurement,** is fundamental to PDCA and is the means by which improvement is gauged. It is also part of every value-added, waste-elimination, and improvement effort.

Though these principles are elemental to JIT philosophy, they should also be considered as principles for enhancing competitiveness in manufacturing operations.

The chapter concludes with a discussion of JIT practices and philosophy, perceived limitations of JIT, and JIT implementation issues.

VALUE-ADDED FOCUS

Value added is the concept that every activity and element of a system (materials, humans, time, space, and energy) should add value to the output of the system. As such, it provides perspective for determining what needs improvement in manufacturing operations.

The value-added concept also relates to the earlier discussion about what constitutes real improvement. Simply improving, say, the efficiency (O/I ratio) of an operation does not mean that an improvement has been made. In particular, improvement applies only to valued-added and necessary non-value-added activities (concepts described next). If you try to improve some aspect of a process that is unnecessary in the first place, then you are wasting your time.

NECESSARY AND UNNECESSARY ACTIVITIES

Combining materials to form a product or doing some service-oriented task that makes a customer happy are examples of value-added activities. These activities *directly* add value to output, whether a product or a service. In contrast, a task such as processing a purchase order is a non-value-added activity, even though it is necessary for doing value-added activities. The value-added approach classifies activities as either value-added or non-value-added. Within the latter category, the absolute necessary activities are separated out, and all the others are candidates for elimination.

Distinguishing necessary, non-value-added activities from the unnecessary, wasteful ones is tricky because unnecessary activities in organizations often *seem* necessary. Purchasing-type tasks are necessary because they procure the materials needed by value-added activities for transformation into the final output. Activities such as inspecting incoming parts for defects or counting materials in inventory also seem necessary; inspection prevents defects from going into a product (a valuable endeavor) and counting ensures that inventories are being kept at the right level (also valuable). The fact that an activity fulfills a valuable purpose, however, should not be confused with its adding value. For inspection and counting, alternatives exist that would obviate the need for either of them. For example, by requiring vendors to deliver only zero-defect parts, the need for incoming inspection is eliminated. By using production procedures that limit inventory levels, the need for inventory counting is reduced or eliminated. Many such valuable purposes can be fulfilled in different ways without necessitating the preservation of a non-value-added activity.

In summary, the value-added concept says to distinguish value-added from non-value-added activities. Among the latter activities, seek out the ones that are unnecessary and try to eliminate them. The remaining activities, which are the value-added and necessary non-value-added ones, then become the focus for improvement.

SUPPORT ORGANIZATION

To distinguish value-added from non-value-added activities, it is useful to think of each organization as being two organizations: one, the **production organization** that makes the product or provides the service; the other, the **support organization** that assists and supports the production organization but does little that qualifies as value added. In common parlance, the production organization is called the **line** (or **frontline**) and the support organization is called the **staff.** In actuality, the two blend together without regard for work function, job level, or job category, and a person's job might readily involve doing things in both organizations.

In many firms, the support organization accounts for a significant proportion of total organizational costs in the form of overhead. Often this cost exceeds by a wide margin the cost of the production organization. Though its ostensible purpose is to assist and facilitate the production organization, the support organization sometimes exists as a self-serving entity, with, at best, tenuous links to the production organization.

The number of activities within the support organization can be quite large and most of them, though necessary, are non-value-added activity. The purchasing, inspection, and inventory counting tasks cited above are examples. The following categories give an idea of the expanse of these activities:[1]

· **Planning, control, and accounting activities:** forecasting, production planning and scheduling, purchasing, master scheduling, requirements planning, production control, customer order processing, order tracking and expediting, responding to customer inquiries, and all associated data entry, bookkeeping, data processing, and follow-up on errors.

· **Logistical activities:** all ordering, execution, and confirmation of materials movement within an organization, including everything associated with receiving, shipping, work orders and expediting, as well as data entry and processing, and follow-up on errors.

· **Quality activities:** all quality-related work such as definition of customer requirements, assurances that necessary activities have occurred, defect prevention, quality monitoring, and follow-up on defects, mistakes, or complaints.

· **Change activities:** all revisions and updates to other activities, value-added or non-value-added, including, for example, customer orders, product designs, and planning and control systems. Change transactions have a multiplier effect: a change in a product design usually requires changes in material requirements, bills of material, and product routings, each of which requires data entry and processing activities to implement them. Although change, per se, cannot be tied to one functional area in the support organization, it requires resources and, hence, contributes to the size of the support organization.

Support activities can often be eliminated by simplifying products and processes, eliminating product defects at the source, improving integration of steps to remove mistakes and duplication of effort, and improving product design and production planning to reduce the number of changes. Aspects of JIT/TQM management philosophies and practices that eliminate the need for parts of the support organization will be discussed throughout this book.

EMPLOYEE INVOLVEMENT

While the value-added approach seems simple in concept, it can be difficult to apply.

HISTORICAL NOTE: Gilbreths and the One Best Way

Among the earliest proponents of eliminating waste were the husband–wife team of Frank Gilbreth (1868–1924) and Lillian Gilbreth (1878–1972). They thought that the role of management is to find the simplest, easiest way to do the job. Their philosophy of "work smarter, not harder" meant that every task should be carefully studied and all wasted motion should be eliminated to arrive at the *one best way* to do the job. During their lifetimes, they applied this philosophy to almost every conceivable kind of work. Frank owned a construction company that specialized in speed building. By applying the one-best-way philosophy to the task of bricklaying, he reduced the number of basic motions for laying a brick from eight to six. At a time when bricklayers were laying about 500 bricks a day,

Gilbreth's bricklayers averaged 2600 a day.

Though important contributors to management thought, the Gilbreths could hardly be called the parents of modern TQM/JIT manufacturing since the latter goes far beyond their way of thinking and in some instances, stands counter to it. The Gilbreths were interested primarily in one particular kind of waste, the waste of motion. As we will discuss later, there are many other sources of waste. Also, in any process there is no such thing as one best way. If there ever was, it would only be temporary and superseded by a still better way (the idea of continuous improvement). Also, JIT/TQM stand by the premise that seeking out waste and finding better ways is the responsibility of *everyone,* not just managers.

For example, there may be only subtle differences between necessary and unnecessary activities *within* a particular job or task. The person best qualified to make the distinction, then, is the one most familiar with the task—the person doing it. Workers usually know what is essential and what is not, and given the opportunity, they will share that knowledge. Getting the workers involved is thus fundamental to every continuous improvement effort.

On the other hand, few people will point out unnecessary portions of their work if they think it will jeopardize their job or continued employment. While the value-added process requires that workers scrutinize their jobs and suggest ways to replace unnecessary activities with necessary, value-added ones, the process must not threaten workers' job security. Getting employees to participate when the covert goal is to eliminate jobs will have only short-lived success and probably preclude any future, meaningful participation from the employees.

SOURCES OF WASTE

Once begun, any manufacturing improvement effort can be sustained by the continuous search for waste. In most organizations waste is rife and easy to find, though finding ways to *eliminate* waste might be difficult. Still, developing lists of wastes and prioritizing them is a logical first step. When all of the obvious sources of waste are removed, continuous improvement efforts switch to searching for hidden sources of waste.

TOYOTA'S SEVEN WASTES

One contribution of Toyota Motor Company to modern manufacturing is its strong advocacy of waste elimination as a strategy for continuous improvement. Toyota defines waste as anything other than the minimum amount of materials, equipment, parts, space, or time which are essential to add value to the product. Though sources of waste vary within and across organizations, the similarities are great. The following sources of waste, identified by Toyota and first described by Taiichi Ohno, are universal in manufacturing:[2]

The Seven Wastes

Waste from **producing defects**
Waste in **transportation**
Waste from **inventory**
Waste from **overproduction**
Waste of **waiting time**
Waste in **processing**
Waste of **motion**

Producing Defects

Defects in any product or service are a major source of waste. Consider defects not remedied by the producer and discovered by a customer. The costs of these defects include warranty or reparation expenses assumed by the producer, aggravation of current customers, and loss of existing and potential customers who hear about the defects.

Product defects are ideally detected and remedied long before products go to a customer; however, detecting and fixing defects are themselves wasteful and costly activities. The simple *expectation* that defects will occur requires that producers devote time and resources to inspecting items and sorting out those that are defective. Defective products accrue additional labor and material expenses related to disassembly and rework. For defective items that must be scrapped, all of the labor, material, and resource expense of producing them is wasted. Products with minor defects might be usable, but must be sold as "seconds" and at reduced prices. The greater the volume is of defective items produced, the more time that must be allocated to correcting and replacing them. Defects in products hold up production and increase production lead times. Multiply every effort to find and correct defects by how often they must be performed to eliminate defects and the result is a tremendous waste of labor, material, and other resources. This is all wasteful and would be unnecessary if products or services were **done right the first time.**

Transportation and Material Handling

In many organizations, items (people, products, parts, supplies, etc.) being processed or serviced must be moved from one location to another over several stages. Two things determine the distance through which items must be moved and the transportation means (conveyors, trolleys, carts, forklifts, overhead cranes, etc.) to move them: the **layout of the facility** (the location of machines, desks, departments, reception areas, shipping and receiving docks, and so on) and the **sequence of operations** required to produce or service the items. For example, Figure 3.1 shows the layout and routing sequencing for processing three items. The facility could be imagined as a factory or an office that processes many kinds of items. Whatever the items, notice the overall distance through which they must move in the course of the process. In many organizations the distance to process items totals *miles,* and the cumulative time involved is very large. Since typically no work is performed on items while they are being moved, time spent en route is wasted. All equipment and labor involved in moving and keeping track of the items is costly and wasteful too.

Figure 3.2 shows an alternative equipment layout, part of which is devoted solely to the three items. By rearranging the layout and putting equipment for sequential operations close together, the distance through which the items move has been reduced to a fraction of the previous distance. The time required to move the items, the associated cost of systems to move and keep track of them, as well as the amount of space required for the processes have all been reduced. Simply, the arrangement is conducive to a more efficient traffic pattern.

Inventory

Toyota calls inventory the root of all evil.[3] That is a strong statement meant to imply that wastes stemming from inventory go far beyond items held in stock. Inventory represents items waiting for something to happen, a waste in that there are costs associated with keeping items waiting and lost time since no value is being added to them. Inventory holding costs increase with size of inventory since it costs more to hold more. Holding costs include the charges for storage space, paperwork and handling, insurance, security, and pilferage. Since the capital needed to acquire or produce the items in inventory cannot be invested elsewhere, there is an opportunity cost as well. If the inventory comprises items procured from borrowed funds, there is also an interest expense. The sum holding costs for all items in all inventories carried by an organization throughout a year can be sizable.

FIGURE 3.1	**FIGURE 3.2**
Routings for three products.	*Alternate layout.*

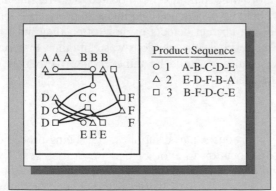 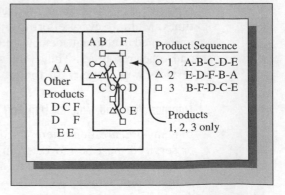

Inventory is also considered evil because it *covers up* other kinds of wastes and encourages, or allows, wasteful practices. Inventory has been called a just-in-case philosophy of management, meaning that managers use it as a hedge against things that might go wrong. While many managers recognize the costs of inventories, they still think of inventory as necessary to overcome other kinds of problems. What they fail to see are alternatives for dealing with these problems. Four such scenarios follow.

1. Inventory is carried to cover fluctuations in future demand. If demand were more accurately forecasted, demand uncertainty and the size of inventory to cover it could be decreased. Even if demand fluctuations and unpredictability persisted, by producing a high-quality product at a more steady rate and offering it at a lower price, other costs associated with forecast error would fall. Demand will less frequently drop below the production rate, and when it exceeds the rate, loyal customers will wait or come back soon.

2. Inventory is carried so that material flow will be uninterrupted in the event of equipment breakdowns or delivery delays. Preventive maintenance programs and close customer/supplier working relationships can eliminate most equipment break-downs and delivery delays, which would obviate the need for protective inventory.

3. Inventory is carried to cover defects in materials and finished products. Making suppliers responsible for the quality of their products and improving product quality through better product design and production processes eliminates defects at the start, which makes inventories unnecessary to cover defects.

4. Large inventories result from large production runs, which managers say are necessary because of time-consuming and costly production setups. If production setup methods were improved and the cost of setups were reduced, then small-batch production would be economical. The byproduct of smaller production runs is smaller inventories.

We can use the analogy of a ship on water to further clarify the point. As Figure 3.3 illustrates, a high water level makes it unlikely that a ship will encounter rocks. When the water level is lowered, the rocks begin to be exposed, and care must be taken to guide the ship around them. Inventory is analogous to the water level: high inventory covers up problems in the system and allows management to cruise without fixing them. As inventory is lowered, problems in the system (poor forecasting, poor maintenance, costly setups, poor product design and quality control, etc.) are exposed, and management has to resolve them in order for the system to work. In JIT, reduction of inventory is not an end in itself; it is a device for exposing problems and wasteful practices in the production system.

Overproduction

Companies sometimes produce more than they have sold or might sell because they want to build inventories (for reasons given above) or because they want to keep their equipment and facilities running (achieve high-level resource utilization). Whatever the reason, making products for which there is no demand is wasteful. If demand does

Figure 3.3

Inventory as a way of avoiding problems (when the inventory tide goes out, the skipper must carefully navigate between the rocks or find ways to eliminate them).

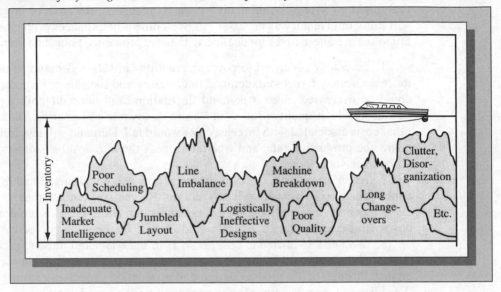

not materialize then at some time the items will have to be discarded or disposed of at reduced price. In the meantime, they are held in stock where they accrue all the costs and waste associated with inventory.

Overproduction is usually shoddy management, instigated as a way to avoid making difficult management decisions. Waste from overproduction is difficult to identify, and unless you compare what is produced with what is sold and shipped, nothing appears wrong. In organizations that habitually overproduce, everyone is busy, and when everyone is busy, no one has time to scrutinize what is happening to find out what is wrong with the system.

The overproduction mindset that more is better is at odds with waste elimination and can ultimately cause an organization to produce itself out of business. During the early 1980s Texas Instruments manufactured large quantities of PCs for the home market, expecting a sales surge. It never kept tabs on PC sales at the retail level, however, and assumed that consumers were buying the product. While its plants were operating at peak capacity, most of its product was going into inventory at various stages of the distribution chain, not to customers' homes. Both the company and its distributors discovered the slow demand too late and had to dump their inventories at a substantial loss. Although this electronics giant was a major player in the early development of home PCs, it took a financial beating and had to drop out of the home PC market.

Waiting

Unlike waste of overproduction, waste of waiting is easy to identify. It takes many forms, including waiting for orders, parts, materials, items from preceding processes, or for equipment repairs. It also occurs in automatic processes or operations, as when an operator loads and turns on an automatic machine, then watches and waits until the machine is finished.

Some companies pride themselves in minimizing the waste of waiting with a policy of keeping workers busy and machines running, regardless of customer demand. In other words, they overproduce. This practice replaces one waste (waiting) with a worse waste (overproduction) since shutting down machines and allowing workers to be idle on occasion is less costly in terms of material, equipment, and overhead than producing inventories for which there are no orders. An advantage to idling workers is that it allows them time to scrutinize operations and search for sources of waste.

Processing

A process may itself contain steps that are ineffective or unnecessary. Take, for example, a product that goes through two steps: cutting, then filing to remove burrs along the cut edge (see Figure 3.4(a)). This process might be altered to reduce wasted time or steps. Automatic filing of the edge is more efficient than manual filing (Figure 3.4(b)); still better is periodic maintenance or replacement of the cutting tool so it gives a smooth edge that doesn't need filing (Figure 3.4(c)). The item might even be redesigned so that the cutting operation is eliminated (Figure 3.4(d)).

Processing waste can be eliminated by taking advantage of natural forces such as gravity. Instead of having a worker remove a finished part from a machine and put it in a bin, the part can be disengaged automatically from the machine and fall down a chute into the bin. Eliminating waste from processing steps can also be achieved by minimizing the motion necessary to perform work.

Motion

People in work settings often confuse being in motion with working. In reality motion and work are not the same. For definitional purposes, **work** is considered a particular *kind* of motion that either adds value or is necessary to add value. A person in constant motion throughout the day (i.e., a busy person) may in actuality be doing little work. Motion that is not necessary to do the work is considered waste. A useful concept for identifying waste of motion is **work content,** or the proportion of all motion in a job that is actually considered useful work:

$$Work\ Content = \frac{Work}{Motion}.$$

For example, a job that takes 10 minutes but involves 6 minutes of work and 4 minutes to pick and place tools and materials has 60% work content.

FIGURE 3.4

Paring waste from a cut-and-burr-removal process.

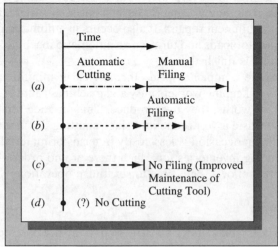

For any job the goal should be to achieve a work content near 100%. This is attained by *eliminating wasteful motions,* not by increasing work. Among wasteful motions in jobs, the most common are searching, selecting, picking up, transporting, loading, repositioning, and unloading. These motions take precious time and increase the cost, but do not add value.

Although it is common for companies to increase output by increasing the number of workers or the number of hours worked, a better way is to attack wasted motion. For example, suppose the work content of a busy worker is 50% (half of the worker's time is spent on wasteful motion) and his daily output is 10 units. To double the output, the company might put on an additional worker or ask the current worker to double his hours. An alternative, however, would be to examine the worker's job and try to eliminate all the wasted motion. This, in effect, would double the work content to 100% and double the worker's output. The worker would still be busy, but he would be busy doing only useful, value-added activities.

CANON'S NINE WASTES

Toyota's Seven Wastes typology emphasizes factory waste; as such it is not the only, or necessarily the best, way to categorize waste. Canon Corporation, for example, uses a broader classification scheme that could be applied even to service companies:

The Nine Wastes

Waste caused by **work-in-process.**
Waste caused by **defects.**
Waste in **equipment.**

Waste in **expense.**
Waste in **indirect labor.**
Waste in **planning.**
Waste in **human resources.**
Waste in **operations.**
Waste in **startup.**

It is useful to classify wastes because it is easier in improvement programs to focus on particular wastes than to try to attack everything at once. Any organization can begin waste elimination using The Seven (or The Nine) Waste categories, then tailor the categories to better suit its purposes and programs.

WASTE REDUCTION AND ENVIRONMENTAL RESPONSIBILITY

Though most organizations take increased competitiveness and profitability as the primary aims of waste reduction, there is another reason for seeking to reduce waste: it makes good sense environmentally. Generally, efforts to reduce waste and improve operations within an organization spill over to reduce environmental damages associated with doing business. Reductions in waste directly result in the conservation of raw materials as well as reduced pollution of air, water, and land from waste byproducts.

While this chapter has focused on waste in manufacturing, waste reduction efforts with the farthest-reaching cost and environmental ramifications must of necessity extend beyond this perspective. **Total waste reduction,** or **industrial ecology,** involves total product life-cycle thinking, starting with a product's design and ending with its disposition at the end of its operational life.[4] Total waste reduction means designing, manufacturing, distributing products, and in general, doing business in ways that utilize less materials, less energy, and a high proportion of recycled materials. The focus is on resource recycling rather than extracting and discarding resources after use. A design philosophy called **design for environment** (DFE) emphasizes environmental consideration in product and process design.[5] A few examples of DFE principles follow:

· Minimize usage of hazardous and bulky materials as well as materials that involve energy-intensive methods of production.
· Maximize usage of materials that are recyclable and environmentally friendly.
· Design products for ease of repair so they are not readily discarded.
· Design products for ease of disassembly after disposal.

Design for disassembly considers how the product will be torn apart at the end of its useful life. The matter of disassembly is becoming more important in design as interest grows in separating out components for reuse and recycling.[6]

Many organizations have developed schemes for recycling scrap and for becoming recyclers of materials they use in their products. Alcoa has long been a recycler of aluminum, as well as a user of recycled aluminum; this is much less wasteful and costly than producing aluminum from bauxite ore. BMW is designing automobiles wherein entire subassemblies can be separated from the vehicle and recycled. Chrysler claims its new LH-model cars were designed so that 90% of the materials in them can be recycled. Xerox designs its products so that most of the materials in them can be recycled or reused. The company reuses machine-parts boxes and pallets, which saves over 15,000 tons of material and $15 million annually (1992). Recycling efforts at its 10 largest US and European sites have reduced waste by more than 25,000 tons.[7]

Like most kinds of waste-reduction efforts, minimizing environmental impacts of industrial waste require long-term planning and commitment because the payback period might be many years. The same is true, however, of most waste-reduction efforts, whether the focus is on internal processes or the overall environment.

JIT PRINCIPLES

Value-added focus and elimination of waste are two cornerstones of JIT management philosophy. To operationalize JIT philosophy in an organization, however, calls for *focus*. A large part of that focus is provided by **JIT principles,** a set of tenets and assumptions that drive decisions and actions about products and processes. The principles, described in this section, address what a producer should do in terms of product and process improvement to increase competitiveness. In a sense, the principles go beyond JIT philosophy and are prescriptions worthwhile for any manufacturer.

SIMPLIFICATION

In virtually any work situation, an action to reduce waste will result in simplification of whatever existed before. The converse is also true; taking action to simplify something usually results in a reduction of waste. Ideas about how to simplify have been around for a long time; consider, for example, the principles of 'motion economy' developed by Frank and Lillian Gilbreth in the early 1900s. Traditional methods like time-and-motion analysis have long been used to improve the efficiency of tasks and processes. In general, however, simplification efforts extend far beyond removing wasted motion or redesigning predefined tasks. They also extend to simplification of products and services, as well as to the overall processes and individual procedures involved in providing these things. Often the best approach is to simplify both the product and the process simultaneously.

Product, Process, and Procedure Simplification

Simplification means accomplishing the same ends but in a less complex, more basic way or with fewer inputs. For any system, whether a process or product, this means critically scrutinizing the components or elements of the system with an eye toward combining, individually streamlining, or eliminating them. Simplification also means cutting out or cutting down on features which do not add value. Consider some examples.

Example   1:   Product/Process Simplification

The component in Figure 3.5(a) is assembled from three kinds of purchased parts—A, B, and C. Part C is a casting (a part formed by pouring molten metal into a mold, solidifying it by cooling, then popping it out like an ice cube from a tray), and the decision was made to alter it into the casting, D, shown in Figure 3.5(b). Though the new casting is slightly more expensive to produce than the original, it eliminates the need for parts A and B. As a result, the assembly operation is eliminated, and since the number of parts is reduced from three to one, costs associated with materials procurement and processing (ordering, inventory, bill-of-materials, inspection, etc.) are also reduced. Further, if the bolts in the original assembly had to be aligned, every assembly risked an alignment error. Redesign eliminates the possibility for this kind of error since the alignment is achieved by the mold.

FIGURE 3.5

Product/process simplification.

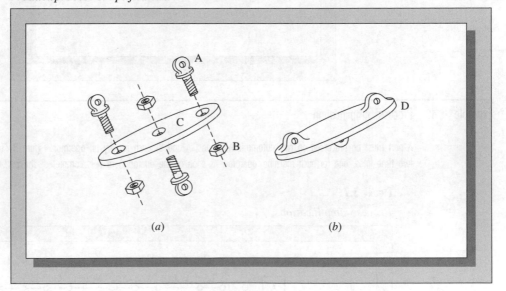

(a)   (b)

Example   2:   Process Simplification

In Figure 3.6(a) we see that moving materials between two successive operations involves the steps of unloading materials from operation A, putting them onto a cart, transferring them to operation B, waiting for operation B to be available, taking them off the cart, and loading them into operation B. The waste in terms of in-process inventory, handling, space, and waiting time is considerable. As shown in Figure 3.6(b), these wastes could all be reduced if the two operations were synchronized and connected with a conveyor system (combining unloading, transporting, and loading into one step). A still better approach would be to synchronize the two and locate them immediately adjacent to each other, which would virtually eliminate all in-process inventory, handling, and lead time between them (see Figure 3.6(c)). (Note that arrangements (b) and (c) result in somewhat less flexibility since it is harder to process items that require *only* A, *only* B, or B *before* A.)

FIGURE 3.6

Process simplification.

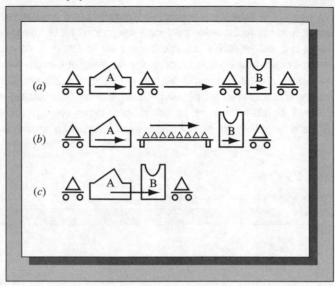

Example   3:   Process Simplification

A part must be processed on two automatic machines, A and B, each run by an operator. Figure 3.7(a) shows two time lines, one for each machine/operator. As soon as the operation at A is completed, the part is

FIGURE 3.7

Process simplification.

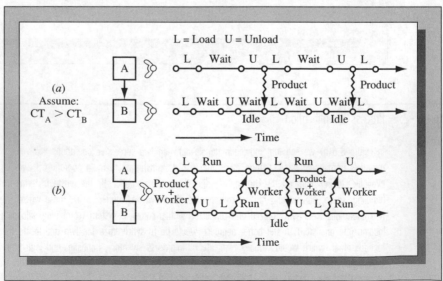

transferred to B, as indicated by the wiggly line. The operators load and unload the machines but otherwise are idle while the machines are running. The machine cycle time (CT) for operation A is slightly longer than for B, so the worker at B periodically has to wait for parts from A. Figure 3.7(b) shows the process simplified by moving the machines together and having one operator run both. (The wiggly line shows points where the operator goes from machine A to machine B with the part, then returns to machine A.) This operator experiences no idle time, though there is still a small amount of machine idle time at B because of the disparity in machine cycle times.

Example   4:   Procedure Simplification

Stamped metal parts are made with a press by using heavy metal forms called dies. A metal sheet is put between the upper and lower matching faces of the die (called "male" and "female" faces) and the two are stamped together to produce a part. A typical press can be used to stamp a variety of metal parts simply by changing dies. The dies, however, are of different sizes, and getting them to precisely fit the press requires delicate adjustment which is time-consuming (see Figure 3.8(a)). A way to simplify the installation procedure is to make a block or fixture for each die to sit upon so that the combined height of the die and its fixture is the same for all dies (see Figure 3.8(b)). When the die and its fixture are installed together, no adjustment for height is necessary, saving much of the time required to set up the dies. This is an example of *setup reduction*, the topic of Chapter 6.

FIGURE 3.8

Procedural simplification.

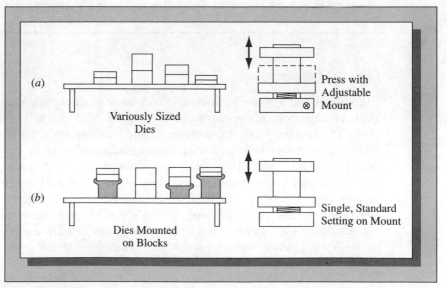

Example   5:   Product/Procedure Simplification

Two different molded plastic parts (A and B) with pegs on the bottom are glued into holes on a board as shown in Figure 3.9(a). The parts look similar so assemblers sometimes glue them into the wrong holes. Also, the parts should be installed with a certain orientation, but assemblers sometimes put them in pointing the wrong way. The solution is

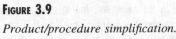

FIGURE 3.9

Product/procedure simplification.

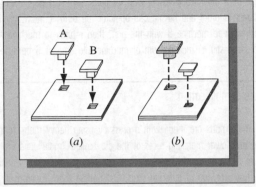

to change the shapes and sizes of the pegs and holes so the parts can only be inserted in the right place and facing the right way (see Figure 3.9(b)). In addition, each part is molded in a different color plastic (one black, one white). Though peg size alone would prevent an assembler from putting a part in the wrong place, coloring prevents the assembler from even *starting* to put a part in the wrong place. These modifications eliminate any possibility of assembly error and, hence, the need for inspection. They also save assembly time since workers need not scrutinize the parts or think about the direction of installation. This is an example of *fool-proofing* covered in Chapter 15.

Concurrent Engineering

Examples 1 and 5 raise an important point worth brief comment here. To make some kinds of improvements requires coordinated effort of people in different functional areas. The improvements in these cases could only happen if people in manufacturing and product design talked to each other. Designers need to know about how the product is to be made if they are to design the product so it can be made simply and well. Such knowledge comes from working closely with people in manufacturing. Yet in many organizations people in different departments (or buildings, professions, wage and salary grades, etc.) tend not to even speak to each other. Instead of having a dialogue, they use a linear process where designers develop a product, then hand the design to the manufacturing group which has to wrestle with the problem of how to make it. The product in Figure 3.9(a) gives assemblers headaches because it inevitably leads to mistakes, no matter how careful they are. The simple changes in Figure 3.9(b) eliminate the mistakes, even if assemblers get careless.

To do something right means incorporating considerations from all the parties affected (manufacturing, design, procurement, finance, marketing, and so on) and incorporating those considerations into the product *before* the production process gets underway. The concept of having a multifunctional team working to design and develop a product, while thinking about how it will be made and simultaneously designing the process for its manufacture, is referred to as **concurrent engineering** and is discussed in more depth in Chapter 12.

CLEANLINESS AND ORGANIZATION

Facilities in many organizations are dirty, cluttered, and disorganized. This is always wasteful because it makes doing work more difficult and often results in poor quality work. Time is wasted looking for misplaced or lost tools and materials; equipment problems are camouflaged by grime and clutter; movement from one place to another is difficult; obsolete and discontinued materials are mixed up with current, needed materials; tools are bent or broken; and gauges and equipment are damaged and out of calibration. In general, messy facilities show an uncaring attitude about the workplace, but even worse they foster similar attitudes about work and the finished product. Disorganization and clutter as shown in Figures 3.10 and 3.11 further suggest a lack of discipline and procedure and the likelihood that waste prevails in other ways throughout the organization. For these reasons it makes sense to begin the continuous improvement process by cleaning and organizing the facility.

Improvement Kickoff

Making housekeeping the responsibility of everyone is a way to ease workers into the improvement process and to prepare them for greater responsibility later on (see Figure 3.12). To this end, managers and workers should get together to clean and organize their workplace *together*. Using the facility as a focus of attention will help

FIGURE 3.10

Inventory clutter and disorganization.

FIGURE 3.11

Scrap and parts clutter.

workers begin to develop the right attitudes and work habits. The facility itself becomes a symbol of the new order, and getting it cleaned up is a way to introduce the
problem-solving skills described in the previous chapter.

More than just getting the facility cleaned up and organized, emphasis must be on
keeping it that way; for this employees will have to exercise continuous discipline,
caring, and attention to detail.

FIGURE 3.12

Proud worker and his work area.

FIGURE 3.13

An organized workplace.

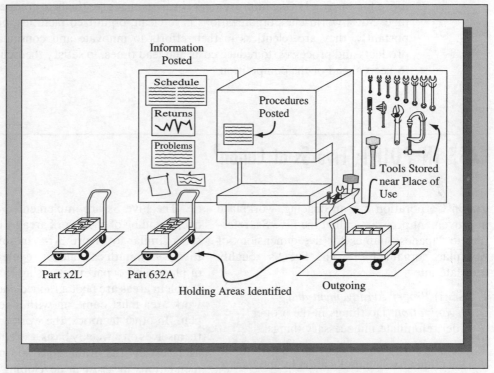

Benefits

Cleanliness and organization are important because without them opportunities for improvement and sources of problems are often obscured. Specifically, a clean workplace makes it easier to see cracks, missing parts, or leaks on equipment; reduces the chance of products being contaminated; improves work safety and reduces the chance for accidents; and makes it easier to spot product defects. Further, a safer, nicer place to work improves morale, and that should reduce absenteeism and turnover. Likewise keeping equipment, processes, and procedures organized makes it easier to find things (tools, parts, materials); makes it easier to assess processes and procedures, to pinpoint trouble spots, and to find better ways; and saves space, saves time, and makes it easier to move from place to place. Figure 3.13 depicts an exemplary work area.

It is worth repeating that housekeeping is a good *starting point* and way to develop and reinforce the work habits, attitudes, and skills important for continuous improvement. This is not the same, however, as saying that having a clean, organized place is an indication that the organization will work well. Cleanliness and organization are only background and mean nothing unless there is also continuous effort to move forward and make improvements in areas that give the firm competitive advantage. Sure, world-class organizations have clean, organized facilities, but, more importantly, they are relentless in their efforts to innovate and continually improve products and processes, to reduce costs and lead times, to satisfy their customers, and to keep ahead of the competition.

CASE IN POINT: Five Ss at Canon[8]

Canon Corporation has an ongoing, workplace improvement program called the Five Ss, referring to Japanese names for five dimensions of workplace organization. The five Ss roughly translate into

1. (Seiri) *Proper Arrangement and Organization.* Do things in the proper order; eliminate unnecessary things.

2. (Seiton) *Orderliness.* Specify a location for everything; designate location by number, color coding, name, etc.; put things where they belong.

3. (Seiso) *Cleanup.* Specify recommended procedures for cleanup; follow the procedures; check over all work.

4. (Seiketsu) *Cleanliness.* Dust, wash, and maintain equipment; keep equipment and the workplace in the best possible condition.

5. (Shitsuke) *Discipline.* Scrutinize practices; expose the wrong ones; learn correct practices and be careful to use them.

(At some Canon factories, the English word "safety" is added as a sixth S.)

The Five Ss are implemented through frequent grading of each work area by using a check sheet similar to Figure 3.14. In some factories, Five-S committees conduct regular inspections of plants and departments using Five-S criteria. Problem areas are photographed and the plant or work area must come up with a solution and a plan. In other factories, the work areas evaluate themselves on a weekly basis. Foremen and managers review the evaluations and make recommendations to assist in developing plans. Work areas that show good housekeeping practices may be awarded recognition plaques. Regardless of performance, all work areas are expected to continuously find ways to improve. Results of evaluations are posted to foster responsibility and pride.

The Five-S movement has helped change attitudes, and employees readily follow workplace rules that previously were difficult to enforce (such as keeping parts and tools in the right place). Performance measures such as number of accidents, equipment breakdowns, and defect rates have all been improved.

FIGURE 3.14

Five-S inspection sheet.

5 S Inspection Sheet	Evaluation Rank			Rank A: perfect score / Rank B: 1-2 problems / Rank C: 3 or more problems
Item	A	B	C	Comments
Proper Arrangement (Sort out unnecessary items)				
Are things posted on bulletin board uniformly?				
Have all unnecessary items been removed?				
Is it clear why unauthorized items are present?				
Are passageways and work areas clearly outlined?				
Are hoses and cords properly arranged?				
Good Order (A place for everything and everything in its place)				
Is everything kept in its own place?				
Are things put away after use?				
Are work areas uncluttered?				
Is everything fastened down that needs to be?				
Are shelves, tables, and cleaning implements orderly?				
Cleanliness (Prevent problems by keeping things clean)				
Is clothing neat and clean?				
Are exhaust and ventilation adequate?				
Are work areas clean?				
Are machinery, equipment, fixtures, and drains kept clean?				
Are the white and green lines clean and unbroken?				
Cleanup (After-work maintenance and cleanup)				
Is the area free of trash and dust?				
Have all machines and equipment been cleaned?				
Has the floor been cleaned?				
Are cleanup responsibilities assigned?				
Are trash cans empty?				
Discipline (Maintaining good habits at Canon)				
Is everyone dressed according to regulations?				
Are smoking areas observed?				
Are private belongings put away?				
Does everyone refrain from eating and drinking in the workplace?				
Does everyone avoid private conversations during work time?				
Rank totals				

Source: Japan Management Association, *Canon Production System: Creative Involvement of the Total Workforce* (Portland, OR: Productivity Press, Inc., 1987) (English translation) Reprinted with permission.

CASE IN POINT: Shrink the Web

Schonberger[9] describes a company of 50 production workers where on Fridays the plant manager makes rounds to rate every employee on six categories of criteria, most of them related to housekeeping and organization. When the results are plotted and connected they resemble a spider web (see Figure 3.15). A perfect score is a zero on all six categories, so the worse the performance, the farther the web is from the origin. Ratings are retained by employees with the presumption that they will work on "shrinking the web."

Each category's rating is an average rating of several subcategories. For example, "arrange-ment of work site" includes subcategories such as "unnecessary things around table," "cleanup of trash and waste," "uncompleted things in the right place," "proper notices on the wall," and so on. Some subcategories might seem picayune but, Schonberger emphasizes, in combination they add up to a system that stamps out sloppiness and mistakes and promotes attention to details.

Even the vigilance of the plant manager is monitored. A special audit team rates him on a regular basis so that, in effect, he too must try to shrink the web of his own ratings.

FIGURE 3.15

Process check sheet.

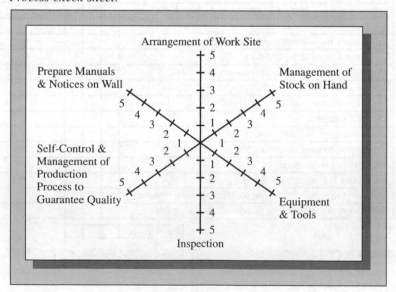

VISIBILITY

Visibility means knowing what has been, must be, or should be done by *seeing* it. The best way to communicate information is to send it directly between the sender and receiver with minimal channels or processing to garble or alter the message.

In traditional manufacturing organizations, information is the bevy of a privileged few. The masses of workers get little information, and they see only what the upper echelons allow. Much of the information generated by an organization is relatively useless, and much of the information that is important and useful never gets to those who could use it.

Visibility is the shop-floor equivalent to *perestroika*. Its essence is to redirect and redefine information so it is visible to workers on the shop floor, and immediately so, whenever they need it. An example is a daily production schedule, prominently posted on the wall or hanging from the ceiling of a production area. Everyone, not just the supervisor, sees what the day's work is. Throughout the day, production results are displayed so everyone knows who is on schedule and who is not.

Charts posted by work areas giving instructions, production standards, and goals are another example. Each department or workstation has charts posted to show workers what should or must be done. Often, the workers themselves prepare the charts and contribute to setting the standards and goals listed on them. This involvement helps to ensure that the tasks are reasonable for workers to accomplish. Special team achievements, quality awards, notices of recognition, and photos of workers and teams are posted too, so people can take pride in and show their successes and accomplishments.

Status of the overall shop floor should be readily visible. Signal lights on machines and on overhead displays indicate when equipment is malfunctioning or out of parts. Workers use signal lights to indicate that they are experiencing problems or that it is time for a setup, tool change, or quality check.

Workplace organization and cleanliness are important to visibility. When there is a designated place for everything, it is easy to see whether everything is in its place. When equipment is kept clean, it is easier to spot abnormalities, malfunctions, or problem indicators such as cracks, leaks, or loose fittings and fixtures.

The very layout of the factory should contribute to high visibility. Equipment, work stations, and stock areas should be situated so workers can easily see what has been or needs to be done. By designing a product line into a U-shape, workers at the start of the line can see what is happening at the end of the line and vice versa. Putting subassembly areas next to final assembly enables everyone to see the final products into which their parts are going; this contributes to higher morale and fewer defects.

Putting inventory stock areas on the shop floor next to workstations allows workers to easily monitor inventory levels. They can anticipate when they will need more parts and can see when they need to produce more parts.

The JIT concept of pull production, discussed in Chapter 8, is a manifestation of the principle of visibility. It relies on workers' observation of simple cards, containers, or inventory stock levels to tell them when to initiate or stop some action or to change what they are doing. The concept of visibility as practiced is called **visual**

management or **visual control,** examples of which will be cited throughout the remainder of this book.

Whereas reports can always be fudged, a physical quantity of inventory tells the truth about the quantity and quality of items supplied, and how well the supply matches demand. Visibility creates immediate feedback, and workers know what to do without relying as much on orders from supervisors or formal pronouncements from management.

CYCLE TIMING[10]

The time interval that elapses between occurrences of something is called the **cycle time.** Cycle time connotes different things, depending on the way it is used. It can be the time

· Between placing job orders or performing different jobs.
· Between preparation of business plans or accounting statements.
· For a machine or person to perform a single operation.
· Between completion of units at an operation or an entire process.

In all cases, the concept of cycle timing suggests the regularity of timing or manufacturing. Regularity of timing benefits productivity and quality because it reduces production uncertainty and permits managers and workers to better anticipate and prepare for the future. Manufacturing regularity ensures that products are produced at a fairly steady rate, which further means that materials flow through the process and are consumed at a steady rate. Thus, there is less confusion about where things go, what needs to done, and when. This directly or indirectly benefits virtually every activity associated with producing, moving, and monitoring material, including material handling, preventive maintenance, machine tooling and setup, material procurement, quality inspection, and personnel scheduling.[11] Note that the emphasis is on a steady, predictable production rate, *not* on increasing that rate. The rate should be whatever the demand requires; if the demand is low, the rate of production should also be low.

Finally, regularity stimulates standardization. If workers set up and operate the same machine at about the same time every day, they are stimulated to develop standardized, simplified procedures for setup.

For all these reasons, the cycle-time concept is fundamental to JIT manufacturing. Specifically, removing wastes from work shortens cycle times and reduces work variation. Shortened cycle times then increase the overall maximum production rate and, hence, the production capacity of the overall process. As work activities are improved, not only is the cycle time shortened, but so is the overall lead time; this, in turn, contributes to another principle of JIT, manufacturing agility.[12]

AGILITY

Chester Richards[13] describes the agile manufacturer in terms of the "OODA-loop" concept in which opponents in a competitive situation must *observe* the situation (absorb information), *orient* themselves (put information in context), *decide* (select a course of action), and *act* (carry out the action). The agile manufacturer is, then, "a lean producer that has extended the concept to improve its ability to function as an open system (observe), change its worldview accordingly (orient), and make timely and effective decisions."[14]

Through rapid execution of OODA loops, companies can quickly increase product variety and attract customers away from competitors. Honda, for example, had lost market share to rival Yamaha for 15 years. In 1981 it began a counterattack, and during an 18-months period replaced its product line twice and introduced three times as many model changes as Yamaha. Honda rapidly surpassed Yamaha and remains today the world's leading motorcycle producer.

Agile manufacturing is not necessarily the same as flexible manufacturing, which is the ability to produce different products using the same line, machine, or process, and to switch over to meet planned changes in demand. It goes beyond that. It is the ability to economically switch back and forth among various products, produce any of them in almost any quantity, and quickly do so in response to unplanned changes in demand.

Automation is not necessarily the way to agility. In fact the expense and time to acquire, install, and program automated lines can actually hamper agility since automated systems tend to be limited in terms of variety of output. Nonetheless, as automation and robotics improve and evolve to incorporate artificial intelligence, automated systems themselves will become more agile.

Many of the JIT techniques described in later chapters for eliminating waste and putting shop-floor workers more in control help speed up the OODA loop. We mention them here briefly.

Reduced Setup Time and Small Production Batches.   Agility is the ability to move quickly from one product to another, one level of production to another, and so on. Short setup times at every stage of the production process are a must. Even with short setup times, however, agility is hampered if large inventories clog the way. Small-batch production is, thus, also necessary.

Equipment Maintenance and Selection.   Equipment must be able to do the work as needed, when needed, so it is essential that equipment be well functioning and reliable. To prevent buildups or shortages, all equipment must run at about the same rate, so high-speed equipment, per se, is not the answer. Probably better than complex, versatile machines through which everything must be routed are multiple, simple machines that can be dedicated to particular products.

Flexible Operations through a Flexible Workplace.   Agility is built into manufacturing by creating operations in which the output can be raised or lowered by simply adding or subtracting machines, people, or workstations. Operations should be designed so they have a low break-even point (Toyota claims to have a break-even objective of only 30% capacity). Operations that must be continuously run (for example, to maintain a certain speed or temperature) should be avoided because they encourage continuous usage (to justify running them), which creates large inventories.

Agile Workers.   Agile production requires agile workers. They must be cross-trained to perform a variety of tasks and do a variety of jobs, many of which are ordinarily done by specialists. Some specialists will always be needed, but even they should be flexible enough to do a variety of things and not feel that nonspecialized work is beneath them.

CASE IN POINT: Agility at Prince Castle[15]

Prince Castle is a leading manufacturer and supplier of foodservice equipment for McDonalds, Burger King, Taco Bell, Hardees, and others. In the past the company was primarily an assembler; that is, virtually all of its products were assemblies of parts and components produced by suppliers.

The company's products are varied, from electronic cooking timers and condiment dispensers to tomato slicers and deep-fryer cleaning equipment. Demand quantities for the products vary widely and change with short notice. Since most industrial suppliers are not willing (or agile enough) to produce parts in small batches, Prince Castle was forced to keep a large inventory of parts and components, even for items with tiny or infrequent demand.

The foodservice equipment business involves periodic demand surges. When a national chain introduces a new product, say a sandwich with a new kind of sauce, it needs a special portion-control dispenser for the product. Before the product can be launched, every restaurant in the chain (from 1,000 to 12,000 or more locations) must have the dispensers. The chains keep new products as carefully guarded secrets, and even long-time suppliers like Prince Castle get only a few months (or weeks) notice. To ensure that it could meet such demand surges, Prince Castle had to carry ample excess stock of finished goods and expensive WIP components.

An additional complicating aspect of the business stems from recent international growth of American fast-food chains. Equipment that looks identical at first glance might have different components because safety requirements and equipment standards vary from country to country, as well as from customer to customer. Ensuring an adequate supply of components to meet all these requirements contributed even more to the parts inventory problem.

In 1992 the managers of Prince Castle embarked on a strategy to increase the company's agility, yet reduce its reliance on inventory. First, they became a full-scale integrated manufacturer; that is, they not only assemble parts but also make most of them in-house. As inventory was reduced to free up cash and space, a variety of manufacturing systems were installed, including a CNC flexible manufacturing system and almost every other kind of machine needed to produce parts, panels, and even fasteners.

They also implemented a three-shift operation. Under normal demand conditions only the first shift is fully staffed, and the others run on skeleton crews. The rationale for maintaining the skeleton crews is that in the event of a demand surge (new product launch), there is an experienced supervisor and core group of workers on each shift to train and oversee temporary workers hired from an agency. On every shift, the full-time workers are multiskilled and can be assigned to different workstations and operations as needed.

The strategy has been a success. Inventories have been cut in half and capital costs have been recaptured. Specially produced products can be brought from concept to customer in substantially less time. Prince Castle retains its leadership position in cost and quality and has enhanced its reputation as an agile manufacturer, which has helped expand its customer base and doubled business revenue. Because customers know that they can count on Prince Castle to fill virtually any sized order for virtually any product, even on short notice, the company has an important advantage over its competition.

Agility calls for flexible scheduling of workers to balance the workload to make it uniform, to raise or lower the production rate, or to change the product output mix as needed. Skill variety not only benefits the plant, it benefits workers too. Work with variety is more interesting and, in a market downturn or shift, workers can be transferred to other jobs instead of being laid off.

VARIATION REDUCTION

Variation (variability) represents the amount by which something differs from some nominal value (standard, target, or expected). While variability in some things and events adds surprise, spice, and novelty to life, in a manufacturing process, surprise and novelty are among the least desirable of things. It is a curse manifested by waste and poor quality. In fact, however, variability runs through every aspect of manufacturing: workers' skills, motivation, abilities, and attendance; equipment and process operating capabilities, cycle times, setup times, and reliability; quality and scheduled delivery of raw materials and components; batch sizes (procured and produced); and innumerable other factors that influence production output.

Because of the persistence of variability, requirements are often defined in terms of a **tolerance range** with upper and lower specification limits and a **target** value at the midpoint. Performance is considered acceptable as long as it lies within the range. Just requiring that every component meets a specification limit, however, does not ensure that a higher-level product or process, one formed by a combination of components, will meet *its* requirement. When one component that is at the extreme of its tolerance range is mated with another component that is at the opposite extreme, the result is a bad fit. This is called **tolerance stackup,** and in products it is observable by gaps between parts that should fit snugly, or tight-fitting parts that should fit loosely. Either way, it's a sign of poor quality.

Variability also has a large effect on production costs and lead times, what Hopp and Spearman refer to as the corrupting influence of variability on system performance. They note that in a steady state system, increasing variability always increases average cycle times and WIP levels and that this effect on WIP and cycle times gets worse the earlier in the routing sequence (in a sequential process) that the variablity appears (that is, variability at an early stage of a process has a greater influence on overall WIP and lead times than variability at later stages).[16]

The traditional ways of dealing with process variability (safety stocks, safety lead times, overtime, and expediting) are costly and disruptive to the schedules of other processes. A better way is to identify the *sources* of variability and to eliminate or reduce them. According to Hopp and Spearman, a manufacturer that does not reduce process variability now will pay for it sooner or later in terms of long cycle times, high WIP, wasted capacity, or lost production throughput.[17]

Reduction in process variability is tantamount to improvement: assuming the standard or target is correct, zero variability equates to zero waste and zero defects. In JIT, variability reduction is enforced through, for example, analysis and standardization of operating routines and procedures, machine setup and preventive maintenance procedures, and leveled, regularized production schedules.

In a meticulously designed product or process, that is, one where target values everywhere have been set to optimize system performance (or, say, to provide total customer satisfaction), *any* amount of deviation from any of the target values will result in less than optimal performance. Genichi Taguchi expressed this less-than-optimal result as a loss to the manufacturer and the customer. Thus, the closer each element of a process (worker, equipment, and input material in a system) comes to meeting its target value, the lower the cost is and the better the overall performance is of the system. The point is, there should be no complacency about meeting specification limits; the goal should be to continuously reduce variability and to achieve the ideal, target value. This principle and its implications for product design and process control are discussed in Chapters 12 and 14.

MEASUREMENT

Another JIT principle is measurement. For whatever we seek to improve or wastes we seek to eliminate, measurement is necessary to know exactly where we are, where we have been, and where we are going. Measurement is fundamental to the PDCA cycle in both the plan stage (collect data) and the check stage (collect data). Any area for which improvement is sought must be initially measured to establish a baseline against which to measure progress. The measurement is either of one's own existing practices or of others who are thought to be doing an exemplary job (a practice known as **benchmarking,** described in the Chapter 4). Once an improvement plan has been approved and implemented, data are collected to assess the extent of progress made and to determine what more needs to be done. Thereafter, data are collected and results are announced to ensure that progress is maintained and to inspire further improvement. This is not some blue-sky prescription; it is a fundamental feature of continuous improvement and JIT/TQM.

Grass Roots Measurement

JIT/TQM organizations utilize measurements in ways unlike many traditional measurement systems. To begin with measurement results are *not* used for the performance appraisal of personnel or work groups. Also, the specific types of data collected are *not* mandated by upper management. Finally, the measurement results are *not* entered into centralized databases for purposes of control. Instead, data are collected to help groups and individuals assess problems, find solutions, and track progress. The workers involved in the problem decide what needs to be measured and how it should be measured; also, as much as possible, they collect the data themselves. Training workers in data collection skills and analysis is part of the improvement process. Having workers track performance and record results is one way of developing the norms of vigilance and attention to detail.

Measurement establishes priorities for workers, departments, and the organization. An unspoken rule in organizations is "If it's measured, it's important," and the corollary is "If it's not measured, it's not important." Of course, in reality many things get measured that never amount to anything (e.g., data are collected, results are filed) and no one ever looks at them. When people discover this, both the rule and the corollary stop applying. Nevertheless, on average, if you give an employee two tasks and only measure one of them, the one being measured will get more attention. Measurement is thus a way of establishing priorities and focusing attention on the areas most needing improvement.

Visual Management: Information Post-Its

The data that workers collect are largely retained by them for their own use. Conforming to the principle of visibility, the results are posted so that anyone can quickly see progress made and problems remaining. One way to gauge an organization's dedication to continuous improvement is to look at how much measurement is going on and how much of it is shared among the people who need it. Organizations serious about improvement have information relating to improvement posted on the walls, next to machines, or wherever it is convenient or expeditious to display it. Information about levels of waste, quality, productivity, and service is collected and posted along with goals so that workers can readily see trends and gaps between goals and practice (see Figure 3.16). This is an important aspect of visual management.

Management has to be careful not to abuse the results of grassroots measurement. The purpose of these measures is to serve PDCA, and management must ensure that the data are used for that purpose. Data collected for any other reasons, such as worker performance appraisal, must be kept separate from these data. If workers find that their measurements are being used for purposes of appraisal or manipulation by management, they will soon learn to misrepresent findings or to measure only those things for which they can readily show progress (neglecting everything else).

FIGURE 3.16

Schedule adherence charts maintained by shop-floor workers.

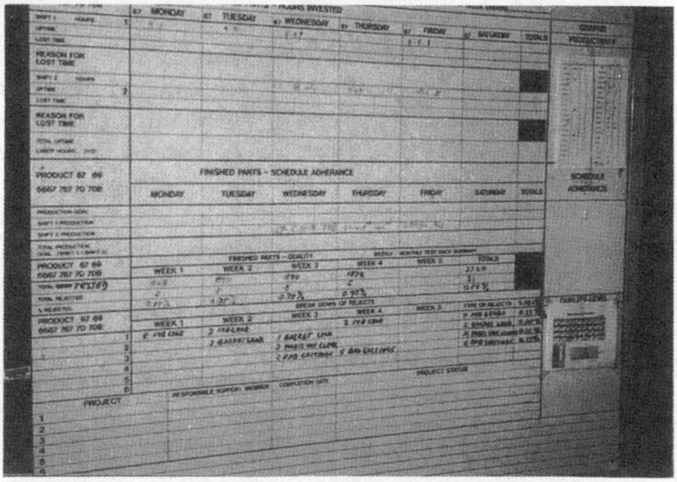

Getting to the Bottom Line

At some point, regardless of the idealism and dedication of the workers and managers, improvement efforts will have to be translated into broader measures of organizational health or competitiveness. To guarantee that continuous improvement and waste reduction are given permanent status in an organization's modus operandi, measures of improvement must ultimately be expressed in terms consequential to everyone. True believers will take it on faith that improvement and waste-reduction efforts will reduce costs and that reduced costs will mean higher profits, but the best way to get everyone united around the cause is to express outcomes in terms they all understand. Canon Corporation, for example, utilizes a system that expresses waste-reduction results in terms of profit and loss.

CASE IN POINT: Cost-Estimating Waste at Canon[18]

Every year Canon Corporation estimates the cost of waste by aggregating the estimates of waste costs from all areas across the corporation. The concept of waste elimination profit (WEP) is used, where

WEP = the degree of improvement over the previous year (in $)

= (*prior waste rate* − *current waste rate*) × *current production*.

Suppose that in 1 year the production output is $100 million. If the cost of waste from product defects is $1 million, the waste rate for defects would be 1%. Suppose in the next year the cost of waste for defects is still $1 million, but production output increases to $125 million. The waste rate for this year would be 0.8%. From one year to the next, the total savings (or earned profit) of reducing the defect waste rate from 1% to 0.8% is

WEP(defects) = (1% − 0.8%) × $125 million

= $250,000.

That is, $250,000 is the cost savings (accrued profit) attributed to waste-reduction efforts focusing on product defects.

The same kind of analysis is performed for all of the previously mentioned Nine Wastes that Canon tracks. The WEPs for the Nine Wastes are added to get total WEP. This figure is divided by the number of personnel in each section, division, factory, or department, to get WEP per person at each level. One reason for Canon's success at waste elimination has been its ability to tie improvement measures to traditional financial accounting measures. Each factory is required to produce an annual waste-elimination plan with high WEP goals. Though the immediate aim of WEP is to improve operations, the result is typically to increase value added and reduce fixed costs. Value added results from reducing wastes from defects, equipment, planning, and operations; lower fixed costs result from reducing wastes from WIP, expenses, and indirect labor. Combining higher value added with lower fixed costs reduces the break-even point and improves product profitability.

THE MEANING OF JIT

PHILOSOPHY, METHOD, OR WHAT?

In this chapter JIT has been referred to as a management philosophy principled on simplicity, organization, visibility, agility, and so on. Part II of the book covers a collection of JIT techniques and methods for small-batch production, setup-time reduction, maintenance, pull production, and the like, and Part IV discusses JIT as a production system. Referring to different concepts like this using the same moniker can lead to confusion. Even in the JIT literature, there is some confusion and debate about what JIT really is—concept, techniques, methods, philosophy, or system.[19] It is pointless to continue this debate here, since JIT can be all of these things, depending on what aspect of it you choose to look at.

In the beginning, JIT was a technique used by Toyota for the purpose of controlling production and reducing inventory. From there, it evolved to include techniques for setups, maintenance, worker participation, supplier relations, and so on. When JIT was then introduced to the rest of the world in the 1970s, it began as a manufacturing technique centered around the kanban method and pull production. Over time, as we have seen, JIT has evolved into a complete management philosophy driven by waste reduction and continuous improvement. Organizations that adopt JIT seem to go through the same kind of evolution: they start using JIT methods to improve shop-floor control, then they adopt the broader principles of JIT philosophy for organizationwide management.[20] Today most managers no longer think of JIT as just a set of implementable manufacturing techniques, but as a philosophy for managing a company and doing business.

JIT LIMITATIONS AND IMPLEMENTATION BARRIERS

Articles abound about the limitations of JIT and the companies that tried to implement JIT and failed. Much of this commentary points to one fact: JIT philosophy involves big changes in traditional attitudes about business relationships, work management, and shop-floor practices, and it requires long-term commitment to quality and waste reduction. Some JIT techniques also require customer-demand stability.

Attitudes

JIT requires a cooperative, participative spirit between managers, workers, suppliers, and their customers. It also requires long-term commitment by top management, as well as trust and mutual respect between managers and workers, and between customers and suppliers. Such concepts are foreign in some companies and industries; to accept them would be nothing short of revolution.

In traditional plants, frontline workers are given limited, singular responsibility for assembling parts or running machines. Contrast that to JIT workers who also have responsibility for continuous improvement. Quality problems and waste arise from many sources and it is impossible to get to all of them without substantial worker involvement. Broadened worker involvement results from a transfer of responsibilities and authority from support staff, supervisors, and managers to frontline workers. The transfer is successful only when staff, supervisors, and managers accept the proposition that workers are capable of handling more authority and that their handling of it is good for the company. The workers, too, must wholly embrace this concept. In companies where resistance to change is widespread and insurmountable, JIT will fail. In companies where such concepts are widely accepted, the few workers and managers who remain opposed and inflexible will either quit or have to be terminated.

JIT is a team-oriented philosophy, and in that regard it is very much like TQM described in the next chapter. In JIT organizations, teams of workers, cross-functional staff, suppliers, and customers are involved in all kinds of projects such as waste reduction, workcell improvement, product and process design, setup reduction, and supplier/customer relations. Every area of the organization is affected, and managers and workers who are unwilling to break down traditional walls between areas and with workers and suppliers will be incapable of implementing JIT.

Time Commitment

Most JIT programs take time to show benefits, especially financial benefits. In one study of companies implementing JIT, 59% indicated they were still 6 months to 3 years from full implementation, and 26% were more than 3 years away.[21] In another study, time required for JIT programs to yield significant benefits and deterioration of top management commitment and support were cited as two major barriers to implementing JIT.[22]

In the short run, the benefits of improved quality, agility, and cycle time are transparent, and, financially, JIT shows up solely as a cost. In terms of payback period, JIT can appear risky, not because of the capital expense involved, but because of the time and expense in training and development programs as well as improvement and waste-reduction projects. In JIT, chronic problems such as machine breakdowns, mistakes in production procedures, and poor organization are eliminated through steady, continual effort and team projects, but that takes time. Some managers do not subscribe to long-term, steady efforts, instead preferring, it seems, large capital expenditures to handle problems that could more effectively be resolved by cheaper means, but which require more staying power. A friend of mine, a successful management consultant, has all but given up trying to sell managers on JIT. He says, "They don't want to hear about JIT. It's too fundamental. What they want is a system, a black box they can plug in to solve their problems. It doesn't matter that the black box is expensive or even that it will introduce new problems of its own."

Quality Commitment[23]

A prerequisite for JIT success is commitment to quality. Among 1035 organizations surveyed in a 1993 study of JIT practices, the largest percentage, 85% were practicing total quality control. Commitment to quality requires changes in policies affecting procurement, production processes, product design, problem troubleshooting, and relationships with suppliers. For example, instead of just price, criteria for suppliers must include guarantees for high-quality products in terms of ability to meet specifications, delivery dates, and delivery quantities. Failure to find suppliers that can meet JIT requirements or that are willing to adapt to them can be a major obstacle to implementing JIT.

Quality must be designed into the product and the production process, and that, in turn, requires adopting a new product/process design methodology. Also, frontline workers must be given time to troubleshoot and resolve quality problems at the source. Companies that espouse quality but fail to support it in terms of quality design and manufacturing practices cannot attain the quality levels assumed for most JIT practices.

Variation Reduction and Stability

JIT seeks to increase stability by reducing variation in inputs, internal processes, and customer demand. It seeks to smooth production because level production is easier to schedule, less wasteful, and less costly than irregular, lumpy production. In turn, it seeks to reduce variation of inputs through improved supplier relationships and of internal processes through preventive maintenance, production leveling, and small-lot and pull production. Demand variation is reduced through better forecasting and closer ties with customers. Sales and production people work together to accomplish these goals.

In some custom-produced and job-shop environments, however, the demands, lead times, and production rates are highly variable, attempts to the contrary notwithstanding. In such environments, JIT practices such as pull production and small-lot production are difficult or impossible to implement. Because of that, however, some critics write off the entirety of JIT, even though most other JIT principles and practices remain applicable and beneficial *regardless of the market or demand environment*. They simply do not understand the full scope of JIT.

Misunderstanding JIT

Because JIT emphasizes inventory reduction, some people believe that JIT's prime focus is inventory, and its goal is small inventory. It is not. The JIT prescription is to reduce inventory slowly, identify problems, then change policies and practices to remove the problems; having done so, then reduce inventory a little bit more, and so on. But confusing means with ends, companies try to reduce inventories *without* resolving the problems. When the production system comes to a screeching halt, as it surely will, they blame JIT.

A further misunderstanding about JIT is that it is a *physical system* to be implemented. The most common mental picture that people have of that physical system is pull production and kanban, topics of Chapter 8. Implementing JIT, they believe, is equivalent to tearing out whatever production system is in place and installing a pull process with kanban cards and small containers. While it is true that a physical pull system with kanban control is an important feature of JIT production, such a system does not represent the entirety of JIT, nor is it a *necessary* component of JIT. A JIT program that focuses on long-term commitment and cultural change devoted to waste reduction and customer-oriented quality can succeed even without a pull system; a JIT program that tries to implement a pull system but exclude all the rest will almost surely fail.

SOCIAL IMPACT OF JIT

Beyond the conduct of business, JIT is having a broader impact, one about which managers might or might not care: the philosophy and practice of JIT returns to workers a degree of dignity, recognition, meaning, and pride of work that has long been absent at the lowest levels of organizational hierarchies. JIT says that the center of wisdom does not reside solely at the top of an organization; rather, it is distributed throughout, though, often, it is only wisdom in potential form, and it needs developing to be realized. The ultimate waste recognized by JIT, then, is the waste of the potential of most workers.

FIRST THINGS FIRST

JIT philosophy and practice is an elaboration on things described in this chapter. A quick review of these things says what JIT is really about—simple, common sense ideas, largely instituted at the shop-floor level by the workers themselves. It also says what JIT is *not* about—automation, robotics, and computerized manufacturing systems designed and installed by engineers and systems specialists. Both JIT and automation are important to manufacturing competitiveness, but while the latter is important in varying degrees to some or many manufacturers depending on industry, the former is important to virtually *all* of them.

JIT is also a matter of priorities. If an organization decides to automate, it had better *first* be well down the road to having eliminated much of the waste in its production system and having improved its product and process designs and procedures for manual systems. Automating something that is wasteful simply casts the waste into cement, and makes it harder and more costly to remove later. General Motors spent *$40 billion* on factory automation, and afterward was still plagued with largely the same quality and productivity problems it faced before. Continuous improvement and elimination of waste through JIT is a movement back to the basics. Having mastered the basics, a manufacturer will be in a better position to take advantage of the benefits offered by computer-integrated manufacturing systems (CIMS), electronic data interchange systems (EDISs), flexible manufacturing systems (FMSs), and the like. Discussing CIM and its disappointingly slow progress in taking hold in industry, Ayres and Butcher note that lean production (JIT philosophy) may be more important to US industry than CIM. The evidence, they say, suggests that unless a company first adopts the basics of lean production, conversion to CIM is likely to fail; cultural change must precede rather than follow technical change.[24]

IMPLEMENTATION: LEARN AS YOU GO

JIT involves so many aspects and is so all-encompassing that top management can be intimidated into avoiding it. Although JIT is so broad and has so many aspects, however, it does not have to be implemented all at once. In fact, rushing headlong into JIT and pushing for change everywhere is likely to be too much, too soon, and to cause increased resistance. On the other hand, introducing it slowly allows problems to be identified and resolved in a more orderly way and resistance to atrophy for lack of cause. Given that management understands the principles of JIT, acknowledges its

---

CASE IN POINT: JIT at ITT McDonnell & Miller[25]

At McDonnell & Miller, a Chicago division of ITT industries that manufactures fluid monitoring and control equipment, elements of JIT philosophy and practice have been slowly implemented since the early 1980s. The McDonnell & Miller plant is divided into focused factories, each with its own mini management team. The focused factories, in turn, are divided into cells, each run and managed by a team of operators. Pull production has been introduced in some parts of the plant but not everywhere. Employees are considered associates. Workers not only operate machines and do product quality inspection, they do job scheduling and rudimentary equipment maintenance. When touring the shop floor, a visitor can easily detect the pride workers have in their jobs and the company as they explain their responsibilities and contributions to improvements. Quality of design, statistical process control, close supplier relations, preventive maintenance, and other key programs in JIT/TQM have become entrenched practices at McDonnell & Miller.

CASE IN POINT: JIT at Strombecker, Inc.[26]

Strombecker, another Chicago-based company, manufactures a variety of toys under the "Tootsietoy" logo. Strombecker became a JIT company starting in 1992. In many ways it is not as far along in JIT as McDonnell & Miller, though in some ways it is considerably ahead. At the Chicago plant, pull production and kanban have been implemented on the major lines, and Strombecker has developed its own pull system for materials procurement. It is experimenting with workcells, defect mistake-proofing, and standard operations, though it has not yet developed a strong preventive maintenance program and has had difficulty in getting its suppliers to subscribe to JIT.

Perhaps the big surprise about Strombecker is that it has undertaken so much change without empowering its workforce. That was not a conscious choice, but rather a result of the fact that many of the company's shop employees speak little or no English. This creates problems for training workers so they can assume broader responsibility. Strombecker realizes the limiting effect this has on quality and process improvement and is committed to increasing worker participation. To that end it has begun an English as a second language program. Though not yet to the extent of McDonnell & Miller, Strombecker workers are treated as associates, and a visitor to the plant with a question is often introduced to a worker who can give an explanation.

necessary long-term commitment and possibly delayed payoffs, then a company can proceed to implement JIT in any of numerous ways. Two companies, McDonnell & Miller and Strombecker are examples.

Summary

Guiding concepts in JIT are value-added and waste elimination. The value-added concept says to identify those activities in a process that directly increase the value of an item and consider all the rest wasteful and candidates for elimination. Only activities that add value, or that do not but are necessary, should be retained. These become the focus of continuous improvement efforts.

One way to distinguish value-added from non-value-added activities is to look at common wastes in organizations such as transportation, inventory, waiting, and setup. These add to cost but not to value, so focusing on them is a logical first step in waste elimination. Once the obvious, prominent sources of waste have been removed, the next step is to pursue the wastes that are hidden. Focus on waste reduction not only improves end-item quality and organizational performance, it is also good for the environment. Broadly construed, less waste in production translates directly into less pollution, conserved resources, and recycled and reused materials.

Decisions and actions in JIT organizations are guided by a set of principles:

· *Simplification.* Given multiple ways to achieve the identical result, simpler is better.

· *Cleanliness and Organization.* A clean, organized workplace promotes discipline and caring attitudes about work and products, reduces waste, and helps pinpoint incipient trouble spots and workplace problems.

· *Visibility.* Information that is immediately visible to everyone who needs it enables people to do their jobs better, motivates them to do the right thing, and eliminates unnecessary and ineffective planning and control activities.

· *Cycle Timing.* Regularity of workplace patterns reduces uncertainty, increases learning and improvement potential, and permits better planning and action toward meeting customer demand.

· *Agility.* Daily, changing customer demand is a fact of life; companies must be able to quickly react to changes, plan for them, and be able to respond even without plans.

· *Variation Reduction.* Reducing the variability by which a process deviates from standards, goals, or expectations uniformly reduces process waste and improves process performance.

· *Measurement.* Continuous improvement and waste-elimination efforts at any level companywide depend on people having data to assess where they are now, where they should be going, and, along the way, how well they are doing.

JIT has been interpreted to mean many different things, such as a method, a system, and a philosophy. The most current interpretation, the one subscribed to here, is that JIT is a management philosophy that addresses not only production practices, but also expectations about roles and responsibilities of managers, support staff, line workers, and suppliers, their relationships to one another and to customers, as well as broader issues about the conduct of business. At some level, JIT principles apply to all organizations—large and small, services and manufacturing. Problems with implementing JIT tend to stem from lack of commitment, resistance to change, or simple misunderstanding about what JIT really means. JIT is a move back to basics, and there can be little argument over JIT from the perspective that the principles behind it make good business sense.

Besides mastering the manufacturing basics (possibly augmented by leading-edge technology), a manufacturing company needs one other thing to be competitive. All of that effort on value added, waste elimination, and continuous improvement, whether by manual or automated means, has to be directed toward the right end, and in competitive markets that end is the customer. Keeping the organization customer-focused is the role of TQM, the topic of the next chapter.

Questions

1. What is the distinction between value-added and non-value-added activities in a process? Give examples of each (other than from this chapter).

2. Distinguish between necessary and unnecessary non-value-added activities. Explain how you differentiate them. Give examples (other than from this chapter). Can a non-value-added activity be considered necessary in some places and unnecessary in others? Explain.

3. Describe typical support activities. Are they value-added or non-valued-added, necessary or unnecessary? Explain.

4. What role do workers play in distinguishing value-added from the non-value-added activities in a process?

5. What are Toyota's Seven Wastes. What are Canon's Nine Wastes. What are categories of waste that neither list includes?

6. Suggest ways to reduce or eliminate each of the wastes listed above (Toyota's, Canon's, and your own).

7. Explain the following JIT principles and give an example of each:
   a. Simplification
   b. Cleanliness and organization
   c. Visibility
   d. Cycle timing
   e. Agility
   f. Variation reduction
   g. Measurement

8. Explain the various interpretations of the term JIT. In its broadest interpretation, what is JIT?

9. A hospital administrator turns down his assistant's request to attend a JIT seminar, saying "We don't make things here. JIT's not relevant to us." Comment.

10. Reference to the term JIT in the popular press, trade journals, and management books seems to be declining.
    a. Is JIT losing relevance? How can you explain less use of the term JIT?
    b. Was JIT a flavor-of-the-month management style that has lost its popularity?

Problems

1. Refer to the processes in problem 6 in the previous chapter. In each of the process flow diagrams:
    a. Classify the activities (steps) as value-added or non-value-added, necessary or unnecessary. Explain how you make the distinction in each.
    b. Based on the way you classified activities in (*a*), what would you do to reduce waste in each process? Would the process be improved in terms of time, cost, quality, agility? Explain.
2. Refer to Examples 1 through 5 in this chapter. Each of these illustrates improvements through product and/or process simplification. For everything, however, there are at least two sides, and decisions about simplification should always consider the trade-offs. Consider in each of the five examples potential drawbacks associated with the proposed simplification in terms of time, cost, quality, or agility. Discuss the improvement/drawback trade-off.

Endnotes

1. T. Vollmann, W. Berry, D. Whybark, *Manufacturing Planning and Control Systems,* 3rd ed. (Homewood, IL: Irwin, 1992), pp. 72–3.
2. T. Ohno, *Toyota Production System—Beyond Management of Large-Scale Production* (Tokyo: Diamond Publishing, 1978) (in Japanese).
3. It has also been called the "flower" of all evil, meaning that inventory is the result of mismanagement of production. *See* R.A. Iman, "Inventory is the *Flower* of All Evil," *Production and Inventory Management Journal* 34, no. 4 1993, pp. 41–5.
4. T.E. Graedel and B.R. Allenby, *Industrial Ecology* (Englewood Cliffs, NJ: Prentice Hall, 1995).
5. B. Patton, "Design for Environment: A Management Perspective," in R. Socolow, C. Andrews, F. Berkhout, V. Thomas (eds.) *Industrial Ecology and Global Change,* (UK: Cambridge University Press, 1994); M.E. Henstock, *Design for Recyclability,* (London: Institute of Metals, 1988).
6. *See* Peter Dewhurst, "Product Design and Manufacture: Design for Disassembly," *Industrial Engineering* 25, no. 5 (Sept. 1993), pp. 26–8.
7. "Xerox Spreading its Recycling Philosophy," *APICS—The Performance Advantage,* August 1992, p. 13.
8. Japan Management Association, *Canon Production System* (Cambridge, MA: Productivity Press, 1987), Chapter 6.
9. R. Schonberger, *World Class Manufacturing*: *The Lessons of Simplicity Applied* (New York: Free Press, 1986), Chapter 2.
10. For elaboration, *see* R. Hall, *Attaining Manufacturing Excellence* (Burr Ridge, IL: Dow-Jones Irwin, 1987), pp. 98–103.
11. R. Hall, *ibid.,* p. 99.
12 For more on cycle-timing, *see* R. Hall, *ibid.,* pp. 103–8.

13. C. Richards, "Agile Manufacturing: Beyond Lean?" *Production and Inventory Management Journal* 37, no. 2 (2nd Quarter 1996), pp. 60–4.

14. C. Richards, *ibid.,* p. 63.

15. Interview with W. Kinney, Sr. V.P. of Sales and Marketing, and J. Esselburn, Sr. V.P. of Operations, Prince Castle Inc.

16. W. Hopp and M. Spearman, *Factory Physics* (Chicago: Richard D. Irwin, 1996), pp. 282–8.

17. Hopp and Spearman, *ibid.,* pp. 296–302.

18. Japan Management Association, *Canon Production System,* pp. 23–5.

19. R. Vokurka and R. Davis, "Just-in-Time: The evolution of a Philosophy," *Production and Inventory Management* 37, no. 2 (2nd Quarter 1996), pp. 56–8.

20. G. Plenart, "Three Differing Concepts of JIT," *Production and Inventory Management* 31, no. 2 (2nd Quarter 1990), pp. 1–2.

21. Touche Ross Logistics Consulting Services, "Implementing Just In Time Logistics," *1988 National Survey on Progress, Obstacles, and Results,* p. 5.

22. K. Crawford, J. Blackstone, and J. Cox, "A Study of JIT Implementation and Operating Problems," *International Journal of Production Research* 26 (September 1988), pp. 1565–6.

23. National Center for Manufacturing Sciences, *Competing in World-Class Manufacturing* (Homewood, IL: Business One Irwin, 1990), pp. 227–8.

24. R. Ayers and D. Butcher, "The Flexible Factory Revised," *The American Scientist* 81 (Sept–Oct 1993), p. 455.

25. Interview with Avi Soni, Manager of Manufacturing Engineering, ITT McDonnell & Miller.

26. Interview with Vern Shadowen, Manager of Plant Operations, Strombecker, Inc.

TQM:
CUSTOMER-FOCUSED QUALITY

To be competitive, a JIT company must be quality oriented. In fact, by not being quality oriented and focusing solely on waste reduction, it would be very easy for a JIT company to create products and services that customers do *not* want. Such a company, says Chester Richards, would then "be stockpiling inventory [of unsold goods] quicker and more efficiently than anybody else," and "if you are truly into Just-in-Time (i.e., produce to demand and minimize inventory), you'll soon build nothing at all."[1] About the relationship between quality and JIT, Steven Ray waxes poetic:

> Without quality improvement, any attempts to implement [JIT] are likely to fail. Even if successful, attaining JIT ideals would be nearly impossible unless there is an ongoing effort to improve reliability throughout the total production system . . . . Achieving the ideals of JIT is the destination, reached by a journey of continuous, fundamental improvement and elimination of waste. Actions centered around companywide quality improvement are the fuels that propel us on that journey.[2]

It is a given that manufacturing competitiveness rests on the producer's ability to make quality products. This chapter argues that to achieve the quality levels mandated in a competitive business environment, organizations must adopt the *total quality approach*. The chapter gives an overview of this approach, and a framework showing the roles that every level and functional area in a manufacturing organization must play. The chapter also describes *employee involvement*, a concept very important to implementing organizationwide total quality, as well as *benchmarking,* a way for setting high, competitive quality standards, and *certifications and awards*, which have become standards for the design of quality programs worldwide. The chapter concludes with a discussion of approaches to implementing organizationwide quality programs and of the barriers to successful implementation.

QUALITY DEFINED

Pirsig's quandary, and ours too, is that quality is a concept that does not lend itself to easy description or simple measurement. Any definition of quality is dependent on the person doing the defining—the customer or the producer—and even within those categories, definitions vary widely. One principle of the **total quality** approach is that any definition of quality must *start* with the customer's perspective. That perspective represents what is termed **customer-focused quality,** which is the way customers view or feel about a product. Obviously, the product customers see is influenced by the way the product is designed, the way it is manufactured, and any service provided to the customer after buying the product. These factors represent **internal quality,** which are the actions or procedures used by the producer to translate customer opinions and requirements into a product design and to monitor and control materials and manufacturing so the final product conforms to customer requirements.

CUSTOMER'S PERSPECTIVE

The customer's perspective of quality is called **fitness for use,** which is how well the product compares to what the customer expects of it. Broadly speaking, the term *customer* refers to the recipient of the output of any process. In manufacturing that can mean a company using materials or parts to produce the product, a person on a production line working on the product, a retailer selling the product, or a person who purchases the product. W. Edwards Deming considered the person who *purchases* the product as the final stage of the production process and the most important customer of all.

David Garvin identifies the following eight dimensions of product quality:[3]

1. *Performance.* Includes operating characteristics like speed, comfort, ease of use, and so on; most products have multiple performance features, and customer preferences determine the relative importance of each (e.g., high acceleration versus high gas-mileage).

2. *Features.* Extras, add-ons, or gimmicks that enable a customer to somewhat customize a product.

3. *Reliability.* The likelihood that the product will perform as expected (not malfunction) within a given time period.

4. *Conformance.* The degree to which the product satisfies or conforms to pre-established standards.

5. *Durability.* The length of time, or extent of use, before the product deteriorates and must be replaced; durability is a function of the product's operating environment and reliability.

6. *Serviceability.* The speed, ease, and convenience of getting or making repairs and the courtesy and competency of repair people.

7. *Aesthetics.* The look, feel, taste, sound, or smell of the product based on personal taste; though subjective, some aesthetic judgments tend to be universal.

8. *Perceived value.* Subjective opinions about the product based on images or attitudes formed by advertising and/or the reputation of the producer.

Besides these are dimensions of *service* quality, for example, product *availability, support* by the manufacturer after the product is purchased, and knowledgeable and courteous sales and support people.

A product does not need to be rated highly by customers on all dimensions, only on those they think are important. Customers weigh the dimensions against the cost of the product and are willing to pay more for higher quality on certain individual dimensions, or for higher quality on a greater number of dimensions. The connection between quality and cost is the concept of *value,* the extent to which customers feel they paid a good price for the quality they received in return.

PRODUCER'S PERSPECTIVE

Once a company has determined the customer's perceptions of quality, it must translate those perceptions into a product design, and then implement the manufacturing process such that the final product meets the design requirements. These two aspects of the producer's perspective are *quality of design* and *quality of conformance.*

Quality of Design

The term **quality of design** represents the ability of a product *as designed* to satisfy or exceed customer requirements. Although quality of design initially focuses on customer requirements, eventually it must also take into account product demand, availability of materials and parts, and capability of the manufacturer to produce the product. There are also matters such as production costs, profitability, and the actions of competitors, which come into play when determining which aspects of a product (say, from among Garvin's eight dimensions) are most relevant to product quality. In Chapter 12 we discuss methodologies such as quality function deployment, design for manufacture, and robust design as ways to integrate the multiple dimensions and perspectives of quality into the product design.

Quality of Conformance

Given that the product design is in fact faithful to the customer requirements, it is then incumbent on the manufacturing function to produce a product that is faithful to the design. **Quality of conformance** is the term used to connote that the manufactured product consistently upholds the requirements as set in the product design. Emphasis in quality of conformance is on two things: defect detection and defect prevention. Here "defect" implies some deviation from the requirements or inability to meet some fitness-for-use criteria.

    · **Defect detection** refers to inspection, test, and analysis of products using (typically) statistical sampling procedures to determine the presence of defects and to draw conclusions about the quality of an overall process or batch. Defect detection helps ensure that the product going to the customer is OK, but it does nothing to improve the quality of the product.

    · **Defect prevention** includes monitoring and controling process variation, again by using statistical procedures, and by identifying causes of variation that, left alone, could lead to defects. The goal is to prevent defects. For some processes, it is possible to institute **error-proofing** or **fool-proofing** procedures, which are procedures that virtually eliminate the occurence of defects caused by errors or inadvertent mistakes.

It should be clear that under TQM philosophy, the emphasis in quality of conformance is overwhelmingly on defect prevention, not defect detection.

    No company can achieve the levels of quality expected by customers without paying attention to both quality of design and quality of conformance. A product must be designed to meet the customer's requirements, yet it must also be designed to fit the capabilities of the production process. After the product is designed to do both, the production process must be controlled to ensure that the output continuously conforms to the requirements of the design. To excel at both quality of design and quality of conformance requires the coordinated efforts of people from all functions and levels of the organization.

FRAMEWORK FOR MANAGING TOTAL QUALITY

Total quality management or **TQM** refers to an integrated approach by management to focus all functions and levels of an organization on quality and continuous improvement. It is considered *total* quality in the sense that it emphasizes customer-focused quality not just for customers of the final product but also for the organization's internal customers. Further it requires total participation and commitment companywide.

TQM PROCESS

TQM is not a program to achieve specific, static goals, but instead is a process committed to *continuous* quality improvement. The reasons why continuous quality improvement is such an important part of TQM have to do with surviving and thriving in a changing and competitive world:

· The competition is not sitting still. No matter what new quality standard a company sets for itself, the competition will eventually meet and exceed that standard.

· Customer expectations are continuously increasing. Brand loyalty for its own sake is a thing of the past. Customers seek out producers that are best able to satisfy their requirements.

· It is difficult to sustain a fixed level of quality. By seeking new, higher-level quality standards, the inclination to fall back to older, lower-level standards is reduced.

Though many companies recognize the strategic importance of continuous quality improvement, many others do not, and as a result the acronym TQM has been overused, abused, and misused. Many self-proclaimed TQM producers have actually done little in the way of improving their processes for quality assurance and quality control; they merely use TQM as a label to convey the image that the company thinks quality is important and as a marketing gimmick to suggest that their products are high quality.

TQM INTEGRATIVE FRAMEWORK

TQM builds quality into the product through continuous attention to quality and improvement by every organizational function, from marketing and design to manufacturing and customer service. Figure 4.1 is a framework illustrating the responsibilities of functional units in TQM and their relationship to the primary tasks of TQM. For example in Figure 4.1, **quality of performance/service** refers to the extent that

FIGURE 4.1

TQM framework: Participants in quality product design, manufacture, and service.

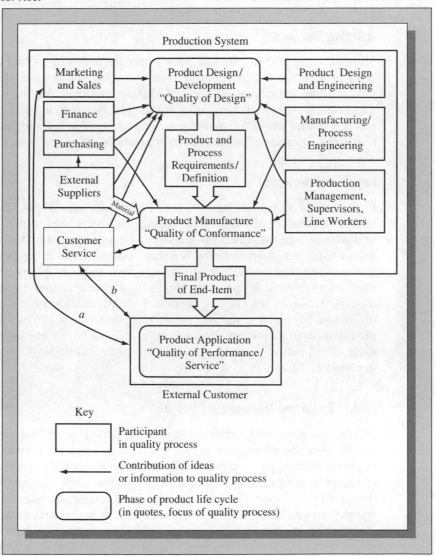

the finished product measures up to the customer's expectations and requirements. The product's ability to do that, of course, depends on how well the company executes the quality-of-design and quality-of-conformance tasks. To the extent that a product fails to meet customer requirements, adjustments are needed to the product's design, manufacture, or both. This suggests the importance of communicating timely, accurate information about product performance from the customer to departments and teams responsible for product quality of design and quality of conformance (represented in Figure 4.1 by arrows *a* and *b*). The responsibilities of functional areas in the TQM process are discussed next.

Marketing and Sales

Marketing and sales are the company's primary points of contact with the customer. Both provide current information from the customer essential for developing new products and improving old ones. Marketing performs consumer research to determine customers' wants, defines customer quality characteristics and requirements, and determines what customers are willing to pay. The sales force provides information about customer opinions of current products and suggestions for future products.

Finance and Accounting

Financial and accounting data are used for strategic analysis and planning. In a TQM company, however, the role of the finance and accounting functions is expanded to find ways to integrate financial measures with operational and strategic measures to give a balanced picture of how well the company is meeting customer-defined requirements.[4] That role includes providing information to support continuous improvement efforts as well as operational and competitive decisions. Performance measurement systems and their role in operational and strategic decision making is the subject of Chapter 21. Finance and accounting also contribute to product design decisions by providing accurate information on costs associated with a product throughout its life cycle. The topics of life-cycle product costs and accurate product costing are covered in Chapters 12 and 20, respectively.

Product Design and Manufacturing Design

Product designers and engineers work with marketing and sales people to translate information about customer needs, wants, and expectations into product technical requirements and physical designs. Since a product is only as good as the process that produces it, product designers must work with manufacturing engineers to ensure the design accounts not only for the customer's requirements, but also for the processes, equipment, and labor skills that will convert the design into an actual product.

In the past, many products were designed without consideration as to how they would be made. Product designers would conceive and design a product in detail, then "toss it over the wall" to manufacturing (see Figure 4.2), the wall being the metaphorical barrier that traditionally separated design and production functions (and that separated all the other functions too). The consequence was that sometimes manufacturing could not make the product conform to the design (the result: high defect rates), or it could make it conform, but only through extraordinary effort (the result: high cost). The point is, issues relating to the production process (workplace equipment, technology, and workers) must be addressed during product design. Among the approaches for integrating both customer requirements and production-process issues

FIGURE 4.2

Over-the-wall product design.

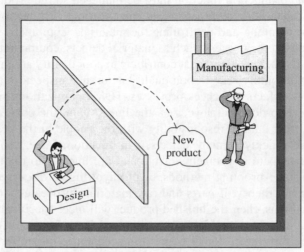

into the product design are **concurrent engineering** and **design for manufacture and assembly,** discussed in Chapter 12.

The emphasis of these integrated approaches is to design *in* quality and to design *out* defects, an aspect of **quality at the source.** Such emphasis is crucial to product-quality improvement since as much as 80% of all defects result from poor design.[5] More time and effort devoted to quality in the early stages of design result in less time and effort in dealing with quality-related problems during production and following sale. It also reduces after-sale defects that cost the company dearly in terms of bad reputation with customers who find or hear about defects, and decreases the chances of losing customers forever.

Purchasing and Suppliers

A high-quality product is achievable only if it has high-quality parts, and for most manufactured products at least half the parts come from suppliers. Purchasing's role in TQM is to ensure that purchased parts and materials meet quality requirements and that suppliers are able to meet delivery and service requirements and guarantee quality parts. Purchasing agents participate in product design by providing design engineers with information about the availability, technology, and costs of parts and materials that go into products.

The purchasing function also serves as the intermediary between the manufac-turer and its suppliers. Common among TQM organizations are *customer–supplier partnerships* wherein managers and engineers from suppliers participate in the cus-tomer's product design process and make recommendations concerning the parts they will be supplying. In turn, suppliers are provided with the training and support they need to better meet customer requirements. Customer–supplier partnerships are cov-ered in Chapter 19.

Production Management, Supervisors, Line Workers

The production function must be managed so the product design is executed and the product is made according to specifications. Production management is responsible for planning and controlling the materials, equipment, and workforce so that variations in the process, such as material defects, equipment breakdowns, order backlogs, and other problems that contribute to poor quality are minimized. Whereas firms have traditionally relied upon quality assurance inspectors (who are not line workers) to spot defects and check processes, TQM organizations give most of that responsibility to shop-floor employees on the line. Again, the concept is quality at the source—putting quality responsibility with the people in the best position to readily identify and quickly remedy defects in production. Supervisors and line workers actively participate in problem solving and are integral to the total quality process. (Use of mistake-proofing methods, or **pokayoking,** is discussed in detail in Chapter 15.)

In theory, if parts and raw materials, processes, and operations all meet specifications, then the finished product will meet specifications, too. Modern customer–supplier partnerships and guaranteed incoming quality have largely eliminated the need for the customer to perform acceptance inspection of procured parts and materials. Also, suppliers and freight carriers working with customers have eliminated most of the defects originating from packaging, delivery, and warehousing. As a result, virtually all of the quality emphasis in the production function is now on monitoring the manufacturing process and using **statistical process control (SPC)** to keep it within required parameters. SPC, which is fundamental to TQM, is the topic of Chapter 14.

Customer Service

Once a customer has acquired the finished product, the producer has responsibility for ensuring that the customer has adequate information, support, and assistance to install, operate, and maintain the product. Good service, an aspect of quality of performance/service in Figure 4.1, further includes the producer's responsiveness to customer complaints and warranty claims and willingness to replace or repair products that fail to meet promised quality levels. Consequently, good customer service directly influences the customer's opinion about the quality of a product.

The customer service function is also an important source of information about quality of performance opinions and customer suggestions for future products. This information should be channeled back to design–production–procurement areas so that sources of quality problems can be eliminated and suggestions for improvement can be designed into new products.

TOP MANAGEMENT'S ROLE

TQM must start at the top and have management's full commitment and backing since its organizationwide scope requires resources and incentives of magnitude that only top management can authorize. It must be understood that quality is pre-eminent on the organization's hierarchy of values. Quality must be part of the organization's vision and mission, and quality initiatives must be included in its strategic plans.

Though TQM must originate and be spread from the top down, its actual implementation is best achieved at the local or departmental level by way of numerous small efforts undertaken by teams of managers, staff employees, and workers. The overall, organizationwide effort should be coordinated by a steering committee comprising representatives from all functional areas and top management. Details of TQM implementation are discussed later in the chapter. References cited in the endnotes discuss additional implementation issues.[6]

EMPLOYEE INVOLVEMENT

Involvement of line and shop-floor workers is fundamental to TQM and quality at the source. For this reason companies should:

· Give ownership for quality to the workers, elicit and listen to workers' ideas about improvement, and empower them to make more decisions and perform tasks that are quality related.
· Organize workers for greater cross-functionality and greater customer consciousness.
· Train and educate workers in quality-related skills and about the importance of TQM to company competitiveness, to their own advancement prospects, and to job security.

EMPLOYEE OWNERSHIP OF QUALITY

Quality is not something that management can mandate or dictate. To gain employee commitment to the quality process, companies must modify their systems of management, control, and rewards to give employees greater responsibility and opportunity to become customer and quality oriented and motivate them to strive for continuous improvement. Many companies tell employees that quality comes first, then send a mixed message by paying them on a quota basis and pressing them to get the product out the door.

Adversarial relations between management and labor will prevent workers from taking a quality-oriented program seriously and will eventually kill the program. In many cases, managers' attitudes about labor and about the way they supervise workers will have to change, too. Specifically, middle- and lower-level managers and supervisors must relinquish some control, give workers more responsibility for running their own jobs, and provide them with opportunity to use their own judgment to solve problems. One sure sign that workers on the shop floor are being afforded (and are assuming) greater ownership of quality initiatives is an abundance of charts on the shop floor created and updated by workers to reflect their own plans, organization, and control activities.

ORGANIZATION FOR QUALITY

Workers in TQM organizations must be process oriented and customer conscious. To that end, companies restructure jobs to put workers in contact with whoever their customers and suppliers are, whether internal or external to the company. As a result, probably the most pervasive organizational feature about TQM organizations is the prevalence of teams.

Cross-Functional Teams

The rule for forming most teams in TQM is to organize them around a process *not* around a function. A cross-functional team is a permanent or temporary group comprising workers who are linked by a common process. One example of such a team is a group of workers who serve each other as internal suppliers and customers. The team includes workers from different areas of the plant who send and receive parts and subassemblies to and from each other. Teams like that raise the consciousness level about customers, both internal and external, and facilitate cross-functional problem solving.

Another team is a customer–vendor team. Workers from both the customer and the vendor plants meet periodically to discuss problems about quality, delivery, and cost and decide jointly how to resolve them. Face-to-face meetings build mutual empathy about the constraints facing workers in both plants and about what each needs to do their jobs better.

Quality Circles

Another common form of worker team in TQM organizations is the **quality circle** (or QC), a concept originated in Japan in the 1960s and introduced to the US in the 1970s.[7] A quality circle is a voluntary group of 6 to 10 workers and a supervisor. The supervisor coordinates and facilitates the group, but the group identifies the problems it wishes to address, collects and analyzes data, produces solutions, and then presents their solutions to management. The problems involve costs, safety, and productivity, as well as quality. Team members are trained in group dynamics and basic data collection and analysis tools like those covered in Chapter 2.

Quality circles have been widely applied and are very successful in Japan. In the 1970s and early 1980s, the number of US companies attempting to implement quality circles reached mania proportions. Most attempts failed, however, because of poor implementation. Specifically, workers were not sufficiently motivated or trained to find meaningful solutions to problems of consequence, and management did not give workers sufficient recognition, resources, or authority to do the job right. Peter Drucker argues that a reason quality circles failed in the US is because they were established without rigorous ways to measure the effects of worker suggestions.[8] In Japan, SPC procedures had already been accepted and widely adopted prior to establishing quality circles, and they became the basis for monitoring work and measuring the effects of improvement suggestions. Nonetheless, quality circle programs have succeeded at many US companies including General Electric, Coors Beer, Lockheed-Martin Aerospace, and Westinghouse. These companies continue to rely on quality circles as a major way for workers to contribute quality improvements.

Process- and Project-Oriented Worker Teams

Worker teams are also formed around either functional processes or project goals.

A departmental workcell or other process-oriented team is a somewhat permanent team formed around a process. Besides performing daily work in team fashion, the team meets briefly daily or weekly to address productivity, quality, and other issues about their workplace. An example is a cellular manufacturing team, a group of workers that handle all tasks in a multioperation workcell. They have purview over everything going into, out of, or happening within the cell. In many cases, they not only perform work tasks but also much of the planning and daily scheduling in the workcell. They investigate problems about machine functioning, equipment setup, product defects, and anything else about their cell.

Project-oriented teams are temporary teams formed around some goal, such as to resolve a specific problem or implement a new process or procedure. Members of a project team are selected for their knowledge, skill, and vested interest in the goal of the project. The team meets on an ad hoc basis and is disbanded when the project is completed.

A common theme in all of these teams is they virtually run themselves. While initially a team might be led or monitored by a facilator, in time worker members are able to function together well enough to take over that role too.

Team meetings are typically well-organized events. Starting and ending times are set, an agenda is set and followed, and action plans are created and followed. Teams regularly discuss their effectiveness and shortcomings. For workers to become team oriented, to know how to perform effectively in a team, and to develop analytical skills for problem solving and technical decision making requires intensive training and education.

QUALITY TRAINING AND EDUCATION

Companies serious about quality are serious about training and educating their shop-floor and line workers. Says Kaoru Ishikawa:

> Quality control begins with education and ends with education. To promote quality with participation by all, QC education must be given to all employees, from the president to assembly-line workers. TQC is a thought revolution in management, therefore the thought processes of all workers must be changed. To accomplish this, education must be repeated.[9]

Educating workers for TQM serves many purposes:

· It informs employees about quality and the company's TQM vision, instills in them a sense of mission, helps persuade them that they will personally benefit, and encourages them to understand and accept the numerous changes that will follow.

· It gives workers tools to collect and analyze information, identify and solve problems, and work effectively both as individuals and as groups.

· It gives workers models and concepts helpful in developing a culture devoted to problem solving, continuous improvement, and teamwork.

JIT-Style Training

The best kind of quality-oriented training is **just-in-time–style training,** that is, training and education which is applied immediately as needed and which happens on the job.[10] Simply training masses of workers for long periods (an unfortunately common practice in many organizations first launching TQM) is not effective. In JIT training, education is implemented as an *ongoing* series of short sessions (a few hours a week, at most) during which workers are taught only what they can apply soon, without suffering information overload. The sooner they can apply the material they learned, the better they will understand it and the longer it will be retained.

In JIT-style training, key concepts and tools for quality are "pulled" up through out the organization. Managers *at each level* require their subordinates to use quality tools and concepts. For example, one vice president at Ford required that his managers use Pareto charts and cause-and-effect analysis during presentations, and that those managers, in turn, require the same from their direct reports. That way everyone, from line workers to executives, shares the usage of common methods for quality improvement and problem solving.

Managers and supervisors need training too, especially about how to manage and supervise the empowered worker. Many of them are lacking in coaching and facilitating skills and need training and reinforcement in participative management, active listening, and collective decision making.

BENCHMARKING

Competitive manufacturers set high quality standards, and one of the best ways to do that is to observe what others have done. **Benchmarking** is the approach of continuously measuring products, services, and practices against tough standards set by competitors or renowned leaders in the field. Through benchmarking, a company knows how far it has to go to be with the best. Xerox originated the concept in the late 1970s when it began to compare its products and processes with those of Japanese competitors. Xerox learned that it would have to achieve annual productivity gains of 19% for the following 5 years just to *catch up* with the Japanese, assuming the Japanese continued to improve at an estimated 6% a year. (They later learned that, in fact, the Japanese were improving at 12% and to catch up and pass them would take a Herculean effort.)

BASIS FOR BENCHMARKING

Benchmarking is not copying. It is a process of studying and learning from others and adapting their best practices to fit your organization. More than just for goal setting, it is used to understand the processes that produce the best results.

Xerox originally limited its comparisons to competitors that were producing copiers and other products of Xerox. It started by asking its main competitors for on-site visits to see their plants and processes, and in return offered them site visits to see what Xerox was doing. Surprisingly, many agreed. (Competitors are typically secretive, so information about their practices usually comes from published materials in trade or professional journals, not from site visits.)

Xerox then looked beyond its competitors to related and unrelated processes in companies in entirely different lines of business. For example, it sent teams to L. L. Bean because Bean had a reputation for quality customer service and efficient order processing and product distribution. Use of noncompetitive businesses for benchmarking is now widespread. Chrysler also went to Bean, but to study warehousing practices. Today, law firms look at accounting firms to learn about billing processes, and hotels look at fast-food chains for hiring and training practices. Internal organizations, other departments, branches, or divisions, are also sources of benchmarking information.

The most ambitious form of benchmarking selects comparison organizations (competitive or noncompetitive) that are recognized world leaders in some process, for example, Federal Express for quick delivery, Disney for employee commitment and quality customer service, American Express for ability to get customers to pay quickly, McDonald's for consistency, and Xerox for benchmarking(!).

Benchmarking is applicable to every *process*—manufacturing, order entry, processing of magazine subscriptions, insurance claims, payroll, food service, maintenance, wherever there is an identifiable process.

BENCHMARKING PROCESS[11]

The benchmarking process commonly involves seven steps.

1. *Determining what to benchmark*. Most things can be benchmarked: an old process that needs improving; a problem that needs solving; a new process being designed from scratch; a process where earlier improvement attempts have failed. A team is formed to investigate the process or problem. The team includes managers and employees who have experience or knowledge about how the process works and about what lies beyond the boundary of the process. The team defines the process, its boundary, tasks it comprises and their sequence, and its inputs and outputs.

2. *Determining what to measure*. The measures chosen to benchmark must be the ones most critical and meaningful to improvement. The team reviews the process tasks in a flowchart and brainstorms about what measures to focus. Examples of measures are overall completion time, completion time for each task, time at each decision point, variations in times, number of loops back or repeats, wages, overhead, and defects and errors at each task. The measures should include the requirements of internal and external customers, even if external customers are distant from the process being benchmarked. The team interviews suppliers and customers of the process about their requirements and links the requirements to measures of in-process performance. It then selects as benchmark measures the ones most critical to significantly improving the process and its outputs, important to supplier and

customers, and about which information can be obtained from benchmarked organizations.

3. *Determining whom to benchmark*. The team selects the organizations that are thought to be the best in the industry.

4. *Collecting data*. The team gathers data about the selected measures for the benchmarked organizations. A typical starting point is published information: product studies, market surveys, customer surveys, trade journals, annual reports, and open meetings. Much information is also available on benchmarking data banks, for example, from the *International Benchmarking Clearinghouse* established by the American Productivity and Quality Center in Houston. The team can also design and send out a questionnaire to the benchmarked companies, either as a sole method for data collection or as a precursor to an on-site visit. During on-site visits, the benchmarking team observes the process using measures that correspond to the internal data it collected before. Several companies should be visited. The assumed agreement is always that the company collecting data will reciprocate.

5. *Analyzing data*. The team compares data from the benchmarked process to data from the internal process to determine gaps between them. It also does a qualitative comparison on systems, procedures, organization, and attitudes. It identifies why the gaps exist and what can be learned from them. The important thing is to avoid denial; if there is a big gap, accept that it exists and that something must be done.

6. *Setting goals and action plans*. The team sets improvement goals for the process. The goals should be achievable and realistic in terms of time, resources, and current ability; as well as measurable, specific, and supported by management and people working in the process. An expanded, multidisciplinary team attacks the problems and develops a plan to establish specific actions to take, time lines, and people responsible.

7. *Monitoring the action*. The team or workers in the process measure progress and identify problems. Measures are evaluated incrementally, and adjustments are made to the plan to overcome hurdles and problems. The team gets feedback from suppliers as well as from internal and external customers about their perceptions of changes.

The gap might never be eliminated since the benchmarked target might itself keep improving. More important than closing the gap is making benchmarking a habit. Some organizations have a department responsible for doing continuous benchmarking studies.

MANDATE FOR BEST-IN-CLASS GOALS

American companies involved in benchmarking use the term **best-in-class** (BIC) to refer to processes known for being the best in the business. When a company pegs improvement goals against a process that is BIC, it is striving to be the best. But BIC standards are moving targets because

> . . . no sooner does a PC board wave-solder operation achieve an old BIC standard of 125 ppm (parts per million) defects than the company discovers that someone else has set the new BIC for comparable boards at 100 ppm or even below 50 ppm.[12]

The process of benchmarking has many benefits. It creates a culture of continuous improvement, devalues the not-invented-here syndrome and develops a strong sense of urgency for ongoing improvement. Additionally, the best practices are shared among benchmarking partners and resources are focused on improvement targets jointly set with employees.[13] Says Richard Dauch, former Chrysler executive VP of Worldwide Manufacturing:

> Benchmarking pays off big. Whereas some of our competitors struggled for months (even years) to get their new, highly automated plants into operation, our launches came off in record time with incomparable precision. Our JIT material delivery system exceeded the Japanese Kanban that inspired it.[14]

QUALITY CERTIFICATIONS AND AWARDS

Short of personal experience with a particular company, there is no sure-fire way of knowing that a company's products or services are high-quality. Part of the trend in TQM and JIT manufacturing is for customers and suppliers to work in a partnership. The number of suppliers is reduced to just a relative few that are willing to work closely with the customer company and are believed to be the best. As an aid to determining which companies are quality conscious, customer organizations rely on certifications and awards as measures of quality management and practices (though not necessarily of quality outputs).

ISO 9000 SERIES CERTIFICATION[15]

In the 1980s members of the European Community (now called the European Union, EU), a free-trade consortium of 12 European nations, created the **ISO 9000 Series standard** as an international benchmark for companies worldwide that wanted to do business with the EU. ISO refers to the International Standards Organization, located in Geneva, Switzerland.

ISO 9000 standards are growing in popularity, and the number of countries adopting them stands at over 80 (from originally 12 in 1987). When a country, industry, or company adopts ISO 9000, it is tacitly accepting the standards and saying that it prefers companies that have ISO 9000 certification. The EU regulates some products, principally health- and safety-related ones whose producers must be able to demonstrate compliance with quality procedures. Though ISO certification is not required, certified companies find it easier to show that they comply. Even for nonregulated products, many producers find they must conform to ISO standards just to be considered suppliers. In the US, organizations such as DuPont, 3M, and the Department of Defense request their suppliers to comply with ISO 9000. ISO has become another criteria for determining who can compete and who cannot.

Certification requires a company to document its procedures. When management decides its company should be ISO certified, the first step is for it to become informed about the standards and the process and to communicate information about ISO companywide. The company arranges to have its quality system audited by an independent, accredited third-party registrar who, for a fee, assesses the quality system documentation and determines whether it complies with ISO 9001, 9002, or 9003 standards. If it does, the registrar issues a certificate and registers it in a book that is widely circulated. Every year the company must have its certification reviewed by the same registrar, and every 3 years it must be reaudited.

Five Standards

ISO includes five separate quality standards, ISO 9000–9004. These standards have technical equivalents in the US and Canada referred to as ANSI/ASQC and CSA, respectively, which stand for American National Standards Institute/American Society for Quality Control, and Canadian Standards Association, respectively.

ISO 9000 (equivalent to the US ANSI/ASQC Q90 and the Canadian CSA Z299.0–86): Quality Management and Quality Assurance Standards—Guidelines for Selection and Use.   This standard provides guidelines for the selection and usage of the remaining standards, ISO 9001–9004.

ISO 9001 (ANSI/ASQC Q91, CSA Z299.1–85): Quality Systems—Model for Quality Assurance in Design/Development, Production, Installation, and Servicing.   This standard gives requirements for a quality management system when the supplier is responsible for design, development, production, installation, and servicing of a product. It sets minimum requirements for contract reviews, design, process control, testing, product handling and storage, packaging, delivery, and so on. It also includes procedures for conducting internal quality audits to assess the effectiveness of the quality management system. ISO 9001 addresses standards in 20 areas that together create an integrated, working quality system. The areas are

Management responsibility	Quality system principles
Contract review	Design control
Document control	Purchasing
Purchaser-supplied products	Product identification
Control of production	and traceability
Inspection and testing	Inspection, measurement, and
Inspection and test status	test equipment
Control of nonconforming	Corrective action
products	Handling, storage, packaging,
Quality records	and delivery
Internal audits	Training
After-sales servicing	Statistical techniques

ISO certification is available in three levels, 9001, 9002, and 9003, each covering a different portion and depth of a manufacturer's quality policies and procedures. ISO 9001 covers all 20 areas and is the highest-level standard in the series. The next two standards involve fewer areas of manufacturing and are less detailed.

ISO 9002 (ANSI/ASQC Q92, CSA Z299.2–85): Quality Systems—Model for Quality Assurance in Production and Installation.   This standard is a subset of ISO 9001; it applies to suppliers that only produce and install a product.

ISO 9003 (ANSI/ASQC Q93, CSA Z299.4–85): Quality Systems—Model for Quality Assurance in Final Inspection and Test.   This standard guarantees integrity of data about the quality of a product from a supplier's final inspection and test procedures. If a supplier is ISO 9003 certified, the customer needs only to be provided with test data and does not have to repeat tests or inspections of the product.

ISO 9004 (ANSI/ASQC Q94, CSA Q420–87): Quality Management and Quality System Elements—Guidelines. This standard provides guidelines and suggestions to help management develop and implement the kind of quality management system required in standards 9001 through 9003. The standard clarifies distinctions and relationships among three quality objectives: (1) achieving and sustaining quality so as to meet the customer's needs; (2) providing confidence to company management that quality is being achieved and sustained; and (3) providing confidence to the customer that quality is being achieved and sustained. The standard formally defines the concepts, elements, and processes associated with quality policy, management, systems, control, and assurance.

CRITICISM AND SUPPORT FOR ISO

Critics argue that ISO standards are based on decades-old (though good at the time) British and US military procurement standards, are expensive to implement and maintain, and have taken root primarily because companies are eager to engage in international business.[16] Companies without ISO certification find it more difficult to compete in the European market, and big international companies that are ISO certified pressure suppliers and subsuppliers to become certified too.

Part of the stimuli keeping ISO in vogue, critics say, are the consultants, seminar providers, international trainers, video producers, and book publishers who profit from "selling" ISO to companies. Registrar charges per location for initial audits can range from as little as $3500 to as much as $40,000. Maintenance audits run between $1200 and $15,000 for each of the 3 years between recertification audits.[17] For one international corporation, the cost of registering 20 of its plants was $20,000 to $30,000 apiece, what the company felt was a necessary expense of doing business.[18] Often registrars do not know the infrastructure or technology of the company they audit, nor do they care about the culture. Says Michael Scotto, an ISO consultant:

> The only good things I can say about ISO 9000 Standards are that they're better than no quality system at all, and that a basic understanding of quality has been introduced to companies that only used the word [quality] before in their advertising.[19]

This statement says something about which both ISO critics and supporters agree. Many firms have no quality system, and ISO certification forces them to address everything they need to get one. If a company already has a good quality system, ISO will require little else than writing reference documentation or rewording procedures to meet ISO standards. A company that has a weak quality system might require several years to develop the standards, educate workers, and integrate the standards into its operations so it can be certified. In the end, it will have a better quality system in place.

Table 4.1   Benefits of Implementing ISO 9000

Consistency throughout the company

Strengthened relationships between suppliers and customers

Strengthened customer confidence

Improved management decision making

Continuous improvement

Institutionalized training

Reduced dependence on individuals

Among the potential benefits from implementing ISO 9000, the most prominent are listed in Table 4.1.[20] ISO 9000 certification focuses on ongoing systems and management for continuous improvement, but not on products, per se. Because certified companies follow well-documented procedures, however, their quality problems are made evident to them and are more likely to be rectified.[21]

Although ISO certification currently offers some competitive advantage in that it raises a company's quality standards to a higher-than-average level, as more companies become certified that advantage will diminish. Further, while ISO certification results in consistent methods of quality tracking and control, it lacks the breadth and continuous improvement focus of companywide TQM systems. TQM systems in firms such as Ford, Xerox, Kodak, IBM, Motorola, and Chevron all have requirements of greater scope than ISO.[22]

Supporters argue that despite ISO being more limited in scope than the Malcolm Baldrige Award criteria (described next) or full-blown TQM systems, most companies find it more feasible and are more likely to have successful results than with either Baldrige or TQM.[23] In 1995 there were 8000 ISO registrations in the US, and that is projected to grow to 115,000 by 1998. ISO provides a standardized quality model upon which a firm can develop its own expanded quality system. It also provides a metric or baseline for quality comparison throughout the 80 countries that have adopted it as a national standard. Says one supporter of the ISO process:

> Whether a firm has a quality system or not, ISO 9000 is an ideal model because it starts at the beginning with management responsibility, and it makes room for all the other quality tools and concepts.[24]

QS 9000 AND ISO 14000

In the US, the three big automakers as well as most large truck manufacturers have instituted the **QS-9000** quality system requirement, which includes all the elements of ISO 9000 plus special requirements for the automotive and truck industry and unique requirements for particular manufacturers such as General Motors, Ford, Chrysler, Mack Truck, Navistar, and so on. QS 9000 replaces all previous automotive supplier quality programs, and eventually all direct suppliers of the major US auto and truck manufacturers will be expected to implement it.[25]

In 1996 the International Standards Organization adopted a series of standards for environmental management systems referred to as ISO 14000. The objectives of the standards are to encourage a common approach to environmental management, strengthen each company's ability to measure its environmental performance, and remove trade barriers. ISO 14000 provides the procedure for certification and registration of an environmental management system (EMS); this procedure is very similar to that for ISO 9000. Two major elements of the series are ISO 14001, which specifies the minimum requirements for an effective EMS, and ISO 14004, which sets guidelines for designing and executing such an EMS.

Among the requirements of the standard are that a company define an environmental policy, that the policy demonstrates a commitment to compliance with environmental legislation and pollution prevention, and that the company continuously improve its EMS. Among issues dealt with by the standards are systems for identifying, controling, and documenting actions regarding material handling, disposal of wastes, and compliance with industry codes of practice and international treaties. The standards are very flexible and allow each organization room to design its own EMS to meet ISO standards and achieve its own objectives.

Supporters of the standard believe that once ISO 14001 gains worldwide acceptance and approval, international suppliers and customers will want to appear environmentally responsible and will seek out organizations that are certified.[26] Already several US companies, including IBM and Monsanto, are working toward either ISO 14001 compliance or registration.

QUALITY AWARDS

Unlike ISO standards, quality awards do not, as a whole, represent a particular quality standard. Like ISO, however, they have been instrumental in spreading quality practices and philosophies that are compatible with TQM throughout the US and the world. A few of these awards and prizes have received world prominence and have affected quality practices and stirred innovative quality approaches.

Malcolm Baldrige National Quality Award

In 1987, President Reagan signed legislation that established the Malcolm Baldrige National Quality Award, an award named after the late secretary of commerce, to be presented annually by the National Institute of Standards and Technology (NIST) to two US companies (at most) in each of the categories of small business, service, and manufacturing. The purpose of the award is to improve quality in American products and make the US more competitive in world markets. Any company that receives the award has an assumed obligation to share its quality methods and strategies.

After establishing eligibility requirements, a company submits an application form. The evaluation process then involves four stages. First, the form is reviewed by a board of examiners most of whom are industry practitioners, but some of whom are academics or consultants. The board selects a subset of the applicants for a second, consensus review. Those companies that pass muster on the second review are personally visited by another group of examiners in a formal site visit to verify the accuracy of information on the application. The site-visit team develops a report for final review by a nine-judge panel, which makes its recommendations for the award to the NIST. Awards are traditionally presented by the President of the United States.

Every year thousands of companies request applications, primarily for the purpose of using the award criteria and guidelines to establish TQM programs. The award criteria are extensive and cover 28 examination items in 8 categories: leadership, information and analysis, strategic quality planning, human resource development and planning, management of process quality, quality assurance of products and services, quality results, and customer focus and satisfaction. Canada has an award very similar to the Baldrige, the *Canada Award for Business Excellence.* At least 35 states also have quality awards, many modeled after the Baldrige.

Although the Baldrige award is in some ways similar to ISO 9000 in terms of quality criteria and audits, it in fact has a much broader scope than ISO. Comparing the Baldrige Award with the ISO registration process, Reimann and Hertz conclude that "overall, ISO 9000 registration covers less than 10% of the scope of the Baldrige Award criteria, and does not fully address any of the 28 criteria items."[27] Whereas ISO certification verifies the execution of quality procedures in a standardized fashion, the Baldrige award also considers worker teams and empowerment, quality issues in company strategy, cycle time reduction, customer requirements and quality results, and more.

Companies have discovered that there is much to be gained simply by conducting the self-assessment required to complete the application. Companies applying must accumulate documented evidence as to having achieved and maintained the requirements listed in the seven categories. In general, companies that have become finalists for the award experience overall performance improvement just by having gone through the application process.

Japan's Deming Prize

Japan's Deming Prize, named after W. Edwards Deming, was created in 1951 to recognize Japanese individuals for achievements in statistical quality theory, Japanese companies for distinctive achievement through quality control, and overseas companies for exemplary quality improvement. In 1960 Genichi Taguchi won the first Deming prize for his work in robust design and design of experiments (as well as three awards, later), and in 1987 Florida Power & Light became the first US company to receive the overseas prize.

Shingo Prize for Excellence in Manufacturing

The Shingo Prize is named after the Japanese quality expert Shigeo Shingo, who made significant contributions to waste elimination through JIT methodology, especially in innovative ways to reduce process setup times and defects from inadvertent mistakes (described in Chapters 6 and 15, respectively). The Shingo award is an American prize

CASE IN POINT: Xerox—Back from the Brink[28]

Xerox in the early 1980s was near disaster, but by 1990 it had turned itself around and into a different company. Financial figures don't tell it all, but they do say something about the size of Xerox's turnaround: in 1984 revenues were $8.7 billion, in 1990 they were $13.6 billion; 1987 return-on-assets was 9%, in 1990 it was 14.6%; most significant was Xerox's market-share gain in installed machines, 12% in 1984 versus 19% in 1990—all at the expense of Xerox's Japanese competitors (each point represents about $200 million).

In 1988, the Baldrige Award was the coveted industry prize. Although Xerox management had no idea whether it had done enough to have a chance at winning, Paul Allaire, president since 1986, thought the application process would be worthwhile as a company motivator and a measure of how good the company really was. Thus, Xerox's goal was not so much to win, but to use the process to energize the company and appraise its quality efforts.

Xerox began the application process in November 1988 by forming a team of 20 members, mostly midlevel managers from throughout the company. The process requires answering a detailed questionnaire which comprises 33 subcategories covering the 12 main categories. Everything had to be quantified and substantiated based upon hard facts and 3 to 5 years of supporting data.

The team dubbed company flaws it encountered as "warts." A total of 503 warts were found (not many, actually, for a company of Xerox's size). Some were minor (paint hallways), some major (find better ways to transfer knowledge between teams). The team discovered that, despite the warts, Xerox was doing a good job. It was one of the only companies that benchmarked its products and processes and that tied executive bonuses to quality.

In May 1989, the application was completed and submitted. In July, Xerox received word that it had made the cut and was getting a site visit. Six examiners descended on the company, meeting with senior managers in Rochester, NY, then visiting facilities in Denver and Los Angeles, where, in 4 days, they spoke to 450 people. They discussed with employees such things as whether they were on teams, what quality tools they used, and what the company policy was on quality.

In November, Xerox got the news: it had won. (By coincidence, Xerox Canada learned a month later that it had won the Canadian National Quality Award.)

As for the warts, some were still there; some are there today. The management team looked at the warts and came up with 50 recommendations, mostly managerial, and most were adopted. The warts were organized into six principles upon which Xerox decided to base its quality efforts in the 1990s:

1. Customers define our business.
2. Our success depends on the involvement and empowerment of trained and motivated people.
3. Line management must lead quality improvement.
4. Management develops, articulates, and deploys clear objectives and directives.
5. Quality challenges are met and satisfied.
6. The business is managed and improved by using facts.

The Baldrige application process had indeed reenergized the company's commitment to quality, and it showed the extent of quality gains made from the early 1980s to 1988; for example defects went from 10,000 ppm to 300 ppm (parts per million), installed product performance went up by 40%, customer satisfaction went up by 38%, labor overhead went down by 50%, and material overhead went down by 40%.

By 1990, Xerox had begun building long-term relationships with its best suppliers, involving them in new product development and training them in quality leadership techniques, SPC, and JIT.

---

awarded annually by Utah State University and is limited to manufacturing firms. The award criteria consider quality management indicators such as quality leadership, strategy, vision, customer satisfaction, worker empowerment, and manufacturing process improvement, though in the last category the emphasis is decidedly on JIT principles such as kanban pull production, inventory reduction, stockless and mixed-model production, setup reduction, and total productive maintenance.

IMPLEMENTING TQM

As the framework in Figure 4.1 suggests, TQM ultimately affects the way people in every function do their jobs. Uniting everyone toward a common, quality-oriented purpose begins with a vision from top management about how the organization will look, act, and compete in the future. Once that vision has been defined, top management must coordinate and channel the efforts to achieve it.

Ways of implementing TQM are almost as varied as the number of companies adopting TQM. One theme, however, pervades all of them: they are intended to change organizational culture and to drive customer focus, continuous improvement, and employee involvement throughout the organization to every level and job. In terms of the way they go about implementing change, several themes are common:

- Top management sets a company vision or broad fundamental objective.
- The vision is broken into narrower, more focused, and shorter-range objectives and plans at every level of the organization.
- The vision and objectives are set high and focus largely on the external customer.
- Objectives are developed by teams at every level so as to involve most of the employee population.

Also common is widespread employee training in problem solving and improvement, and frequent use of prespecified metrics to assess progress toward process improvement and meeting targets. But simple achievement of targets is not enough in TQM; it is important to ensure that the process that leads to meeting targets is itself continuously improved. Targets are set primarily as a means to provide concrete direction and motivation for improvement efforts.

Two illustrations of TQM implemention follow: (1) a generic TQM implementation approach called **policy deployment** and (2) an example of an approach used by Texas Instruments.

POLICY DEPLOYMENT[29]

Policy deployment is an approach to orchestrating continuous improvement through TQM; it is an application of PDCA on a large-scale to strategic management. *Policy* refers to the company vision, long-range plans, and targets: *deployment* refers to the way top management conveys the vision and plans to managers and encourages their participation in deploying vision-related goals and plans throughout the organization. Policy deployment has six key steps.

Step 1: Develop a Long-Term Vision for the Company.   Top management creates a vision of the company's position, say, 5 years hence in terms of improvements in quality, costs, and service. The vision should consider the external environment, especially customer needs and the competition. Benchmarking against best-in-class companies is one way to ensure that the vision is set high. The vision should not be financially oriented, but should be tied to customers, and should be a motivator for people to work together. Examples of objectives in a vision statement are to improve product dependability and to be the producer of highest quality product-family X in the US.

Step 2: Determine Annual Policies to Support that Vision.   The vision is defined in terms of a series of successive annual improvement policies and plans. Included in the annual plans are items carried over from the previous year, issues about emerging developments or opportunities, actions yet to be taken, and data obtained from benchmarking. Examples of annual objectives are to improve product dependability by 50% and to improve product-family X in terms of reliability by 30%, serviceability by 20%, conformance by 50%, and so on.

Step 3: Deploy the Policy Organizationwide through Participation in Planning.   Each level of the organization develops plans and measures for activities in support of targets at the level above it. The plans are hierarchical, starting from top management's plan and cascading down. Thus, action plans to a target at one level are the link to targets at the next higher level. This is illustrated in Figure 4.3.

Plans at each level are progressively more focused and detailed. This planning process happens simultaneously throughout the organization at every division and department. The preferred focus of targets and plans at every level remains external and on the customer; for instance, the engineering department seeks external benchmarks for product development and customer assessment of products. Other examples of externally focused benchmarks are customer billing, customer service, order processing, product distribution, and product standardization.

The Pareto principle is applied to set priorities at each organization level as to what most needs improvement and is most related to the vision. Management must be tolerant of plans that address employees' internally focused needs, for example, the layout of the cafeteria. Such plans, however, are not considered part of policy deployment unless they are specifically tied to the vision of the firm.

A useful tool for assessing alternative plans and the degree to which they are tied to vision-related targets is a matrix such as Figure 4.4. The symbols inside represent the strength of relationships between plans (means) and targets (ends). For example,

FIGURE 4.3

Policy deployment process through successive organization levels.[30]

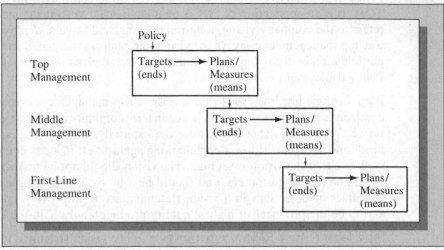

FIGURE 4.4

Matrix for relating plans to attainment of objectives and targets.

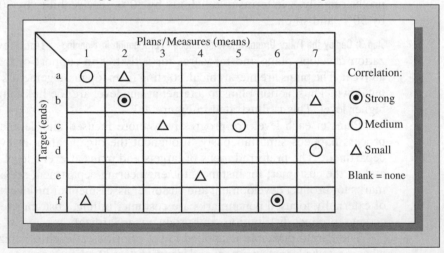

suppose the first two targets in the matrix in Figure 4.4 are to increase serviceability by 20% (target *a*) and to decrease service response time by 10% (target *b*); suppose also the first two plans in the matrix are to survey mechanics for suggestions about improving serviceability (plan 1), and to put service representatives in direct contact with field crews (plan 2). If it is believed that plan 1 would contribute somewhat to achieving target *a* though certainly not to target *b*, and that plan 2 would contribute greatly to achieving target *b* and only somewhat to target *a*, the correlations would be as indicated in the upper left four cells of the matrix in Figure 4.4.

The scope of the targets and plans in the matrix depends on the organizational level and functional area for which they are developed. For example, given the target at one level of increasing serviceability by 20%, the target at another, lower level might be to reduce replacement time for worn components in less than 10 minutes. In general, the matrix is useful for checking the impact of plans on targets and the completeness of plans as well as for preventing things from falling through the cracks.

Step 4: Implement the Policy.   Employees at all levels participate in generating action plans to attain the vision. Plans are prepared in great detail to identify and address root causes of problems, not symptoms, and to anticipate problems of implementation. Responsibilities, deadlines, and progress measures are specified in each action plan. To ensure that improvement efforts are all directed toward the same general ends, everyone should be aware of management's five or so top policy goals.

Step 5: Audit the Process and Plans Monthly.   Plans are evaluated and modified on a monthly basis by divisional and departmental managers based on scheduled audits. The emphasis of evaluation is on *process* improvement, not just progress toward meeting targets. Corrections and adjustments to plans are made midstream as necessary based on information collected.

Step 6: Audit the Process Annually by Top Management.   At least once annually top management personally audits progress of the deployment process, again focusing on improvements in individual processes as well as achievement of targets. Results of the audit provide information to set policy and plans for the upcoming year.

BARRIERS TO SUCCESSFUL TQM

The barriers to implementing TQM somewhat mirror those for JIT because both JIT and TQM involve what are, for many companies, dramatic changes in the ways they set goals and try to achieve them. Additionally both TQM and JIT necessitate a cultural transformation that must be spearheaded by top management. Thus, two main reasons for JIT failure and TQM failure are the same: lack of long-term commitment and leadership from management, and insufficient empowerment of workers.

The literature gives other reasons for TQM failure:

· Misdirected focus—emphasis on the trivial many problems facing a company rather than the critical few.
· Emphasis on internal processes to the neglect of external (customer-focused) results.
· Emphasis on quick fixes and low-level reforms.
· Training that is largely irrelevant and lacks focus.
· Lack of cross-disciplinary, cross-functional efforts.[31]

Managers often see improvement programs as solutions to particular problems (e.g., JIT to make certain operations lean and less wasteful, TQM to improve product

CASE IN POINT: Texas Instruments—Learning and Leading by Example[32]

The quality strategy at Texas Instruments' Defense Systems & Electronics Group addresses the main areas illustrated in Figure 4.5. The first is the objective to please the customer, an objective that has been in place since the mid-1980s, but which, nonetheless, Texas Instruments (TI) found challenging and frustrating to relate to its 14,000 people at 10 work sites.

The second main area comprises improvement thrusts generated as a result of TI's application for the Baldrige Award in 1990. When TI entered the contest, management believed TI was already good, being the first and second in its markets. What shocked them was that the Baldrige report indicated 89 areas in need of improvement. Most of these areas now serve as a road map for changes needed and as an aid to developing the improvement thrusts.

The third area is performance metrics, the way TI sets goals and measures progress across the organization. Part of TI's measurement success has been in its employees' ability to answer questions such as

· Who are my customers?
· How do I know when I have pleased them?
· What is my error rate?
· What is my personal training plan?
· What am I going to do to improve my job?

To drive quality from the top, TI established a quality improvement team (QIT) of top managers that meets every week to discuss quality issues. From QIT meetings, management learned it is important to share all information with employees, even information previously considered confidential or for management only. Management must try to foster an environment where employees feel empowered, free to offer opinions, and part of the continuous improvement team. The president now makes site visits once a week and talks to employees.

TI also learned from the Baldrige application the importance of connectivity. For example, TI now bases its human resources initiatives on five areas from the Baldrige human resource category:

· Planning and management
· Employee involvement
· Education and training
· Performance and recognition
· Well-being and satisfaction

TI named members of the QIT to oversee each of the initiatives in each of these categories and included them on its management team to encourage cross-functional planning and coordination.

Though TI has long had a team culture, the new emphasis is on self-directed and self-managed teams. These new teams are intended to significantly reduce the number of levels of management in the organization.

In 1990 TI was averaging 3 days of training per person, and about 25% of the workers had less than a day of training. Management thought this was OK until it looked at Motorola, which had a minimum of 40 hours and an average of 80 hours of training. TI management set a goal of a minimum of 2 days training for every employee, with an increase of 1 day a year.

The key to employee development and quality improvement, TI management believes, is to lead by example. So management decided to attend the training first; this, they believed,

FIGURE 4.5
Texas Instruments' quality management strategy.[33]

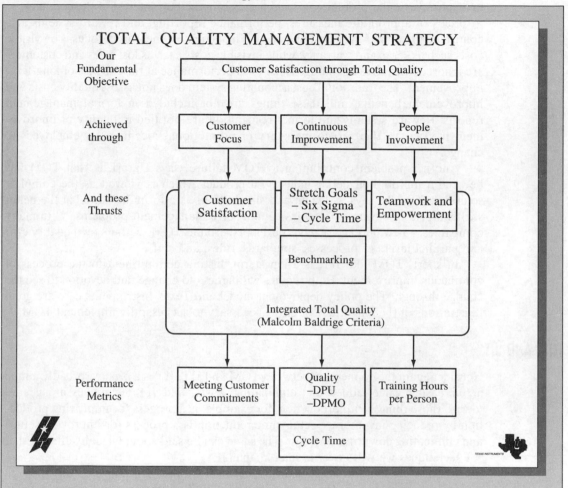

would send a strong message to everyone about the importance of training. Management also decided it would set for itself twice the level of whatever training goal it set for employees to send the message that TI is a learning organization and everyone learns as a team.

Says Mike Cooney, Vice President and Manager, Quality Assurance, "The whole TQM program is driven by our need to sustain our competitive edge. We ask ourselves regularly whether what we are doing will give us sustained competitive advantage and satisfy our customers."

quality) rather than as stepping stones to cultural change and improved competitiveness.[34] Thus, they give little forethought to whether the allocation of scarce resources to resolve particular problems or weaknesses is in the best interest of the company.

Lack of appropriate measures, performance reporting, and reward systems also contribute to failure.[35] The cost of quality is inadequately measured; focus is on visible costs such as scrap and warranty, while invisible costs such as lost sales and customers are ignored. Measures encourage short-term performance at the expense of long-term improvement. The traditional cost accounting system does not assess quality costs and improvement benefits, and these things are not included in formal management reports. Reward systems and formal recognition are not tied to quality or improvement metrics, so there is no monetary or promotional incentive for employees to change.

Another problem contributing to TQM failure, says Harari, is that TQM has become a multibillion dollar industry, a product which is viewed as the complete solution. TQM, he says, is "plain and simple, sold as a formula," and "in the helter skelter world of business, formulas cannot solve management problems."[36] In many companies, a new bureaucracy has developed around TQM, with its own quality czar and parallel layers of processes, standards, rules, and staff.[37]

In short, TQM like JIT, is a long-term, lasting commitment to the process of continuous improvement. Both require willingness to change and devotion to see the change through. The policy deployment model and Texas Instruments case are good illustrations of the magnitude of effort necessary to successfully implement TQM.

TQM AND JIT

Consider again the connection between TQM and JIT. JIT is a *process* broadly aimed at increasing value–added and eliminating waste, and JIT techniques are geared toward those things. Pull production, for example, is a process for improving production by reducing inventories; setup-time reduction is a process for improving setups and eliminating downtime and cost. The same can be said about virtually all the other JIT techniques we will cover in later chapters.

Eliminating waste in manufacturing, however, cannot be achieved *solely* through efforts in manufacturing. Process improvement and waste reduction require a companywide, integrated effort that includes all functions—marketing, sales, finance, product engineering, purchasing, customer service, accounting—as well as manufacturing. This is where TQM and its companywide commitment to quality come in. While JIT seeks improvement through reduction of waste, TQM ensures that the improvements are fundamental and not superficial. As an example, manufacturers used to think that inspection to sort out defects was an improvement because it reduced bad products going to the customer. It *did* reduce waste and it *was* an improvement. Nonetheless, since sorting out defects did not require finding the root causes of defects (and allowed the causes to stay in the system), the improvement was not *fundamental*. Fundamental improvement means eliminating the sources of problems, not just the symptoms and it requires changes other than in manufacturing, for example, in the product design and in purchasing practices. JIT is known as lean production because, theoretically, it allows no excesses or wastes that might mask problems, but within JIT, TQM is the mechanism for seeking out the causes of excesses so they can be eliminated.

Because JIT systems run very lean, the production process must be reliable, stable, and predictable. In most processes, the biggest detractor from reliability and stability is uncontrolled process variability in production schedules, procedures, materials, tools, machine functioning, and worker skills. TQM provides procedures and tools for identifying and eliminating the sources of variability. Since companies are always changing products and processes and since the manufacturing environment (both internal and external to the company) is always changing, any source of variability, once identified and removed, will soon be replaced by others. As long as TQM is in place, however, new sources of variability will be identified and dealt with before they cause problems. TQM tools for identifying and eliminating sources of variability are discussed in Chapter 14.

Summary

Quality can be defined from two perspectives, that of the customer and that of the producer. The total quality approach starts by understanding the customer's perspective, then translates that into the producer's perspective, that is, considerations about the product design and manufacturing process that will result in a product that meets or exceeds customer requirements. Orienting the design and manufacture of products toward meeting these requirements is referred to as quality of design and quality of conformance, respectively.

Total quality management is an organizationwide commitment to quality and continuous improvement. It is also a process in which an organization is continually aware of the changing needs and expectations of customers, of challenges posed by the competition, and of threats and opportunities in the business environment. TQM is also a management framework for integrating the efforts of sales, marketing, finance, engineering, manufacturing, purchasing, suppliers, and customer service around knowing what customers want and need, as well as what the organization must do with its products and services to satisfy them. TQM is a concerted, continuing effort to broaden and deepen worker involvement in quality and improvement efforts and to give workers the support, training, education, and rewards necessary for them to meaningfully contribute to those efforts.

Setting goals is a step toward improvement. The benchmarking process sets goals by comparing current standards and practices to organizations that are known leaders in the field. Benchmarking is studying and learning what others have done, then adapting their best practices to fit your organization.

Quality certifications and awards help companies know which producers and suppliers have quality-oriented procedures and processes. ISO 9000 is a series of standards that requires a company to create and document procedures for an integrated, working quality system. As such, it provides a common baseline for comparing the quality procedures of different organizations. ISO certification means that a company has been audited and found to meet the standards.

Applying for quality awards is another way to establish a reputation for quality. In the US, the most prestigious award is the Malcolm Baldrige Award. As part of the application process for the award, a company must show evidence of having achieved and maintained requirements in several categories such as quality leadership, quality strategic planning, process quality, product quality assurance, and customer focus. The assessment process itself is valuable for helping a company to determine just how good its quality efforts are and where improvements are most needed.

Implementing TQM requires long-term commitment from management, starting with a company quality vision and deploying that vision systematically to all functions and levels in the organization. Deployment involves managers and workers breaking down higher-level objectives into detailed, focused objectives for their areas.

Any organization that considers adopting JIT should already be involved in TQM initiatives. While JIT provides techniques and philosophy for process improvement through waste reduction in manufacturing, TQM provides the tools, teamwork, organizationwide participation, and customer focus necessary to guarantee that improvement efforts address fundamental problems and have the greatest benefit for organizational competitiveness.

Questions

1. What is meant by the customer's perspective of quality? The producer's perspective? How do these perspectives relate to customer-focused quality?

2. What are the eight dimensions of quality as identified by Garvin? What are other possible dimensions of quality? Select three products and discuss how the dimensions apply to each.

3. What is the meaning of quality of design? Quality of conformance? Quality of performance/service?

4. In what ways are employee involvement and employee ownership in the quality concept cultivated in TQM organizations?

5. Many large corporations have demonstrated their commitment to TQM by requiring that every employee attend seminars on quality concepts and know the tools for problem solving and SPC. Everyone belongs to a problem-solving group, and groups are expected to meet once a week. Comment on this approach to TQM.

6. In 10 words or less define benchmarking.

7. How does a company determine which things to benchmark?

8. Describe how you might use benchmarking in your job. Describe processes in your company where benchmarking might be appropriate. Why did you pick those processes?

9. Comment on the comment: "A company makes bicycle tires; thus, for benchmarking, it should look at other companies making bicycle tires."

10. A company is ISO certified. What does that say about the company?

11. Comment on the comment: "This company has no hope of ever winning the Malcolm Baldrige Quality Award, so there's no point in going through the application process for the award."

12. How does the criteria for the Malcolm Baldrige Quality Award differ from the criteria for ISO 9000? In what ways are the scope and focus of Baldrige and ISO similar or different?

13. Research question: In the Baldrige Award, 30% of the points address customer satisfaction. Name some companies that regularly survey their customers for satisfaction with products and service. How are the surveys done? How often? What happens to survey results?

14. Research question: List some companies that have won the Baldrige Award, then look at each company's financial and market performance before and after it won the award. Does there seem to be a relationship?

15. What do you think are the difficulties in implementing TQM? What distinguishes companies that *say* they are TQM companies from those that *are* TQM companies?

16. Why be a TQM-*and*-JIT company? Why not be JIT only?

Endnotes

1. C. Richards, "Agile Manufacturing: Beyond Lean?" *Production and Inventory Management* 37, no. 2 (2nd Quarter 1996), p. 63.

2. S. Ray, "JIT and Quality," *Total Quality: An Executive's Guide for the 1990s* (Homewood, IL: Dow-Jones Irwin, 1990), p.190.

3. D. Garvin, "Competing on the Eight Dimensions of Quality," *Harvard Business Review,* November–December 1987, pp. 101–9.

4. *See* C.L. McNair, *World-Class Accounting and Finance* (Homewood, IL: Business One Irwin, 1993).

5. B. Flynn, "Managing for Quality in the U.S. and in Japan," *Interfaces* 22, no. 5 (1992) pp. 69–80.

6. For example: D. Gavin, *Managing Quality: The Strategic and Competitive Edge* (New York: The Free Press, 1988); G. Bounds, L. Yorks, M. Adams, G. Ranney, *Beyond Total Quality Management* (New York: McGraw-Hill, 1994); Ernst & Young Quality Improvement Consulting Group, *Total Quality: An Executive's Guide for the 1990s* (Homewood, IL: Dow-Jones Irwin, 1990); S. George and A. Weimerskirch, *Total Quality Management: Strategies and Techniques Proven at Today's Most Successful Companies* (New York: John Wiley & Sons, 1994).

7. *See* L. Fitzgerald and J. Murphy, *Installing Quality Circles: A Strategic Approach* (San Diego: University Associates, 1982).

8. P. Drucker, "The Emerging Theory of Manufacturing," *Harvard Business Review,* May–June 1990, pp. 94–102.

9. K. Ishikawa, *What Is Total Quality Control: The Japanese Way* (Englewood Cliffs, NJ: Prentice-Hall, 1985), p. 37 (translated by David Lu).

10. D. Muther and L. Lytle, "Quality Education Requirement," in Ernst & Young Quality Improvement Consulting Group, *Total Quality: An Executive's Guide for the 1990s,* pp. 105–7.

11. Adapted from *Competitive Benchmarking: What It Is and What It Can Do for You,* (Stamford, CT: Xerox Corporate Quality Office, 1984); and R. Chang and P. K. Kelly, *Improving through Benchmarking* (Irvine, CA: Richard Chang Assoc., 1994).

12. R. Hall, H.T. Johnson, P. Turney, *Measuring Up: Charting Pathways to Manufacturing Excellence* (Homewood, IL: Dow-Jones Irwin, 1991), p. 56.

13. R. Fortuna and H.K. Vaziri, "Orchestrating Change: Policy Deployment," in Ernst & Young Quality Improvement Consulting Group, *Total Quality: An Executive's Guide for the 1990s,* p. 51.

14 R. Dauch, *Passion for Manufacturing* (Dearborn, MI: Society of Manufacturing Engineers, 1993), pp. 209–10.

15. A good introduction to ISO is W. Lutman, "ISO 9000: Can America Demonstrate a Commitment to Quality?" *Production and Inventory Management Journal* 35, no. 2 (2nd Quarter 1994), pp. 81–5.

16. *See* M. Scotto, "The Trouble with ISO, or the International Shell Game," *Target* 12, no. 1 (1996), pp. 6–7.

17. *Ibid.,* p. 7; B. Bishop, "Reader Response," *Target* 12, no. 3 (1996), p. 51.

18. G. Lofgren, "Quality System Registration: A Guide to the Q9000/ISO 9000 Series Registration," *Quality Progress* (May 1991), p. 37.

19. M. Scotto, "The Trouble with ISO . . . ," p. 7.

20. Adapted from A. Davin and A. McCampbell, "Foxboro's ISO 9000 Experience," *Production and Inventory Management* 37, no. 3 (3rd Quarter 1996), pp. 1–3.

21. G. Lofgren, "Quality System Registration . . . ," p. 37.

22. R. Yates, "U.S. lags in rigorous new quality standard," *Chicago Tribune,* Nov. 16, 1992.

23. R. Schueppert, "Reader Response," *Target* 12, no. 3 (1996), p. 52.

24. B. Bishop, "Reader Response," p. 51.

25. J. Banddyopadhyay, "Quality System Requirements QS-9000: The New Automotive Industry Standards," *Production and Inventory Management Journal* 37, no. 4 (1996), pp. 26–31.

26. F. Alexander, "IS 14001: What Does It Mean for IEs?" *IIE,* (January 1996), pp. 14–8.

27. C. Reimann and H. Hertz, "Understanding the Important Differences Between the Malcolm Baldrige National Quality Award and ISO 9000 Registration," *Production and Operations Management* 3, no. 6 (1994), pp. 171–85.

28. From D. Kearns and D. Nadler, *Prophets in the Dark* (New York: HarperBusiness, 1992), pp. 246–56.

29. Adopted from R. Fortuna and H.K. Vaziri, "Orchestrating Change: Policy Deployment," in Ernst & Young Quality Improvement Group, *Total Quality: An Executive's Guide for the 1990s,* pp. 39–53; For full coverage of policy deployment concepts and implementation, see also Y. Akao (ed.), *Hoshin Kanri: Policy Deployment for Successful TQM* (Cambridge, MA: Productivity Press, 1991).

30. Adopted from R. Fortuna and H.K. Vaziri, "Orchestrating Change . . . ."

31. R. Chang, "When TQM Goes Nowhere," *Training and Development Journal* 47 (January 1993), pp. 22–9; O. Harari, "Ten Reasons Why TQM Doesn't Work," *Management Review* 82 (January 1993), pp. 33–8.

32. Adopted from M. Cooney, "Learning and Leading by Example," *Lessons Taught by the Baldrige Winners* (New York: The Conference Board, Report 1061-94-CH, 1994), pp. 23–25.

33. *Ibid.,* reprinted with permission, The Conference Board.

34. R. Hayes and G. Pisano, "Beyond World Class: The New Manufacturing Strategy," *Harvard Business Review,* January–February 1994, pp.77–86.

35. L. Tatikonda. and R. Tatikonda, "Top Ten Reasons Your TQM Effort Is Failing to Improve Profit," *Production and Inventory Management* 37, no. 3 (3rd Quarter 1996), pp. 5–9.

36. O. Harari, "The Eleventh Reason Why TQM Doesn't Work," *Management Review* 82 (May 1993), pp. 31–6.

37. L. Tatikonda and R. Tatikonda, "Top Ten Reasons . . . ."

ELEMENTS OF LEAN PRODUCTION

Consider again the wastes listed in Chapter 2:

defects	waiting time
transportation	processing
inventory	motion
overproduction	

In a typical manufacturing plant it is easy to find these wastes by just walking around. It is also relatively easy to identify many of the **contributors** or **sources** of these wastes by observing management directives, shop-floor practices, and working conditions.

Among the sources of these wastes are

· Large lot production.

· Inefficient setup procedures and long changeover times.

· Poor operating performance and breakdown of equipment.

· Poor layout of equipment for the processes required.

· Inefficient procedures and lack of performance standards.

· Poor shop-floor coordination and control.

Some of the sources of waste are the result of outdated or incorrect notions about relationships between production costs, quality, efficiency, and demand. For example, when changeovers are costly and time-consuming, large-lot production is favored as a way to keep some costs down, in spite of the fact that large lot sizes contribute to overproduction and large inventories, which keep other costs up.

Some of the sources of waste are the result of neglect. Consider the following instances:

· Process and equipment changeovers and setups take a long time because no one tries to find ways to do them better or faster.

· Machines run poorly and are unreliable because no one attends to them until they are barely running or break down completely.

· Processes consist of wasteful steps and inefficient procedures because no one investigates them, prescribes improved procedures, or provides standards to which the operations should conform.

· Materials on the shop floor have to be moved long distances and then wait for long times between operations because equipment is poorly situated for the process, and no one rearranges the equipment to make it better.

Sometimes the source of wastes is not neglect, errors in judgment, or outdated notions, but simply because the system of production planning and control is inadequate to meet the requirements of the production process and customer demand.

To the extent that all of these waste contributors are somewhat interlinked, eliminating waste and improving processes in manufacturing requires that *all* of them be addressed. For example, start with the premise (argued in Chapter 5) that small-lot production is generally preferable to large-lot production: If, then, you want to reduce the size of production batches, you probably first have to reduce the time and effort of production changeovers, possibly dramatically. And to be able to economically process those many small batches (as opposed to a few large ones) through multiple operations, you probably also have to rearrange factory facilities so operations are closer together. Small-lot production reduces inventory, but that leaves less stock to buffer against equipment problems and machine-induced defects, so you also have to improve equipment reliability and performance.

Because the topics covered here deal directly with sources of manufacturing waste, including waste from defects and quality problems, they are considered the fundamental elements of lean or wasteless production. They all relate primarily to issues on the shop floor, and many of them require significant changes to the roles and responsibilities of shop-floor workers, supervisors, and machine operators. The topics are

CHAPTER 5
SMALL-LOT PRODUCTION

Everything is produced, procured, and handled in lots. A **lot** is a batch of something; in fact, the terms lot and batch are used interchangeably. The smallest lot-size alternative is one unit, for example, pick up one lobster from the market, make one pizza from scratch, or shape one metal part on a press. The alternative is multiple-unit lots—pick up 10 lobsters at once, make 10 pizzas, or shape 1000 parts one after another. Either alternative makes sense depending on factors such as time, cost, and demand. Determining the right lot size is called **lot sizing**.

Traditional manufacturing has had an affinity for large lot sizes. It just seems more practical to do things in large numbers. Sometimes it *is* more practical, though by no means always. Many of the costs associated with lot sizing are not initially obvious. Besides cost, lot size has a major impact on overall production throughput, lead time, manufacturing flexibility, and product quality. It also impacts manufacturing wastes such as inventory, waiting time, and transportation. In short, lot sizing is important because it impacts manufacturing speed, cost, quality, and agility. As this chapter will illustrate, a manufacturer and its customers potentially have much to gain by using smaller **lot sizes.**

The chapter reviews the factors relevant to lot sizing decisions and the traditional approaches for lot sizing. General benefits of small-lot production are discussed, as well as situations that merit large lot sizes. Practical and economical issues of using small lots in production, procurement, and shipping and the role of lot-size reduction in continuous improvement are also covered.

LOT-SIZE BASICS

The effort required to go to the market, to gather together ingredients to make pizzas, or to changeover a machine to make a kind of part is called **setup.** The desire to save on setup time and cost leads to working with larger lots—like buying multiple lobsters at once to save trips to the market, making multiple pizzas to save time on gathering ingredients, or manufacturing many parts at once to save time and cost associated with ordering materials and setting up a machine. Intuition says it's more efficient to do things in large lots.

But unless the demand is large enough to rapidly consume all the units in a large lot, many of them have to be stored. Excess lobsters and pizzas crowd the freezer, making it hard to put in or take out other things. If we eat 5 lobsters a year and have 10 in the freezer, half will remain a year later. They might be edible, but how will they taste? Large-sized lots offer savings in some ways, but they increase costs in others.

DOLLAR COSTS ASSOCIATED WITH LOTS[1]

The two principal dollar costs associated with lot sizing are *setup costs* and *holding costs*. In the lobster case, setup cost is the cost of going to the market (time, fuel, etc.); holding cost is the cost of storing the lobsters (space occupied, taste deterioration, etc.). Formally, the costs are defined as follows:

Setup cost, *S*, is the cost of preparing to make a batch *or* of ordering a batch. When applied to *manufacturing, S* is the cost of changeover from making one kind of item to another kind. It may include the cost of lost production while the machine is being changed and the cost of scrap incurred while adjusting the machine. When applied to *purchasing, S* is called the **order cost** and is the cost of placing and receiving an order from a supplier. For purposes of lot-sizing analysis it makes no difference whether *S* represents setup cost or order cost. We consider *S* as a fixed cost, independent of the size of the batch produced or ordered.

Holding cost, *H*, is the cost of *holding* a unit in inventory for a given time period. *H* includes expenses such as storage (rent, lease, mortgage, utilities, maintenance, etc.), tracking and monitoring of inventory, damage and pilferage, insurance, interest on money to produce or procure the items in inventory, and the opportunity cost of money tied up in inventory (and not available for use elsewhere). Usually items that are more valuable or costly to produce are also more costly to hold; that is, *H* is a percentage of the value of the item held in stock:

$$H = rP,$$

where

   $P =$ **unit production cost** or **unit procurement cost,** the cost of
        manufacturing (materials, labor, overhead) or purchasing one unit,
   $r =$ percentage based upon rates for borrowing, insuring, investing
        (opportunity), and so on.

LOT SIZING AND SETUP REDUCTION

Small-batch production and **delivery** is a principal feature of JIT manufacturing. Yet stand in a typical US factory and look around. What you see too often are crates, boxes, bins, and pallets of materials stacked floor to ceiling. This is a consequence of US managers' preference for large-batch production and procurement, which stems, in part, from their tendency to view material ordering, handling, and setup as fixed activities.[2] If you take the time and cost of a setup activity as given and fixed, then that time and cost will dictate your thinking about lot sizes: If *S* is large, then the lot size should be large; if S small, then the lot size can be small, too. Traditionally, however, S has been large.

This concept of starting with S, assuming it is fixed, then determining the lot size as a function of S is a sharp contrast with the JIT approach to lot sizing. JIT views all activities associated with setup, ordering, and handling of materials as non-value-added activities, wasteful things that should be minimized and eliminated. Thus, not only does JIT treat S as *not* being fixed, but in JIT the explicit goal is to reduce S to zero if possible. JIT emphasizes **setup reduction** as a form of continuous improvement; it is the continuous reduction of the time and cost of setup, ordering, and handling of materials. As the time and cost of these activities is made smaller, production and procurement in small lots is easier to justify, even in high-demand situations. The next chapter discusses setup procedures and the topic of setup-time reduction.

KINDS OF LOTS

A **lot** is a quantity of items purchased, produced, or transported. When a lot is the quantity of items manufactured as the result of a single setup it is referred to as a **production** or **process batch.** When it is the quantity of materials purchased from a supplier it is called a **purchase** or **order quantity.** A lot moved or transferred from one operation or workstation to another is called a **transfer batch.** Finally, a lot shipped between supplier and customer is called a **delivery quantity.**

As examples of these concepts, consider a machine that is set up to produce 100 units. As every 10 units are completed, they are moved to the next operation. In this example, the size of the process batch is 100 units, and the size of the transfer batch is 10 units. Similarly, suppose a purchase order is sent to a supplier for 500 units, and the supplier fills the order by making 10 deliveries of 50 units each. In that case, the purchase order quantity is 500 units, and the delivery quantity is 50 units.

LOT SIZING

Deciding the appropriately sized lots is important to good manufacturing management. Regardless of the kind of manufacturing scheduling and control system used, whether an MRP-type push system or a JIT-type pull system, lot sizing has a major impact on the efficiency, cost, and flexibility of production.

Organizations use different guidelines and procedures for determining lot sizes, from simple rule-of-thumb methods ("order enough to last the month") to analytical procedures. This section reviews some common analytical models for lot-sizing process batches and purchase-order quantities. Lot sizing of transfer batches is treated later.

PROCESS AND PURCHASE BATCHES

Following are four traditional lot-sizing approaches. We first explore the impact of these models on dollar-costs, then discuss the non-dollar-cost ramifications.

Lot-for-Lot

In lot-for-lot (LFL) lot sizing, the size of the lot or batch corresponds exactly to the amount required (ordered or forecasted) during a particular time period. If, for example, total customer orders for 4 successive weeks are 600, 10, 120, and 200 units, respectively, then the product would be manufactured over the 4 weeks (or as close to then as possible) in process batches of lot sizes 600, 10, 120, and 200, respectively.

	Week			
	1	2	3	4
Demand	600	10	120	200
Lot size	600	10	120	200

If the batches are shipped immediately upon completion, holding costs will be zero because each lot will be consumed immediately and never held in stock.

An advantage of LFL lot sizing is that it generally works well in both pull production systems and push production systems (both discussed in later chapters).

LFL also works well whether demand is independent or dependent. **Independent demand** means the demand for an item is generated exogenous to the production system, that is, demand is customer or market driven. For lot-sizing purposes, independent demand is determined either from a forecast, from actual sales, or from a combination of both. **Dependent demand** means the demand for an item is generated internal to the production system, usually as a function of the demand for a higher-level item. For example, the demand for headlights and steering wheels in automobile production is a function of the number of cars produced (1000 cars require 2000 headlights and 1000 steering wheels). Headlights and steering wheels are dependent-demand items; the autos themselves are independent-demand items. The items can be procured from suppliers (headlights) or produced internally (fenders, trunk lids, and so on). These concepts are discussed in depth in the Appendix on MRP.

LFL dictates production or procurement whenever there is nonzero demand (whether demand is independent or dependent), even if the demand is small. Demand that occurs in frequent, discrete amounts will cause frequent setups or orders (assuming one setup or order for every discrete amount). As a consequence, LFL can result in high setup costs or high order costs.

Period Order Quantity

The **period order quantity** (POQ) method reduces the number of setups or orders by putting restrictions on the frequency of orders. The POQ method starts with a predetermined **order frequency**, then determines the lot size according to the demand occurring between successive orders. As an example, suppose in the above situation the order frequency is 2 weeks, that is, one setup or purchase order is allowed once every 2 weeks. If orders are placed in weeks 1 and 3, then the sizes of the two lots would be as shown below:

	Week			
	1	*2*	*3*	*4*
Demand	600	10	120	200
Lot size	610		320	

While the POQ method results in fewer number of setups or orders than LFL (in the above case, half), it also usually results in inventory being carried. In the example above, 10 units are carried from week 1 to week 2 and 200 are carried from week 3 to week 4. Compared to LFL, POQ results in a reduction in setup costs, but that is traded off with an increase in inventory carrying costs. The next two lot-sizing methods balance setup and holding costs, and give the optimal trade-off.

Economic Order Quantity

The **economic order quantity** (EOQ) model gives the lot size that most economically satisfies forecasted demand for a given time period; it minimizes the sum of setup costs and carrying costs over a specified time period. The model was developed in 1915 and for 70 years was considered by academics as the fundamental method for determining lot size (managers had learned from experience not to trust its results).

As suggested in the LFL and POQ examples, there is an inherent trade-off between setup costs and carrying costs in inventory systems; as one goes up, the other goes down. If a few large lots are produced, setups will be few and overall setup costs will be low, but it takes longer to deplete the lots, so carrying costs will be high. If many small lots are produced, carrying costs will be low because each lot is small and is used quickly, but overall setup cost will be high because of the many setups. This trade-off of costs as a function of lot size Q is shown in Figure 5.1. The EOQ model gives the lot size Q that minimizes the sum of the two costs:

$$\min\left[TC = total\ setup\ cost\ +\ total\ carrying\ cost\right]$$

where TC represents total cost over a given time period (we assume here the time period is annual). In general, total annual cost is

$$TC = \frac{SD}{Q} + \frac{HQ}{2}.$$

FIGURE 5.1

Inventory costs and lot sizes.

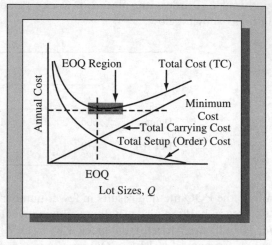

The lot value, Q, that minimizes this cost is

$$Q = EOQ = \sqrt{\frac{2DS}{H}},$$

where

EOQ = optimal (least cost) lot size,
D = average demand for a year,
S = setup (or order) cost as defined earlier,
H = unit holding cost per year, rP, as defined earlier.

(Derivations of the *TC* and *EOQ* formulae are provided in the chapter supplement.)
The model holds for the following assumptions:

1. Demand is constant, continuous, and known.

2. Demand is *independent*.

3. Setup (order) cost S is fixed, regardless of lot size.

4. Unit carrying cost H is known and constant; total carrying cost is a linear function of lot size.

5. The entire lot arrives (is produced or delivered) all at once.

6. Unit purchase (manufacturing) cost P is fixed, regardless of lot size (no quantity discounts or production economies).

7. Stockouts (or subsequent backorders) do not occur.

Example   1:   Application of the EOQ Model

An item has an annual demand of 10,000 units, annual unit carrying cost rate of 20%, order cost of $150, and unit purchase cost of $5.

The annual unit holding cost is $H = rP = .20(\$5) = \$1$. Thus, the lot size is

$$EOQ = \sqrt{\frac{2(10,000)(\$150)}{\$1}} = 1732.$$

Given $Q = EOQ$, the total annual cost of ordering and carrying is

$$\frac{10,000(\$150)}{1732} + \frac{\$1(1732)}{2} = \$866 + \$866$$

$$= \$1,732.$$

We can also determine the average purchase **order (or production) cycle** time, which is the time between orders: $Q/D = 1732/10,000 = 0.173$ yr $= 63$ days. This says that, assuming constant demand, we will order a batch of 1732 units about every 63 days.

Notice in Figure 5.1 that in the region near EOQ the TC curve is somewhat flat, which says that values of Q in the vicinity of EOQ all have relatively low cost. The above example indicates that Q should be 1732; however, because of the flatness of the curve, lot sizes of, say, 1500 or 2000 could be used instead with, probably, only a small deviation from the minimum cost. (The exact effect is determined by substituting these values for Q in the TC formula.)

Economic Manufacturing Quantity

The above EOQ model assumes that the entire lot arrives at one time. An example is when a lot size Q, ordered from a supplier, is shipped all in one delivery. When the lot arrives, the inventory is increased by the amount Q. Now, although that can happen with a batch of procured items, when the items represent a batch being manufactured, all-at-once delivery does not happen. Since the items are manufactured unit-by-unit, say at the **production rate** p, the inventory will *gradually* grow as the completed items are moved into finished inventory. To account for this gradual increase in inventory level, the EOQ model must be modified, and this modified model is called the **economic manufacturing quantity** (EMQ). The shape of the TC curve for the EMQ situation is similar to that in Figure 5.1; thus, the procedure to determine the minimum-cost lot size (described in the chapter supplement) is the same as for EOQ. The result is

$$Q = EMQ = \sqrt{\frac{2DS}{H[1 - (D/p)]}}.$$

With the exception that items are put into stock at the rate of p instead of all at once, the assumptions of the EMQ model are the same as for the EOQ model.

Example   2:   Application of the EMQ Model

A manufactured item has annual demand of 10,000 units. The production cost is $5 per unit; the annual unit carrying cost rate is 20%. The production rate is 500 units a week.

Converting to an annual figure, p becomes

$$p = 500 \times 52 \text{ weeks} = 26,000.$$

Thus, $1 - (D/p) = 0.616$, so

$$EMQ = \sqrt{\frac{2(10,000)(\$150)}{\$1(0.616)}} = 2207.$$

According to this model, production batches should be of size 2207. This lot size will satisfy demand for $Q/D = 2207/10,000 = .2207$ yr $= 11.5$ weeks, so a new batch of 2207 units must be run every 11.5 weeks.

The EMQ model is more applicable than the EOQ model for determining the lot size of production batches, though, obviously, EMQ is but a variant of EOQ that allows for a different assumption. Still other variants of EOQ have been developed to account for other assumptions such as variable P (quantity discounts), multiple-item orders, back orders, and planned shortages.[3]

EOQ-BASED METHODS: DISCUSSION

Even before JIT came along and started people thinking about the waste in inventory, the validity of EOQ-based methods for making lot-sizing decisions was in question. Though the logic of the models is correct, the assumptions inherent in them delimit the models' applicability.[4]

One problem is demand. Virtually no industry has continuous, fixed demand; many industries have strong seasonal or even erratic demand. Practically speaking, with each change in D, the EOQ must be recomputed. That is easy enough to do, but the result is wide swings in lot sizes over time, which complicates planning, ordering, and scheduling. If demand fluctuates slightly and has no trend, then an average value for D can be used. If the fluctuations are large, however, EOQ-derived lot sizes based on average demand will result in either excess inventory or stockouts.

A second problem with using EOQ models is in the costs. Much has been written about cost determination, though the bottom line is that it takes considerable accounting finesse to accurately determine the holding and setup costs and to keep them current. Few companies can do it. (Some books on inventory management actually suggest working it backwards: start with a desired EOQ, figure what the costs are, then try to achieve those costs!)

Consider the difficulty in determining carrying costs, H. Even when all dollar costs in H are known and accounted for, H still understates the true cost of carrying inventory because it fails to account for the detrimental effect of inventory on production quality and lead time. Generally, the larger the inventory carried, the more detrimental the effect. There is a similar difficulty with setup cost, S. Even when all dollar costs in S are accounted for, S is still potentially too low because it does not account for the effect of setup on idling the operation. If the operation is a bottleneck (i.e., scheduled work exceeds work capacity), the effect of the setup is equivalent to the cost of all throughput lost as a result of the operation being idled.[5] If, however, the operation is a nonbottleneck, the effect of the setup on throughput is zero because the operation has excess capacity anyway. The EOQ models do not distinguish bottleneck from nonbottleneck operations. These issues will be revisited later.

This is not to say that EOQ lot sizing is nowhere applicable. There are situations where EOQ-based lot sizing works, though they tend to be in nonmanufacturing situations like distribution and retailing, where inventories of different items are independent, batches of materials do not flow between operations, and where issues of production lead time and flexibility are irrelevant. In those cases EOQ is useful for determining the appropriate magnitude of orders, even when H and S are not precisely known. If EOQ says order 523, that probably means the lot size should be between, say, 200 and 800, and not be 50 or 5000. The flatness of the TC curve in the region near $Q = EOQ$ implies you will be near the minimum cost in that lot size region.

TRANSFER BATCHES

Many of the problems of large process batches come from the fact that a large batch takes a long time to process, which ties up the operation, prevents it from doing other jobs, and causes WIP inventory to build up both in front of and behind the operation. This increases the time all jobs must wait at the operation, which increases total production lead time for the job. One way to reduce production lead time and WIP for a process batch of any size is to use *lot splitting* and move the lot to subsequent operations in smaller **transfer batches.** Say, for example, 1000 parts are being machined at an operation; as they are completed, they are put in containers that each hold 100 parts, and, upon being filled, each container is moved to the next operation. Thus, the transfer batch size is 100 units, and 10 transfer batches are required to move the entire process batch of 1000 units.

In general, using transfer batches that are smaller in size than the process batch reduces lead time because items do not have to wait as long before being moved to the next operation. As an illustration, assume 1000 units must be processed in the routing sequence of operation A, operation B, then operation C. Each operation requires 1.0 min/unit processing time and has a process batch size of 1000. The left side of Figure 5.2 shows the resulting effect of using a transfer batch size of 1000. The right side of the figure shows the effects of using transfer batch sizes of 200, 500, and 500 units at operations A, B, and C, respectively.

The top of Figure 5.2 shows the accumulated WIP output for each operation, and the bottom shows elapsed time. The dashed triangles on the right represent the

FIGURE 5.2

Left: transfer batch = process batch = 1000.
Right: transfer batches are 200, 500, 500, respectively at A, B, C, and process batches = 1000.

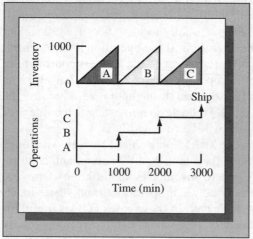
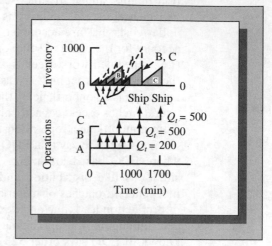

combined inventory at operations A, B, and C. The difference between the size of the triangles on the left and those on the right reveals how the smaller transfer batches reduce WIP. Using the smaller transfer batches also reduces the production lead time from 3000 minutes to 1700 minutes.

There is a caveat: using small transfer batches provides the benefits exemplified *only* if the transfer batches can be processed as soon as they arrive at the next operation. In Figure 5.2, the transfer batches from operations A and B are processed immediately at operations B and C, respectively, because (we assume) there is no pre-existing WIP ahead of those operations and the setup time is zero. The greater the WIP in front of operations and/or the longer the setup times, the smaller the benefit of using small transfer batches. To prevent large WIP buildup in front of operations, the setup times and the size of process batches used at operations *throughout* the plant must be small. Reducing the setup times or process lot sizes at just a few operations will have little overall effect; it just speeds up the flow of jobs through some operations, only to have them arrive sooner at subsequent operations (where they just wait longer until they can be processed)!

In general, the smaller the transfer batch, the larger the number of transfers (moves) required. Because of that, any initiative to reduce transfer batch sizes must be accompanied by a program to reduce the time and cost of material handling.

As the previous example illustrated, transferring materials between operations in batches that are smaller in size than the process batch can significantly influence production lead times and WIP quantities. Reducing the lot size of process batches has a similar influence, as explained next.

LOT-SIZE REDUCTION

EFFECT OF LOT-SIZE REDUCTION ON COMPETITIVE CRITERIA

To illustrate the effect of reducing the lot size of process batches, consider two products, X and Y. Assume that both must be processed through three operations, A, B, and C, in that sequence, that the setup times to changeover between products is negligible, and the daily production rates at the operations are as follows:

	Operation (units/day)		
Product	*A*	*B*	*C*
X	1000	2000	1000
Y	2000	2000	2000

Now suppose that 8000 units each of products X and Y must be produced; X first, then Y.

Figure 5.3 shows the schedule using process and transfer batches of 8000 units for both products. Figure 5.4 shows the schedule when the process batch size is reduced to 4000 units and the transfer batch size is reduced to 2000 units. In the figures, batches of products X and Y are represented by x and y, respectively. Comparing Figures 5.3 and 5.4, we can draw some general conclusions about the effects of reducing process lot size on speed, cost, quality, and flexibility of production.

FIGURE 5.3

Schedule with process batches = transfer batches = 8000.

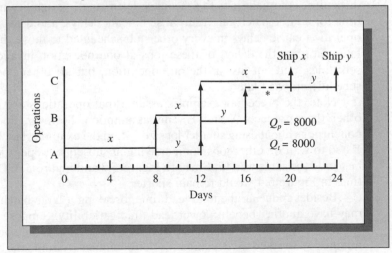

Note: Product Y is temporarily blocked from processing at operation C.

FIGURE 5.4

Schedule with process batches = 4000, transfer batches = 2000.

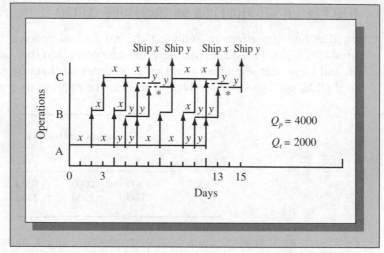

Note: Product *Y* is temporarily blocked from processing at operation C.

Lead Time

Production lead time (start to finish) for product *X* is reduced from 20 days to 13 days; for product *Y* it is reduced from 24 days to 15 days. With the smaller batches, product *X* finishes 7 days earlier, and product *Y* finishes 9 days earlier. In general, the smaller the process batch size of a job, the less time the job ties up an operation, and the less time other jobs at the same operation have to wait to be processed. Conversely, the larger the process batch size, the longer a job ties up an operation, and the more difficult it is to hold jobs to schedules. Even small variability in per-unit processing time for a large batch can result in significant delays, and delays in any one job at an operation cause delays in every other job scheduled to move through that operation later. In turn, the delays of these jobs at one operation invalidate their production schedules, and not just at the one operation, but all other operations the jobs are scheduled to visit later.

Note, the preceding examples assume that operations are never busy with jobs other than products *X* and *Y*. This assumption, however, does not invalidate the conclusions about using smaller lot sizes. If, in the example, batches of products *X* and *Y* had to wait on other jobs upon arriving at subsequent operations, the effect would be to add the same wait time in both Figure 5.3 and Figure 5.4. Obviously, the elapsed time in Figure 5.4 would remain shorter.

Besides reducing the total lead time, breaking a large batch into smaller batches may have another benefit: lower lead time variability. Suppose for example that the usual batch size is 200 units and that it requires a process time on average of $t_L = 200$ minutes, with standard deviation $\sigma_L = 40$ minutes. Assume the batch can be split into four batches of 50 units, each requiring a process time on average of $t_S = 50$ minutes, with $\sigma_S = 10$ minutes. If the four batches are independent, then the total process time average for the four batches remains 4(50) = 200 minutes, but the standard deviation for the combined four 50-unit batches is $\sqrt{4\,\sigma_S^2} = \sqrt{4(100)} = 20$, which is only half the standard deviation of the 200-unit batch.[6] This example is only an illustration of the *potential* of small-batch production to reduce variability, and it assumes, among other things, that small batches are processed independently of each other and that the ratio of the average time to standard deviation, t/σ, is the same for each small batch as for the large batch (i.e., average time for a small batch t_S is one-fourth the large batch t_L, and standard deviation for a small batch σ_S is also one-fourth the large batch σ_L).[7] It does illustrate, however, that dividing big jobs into small, uniform jobs can reduce the time variability of the overall process.

Carrying Cost

For a given production volume, WIP is proportional to production lead time. The longer items are at an operation or in the system, whether in process, in transit, or waiting, the greater the accrued carrying costs. Figures 5.5 and 5.6 show the accumulated output inventory for each operation and for the entire process. The dashed lines in the processwide inventory represent the average inventory: for the larger batches,

FIGURE 5.5

(Bottom) *Inventory level of completed units following each operation when process batches = transfer batches = 8000.* (Top) *Inventory level, processwide.*

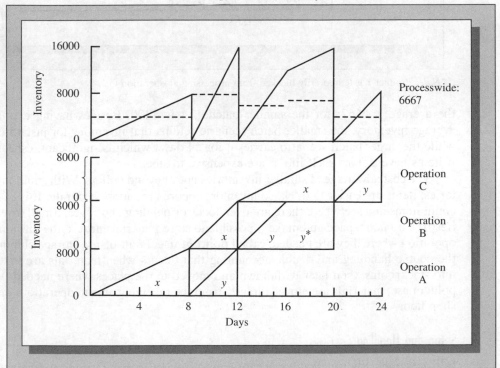

Note: Product *Y* is temporarily blocked from processing at operation C.

Figure 5.6

(Bottom) *Inventory levels of completed units following each operation using process batches = 4000, transfer batches = 2000.* (Top) *Inventory level, processwide.*

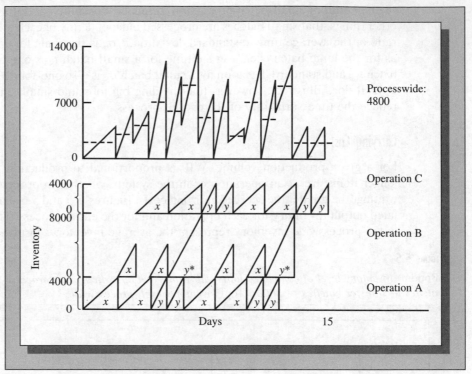

*Note: Product *Y* is temporarily blocked from processing at operation C.

the average is 6667; for the smaller batches, it is 4800. Besides having a smaller average inventory, the smaller batch scenario retains that inventory for just 15 days, while the larger batch scenario carries it for 24 days, which is significant, especially if items have a short shelf life or are expensive to stock.

The cost advantage of smaller inventories goes beyond dollars. With small inventories, items are easier to track, so inventory records are more accurate. It is easy to count items and see where there are overstocks or pending shortages. Small inventories free up floor space and make it possible to store materials next to the machine or operation where they are needed, called **point of use.** Point-of-use storage eliminates the double handling and double accounting that occurs when materials are first put into stockrooms, then later withdrawn and moved to the places where needed. With point of use, materials are moved directly from the receiving area to operations on the shop floor.

Setup and Handling Cost

In the example, the smaller-batch case requires twice as many setups and four times as many material transfers as the larger-batch case (Figure 5.3 versus Figure 5.4), which overall equates to a doubling of setup cost and a quadrupling of handling costs. It should thus be clear that if process and transfer lot sizes are to be reduced, the time and cost associated with setups and material handling must also be reduced to make small-lot production practical and economically feasible. Fortunately, reducing setup and handling costs is not necessarily as difficult as might first be presumed. Ways of reducing costs and wastes associated with setups and material handling are addressed later in this chapter and elsewhere throughout the book.

Quality

Defects are often batch specific; they result from a particular setup or method unique to the production batch. As a result, the larger the batch, the more units affected. In the example, 8000 units would be affected in the large-batch scenario, versus only 4000 units in the small-batch one.

Often a defect is not discovered until subsequent operations. With larger batches it will not be discovered until much later: by that time, the cause of the defect might be hard or impossible to find. Suppose a defect is introduced in product X at operation A but is not noticed until operation C. Referring to Figure 5.3, the defect will not be discovered until 12 days after it occurred, at the earliest. With the reduced-size batches (Figure 5.4), it would be discovered in just 3 days. The smaller WIP from the reduced-batch scenario (Figure 5.5 versus Figure 5.6) also contributes to fewer defects since items wait less on the shop floor and are less subject to damage and deterioration. With smaller lot sizes, engineering changes and redesign improvements can be introduced sooner and incrementally, instead of waiting until all of a current large batch is completed. For products where the required changes are released *after* production has begun, smaller process batches will result in fewer items needing rework.

CASE IN POINT: Effect of Smaller Lot Sizes on Quality[8]

Inman surveyed 114 manufacturing firms to assess the relation between reduction in lot sizes and reduction in scrap and rework. Taking into account both in-house and vendor lot sizes, he found roughly a 1:1 relationship between lot-size reduction and quality improvement (suggesting, for example, that a 50% reduction in lot size corresponds to a 50% decrease in scrap and rework). However, most of the surveyed firms had also implemented quality programs (supplier certification, SPC, quality circles), and some experienced reduced scrap and defect rates even when they did not reduce lot sizes. Inman concluded that lot-size reduction surely does improve quality (through reduced scrap and rework), though probably the improvement is less than proportionate to the lot-size reduction.

Flexibility

Large WIP ahead of every operation reduces the ability of a process to adjust to changes in products or demand. Whatever the nature of the change, it takes longer for large-batch operations to respond because the change is not felt until the pre-existing WIP is processed first. With large-batch production, the only way to achieve flexibility is through measures such as expediting, overtime, or subcontracting. Such measures can be costly, dispiriting to workers, and disruptive to work schedules. With smaller batches, it is easier to change job schedules, and to insert new jobs with less effect on the schedules of other jobs.

To illustrate, suppose in the prior example a special order for 4000 units of product Z arrives. Product Z requires processing times identical to product Y on operations A, B, and C. Assume products X and Y must be completed by days 20 and 24, respectively. If product Z were introduced into the schedule in Figure 5.3, it could not be started at operation A until day 12 at the earliest (else products X and Y would miss their due dates) and would not be finished at operation C until day 26. Specifically, product Z would be processed as follows:

1. Start job Z at operation A on day 12; finish on day 14 and transfer it to operation B; wait.
2. Start at operation B on day 16; finish on day 18 and transfer it to operation C; wait.
3. Start at operation C on day 24; finish on day 26.

Now, if product Z were introduced into the schedule in Figure 5.4, it could be started at operation A as early as time 0 (before the first batch of product X) or at some time later *between* any of the process batches for products X and Y, because with process batches of 4000 and transfer batches of 1000, the product Z order would take 5 days to process, meaning it could be completed in day 5 at the earliest and day 17 at the latest. Regardless where in the schedule in Figure 5.4 product Z is inserted, products X and Y will still be completed before their respective due dates of day 20 and day 24.[9]

In general, large batch sizes impede the ability to make necessary changes to production schedules and priorities. They contribute to large WIP and large lead times, which require all jobs to be released to production far in advance of their due dates. If a customer order arrives inside the lead time, then it will not be filled by the required due date. Orders representing forecasted demand must be forecasted farther into the future, which decreases the accuracy of the forecast.

These examples illustrate a property named after John D.C. Little, known as Little's Law:

$$WIP = [Lead\ Time] \times [Throughput\ Rate]$$

or

$$Lead\ Time = \frac{WIP}{Throughput}.$$

This says that, assuming constant throughput (in the example, production rate in terms of units/day), lead time can be reduced by reducing WIP. In fact, that is what happens when the batch sizes are reduced.

The examples provided are very simple so as to easily illustrate the effects of lot-size reduction. For a more complex situation, such as a plant in which a large variety of products is processed through a large number of operations, the effects of lot-size reduction are more difficult to assess and analysis requires tools that are more sophisticated. Computer simulation is useful in this regard, especially for assessing the impacts of lot-sizing decisions at particular jobs and operations on plantwide lead times and WIP.

In most cases, reduction of lot sizes brings improvements in cost, lead times, quality, and plant flexibility, but there are situations that call for larger lot sizes, or where constraints make small lot sizes infeasible or impractical.

CASE FOR LARGER PROCESS BATCHES

In the past (before people started looking at ways to reduce setup times), the size of process batches was often set solely to minimize the number of setups. Less time consumed by setups allows more time for production. To guarantee ample time for production, it was reasoned, setups should be spaced far apart so process batches could be large. That rationale is still valid when the time required for setup is lengthy, especially when the setup is at a bottleneck or almost-bottleneck operation.

A **bottleneck** operation is one where the production capacity is less than the demand placed upon it; it is a resource where the scheduled work exceeds the work capacity. It is overloaded. An almost-bottleneck operation is one where capacity is barely adequate, one which could readily become a bottleneck if additional jobs are imposed on it or current jobs are rescheduled carelessly.[10]

At bottlenecks, larger process batches might be desirable because larger batches take fewer setups, which allows more time for processing and higher throughput. To create larger batches, several different jobs that all require the same kind of setup might be combined into one large batch, ignoring priorities or due dates on the jobs.

At almost-bottlenecks, process batches can be somewhat smaller than at bottlenecks, though the feasible minimal size of the batches depends on the resulting number of setups and the time remaining for production. In choosing the process batch size, care must be taken so the number of resulting setups does not turn an almost-bottleneck into a sure bottleneck.

MINIMAL LOT SIZE

The minimal lot size for a given demand is constrained by the production capacity and setup time. Suppose an operation makes five different parts and runs 40 hours a week; after subtracting out the time necessary for production and maintenance, 7.5 hours a week remain for performing setups. If each setup takes 0.5 hour, then

$$The\ Number\ of\ Possible\ Setups = \frac{Time\ Available\ for\ Setup}{Time\ to\ Perform\ Setup} \tag{1}$$

$$= 7.5\ \text{hrs}/0.5\ \text{hr} = 15\ \text{setups a week.}$$

This means that, on average, there is time to do 15 setups per week for five parts, or three setups per part per week.

To satisfy demand for the given number of setups,

$$Minimal\ Process\ Lot\ Size = \frac{Average\ Weekly\ Demand}{Number\ of\ Setups}. \tag{2}$$

So, if the average weekly demand for each part is, say, 1500 units, then

$$Minimal\ Process\ Lot\ Size = \frac{1500}{3} = 500\ units.$$

The *time to perform setup* in formula (1) is the **internal setup time,** which is the time the machine or operation must be stopped to perform the setup. Another factor that could affect lot size is the **external setup time,** which is time devoted to performing the setup *while* the operation is running (e.g., getting a tool to set up a machine for the next job while the machine is performing the current job). If, in the above example, 5 hours of external setup are required *in addition* to the 0.5 hour for internal setup, then the total time per setup is 5.5 hours. Thus, during the 40-hour work week the maximum number of setups that can be done is 40/5.5 = 7.2, or 7 setups.[11] For five parts, that allows 7/5 = 1.4 setups per part per week. Therefore, the minimal theoretical lot size for weekly demand of 1500 is

$$\frac{1500}{1.4} = 1071.$$

The external setup time constrains the minimal process lot size only when it mandates a smaller number of setups than does the internal setup time alone. In the above example, if the external setup time were only 1 hour, there would be enough time in the 40-hour workweek for 40/1.5 = 26.6 setups. But since the internal setup time of 0.5 hour allows a maximum of only 15 setups, the internal setup time is the constraining factor, and the external setup time can be ignored.

Besides setup time, product demand and production rate are the other major determinants of minimal process lot size. Smaller demand can be satisfied for a fixed number of setups with smaller lot sizes. Processes with faster production rates require less time for processing, which allows more time for setups and permits smaller process lot sizes. In other words, lot size can be varied dynamically depending on (or to take advantage of) the immediate circumstance.

A further consideration in lot-size determination is delivery size. In the above examples the average weekly demand was 1500 units. Suppose shipments are made weekly to a customer in quantities that average 1500. If the computed batch size is 1071, then to meet the weekly shipment would require two setups (produce 1071, then produce 429). However, since the maximum feasible number of setups is only 1.4, usually only one setup can be performed a week, not two. Thus, to meet the shipment size of 1500, the process batch size should be 1500, not 1071.

SMALL BUFFER STOCK

Buffer stock (also called **safety stock**) is the excess inventory held between stages of a process to avoid running short. The two reasons for carrying buffer stock are uncertainty about demand and uncertainty about lead time.

If you know exactly what the demand is, then you can plan to make or order exactly what you need. On the other hand, if you are uncertain about demand, then to be safe you order, make, or stock *more* than you think you will need. The excess is the buffer stock.

The same rationale applies to lead time. If you know exactly the time to produce or take delivery of something, then you can schedule orders such that items will be completed or arrive exactly when needed. If, however, you are uncertain about the lead time, then to be safe you keep some extra on the side so you do not run short if the lead time is longer than expected.

Buffer stocks everywhere in the plant contribute to large inventories, with all the time, cost, quality, and agility consequences mentioned before. Since the purpose of buffer stocks is to protect the process against variability, to reduce buffer stock it is necessary to reduce variability.

Demand Variability

One way to reduce demand variability is to level the production schedule, that is, to produce the same quantity of an item in each time period. With a somewhat uniform schedule, there is no (or less) variability and, hence, no (or less) need for buffer stocks. When demand cannot be leveled, then production should mimic demand, that is, stop–go, stop–go, producing as close to demand as possible. To do that, you need very agile production capability. (Chapter 16 discusses production leveling and ways to reduce dependency on buffer stock when leveling is not possible.)

Lead Time Variability

Variability in internal (process) lead times stems from variability in equipment functioning, setup times, worker absenteeism and skill level, material and product defects, and innumerable other sources. Variability in external lead times stems from unreliable delivery. To reduce buffer stocks while protecting against lead time variability, it is again necessary to eliminate the sources of variability. This can be achieved via preventive maintenance of equipment, setup improvement, production quality control, standardized operations, and contracts with very dependable suppliers. (These topics are covered in the next six chapters on lean production and in Chapter 19, supply chain management.)

FACILITATING SMALL LOT SIZES

There are many ways to make small-lot production practical and economical, though they require making changes in shop-floor practices and procedures and, often, in manufacturing planning and control systems as well as management philosophy and outlook. These ways are covered in various chapters throughout this book. This section gives an overview of issues relating to the feasibility and practicality of small lot sizing as applied to process, purchase, transfer, and shipping batches.

PROCESS BATCHES

The key factor in the feasibility of small-lot process batches is setup time. Ceteris paribus, shorter setup times enable smaller production batches. Though the topic of setup has been mentioned before, the topic of setup *reduction* is so important to JIT that the entire next chapter is devoted to it.

PURCHASE QUANTITIES

Reducing the size of purchase quantities requires reducing the cost of order placement and processing. Order costs are analogous to setup costs in that they are independent of the size of the purchased quantity. One way to reduce order costs is to move some (or much) of the responsibility for purchasing from the purchasing department to the production department and even to the shop floor, where supervisors and workers place the orders (this topic is discussed later in the chapters on workcells, pull production, and shop-floor control). This way reduces purchasing overhead costs and order lead times.

Another way to reduce order costs is to reduce the number of suppliers and to develop standard agreements and trusting partnerships with them. With fewer suppliers, the overhead cost associated with purchasing is less; remaining suppliers get a larger share of the business and, hence, are more committed to providing better service, including more frequent, smaller-quantity deliveries. Further, with supplier partnerships, suppliers take on much of the responsibility for the quality of incoming materials, which reduces or eliminates costs associated with the customer having to perform incoming inspection.

Additionally, suppliers and customers in a partnership work to determine ways to mutually reduce ordering, transportation, and receiving costs. The two parties can agree on standardized containers so that incoming items can be moved directly into the customer's production process, to the point-of-use, rather than being unpacked and transferred to different containers. Hewlett-Packard, for example, worked with one supplier to develop dual-purpose packaging: the package in which incoming parts are received becomes the package for the finished product. In many cases the vendors also take responsibility for determining the customer's order requirements. With each delivery, the driver checks the customer's stock level to determine the sizes of the order quantities for subsequent deliveries. Paperwork is reduced through blanket purchase orders covering a given time period, and the customer is billed once at the end of the period. (This subject of customer–supplier relationships is covered in more detail in Chapter 19.)

TRANSFER BATCHES

The economics of small transfer batches depends on the cost of material handling: as the cost goes down, smaller transfer batches become more economical. The cost of material handling is principally a function of three things: (1) the distance over which materials are moved, (2) the number of steps or transactions involved in the move, and (3) the complexity or sophistication of the material handling system.

Distance is reduced by locating workstations and machines close together and in sequence so as to eliminate backtracking and to minimize cross-traffic and congestion of material flow. This is one advantage of using focused facilities and workcells (described in Chapters 9 and 10). With workcells, the need for expensive conveyance systems, forklifts and sophisticated material tracking systems is reduced or eliminated. Heavy, bulky items still require mechanical handling systems, but shortened distances keep the cost of such systems to a minimum.

DELIVERY AND SHIPPING BATCHES

To make small deliveries from suppliers practical, the per-unit transportation cost must be reduced. One way to do this is to use smaller trucks and vans for short-distance deliveries or to use large trucks, but visit more customers on each trip. For example, instead of having a large truck make one big delivery a week to each of three customers, the same truck makes three trips a week, on each trip visiting all three customers. Each trip, customers would get one-third of the average weekly quantity. Of course, the practicality and cost benefit of doing this depends on the relative proximity of customers to each other and to the supplier. (This subject is covered in depth in Chapter 19.)

As more companies become JIT suppliers, more trucking firms and for that matter the entire logistics industry are taking greater responsibility for working out the details of delivery routes and schedules, and for coordinating deliveries between groups of suppliers and groups of customers so that frequent delivery of small quantities is economical. Many companies contract with third-party distributors to handle the logistics for them. When transportation costs stay the same or even increase slightly, smaller shipments result in overall savings from smaller inventories of incoming and finished materials, higher quality materials, and better responsiveness to short-term demand.

CONTINUOUS IMPROVEMENT

The premise of this chapter is that *in general* smaller lot sizes (process, transfer, and buffer stock) lead to better manufacturing performance and greater customer satisfaction. Yet, as explained, there are valid reasons for using large lot sizes and carrying large buffer stocks. Thus, if a company sets out to significantly reduce lot sizes and buffer stocks, it will not be able to do it all at once. Nor should it try. In JIT, reduction of lot sizes and buffer stocks is part of the continuous improvement process. It is, like PDCA, a process. The idea is to reduce lot sizes and buffers a little bit at a time to see what happens. As soon as the reduction begins to cause a problem, the next step is to find the source of the problem, prescribe a solution, and implement it. When the problem source has been eliminated, the lot sizes and buffers can again be reduced until new obstacles arise, and so on.

Some problem sources can be eliminated right away. For example, a machine that is unreliable might require only periodic, scheduled recalibration; in that case, the source of uncertainty can be removed as can all buffers surrounding the machine. Other problem sources will be much more difficult to resolve, for example, a supplier that is habitually late, not willing to change, and for which there is no alternative supplier. Even with difficult problems, however, the principle is the same: keep trying no matter how long it takes, and eventually a way to eliminate the problem source *will* appear (a different, more reliable supplier will be located, or production of the item will be transferred in-house). Like continuous improvement, reduction of lot sizes and buffer stocks should proceed methodically and perpetually.

Summary

Lot sizing affects manufacturing competitive advantage because it influences the cost, quality, lead time, and flexibility of production. Traditionally, US managers have favored larger lot sizes, primarily because of the large expense associated with setting up production, placing orders, and making deliveries. Large lots are also the result of large setup expenses in EOQ-based models, which give the economic optimum, but only in terms of dollar costs. The drawback of large lot sizes is that even when they minimize dollar costs, they lead to greater nondollar costs associated with increased production lead times, hidden defects, and reduced scheduling flexibility.

JIT acknowledges the problems and wastes connected with using large lot sizes. Small-lot production is achieved by giving more purchasing responsibility to shop-floor workers, by reorganizing the facility layout to reduce material transfer distances and cost, by locating materials at the point of use, and by working with suppliers to find ways to increase the frequency of deliveries, reduce the need for incoming inspection, and reduce the costs of handling, purchasing, and transportation. Even when process lot sizes must be somewhat large, speed and flexibility can be increased by using small transfer batches.

To the extent that large lot sizes and buffer stocks are maintained to absorb process variability and allow continued production in the face of problems, lot-size and buffer-stock reduction is a method of continuous improvement. It is a way to reveal the sources of variability and problems and to force their removal.

The minimal lot size of a process batch depends not just on costs, but also on demand, production capacity, and setup times. Sometimes these factors in combination mandate larger lot sizes, particularly at bottleneck or almost-bottleneck operations. However, for a given demand and production rate, the major determinant of process lot size is the setup time. Changeovers and equipment setups that are long and inefficient are the major barrier to small-lot production. Like many other wastes on the factory floor, however, setups are inefficient and time-consuming not because they *have* to be, but because seldom does anyone look carefully for ways to improve them. The next chapter describes a methodology for analyzing setups as well as procedures for reducing setup time.

Chapter Supplement

DERIVATION OF EOQ AND EMQ MODELS FOR LOT SIZING

EOQ MODEL

To arrive at the minimum-cost lot size, setup and ordering costs are first expressed in terms of lot size. Let

Q = lot size,
D = average demand for a year (or other time period),
H = carrying cost as defined earlier,
S = setup or order cost as defined earlier.

Since

$$TC = Total\ Setup\ Cost + Total\ Carrying\ Cost$$

we start by defining the (1) total setup cost and (2) total carrying cost as a function of lot size Q:

1. *Total setup cost.* Since the number of annual setups is equal to the average demand divided by the lot size (D/Q),

$$Total\ Setup\ Cost = S(D/Q).$$

2. *Total carrying cost.* Since D is constant and continuous, the inventory level fluctuates like the sawtooth curve shown in Figure 5.7. The inventory level peaks when each lot arrives (the lot is delivered), then decreases uniformly at rate D until it reaches zero; at that time another lot arrives. The order (or production) cycle, Q/D, which is the time between orders, is also shown in Figure 5.7.

As the figure shows,

$$Average\ Inventory = Q/2.$$

FIGURE 5.7

Inventory versus time.

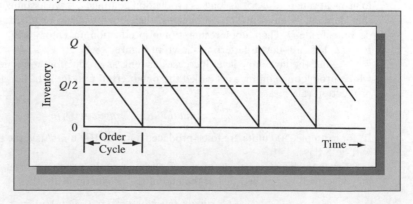

Assuming total carrying cost is based on average inventory,

$$Total\ Carrying\ Cost = H(Q/2).$$

In summary, total annual cost is

$$TC = \frac{SD}{Q} + \frac{HQ}{2}.$$

Plotting *TC* for values of *Q* gives the curve shown in Figure 5.1. Using calculus, the formula for *Q* that corresponds to the minimum point on the total annual cost curve (slope = 0) is found by taking the derivative of *TC* with respect to *Q*, setting it equal to 0, then solving for *Q*:

$$d(TC) = \frac{-SD}{Q^2} + \frac{H}{2} = 0$$

so

$$Q = EOQ = \sqrt{\frac{2DS}{H}}.$$

EOQ is the lot size that minimizes costs.

The same solution can be derived without calculus. Referring back to Figure 5.1, it is noted that the EOQ occurs at the place on the graph where (total setup cost) = (total carrying cost), that is,

$$(DS)/Q = (QH)/2.$$

Restructuring this equation gives

$$Q = \sqrt{\frac{2DS}{H}}.$$

EMQ MODEL

Figure 5.7 illustrates the periodic all-at-once arrival of a lot *Q* by the periodic vertical rise in inventory level. But when additions are made gradually to inventory, as in the EMQ case, the inventory level grows at a rate that is the *difference* between additions to inventory at production rate *p* and subtractions from it at demand rate *D*, or $p - D$. The inventory level continues to grow at rate $p - D$ for as long as production continues. If we assume, as in the EOQ model, that demand is uniform and continuous, then upon ceasing production, the inventory will decline at rate *D*. Then, upon resumption of production, inventory will again grow by the rate $p - D$. This up–down pattern is shown in Figure 5.8.

Again, the inventory level increases as long as production continues. The duration over which production continues is called the **production run length.** For a given lot size *Q* and production rate *p*,

$$Production\ Run\ Length = Q/p.$$

If, for example, 500 units are to be produced and *p* is 100 units/day, the production run length will be 5 days.

Since inventory increases at $p - D$ throughout the production run, the maximum inventory level will be reached just at the end of the production run; thus,

$$Maximum\ Inventory = (p - D)(Q/p).$$

FIGURE 5.8

Inventory versus time.

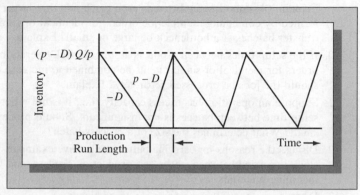

In that case,

$$Average\ Inventory = \frac{(p - D)(Q/p)}{2} = \frac{[1 - (D/p)]Q}{2};$$

multiplying this formula by H gives the annual carrying cost. The annual setup cost is not affected by the gradual additions to inventory, and so is the same as in the EOQ model.

The *TC* formula for gradual additions is thus

$$TC = \frac{SD}{Q} + \frac{H[1 - (D/p)]Q}{2}.$$

The shape of this TC curve is similar to that shown in Figure 5.1. To determine the formula for the minimum-cost lot size, use the same procedure as to get EOQ. The result is

$$Q = EMQ = \sqrt{\frac{2DS}{H[1 - (D/p)]}}.$$

Questions

1. What factors are included in order and setup costs? What about holding and carrying costs? Give examples. Why is it difficult to attach a precise dollar value to these costs?

2. How does the batch size affect the average inventory?

3. Explain the trade-off between setup cost and carrying cost.

4. Comment on the following statement: the EOQ and EMQ models are not appropriate for determining the batch size of items processed through a sequence of multiple operations, but they might be appropriate for determining the batch size of items fully produced at one operation or procured from a supplier.

5. What factors/costs do the EOQ and EMQ models ignore?

6. How does the process batch size affect quality?

7. Discuss the effects of reducing the size of process batches.

8. Discuss the effects of reducing the size of transfer batches.

9. In general, should the process batch size at a bottleneck operation be large or small? Explain. (Assume a setup between each batch and that larger process batches can be formed by combining multiple job orders for identical or similar items.) Should the transfer batches at a bottleneck be large or small? Explain.

10. If the setup times between products at a bottleneck operation are negligible, should job orders for identical or similar items be combined to increase the process batch size, or should the jobs be processed separately? Explain.

11. Suppose an operation has excess capacity (i.e., it is not a bottleneck), however the setup time between batches is *not* insignificant. Should process batches be large or small? What determines the size of a process batch?

12. Discuss the reasons for carrying buffer stock. Give examples illustrating why buffer stock is carried between stages of a production process, and why it is carried for incoming materials.

13. Discuss how the following costs can be reduced:
    a. Order placement and processing
    b. Material handling
    c. Shipping and delivery

Problems

1. A product has the following weekly demands:

	Week							
	1	*2*	*3*	*4*	*5*	*6*	*7*	*8*
Demand	20	70	100	190	50	20	80	120

Assume: no initial inventory

    carrying cost = $2.00/unit/week

    setup cost = $130

    lead time = 1 week

Using the above table, determine the lot sizes and calculate the total cost using
    a. Lot-for-lot.
    b. Two-week period order quantity (assume inventory is the amount remaining after the first week of every two-week order period).

2. A manufacturer buys cardboard boxes from a supplier. The annual demand is 36,000 boxes and is uniformly distributed. The boxes cost $4 each. The estimated order cost is $6, and the carrying cost rate is 30% per year.
    a. What are the EOQ, and the annual order and carrying cost?
    b. How many times a year are orders placed, and what is the average time, in weeks, between orders?

   c. Using the answer from (*b*), if you round the average time between orders to the nearest week, what should the order quantity be? Would you recommend using this order quantity and time interval?

3. Suppose for problem 2 the actual demand turns out to be 72,000 boxes instead of 36,000 boxes. If you had used the EOQ from the previous problem, what would the annual order and carrying cost be? What percent larger is this cost than the cost estimated above in (*a*)? What can you conclude about the cost of an incorrect demand estimate?

4. Referring to problem 2 again, suppose the box supplier is located close to the manufacturer's plant. For any quantity ordered from the manufacturer, the supplier fills it by making daily deliveries of up to 200 boxes per day for as many days as it takes to fill the order. Both the supplier and the manufacturer use a 5-day workweek.
   a. What is the economic order quantity and the annual order and carrying cost? (Hint: Use EMQ.)
   b. What is the manufacturer's annual savings in carrying cost by using this system instead of the one in problem 2?
   c. What is the average time, in weeks, between orders?
   d. Suppose the manufacturer places orders at 2-week intervals. What should the order quantity be? How many days will it take the supplier to fill the order?

5. A machining area produces part QR for use in an adjacent assembly area. Estimated annual demand for the part is 20,000 units. The value of the part is $50 per unit. The annual carrying and handling cost rate is estimated to be 16%. The plant operates 250 days a year. The assembly area uses one part QR for each product, and it produces 100 products per day. When producing part QR, the machining area can produce 200 units per day. The cost of ordering and setup for part QR is $200.
   a. What is the economic order quantity?
   b. Suppose the assembly area places an order when the on-hand amount of part QR reaches a certain level, the **reorder point.** If it takes the machining area two weeks to begin filling any order, and if the assembly area wants to maintain a minimum, or **safety stock** of 200 units, at what on-hand quantity should an order be placed (i.e., what is the reorder point)?
   c. If part QR were ordered from a supplier for the same costs as above, and the supplier delivered the entire order all at once, what would the order quantity be?

6. Redo the analysis illustrated in Figures 5.3 and 5.4, except that assume processing of product Y must precede processing of product X. What effect does this have on the shipping dates?

7. A product moves in sequence through five operations, V, W, X, Y, and Z. The processing time at each operation (min/unit) is 10, 20, 10, 20, and 10. Use a chart like Figure 5.2 to show the flow of the product through the five operations and the inventory accumulation after each operation. Determine the total production lead time and average inventory. Assume the production quantity and the process batch size is 100. Use transfer batch sizes of (a) 100, (b) 50, and (c) 25.

8. For problem 7, assume the inventory carrying cost is $50/unit/day, and the material handling cost is $10/transfer. Determine the total carrying and total transfer costs for the three cases. Assume carrying cost is based on average inventory.

9. An operation is used to machine 10 kinds of parts. The total weekly requirement for all ten parts is 900. Each part requires 20 sec. machine time. Assume the machine is to be scheduled for no more than 90 percent of its total available time. A normal workweek

is 40 hours/week, but 4 hours a week are reserved for normal machine preventive and repair maintenance. If the setup for each kind of part is one hour:

a. What is the maximum number of setups per week?

b. What is the smallest allowable lot size, assuming all batches are the same size?

c. To reduce the lot size in (b) by 50 percent, what must the setup time be reduced to?

10. Three parts are routed through the same operation. The daily production volume and processing times are shown in the table below. The operation is available 400 min/day, and the setup time between parts production is 10 minutes. If the amount of time each day devoted to setup is to be equally allocated among the three parts, what are the minimum lot sizes of the three parts?

Part	Processing Time (sec/unit)	Average Daily Volume (units)
GB	10	1050
QED	7	550
RBW	13	300

11. Four products use the same machine. Processing times, daily production volumes, and setup times for the products are shown below. Assume the machine is run for two shifts, and is available for 800 min/day. The products are to be produced in a sequence that is repeated throughout the day until the required volume is filled. How many times a day can the sequence be repeated, and what is the resulting lot size of each product?

Product	Processing Time (sec/unit)	Average Daily Volume (units)	Setup Time (minutes)
B	20	450	15
G	15	800	18
R	10	600	6
H	25	250	10

Endnotes

1. There are many costs besides dollar costs associated with lot sizing. These costs ultimately affect the quality of output and functioning of the organization (and so the bottom line), but are difficult or impossible to quantify. These nondollar costs are discussed later.

2. That is, fixed-cost has been confused with fixed procedures. Indeed, setup and ordering are fixed-cost activities (S remains constant regardless of the size of the lot), however, they are not fixed procedures in the sense that the steps involved in setup or ordering cannot be changed.

3. J. Evans, D. Anderson, D. Sweeney, and T. Williams, *Applied Production and Operations Management* (3rd ed.) (St. Paul: West Publishing, 1990), Chapter 13.

4. G. Woolsey, "A Requiem for the EOQ: An Editorial," *Production and Inventory Management Journal* 29, No. 3 (1988), pp. 68–72.

5. M.M. Umble and M.L. Srikanth, *Synchronous Manufacturing* (Cincinnati: South-Western Publishing, 1990), pp. 113–14.

6. Assuming the batches are independent, the standard deviation of the times for a group of batches is the squared root of the sum of the variances of the times for each of the batches.

7. W. Hopp and M. Spearman, *Factory Physics* (Chicago: Irwin, 1996), pp. 258–60.

8. R.A. Inman, "The Impact of Lot-Size Reduction on Quality," *Production and Inventory Management Journal* 35, No. 1 (1st Quarter 1994), pp. 5–7.

9. The example assumes savings in lead times have not been filled up with other jobs. A principle in JIT production is to never schedule for full capacity. Some excess capacity is always allowed for disruptions, problem solving, or, as in this case, special requirements.

10. The subject of bottleneck scheduling includes considerations much beyond production lot sizing, and is a topic in synchronous manufacturing and the theory of constraints. *See* E. Goldratt and J. Cox, *The Goal* (revised ed.) (Croton-on-Hudson: North River Press, 1987); E. Goldratt and R. Fox, *The Race* (Croton-on Hudson: North River Press, 1986); M. Umble and M. Srikanth, *Synchronous Manufacturing.*

11. Since most of the setup time in this case is external time, the full 40-hour workweek can be used to determine maximum number of setups.

SETUP-TIME REDUCTION

One challenge facing modern-day production is to meet growing demand for ever more-diversified products. With increased product diversification, product order sizes tend to get smaller and product life cycles tend to get shorter. To meet the demand, companies must be able to profitably produce in small quantities and make frequent product/model changeovers. Yet even in industries that produce fewer kinds of products in large volumes, there is something to gain from small-batch production in terms of costs, quality, lead times, and agility. Whether a company makes-to-order or makes-to-stock, the realities of today's markets and competition call for production methods that require doing a growing number of setups. Customer service and product quality are directly affected by setup procedures. The lowly setup now occupies a central place in competitive manufacturing.

This chapter reviews the ways that companies have traditionally dealt with setups, and the consequences. Simplification, an alternative approach to setup, is discussed, and a methodology is presented for analyzing and improving setup procedures. The chapter also profiles techniques for minimizing setup time and effort and discusses the organizational and procedural aspects of conducting setup-reduction projects.

IMPROVE SETUPS? WHY BOTHER?

TRADITIONAL APPROACHES

Companies have traditionally sought to keep the *number* of setups to a minimum. After all, a setup operation takes time, costs money, and produces nothing. It is a non-value-added activity.

Setup time is time spent in preparation to do a job. In manufacturing, setup is the elapsed time between when the last unit of one lot is produced and when the first *good* unit of the next lot is produced. It includes time to replace fixtures and attachments on a machine and to adjust the machine until it produces a part that meets specifications. During much of the setup time the machine is shut off and produces nothing. During the rest of the setup time the machine is running and producing parts, but until the machine is fully adjusted, the parts are nonconforming and must be scrapped or reworked.

The usual ways that companies deal with setups are to (1) increase the skills of setup personnel, (2) minimize product variety, (3) combine different jobs with similar setup requirements, and (4) use large lots. All of these ways bow to the fact that setups are often complicated, time-consuming, and costly. The first way puts setup responsibility into the hands of a few highly skilled workers; the other ways minimize the number of required setups.

Most traditional setups require special knowledge of machines, tools, fixtures, and materials as well as special skills for changing over and adjusting equipment so it can produce to meet requirements. As a result, companies assign setup operations exclusively to skilled workers who have the title "setup person" or "setup engineer." When setup workers are scarce, equipment sits idle until they arrive. As machines are being changed over, machine operators sometimes help with the setup or work at other machines (if they are cross-trained), though often they simply wait until the setup is finished. Of course, restricting setup operations to a relative few workers limits the number of setups to only what those workers have time to do.

The smaller the difference between products, the smaller the difference in the processes and operations that produce them. Companies can, thus, reduce the number and types of setups by making products that are largely the same. Reducing product variety makes sense if a company can profitably survive by making just a relative few, similar products, though for many companies that will never be the case. At one extreme are companies that offer high-volume, standardized products that each come in numerous models with endless options; at the other extreme are companies that produce small-volume, virtually unique products, made-to-order. Either way, total production volume depends on the ability to offer variety, even though the unit volume for each model/option combination or each customer order might be small.

The number of setups required to process a list of current jobs can be reduced by scheduling the jobs in a sequence so that all jobs with similar or identical setups are produced back-to-back. This method uses similarity-of-setup as the criterion for work scheduling. It ignores other scheduling priorities, such as due dates, and results in jobs being finished earlier or later than needed (i.e., causing either WIP or shortages, respectively). Scheduling jobs this way also precludes any chance of smoothing work flow through multiple operations, since jobs waiting at each operation will be preempted by any job that arrives and does not require a change of setup.

The relative effect of setup time on each production unit can be mitigated by increasing the production lot size. The larger the lot size, the smaller the effect of the setup on each unit. As an example, suppose setup time for an operation is 4 hours and unit processing time is 1 minute. If the lot size is 100 units, the unit operation time is

$$\frac{4(60) + 100}{100} = 3.4 \text{ min/unit.}$$

If the lot size is 1000 units, the unit operation time is only

$$\frac{4(60) + 1000}{1000} = 1.24 \text{ min/unit.}$$

The 1000-unit batch yields an approximate 63% reduction in unit operation time over the 100-unit batch. Generally, the longer the setup time, the greater the impact of producing larger lots on reducing unit operation time.

FIND ANOTHER WAY!

The above ways of handling setups are acceptable if you start with the premise that setup time and cost are *immutable, inflexible,* and *unimprovable.* But if your goal is to minimize production costs and maximize quality and customer service, then all four of the above ways have major drawbacks. For the most part, the traditional ways hamper product diversity, quality, and production flexibility for the sake of one thing: minimum number of setups. If, instead, you consider setup time as variable, flexible, and improvable, then you will find another way; you will *change the setup procedure.*

Suppose, using the previous example, you want to produce in small batches, say batches of 100 units. Also, say you don't want the operation time/unit (setup + processing time) to exceed 1.24 minutes. The solution is to reduce the setup time. If the processing time is 1 min/unit, then the setup time must be reduced from 4 hours to

$$x = 1.24(100) - 100 \quad \text{or} \quad x = 24 \text{ minutes.}$$

You can achieve this reduction by reducing the number of setup steps and making the setup procedure so direct that operators can do it themselves. You might think this example (reducing setup time 90% from 4 hours to just 24 minutes) is unrealistic. In fact, it's very realistic. Improvements of that magnitude happen all the time in companies where setup-time reduction is a priority. Despite infinite variety in the kinds of setup activities, all share commonalities, and that enables use of a common methodology for analyzing setup procedures, simplifying them, and reducing setup time.

BENEFITS OF SIMPLIFIED SETUPS

Simplifying setup procedures and reducing setup time provide the following benefits:

1. *Quality.* As a rule, people make fewer mistakes when they follow simpler procedures. That applies to setup procedures, too. A setup mistake has potential to cause defects in every unit in a batch. Simplifying a setup procedure can thus improve product quality. With standardized setup procedures, trial-and-error adjustment and inspection are eliminated.

2. *Costs.* When changeover time is small, batches can be produced on a daily basis, which, in turn, virtually eliminates WIP and finished goods inventory investment. Simpler setups reduce the required labor hours and skill level for setups and eliminate scrap produced during the setup procedure. As a result, setup-related costs are reduced.

3. *Flexibility.* With quick setups, manufacturing has more flexibility to adjust to changing levels of demand or changing demand for different products.

4. *Worker Utilization.* Simple setups do not require special setup skills and can be done by equipment operators, which in turn reduces their idle time. This gives setup specialists more time to devote to working on technically difficult setups and on ways to improve setup procedures. For instance, there is clear benefit when a setup that used to take 90 minutes for a specialist can be done in just 10 minutes by an operator. Simpler setups are also safer.

5. *Capacity and Lead Times.* Shorter setup times increase production capacity. When current capacity is nearly filled, reducing setup time is an alternative to using overtime or making capital equipment acquisitions to increase capacity. With short setup time, make-to-order becomes possible even in a traditional make-to-stock business. Also, production lead time is reduced because of the combination of smaller lot sizes and less time spent waiting for setup.

6. *Process Variability.* Because each setup is itself a process with several discrete steps, it exhibits time variability.[1] The variability stems from looking for tools and fixtures necessary for the setups, tearing down the old configuration, inserting new fixtures, and adjusting parts so they line up properly. To the extent that procedures for all of these steps might be ill-defined, they result in large variability in the actual setup time. Variability in setup time obviously contributes to variability in available production capacity. The ultimate setup reduction is to eliminate the setup entirely, which eliminates the setup contribution to process variability.

As an example of the benefits of reduced setup time, consider the following example: a 40-hour operation produces five different parts, each with weekly demand of 240 units and a processing time of 1 minute per unit. If the setup time to changeover between parts is 4 hours, then half the workweek (20 hours) is spent on changeovers. During a 5-day week, each day must be wholly devoted to producing a different part—4 hours for setup, 4 hours for production.

Now, suppose the setup procedure is simplified and standardized, and the time is reduced to 24 minutes. It is then possible each day to produce one day's demand, 48 units, of *every* part. Total setup time each day is $5(24) = 120$ minutes, and total processing time is $5(48)(1 \text{ min/unit}) = 240$ minutes. Average inventory per part is reduced from 120 units to 24 units. Besides that, since each day's setup and production take only 6 hours ($120 + 240 = 360$ minutes), 2 hours remain in an 8-hour workday for producing other parts, problem solving, equipment maintenance, and so on. In addition, the quality of the parts is better because of the simplified, standardized setup technique; the actual extra time available will usually be close to 2 hours because of the low setup time variability.

SETUP: A CASE IN NEGLECT

Although setup reduction is important, companies didn't start doing it until recently. Harmon and Peterson offer the following reasons for the delay:[2]

1. Not until recently were full-time teams given responsibility for making improvements in machines, tools, and fixtures. Setup reduction takes dedicated effort from people who know the operation and equipment best, the setup people and

machine operators. In many plants these people have never been asked to do analysis, contribute suggestions, or take responsibility for anything beyond their rather narrow job classifications. Setup improvement requires their concerted effort and the support of a team of specialists that includes tool makers and process and manufacturing engineers.

2. Managers prefer to buy new equipment rather than to improve existing equipment. Setup-reduction projects focus on existing operations, machines, tools, and fixtures, so the primary motivation must be to improve the things you have, not to replace them.

3. Engineers with training and experience in factory automation come up with complex, setup-reduction solutions, which are rejected as too costly or impractical. In fact, most setup improvements can be achieved by relatively simple means and low cost.

4. Improvements to machines and tools often require the skills of machinists and tool makers, who are usually busy fixing broken machines or preparing tools for new products. Setup reduction requires that these people be allocated time for setup projects.

5. Reducing setup on just a few machines or processes has little impact, so individual setup-reduction projects are hard to justify. Management must take a global, plantwide view, recognizing that major benefits of setup reduction accrue only as the result of a dedicated, continuous, plantwide effort. Setup reduction cannot be achieved everywhere, all at once; it happens setup by setup, machine by machine, and it takes a while to see the benefits.

It is interesting to note that companies often go to extremes to design products so their customers can easily set up and use them, yet at the same do nothing to improve the ease of setup and operation of their own production equipment.[3]

SETUP-REDUCTION METHODOLOGY

SHINGO AND SMED

Probably the foremost authority on setup reduction is Shigeo Shingo.[4] Shingo, over many years working as a consultant to Toyota and other Japanese manufacturers, developed a methodology to analyze and reduce the changeover time for dies on huge body-molding presses. With the methodology, which he called **SMED** for *single-minute exchange of dies,* Shingo was able to achieve astonishing improvements; for example, he reduced the setup time on a 1000-ton press from 4 hours to just 3 minutes. Although developed primarily for metal-working processes in the automotive industry, SMED, it turns out, can be universally applied to changeovers and setups in all kinds of processes and industries like woodworking, metal forming, plastics and electronics, pharmaceuticals, food processing, chemicals, and even services.

In any particular application, most of the experience gained in reducing setup times at a few operations or machines can be readily transferred to setup-reduction projects on other operations and machines. Setup procedures are infinitely varied, depending on the particular type of equipment and operation involved, yet because all setup procedures consist of similar steps, they can be dealt with similarly.

The following types of steps are common to most industrial setup procedures:

· *Type 1:* Retrieving, preparing, and checking materials, tools, and so on before the setup; cleaning the machine and workstation, and checking and returning tools, materials, etc. after the operation is completed.

· *Type 2:* Removing tools, parts, etc. after completion of the last lot; mounting tools, parts, etc. prior to the next lot.

· *Type 3:* Measuring, setting, and calibrating the machine, tools, fixtures, and parts to perform the operation.

· *Type 4:* Producing a test piece after the initial setting, measuring the piece, adjusting the machine, then producing another test piece, and so on, until the operation meets production requirements.

By studying, classifying, and organizing steps such as these, it is often possible to reduce the total setup time through a combination of eliminating the unnecessary steps, improving the necessary steps, and doing some steps in parallel rather than in sequence. Shingo's SMED approach, described next, is a four-stage methodology for doing just this.

SMED METHODOLOGY FOR SETUP REDUCTION

Stage 1: Identify Internal and External Steps.   An **internal setup** is a step that must be performed while the machine or operation is stopped; internal setup time is the same as downtime. An **external setup** is a step that can be performed while the operation is running. Referring to the types of steps listed above, most Type 1 steps are external, while most Type 2, 3, and 4 steps are internal.

The primary focus in setup-time reduction is not on total setup time (internal + external) nor on setup labor time, but on internal time alone. While reducing total setup time and labor hours is desirable, it is only of secondary importance.

Learning the setup steps and classifying them requires an actual study of each setup procedure. The study is performed by detailed observation of the procedure and may involve stopwatch analysis of steps, interviews with workers, and videotaping the operation. During this analysis certain steps might be identified as obsolete or no longer practical for the current application. Such steps are classified as *unnecessary* and are eliminated from the procedure. The results of the study are recorded on a worksheet like the one shown in Figure 6.1.

In the average factory, no distinction is made between internal and external steps; everything is treated as if it must be internal. For example, although material, jigs, and tools for the next job *could* be brought to a machine while the current job is running, these things are not done until after the current job is completed and the machine is stopped. The machine then sits idly while the operator or setup person fetches the tools and fixtures to do the setup. This is illustrated in Figure 6.2 for the seven setup steps in Figure 6.1.

FIGURE 6.1

Setup worksheet.

Setup Worksheet

Operation:	Total Setup Time:		Elapsed Setup Time:
10-t press	80 minutes		65 minutes

Step Number	Step	Internal/External	Time (min)	Performed by
1	Check in at operation, go to die storage	E	5	Setup person
2	Transfer new die	E	8	Setup person
3	Remove old die	I	10	Setup person
4	Return old die to storage	E	10	Setup person
5	Get new material	E	15	Operator
6	Attach new die	I	12	Setup person
7	Adjust machine	I	20	Setup person
			42 38	

FIGURE 6.2

Setup procedure: no distinction between internal and external setup steps (times from Figure 6.1).

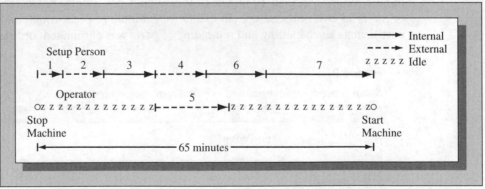

In Figure 6.2, note that every step, whether potentially classified as internal (solid lines) or external (dashed lines), is done after the machine is stopped. Notice that except for step 5, the operator is not involved and is idle during the setup procedure (Zs).

Stage 2: Convert Internal Steps to External.   The initial principal objective of setup improvement is to *reduce internal setup time.* The more setup steps, decisions, adjustments, whatever, that can be done on external time, the better. To that end, wherever possible setup steps formerly done while the operation is stopped (on internal time) are now done while the operation is running (on external time). This usually results in a dramatic reduction in internal setup time, frequently by as much as 50%.

Figure 6.3 shows the setup time for the operation in Figure 6.1 when external activities are done by the operator, some while the machine is running. (Assumed here is that the operator can leave the machine to do steps 1 and 2.) In this case two of the external steps, 4 and 5, are done while the machine is stopped, but that is because the operator would otherwise be idle, and because doing them while the machine is stopped does not affect elapsed setup time anyway. Elapsed setup time is affected only by the internal setup time, 42 seconds.

All internal setup steps should be reexamined to determine if any of them can be reclassified as external. For example, in producing metal castings, the casting mold must be raised to a certain temperature, otherwise the castings are defective. The usual way to raise the temperature is to attach the mold to the machine, then inject it with molten metal. This raises the temperature of the mold, though until the temperature gets high enough the castings produced are defective and must be melted and re-molded. Heating up the mold can be converted into an external step by using gas or electricity to preheat it before attaching it to the machine. The mold would then produce good castings immediately. One company found that by preheating the molds using heat from the oven that melts the metal saved 30 minutes of internal setup time. The only cost to the company was the expense of building a special rack to hold the molds.[5]

Stage 3: Improve All Aspects of the Setup Operation.   Converting internal steps to external steps reduces setup time considerably, although usually not enough to be in the single-minute range (less than 10 minutes). It also does not usually reduce the actual labor or material cost of the setup. (In the above example of preheating molds there *was* a cost savings since melting and remolding of parts was eliminated; ordinarily however,

FIGURE 6.3

Setup procedure: internal and external steps performed separately.

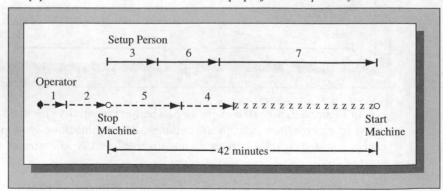

simply converting an internal activity to an external activity changes only the time to do the activity, not the cost of doing it.) As long as the average total internal and external setup time exceeds the average run time, the setup time constrains the number of lots (and the minimum size of lots). Setup-reduction efforts must thus focus on both internal and external activities, or at whichever most constrains the minimum lot size (and hence the maximum number of setups) for a particular operation.

The emphasis in the setup in Figure 6.1 should be on decreasing internal task time because that time reduces by 42 minutes per setup the daily time remaining at the operation for processing. With the operator doing the external tasks, a minimum of 13 minutes is needed for tasks 1 and 2 while the machine is running. If the machine run time is *less* than 13 minutes, then the time for tasks 1 and 2 must be reduced so as not to exceed 13 minutes.

Reducing setup time focuses on simplifying and standardizing procedures on *existing* equipment. While procuring new equipment that requires little setup is an option, it is often less costly and more effective to improve the setups on existing equipment.

Setup simplification should reduce setup time to the point where setup is no longer an issue in lot-size determination, that is, to the point where the cost associated with setup is minuscule compared to inventory carrying costs. To minimize lot sizes, setup times must be small enough such that virtually any small lot size—whatever is necessary to meet demand, smooth the production flow, or meet other requirements— is practical to produce. For that to happen, the rule-of-thumb is that a setup should take less than 10 minutes and involve no more than a single touch procedure. Shingo has dubbed the latter part of this goal **OTED** for *one-touch exchange of dies.*

The setup procedure should be simplified enough so that eventually machine operators or workcell workers can do it themselves. This deskilling of setup proce- dures takes setup out of the hands of a few skilled specialists and enables changeovers to be performed as needed, without schedules. As discussed in later chapters, this is one requirement for pull production.

Stage 4: Abolish Setup.   Beyond OTED comes the ultimate setup improvement: complete abolishment of the setup. Here are some way to eliminate setups:

1. Reduce or eliminate differences between parts. Fewer or no differences be- tween parts means fewer or no changeovers to manufacture the parts. This is a product design approach to eliminating setups. For each new product the designer raises the question, "Are we currently producing parts for other products that could be used in this product?" or "How can I design this product to minimize the number of new parts (without sacrificing product functionality and customer appeal)?" For existing prod- ucts, the designer asks, "Which existing different parts can be standardized and used on all or many products?" Answers to such questions are addressed by techniques in *group technology* and *design for manufacture,* discussed in later chapters.

2. Make multiple kinds of parts in one step; for example, form two kinds of parts from the single stroke of a press (rather than forming the two parts sequentially, with a setup between).

3. Dedicate machines to making just one item. If only one item is ever made on a machine, then the machine never needs changeover. Obviously, this approach is practical only when machines are relatively inexpensive compared to the costs of setups or when the number of different kinds of items produced is small.

It should be noted that to abolish a setup, it is not necessary to have gone through the other three steps. The alternatives for abolishing setups are very doable, and it might be possible to do them right away.

The goal of setup reduction is to maximize the transfer of setup responsibility to operators, to minimize the machine downtime, and to abolish setup; it is *not* to eliminate the jobs of setup specialists. Specialists are still needed but to do different things such as to standardize setup procedures, to modify procedures, machines, tools, and fixtures to improve setups, and to perform difficult, first-of-a-kind and one-and-only setups.

TECHNIQUES FOR SETUP REDUCTION[6]

There are many techniques for setup reduction. This section reviews common techniques with wide-ranging application. Techniques beyond these, those which apply only to a specific setup situation, are developed as the result of detailed analysis and brainstorming during each setup-reduction project. Setup-reduction projects are described later.

This section makes frequent mention of the terms machines, fixtures, and tools; they are defined and distinguished as follows:

· A **machine** is the piece of equipment that is fundamental to the operation; it is the one constant in a changeover or setup in that it is always there regardless of the kind of item to be produced. Setup involves doing something on or to the machine so that it can produce a different item. A food processor is an example of a machine. You can do many different things with the same food processor just by changing its setup. One way to change the setup on a food processor is to alter the setting (blend, chop, stir); another way is to change the fixtures.

· A **fixture** is a device attached to a machine to adapt it for a particular purpose. Fixtures include dies, nozzles, blades, drill bits, cutting heads, and extensions. An example of a fixture is the cutting blade on a food processor; if you want your food cut with a particular characteristic, you select and attach the appropriate blade.

· A **tool** is a device for adjusting fixtures and machines or for attaching fixtures to a machine. Screwdrivers and wrenches are common tools. One way to reduce the time and skill required for setup is to minimize the need for special tools. (For example, food processors are usually designed so the setup can be done without tools; just press a button to slip different blades out and in.)

The following subsections describe procedures and techniques for setup improvement according to the stages of the SMED process: separate internal and external setup activities, improve internal setup, improve external setup, and abolish setup.

SEPARATE INTERNAL AND EXTERNAL ACTIVITIES

Checklists

In many companies, prescribed standard setup procedures are followed only for the most common or most frequently done setups. For setups that are infrequent, the procedure is not prescribed and tends to vary, depending on who's doing the setup. The problem is that an operation's output depends on the setup, so different setup procedures will result in variation in the same items from one batch to another.

For every setup on every machine and at every workstation, there should be a reference checklist for operators or setup people. The checklist should give all necessary information about the setup: the setup steps and their sequence; all parts, tools, dies, and other items required; numerical values of all settings, dimensions, and measurements for the machine, tools, fixtures, and materials; and specifications for the product. One purpose of the checklist is to make explicit the logic of the setup procedure and aspects of it that need improvement. Another purpose is to ensure that no steps, parts, tools, or requirements are overlooked in the setup operation.

Every time a setup is done, a worker checks off steps on the checklist to ensure that everything is done correctly. When the number of different possible setups for a machine is not large, the procedures for all of them can be posted at the machine. Infrequently used checklists can be accessed and displayed on a nearby computer monitor. The checklist should be reviewed prior to each setup so that as soon as the machine or operation stops, the internal part of the setup procedure can be started without hesitation. Checklists are maintained by operators and others responsible for setups and are revised whenever the setup procedure is modified.

Equipment Checks and Repairs

Machines, tools, and parts must be in top working condition, otherwise they will delay the setup operation. Often the fact that equipment is malfunctioning or inadequately repaired is not discovered until the time of internal setup, in which case repairs must be hurriedly ordered or the setup must be replaced by a different one. Equipment performance should be routinely checked as part of the external setup, and these checks should be included with the steps listed in the checklist. All fixtures and tools should have assigned storage locations. Tools or fixtures that are damaged during an operation should not be returned to the storage location without first being repaired, cleaned, and checked.

Setup Schedules

Often equipment and workers sit idly because the special tools or workers needed for the setup are not available. Setup operations should be scheduled in advance so that machines, tools, parts, materials, and workers will be ready when needed. The schedule shows the time when internal setup is to begin, which enables workers to determine when to begin the external setup so it can be completed on time. Daily setup schedules are prepared by departmental supervisors and take into account current job orders received from production schedulers. They might have to be revised on short notice if additional, unanticipated jobs or changes in job priority are inserted into the production schedule. In pull production systems, where workcenters do not have daily production schedules, the supervisor or workcell team leader prepares setup schedules based on current or anticipated orders sent from downstream operations.

Later in this book the concepts of level production and mixed-model production are discussed. In those production methods, daily setups occur in a repetitive daily pattern, which greatly simplifies scheduling of setups.

IMPROVE INTERNAL SETUPS

Parallel Setup Tasks

The internal setup can sometimes be reduced by having multiple workers do setup tasks simultaneously. As Figure 6.4 shows, setup on some large machines requires adjustments at both the front and the back, and the setup person must walk back and forth around the machine. Much of this walk time is eliminated by assigning more than one worker to the setup. The trade-off between the cost of adding extra workers and the time saved must be considered; for instance, by assigning two workers to a setup, *ideally* the internal setup time should be reduced by a minimum of 50%.

A multiple-person setup is a team effort, which means that the entire team must be assembled for each setup. This is a potential source of delay if workers are scattered throughout the plant. Any setup that requires a team should thus be considered a temporary solution to be ultimately substituted by a procedure that requires only one worker.

Workers doing parallel setup steps often need to coordinate actions and signal each other about when to wait and when to go. Sometimes shouting back and forth

FIGURE 6.4

Parallel setup operations.

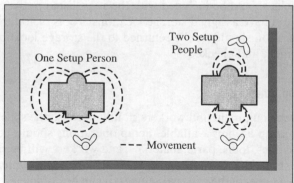

works, though in a noisy factory buzzers and lights are better. For safety, foolproof mechanisms must be installed to prevent one worker from doing a step or starting an operation that might injure other workers.

When the operator is to become the primary setup person, or even the assistant as in Figure 6.3, it is necessary to provide training. Usually setup specialists do the setup training. It is also necessary to upgrade the job description and pay system for operators to account for the additional responsibility and skill level of the job.

Attachment Devices

Much internal setup time is spent attaching and securing fixtures and materials to machines. Any attachment method that requires more than one tool, more than one person, or more than a single motion is a good target for improvement. The variety of devices used to simplify attachment is limitless, as there seems to be no end to the innovation and creativity of the setup teams that design them. This section covers but a handful of these techniques.

Bolts are a widely used method of attachment, but they are very setup-inefficient. The time required with bolt attachment increases with the number of bolts needed and their lengths. The number of bolts in a setup should be questioned since often the number used far exceeds what is necessary to secure a part. All nuts and bolts used should be the same size so only one tool is needed to tighten/loosen them. In fact, just **standardizing** the kind of fasteners used in the setup can greatly reduce the setup time because the setup person doesn't have to figure out for each fastener which tool to use, search for and pick out the tool, then repeat the process if the wrong tool was picked.

The longer the bolt, the more turns needed to tighten it. In reality, however, it is only the last turn that truly tightens the bolt and only the first turn that loosens it. Given that reality, setup time can be shortened by the use of innovative one-turn bolt attachments. Figure 6.5 shows the following types of attachment devices:

FIGURE 6.5

One-turn bolt attachment devices.

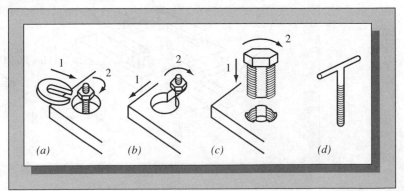

(a)   *(b)*   *(c)*   *(d)*

a. **U-shaped washers.** The fixture to be attached has a hole bigger than the bolt. The hole on the fixture is placed over the bolt, a U-shaped washer is slipped around it, and the bolt is tightened with one turn. To remove the fixture, the bolt is loosened with one turn and the washer is slipped off.

b. **Pear-shaped holes.** To attach a fixture, the wide part of the hole on the fixture is placed over the bolt, the fixture is slipped so the bolt covers the narrow end of the hole, and the bolt is tightened with one turn. To remove the fixture, the bolt is loosened with one turn, the fixture is slipped so the bolt is at the wide end of the hole, and the fixture is removed. (Wall telephones, small appliances, and smoke detectors often have pear-shaped holes in back for easy mounting.)

c. **Split-thread bolts.** This is a bolt that has grooves cut along three sides so as to divide it into three sections. The hole for the bolt also has grooves cut to correspond to ridges of threads on the bolt. By aligning the threaded parts of the bolt with the grooved parts of the hole, the bolt can be slipped all the way into the hole. The bolt is tightened with just a one-third turn.

d. **T- or L-shaped heads.** When high torque is not required, hexhead bolts can be replaced by bolts and screws with T- or L-shaped heads (and hexnuts can be replaced with wing nuts) for easy tightening by hand. The special head eliminates the need for a tool and when combined with one-turn features can reduce the tightening time to almost zero. When the setup calls for many bolts that require high-torque turns, power tools should be used.

Parts and fixtures can also be held in position by **standard-sized holders** and **pins.** Figure 6.6 shows an example. The locking pin is pulled outward, and the fixture (a die in Figure 6.6) is slipped between the holders until it reaches the stop. This step aligns the hole on the fixture with the locking pin. When the pin is released, the spring

FIGURE 6.6

Attachment with fixed holders and pins.

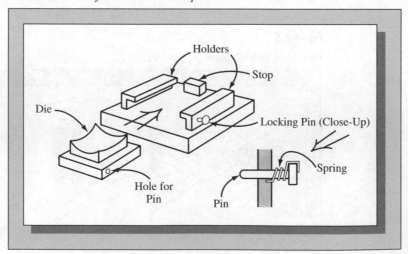

pulls it back into the hole in the fixture. (Spring locking pins are often used to hold screens and storm windows in place.)

Other simple means of attachment are one-motion devices such as **clamps.** Clamps are especially useful for securing machined parts because, unlike bolts, they don't require a hole in the thing to be attached. The clamp remains affixed to the machine while the fixture or part is inserted or removed. Two clamping devices are shown in Figure 6.7. With the first clamp, the part or fixture is secured by tightening a one-turn bolt that pressures the clamp onto the fixture. Clamps like this can be used to secure only certain, standard-sized parts or fixtures; other clamps, like the second one in Figure 6.7, are flexible and can secure parts or fixtures of different thicknesses. This clamp uses a cam. After slipping the part or fixture under the clamp, the handle is raised. This turns the cam, pushes the clamp down, and secures the part. A pin or other device locks the handle in place. The purpose of the spring is to raise the clamp when the locking pin is removed.

Most clamping devices are simple and inexpensive, though more-sophisticated (and costly) automated or hydraulic clamping systems can also be used. The best device to use is the one that provides the simplest, least expensive, and least time-consuming solution.

FIGURE 6.7

Examples of simple clamping devices.

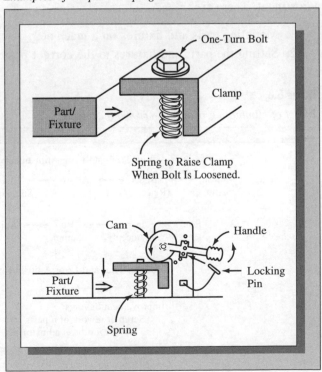

Eliminate Adjustments

Most setups include a period of adjustment. Following the installation and initial setting of the fixture or part is a lengthy trial-and-error process that includes production of sample parts, measurement of the parts, and readjustment. This process occurs no matter how skilled the setup person is. The run-measure-adjust cycle, repeated until every setting is correct, is often the most time-consuming portion of the internal setup procedure. Until all the settings are right, the sample parts are defective and must be scrapped or reworked. Figure 6.8 illustrates how eliminating the trial-and-error adjustment cycle improves the setup procedure.

Machines, fixtures, and tools often have variable-setting meters, scales, and gauges that are inaccurate or are illegible because of grime and grease. The trial-and-error cycle can be reduced by just keeping measurement and setting mechanisms clean and calibrated. When only a few different kinds of parts are made, the setting for the different parts can be marked or inscribed on the meters and gauges. For machines and fixtures used to make just one part, the setting mechanisms should be semipermanently fixed at the right setting so they cannot shift from vibration, heat, or pressure, or be accidentally moved.

When an adjustment is necessary, the goal should be to achieve it through no more than a single motion. Often internal setup time can be reduced as much as 50% simply by improving adjustments.

The best method for reducing the time for adjustment depends on the kind of adjustment. There are three:[7]

1. Mounting parts and fixtures on a machine.
2. Setting the parts and fixtures to the correct position.

FIGURE 6.8

Effect of eliminating trial-and-error adjustment.

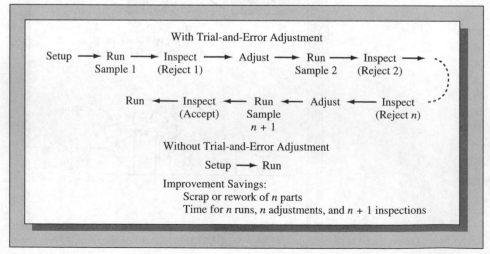

3. Setting the right combination of speed, pressure, feed rates, temperature, and so on, so a part meets specification.

Mounting parts and fixtures on machines can be simplified by using standardized fasteners, clamps, and holders. Using **shims** and **inserts** greatly simplifies the mounting of varisized tools and fixtures into fixed-position holders and clamps (see Figure 6.9). To hold smaller fixtures and dies, special **cassette-type holders** should be designed and fabricated. The cassette holder serves the same function as the holder used to play 8mm videotapes on standard VCR machines. The fixture/die goes into the holder, and the holder slips into a fixed-position clamp or other attachment. No adjustment required. Variable or sliding shims can be used to mount varisized pieces. For example, duplicating machines with multiple-page feeders have sliding ledges to hold the sides of paper, like shims, that are adjustable to the paper size. Any shims, inserts, or cassettes necessary for the setup should be specified in the setup checklist.

Quick-change procedures have been developed for securing dies to machine presses. A **die** is a fixture like a mold for shaping metal (or other malleable material). Most dies have two parts, called male and female. On a typical machine press, one die is mounted on a stationary surface called the **bed,** while the other die is mounted on a movable surface called the **ram.** When a sheet of metal is placed between the ram and the bed, the ram is lowered and the dies are pressed together, forming and/or cutting the metal to the desired shape.

Figure 6.10 shows a way to secure dies of different heights with a standard clamp on a fixed-bed press. The usual way to deal with variable-height dies is to raise-lower the machine bed or adjust the stroke of the ram press so the male and female dies match up at the right height when shut. Raising and lowering the bed and the stroke is time-consuming, and often several sample pieces have to be produced before the height setting is correct.

FIGURE 6.9

Use of shims and cassette-type holders with fixed-position holders on machine.

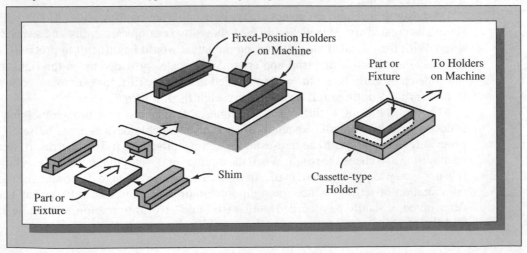

FIGURE 6.10

Accommodating variable-height dies without making adjustments.

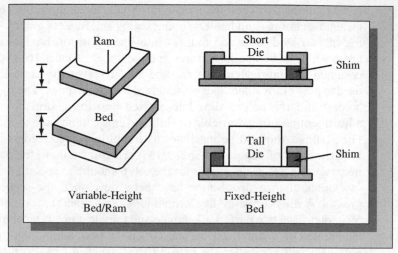

A better way is to keep the bed or ram stroke fixed and to accompany each die with right-sized shims so the dies and shims combined give the correct shut height without any adjustment.

Machines and fixtures typically have adjustable mechanisms (cranks, handles, levers, switches) that must be turned or positioned to a specific setting; sometimes the setting mechanisms are damaged or broken off. For just one setup, it might be necessary to perform repeated adjustments on numerous such mechanisms. This can be very time-consuming. It is therefore important that once the correct settings have been determined for all the mechanisms, those settings are recorded and included in the setup checklist.

Adjustable mechanisms do not always have calibrated setting scales. If not, scales should be created and affixed. Figure 6.11 shows two examples, a crank and a variable lever. With the unscaled mechanisms on the left it would be difficult to precisely set the machine without using trial and error. With scales provided as on the right, the machine can readily be set to values specified in the checklist, for example, "set lever to 6.7; turn crank three full turns and five-eighths of a turn."

Getting the right settings for a machine or fixture the first time something is produced can be difficult, especially if several adjustable devices must be set. The procedure is to start with the best-estimate settings, then use trial and error to tweak each setting and check the result. When the number of devices that must be set is large, it is necessary to perform systematic, designed experimentation to determine the right combination of settings. Once the right combination of values for settings has been determined, it should be recorded so that trial-and-error information will not be lost and the experimentation process will not need to be repeated.

FIGURE **6.11**

Examples of methods for showing settings on adjustment devices.

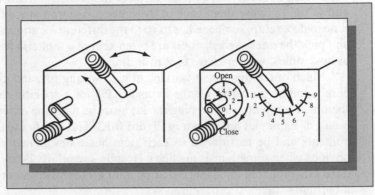

IMPROVE EXTERNAL SETUPS

Storage

Everything needed for a setup (fixtures, dies, tools, raw materials, and documentation) should be stored as close as possible to where the setup is done. This can save a great deal of external setup time. The more dedicated the items stored are, the more setup time can be reduced. Of course, dedicating equipment to one use precludes it from other uses, which reduces flexibility of operations elsewhere. Thus, dedicating equipment often means procuring more equipment, and that can be expensive. As a result, decisions about dedicating equipment must weight the benefit of reduced setup time at one operation against the cost of purchasing additional equipment or of reducing flexibility at other operations. Items used frequently at one machine or cell should, ideally, be kept *at* the machine or cell; items used less frequently can be shared, but should be located centrally to all the places where they are used.

Everything about the storage location should be reviewed in terms of effect on setup time. For example, so that heavy tools and fixtures do not have to be moved up or down, the racks on which they are stored should be the same height as the carts used to transport them. (And the height of the carts, in turn, should be about the same as the location on the machine where the tool or fixture must be attached.) It is better yet to dedicate one cart to each fixture so fixtures do not have to be moved to or from a storage rack.

When the number of different fixtures and tools is large, cost and space limitations might dictate that they be stored together. Storage should be arranged so everything can be found and moved easily. Tools and fixtures can be painted different colors or marked with large labels. Storage places on the floor, shelves on a rack, drawers, hangers, and so on can be painted in colors or labeled to correspond to the items stored in them. That way items are easy to find and hard to misplace.

Setup Kits and Carts

Most setup operations require an array of items such as fixtures, tools, clamps, bolts, and so on. In many shops each of these items is stored at a different place. When it's time to do a setup, someone has to go to the different locations, sort through the items, and pick the ones needed. Tools are often kept in a tool crib and must be checked out; at busy times, workers have to wait in line.

Much of the time spent walking to get, waiting for, and picking out items can be eliminated by gathering all the items needed for a specific setup procedure, putting them in a setup kit, and keeping the kit near the machine or workstation where it will be used. Examples are shown in Figure 6.12. The kit should also include a list of its contents and be partitioned so each item has a designated place (and so it will be obvious when something is missing). Hospitals regularly do this, using surgical procedure kits prepared in advance that contain all the instruments necessary to perform a particular medical procedure.

When tools cannot be dedicated to a kit, or when kits cannot be kept at machines, then the setup tools or kits can be put on carts, and the carts can be partitioned with shelves and dividers so items can be quickly found. There should be a designated place for everything on the cart, and everything should be in its place. This is important not only to speed the setup, but to keep track of tools and to hold workers accountable for the tools.

Material Handling

Equipment used for *transporting* tools and fixtures for setup should be dedicated to that purpose (again, taking into account the matter of flexibility of use and of the cost of procuring additional handling equipment). Hand or motorized carts, pallets, bins,

FIGURE 6.12

Examples of setup tool/fixture carts.

and overhead cranes employed in setups should not be used for other purposes like transporting WIP, raw materials, or machinery. Fixed-place machines should be arranged with enough space around them so as to avoid impeding the movement of material handling equipment.

Equipment should be customized to facilitate setup. Three cases are shown in Figure 6.13. For example, carts that have rollers on top and are the right height make it is easy for items to be rolled off the cart and onto the machine, and vice versa. In Figure 6.13, left, a fixture is being moved from a cart onto a machine. Presumably, the fixture from the previous job was moved onto another cart. If a large-enough cart were used, then only one cart would be needed: the previous fixture could be slid onto the cart next to the new fixture, then the new fixture could be slid onto the machine.

Figure 6.13, center, shows a manual or motorized cart with forklifts to handle fixtures for machines that are of different heights. The cart shows two sets of forks, one set holds the new fixture while the old fixture is being slid onto the second set. The forklift is raised or lowered using manual, hydraulic, or electrical force.

When fixtures are heavy and must be transported with a forklift or overhead hoist, holding tables with rollers adjacent to the machine (Figure 6.13, right) enable workers to slide one fixture off the machine and another onto it without a forklift or hoist. The scheduled use of the forklift or hoist to transport the fixture to/from the machine does not have to coincide exactly with the scheduled time of setup; as long as the forklift or hoist can deliver the next fixture to the holding table *anytime* prior to the scheduled setup, no time is wasted waiting for them.

As much as possible, need for forklift trucks and special hoists to move fixtures in setups should be eliminated. They take up space, must be scheduled in advance, and cannot be dedicated to setup operations.

FIGURE 6.13

Examples of material-handling equipment.

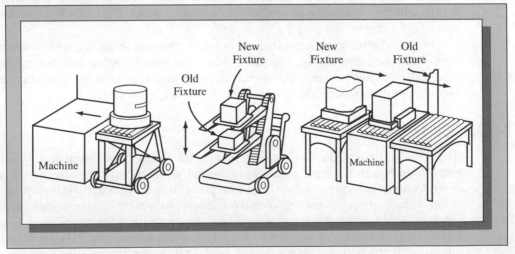

ABOLISH THE SETUP

One way to eliminate setup is to use the same, standardized parts and components for different products. The smaller and fewer the differences between things to be produced, the smaller the changeover between them. Through the cooperation of people in marketing, product design, and production, parts proliferation can be stopped, and the amount and difficulty of setup required to produce different parts can be reduced. Parts should be differentiated only to the extent that they add to product performance, functionality, or appeal as required by customers. (These quality-of-design matters are discussed in Chapter 12.)

Application of group technology and production by part families (discussed in Chapter 9) can also reduce setup times. William Sandras gives an example at NCR where the production of 22 different shafts was sequenced in a cell such that the first shaft required a complete setup, but the subsequent 21 required setups only one-third or less the time of the first one. Essentially, only one full setup was necessary; the other 21 were adjustments.[8]

Another way to eliminate setups is to produce multiple kinds of things during each operation. For example, every automobile has right- and left-side doors and fenders. Instead of producing each side separately with a changeover between, produce both right and left sides at once. Dies for both left- and right-side door panels are installed in the press and with a single stroke both parts are produced. Similarly, both the hood and the trunk can be formed at once. In general, simultaneous production of n different items by a single machine reduces the number of setups on the machine to $1/n$ the number if they were produced individually.

Simultaneous production and, consequentially, fewer setups can also be achieved by using multiple, dedicated machines. Instead of using a single, expensive machine that can produce many kinds of parts, several less-expensive machines are used, each dedicated to a single part (e.g., a machine that makes *just* right-door panels or *just* left-door panels). When machines are devoted to one part (or similar kinds of parts), changeover between parts is eliminated or is reduced to trivial steps. Group technology coding can help determine which parts to assign to which machines to eliminate or reduce setup times.

Projects for reducing setup time, discussed in the next section, can themselves be time-consuming and costly. Especially when the existing setup procedure cannot practically be reduced, but where further improvement is needed, the only alternative might be to procure additional equipment and abolish the setup.

SETUP-REDUCTION PROJECTS[9]

The goal of setup-reduction projects is to reduce individual setup times so that small-lot production is feasible. Beyond this goal, setup-reduction projects are a good place to begin carrying out JIT. Like workplace organization and cleanup projects, setup reduction requires participation from shop-floor workers. Setup-reduction projects are highly visible to shop-floor workers, and early setup successes help to gain buy-in from workers and supervisors necessary to implement other JIT ideas such as small-batch production, pull production, and total productive maintenance.

SCOPE OF PROJECT

Each setup-reduction project must be undertaken in the context of a larger, ongoing setup-reduction program. This is because a few, standalone setup improvements will have little effect on overall operating performance. In general, reducing setup times at an operation increases the operation's throughput. However, unless the operation is a bottleneck that has caused downstream operations to be starved for work, increasing the operation's throughput might only serve to speed up the growth of WIP waiting at downstream operations.

The eventual focus of setup reduction should be plantwide. Although initial setup projects should be limited to operations and products having the greatest need—bottlenecks and operations with the largest waiting WIP—eventually setup projects must be directed at other machines, operations, products, and, ultimately, to other processes and areas of the plant.

Setup reduction has the most immediate impact at a bottleneck operation because at that point setup delimits production capacity. As setup times are reduced, more time is available for production. Eventually if the setup reduction is great enough, small-batch production becomes possible, even at operations that were formerly bottlenecks.

The alternative to reducing setup times at bottlenecks is to increase capacity either by duplicating the operation, outsourcing production, or using overtime. However, if the portion of existing capacity dedicated to setup time is large, then it is usually more effective to reduce the setup times rather than to increase the capacity. In general, a principle for selecting setup projects is to initially focus on operations that spend the greatest proportion of time doing setups, then strive at these operations to achieve the maximum-possible reduction in setup time.[10]

A setup project focuses on a given machine or operation and the setup for a particular part/product at that machine. Every piece of equipment and operation must be handled individually. Because of even small variations in seemingly identical equipment, products, or operations, every setup procedure is different. Even if exactly the same model machine is used in many places, the setup at each must be studied separately.

To be considered as a candidate for setup reduction, there must be some need to improve the setup of the machine for a product. Need is identified analytically from computer models or empirically from shop-floor information by using as criteria the product/machine combinations that have the highest utilization rates, longest setup times, highest amounts of WIP, largest batch sizes, and largest product diversity.

Candidate projects should focus on machines and products that have a future, that is, products/machines that will continue to be important and will not soon be changed or eliminated. The best setup-reduction projects help to improve manufacturing flexibility. For all the different items produced at an operation, a good project will result in an improved setup between any ordered pair of the items. For example, if a machine can produce three items, X, Y, and Z, the setup improvement should affect the six possible setup combinations (X to Y, Y to X, X to Z, and so on). Improved setup between just one possible pair and not the others does little to improve flexibility.

A final, important criterion for selecting early setup projects is high-success potential. Successful projects generate interest, enthusiasm, and motivation to continue; more-difficult and risky projects should be saved until later after learning and confidence levels have increased. This holds true for virtually all projects to implement aspects of JIT and TQM.

The above considerations result in a list of candidate projects for setup improvement. The list is based on information from setup people, operators, supervisors, production planners, schedulers, and engineers. To decide which projects have priority and should be started first, the list should be given to shop-floor supervisors.

SETUP-REDUCTION TEAM

Once the machine/product combination has been decided, the project team is selected. The team must include people who know the most about the machine and the problems of setup, who will be affected by changes, and who have ideas for improvements; usually, these are the setup people and machine operators. Their participation in developing new procedures is important because they must be motivated to follow them. Also, setup people and operators tend to propose good ideas that are simpler and less costly to implement than ideas from engineers and other staff personnel. At some point, when the average batch size gets small enough, operators will spend more time doing setups than operating machines; eventually, as machines become automated, they will spend most of their time doing setups and solving problems.

The team should also include others, for example, tool and die makers, or industrial and manufacturing engineers, depending on the analytical and technical expertise required for the project. The team is informed about the goals and focus of the setup project and is trained in setup-reduction methodology, methods analysis, and setup-reduction techniques. Workers with prior experience in setup reduction should help do the training.

GET READY, GET SET, SHOOT!

The team documents features of the current setup operation by using technical reports and blueprints for the product/part, the machine, and tools and fixtures. They then prepare a plan for the major information-gathering event of the project, videotaping the setup. The purpose of videotaping the setup is to get a detailed picture of the current setup procedure. To that end, the videotaping should be scheduled for normal production hours and within the normal production schedule.

In case the operators and setup people are not members of the setup-reduction team, they should be informed in advance about the purpose of the videotaping so they are aware that they personally are not being evaluated. The videotaped procedure must be identical to the usual modus operandi, and the people in the setup must do everything they normally do. The entire setup operation—from the time the last part of the last batch is produced until the time the first good part of the next batch is produced—should be taped, even if the elapsed time takes hours; throughout, the time display on the video camera should be turned on. While one person operates the camera, another takes notes. Neither interrupts the operator or setup person with repeated questions.

ANALYSIS OF VIDEOTAPE

The videotape is closely reviewed, and the individual or elemental (micro) steps and their elapsed times are identified. The duration of the elemental steps might range from just a few seconds to several minutes. It is important to identify microsteps in detail because the smaller the steps, the easier it is to define their purpose and decide how to simplify, eliminate, or transfer them to external time.

The elemental steps are clustered into setup categories. For example, the initial 20 or so steps might all be clustered as "removing old fixture," the next 30 steps, "obtaining and preparing new fixture," the next 50 steps, "attaching new fixture and materials," and so on. Steps are clustered because it is easier for workers, supervisors, and managers to discuss six or so procedural categories than, say, 430 elemental steps. The sum of the elapsed times of elemental steps in each category is the total time for that category; the sum of the category times is the total setup time.

GENERATING AND SELECTING IDEAS

Throughout the videotape analysis as well as in subsequent meetings and informal discussions, the team develops ideas about how steps can be eliminated, simplified, or transferred to external time and from setup person to operator. The ideas are shared with (and advice sought from) operators, setup people, engineers, production planners, supervisors, and vendors of the machines, fixtures, and parts/materials involved. The impact of these ideas and suggestions on reducing times for elemental steps and categories is estimated. Not every idea can be adopted, so a biggest-bang-for-the-buck approach is used. Ideas that have the greatest ratio of *internal* setup time savings to cost of implementation are considered first, then those with less savings per cost are considered next. The same is done for savings in total setup time. This concept of marginal improvement in setup time versus cost of improvement is shown in Figure 6.14. As illustrated, initial improvements usually result in big time savings at relatively low cost, while additional improvements are smaller and come at higher cost.

Pareto analysis can be used to separate the steps that take the most time and, within each step, the microsteps that take the most time. The most time-consuming microsteps of the most time-consuming steps are the first targets of elimination or time reduction.

The proposed new procedure and its impact are discussed with people who have relevant expertise, will be affected by, or have valid opinions about the solutions. The team then presents the new procedure and the cost/benefit analysis to management. After getting approval and suggestions from management, the new setup procedures are implemented. A follow-up study is performed to assess the impact of the new procedures on setup times and to determine whether further modifications are needed.

FIGURE 6.14

Setup-time improvement versus implementation cost.

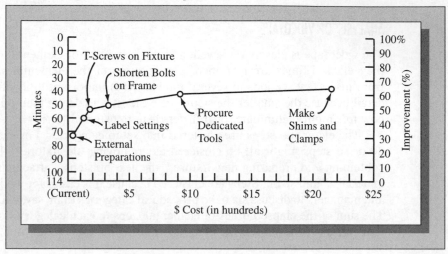

There are hundreds of published examples of the results of setup-reduction projects. A few follow as cases in point.[11]

CASE IN POINT: Setup-Time Reduction at Plastic Design Inc.

At Plastic Design, Inc., a 110-ton injection molding press took 135 minutes to changeover. A team videotaped the setup procedure, then made several improvements. First, they externalized setup tasks and created two carts; one cart holds all the tools with silhouette locations, setup procedures, and quality criteria needed for setup, and the other cart holds hoses and fittings for changeover. Within 3 days the team reduced the setup time to 16 minutes. Aside from the team members' time, the setup-reduction project cost virtually nothing.

CASE IN POINT: Setup-Time Reduction at CSSI

At Connecticut Spring and Stamping, Inc. (CSSI), 200- and 300-ton metal stamping presses were producing lot sizes of 200 to 50,000 pieces, which is 4–8 weeks of customer demand. A team analyzed the setup of the presses, then implemented standardized die-positioning techniques such as quick-clamps, locator pins, and shut-height blocks. They also externalized many tasks, put a parts storage area next to the presses, and developed an Indy 500 pit crew concept for team setup. Within only a few days, the team had cut changeover time by 50%.

In another area of the CSSI plant, a team investigated changeovers on three medium coiler machines for eight high-volume parts. The team created a standard work setup procedure and posted it in the work area. The procedure cut changeover steps from 108 to 28 and reduced changeover time from 3 hours to 15 minutes. The reduced time now allows all eight parts to be run daily and has cut inventory enough so that parts can be stored at point-of-use in the work area.

Intermediate parts storage and movement from the warehouse have been eliminated.

In the foot-press area of the CSSI plant, average setup time on six presses used to be 40 minutes. After videotaping and timing the old procedure, the team eliminated many adjustment steps on the presses by using standardized bases with stop positions and quick clamping. The new setup time is 6.8 minutes.

CONTINUOUS IMPROVEMENT

Setup times should be tracked, charted, and posted as evidence that management considers performance in setup important. This tracking and charting also prevents backsliding and motivates workers to find additional, simple, low-cost ways to continue to improve the setup. However, repeated data collection for charting is time-consuming, and tracking and charting should not be held a stick over workers' heads to make sure they follow procedures. The setup-reduction project should not just result in a cost-effective procedure to reduce setup time, but in a procedure that workers will readily follow without supervision.

For each setup project, an initial goal should be set to reduce setup time by 50%. Usually the resulting time will still exceed an hour, so the next goal should be to reduce it to, say, 30 minutes, then, later, to less than 10 minutes. Less than 10 minutes might seem extreme, but short setup time is essential for flexibility, particularly in processes that use pull and mixed-model production. To achieve the series of goals of ever-smaller setup times requires a succession of setup-reduction projects. Given that the average factory has many machines, it is obvious that a setup-reduction campaign must be continuous. According to Harmon and Peterson, that is just the way it should be: [Since]

> setup reduction is one of the most important foundations of superior manufacturing, . . . every company should have an aggressive program [devoted to] developing simple, low-cost solutions and to training management and technical personnel in the techniques of one-touch changeover.[12]

Summary

Simplified setup and reduced setup time permit reduced lot-size production and result in increased production capacity, flexibility, and resource utilization, as well as improved product quality and customer satisfaction. Although setup procedures vary widely with type of equipment and equipment application, the methodology to improve setups developed by Shingo, called SMED, can be applied to virtually any setup procedure. The principle objective of improvement is to reduce the internal setup time, that is, the setup time during which the machine or operation must be stopped. SMED has four stages:

1. Analyze steps in the setup procedure to distinguish which are internal and which are external.
2. Convert as many internal steps as possible to external steps.
3. Improve all steps to the extent that virtually any lot size is practical to produce.
4. Seek ways to eliminate the setup.

Setup improvement begins with identifying, standardizing, and listing setup procedures on a check sheet. Internal setup time is reduced by using rapid-attachment devices as well as standard fixtures and tools to eliminate trial-and-error adjustment. External time is reduced by keeping tools, fixtures, and parts near the place of setup or putting them on convenient, movable carts. Everything needed for setup should be organized and stored so as to minimize time and effort in selecting and transporting them to the place of setup.

Setup reduction is implemented setup by setup, starting with operations and setups showing the greatest need, which are usually instances where setup time constrains production capacity and flexibility. The setup-reduction project is conducted by a small team of operators and setup people, assisted by engineers, tool makers, and other specialists. The team systematically analyzes the existing procedure, develops ideas for improvement, then uses cost/benefit analysis to cull ideas that enable the largest marginal time reduction for given cost.

Although the primary goal of setup reduction is to increase flexibility and make small-lot production practical, the process of reducing setups is itself a useful way to start increasing shop-floor workers' participation in problem solving and decision making, which is necessary for other aspects of JIT such as pull production, pokayoke, and product/process quality monitoring. To the extent that it involves factory workers participating jointly with staff experts to improve conditions and remove waste on the shop floor, setup reduction is similar to another element typical of JIT, equipment maintenance, the subject of the next chapter.

Questions

1. Describe ways that companies have traditionally dealt with equipment setup. What are the advantages of each? From a JIT perspective, what are the drawbacks of each?
2. Discuss the cost, quality, time, and flexibility ramifications of reducing setup times.
3. What is the difference between internal and external setup procedures? Give examples of both.

4. Suppose that in the setup procedure shown in Figure 6.1 step 5 takes 25 minutes and step 6 takes 15 minutes. How long *should* the setup procedure take?

5. List and discuss the steps in Shingo's SMED methodology.

6. How does the external setup time constrain the minimum process lot size?

7. What is the purpose of a setup checklist? How is it used? How is it created?

8. Give industry and household examples from your experience of devices that simplify installation and attachment and that eliminate trial-and-error adjustment. Give examples from your experience of situations where trial-and-error adjustment could be eliminated by simple means.

9. On what operations should the first setup-reduction efforts focus?

10. Who should participate in the setup-reduction team?

Problems

1. As part of a JIT effort, a manufacturer has reduced the setup cost for machining a component from $200 to $12.50. As a result, the new economic lot size is 10 units.
   a. The former economic lot size had been much larger. What was it? (Hint: look at EOQ in Chapter 5.)
   b. If the goal is to reduce the economic lot size to 1 unit, what must the setup cost be reduced to?

2. A setup reduction team has been working on a punch-press machine that currently takes 75 minutes for internal setup. Each part requires 1.5 minutes on the machine. The machine is not a bottleneck, and the motivation for reducing setup time is to reduce the unit cost of the part and to have the machine operator perform the setup. The labor rate for the operator is $12.50 per hour. What must the setup time be reduced to for the lot size to be 10 units and the average labor cost per unit to be $0.75?

3. In the above problem, the setup team has set the target production lot size to 5 units. The production rate on the machine is 40 units/hour, the demand for the part is 10 units/hour, and the carrying cost of the part is $ 4.25 per unit per year. Assume annual demand is 8000 units. What must the setup time be reduced to for this part? (Hint: Look at EMQ in Chapter 5.)

4. The official setup time for a machine is 40 minutes. Suppose a workday is 420 minutes, the machine must process 200 parts a day, and the processing time is 0.5 min/unit.
   a. What is the minimum batch size?
   b. Suppose the operation is run for 1 day using the batch size from (a) above, and at the end of the workday only 133 units have been produced. Assuming the processing time per unit was 0.5 minutes, and there were no stoppages except for setup, how much time was used for setup? What was the average time per setup? Explain how the actual setup time might be so much longer than the official setup time.

5. Changeover of fixtures on a machine takes 35 minutes. Following the changeover, an average of four parts must be produced and discarded before the correct setting is

achieved. For each part the processing time is 2 minutes and the material cost is $1.50. The labor cost for a skilled setup person to do the changeover and adjustment is $15.50 per hour. The labor cost of the machine operator is $10.50 per hour. Currently, the part is produced in batches of 50 units. Suppose the setup procedure could be simplified so that the operator would be able to do it and not have to make any adjustment in the setting. What must the fixture changeover time be reduced to so that a batch size of 20 units could be produced for the same average per-unit cost as the present cost? Assume the per-unit cost includes labor and material costs of setup and production; also, assume the machine's excess capacity is ample and is not a consideration.

6. Don Knotts, the new assistant manager of manufacturing, has sent a proposal for a setup-reduction project on the DMK-020 press to his boss, Wilie Fox. The DMK press is not currently a bottleneck, but it is used on a large number of products and typically is run at near-capacity levels. Fox says, "Before you start anything like this, I want to see some cost figures." Knotts estimates that the setup time could be reduced 50% by analyzing procedures, separating internal and external procedures, and simplifying internal procedures so the operator can do them himself. With the reduced setup time, the press would be able to produce in batches of 75 units (average size) instead of the current 450 units. The combination of reduced setup time and the operator performing the setup would reduce the labor cost of each setup by about $40. He also estimates it will take a team of three workers, a machinist, the operator, and himself, about a day for the project. Knotts gives his cost analysis to Wilie, whose response is, "You propose to spend a day on a project that will save only $40! Compared to the cost of your team, the $40 savings is insignificant. Besides, the person who does the setup now will still be on the payroll, so you're not going to save anything, really." If you were Knotts, what would your response to Wilie be?

Endnotes

1. S. Melnyk and T.T. Christensen, "Understanding the Nature of Setups," *APICS–The Performance Advantage,* March 1997, pp. 77–8.

2. R. Harmon and L. Peterson, *Reinventing the Factory* (New York: The Free Press, 1990), pp. 181–2.

3. R. Hall, *Zero Inventories* (Homewood, IL: Dow-Jones Irwin, 1983), p. 109.

4. S. Shingo, *A Revolution in Manufacturing: The SMED System* (Cambridge, MA: Productivity Press, 1985) (translated by A. Dillon).

5. A. Robinson, *Modern Approaches to Manufacturing Improvement* (Cambridge, MA: Productivity Press, 1990), pp. 320–1.

6. For more setup-reduction techniques and examples *see* S. Shingo, *A Revolution in Manufacturing: The SMED System;* R. Harmon and L. Peterson, *Reinventing the Factory,* pp. 186–200; and R. Hall, *Zero Inventories,* pp. 84–111.

7. H. Steudel and P. Desruelle, *Manufacturing in the Nineties* (New York: Van Nostrand and Reinhold, 1992), pp. 200–2.

8. W. Sandras, *Just-in-Time: Making It Happen* (Essex Junction, VT: Oliver Wight Publications, 1989), p. 116.

9. Portions of this section are adopted from H. Steudel and P. Desruelle, *Manufacturing in the Nineties,* pp. 179–191.

10. These conclusions are based on propositions developed by C.K. Hahn, D.J. Bragg, and D. Shin, "Impact of Setup Variable on Capacity and Inventory Decisions," *Academy of Management Review* 35, no. 9 (September 1989), 91–103.

11. From G. Galsworth and L. Tonkin, "Invasion of the Kaizen Blitzers," *Target* 11, no. 2 (March/April 1995), pp. 30–36.

12. R. Harmon and L. Peterson, *Reinventing the Factory,* p. 202.

MAINTAINING AND IMPROVING EQUIPMENT

A US steelmaker and a Japanese steelmaker were negotiating to start a joint venture. The Japanese firm sent a delegation of executives to tour the US plant. One executive in the delegation had a small hammer, and as the group walked through the plant, he would sometimes gently tap bolts on the machines they passed. This slightly unnerved the US managers conducting the tour. They had no idea what he was doing, but of course they dared not ask and reveal their ignorance. Throughout the tour the question nagged them, Why is he *doing* that?

This chapter is about the executive's concern and the reason for the hammer: it is about equipment **maintenance.** Like small batch sizes and short setups, equipment maintenance is a key element of JIT and is fundamental to competitive manufacturing. The first section of this chapter explains reasons why and gives a preview of total productive maintenance (TPM), which is the philosophy that makes equipment part of a company's competitive capability. The later sections describe concepts and measures associated with equipment effectiveness, the role of preventive maintenance and TPM in increasing equipment effectiveness, and issues associated with implementing TPM.

EQUIPMENT MAINTENANCE

Throughout most of the last 4 decades manufacturing was seen by many US managers as a low-status, low-glamour function; somewhere below it was maintenance—the no-status, no-glamour function. Maintenance departments in most US companies were understaffed and underfunded. Maintenance was viewed as an overhead cash pit, and certainly never as a way to increase profits or competitiveness. Its role was largely one thing: breakdown repair.

BREAKDOWN REPAIR

Breakdown repair is the practice of caring for equipment when and only when it breaks (if it ain't broke, don't fix it).

If you only tend to equipment when it breaks, and if you have a great deal of equipment, then you will always be tending to breakdowns. Breakdown repair is playing catch-up; you're constantly trying to find where the breakdown occurred, nedying the breakdown, then shuffling to make up for lost production time. In mpanies where the breakdown rate is high, the maintenance staff works overtime try to keep pace, though being understaffed, they cannot. Repairs are done hastily, ometimes poorly. Vital production time is lost as equipment and workers sit idle.

Breakdown repair (also referred to as repair maintenance) is the worst kind of maintenance. Like inspecting for product defects, it focuses on problems after they've occurred, not on diagnosing the problems to keep them from happening again. Equipment breakdown and malfunction directly contribute to wastes such as waiting, inventory, and product defects. In a competitive environment, manufacturers need to move beyond breakdown repair.

EQUIPMENT PROBLEMS AND COMPETITIVENESS

Equipment problems have a direct effect on production cost, quality, and schedules (see Figure 7.1). With each breakdown, one or more operations are idled, and scheduled completion times are delayed. If a machine needs a new part, it will be idled for as long as it takes to get the part, which could be days or weeks. Meanwhile, production must be transferred to other machines or covered by overtime, which disrupts schedules at other operations and increases costs. The machine might malfunction for a while before it finally breaks and produce defective parts in the meantime, which, if detected, would have to be scrapped or reworked.

One way to enable the rest of the process to continue if one machine breaks down is to carry inventories of whatever that machine produces. Subsequent operations can continue working for as long as the inventory lasts. To speed up repairs, inventories of spare parts are carried too. But the more chronic the machine's problems, the more inventory needed to cover for them. Further, while the machine is broken down, materials accumulate as WIP, which results in still more inventory.

It is evident that by reducing equipment problems, a company can also reduce the inventories, schedule disruptions, defects, and the costs associated with these

FIGURE 7.1

Consequences of equipment problems.

Machine Problems	Possible Immediate Effects	Ultimate Cost/ Consequences
Malfunction	Machine deterioration	Shortened machine life
	Machine inefficiency	High repair cost
	Output variability	Scrap and rework
Breakdown	Safety hazards	Injuries
	Idled workers	Inventories
	Idled facilities	High production cost
		Schedule delays

problems. At the same time, it can improve safety and reduce injuries from equipment malfunction.

PREVENTIVE MAINTENANCE

Preventive maintenance (PM) is the practice of tending to equipment so it will not break down and will operate according to requirements. It entails understanding and maintaining all the physical elements of manufacturing—machine components, equipment, and systems—so they consistently perform at the levels required of them.

Although reliable, well-functioning equipment is a good thing in general, it is a *prerequisite* for JIT and TQM. A hallmark of JIT production is ability to function with little inventory, and a JIT process simply does not have enough WIP inventory to buffer against chronic equipment problems. Equipment that performs erratically or breaks down will soon bring the entire process to a halt.

A hallmark of TQM is its ability to hit product or service targets, which means no significant deviation from them. In manufacturing that happens only when equipment is reliable and well-functioning. Regardless of what else a manufacturer is doing to improve product quality, few things will have as much impact as improved equipment functioning. For many companies PM is but a stepping stone to another, higher level of equipment maintenance, TPM.

TOTAL PRODUCTIVE MAINTENANCE[1]

Preventing equipment breakdowns is good, but even better is squeezing the ultimate potential from equipment. That is the purpose of **total productive maintenance (TPM).** The ultimate potential of a piece of equipment depends on its unique function and operating environment, and, in particular, on how well the equipment meets requirements such as availability, efficiency, and quality. Briefly, *availability* means that equipment is in operational (working) condition when it is needed; *efficiency* means that it performs at its standard or rated speed; and *quality* means that it produces no nonconformities or defects. TPM moves beyond preventing breakdowns and includes equipment restoration and redesign. A goal of TPM is to upgrade equipment so it performs better and requires less maintenance than when it was new.

Equipment responsibility in TPM is spread throughout many departments such as production, engineering, and maintenance, and to a range of people, especially equipment operators and shop workers. In TPM, operators perform basic equipment repairs and PM; meanwhile, teams of maintenance staff, engineers, machinists, and operators redesign and reconfigure equipment to make it more reliable, easier to maintain, and better performing. TPM is another never-ending facet of continuous improvement in manufacturing.

Benefits of TPM

TPM aims for greater manufacturing competitiveness through improved equipment effectiveness. By tailoring equipment to better suit a particular production environment, and by making it better-than-new, TPM increases production capacity and process reliability and reduces the costs of lost production time, defects, repairs, shortened equipment life, and inventory. Since it involves everyone in the process, TPM also contributes to improvements in safety, morale, and pollution. The following TPM results were reported by Seeiich Nakajima:[2]

- Productivity: Breakdowns were reduced by 98% (from 1000 to 20 times/month).
- Quality: The defect rate was reduced by 65% (from 0.23% to 0.08%).
- Cost: Labor cost was reduced by 30%; maintenance cost was reduced by 15%–30%; energy consumption was reduced by 30%.
- Delivery: Inventory turnover increased by 200% (from 3 to 6 times per month).
- Morale: Improvement ideas increased by 127% (from 36.8 to 83.6 ideas/person per year).
- Safety: There were no accidents.
- Environment: No pollution was created.

Managers are often unaware of the improvement potential of better maintenance because they do not know the costs of equipment-related problems. Records of the causes and frequency of breakdowns, amount of downtime, kinds and costs of repairs, and product defects from equipment are inaccurate or nonexistent. TPM starts by assessing the state of equipment effectiveness and its impact on production.

EQUIPMENT EFFECTIVENESS

Equipment effectiveness (EE) refers to the multitude of ways equipment influences productivity, costs, and quality. The term can be used in reference to individual pieces of equipment, or, when aggregated, to all equipment in a plant or company. High-average equipment-effectiveness indicates a plant or company has minimized or eliminated wastes that stem from equipment-related problems.

EQUIPMENT LOSSES

Think for a moment about the equipment-related sources of waste discussed before—inventory, waiting, defects, and so on. Besides these are wastes associated with machine operation, idling, and repairs. Nakajima[3] has categorized these equipment wastes into what he terms the **six big losses:**

1. Downtime from equipment setup and adjustments.
2. Downtime from sporadic or chronic equipment breakdowns.

These two losses affect the **availability** of a piece of equipment to perform work. The more time equipment is stopped for setups or repairs, the less time remaining for it to do work.

3. Idling and minor stoppages (equipment is running, but parts flowing to it periodically jam or parts flowing from it are momentarily blocked because the next machine is broken down).

4. Reduced speed of operation (equipment is running, but at a reduced speed because it is worn out or needs adjustment).

These two losses in combination affect equipment **efficiency.** Equipment that is periodically interrupted by shortages, or that produces at a rate less than its standard capability takes longer than necessary to do the work.

5. Defects caused by variability in equipment performance.

Equipment that is worn-out or near breakdown causes defects and increases process variability. The result is reduced **quality** from nonconforming output that must be reworked or scrapped.

6. Reduced yield caused by nonoptimal operation.

Every time a machine is stopped because of setups, breakdowns, or minor interruptions and then restarted, it takes a while for the machine to reach its normal operating conditions (speed, temperature, etc.). Until then, it produces more slowly or causes a greater proportion of defective output.

The following sections discuss criteria for measuring the impact of these losses on manufacturing productivity.

MAINTAINABILITY

Maintainability is the effort and cost of performing maintenance. It is affected by, for example, the ease of access to equipment for maintenance, the skill level required to do the maintenance, and the availability and convenience of getting spare parts and service. One measure of maintainability is **mean time to repair** (MTTR); high MTTR is an indication of low maintainability. MTTR is the average time a machine is down:

$$MTTR = \frac{\Sigma(\text{Downtime for Repair})}{\text{Number of Repairs}},$$

where downtime for repair includes time waiting for repairs, time spent doing repairs, and time spent testing and getting equipment ready to resume operation.

In some organizations, repair time is used as the downtime for repair, however they are not the same, as indicated in Figure 7.2.

RELIABILITY

Reliability is the probability that equipment will perform properly under normal operating circumstances. One measure for reliability (R) is the probability of successful performance, or

$$R = \frac{Number\ of\ Successes}{Number\ of\ Repetitions},$$

FIGURE 7.2

Repair-related downtime verses repair time.

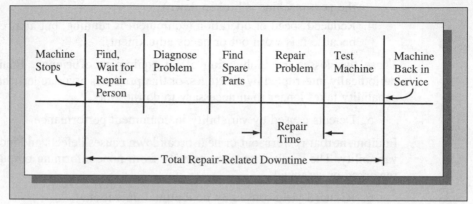

Source: Adopted from J. Moubray, *Reliability-centered Maintenance* (New York: Industrial Press, 1992), p. 64.

where number of repetitions is the number of times the equipment does something. For example, if a machine produces 1000 parts of which 960 are good, then the machine is 96% reliable. Similarly, if a machine used to test circuit boards for defects works 99% of the time (it misses 1% of all defective boards), then the machine is 99% reliable.

The opposite of successes is defects or failures. Failure here simply means that equipment performance is not satisfactory. It can mean that equipment is malfunctioning in some aspect or is completely broken down.

Failure Pattern

The more reliable equipment is, the less likely it will fail. The likelihood of equipment failure is shown with the **failure pattern.** The appearance of the failure pattern depends on the piece of equipment as well as its usage and environment. Figure 7.3 shows three common failure patterns.[4]

In pattern A, the failure potential (probability of future failure given that so far failure has not occurred) is a function of age. The older the item, the more likely it will fail. The failure potential in pattern B has the so-called bathtub shape. Items having this pattern go through an early burn-in period in which failure potential (infant mortality) is relatively high. This pattern is common for electronic components. Manufacturers of such components operate or run them for a while before shipping, or provide customers with a 90-day warranty to account for infant mortality. Items that survive burn-in then have a failure pattern similar to pattern A.

Some things continue to function well regardless of age. This is represented by the constant, uniform failure potential in pattern C. Although eventually all things fail, with this pattern the point of increasing failure potential is unknown. For an item having this pattern, there is often insufficient statistical information because managers

Figure 7.3

Three common failure patterns.

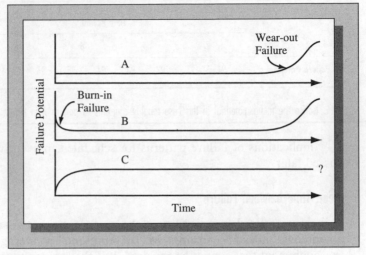

get nervous and replace the item before it ever fails. Even if theoretically the item has failure pattern A, insufficient information about the far right-hand part of the curve results in pattern C.

The following example illustrates how the failure potential curve is interpreted and developed from empirical data.

Example   1:   Failure Potential Curve

Suppose we start with 110 components and observe the time periods within which they fail. We observe the following:

						Time Period						
	0	**1**	**2**	**3**	**4**	**5**	**6**	**7**	**8**	**9**	**10**	**11**	**12**
No. Failures	0	1	1	1	1	1	1	1	2	15	46	30	10
No. Survivors	110	109	108	107	106	105	104	103	101	86	40	10	0

Now, the failure potential is a **conditional probability.** It specifies for an item *that has survived* up until a given time period, the probability that it will then fail during that time period. It is computed as the number of items that fail in a period, divided by the number of items that started the period. For example, using the above numbers and looking only at period 11, the number of observed failures is 30 and the number of items started is 40, so the failure potential in period 11 is 75%.

Performing the same computation for all periods and rounding to one decimal, gives

	Time Period											
	1	*2*	*3*	*4*	*5*	*6*	*7*	*8*	*9*	*10*	*11*	*12*
% Failure Potential	.91	.92	.93	.93	.94	.95	.96	1.94	14.9	53.5	75.0	100

Notice the failure potential in this case roughly conforms to pattern A in Figure 7.3.

Implications of failure patterns for scheduled, preventive maintenance are discussed later.

Mean Time between Failure

A measure related to reliability is the **mean time between failure** (MTBF). For equipment that can be repaired, MTBF represents the average time between failures. For equipment that cannot be repaired, it is the average time to the first failure. The greater the MTBF for a piece of equipment, the greater its reliability. If we assume a constant failure rate, such as pattern C, then

$$MTBF = \frac{Total\ Running\ Time}{Number\ of\ Failures}.$$

The MTBF can be used to estimate the reliability of an item. In this case, the reliability $R(T)$ is defined as the probability that the item will not fail before time T:

$$R(T) = e^{-\lambda T},$$

where

$0 \le R(T) \le 1.0$,
e = natural logarithm base (about 2.718),
T = specified time,
λ = failure rate = 1/MTBF.

The following examples illustrate this concept.

Example   2:   MTBF

Twenty machines are operated for 100 hours. One machine fails in 60 hours and another fails in 70 hours. What is the MTBF?

Eighteen of the machines ran for 100 hours, while two others ran for 60 hours and 70 hours each. Thus, the total running time is $18(100) + 60 + 70 = 1930$, and

$$MTBF = \frac{1930}{2} = 965 \text{ hours/failure.}$$

Example   3:   Reliability for a Given Time of Operation

What is the reliability of the same machines from Example 2 at 500 hours? At 900 hours?

$$\lambda = 1/965 = .0010362 \text{ failure/hour.}$$

$$R(500) = e^{-.0010362(500)} = 0.596.$$

$$R(900) = e^{-.0010362(900)} = 0.394.$$

Thus, there is nearly a 60% probability that the machine will run 500 hours (without failure), and a nearly 40% probability that it will run for 900 hours.

Suppose the machine's performance is entirely dependent on one particular component. Each time the component is replaced, the machine's reliability returns to 100%. How often should the component be replaced so the machine's reliability is never less than 90%?

$$R(T) = e^{-\lambda T}$$

$$0.90 = e^{-.0010362(T)}.$$

Transposing the formula, $T = -1000 \ln(0.90)$, so $T = 109.2$. The component should be replaced every 109.2 hours.

Results from this kind of analysis are not necessarily intuitive. For example, if we wanted to increase the reliability to 95%, the computation gives 51.3, which indicates we must replace the component every 51.3 hours, despite the fact that among the 20 machines tested, none failed in less than 60 hours, and 18 were still running at 100 hours.

AVAILABILITY

Availability is the proportion of time equipment is *actually* available to perform work out of the time it *should* be available.

Availability and Downtime for Repair

One measure of availability (A) is

$$A = \frac{MTBF}{MTBF + MTTR}.$$

As this formula suggests, availability is increased through a combination of increasing MTBF, decreasing downtime for repair, MTTR, or both. This is illustrated in Figure 7.4. Strategies for lengthening MTBF and shortening MTTR are addressed later.

Availability and All Downtime

The above measure rightfully shows that by improving MTBF and MTTR, availability is improved too; however, as a formula for determining availability it is misleading

FIGURE 7.4

Impact of increasing MTBF and of decreasing MTTR on availability.

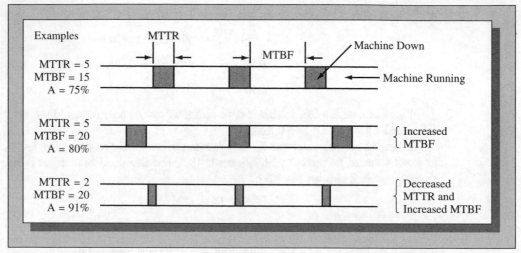

because, while it considers repair-related sources of downtime (MTTR), it ignores *nonrepair sources* of downtime. As such, it overstates the actual equipment availability. A more accurate measure of availabilty, because it includes *repair and nonrepair* sources of downtime, is the following:

$$A = \frac{Actual\ Running\ Time}{Planned\ Running\ Time},$$

where

planned running time = (total plant time − planned downtime),
actual running time = (planned running time − all other downtime).

In the above definitions, planned downtime includes all planned nonworking time: meals, rest breaks, meetings, and scheduled PM. No workers or equipment are considered idled by planned downtime. All other downtime refers to all the other times when the machine is down (internal setup, equipment breakdown (MTTR), etc.) and during which workers and equipment are considered idled.

Suppose a plant runs two-shift (16-hour) workdays, and during each shift there are 2 hours of planned downtime. The **planned running time** is thus

$$16 - 2(2) = 12\ \text{hours.}$$

To determine the **actual running time,** subtract from this the time the machine is down due to setups (die changes, adjustments), equipment failures, and so on. If the machine is stopped each day an average of 110 minutes for setups and 75 minutes for breakdowns and repairs, then the actual running time is

$$12(60) - (110 + 75) = 535\ \text{minutes.}$$

The **availability** of the equipment is thus

$$A = \frac{Actual\ Running\ Time}{Planned\ Running\ Time} = \frac{535}{12(60)} = 0.7431.$$

This measure of availability might be preferable to the other because it gives incentive to reduce *both* MTTR and internal setup time. Though setup time might be independent of MTTR, the two are often interrelated to the extent that poorly maintained equipment is harder to change over and adjust.

Repair Downtime Variability

The above measures of availability are average measures. They indicate nothing about the impact of unscheduled downtime on process variability, which, for making equipment decisions, is an important matter. Suppose, for example, you have two machines, one with MTBF of 100 hours and MTTR of 10 hours, the other with MTBF of 10 hours and MTTR of 1 hour. Though both have availability of approximately 0.91, they should not be considered equivalent. Assuming breakdowns occur randomly, the first machine requires a minimum of 10 hours of WIP buffer stock to protect the process from shutdown, whereas the second requires a minimum of only 1 hour of WIP. Considering only the cost of buffer stock, the second machine is preferable. In general, all else equal, machines with more frequent but less severe breakdowns are better in terms of process stability and inventory cost than machines with less frequent, more severe breakdowns (logic somewhat similar to preferring smaller batches and short setups over larger batches and long setups).

Accurate assessment of availability and variability calls for high data integrity of equipment records. Equipment records must show *all* time that equipment is down for internal setups and failures. In many companies records are inaccurate because they show only major breakdowns; breakdowns lasting only 10 or 20 minutes are not recorded, even when they occur frequently during the day. A chart should be kept at each machine for the operator to record every instance of machine downtime.

Data for the next two equipment measures, efficiency and quality, must be collected by a team of skilled observers (engineers or trained shop people). To ensure that the data accurately measure machine performance, they should be collected over a period of many days or instances of machine operation.

EFFICIENCY

Efficiency is a measure of how well a machine performs while it is running. It requires answering two questions: (1) the machine is running, but is it producing *output* (i.e., what is the rate efficiency)? and (2) the machine is producing output, but is it producing output at the right *speed* (i.e., what is the speed efficiency)?

Rate Efficiency

Suppose parts that move down a chute feeding into a machine periodically jam. Every time parts jam, the flow of parts into the machine (which is running) is disrupted (see

Figure 7.5

Minor disruption from parts jamming.

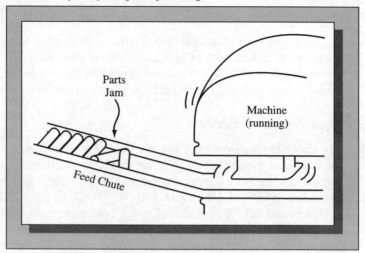

Figure 7.5). The machine operator has to dislodge the parts to resume flow. In the course of a day these disruptions add up and reduce machine output considerably. They contribute to reduced yield loss, the last of Nakajima's six losses mentioned previously. Suppose this is the same machine as in the previous example, which (from above) runs 535 minutes a day. Also suppose the average daily throughput of the machine is observed to be 830 units, and the actual cycle time is observed to be 0.6 min/part. In theory, it should take $830 \times 0.6 = 498$ minutes per day to produce the parts. However, since the machine is running for 535 minutes a day, its **rate efficiency,** RE, is

$$RE = \frac{Actual\ Production\ Volume \times Actual\ Cycle\ Time}{Actual\ Running\ Time}$$

$$= \frac{830 \times 0.6}{535} = \frac{498}{535} = 0.9308.$$

Thus, the machine is processing parts only 93.08% of the time it is running. Parts jamming in the chute plus other interruptions are consuming 6.92% of the machine's running time.

Speed Efficiency

Suppose the machine is *designed* to produce two parts per minute, the equivalent to a 0.5 min/part cycle time. Since, in actuality, the machine's cycle time was observed to be 0.6 min/part, then the **speed efficiency,** SE, of the machine is

$$SE = \frac{Design\ Cycle\ Time}{Actual\ Cycle\ Time} = \frac{0.5}{0.6} = 0.8333.$$

The machine is running at 83.33% of its rated speed.

RE and SE are independent measures of efficiency. Multiplied they give the overall **performance efficiency,** PE, of the machine:[5]

$$PE = RE \times SE.$$

For the example,

$$PE = 0.9308 \times 0.8333 = 0.7756.$$

Sometimes it is difficult or impossible to compute SE because the design cycle time is unknown or because the machine makes different parts with different cycle times. In that case SE is ignored and PE is computed solely as a function of lost time from interruptions (i.e., machine is running but not doing work):[6]

$$PE = \frac{Actual\ Running\ Time\ -\ Time\ for\ Interruptions}{Actual\ Running\ Time}.$$

QUALITY RATE

The **quality rate,** Q, is an index of the equipment's ability to produce output that is nondefective or conforms to requirements:

$$Q = \frac{Actual\ Production\ Volume\ -\ Defect\ Output}{Actual\ Production\ Volume}.$$

Suppose the machine in the example produces an average of 30 defective units out of 830 units/day. The quality rate is

$$Q = \frac{800}{830} = 0.9639.$$

OVERALL EQUIPMENT EFFECTIVENESS

A measure of equipment effectiveness that incorporates availability, performance efficiency, and quality rate is the **overall equipment effectiveness,** OEE:

$$OEE = A \times PE \times Q.$$

For the example,

$$OEE = 0.7431 \times 0.7756 \times 0.9639 = 0.5555.$$

OEE can dramatically affect plant productivity and choices for improving productivity. In the example, the machine produced 830 units in two shifts. Were demand to double to 1660 units it would be necessary to add a second (theoretically identical) machine to meet demand. An alternative, however, would be to improve the OEE of the current machine 50% to 0.8333.

Improving the OEE not only increases production throughput, it also reduces variability in product quality and schedules, and, as a result, need for inventory, overtime, rework, and other costly ways of dealing with output variability. This is why JIT and TQM manufacturing plants strive for high OEE *plantwide,* that is, high effectiveness of *all* equipment.

In many traditional plants the only equipment treated as if effectiveness matters are bottleneck machines. They get regular preventive maintenance because any breakdown would have immediate and severe impact on plant throughput. However, when preventive maintenance is focused *exclusively* on a few high-use, bottleneck machines, all other machines are neglected. Eventually, these other machines fall into a state of disrepair, causing innumerable bottlenecks by virtue of their low availability, efficiency, or rate of quality. High-use equipment should receive maintenance priority, but *all* equipment should receive preventive maintenance and be able to meet minimal standards of availability, efficiency, and quality. With small WIP inventories, every piece of equipment is a bottleneck waiting to happen.

PREVENTIVE MAINTENANCE PROGRAM

The aim of preventive maintenance (PM) is to improve equipment performance. This is done through a number of steps and practices that address and rectify the major causes of equipment problems.

CAUSES OF EQUIPMENT PROBLEMS

Chronic equipment problems often stem from more than one cause. Kiyoshi Suzaki[7] gives the following five causes that act individually or in some combination to cause equipment problems:

1. *Deterioration.* The fact is, parts wear out. Moving parts like gears, bearings, and belts wear down or break, and electrical components burn out. Most kinds of operational equipment eventually deteriorate, but neglect or abuse hastens their deterioration.

2. *Equipment ill-suited for the purpose.* The equipment is utilized for purposes other than those for which it was designed. The material, size, or operation of the equipment cannot handle the expected load, which causes accelerated deterioration, breakage, and product defects.

3. *Failure to maintain equipment requirements.* The equipment is dirty, lubricant is not replenished, dust and grime foul the mechanism, and so on.

4. *Failure to maintain correct operating conditions.* The equipment is operated at speeds, temperatures, pressures, etc., in excess of recommended design levels.

5. *Lack of skills of operators, maintenance crew, and setup people.* Operators don't know standard equipment operating procedures and cannot detect or don't care about emerging equipment problems; maintenance people replace parts but don't question why breakdowns occur; setup people use the wrong tools, fixtures, or adjustment settings; operators, maintenance staff, setup people, and engineers seldom talk to each other about equipment problems, causes, and solutions.

To address these problems, PM programs emphasize the need to:

· Maintain normal operating requirements.
· Maintain equipment requirements.
· Keep equipment and facilities clean and organized.
· Monitor equipment daily.
· Schedule preventive maintenance.
· Manage maintenance information.
· Use predictive maintenance.

MAINTAIN NORMAL OPERATING CONDITIONS

All machines have design limitations. Often, purchased machines come with operating manuals that list recommended, normal, and maximum operating conditions. Companies often operate equipment at the maximum condition; though theoretically the equipment is designed to handle that condition, continual operation at that level forces accelerated deterioration. Preventive maintenance starts with knowing the *normal* operating conditions (speed, pressures, temperatures etc.) and not running equipment in excess of those conditions. Normal operating requirements should be posted at every machine, and operators should run equipment and monitor conditions to make sure these requirements are not exceeded. Derating the equipment (running it at below normal operating conditions) further reduces deterioration and extends the equipment's useful life. The life of a bearing, for example, is inversely proportional to rotational speed, so reducing the speed by one-half can double the life of the bearing.

MAINTAIN EQUIPMENT REQUIREMENTS

Equipment has physical needs. These needs are, like operating conditions, sometimes listed in manuals which accompany the equipment; sometimes, however, they must be determined by operational experience.

An example of an equipment requirement is lubricant. Most equipment with moving parts requires oil, grease, silicone, and so on, which must be checked and periodically replenished or replaced.[8] In one General Motors plant, 70% of the operators felt that the main reason for machine downtime was inadequate lubrication.[9]

Another equipment requirement is tight bolts and fasteners. Bolts and fasteners that become loose during machine operation induce greater vibration, which introduces defects in products and hastens equipment deterioration. One Japanese factory estimated that it reduced equipment breakdowns by 80% just by frequently retightening tens of thousands of bolts on its equipment.[10] Some managers would say that loose bolts on equipment is a sure sign of poor PM.

Another equipment requirement is the use of proper tools and fixtures in machine setup. Machines malfunction when they are incorrectly adjusted or configured during setup. Reviewing setup procedures, training operators and setup people in proper setup techniques, and using setup checklists are ways to reduce machine problems from setup mistakes.

KEEP EQUIPMENT AND FACILITIES CLEAN AND ORGANIZED

Cleanliness and organization are essential to preventive maintenance. Noise, oil leaks, wobbling fixtures, cracks, discolorations, and other sources of problems that might otherwise be concealed by dirt, show up readily on a clean machine. Calibrations and settings on clean machines are readily visible, making it easier to see when they need resetting.

Dirt and disorganization are themselves major causes of equipment problems. Grime gets into working parts and causes scratches and friction, which slows down or jams machinery. Clutter in the shop leads to confusion, difficulty in locating repair parts and tools, and mistakes in setting up, operating, and repairing machines. Clutter impedes efficient response to breakdowns and increases MTTR.

Responsibility for keeping machines and workplaces clean and organized is assigned to machine operators, and this assignment is an early step in increasing employee involvement in managing the shop floor. Involvement is essential if operators are to be trusted to operate the equipment properly, maintain basic equipment requirements, and monitor equipment for problems. It is also important for developing employee attitudes regarding the importance of paying attention to details and caring about the workplace, which correlate with their attitudes about product quality and the impact of their work on quality. Of course, management must recognize that cleaning takes some time and allow for it. Workers with tight production quotas ordinarily will not take the time to do anything that detracts from meeting their quotas.

MONITOR EQUIPMENT DAILY

Periodic cleaning of equipment is not enough. Equipment must be monitored daily or, ideally, in real time so that early signs of problems are promptly detected and fixed. Operational monitoring for subtle signs of problems, such as increased heating, vibration, jamming, defects, and so on, provides advance warning of emerging problems (see Figure 7.6). Often, quick detection of an emergent problem allows a simple solution like tightening a bolt, adding oil, or inserting a new part, whereas, without detection, the problem could grow into an expensive, catastrophic failure.[11]

The most practical way to monitor and maintain equipment in real time is to have the operators do it. Giving operators responsibility for basic machine upkeep helps ensure that problems will be detected early, minor problems will be fixed quickly, and major problems will be avoided. Giving them this responsibility also helps justify why they must keep machines clean and organized. Again, management must set aside some time each day so workers are able to exercise this responsibility.

SCHEDULE PREVENTIVE MAINTENANCE

Even machines that are properly operated and maintained need periodic attention from the experts. Instead of waiting until machines break down, PM programs allow for periodic, scheduled downtime during which experts can inspect, replace parts in,

FIGURE 7.6

Signs of emerging equipment problems.

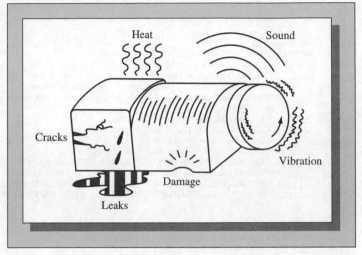

and overhaul equipment. As a rule, the trade-off is that relatively little scheduled downtime for PM affords big benefit in terms of fewer random, unscheduled machine breakdowns. With scheduled PM, everything is stopped at the same time, and production schedules are not disrupted. Overtime and missed deliveries from breakdowns are averted.

Ways of Scheduling PM

Scheduled time for PM can be based on the following:

• *Clock or calendar time intervals.* Some examples follow: Run a two-shift operation, then devote the third shift to PM; run a three-shift operation, using 30 minutes at the start and finish of each shift for PM; perform PM tasks monthly, quarterly, and annually (Figure 7.7 shows an example).

• *Cycles of usage.* For example, schedule PM for every 1000 hours of machine operation, every 5000 units produced, or every 50 setups.

• *Periodic inspection.* Schedule PM whenever a periodic inspection indicates impending or possible malfunction or failure.

Typical scheduled PM includes opening up equipment for thorough cleaning and replacing major internal components such as motors, bearings, valves, seals, and belts. All of this is performed by skilled maintenance workers, and is *in addition* to the daily and weekly cleaning and inspection activities performed by operators.

With scheduled PM there must be ample time kept open every day and week for maintenance. Never, or only rarely, should production work be scheduled to consume an entire 8-hour shift and three full shifts.

Monthly, quarterly, and annual PM tasks.

Description:
MONTHLY MACHINE PREVENTIVE MAINTENANCE
_____1. Complete all weekly checks.
_____2. Check all flexible lines and cables. Repair or replace any that are cracked or damaged.
_____3. Remove and clean the air intake filter to the hydraulic power supply.
_____4. Make a visual inspection of the hydraulic oil; either excessive darkening or milkiness indicates a need to
                replace the oil.
_____5. Check edge locators parallel to X and Z axis.
_____6. Check sliding covers and curtains. Replace if necessary.
_____7. Tighten contacts at all terminals.
_____8. Clean relay contacts with contact cleaning spray.
_____9. REMOVE Z AXIS COVER AND CLEAN CHIPS FROM CAVITY.
_____10. REMOVE B AXIS COVER AND INSPECT GEARS FOR SMOOTH OPERATION.
_____11. INSTALL BOTH COVERS AND SILICONE THE LEADING EDGE OF THE Z AXIS COVER.
_____12. INSPECT TOOL CHANGER ARM FOR ANY WEAR AND FREENESS.

Description:
QUARTERLY MACHINE PREVENTIVE MAINTENANCE
_____1. Complete all monthly checks.
_____2. Check hydraulic supply relief valve pressure setting - 48.2 bar 700 psi.
_____3. Check hydraulic pump pressure setting 41.4 bar (600 psi).
_____4. Check all axes reference positions.
                X Axis_____   Y Axis_____
                Z Axis_____   B Axis_____
_____5. Check operation of tool changer. Confirm all switch adjustments and tool changer travel motions
                and speeds.
_____6. Check axis and spindle drive electronic adjustments.
_____7. Check axis lost motion and correct as needed.
_____8. Take oil samples for analysis.
_____9. Replace oil filter element.
_____10. Run DCS fingerprint.
_____11. CLEAN CONDENSOR AND EVAPORATOR.

Description:
ANNUAL MACHINE PREVENTIVE MAINTENANCE
_____1. Complete all semi-annual checks.
_____2. Check the axes drive belts for looseness or wear. Adjust or replace if necessary.
_____3. Replace wipers of guideway bearings.
_____4. Replace tool magazine drum rollers if worn.
_____5. Check spindle bearings for temperature. (Run spindle at 1200 rpm until temperature of spindle
                nose casting stabilizes. Temperature should be 110 deg F. to 160 deg F. maximum.)
_____6. Check the machine geometry. Correct as necessary. Refer to Section 9.0 of manual for instructions.

Source: Courtesy, ITT McDonnell & Miller Corporation.

Scheduled PM and Failure Pattern

Preventive maintenance often involves replacing components that are functioning perfectly. This is because the component is believed to be approaching the end of its estimated **useful life,** the point at which the probability of the component failing greatly increases. The estimated useful life on the three failure patterns discussed earlier is shown in Figure 7.8.

FIGURE 7.8

Useful lives in common failure patterns.

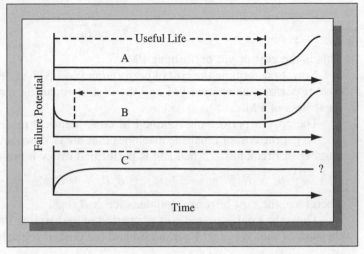

Components with patterns A and B in Figure 7.8 have a somewhat obvious useful life, which is used in PM to determine when they should be replaced or refurbished. For example, components on the airframes and engines of aircraft are replaced at a specified number of operational hours, which is their estimated useful life. Though still functioning, replacing them at that time is obviously safer than waiting until they fail. In many cities, crews replace street lights block by block, street by street because (assuming the lights were all installed at the same time) all are near the end of their normal lives. Replacing them then, all at once, is less costly than replacing them individually as they burn out. The same rationale applies to PM of all kinds of equipment in all kinds of facilities.

To extend the useful life of equipment approaching the wear-out zone, equipment can be run at lower-than-normal speed (derating), or exposed to less-than-normal workload or stress level.

One way of deciding when to perform PM, including replacement or renovation of components, is to analyze the trade-off of costs between letting equipment break down and performing PM on equipment. Assume the cost of PM on a machine is c_P, and the cost of repairing a broken down machine is c_B. To get the expected cost of letting machines break down, first determine the expected time between breakdowns, $E(n)$, or

$$E(n) = \sum nP_n,$$

where

n = time period when a breakdown may occur,

P_n = probability of a breakdown in time period n,

$\quad = \dfrac{b_n}{\sum b_n} = \dfrac{\textit{Number of Machine Breakdowns in Period n}}{\textit{Total Number of Breakdowns in All Periods}}.$

The expected number of breakdowns is then $1/E(n)$, so the expected cost of letting N identical machines break down, C_B, is

$$C_B = \frac{N c_B}{E(n)}.$$

This is the cost of *not* performing PM.

Now, to determine the cost of *performing* PM involves determining two costs: the cost of performing routine PM and the cost of repairing machines that break down regardless of PM.

The cost of performing routine PM on N identical machines is $N(c_P)$.

To get the cost of repairing machines that break down anyway, let B_n = expected number of breakdowns when PM is performed every n periods:

$$B_n = N(P_1 + \cdots + P_n) + B_1 P_{n-1} + B_2 P_{n-2} + \cdots + B_{n-1} P_1.$$

Therefore, the cost of repair maintenance is $B_n(c_B)$.

Thus, the total expected cost per period of performing PM every n periods, C_n, is the sum of the cost of PM per period and the cost of repair maintenance per period, or

$$C_n = \frac{N c_P}{n} + \frac{B_n c_B}{n}.$$

When $C_n < C_B$, then PM every n periods is less costly than letting equipment break down. Following is an illustration.

Example   4:   Determining Maintenance Costs and Schedules

Suppose a group of 25 identical machines is monitored for 5 months, and without PM the number of breakdowns in each month is as follows:

Months of Operation before Breakdown, n	1	2	3	4	5
No. of Breakdowns, b	3	4	3	5	10
Therefore, P_n	0.12	0.16	0.12	0.2	0.4

This indicates that the longest time a machine runs before breaking down is 5 months, and that, for example, 4 machines ran 2 months before they broke down.

The cost of repairing a machine after breakdown is $500 ($c_B$), whereas the cost of PM on a machine is $100 ($c_P$). Preventive maintenance does not eliminate breakdowns.

1   What is the monthly cost of breakdowns?

2.   If PM used, how often should it be done?

Solutions:

1. With no PM, the expected time between breakdowns is

$$E(n) = \sum nP_n = 1(.12) + 2(.16) + 3(.12) + 4(.2) + 5(.4) = 3.6 \text{ months.}$$

Thus, the monthly expected cost of not performing PM is

$$C_B = \frac{NC_B}{E(n)} = \frac{25 \text{ machines } (\$500 \text{ per machine})}{3.6} = \$3472.22.$$

2. The expected number of breakdowns with PM performed every n months, B_n, is $N(P_1 + \cdots + P_n) + B_1 P_{n-1} + B_2 P_{n-2} + \cdots + B_{n-1} P_1$:

$$B_1 = N(P_1) = 25(.12) = 3,$$
$$B_2 = N(P_1 + P_2) + B_1(P_1) = 25(.28) + 3(.12) = 7.36,$$
$$B_3 = N(P_1 + P_2 + P_3) + B_1(P_2) + B_2(P_2)$$
$$= 25(.4) + 3(.16) + 7.36(.12) = 11.36,$$
$$B_4 = N(P_1 + P_2 + P_3 + P_4) + B_1(P_3) + B_2(P_2) + B_3(P_1)$$
$$= 25(.6) + 3(.12) + 7.36(.16) + 11.36(.12) = 17.9,$$
$$B_5 = N(P_1 + P_2 + P_3 + P_4 + P_5) + B_1(P_4) + B_2(P_3) + B_3(P_2) + B_4(P_1)$$
$$= 25(1.00) + 3(.2) + 7.36(.12) + 11.36(.16) + 17.9(.12) = 30.45.$$

The remainder of the analysis is summarized below:

Months between PM Service, n	Expected Breakdowns in n Months, B_n	Expected Breakdown Cost $= \$500(B_n)$	Expected Breakdown Cost/Month $= \$500(B_n/n)$	Expected PM Cost/Month $= \dfrac{25(\$100)}{n}$	Expected Total Cost, C_n (Breakdown + PM)
1	3	1500	1500	2500	4000
2	7.36	3680	1840	1250	3090
3	11.36	5680	1893	833	2726
4	17.9	8950	2238	625	2863
5	30.45	15225	3045	500	3545

Except for PM every month or every 5 months, ($n = 1$ or 5), the expected cost of PM service per month is always less than the expected cost of not performing PM ($\$3472$). Using the least costly schedule of PM every 3 months instead of no PM, the expected savings is $\$3472 - \$2726 = \$746$ per month.

For several reasons, it is not always so easy, or even desirable, to schedule replacement or renovation of equipment using the concepts of useful life or expected breakdowns as illustrated above. First, periodic scheduled replacement of components can actually *increase* the risk of failure in complex machines or processes. Every replacement of a component that has a bathtub failure pattern (pattern B) at first reintroduces to the machine or process an increased risk of failure stemming from the infant-mortality risk of the component.[12] Other than that, however, component replacement in machines and processes comprising numerous components results in pattern C for the overall system since it has a combination of new and old parts with a range of expected useful lives.

Finally, the useful life of an item is commonly estimated by statistical analysis of failure of the item and the resultant failure pattern. But for most components and equipment the failure pattern is *unknown* and will always be unknown! To derive the failure pattern, a component must be allowed to fail many times (alternatively, many units of the component must be allowed to fail once). But as John Moubray points out, the reason companies do PM is because they cannot *allow* components to fail, ever. This poses a contradiction, he says, in that "successful preventive maintenance entails preventing the collection of data which we think we need in order to decide what preventive maintenance we ought to be doing."[13]

On the other hand, there is usually a great deal of information about equipment failures that have only minor consequence, because these failures are allowed to happen. The result is that the less important a piece of equipment (in terms of its breaking down), the easier it is to determine its useful life; the more important the piece of equipment, the harder.

Because of these difficulties, replacement or overhaul in PM is often predicated on periodic equipment *inspections* to reveal impending or possible failure or malfunction. This practice of relying on inspection and close monitoring of equipment to determine when and what kind of PM tasks to perform is referred to as *condition-based* or predictive maintenance, and is discussed later.

Scheduled PM cannot prevent every breakdown or malfunction, and there will always be the need to perform unscheduled repair maintenance. Need for repairs is identified by workers or automated equipment sensors that monitor equipment performance using standards or control charts, or that detect signs of problems such as oil leaks and cracks. While some repairs can be delayed until the next scheduled maintenance period, often they must be performed immediately. Regardless of the amount of effort devoted to scheduled PM tasks, there must always be adequate expert support staff to meet on-demand (unscheduled) requests for breakdown repairs.

MANAGE MAINTENANCE INFORMATION

Preventive maintenance requires keeping good records about the performance and breakdown history of equipment and the costs of operations and repairs. In many companies no one keeps track of frequency of repairs, kinds of repairs requested, sources of problems, or costs. In a big company that has much equipment, the maintenance people might keep track of only the key machines. The operators know about the problems on their machines, but do not know the sources of the problems or solutions to them. No one asks them anyway. In a multishift plant, the operators on one shift are often unaware of equipment problems that happened on other shifts.

Effective PM requires a good system for tracking equipment performance and breakdowns, repairs, and related costs. The tracking system should be part of a larger

FIGURE 7.9

Monthly PM summary report for a machine.

```
                              WORK HISTORY FILE REPORT
Work Category equal to:  PM
Date Issued greater than or equal to:  06/01/95
Equipment No. equal to:  05010
Job # greater than or equal to:  0002

             WO Number    06199504041              Parts Available?  Y
           Work Category  PM                             WO Status
            Failure Code                          Number Printed  1
                Priority          Job # 0002         Requested By
             Date Issued  06/19/95  07:18                  Account # WO1111
           Date Required  07/14/95  00:00              Schedule Date 00/00/00
          CAUSE CODES                             Earliest StarFolder Name Shift 0
           Equipment No.  05010                  Date completed 07/21/95 Actual 00/00/00
                   Name   CNC M/C, HOR, K&T                            Time 07:17
                 Dept/FF  FF-1                      Meter Reading      0.00
                Location  K-11                    Previous Reading     0.00
           Warranty Date  00/00/00                      Downtime       0.00 % Productive  0
                   Cost   LTD  74144.33          Lost Operating Cost   0.00
                Problem:

                                                      Labor Cost     1097.14
                                                    Outside Costs       0.00
                                                Projected WO Cost       0.00
                                                        Parts Cost      0.00
                                                  Work Order Cost    1097.14

Corrective Action:
   MONTHLY K&T PREVENTIVE MAINTENANCE
Text Codes:
      Text Code  Text Code Name
   1  WKTM     K&T MONTHLY PM
Tools:
Parts:
      Part #/Name/Location
Labor:
      Clock#    Craft      Date      EST Hrs     Reg Hrs    OT Hrs    DT Hrs     CI Hrs
   1  004       HELP     07/06/95      0.00        10.50      0.00      0.00       0.00
                                         ACTION CODE                 Craft Cost  103.74
   2  004       HELP     07/05/95      0.00         6.50      0.00      0.00       0.00
                                         ACTION CODE                 Craft Cost   64.22
   3  091       MECH     07/08/95      0.00         2.00      0.00      0.00       0.00
                                         ACTION CODE                 Craft Cost   31.20
   4  091       MECH     07/11/95      0.00         8.00      0.00      0.00       0.00
                                         ACTION CODE                 Craft Cost  183.30
   5  055       MECH     07/18/95      0.00         6.50      0.00      0.00       0.00
                                         ACTION CODE                 Craft Cost  101.40
   6  055       MECH     07/20/95      0.00         8.50      0.00      0.00       0.00
                                         ACTION CODE                 Craft Cost  132.60
   7  230                07/21/95      0.00         6.50      0.00      0.00       0.00
                                         ACTION CODE                 Craft Cost   89.57
   8  055                07/21/95      0.00         1.00      0.00      0.00       0.00
                                         ACTION CODE                 Craft Cost   15.60
   9  230                07/18/95      0.00         8.50      0.00      0.00       0.00
                                         ACTION CODE                 Craft Cost  117.13
  10  230                07/19/95      0.00         8.50      0.00      0.00       0.00
                                         ACTION CODE                 Craft Cost  117.13
```

Source: Courtesy, ITT McDonnell & Miller Corporation.

computerized maintenance management system (CMMS) that processes workorders for repair maintenance, maintains PM procedures and schedules, releases workorders for all scheduled preventive, predictive, and repair maintenance, and prepares summary reports. Figure 7.9 shows an example of a summary report giving the tasks and costs for monthly PM on one machine.

Information retained by the CMMS about machine performance, breakdowns, and costs is used to compile statistics on equipment availability, MTTR, efficiency, and quality, and to assess current maintenance activities. The statistics are useful for determining maintenance requirements and schedules for components and equipment and for improving maintenance procedures. The CMMS reports hours lost and costs of both repair and prevention activities and shows the trade-offs. Company engineers use this information to upgrade old equipment and procure new equipment. Maintenance staff use it to establish PM procedures and schedules, determine operator and expert training, and know what kinds of spare parts to carry.

Creating a CMMS begins with a plant register or inventory that lists all equipment. For all equipment in the register, the following information must be compiled:

Type of machine	Serial number
Date put in service	Manufacturer
Dates of upgrade or changes	Location in plant
Location of manuals, schematics and drawings, spare parts	

For all equipment in the register the CMMS should also include information such as standards of performance, ways in which equipment could fail to meet those standards, potential causes of failure, and consequences. The consequences determine the *criticality* of PM. Equipment in which malfunction would result in process shutdown or safety hazards is the most critical; equipment where the consequences are not immediate or less significant is less critical. Such information is necessary for developing PM procedures, priorities, and schedules.

When establishing an equipment database, the best sources of information are people most knowledgeable about the equipment's functioning, operation, and uses, usually the operators, supervisors, and repair staff. A way to tap that information is to form small discussion groups that each focus on the equipment in a process (a line or cell) or department. Equipment manufacturers sometimes recommend PM procedures and time intervals; often however, PM schedules and procedures are better determined from the experiences and knowledge of the people who work with the equipment.

One problem with scheduling periodic PM is that scheduled PM tasks must take into account the workload of the maintenance staff. A good CMMS sets PM schedules such that not only are the PM requirements of equipment fulfilled, but the workload imposed on the maintenance staff is also leveled and uniform.

USE PREDICTIVE MAINTENANCE

For cases where it is difficult or impossible to determine the useful life of a component or piece of equipment, a common practice is to employ **predictive maintenance** to give warning about potential failures. Rather than perform periodic scheduled maintenance tasks, predictive maintenance performs periodic, scheduled *inspections,* the results of which are used to determine specific PM tasks and replacement of components. The periodic inspections might be done by workers, though usually they require high-level skill and must be done by the maintenance staff.

Predictive maintenance is sometimes classified as a function separate from PM, though it is always performed in conjunction with PM. However, to the extent that predictive maintenance is another way to prevent breakdowns and malfunctions, we consider it here to be an element or aspect of PM.

Most failures give some kind of advance warning, and in predictive maintenance the advance warning indicates that a replacement or overhaul is necessary. The advance warning might give enough time to order replacement parts (when not stocked), transfer production to other machines, or schedule maintenance tasks. Predictive maintenance is also called **condition-based** maintenance because items remain in service on the condition that potential failure is not detected. When inspection indicates an impending problem, a closer inspection or immediate remedial action is scheduled.

Predictive maintenance often involves monitoring the vibration, speed, temperature, sound, and other physical phenomena of machinery. For example, failure of spindle bearings is a common cause of defects and breakdowns in all kinds of rotating machinery, and vibration can be an indication that a bearing fault is developing. In addition to monitoring the machine directly, measures of the *output* of the machine can sometimes be used to predict machine malfunction. For example, points on an SPC control chart for product quality that show a process is moving toward an out-of-control situation might also be indicating a nascent machine problem.

Human sensory inspection often provides adequate results, though sometimes it does not because signs of emerging problems are too subtle. This is where detection technology comes in. One example of this technology is X-ray radiography. The human eye can easily see stress cracks on a machine, but it cannot see where metal is fatigued and about to crack. From X-raying the metal (in a manner similar to X-raying people), it is easy to see on exposed film areas of discontinuity in the metal. Two other examples of technologies for predictive maintenance are infrared thermography and ultrasound.[14] All equipment has thermal patterns that are easily detected with thermal imaging devices; some devices can detect temperature differences smaller than 1/10°F. Thermal devices are useful for finding hot spots caused by high resistance in electrical connections and friction in bearings and couplings. With a portable infrared thermography machine, thousands of bearings in a hundred yards of conveyor can be inspected in a matter of minutes. All operating equipment also produces a broad range of sounds, though leaks in valves, pumps, gaskets, and seals in high-pressure and vacuum systems produce only high-frequency, short-wave sounds. Though these high-frequency sounds are inaudible, ultrasound instruments easily separate them out from background noise and determine their origin.

The amount of warning from inspection can vary from microseconds to weeks or more. Shorter warning time mandates more frequent inspections, and some equipment requires 24-hour surveillance using sensors linked to a computer. On-line computerized monitoring can be expensive but sometimes it is a cost-effective alternative to human inspection and data logging, especially when the inspection is for components located in hidden or inaccessible places or when the inspection results must be highly accurate.[15]

Corporations like GM, Eaton, and Monsanto rely heavily on on-line monitoring. GM monitors the wear of bearings on ventilation fans on heat-treatment furnaces and tool wear and breakage on production equipment. At GM's wind tunnel, which runs 24-hours a day, 5 days a week, bearings on motors and blowers are monitored. To replace a main drive motor bearing means 28 weeks of downtime since the building must be partially disassembled to reach the motor; however, with advance warning, as much as 20 weeks of this downtime can be avoided.[16]

ROLE OF OPERATORS

Though equipment monitoring sometimes requires sophisticated technology, the watchful eye of an operator is often sufficient to determine when equipment is performing abnormally and needs adjustment or repair. To achieve and retain high equipment effectiveness, there is no substitute for operators who believe in the importance of keeping equipment well-functioning.

Most plants have hundreds or thousands of pieces of equipment—production and materials handling equipment, support machinery, fixtures, and tools. Expecting a small pool of experts from maintenance and engineering to keep up with all this equipment is illogical. On the other hand, operators deal with the same equipment daily. If they care about the equipment, they will treat it well; and if something goes wrong, they will notify someone to fix it. If they don't care about the equipment, they will abuse or misuse it; if something goes wrong, they will ignore it, try to work around it, and not report it until the problem is serious or catastrophic.

When equipment cleaning and basic upkeep are included in the responsibility of operators and line people, when every eye is watchful of equipment problems, then the frequency of undetected problems will drop and the plant OEE will rise. Even if a worker sits at one machine all day, her responsibility will be increased enormously by simply transferring to her custodial care and basic upkeep of her machine. She will have more control over her work and she will likely be more proud of her work. In many JIT companies operators proudly put their names on equipment.

Additional responsibility must be accompanied with training in additional skills. Workers should be trained to perform basic maintenance procedures (cleaning, lubricating, tightening fasteners and connections, replacing filters, etc.). Most of the training is conducted by staff from the maintenance department.

Of course, just giving operators partial responsibility for machine upkeep will not eliminate machine problems. Management must acknowledge the time and skill associated with the responsibility and upgrade job descriptions and pay accordingly. Experts from maintenance, engineering, and equipment manufacturers must be ready to give quick, reliable service to deal with serious and complex equipment problems.

Initially, the operators are guided by maintenance people and rely on their instructions. Eventually as the operators develop their skills, they will move on to the next step, at which time they are given greater autonomy to participate in performing basic preventive and repair maintenance, develop improved maintenance procedures, develop their own inspection check sheets, and meet in groups to discuss, diagnose, and resolve equipment problems. This next step is but one aspect of total productive maintenance.

TOTAL PRODUCTIVE MAINTENANCE[17]

Total productive maintenance (TPM) is a commitment to maintenance that goes beyond preventive and predictive maintenance. In some ways TPM is similar to TQM:

· All employees are involved in satisfying customer needs, where the customer is the person at the next stage of the process. For TPM, this translates into providing maximum support and service to all of the users of equipment.

· A machine breakdown is seen as a form of defect, and TPM is committed to *preventing* breakdowns and malfunctions from happening in the first place.

· TPM is a further aspect of continuous improvement. It is an ongoing *process* of educating and involving workers, upgrading and redesigning equipment, instituting foolproofing devices, monitoring equipment performance, and eliminating sources of equipment waste.

TPM uses a life-cycle perspective of equipment. The likelihood of equipment not performing during its useful life is a function of many factors, including the equipment's design, construction, operation, and upkeep. Equipment deteriorates with usage, and with deterioration comes diminished reliability and effectiveness. TPM seeks to reduce deterioration and increase effectiveness and useful life by focusing on *all* the factors that govern equipment life, which not only includes upkeep and operation, but also construction and design. In TPM, the emphasis and spending switches from procuring new or more equipment to monitoring and upgrading existing equipment.

Just as TQM seeks zero defects, TPM seeks zero machine malfunctions and breakdowns. A malfunction is the end of a series of linked causes: lubricant runs low or dust and dirt accumulate, which causes scratches and friction, which cause loosened, cracked, or fatigued parts, and so on. As long as the initial and intermediate causes go undetected, they remain untreated, which eventually leads to malfunction. Nakajima[18] suggests the following steps for revealing and treating the hidden causes of equipment problems:

· Perform TPM preventive maintenance.
· Develop in-house capability to restore and redesign equipment.
· Eliminate human error in operation and maintenance.

PERFORM TPM PREVENTIVE MAINTENANCE

TPM preventive maintenance includes all the PM features described earlier, with the addition that *operators* bear more responsibility for performing PM tasks and basic repairs. Operators are trained to take on many of the maintenance tasks formerly done by maintenance experts. They follow PM procedures listed on daily and weekly checklists. Like setup tasks, PM tasks can be separated into those that can be done

CASE IN POINT: Tennessee Eastman Co.[19]

Some machines at Tennessee Eastman have a small rubber disk that ruptures and shuts down the machine if the vacuum pressure gets too high. It used be that a ruptured disk was the start of a long chain of events: the operator informed the production manager, who informed the maintenance manager, who located and called away from another job a maintenance expert, who went to the stores area for a replacement disk, then went to the machine, removed four bolts, replaced the disk and aligned it, and reattached the bolts. The average down time was 4 hours.

This happened about 200 times a year, so total downtime was 800 hours.

With TPM, operators were trained to do the repair themselves, and it took them only 1 hour. However, since they did not like doing the repair, they started monitoring the vacuum pressure more closely so the disk would not rupture. With this, the number of ruptures dropped to just 10 a year—a 95% reduction. The machines now have 790 more hours annually to produce, and the maintenance department has 800 more hours to do other things.

safely while the machine is running (inspections and cleaning of external components) and those that must be done while it is stopped (checking movable or internal components). This operator involvement enables basic PM tasks and minor repairs to be performed more frequently and, often, more efficiently than the maintenance staff is able to do. This results in less equipment downtime and frees up the maintenance staff to take on other responsibilities, such as equipment renovation and redesign.

In traditional union shops with rigid trade classifications, all equipment-related work is handled by trade specialists. Although this is supposed to result in better quality and more efficient work, for equipment maintenance and repair it can be counterproductive. A breakdown problem is often better resolved by someone with a good general understanding of a machine than by a group of specialists, each of whom understands only a limited part of it. Being well-rounded, however, should not preclude maintenance staff members from also being specialists in any one area. Trained electricians, machine technicians, and plumbers are still needed to keep the factory running.

The maintenance staff's new role influences equipment-related procedures and decisions in important ways. The new role includes teaching operators skills in basic maintenance, assisting them with maintenance activities, restoring deteriorating equipment, assessing weaknesses in equipment design, upgrading equipment, and developing new operating and maintenance requirements for the equipment. Figure 7.10 summarizes the new roles of operators and maintenance staff in TPM.

DEVELOP IN-HOUSE CAPABILITY TO RESTORE AND REDESIGN EQUIPMENT

Another way that TPM differs from simpler PM is that TPM includes emphasis on developing in-house capability to restore, redesign, and fabricate equipment, fixtures, and tools.

FIGURE 7.10

New role of operators and maintenance staff.

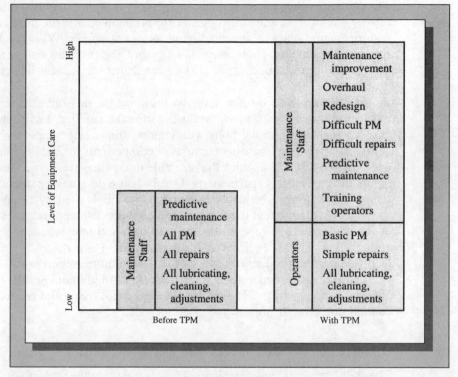

Many companies subcontract equipment maintenance, restoration, and design so they can better focus on equipment *usage* (i.e., on manufacturing). But equipment usage, design, and upkeep cannot be divorced. Companies that rely entirely on suppliers to produce and maintain equipment and tools never truly understand their own equipment needs. These manufacturers are at the mercy of their suppliers for recommendations about new equipment and for repair or PM services, even though those recommendations or services might not best suit their needs.

A company that develops in-house technical capability is in control of the useful life of its equipment, and it often can perform most of its own PM and repair maintenance more effectively than equipment suppliers. When people in the company become involved in the upkeep and renovation of equipment, they develop an understanding of the workings and technology of that equipment, and that enables them to alter the design of the equipment to better suit the unique needs of the company. In many companies, the same equipment is used for 40 or 50 years, over which time there is ample opportunity to upgrade the equipment in terms of maintainability and operating performance. As they upgrade equipment, engineers and technicians in the company are also utilizing and upgrading their technical skills.

The ultimate outcome of in-house design capability is that the company can redesign its own machines, tools, and fixtures to improve equipment performance, problem detection, and maintainability. One example is maintenance prevention, that is, equipment that itself performs functions which eliminate or speed up maintenance. The common office copier is an example. Most copiers detect potential problems and display the location and error code for the problem. Often the problem is small (e.g., add toner) and quickly remedied by users of the copier. When problems are more serious, the machine shuts itself down before the problem can spread. Even then, downtime is reduced because an error code tells the service specialist where to find the problem.

Most companies do not have the resources to do sophisticated or large-scale redesign, though they do have resources to make smaller, less sophisticated design changes such as replacing bolts with clamps, improving access to internal components, and attaching permanent fixtures or components to simplify machine operation and changeovers. Companies that are able to do this, even on a small scale, gain a competitive advantage, particularly if the in-house design is a patentable process or is a machine that exceeds the performance of machines used by competitors.

Effective equipment overhaul, design, and procurement requires that all aspects of the equipment life (operational uses, setups, and maintenance) be considered together. To this end, equipment decisions in TPM are made by teams comprising technicians from production, engineering, and maintenance, as well as setup technicians and equipment operators. Though operators might not know how to make design changes in equipment, they know about equipment usage and related problems, and can tell others what improvements are needed.

ELIMINATE HUMAN ERROR IN OPERATION AND MAINTENANCE

The TPM view of equipment problems is that problems don't just happen, they happen because managers, workers, maintenance staff, and engineers are either doing things incorrectly or are not doing things that *should* be done. The TPM solution is threefold: education/training, foolproofing, and improving maintenance procedures.

Education and Training

Besides being trained to operate equipment properly and to perform basic PM and simple repairs, operators are trained on how to inspect for and recognize signs of deterioration and hidden causes of problems. They also learn the basic tools for data collection, analysis, and problem solving, which they apply individually and in small-group sessions. Training is based upon equipment needs, trainability and motivation of the operators, as well as on time and resources available. Training is provided in a variety of ways such as 30-minute minisessions on the plant floor, in-house seminars and workshops, take-home videos, and courses at junior colleges and trade schools. Some training might be done by TPM consultants and equipment vendors, but most is done by in-house trainers and maintenance staff.

To help motivate operator participation in TPM and to ensure adequate skill development, operators should be tested for certification upon completing a course of training. The certification formally acknowledges that an operator has mastered some

FIGURE 7.11

Operator certification levels and displays.

Machine	LU29		
		TPM Certification Level	
Operator	1	2	3
Gary Owen	✓		✓
Marge Jones	✓	✓	
Renee Lopez	✓	✓	
Horst Jankowski			

Machine___LU29___
Operator___Gary Owen___   TPM
Skill set   Certification

External lube ___✓___
Replace filter ___✓___   Level 1
Adjust belt ___✓___   Basic
Adjust fairing ___✓___

Internal lube ___✓___
Adjust sprocket ___✓___   Level 2
Adjust drive _____   Intermediate
  oil seal & bushing _____

Replace sprocket _____
Replace drive   Level 3
  seal & bushing _____   Advanced
Adjust magazine
  camber _____

Dept. 24	Machine, TPM Certification Level				
Operator	LU26	LU29	GOB1	GRB13	GRB15
Gary Owen		1	2	2	2
Marge Jones	3	3			
Renee Lopez	1	2	2		
Horst Jankowski			3	2	2

skill requirement. The certification can be general (e.g., lube all GRB-type machines) or for a particular machine (see Figure 7.11, left). In many plants, operator certifications are displayed at each machine, department, or workcell (see Figure 7.11, right).

Likewise, maintenance staff are trained so they are able to take on a new, expanded role that emphasizes increased maintenance speed and efficiency, fewer maintenance errors, and greater usage of their technical skills. Increased speed and efficiency requires that all maintenance people, in addition to being skilled in some special trade, have *general skills* in electronics, hydraulics, and so on, as well as knowledge of basic equipment technology, equipment functioning, and new technology. The purpose is to make them more well-rounded at diagnosing equipment problems, repairing equipment, and performing PM procedures with fewer mistakes, no matter what equipment they work on. It also prepares them for assisting in in-house design and renovation of equipment. Some of these skills come via in-house seminars and on-the-job training, while others come from special outside seminars, courses, and workshops.

Foolproofing

Not all equipment problems caused by human error can be resolved by training. Some errors are inadvertent, and the way to eliminate them is to determine their root causes and install ways to prevent them from happening. Any mechanism, device, or procedure installed to preclude an inadvertent error is called a **pokayoke** device. Pokayoke

CASE IN POINT: TPM at ITT McDonnell & Miller Corporation[20]

McDonnell & Miller (M&M) formerly did only repair maintenance; now it does PM on every machine, both daily and weekly basic PM by operators, as well as computer-scheduled expert PM by maintenance specialists. Every machine and workcell has its own PM procedures, which in some cases the operators helped prepare, as well as daily and weekly checkoff sheets for operators to follow (see Figure 7.12). In each workcell is a binder showing procedures for every machine, including machine drawings that show places requiring adjustment and lubrication. Each machine or workcell also has the tools necessary for simple repairs. Tools are kept in locked cabinets, but the operators have the keys.

Now in its second year of TPM, M&M is developing a routine for doing PM and predictive maintenance. Information about PM procedures, breakdown repairs, labor time, and costs is stored, processed, and reported using a CMMS. The system generates monthly, quarterly, semiannual, and annual workorders for all equipment needing PM. To allow adequate time for PM and to minimize interference with production schedules, most PM is performed on the third shift.

Lubrication is taken seriously. Prior to TPM, equipment at M&M was seldom lubri-

FIGURE 7.12

Daily and weekly maintenance checklists.

```
                        ACTION CODE WKTD
                   Text Code Name DAILY K&T PM
Description:
                      DAILY K&T CHECK LIST
     TASK                                      M    T    W   TH    F    S
 1. CHECK AIR PRESSURE GAGE (NORMAL-30-60PSI)  __   __   __   __   __   __
 2. CHECK FLOOD COOLANT LEVEL AND REFILL
    IF NECESSARY                               __   __   __   __   __   __
 3. CLEAN ALL MAGAZINE SOCKETS AND TOOLS       __   __   __   __   __   __
 4. CLEAN TOOL CHANGE ARM TOOL PICKUP AREA     __   __   __   __   __   __
 5. CLEAN AREA BETWEEN TABLE AND COLUMN WAY    __   __   __   __   __   __
 6. CHECK FOR NORMAL AIR BLAST AT THE SPINDLE
    NOSE WHILE SPINDLE IS RUNNING              __   __   __   __   __   __
 7. CHECK ALL LIGHTS FOR PROPER OPERATION      __   __   __   __   __   __
- - - - - - - - - - - - - - - - - - - - - - - - - - - - - - - - - - - - - -
                        ACTION CODE WKTW
                   Text Code Name K&T WEEKLY PM
Description:
WEEKLY MACHINE PREVENTIVE MAINTENANCE:
____1. Review machine log book since last PM. Resolve problems noted.
____2. Wipe down entire Machine, Power Supply, and Control Unit. Clean all exposed limit switches and their trip dogs.
____3. Listen to hydraulic unit. Is the sound normal?
____4. Check hydraulic oil for coolant contamination (milkiness).
____5. Check system pressure - 41.4 bar (600 psi). Relief valve setting - 48.2 bar (700 psi).
____6. Check all exposed oil lines and repair any existing leaks.
____7. Check the tool transfer and magazine index. Did all of the tools index and change properly?
____8. Clean or replace the air intake filter for the control.
____9. Clean tape reader.
```

Source: Courtesy, ITT McDonnell & Miller Corporation.

cated; some had not been lubricated since purchase. Now, on every machine there is a list showing all required lubrication, as well as small color-coded stickers indicating points of lubrication and type of lubricant (see Figure 7.13). Every machine or workcell has containers for every kind of lubricant. When containers run low, operators go to a store area in the plant and take whatever lubricant they need from 12 huge barrels.

Resistance to TPM at M&M stems largely from misconception about the necessity to perform rigorous PM, especially when it interferes with production. For some machines, maintenance takes longer than the third shift, and the production department balks at machines being held up for PM during scheduled production hours. The acceptance of TPM by operators has been good, in some cases too good. A few overzealous operators want to do more PM than required, including things such as electrical work

for which they are not trained. The concern is that this is hazardous and can result in operators being injured.

Has TPM paid off? Prior to TPM M&M did not have a good system of maintenance record-keeping, so comparisons of breakdowns, MTBF, and costs are impossible. But there are other indicators of TPM's effects. The maintenance staff used to have nine people, and they were faced with a continuous backlog of repairs. Now, less than 2 years after the start of TPM the backlog is gone and requests for breakdown repairs are readily dispatched. Even with all the PM being performed, the staff has had enough extra time to construct and equip a new central spare parts store, install a new CMMS, train operators, and develop PM procedures for every machine. They have been able do all this even though, as a result of two people retiring, the current maintenance staff is smaller than before.

Figure 7.13

Diagrams on machines showing points for necessary lubrication and kinds of lubrication.

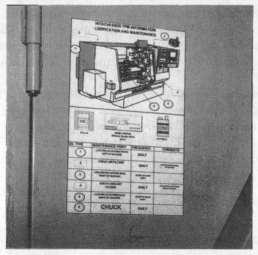
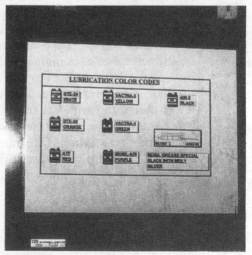

is Japanese for foolproofing. For example, suppose a source of equipment breakdown is the operator occasionally forgetting to check the oil level in the reservoir. When the oil level is too low, the shaft on the machine freezes. As a result, the cutting tool is damaged and the part being machined is destroyed. A simple, inexpensive foolproof device is a float in the oil reservoir connected to a light and a switch. When the oil drops below a certain level, the light goes on and the switch prevents the motor from being turned on. Most pokayokes are inexpensive and originate from worker suggestions. Pokayokes and foolproofing are the subject of Chapter 15.

Improving Maintenance Procedures

Eliminating human error in equipment problems also requires attention to improving maintenance procedures, a concept analogous to improving equipment setup procedures. Like setup, maintenance is often done in a somewhat disorganized and ad hoc fashion. Both can be time-consuming and decrease production capacity and quality. Like setups, maintenance procedures should be analyzed, simplified, and standardized so they will (1) be done more quickly (short MTTR) and (2) result in fewer or no mistakes. The same practices used to reduce setup times can be applied to improve preventive maintenance: keep tools and spare parts organized, labeled, and easily accessible; use repair carts; keep instructions, tools and parts next to machines needing frequent maintenance; and train workers to do basic repairs themselves. A study team comprised of maintenance workers, operators, and engineers analyzes machine records, videotapes frequently used maintenance procedures (such as for PM), and determines how to streamline or eliminate the procedures.

IMPLEMENTING TPM

If TPM is eventually to be spread plantwide and impact management policy, worker responsibility, and staff roles in the functions of production, maintenance, and engineering, then TPM implementation must be guided by a **steering committee** that consists of managers from those functions. The purpose of the steering committee is to formulate TPM policies and strategies and to give advice. A top-level executive should serve on the committee to show management's endorsement of TPM and serve as champion for the TPM program.

The actual oversight and coordination of implementation activities are done by a **TPM program team.** The team includes managers, staff, and technicians from the production and maintenance departments, a TPM program manager, trainers, and sometimes a consultant. This team oversees the TPM program feasibility study, sets detailed program objectives, selects target areas, and prepares a master plan for implementation. The groups and their relationship are shown in Figure 7.14.

PROGRAM FEASIBILITY

Prior to initiating the program, a feasibility study is performed to gather baseline data for planning the program and for assessing the program's likely costs and benefits. The study is performed by a small group of operators, maintenance experts, and engineers. Through observation, interviews, and records, the study group gathers data about the current state of equipment in terms of EE, production losses, downtime, MTBF, and so on. The team assesses current skills of plant personnel, other skills they will need for TPM, and their ability and motivation to learn additional skills. The assessment

FIGURE 7.14

Groups involved in TPM program implementation.

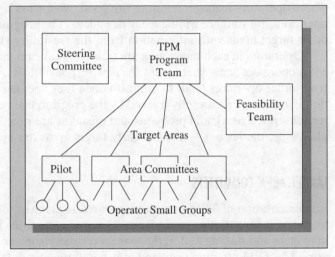

can be done with the assistance of small groups of operators in individual work areas. The study team assesses all matters relating to maintenance—current housekeeping, PM efforts, procedures for scheduling and managing PM and repairs, and so on—and the organization's culture and ability to adapt to change.

PROGRAM OBJECTIVES AND MASTER PLAN

The program team sets definitive annual objectives for the TPM program.[21] The objectives might address specific performance measures such as MTBF, MTTR, equipment availability, performance efficiency, rate of quality, EE, number of accidents, percentage of employees participating in TPM, and skill level acquired by participants. An example of an objective is to reduce the amount of downtime from equipment failure by 30% within a year of TPM kickoff.

The program team also prepares a master plan for implementing TPM plantwide. Rather than dictate precise events in the program, the purpose of the master plan is to lay out a general sequence of activities for implementing TPM in particular target areas and for implementing plantwide tasks such as training managers and maintenance staff, setting up or upgrading the CMMS, and reorganizing the maintenance function.

TARGET AREAS

Although ultimately TPM will be practiced in every area of every plant, the implementation should begin with just a few target areas—particular departments, focused factories, or processes in the factory. The first target area will serve as a *pilot* area, both for trying out TPM ideas and for demonstrating TPM concepts and results to the other target areas. A pilot target area should be selected based on high likelihood of success, that is, an area that has important but resolvable maintenance problems, where operator–manager relations are good, where workers are trainable, and where operators and staff are willing to try new ideas. The program team selects the pilot and other target areas with information from the feasibility study.

Operators in each target area are trained to take on maintenance responsibilities. Most operators somewhat accept the new responsibilities, and much of the resistance from other operators tends to diminish once they see how TPM works. Implementation in each area is carefully tracked by the program team and the target area committee (described next), and problems and mistakes are noted. As the program is spread plantwide, the lessons learned in early target areas are applied.

TARGET AREA COMMITTEES

Implementation of TPM in each target area is planned jointly by the TPM program team and a **target area committee.** The area committee is made up of maintenance managers and staff as well as the manager, supervisors, and operators from the target area. The TPM program team and area committee work together to determine particular TPM tasks to implement, schedules for implemention, and people who will be responsible for the tasks. The following specific tasks are assigned:

· Determine for every machine how much improvement is needed; also identify sources of problems and ways to eliminate them. (To avoid improvement for improvement's sake, the initial focus is on high-priority machines—bottlenecks, near bottlenecks, or machines that delimit the capacity or quality of the target area.)

· Decide which PM and repair tasks can be transferred to operators; consider which tasks (a) operators *want* to do, (b) operators are *capable* of doing, and (c) the maintenance department is *willing* to relinquish.

· Train operators in basic PM, then set daily and weekly PM procedures for the operators in addition to monthly, quarterly, and annual PM procedures and schedules for the maintenance staff. (The time required for PM must be estimated and compared to available labor hours; PM procedures and schedules must allow adequate time for the operators and maintenance staff to do a good job of PM maintenance.)

· Determine equipment that requires predictive maintenance; define inspection procedures, frequency of inspection, and any special inspection equipment and skills needed for inspection.

As additional areas of the plant are targeted for TPM implementation, the program team coordinates tasks with the target area committees to maximize sharing of lessons learned and minimize conflicts.

PLANTWIDE ISSUES

The TPM program team initiates and oversees umbrella activities that will affect every department or focused factory in the plant. The following activities are included:

· Reviewing and revising existing company policies and procedures to include maintenance issues in future decisions concerning equipment renovation, redesign, and procurement.

· Educating maintenance staff about the philosophy and focus of TPM; broadening and enhancing their maintenance skills to enable them to fulfill their new roles.

· Determining maintenance-related issues that need special attention, then forming project teams to address them; for example, selecting particular equipment for renovation or redesign; deciding whether to renovate, redesign, or buy equipment; and investigating ways to reduce the time to perform breakdown repairs and PM.

· Determining how best to reorganize the maintenance department. If the department is to be decentralized, the roles of newly formed decentralized units, as well as of the remaining central maintenance function must be determined.

· Setting up a new (or enhancing the existing) CMMS system. This involves establishing system requirements, procuring and installing hardware and software and developing procedures and schedules for data collection, as well as determining how to improve efficiency of data collection (for example, putting bar codes on all machines and on the name badges of maintenance workers to reduce the tedium of data entry for every PM or repair task). If the maintenance function is to be decentralized, responsibility for the CMMS must be apportioned to the decentralized units.

· Breaking down TPM program objectives into objectives for target areas, operators, and pieces of equipment and establishing a system so work areas and operators are rewarded/recognized when they meet or exceed objectives (e.g., pins, luncheons, banquets, and photos of operators and teams in the company newsletters; one company awards Gold, Silver, and Bronze decals, which operators proudly display on their machines).[22]

· Coordinating TPM with other improvement efforts such as setup-time reduction, process or layout changes, process capability studies, standard work studies and documentation, and employee involvement. There is often considerable overlap in these activities in which case they should be implemented as a coordinated package.

During implementation, the program team meets with the target area committees to assess progress as well as to identify barriers and find ways to resolve them. In the beginning, TPM will appear as little more than a source of expenditures (and headaches). It will be a while before TPM benefits are seen, and until then many will argue against the program and resist the necessary changes. For the first year or two, a major task of the TPM program team is to work toward minimizing resistance, maximizing support, and helping the program gain inertia. Once the benefits of TPM start to appear and the program does gain momentum, the program team can be dissolved, and responsibility for planning and daily coordination of the remaining implementation tasks can be transferred to the maintenance department.

MANAGEMENT SUPPORT

TPM cannot succeed without the support of top management. Workers, supervisors, and staff need to know that top management is committed to the change. During a kickoff meeting involving everyone ultimately to be affected by the TPM program, top management explains the overall TPM philosophy, the mission of the TPM program, the organizational changes required as part of the program, and the time and resources it will commit in support of the program. Throughout implementation, the program champion and steering committee work together to retain that commitment and to show that management stands behind the program.

MAINTENANCE ORGANIZATION

In traditional plants, a single pool of maintenance people services the entire factory. As a result, maintenance workers never master skills for particular equipment because they are too busy maintaining all equipment; this is especially true in large plants. For the same reason, maintenance workers never develop cordial working relationships with operators or managers in particular work areas. They never come to understand the needs of production people. Of course, the production people never come to understand the necessity for maintenance (other than breakdown repairs), either. Each feels the other gets in the way, and there is often animosity. TPM requires breaking down the barriers between maintenance and production departments.

Decentralization

A good arrangement for breaking down interdepartmental barriers is to decentralize the maintenance function, that is, to assign maintenance workers to particular areas, processes, or departments in a factory. Being affiliated with a particular production area enables maintenance workers to learn more about particular processes and machines, become better acquainted with individual operators and supervisors, and better understand their equipment needs. They learn the idiosyncracies of each machine, and when something needs attention, they are there on the spot. Though maintenance workers still *report* to the maintenance department, most days they work in the same preassigned production areas next to the same supervisors and operators. Eventually they are viewed no longer as outsiders, but as members of the production team, there to help resolve equipment-related problems.

One drawback of decentralizing the maintenance staff is that equipment problems are not uniformly dispersed throughout a factory, so staff assigned to some areas are overworked, while those in other areas have little to do. Thus, decentralized staffing should be based on need: high-maintenance areas have a dedicated staff, but low-maintenance areas share a common staff.

Central Maintenance

Even with decentralization, a central maintenance function is still necessary to handle maintenance issues that are plantwide or that fall within no particular department of the plant. In smaller plants, this central maintenance function schedules equipment inspection and PM and manages the store of spare parts. (In larger plants, much of this scheduling and spare parts management is handled in a more decentralized fashion). For parts storage, the central area is responsible for certain, expensive items, while most other parts are stored at areas near the point of use; inexpensive, high-use items (like fasteners, fittings, and lubricants) can be kept in areas where needed and made freely available without requisition.

The central maintenance department also has responsibility for monitoring the overall TPM program and assessing its strengths, weaknesses, and opportunities. To keep TPM current and focused for competitive advantage, the central maintenance department identifies the best maintenance practices of other organizations and uses them as benchmarks for improvement.

Summary

Despite the fact that equipment functioning has a big impact on production cost, quality, and schedules, equipment upkeep is traditionally afforded low priority, and inventory is maintained to buffer against breakdowns and malfunctioning. Like other wastes, JIT seeks to identify sources of equipment-related waste and eliminate them. Eliminating equipment wastes begins with determining measures for equipment effectiveness, which is the degree to which a piece of equipment is available to do work, perform at an expected level of efficiency, and produce no defects. The measures are used as indices for assessing levels of equipment-related waste and for setting goals for equipment improvement.

Fundamental to achieving high equipment effectiveness is a program of preventive maintenance (PM). The program must emphasize maintaining equipment requirements and operating conditions, keeping equipment clean, monitoring daily for signs of potential malfunction, performing regularly scheduled preventive maintenance and predictive maintenance tasks, and keeping good equipment records. Effective PM requires that operators take responsibility for proper equipment operation, daily cleaning, monitoring, and basic equipment upkeep.

Total productive maintenance (TPM) represents a commitment to equipment performance beyond original equipment design parameters and a move to make equipment a source of competitive advantage. One goal of TPM is zero breakdowns, the virtual elimination of equipment malfunction and equipment-related sources of products defects. A second goal is equipment restoration and redesign such that equipment performs better than new and in ways that competitors' equipment cannot. TPM shifts much of the responsibility for maintenance to operators, which frees up the maintenance staff to train operators, perform additional scheduled PM, and to participate in equipment redesign and restoration projects.

Implementing TPM plantwide is a major project that requires support from top management. Large-scale TPM is best implemented piecewise through a series of initiatives directed at small target areas such as departments or work areas. Implementation in each of these areas is managed directly by a target area committee, with assistance from the TPM program team. The TPM program team oversees initial planning and coordination of all TPM efforts, though ultimately this responsibility is transferred to the maintenance department. As part of TPM, the maintenance department itself might undergo restructuring, including decentralization and deployment of maintenance workers to assigned areas of the plant.

This and the previous chapter explained aspects of equipment that, historically, many managers have all but ignored. Though both chapters stressed the importance of plantwide, systemwide efforts to reduce setup times and improve equipment effectiveness, the immediate point of focus in both setup reduction and equipment maintenance is on improvement of *individual pieces* of equipment. Now here is the rub: To improve the overall production system, improvement of equipment *is not enough*. In fact, systems theory relates that if you try to improve the elements of a system and do not *first* look at them in the larger context, you could end up worsening the system. Thus, despite the necessity of equipment maintenance and setup efforts, they alone are not sufficient to improve a manufacturing process enough to make it more competitive. Pieces of equipment are elements of the larger production process, and it is necessary to look at them in this larger context. The purpose of the next three chapters is thus to shift focus from equipment to the *processes* within which it is used.

Questions

1. List the consequences of equipment malfunction and breakdown in terms of cost, quality, safety, and lead time.
2. Contrast the following kinds of maintenance: repair, preventive, and total productive.
3. How does investing in maintenance help an organization?
4. What are the six sources of equipment waste?
5. Define and give examples for each of the following terms:

   Maintainability
   Reliability
   Availability
   Equipment efficiency
   Equipment quality rate

6. What is the difference between repair time and downtime for repair?
7. What are the five principal causes of equipment problems.
8. What is the failure pattern of a system or component?
9. What is the bathtub function? What is the burn-in period? What is the wear-out period? How does knowledge about these help in maintenance scheduling?
10. Why should a component that is functioning well be replaced?
11. Where does probability data come from for determining failure potential?
12. What is meant by predictive or condition-based maintenance?
13. A warning light on a copier indicating the toner level is low is an example of a device for condition-based maintenance. Give some other examples.
14. Discuss at least five common practices in PM programs.
15. What role do equipment operators serve in PM?

16. Describe the meaning of in-house equipment restoration and redesign. What potential advantages docs it offer over outsourcing of equipment restoration and redesign?

17. What steps are taken in TPM to eliminate human error in equipment operation and maintenance?

18. In the implementation of companywide TPM, what roles do the following groups serve:

> Steering committee
>
> TPM program team
>
> Target area committees

19. Discuss the difference between centralized and decentralized maintenance staff. What are reasons for decentralizing the maintenance function?

Problems

1. During a three-week period, two identical machines have the following record of downtime (in minutes) for repairs:

Machine	Week 1	Week 2	Week 3
1	45, 18, 30	32, 55, 20, 15, 12	22, 38, 19, 15
2	136, 98	166, 124, 56	98, 107

a. Which machine is better in terms of maintainability?
b. Which is better in terms of other criteria? Explain "other" criteria.

2. The manufacturer of a machine component states that its MTBF is 4000 hours. When should the maintenance staff schedule replacement of the component? What reliability did you use? Discuss the result.

3. A valve for a hydraulic press has an average failure rate of once every six months. The press is to be used for a critical job that will require two weeks operation, during which everything possible must be done so the press does not break down. What is the reliability of the valve during this period of operation? What are the options to increase its reliability?

4. A machine has 30 belts that are difficult to access. Whenever a belt snaps, a warning light goes on. Each time a belt has to be replaced, it costs $50 labor and machine downtime to open up the machine. Once the machine is opened, the belts are easy to access and cost about $10 additional to replace (thus, the cost of installing one belt is $60, whereas the cost of replacing all 30 belts is $350). The maintenance department has logged the following data about the times of operation at which the belts break:

Hours of Operation	1000	2000	3000	4000	5000	6000
No. Broken Belts	1	2	5	7	7	8

If the maintenance department chooses to replace all the belts at once to minimize downtime and replacement costs, after how many thousand hours of operation should they be replaced?

5. Bill Sworn supervises an operation that habitually requires readjustment by a skilled machinist once every three weeks (120 hrs). It takes the machinist two hours to make the adjustment. In addition, the operation is usually idled for two hours before the machinist arrives. Bill thinks that the operator should be taught to do the adjustment. Assuming the operation is not held up for anything other than the adjustment:
   a. What is the availability of the operation?
   b. What are the issues in the operator doing the adjustment?

6. In the course of subjecting 100 components to 5000 hours of operation, five of the components had failed as of 2500 hours but the remainder survived the entire time. What is the failure rate in terms of
   a. Percent failure?
   b. Number of failures per hour?
   c. If each component is utilized 1750 hours per year, what is the average number of failures per year per component?
   d. If 500 of this kind of component are to be installed in machines in a plant, how many can be expected to fail during the next year?

7. Shamway Maintenance Company charges Burgess Company $500 per week for preventive maintenance on 22 machines. The cost to Burgess of each breakdown and repair is $1225. Before signing with Shamway, Burgess had collected the following data:

Weeks of Operation (n)	1	2	3	4	5
No. of Breakdowns (b)	4	5	7	4	2

In terms of costs, was it a good idea for Burgess to sign up for weekly PM with Shamway? Would PM once every two weeks or greater be more cost effective?

8. Suppose the downtime and repair cost of a broken machine is $2000, whereas comprehensive preventive maintenance costs $800 per machine. Records show the following frequencies of breakdowns for a group of the machines:

Weeks between PM	Average Breakdowns between PM
1	.6
2	1.5
3	2.9
4	5.5
5	8.0

Recommend how often PM should be performed.

9. Sonya Marx operates a machine 340 minutes a day. The actual cycle time per part on the machine is measured to be 0.8 minutes, and the machine produces 560 parts a day.

The machine specifications indicate that it should have a cycle time of 0.75 min/part. What is the performance efficiency of the machine?

10. Sonya's machine (described in problem 9) is scheduled to operate 390 minutes a day. About 6 parts per day from the machine are rejected as non-conforming. What is the machine's overall equipment effectiveness?

11. A certain manufacturing process requires a continuous supply of water. The water comes from a tank, and is maintained at a constant level with a pump. Should the pump stop, an alarm sounds, and the tank has enough water to last 2.5 hours. If the tank runs dry the process must be stopped, and the cost is $8000 per hour. Suppose the most common failure mode of the pump is a seized bearing. A seized bearing has an MTBF of three years and requires four hours to replace. It is possible to anticipate a bearing that is about to fail by checking the sound of the pump once a week. Such a bearing can be replaced during a shift when the process is not running. It takes 20 minutes for a $30-an-hour inspector to perform a sound check. The process runs 50 weeks a year.

    a. Is it cost effective to perform the weekly sound check?

    b. A common way to avoid system failure is with backup equipment. Suppose a standby pump is to be installed for use when the first pump fails. Is the standby pump a good idea if its annual cost (capital and operating) is $800?

12. A machine has a failure pattern like curve A in Figure 7.8. The useful life of the machine can be extended 18 months if overhaul is performed at 18 months; assuming no machine overhaul, the MTBF is 24 months (to prevent most failures, an overhaul must be done within 18 months; failure within 24 months is otherwise assured). Suppose the downtime and repair cost of failure is $6000; the cost of overhaul is $2000.

    a. Assuming it is done every 18 months, is the overhaul cost effective?

    b. Assume that daily PM (annual cost: $1200) extends the MTBF of the machine to three years. Assuming everything else remains the same, is PM cost effective?

Endnotes

1. Adopted from S. Nakajima, *Introduction to TPM: Total Productive Maintenance* (Cambridge, MA: Productivity Press, 1988).

2. S. Nakajima, *Continuous Improvement in Operations,* Alan Robinson (ed.) (Cambridge, MA: Productivity Press, 1991), p. 295.

3. *Ibid.* p. 302.

4. There are actually six possible failure patterns. For discussion of these, *see* J. Moubray, *Reliability-centered Maintenance* (New York: Industrial Press, 1992), Chapter 5.

5. A simpler method for calculating performance effectiveness, derived from the product of the formulas for SE and RE, is

$$Performance\ Efficiency = \frac{Design\ CT \times Actual\ Production\ Volume}{Actual\ Running\ Time}$$

$$= \frac{0.5 \times 830}{535} = 0.7757$$

(The tiny difference between this result and that of the other formula is due to rounding error in the first approach.)

6. E. Hartmann, *Successfully Installing TPM in a Non-Japanese Plant* (Pittsburgh: TPM Press, 1992), pp. 61, 63.

7. Adapted from K. Suzaki, *The New Manufacturing Challenge* (New York: Free Press, 1987), p. 116.

8. Frequently cited in automobile literature is that the single most important thing owners can do to minimize engine problems is to change oil periodically. *Consumer Reports* recommends a change every 7500 miles, even in normal or light driving conditions.

9. R. Schonberger, *World Class Manufacturing: The Lessons of Simplicity Applied* (New York: The Free Press, 1986), p. 68.

10. K. Suzaki, *The New Manufacturing Challenge,* p. 119.

11. "Catastrophic" here means the condition where failure of one component leads to failure of another, sometimes in a chain-reaction fashion. For example, when a turbine blade in a jet engine fails, parts of it can fly off and go crashing into other components, including other blades, causing destruction of many components and possible loss of the entire engine.

12. J. Moubray, *Reliability-centered Maintenance,* p. 13.

13. J. Moubray, *Reliability-centered Maintenance,* p. 221.

14. See J. Snell, "Infrared Thermography: New Solutions for Both Maintenance and Production Problems," *P/PM Technology* 8, No. 5 (October 1995), pp. 54–8; G. Mohr, "Technology Overview: Ultrasonic Detection," *P/PM Technology* 8, No. 4 (August 1995), pp. 56–61.

15. E. Page, "Spurring Wider Use of On-Line Condition Monitoring for Predictive Maintenance," *Industrial Engineering,* (November 1994), pp. 32–4.

16. *Ibid,* p. 33.

17. Adopted from J. Moubray, *Reliability-centered Maintenance,* Chapter 10; J. Wright, "Unleashing a Maintenance Department's Full Potential Through Reliability-centered Maintenance," *P/PM Technology,* No.1 (February 1996), pp. 50–60; E. Hartmann, *Successfully Installing TPM*; H. Steudle and P. Desruelle, *Manufacturing in the Nineties* (New York: Van Nostrand Reinhold, 1992), pp. 330–4, 337–40.

18. S. Nakajima, *Introduction to TPM*.

19. E. Hartmann, *Successfully Installing TPM,* p. 46.

20. Conversation with Lawrence Kocen, Plant Engineer, ITT McDonnel & Miller.

21. John Wright argues that besides objectives, maintenance programs should have a mission statement that tells everyone what the program wants to accomplish and how it will do it. Some examples follow:

    Being responsive to customer needs; maintaining equipment to allow continuous operation to meet material requirements; applying predictive and preventive maintenance and evaluating their cost effectiveness; providing resources for all crafts to keep up with expanding technologies; fostering a work environment that will enhance morale and pride in a job well done.

    See J. Wright, "Unleashing a Maintenance Department's Full Potential . . . ", p. 52.

22. E. Hartmann, *Successfully Installing TPM . . . ,* p. 206.

PULL PRODUCTION SYSTEMS

No sooner said than done.

Don't give your advice until it is called upon.   *Desider*

A manufacturing process typically involves numerous stages, all of which must be coordinated such that materials produced at some stages arrive in the right quantities and at the right times at other stages that need them. Ensuring that the right quantity gets to the right place at the right time—the function of **production control**—is not trivial because equipment breakdowns, material shortages, absent workers, production bottlenecks, and other unanticipated problems keep changing the rates of supply and demand everywhere in the process. Even well-run companies that have minimized these problems find production control no simple matter. One way to keep materials moving through the process regardless of problems is to build in a cushion. Traditionally that cushion is provided by inventories held between stages of the process. In plants that manufacture products that have numerous parts and production stages, however, the inventory cushion can be huge.

As part of his work on the Toyota production system, Taiichi Ohno spent years looking for a way to improve production coordination without the need for large inventories. The solution he finally adopted was based on his observation of American supermarkets. He noticed that rather than stock large amounts of food at home, Americans made frequent trips to the supermarket to buy items as needed. Similarly, rather than carry large inventories, the supermarkets replenished food items according to the rate at which they were removed from the shelves. Since customers take only what they immediately need from the shelves, and since supermarkets order just what they need to replenish stock on the shelves, the customers, in effect, *pull* material through the system. This is the concept of **pull production.**

This chapter elaborates on pull production—its methods, advantages, limitations, and how it compares to the more-traditional form of mass production, called **push production.** The chapter describes various pull methods for controlling inventories and authorizing production, including **Kanban,** the system developed by Ohno at Toyota.[1] The chapter discusses the central role of pull production in continuous process improvement and elimination of waste. Situations where pull production works best and worst are also reviewed.

PRODUCTION CONTROL SYSTEMS

The purpose of production control is to ensure that production output meets or closely conforms with demand. Ideally, it ensures that products are made in the *required quantities,* at the *right times,* with the *highest quality*. It should do these things for the lowest cost, which means for the least non-value-added activity, and enable production problems to be easily identified and remedied.

Most production control systems accomplish these ends, though sometimes just barely. Take a simple example, a product that can be produced in many possible configurations and where almost every product order is somewhat unique. Personal computers are like this. Because of variations in product demand and product configuration, it is impossible to completely manufacture such products on an assembly line. When a customer order arrives, the operations routing sequence for the particular product configuration must be determined, and a schedule must be prepared showing the expected date of processing the job at every operation in the sequence.

With a **push production** system, the schedule is based upon when the order is expected to arrive at an operation, plus the time when the operation is expected to complete any pre-existing jobs and be available. Typically the schedule is performed by a central staff responsible for scheduling all operations for all job orders. As a job order moves from operation to operation, work is performed in batches where, often, the size of the production batch is the same as the customer order. Accompanying the job through the plant from one operation to the next are a route sheet, schedules, and work instructions for every operation. When there are several jobs waiting at an operation, the supervisor often has to decide which gets priority, though the priority will not necessarily be the same as that assumed by the central staff when they created the schedules. Changes in priorities and delays from parts shortages, machine breakdowns, and other unexpected events make the production schedules obsolete almost as soon as they are created so they must be constantly revised.

Besides the problems associated with maintaining valid schedules are the problems of batch-oriented production. The schedules not only specify when something must be done, but how much. In traditional production control, the assumption is that the batch size is constant throughout the process, that is, the process and transfer batch sizes remain the same for every operation. Problems with that in terms of waiting time, carrying costs, and product defects were discussed in Chapter 5.

The traditional control process is itself costly and wasteful considering the time and effort required to create schedules for every operation and job order, track orders through the plant so none get misplaced or forgotten, monitor and update schedules, and switch priorities when jobs fall behind. Of course, switching a job's priority by putting it ahead of others so it gets back on schedule (called expediting) disrupts the schedules of other jobs and operations, and makes it likely that, later, other jobs will have to be expedited, other operations will have to be rescheduled, and so on.

Many of the difficulties associated with push production come from trying to schedule every operation for a job in advance and from relying on a remote central staff to update schedules to account for current shop-floor conditions. It is a fact that the central staff is too far removed from the shop floor, physically and temporally, to ever be able to keep schedules current. It is also a fact that workers often do not need the schedules anyway and tend to ignore them. In **pull production,** detailed production schedules for every operation are eliminated, and immediate decisions about quantities and timing of work are made by workers using a simple signal system that connects operations throughout the process.

PULL SYSTEMS AND PUSH SYSTEMS

As an example of how a pull system works, consider the chain of events initiated by a child drinking milk. Whenever the child, call him Josh, wants a drink, he goes to the refrigerator. He is never concerned about there being enough milk because his mom takes care of that. When the milk gets down to, say, 0.25 gallon, she goes to the store for more. The Josh/mom process is an example of a two-stage, producer–consumer **pull system** with a stock point between the stages. Josh is the consumer, mom is the producer, and the stock point is the refrigerator (see Figure 8.1). In pull systems, the inventory in the stock point is kept as small as possible, usually by carrying it in **containers** of standardized size and by restricting the number of containers. In this example, the inventory at the stock point is held to a maximum of 1 gallon.

The process is a pull system because it is *initiated at the downstream location* by the consumer. The consumer withdraws whatever material is needed from stock, and when the amount in stock reaches some minimum level, that signals the producer at the upstream location to replenish it. The producer then makes or procures the material in some prespecified quantity and puts it into stock.

The charm of the pull system is its effectiveness and simplicity. With relatively little inventory and only minimal information requirements, the system keeps material flowing to meet demand. If the fluctuation in demand (when it's hot, Josh drinks more; when it's cold, he drinks less) is not too great, the amount held in the stock area is sufficient to satisfy demand. It is the responsibility of the producer to keep enough in the stock area. In the simplest form of pull system, the producer knows when to make or procure more by simply *looking* at the current inventory in the stock point; that amount of inventory is one of the few bits of information needed to regulate the system. In the example, mom does not have to anticipate Josh's thirst or schedule how much to buy. The replenishment decision is based on the level of milk remaining. When the level is high, mom does nothing; when the level reaches some minimum (say, 0.25 gallon), she goes to the store. Only rarely, when there is an anticipated shift in demand (Josh having friends over or the family leaving for a vacation) or supply

FIGURE 8.1

Pull system example.

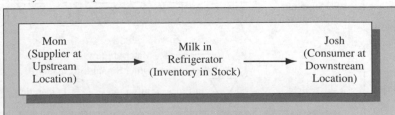

(milk drivers going on strike) does mom need to schedule, that is, go to the store in advance or change the replenishment amount (say, buy 2 gallons, or buy none).

PULL PRODUCTION PROCESS

The above example of a two-stage process with a stock point between can be extended to processes with *any* number of stages since, conceptually, any process can be viewed as a string of successive two-stage pairs. Figure 8.2 shows a production process consisting of four operations with a buffer stock between each pair of them. The term buffer refers here to a small amount of in-process material held between workstations to offset small imbalances between them in terms of production rate and demand rate. Think of each buffer as consisting of a certain number of standard-sized containers holding materials.

The process in Figure 8.2 works as follows. The last or most downstream stage, final assembly, produces the finished product. When a customer order arrives at that stage, operation D, material is withdrawn from buffer 4 to assemble just enough of the product to fill the order. When the size of buffer 4 drops to a certain level (which might be determined by the number of full containers there dropping to a prespecified minimum), operation C begins production to replenish the buffer. For its own production, operation C withdraws material from buffer 3, and when that buffer drops to a certain level, operation B begins production to replenish it. Operation B withdraws material from buffer 2, and when buffer 2 drops to some level, that signals production to start at the first or most upstream stage, operation A. Buffer 1 contains raw materials, which upon dropping to some minimum, is replenished by a supplier. Throughout the process, material is pulled from operation to operation.

The solid arrows in Figure 8.2 represent the flow of materials from left to right, from supplier operation to consumer operation, just like an assembly line. The difference between a pull system and an assembly line is that in the latter every operation continuously produces, so material flows continuously. Also, the kinds of materials

FIGURE 8.2

Flow of material and signals in a pull system.

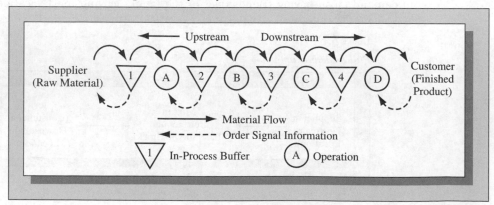

flowing between pairs of operations in an assembly line tend to stay the same since the final product stays the same (assuming the line makes only one kind of product).

In a pull system, production at each operation is contingent on a **signal,** or authorization, coming from a downstream operation. Thus, material flows only when authorized from a downstream stage (in effect, the authorizations move upstream, as indicated in Figure 8.2). Also, the kind of material moving between each supplier–consumer pair can vary. If the supplier operation is capable of producing different kinds of products or parts (such as in a workcell or a multiproduct line, described in later chapters), then it will make whatever is requested from downstream. (In the example, sometimes mom buys milk, sometimes juice or pop, depending when the level for each in the refrigerator buffer gets low.) There are various ways to authorize replenishment of a buffer, the simplest being when the buffer level drops to some predetermined point.

WHY PULL PRODUCTION CANNOT BE STOCKLESS

Pull production is sometimes called **stockless** production because its goal is to eliminate in-process inventory, that is, to function with zero inventory in the buffers between operations. Pull production is also called **just-in-time (JIT) production** because it seeks to have every stage in a process produce and deliver materials downstream in the exact quantities and at the exact times requested.[2] Although it is possible with pull production to operate with very little in-process inventory, and certainly, for most companies, to greatly reduce the amount of in-process inventory necessary to function, it is not possible to produce just-in-time with no in-process inventory. Some inventory must be held in the buffers.

As an example why, refer back to Figure 8.2 and suppose that the production and delivery lead time for any size of order at any operation is 0.5 day. Consider first what happens if all the buffers are empty (no in-process inventory). When a customer order arrives, operation D has nothing to work on since buffer 4 is empty; thus, it must order material from operation C and wait for the order to be filled. Since buffer 3 is empty, operation C has nothing to work on either, so it must send an order back to operation B. Operation B has nothing to work on, since buffer 2 is empty, so it has to wait for operation A. Since there is no raw material in buffer 1, an order must be sent to the supplier, and operation A must wait. Even if all of this ordering happens instantaneously, since every one of the five stages of the process (four operations plus the supplier) takes 0.5 day, then the soonest the process can complete the order is 2.5 days after the order is received. Every operation must wait for the operations upstream to produce material so it has something to work on. All this waiting is not exactly what would be called just in time.

Now, if there were *some* stock in each buffer, then none of the operations would have to wait. Each could begin production as soon as it received an authorization. Every operation would be working, using material from its upstream buffer to produce material to replenish the downstream buffer. Of course, the ability for each operation to keep producing without running short depends on the amount of material in the buffer and the upstream operation's ability to replenish that buffer. These topics are covered later. The paradoxical point is that *to achieve stockless production, you must carry stock*.[3]

The following example is an illustration of the application of pull production in a plant that manufactures multiple kinds of products.

Example 1: Pull Production for Multiple Products

A product is manufactured in four different configurations: models W, X, Y, and Z. The production process for all of the products involves four workstations: stations 1, 2, and 3 make parts and subassemblies for the models; station 4 assembles the parts and subassemblies to produce finished products.

Figure 8.3 shows the product structure for the four products, the major subassemblies, and their parts. It also shows the following:

- Components A and C are subassemblies produced at workstation 2 from parts M, N, and O.
- Components B and D are molded parts made at workstation 3 from parts S, V, and T.
- Parts M, S, and V are produced at workstation 1 using raw material R.
- Parts N and O, and raw materials R and T are purchased from suppliers.

FIGURE 8.3

Product and parts structure diagram.

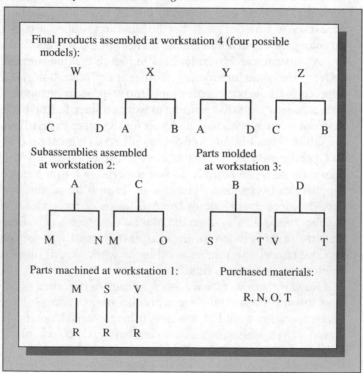

FIGURE 8.4

Layout of workstations and buffers.

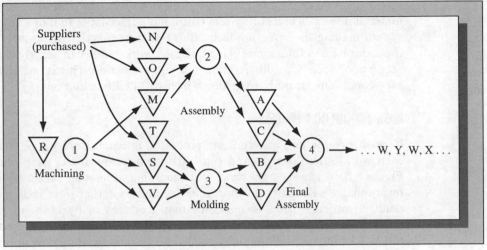

Figure 8.4 shows the locations of the workstations and inventory buffers between them (remember, some amount of material must be held in the buffers). When a process produces multiple kinds of products, the buffers must hold some of *every kind* of part needed for every product. Think of the buffer for each part as consisting of a small number of standard-sized containers of the part.

For simplicity, presume that the final workstation, station 4, has a schedule that specifies the quantity of each of the four products required. Unlike push production, which would have a schedule for every workstation, station 4 is the *only* station in the process with a schedule.

The system would work as follows. Suppose the final assembly schedule first specifies some quantity of model W. Workers at station 4 withdraw components from the buffers for components C and D as needed to complete the assemblies of model W. If the schedule next calls for a quantity of model X, workers will withdraw appropriate quantities of A and B from the buffers. When the buffers for any of the A, B, C, or D components reach a predetermined minimum level, then workstations 2 and 3 will begin to produce in prespecified quantities to replenish the buffers. To do this, of course, workstations 2 and 3 will withdraw materials from their own buffers, and when these reach predetermined levels, replenishment will begin for them, either from workstation 1 or from parts suppliers. The suppliers might be notified electronically that a buffer minimum is impending and replenishment is needed, or they might determine the need on their own from periodic inspections.

Smooth running of a pull system requires buffers between the stages, one for each kind of part used in production. Given that there can be innumerable parts, you might wonder how a pull system is any less costly or wasteful than a traditional batch-oriented push system. Part of the answer is in the overall quantities of inventory held in the buffers. If the buffer consists of standard-sized containers, the number of containers and their size are determined so that only the *minimum* necessary amount of material is held. The size and number of containers in the buffer are based upon production rates and setup times and are described later.

The point is, although pull production might require numerous buffers, each is tightly controled and kept at the minimal level necessary for the system to operate smoothly. As a result, even with all of these buffers, the overall in-process and raw material inventory in a pull system is still but a fraction of that in a comparable push system making the same products. Being able to function with only small buffers depends on many things, one being that each workstation can quickly change over and set up upon receiving authorization to begin production. This is one of several necessary conditions for pull production which will be discussed later.

PUSH PRODUCTION PROCESS

In **push production,** materials are processed in batches according to a schedule for each workstation, then moved (pushed) downstream to the next workstation (see Figure 8.5) where they are processed according to another schedule. The materials must usually wait until the workstation completes earlier jobs, changes over, and is ready to process them. In a factory that produces many kinds of products with different routing sequences and demand rates, the wait can be unpredictable. As a result, schedules are substantially padded to offset the waiting time uncertainty and to account for material shortages, machine breakdowns, and so on. This uncertainty and the consequential padding of schedules leads to long lead times, high variability in lead times, and large in-process inventories as the following example illustrates.

FIGURE 8.5

Typical push system.

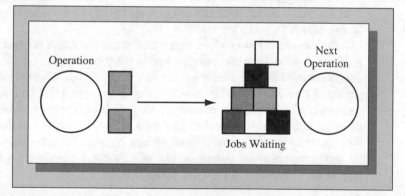

Example   2:   Push Production

Consider a push production system for making the four product models described earlier. Job orders are batch processed according to the production sequence in Figure 8.4, that is, they are processed starting at workstation 1, then moved to workstation 2 or 3 for the next operation, then to workstation 4 for final assembly. Given that each station processes several types of jobs, each job requires a workorder and schedule. Schedules for every job at every workstation are centrally prepared, possibly with a **material requirements planning** (MRP) system. (The MRP scheduling process is reviewed in the Appendix.)

The scheduling process starts with the desired completion date for each order of finished product, then works backward using production or delivery lead times to determine when each workstation (or supplier) should commence production (or delivery) of a part or component. Though processing times might be short, a few hours or less, schedules are usually prepared using daily or weekly time buckets because of the uncertainty about how long each job will wait at an operation before it is processed. The result is that jobs requiring only hours or minutes to process will be assigned, at minimum, a day or a week at each operation. Although computers now have the capability to schedule and update jobs daily or even hourly, the time it takes to get information from the shop floor into the computer is much longer than that, so scheduling has remained at the daily or weekly level for most companies. In fact, given that there is so much work waiting at every operation, companies often prefer to allow a 1-week minimum lead time on everything.

For an example of push scheduling, refer to Figure 8.6, which shows the product structure diagram for one of the products, model W. The figure also shows the workstations that perform the operations.

FIGURE 8.6

Product structure diagram and work sequence for model W.

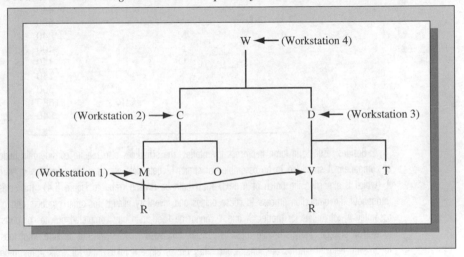

Suppose an order is received for a quantity of 400 units of model W to be shipped at the start of day 6, and suppose the nominal lead time for every operation and purchase is 1 day. The schedule will thus indicate that final assembly (workstation 4) will process the order on day 5 (a day before the ship date). Similarly, the schedule will show workstation 2 and workstation 3 working on the order on day 4, workstation 1 and the purchase of materials O and T on day 3, and the purchase of raw material R on day 2.

Suppose the orders for the other three models to be shipped on day 6 are as follows:

Model	Quantity
X	200
Y	200
Z	40

Work for models X, Y, and Z is scheduled by the same procedure, though with multiple products it is necessary to cross-check the schedules to ensure that every workstation has enough capacity to produce the parts, components, and final assemblies for all the products. (This procedure, **capacity requirements planning**, is described more fully in the Appendix.)

If the production system uses a **lot-for-lot** order policy, then the weekly gross requirement for parts and components will be as shown in Table 8.1. These quantities represent roughly the maximum inventory for each item in the system in a given week. Of course, the inventories will be diminished throughout the week as materials are processed into higher-level items and, eventually, into finished products. Still, the average weekly inventory will be about half of the amounts in Table 8.1.

Table 8.1

Component	Part	Material	Quantity
A			400
B			240
C			440
D			600
	M		840
	N		400
	O		440
	S		240
	V		600
		R	1680
		T	840

Besides resulting in large in-process inventories, the schedules also require considerable updating effort. If a batch of component A scheduled to be assembled at station 2 gets delayed, then the schedules at station 2 and at station 4 (which is expecting the batch of A next) must both be revised (refer to Figure 8.4). This revision will ripple throughout the production process to cause delays and inventory pileups for other products and other stages. Without assembly A, job orders for models X and Y cannot be filled, and any completed batches of parts B and D will have to wait in storage. Every schedule must be revised, otherwise workers will not be sure what jobs to do next or what to do with delayed batches of material once they arrive. Since it takes time for work-status information to get from the shop and into the schedules, by the time new schedules are released they might again be outdated. Thus, in using long lead times (daily or weekly time buckets) to pad the schedules, the schedules become somewhat insensitive to short-term (daily and hourly) changes.

PULL AND PUSH PRODUCTION CONTRASTED

In practice, some aspects of push systems and pull systems are identical or similar. Pike and Cohen examined **Kanban** (pronounced conbon), the card signaling system used at Toyota, which is considered the classic pull system and **MRP** (described in the Appendix), which is considered the classic push system. They found the following.[4]

· *Timing* (time when production or transfer of batches is signaled). This is the *only* aspect that is completely different for the two systems.

MRP systems specify order releases of production schedules using lead times and global information from the master schedule (global information is information that relies upon factorywide inputs and is processed through a central system).

In Kanban, an order release does not occur until the level of stock at the downstream buffer reaches a prespecified minimum. Thus, the actual withdrawal of material from the buffer eventually results in an authorization signal being sent upstream to produce a new batch.

· *Batch Size* (size of production batches and order shipments). Batch sizes in MRP systems are determined in advance by a central planning staff using lot-sizing rules and requirements from the master schedule. Batch-sizing decisions are based upon global information such as demand forecasts, available capacity, existing stock levels, job routings, and bills of materials.

Batch sizes in Kanban are determined at the shop-floor level according to the demand and replenishment requirements of downstream inventory buffers. However, the size of containers for carrying inventory and the number of containers (or kanban cards) are based on the schedule of the final operation, which is determined from global demand information—the same as in push systems.

· *Priorities* (basis for priority of orders when there are multiple orders for production and/or shipment). Schedules in MRP systems may incorporate priorities based on rules (e.g., earliest due date, shortest processing time, or first-come-first-serve). Often, however, final decisions about priorities are made on the shop floor depending on the status of work at each workstation. This is the same as in pull systems.

Workstation operators in Kanban use categories on a sequence board (described later) to determine job priority. The size of the categories, however, is determined a priori using global information. When multiple orders all fall in the same category, the supervisor at the upstream operation decides which gets priority, just as in push systems.

· *Interference* (procedure for handling unanticipated orders that require immediate attention). In MRP systems, decisions about unanticipated orders rest with upstream workstations, though ordinarily the schedule is frozen so that no new requests will be honored. Sometimes, however, the schedules are regenerated and priorities are reset, in which case the decisions are based upon plantwide information.

Kanban systems conform to daily quotas using somewhat-stable schedules for the final operation, although daily production at each workstation always depends on decisions about requirements at downstream workstations. When an emergency order arrives, however, it will be honored. Just like in push systems, some policy must be established a priori to determine how and where production capacity should be allocated when there are multiple, competing requests from downstream.

Given the similarities between the most common kinds of push and pull systems, it can be stated that, in reality, there are no *pure* pull or push production systems. Every production control system has elements of both push and pull, though some, like MRP, are more push-like, while others, like Kanban, are more pull-like. The remainder of this chapter focuses on systems that are more pull-like.

CONTAINERS AND CARDS

In a pull production process, often the same standard-sized containers are used throughout all or most of the process. In the process illustrated in Figure 8.4, all of the buffers might utilize the same-sized container to hold parts, components, and assemblies. To clearly distinguish the contents of containers, however, a card must be attached to each. The card provides information such as the kind of material in the container, the quantity of material, the origin or producer of the material (upstream source), and the consumer of the material (downstream destination). An example of containers and accompanying cards is shown in Figure 8.7.

Besides describing the contents of containers, the cards serve the purpose of restricting the amount of inventory in the system. In pull systems that use cards, every container of material must have an attached card. Without a card, no material can be put into a container. Once the minimal amount of material needed in the buffers to keep the system functioning has been determined, then the number of containers is also determined. One card is created for each container. Thereafter, no container in the system can be filled or moved unless it has a card. By restricting the number of containers in the system to the prespecified number of cards, the quantity of in-process inventory in the system never exceeds a predetermined maximum.

Another, related, purpose of the cards is authorization. When materials in a container are first withdrawn at a downstream operation, the operation posts the card as a signal to replenish the container. The posted card authorizes the upstream operation to produce (or procure) a container of material and move it downstream to replenish the buffer.

The best known card signaling system is **Kanban.** Kanban is the Japanese word equivalent for "card" or "visual record." In the Kanban system, a card signals the need

FIGURE 8.7

Standard containers of material with accompanying cards.

for and subsequent authorization to produce and move a container of materials, parts, or subassemblies. The number of kanban cards corresponds to the number of containers in each buffer. In the following discussion, Kanban (with an uppercased K) refers to the Kanban system of pull production, while kanban (with a lowercased k) refers to the card.

RULES FOR PULL PRODUCTION

Successful functioning of the card-based pull system requires understanding and conformance to certain rules. Table 8.2 lists the rules of Kanban pull production systems.[5]

The first rule specifies how, when, and in what order materials are moved between stages of the process. Each stage withdraws only the materials it needs from previous stages. The quantity of parts withdrawn is determined by the number of kanbans (and containers) in circulation.

The second rule specifies the amount and priority in which items are produced. People at each stage produce only enough to meet the demand requirements of downstream processes. The quantity and sequence of production are determined by the number of cards. When multiple kinds of material are requested, they are produced in the order in which the demand occurs (i.e., order in which containers are emptied or cards are sent upstream).

The third rule prevents the overproduction or the movement of items not required.

The fourth rule encourages cooperation and defect prevention. A defective item discovered downstream is never used but is returned upstream, where it is analyzed and the defect source is identified. Defects are corrected and replaced on the day they occur.

The fifth rule mandates a level rate of production. This eliminates the need for each operation to be capable of operating at the high-end of its capacity, which is what

---

TABLE 8.2   Rules of Pull Production*

1. Downstream operations withdraw only the quantity of items they need from upstream operations. The quantity is controlled by the number of cards.

2. Each operation produces items in the quantity and sequence indicated by the cards.

3. A card must always be attached to a container. No withdrawal or production is permitted without a kanban.

4. Only nondefective items are sent downstream. Defective items are withheld and the process is stopped until the source of defect is remedied.

5. The production process is smoothed to achieve level production. Small demand variations are accommodated in the system by adjusting the number of cards.

6. The number of cards is gradually reduced to decrease WIP and expose areas that are wasteful and in need of improvement.

---

* The term "card" in the following assumes cards are used in conjunction with containers; when cards are not used, the rules apply to the containers themselves.

happens when demand vacillates. The greater the potential vacillation, the more excess capacity that must be available. The final stage of the process is the only one that has a daily schedule, and all operations elsewhere in the process respond to that schedule using only cards. When demand level changes, the daily schedule is adjusted, but adjustments are kept small so the impact on upstream processes will be manageable.

The sixth rule is based on the premise that inventory hides problems, and that progressively reducing the number of kanbans reduces inventory and enables more problems to be exposed and resolved. Reducing the number of cards is a mechanism for continuous improvement.

These are *rules,* not recommendations. For successful pull production they must be observed. According to Taiichi Ohno, attempting pull production without obeying the rules "will bring neither the control expected . . . nor the cost reduction . . . [A] half-hearted introduction of Kanban brings a hundred harms and not a single gain."[6] He should know; he devoted over 2 decades to perfecting Kanban at Toyota.

PROCESS IMPROVEMENT

In pull production, continuous improvement is enacted by continuously reducing buffer sizes—the point of rule number 6 in Table 8.2. By reducing the number of kanbans, buffers are reduced, and problems with the production system are exposed. To enable the production system to function with ever-fewer kanbans, management has to face up to and resolve the problems exposed by less inventory.

Suppose the buffer between two operations consists of eight containers with 10 units each, or a total of 80 units. Now, slowly reduce the number of containers until shortages begin to occur. Suppose that with seven containers the process works fine, but with six the buffer occasionally runs out and downstream operations have to wait. The buffer level would then be set at seven containers, and an analysis would be done to determine reasons for the shortages when there are only six containers. Suppose the main reason is that setup time at the upstream operation takes too long. Suppose the setup time is shortened, and with that it is then possible to reduce the size of the production batch from 10 units to 9. Further, suppose that when the standard quantity per container is also reduced to nine units, no shortages occur. Thus, the new buffer size will be 63 units (seven containers, nine units each). The next step is to try to further reduce the buffer size, look for more problems, solve them, and so on.

Some organizations establish a pull production system, then afterward never try to reduce the size of the buffers. The managers are ecstatic because they got the pull system to "work," and because it resulted in, say, 50% reduction in inventory. Of course, 50% of a large quantity is still a large quantity, so the organization still retains much more inventory than necessary, not to mention the problems that inventory covers up and which never get resolved. Aside from permitting managers to boast that they have implemented pull production, a pull production system wherein the buffers are never reduced misses one of the major opportunities offered by pull production: the opportunity to expose sources of waste and eliminate them.

NECESSARY CONDITIONS FOR PULL PRODUCTION SYSTEMS

Pull production systems are demanding in terms of requisite conditions. Among the conditions that should exist *before* a pull production process is instituted are the following:

1. More **planning and control responsibility** must reside in the hands of shop supervisors and worker teams (and less of it in the hands of centralized staff).

2. Production emphasis must switch from producing for producing's sake to **producing to meet demand** (no overproduction).

3. Throughout the process, the motivation everywhere must be to **reduce in-process inventories** and remove unnecessary stock.

4. Equipment **preventive maintenance** efforts must be ongoing and geared to eliminate breakdowns, since breakdowns will halt an operation (and, soon after, the entire process). Ample time must be scheduled to allow for PM.

5. **Quality assurance** efforts must be aimed at preventing defects from happening. Since pull systems carry minimal buffers and allow no defective items to proceed through the process, defects and quality problems will halt production flow. Process capability studies, SPC, source inspection, pokayoke, and worker inspection and feedback, topics of Part III, must be built into the production process.

6. **Setup times** must be **small,** otherwise operations that produce a variety of outputs will require too much time for changeovers and not have enough time for production. Every operation in pull production must be capable of responding quickly to orders from downstream, and of economically producing in small batches.

7. Plant layout must facilitate **linking** of all **operations** into the process. Even autonomous workstations or cells must be imagined as elements of a linked, synchronized system. For smooth material flow between operations, every operation must have roughly the same capacity and be capable of producing at the rate dictated by the final stage of the process.

8. **Production plans and schedules must be somewhat uniform.** Large variations and seasonal patterns that can be anticipated are leveled in advance to minimize the impact on upstream processes. This is necessary since a Kanban system with a given number of cards can effectively deal with demand variations in the range of only plus or minus 10%. The leveling process is described in Chapter 16.

9. The training, job descriptions, and compensation of workers must be geared toward **developing cooperative work attitudes** and **teamwork** since much of the planning and control decision making in pull production is done by worker teams on the shop floor. Management's role regarding workers is important too; managers must provide workers with the opportunity to develop and expand their skills and utilize their capabilities, and they must show workers respect and recognition for their ability as problem solvers.

From this list it should be obvious that pull production will be a long time in coming for some organizations, and will never come for others. Many organizations have begun to turn the corner in terms of attitudes about worker involvement and product quality, and that is an important start. Some of the conditions listed above can be achieved incrementally and require changes in policy rather than big capital investments (e.g., reducing inventories and moving from repair to preventive maintenance). Others, however, are more difficult to meet. Engineering studies and projects for reducing setup times, preventing breakdowns, and rearranging facilities as well as training programs to give workers skills in equipment setup, basic maintenance, inspection and quality, and scheduling and control are all costly and time-consuming. Management must understand, however, that these costs are short-term and justifiable given the long-term benefits of reduced inventory and improved flexibility, responsiveness, and quality.

It should be noted that nothing in the above conditions pertains exclusively to pull production. Efforts toward achieving these conditions in any kind of production system will have the same result: improvement! Even in traditional job shops and push production systems, efforts to improve quality control, reduce setup times, enhance preventive maintenance, and improve worker skills can only make the system better. It can be argued that by initiating these efforts, even if pull production fails, an organization will be better off than before it started.

HOW TO ACHIEVE PULL PRODUCTION

Several questions need to be answered in setting up a pull production system: (1) When and how should authorization signals for replenishment of buffers be sent upstream? (2) What size should the buffers be? and (3) How should operators keep track of what they are supposed to do? The last question arises whenever an operation produces multiple kinds of items, or when it is located in a place where the operators cannot see the buffers they are supposed to replenish (analogous to mom having to decide when to replenish milk without being able to look in the refrigerator first). These questions can be answered in different ways; we will consider several, taking them in order of increasing complexity.

PULL SYSTEM AS A FIXED-QUANTITY/REORDER-POINT SYSTEM

The pull system is, in effect, a variant of the simple reorder-point system where a replenishment order is placed whenever inventory falls to a critical level. This level, the **reorder point** (ROP), is based upon the estimated amount of material used between the time when an order is placed and when the replenishment batch is received. The formula for ROP is

$$ROP = D(LT) + SS,$$

where

D = demand (consumption rate),
LT = lead time (elapsed time between order and replenishment),
SS = safety stock.

Safety stock, discussed in Chapter 5, is a small amount of stock to buffer the variability in D and LT. The greater the variability in D or LT, the larger the SS. When D and

LT are relatively constant, SS can be zero. We will start with the assumption that LT and D between any two stages of a production process are relatively constant.

An application of the reorder–point system is the **two-bin** system. Material is held in two bins—one large, one small. The capacity of the small bin is the specified ROP quantity. To satisfy demand, material is withdrawn from the large bin first. When the stock level in the large bin reaches the bottom, a requisition is sent ordering more material. Meanwhile, material is withdrawn from the small bin to satisfy demand. At just about the time when the small bin runs out, the replenishment arrives with enough material to fill both the large and small bins. The process repeats.

In a pull production system, the LT is the total time required to replenish a buffer. Usually LT is separated into two categories, **production time** (P) and **conveyance time** (C), that is, $LT = P + C$. P is the total time to produce the quantity ordered, including the setup time, processing time, and any planned waiting time. C is the time to convey the order to the upstream operation that will fill it, plus the time to move the materials to the downstream operation that initiated the order.

Suppose demand for an item is 105 units per week; given a 5-day week, demand is 21 units per day. If production time is 0.1 day and conveyance time is 0.4 day, then

$$ROP = 21(0.1 + 0.4) = 10.5 \text{ units; rounding up, } ROP = 11 \text{ units.}$$

This says that whenever the inventory level in the buffer drops to 11 units, an order should be placed. In a two-bin system, the small bin would hold 11 units.

Containers in a Buffer

Common practice in pull production is to use **standard-sized containers** for holding and moving parts. The answer for when to order still uses ROP, but the ROP is expressed as the number of containers instead of number of units. Suppose Q represents the capacity of a standard container, then the ROP as expressed in terms of the number of containers, K, is

$$K = \frac{D(P+C)}{Q}.$$

The term K represents the maximum number of *completely* full containers in a buffer. As soon as even one unit is withdrawn from one of these containers, an order for replenishment is sent upstream.

As mentioned, pull systems often use **cards,** and in that case K refers to the number of cards. (If you like, think of K as representing the number of kanban cards.) Given that usually there is one card for each full container, it does not matter whether K represents the number of cards or containers. The manner in which these cards are used to authorize production and/or the movement of materials is discussed later.

Fixed-Quantity Order Rule

As a rule, the container size Q is also the size of the **order quantity,** or the quantity to be replenished with each order. If Q is fixed, then the order quantity for each replenishment is also fixed. According to the order rule, every time one container is emptied and another is accessed, an order must be placed upstream to refill the empty container. A simple way to place the order is to send the empty container and its card upstream to the operation that will refill it.

Container Size

In pull production the size of buffers is kept small by using containers that are small. Another reason for small containers it that they are easy to move and materials inside them are easy to access. This keeps material handling costs as well as time and motion wasted from picking and placing parts to a minimum. (Small containers require shorter reach to access parts inside, and they can be placed on tilted stands to further improve access.) Smaller containers take up less space, which means more room in aisles, closer location to workstations, and shorter assembly lines (the length of a line is often set by the length of the row of containers of parts needed to supply the line). The range of varisized containers is also kept to a minimum, usually between three and nine for an entire plant.

A rule of thumb is that a container should have the capacity to hold about *10% of the daily demand* for the material it holds. Using the previous example, if $D = 21$ units/day, then $Q = 0.10(21) = 2.1$ units. Allowing for upward fluctuations in demand, we would specify that a container hold a quantity of 3 units.

Example   3:   Simple Pull System

To put all this together, let $P = 0.1$ days, $D = 21$ units, $Q = 3$ units, and $C = 0$ (assume the buffer rests snugly between two close workstations, and move time is zero); then,

$$K = \frac{21(0.1)}{3} = 0.7 \text{ kanban, rounding up, } K = 1 \text{ kanban.}$$

Therefore, the buffer should hold *one full* container. In practice, we need at least two containers between workstations, one initially empty, the second initially full. The upstream station puts new stock into the one while the downstream station withdraws old stock from the other. In this simple two-container system, one container is ideally fully replenished just as the other is fully depleted. Because of the necessity to round up in the computation of K (in this example, but in most cases as well) to get an integer (here, from 0.7 to 1), the one container will be fully replenished at some time *before* the other is fully depleted. In the meantime, before the other is depleted, there will be two containers having some material in them.

Next consider the case where containers must be moved between operations for replenishment (i.e., $C > 0$). In that case, workers at either the downstream or upstream operation can be given responsibility to move the containers. For instance, in the example in Figure 8.4, whenever one container is emptied in the buffer for material D, an operator from workstation 4 would take it to workstation 3. As soon as workstation 3 fills the container, an operator from there takes it back to the D buffer at workstation 4. Another way is to have material handlers, workers whose sole responsibility is to monitor the buffers and transfer containers back and forth throughout the plant.

Suppose the producer and the consumer workstations cannot be located right next to each other, or suppose that inventory buffers cannot be located right next to workstations. For example, a buffer that holds a part used by several workstations might be located in a place central to all of them, yet not be close to any of them. The time it takes to transmit replenishment orders between workstations, or to move the materials between workstations and buffers, then becomes an important matter. Additionally, suppose each buffer holds several kinds of materials, in which case some method is needed to keep track of which materials require replenishment, and which materials get priority. Such situations are common, as described next.

Outbound and Inbound Buffers

Workstation 1 shown in Figure 8.4 makes parts M, S, and V, which are used by workstations 2 and 3. Suppose the three workstations are situated some distance apart, so it is not possible to put the buffers between them in a location that is close to all of them. In such a case it would be necessary to have *two kinds* of buffers for each part, an **outbound** buffer and an **inbound** buffer. This is shown in Figure 8.8, where the outbound buffer (or outbound stock point) holds the output material of workstation 1 (the producer station), and the inbound buffer (or inbound stock point) holds the input materials for workstation 2 and 3 (the customer stations).

Both outbound and inbound buffers consist of one or more containers for each kind of part. In Figure 8.8, workstations 2 and 3 *withdraw* parts from containers in their respective *inbound* buffers, while workstation 1 *deposits* parts into containers in its *outbound* buffers. Whenever workstations 2 and 3 need more parts, full containers are withdrawn from the outbound buffers at workstation 1.

Now, to ensure there are enough containers of the different parts in the outbound buffer of workstation 1 to meet demand at workstations 2 and 3, and to ensure the production process proceeds smoothly, some form of communication mechanism is needed to **signal** to workstation 1 when to (1) *move* a full container downstream and (2) *produce* items to fill another container. Also, in case multiple move or produce signals are sent upstream at once, a scheme is needed to tell operators and material

FIGURE 8.8

Outbound and inbound buffers.

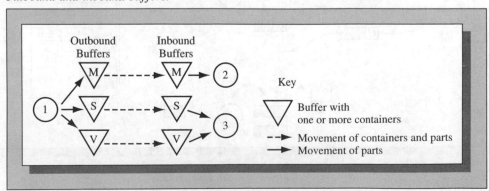

handlers at workstation 1 which to attend to first. A simple way to do all this is to use kanban cards. The following sections discuss three different kinds of kanban cards.

CONVEYANCE KANBANS[7]

A **conveyance kanban** or **C-kanban** (also termed a *move* or *withdrawal* kanban) is an authorization to *move* a container from an upstream, outbound buffer to a downstream, inbound buffer. No container can be withdrawn from an outbound buffer unless a C-kanban has been issued. The conveyance process as illustrated in Figure 8.9 works as follows:

Step 1. When operators at station 2 first access a full container, they take the C-kanban from it and place it in a *kanban mailbox*. (The mailbox is the place where cards are kept or posted, as shown in Figure 8.10.) The C-kanban specifies the kind of material needed and the upstream station from which to get it.

Step 2. A material handler reads the C-kanban and takes it to the specified upstream station (here, station 1).

Step 3. The material handler affixes the C-kanban to a full container (located at the outbound buffer of station 1), then takes the container back to station 2.

FIGURE 8.9

Single-card Kanban system using only C-kanbans (example of card shown on right).

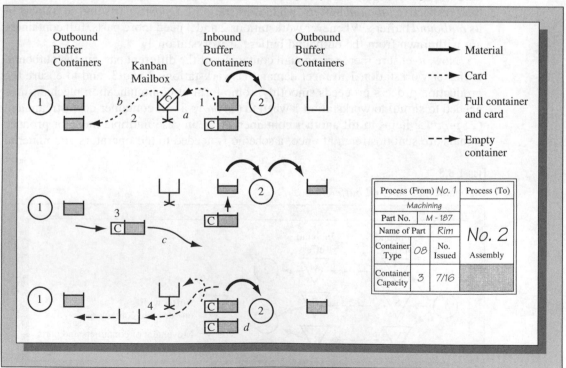

Step 4. Whenever station 2 empties a container, the material handler takes the container upstream to station 1. (Often steps 2 and 4 are combined so that the material handler takes the card and empty container in a single trip.) The process then repeats.

The example in Figure 8.9 is called a **single-card Kanban system** because it uses only one kind of kanban, the C-kanban. Upstream workstations (e.g., station 1) produce according to an order list or a daily schedule, possibly one generated by an MRP system using an expected daily demand rate. To prevent buildup of outbound stock in the event of downstream interruptions, production is limited to a prespecified number of full outbound containers.

A downstream workstation (station 2) can accumulate no more material in its inbound buffer than it has immediate need for because containers of material cannot be moved to it without a C-kanban. Therefore, the maximum number of full containers at the inbound buffer corresponds exactly to the number of C-kanbans. Recall the formula for the number of containers between two processes:

$$K = \frac{D(P + C)}{Q}.$$

To determine the number of C-kanbans, K_C, focus only on C, and ignore P. Thus,

$$K_C = \frac{D(C)}{Q},$$

where C is the total time between when workers remove a C-kanban from a full container at the inbound buffer and when they remove a C-kanban from the *next* full

FIGURE 8.10

Kanban mailbox and posted cards.

container. The time, called the **conveyance cycle time,** is the sum of the times shown by the lowercased letters in Figure 8.9. Specifically this is the time that the C-kanban

a = waits in the mailbox,

b = moves to the upstream station,

c = moves back to the downstream station (in Figure 8.9, with a full container),

d = waits in the downstream buffer until the container is accessed and the kanban is put back in the mailbox.

Example   4:   C-kanban Computation

Suppose $D = 21$ units/day, $Q = 3$ units, and, in minutes, $a = 32$, $b = 52$, $c = 60$, $d = 48$, and 1 day $= 480$ minutes. Then,

$$C = (32 + 52 + 60 + 48)/480 = 0.4 \text{ day}$$

so

$$K_c = \frac{21(0.4)}{3} = 2.8 \text{ C-kanbans; rounding up, } K_c = 3 \text{ C-kanbans.}$$

Thus, the inbound buffer of workstation 2 will at most consist of three full standard containers.

PRODUCTION KANBANS

Besides the C-kanban, another principal kind of kanban is the **production kanban,** or **P-kanban,** which is used to authorize production of parts or assemblies. In a system that utilizes this kind of card, *no* production is allowed without it. Except at the final station in the process, there are no production schedules, just P-kanban authorizations. A system that uses both C-kanbans and P-kanbans is called a **two-card** pull system. As shown in Figure 8.11 this system works as follows:

Step 1. When operators at station 2 access a full container, they remove the C-kanban and place it in the *C-kanban mailbox*. The C-kanban specifies the material needed and the upstream station that produces it.

Step 2. A material handler takes the C-kanban *and* an empty container to the specified upstream location (in the figure, station 1).

Step 3. The material handler removes the P-kanban from a full container at station 1, puts it in the *P-kanban mailbox*, then affixes the C-kanban to that container.

Step 4. The material handler leaves the empty container at station 1 and takes the full container downstream to station 2.

Step 5. The P-kanban in the mailbox authorizes station 1 to produce enough material to fill an empty container. An operator removes the P-kanban from the mailbox and affixes it to an empty container.

Step 6. Station 1 produces just enough material to fill the empty container.

FIGURE 8.11

Two-card kanban system (P-kanban example shown on right).

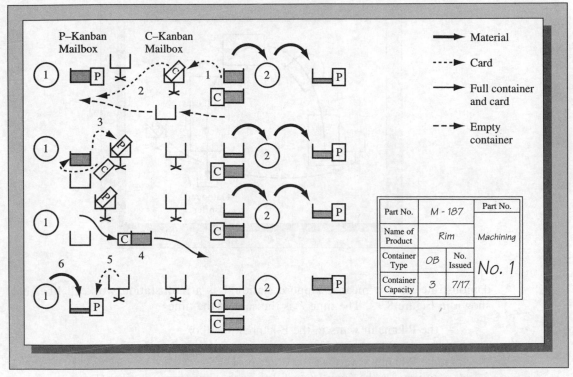

(Meanwhile, the same procedure happens at station 2, that is, production will not begin until a P-card is posted in its own P-kanban mailbox. When a card is posted, station 2 then begins producing, which requires that it access a full inbound container. The C-kanban from that container is posted, and the process repeats.)

The two-card system gives tight control over buffer inventories. No container can be *moved* or *filled* unless there is a C-kanban or P-kanban, respectively, authorizing it. Since standard-sized containers are used everywhere in the buffer, the size of both the transfer and the production batch is the container capacity, Q.

Just as the number of C-kanbans specifies the maximum number of full containers at an inbound buffer, the number of P-kanbans specifies the maximum number of full containers at an *outbound* buffer. The number of P-kanbans is

$$K_P = \frac{D(P)}{Q},$$

where P is the total time elapsed from when workers or material handlers remove the P-kanban from a full container and post it at the outbound buffer until the time they remove the P-kanban from the *next* full container. P is the **production cycle time.** To

FIGURE 8.12

Time elements in computing P.

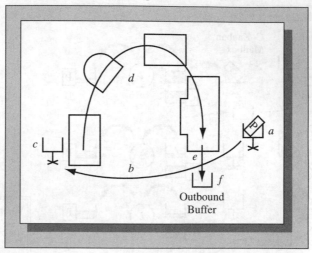

demonstrate what it means, suppose station 1 is a multistation workcell like that shown in Figure 8.12. The time P is the sum of the times

a = the P-kanban waits in the P-kanban mailbox,
b = for the P-kanban to be moved to the order post at the first station,
c = the P-kanban waits at the order post
d = to process the quantity to fill the container (= setup time + run time + in-process waiting time),
e = to move the full container to the outbound buffer,
f = the container waits in the buffer.

Often there is no separate order post, so times b and c are zero.

Example   5:   P-kanban Computation

Suppose D = 21 units/day, Q = 3 units, and, in minutes, a = 15, b = 0.5, c = 0.5, d = (setup = 6, run = 3/unit, in-process wait = 0), e = 0, f = 17, and 1 day = 480 minutes.

Thus, $P = [15 + 0.5 + 0.5 + (6 + 3(3) + 0) + 0 + 17]/480 = 0.1$ day, so

$$K_P = \frac{21(0.1)}{3} = 0.7 \text{ P-kanban; rounding up, } K_P = 1 \text{ P-kanban.}$$

Thus, there will be at most one full standard container of this material at the outbound buffer.

Combining this result with the result of the previous example yields $K = K_P + K_C = 4$ kanbans for the outbound and inbound buffers separating stations 1 and 2. Technically, this stage of the process should be able to operate with four full containers of materials (and one empty container).

Safety Factor

It is common in determining K to include a **safety factor,** X, to account for minor fluctuations in demand. The more leveled the demand, the less the need for a safety factor, though some margin should be included to cover minor glitches and break-downs in the system. The safety factor results in the earlier-mentioned safety stock being added to the buffer. The more problems there are in the system, that is, the more factors contributing to fluctuations in supply and demand between workstations, the larger X has to be to offset them. To explicitly account for X, the K formula is modified:

$$K = \frac{D(LT)(1 + X)}{Q},$$

where

LT is P, C, or the sum, $P + C$.

Given that the value for K is frequently rounded up to arrive at an integer value, the safety factor is often accounted for even when X is *not* included in the original computation. In a previous numerical example, K_C was computed as 2.8. Though a safety factor was not initially included, when the number was rounded up to 3, a factor of $(3 - 2.8)/2.8$, or 7.1% was built in. If managers think this margin is too small, the number of containers can be increased to four. For K_P the computed value was 0.7. When rounded up to 1.0, this gives a factor of $(1 - 0.7)/0.7 = 43\%$. The rule of thumb is to start with a safety factor of about 10%, then try to decrease it to whatever practical experience shows is most workable.

SINGLE-CARD SYSTEM, NO. 2

If workstations are located closely adjacent with a buffer stock between them, then only one card, a P-card, is needed. Since the move time is almost zero, C-kanbans are not necessary. When the station downstream accesses a container in the stock area, it posts a P-kanban from the container, which authorizes the upstream station to fill another container with the item on the card.

Even when workstations in a process are not adjacent, it is still possible to use a single, P-card system. Imagine a rack of shelves that holds a large number of different components used by two workstations that each assembles a different product. Suppose all the components on the shelves are produced by four upstream operations. Each of the two assembly areas withdraws the type and quantity of components it needs to make products according to a daily production schedule. The components are boxed, and inside each box is a card. Whenever an assembler accesses a new box of components, he posts the card in a nearby mailbox. Someone stops by frequently, removes all the cards from the mailbox, sorts them by upstream operation, then puts them into the mailbox by each of the four upstream operations. Each card is a P-kanban, an authorization for the operation to produce another box of the specified component.

SIGNAL KANBAN[8]

A signal kanban is a special kind of production kanban. There are actually two kinds of signal kanbans. The first, an **SP-kanban** or **production signal kanban,** is for ordering production of larger batches, or quantities in excess of one container. Large-batch production is necessary when the changeover time between products is time-consuming enough so as to restrict the number of daily production runs to a relative few. This is the case for processes such as punch pressing, die casting, forging, and injection molding.

Whereas a P-kanban restricts the batch size to the capacity of a container (Q), with an SP-kanban the batch size can be any *multiple number of containers*. Using an SP-kanban is like collecting several P-kanbans before starting production. If, for example, a process involves a batch size of 12 units and the container size is 3 units, then four P-kanbans would have to be accumulated before starting; for the same case, only one SP-kanban is needed.

The other kind of signal kanban is an **SM-kanban** or **material signal kanban.** It is like a C-kanban in that it is used to authorize movement of materials, except the SM-kanban is used *in conjunction* with an SP-kanban to authorize the transfer of materials needed to produce the batch authorized by the SP-kanban.

Use of signal kanbans is predicated on the requirement that batch sizes exceed one container. In general, the minimal batch size, B, for an item is determined by the maximum number of times a process can be switched over; that, in turn, is a function of **total** (**internal** + **external**) **setup time**[9] and the number of different items to be produced.

Suppose workstation 3 is a molding machine that requires a total time of 2 hours for each changeover. Also suppose the machine must produce two different kinds of parts each day. Assuming an 8-hour workday,

$$Maximum\ Number\ of\ Setups = \frac{8\ hrs/day}{2\ hrs/setup} = 4\ setups/day.$$

If two kinds of parts must be produced each day, then for each part the maximum number of setups per day is

$$S = \frac{4\ setups/day}{2\ parts} = 2\ setups.$$

Assume that demand for just one of the parts is 30 units per day. Thus, the minimum batch size for this part must be

$$B = \frac{D}{S} = \frac{30\ units/day}{2\ setups/day} = 15\ units.$$

To allow for a 10% minimum safety factor, increase this to 17. Now, the batch size must be expressed in terms of the container size, Q, and if $Q = 3$ units, then B, rounded up, must be 18 units, which is six containers. Thus a batch size of six containers should be produced whenever production is authorized using an SP-kanban.

FIGURE 8.13

Signal kanbans and their locations.

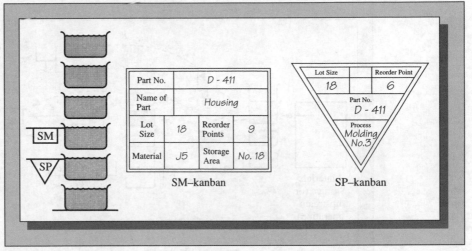

To show how SP- and SM-kanbans are used, imagine a buffer where full containers are stacked one atop another. For each kind of item there is a stack, and for each stack there are one SM-kanban and one SP-kanban. These are attached to containers as shown in Figure 8.13. As containers are withdrawn from the buffer, the stack gets smaller. When the level of the stack reaches the container with the SM-kanban, that kanban is sent to the indicated upstream location (operation or parts storage) as authorization to withdraw and move materials. When the level of the stack is further depleted to the container with the SP-kanban, that kanban is posted to authorize production. The materials authorized by the SM-kanban will arrive at just about the time they will be needed for production.

The whole process must be synchronized, and for that to happen the SM- and SP-kanbans must be located at the right locations in the stack. These locations are determined using variants of the familiar formula

$$K = \frac{D(LT)}{Q},$$

except that here K represents the level of full containers in the stack at which the SM- and SP-kanbans will be located.

Consider first the SP-kanban. Its position in the stack is that level where enough containers remain to satisfy demand for the item while a batch of additional items is produced and transferred to the buffer. This, the number of full containers in the stack where the card is located, is

$$K_{SP} = \frac{D(P)}{Q},$$

FIGURE 8.14

Example of SP- and SM-kanbans.

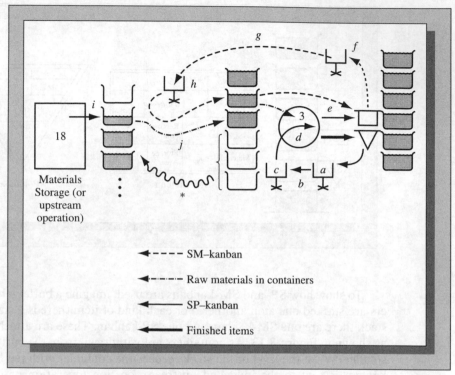

where D is the consumption rate, Q is the container size, and P is the time between when the batch is ordered and when it is received at the buffer. The time P, here being the **SP cycle time** (refer to Figure 8.14), is the sum of the times

a = the SP-kanban waits in the mailbox,
b = for the SP-kanban to be moved to the order post prior to the first operation,
c = for the SP-kanban to wait at the order post,
d = to process the specified batch quantity (setup time + run time + in-process waiting time),
e = to move the batch of full containers, along with the SP- and SM-kanbans, to the outbound buffer.

(Note: times for f through j are explained in the next section.) When there is no separate order post, times b and c are zero.

Example   6:   Computation of SP-kanbans

Suppose D = 30 units/day, Q = 3 units, and, in minutes, a = 15, b = 0.5, c = 0.5, d = (setup = 16, run = 2 per unit, in-process wait = 2), e = 5, and 1 day = 480.

From above, assume the batch size is 18 units; then, the SP-kanban cycle time is

$$P = 15 + 0.5 + 0.5 + (16 + 18(2) + 2) + 5 = 75 \text{ min.}/480$$

$$= 0.15625 \text{ day.}$$

Therefore,

$$K_{SP} = \frac{30(0.15625)}{3} = 1.5625 \text{ containers.}$$

Since the position of the SP-kanban must be an integer, round up to 2 containers; this rounding affords a safety margin of 0.4375/1.5625, or 28%.

In summary, when the buffer level reaches two full containers, a production order for a new batch (six containers) will be placed in the kanban mailbox.

Next, determine the location of the SM-kanban in the stack using

$$K_{SM} = \frac{D(C - P')}{Q} + K_{SP},$$

where D and Q are the same as before, C is the total time between when materials are first ordered and when they arrive for usage, and P' is the time between when production is first ordered and when setup begins. Setup here refers to *internal* setup tasks only (that portion of the changeover procedure that must be performed when the machine or process is stopped). If the internal setup procedure requires adjustments through trial and error, then material must be delivered in time for the adjustment procedure.

The time P' is the sum of the first three time elements in the **SP cycle time,** described above. In Figure 8.14 it is the sum of the time that the SP-kanban

a = waits in the mailbox,
b = moves to the order post prior to the first operation,
c = waits at the order post.

If there is no separate order post, times b and c are zero.

The time C is called the **SM cycle time.** From Figure 8.14, it is the sum of the times

f = the SM-kanban waits in the mailbox,
g = for the SM-kanban to be moved upstream (to parts storage or previous operation),
h = for the SM-kanban to wait at the order post,
i = to fill the order (withdraw or produce parts),
j = to convey filled containers to the place of usage.
$*$ = Empty containers are taken back upstream on the return trip. The time for this is irrelevant.

If $(C - P')$ has a negative value, round to the lowest negative integer (e.g., -0.4 becomes -1).

Example   7:   Computation of SM-kanbans

Suppose $D = 30$ units/day, $Q = 3$ units, and, in minutes, $a = 15$, $b = 0.5$, $c = 0.5$, $f = 6$, $g = 10$, $h = 1$, $i = 15$, $j = 10$, and 1 day $= 480$. Thus,

$$C - P' = (6 + 10 + 1 + 15 + 10) - (15 + 0.5 + 0.5) = 26 \text{ min.}/480$$
$$= 0.0542 \text{ day.}$$

From before, $K_{SP} = 2$ containers, so

$$K_{SM} = \frac{30(0.0542)}{3} + 2 = 2.542 \text{ containers; rounding up, } K_{SM} = 3 \text{ containers.}$$

Summarizing, the signal system in this and the previous example works as follows: authorize materials transfer when only three full containers remain; then authorize production when only two full containers remain; each time, authorize enough material transfer and production to make 18 units (six containers).

These are the basics of Kanban pull production. To illustrate how different cards and containers move through the system, all the kinds of cards discussed in this section using the original example in Figure 8.4 are illustrated in Figure 8.15. With the exception of the last operation, station 4, which operates according to a schedule that specifies the products to be assembled and their sequence, the production and movement of material everywhere in the system is dictated by cards. Creating the final assembly schedule is covered in Chapter 16.

Another important kind of kanban card that has not been discussed is the **supplier kanban.** If suppliers of the raw materials and parts in Figure 8.15 are **just-in-time suppliers,** then the card system can be extended to them using supplier kanbans, or **S-kanbans,** cards which link buffers of raw materials and parts to external suppliers (the *S* loops in Figure 8.15). S-kanbans are discussed in Chapter 19.

One other place in the process where the pull concept can be applied is to link the organization to its customers. If the organization represented in Figure 8.15 is itself a just-in-time supplier, then the finished products storage (on the lower right) can itself be considered an outbound buffer, with replenishment dictated by authorizations (kanbans) coming from customers. This concept is also discussed in Chapter 19.

Whether or not a pull-producer is a just-in-time supplier, its final assembly operation must operate to keep pace with demand. Pull systems work best when demand is fairly uniform; they are somewhat limited in ability to adjust to large, short-term fluctuations in demand. As a result, pull system producers must carry some amount of finished goods inventory to absorb demand fluctuations. These and other matters about accommodating pull systems to demand are discussed later in this chapter, and in Chapter 16.

CONWIP METHOD OF PULL PRODUCTION

An interesting pull production variant is CONWIP, which stands for *con*stant *work in p*rocess. The CONWIP procedure is illustrated in the production process in

FIGURE 8.15

Kanban cards, routes, and buffers.

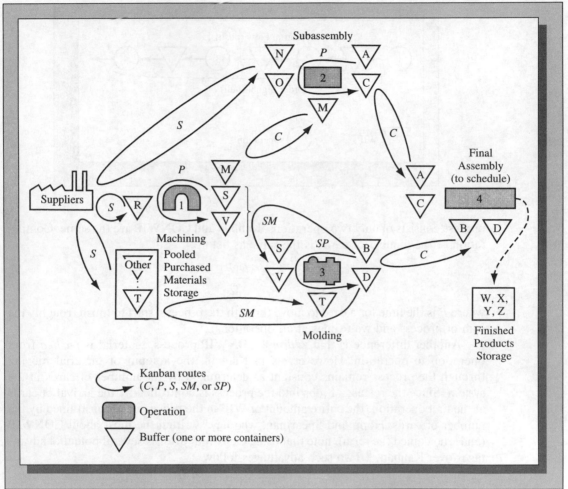

Figure 8.16. In the entire process, the only place that sends an order signal is the last operation, and the only place that receives an order signal is the first operation. With each job completing the process at operation 4, a kanban card is sent back to the start of the process at operation 1 as authorization to release a new job into the process. The similarity between CONWIP and Kanban is, obviously, the use of cards to authorize production. In other ways, however, CONWIP and Kanban are somewhat different, the biggest way being that authorization cards in CONWIP move only from the last operation back to the first operation, whereas in Kanban they move between each and every successive pair of operations (compare Figures 8.2 and 8.16). If the entire

FIGURE 8.16

CONWIP production process.

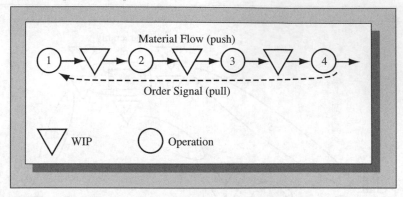

process consists of only two operations, Kanban and CONWIP are the same. Computation of the number of cards is the same as before:

$$K = \frac{D(P)}{Q},$$

where P is the time for a card to move through the process, start to finish (roughly the sum of process and wait times at all operations).

Another difference is that *within* a CONWIP process, material is *pushed* from operation to operation. However, as in Kanban, the amount of material moving through the process remains constant as determined by the number of cards in the system. Since the release of jobs into the process is controlled by the arrival of cards at the first operation, the entire amount of WIP in the processes is constrained by the number of cards. Hopp and Spearman, who have written the most about CONWIP (and who coined the term), note that using CONWIP affords several potential advantages over Kanban.[10] Two such advantages follow.

Card Count

In Kanban, each card specifies the kind of material (part or product) to be made or moved. Thus, in a multiproduct process such as illustrated before, there will be numerous kinds of cards and containers—in effect, a set of each for every *kind* of material at every stage of the process. This was shown in Figure 8.15 by the multiple buffers at each workstation (buffers for parts M, S, and V at station 1, for parts A and C at station 2, and so on). Thus, for a process that produces numerous products, there must be numerous buffers to hold all the different kinds of parts needed.

In contrast, the cards used in CONWIP do not specify the kind of part or product to be made in the process. The card has one function: to authorize production of a certain quantity (standard container) of *something*, but the something is left blank on the card. That something is determined from an *order list* held at the first operation.

When the card arrives at the first operation, the order list is referenced, and the job at the top of the list is released into the process. The order list is created in advance and consists of firm customer orders or a mix of mostly firm orders plus likely anticipated future orders. This production-authorization procedure is illustrated in Example 8.

Example   8:   Multiproduct Production Using CONWIP

Figure 8.17 shows a three-stage process with two WIP stock areas between. The process produces different kinds of parts according to an order list. Each time a finished container of parts leaves the process, a card is sent to station 1 to authorize it to start work on the next job on the order list. The card then moves with the job through the three operations. Suppose the specified number of cards for the entire process is three, and each card represents one *full* container. Thus, the process never has more than three full containers of material. (Figure 8.17 shows six containers — a, b, c, etc., two for each operation, one to the left and one to the right. Material from the left container is processed at the operation and put into the right container. In combination, the two containers have one container's quantity of material.) In addition, suppose the process can produce items A, B, C, and D, and that

- Stock area 1 has partially filled containers for items D and B.
- Stock area 2 has partially filled containers of items B and A.
- Operation 1 is in the process of producing item Ds.
- Operation 2 is in the process of producing item Bs.
- Operation 3 is in the process of producing item As.
- The sequence of the next 11 production jobs (for items A–D) on the order list is C, B, A, D, C, A, B, D, B, B, A.

FIGURE 8.17

Production sequence.

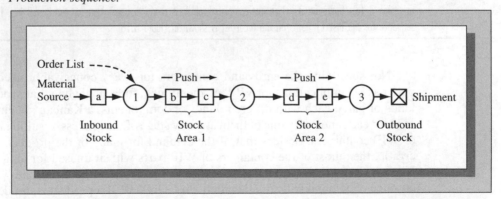

Now, as Figure 8.18 illustrates, as soon as operation 3 completes its item-A job, a card is sent back to operation 1. The card authorizes operation 1 to begin the next job on the list (which is for item C) as soon as it finishes its current job for item D. When operation 1 does finish, it will push the item-D job to operation 2 (c). Material for the item-C job is put at the inbound (a) stock area and made ready for operation 1.

FIGURE 8.18

Multiproduct sequence example for CONWIP.

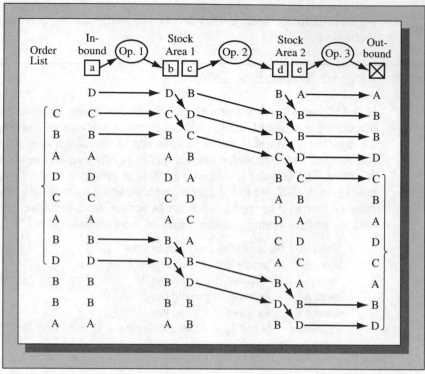

Operation 2 will begin the item-D job as soon as it finishes its current job on item B, which it will push to operation 3 (e). Operation 3, which just completed job A, is ready to begin work on the item-B job. The production sequence for the first 11 items on the order list is shown in Figure 8.18.

Not specifying the cards and containers for every conceivably needed kind of part has big implications for WIP. As mentioned, for a single line that produces many kinds of parts, each with different kinds of components, a Kanban system requires a card for each and every one of them at every stage of the process, resulting in hundreds of WIP containers. Besides that, if the demand for many of the products is small or erratic, then most of the containers of WIP parts will sit unused for long periods. In Kanban, every time a container is emptied, it is replaced by a full one, which in the absence of demand will sit indefinitely. In CONWIP, if a product is not demanded, it will not show up on the order list, and, hence, it will not be released into the process.

Floating Bottlenecks

A second advantage of CONWIP over Kanban is that CONWIP is much more toler-ant of changes in product mix and shifts in volume. Suppose the process times at each operation in the production sequence are different, in which case the throughput depends on the slowest operation, the bottleneck. To ensure maximal throughput, the bottleneck should never be permitted to be *starved* for work (i.e., it should never be idle because other, preceding operations have been interrupted). Ordinarily, the way to guarantee that a bottleneck keeps busy is to hold excess stock in front of it. In terms of Kanban, that means creating additional cards at the bottleneck operation.

In a multiproduct production situation, however, the location of the bottleneck can shift, depending on the current product. In other words, the bottleneck location is variable. In that case, it is necessary to elevate the number of cards at *all* operations, that is, carry enough WIP such as to always protect the bottleneck, wherever it happens to be at the moment. With CONWIP, however, because it uses a push system between operations within the process, excess WIP naturally builds up in front of the bottleneck, wherever it is. When the bottleneck shifts, so will the WIP buildup. Thus it is not necessary to create extra cards to protect bottlenecks. Protection happens on its own.

CONWIP does not work everywhere. For example, all the above cases assume that products follow the same routing sequence of operations. Products sharing operations, but moving through different routing sequences, must use the traditional Kanban method (though, as Hopp and Spearman note, even in such cases CONWIP can often be applied to portions of the routing).[11]

WHAT, MORE CARDS?

Move, production, and signal kanbans cover most but not all of the shop-floor authorizations in pull production. Others are needed for producing or moving items not included in the normal production sequence or for compensating for unanticipated situations. Pull production is not immune (and is perhaps prone) to unanticipated events, so there must be cards to cover every eventuality.

Express Card

This card is used whenever problems cause a shortage of items (e.g., defective parts) or threaten to seriously interrupt production (e.g., equipment breakdowns). It is issued to expedite production or to move "emergency" items.

Temporary Card

This card is issued whenever production must temporarily deviate from the normal pull pattern. It is issued to authorize a temporary increase in production necessary when, for example, downstream operations need more materials to fill special orders, or outbound buffers must be built up to cover temporary machine downtime for maintenance. A temporary card is also issued to authorize production of trial parts for new products or special parts for test, engineering, or purposes other than customer demand.

Odd-Number Card

Defective items discovered in a container are not used; the result is that the number of usable items will be less than the standard quantity. When that happens an odd-numbered card is issued to authorize production of just the quantity needed to fill the container. That container is then given priority for the next withdrawal.

The different kinds of cards have different colors for quick identification: green for normal work, orange for rework, blue for temporary work, yellow for higher-than-normal production, red for express, and so on.

PRACTICAL MATTERS

Many managers do not rely too much on the results of formulae to determine the number of kanbans, either because they do not trust the results or they know the production system has many problems, and the formulae results are not reliable. When they begin to install a pull system, they are skeptical that a process can operate effectively with so little in-process inventory. As a result, they often start with a number of kanbans that they are sure will work, which is usually around three or four times the number the formulae will give. (Even with that, the overall quantity of inventory in the system is much less than managers are accustomed to.) As they gain confidence and tinker with the process, they gradually reduce the number of kanbans. It is common, however, that the number of kanbans settled on is about *twice* the number suggested by the formulae (just to be safe), though in many cases that is not a bad idea since the plant must deal with somewhat unpredictable demand, long setup times, equipment unreliability, and so on, problems for which the formulae do not account. But as mentioned, the fact that large inventory buffers are necessary is a symptom that the system has many unresolved problems.[12] It is a practical matter that pull systems start out with large buffers, but it is bad management when no continuing attempt is made to reduce the size of those buffers by resolving the problems that make them necessary.

OTHER MECHANISMS FOR SIGNAL AND CONTROL

Kanban cards are just one of many possible ways for signaling and controlling pull production, and often they are not even necessary. If an operation produces only one kind of part, the mere presence of an empty container can be the signal to authorize production to replenish it. Even when multiple kinds of items are being produced or moved, information from the cards (the type and quantity of the items inside the container, and the workstations between which it is moved) can be written on the containers themselves, and the cards can be eliminated. Operators often become so familiar with the procedure that, as a matter of course, they do not even need the information on the cards or containers to know what to do. Still, it is a good idea to continue to use cards or clearly marked containers to prevent workers from making mistakes or getting careless. Since the number of cards and containers controls production and buffer stock levels, putting this information where it can be easily cross-checked ensures the correct levels will be maintained.

Though the concept of container might conjure an image of a handheld shopping-basket thing, actual containers can be of any size and configuration—whatever effectively contains the quantity of the item produced and moved. A container can be a small box that is manually lifted and moved or a larger pallet or skid transferred using a forklift. One manufacturer of farm equipment uses large, wheeled iron frames, called dollies, as containers. Each frame serves both as a support structure for assembling the equipment chassis and as the vehicle for moving the chassis from operation to operation.

In addition to cards and containers, there are many other ways to authorize and control production in pull systems. Some of these are explained next; the first three are illustrated in Figure 8.19.

WHEELED CARTS

Wheeled handcarts or pallet carts are lined up in lanes painted on the floor. Each kind of item has a separate lane, clearly marked, just long enough to hold a certain number (K) of carts. Typically each cart has a kanban card attached to show its contents and the necessary production/move information. Each lane might also have a line painted

FIGURE 8.19

Different kinds of pull signal mechanisms.

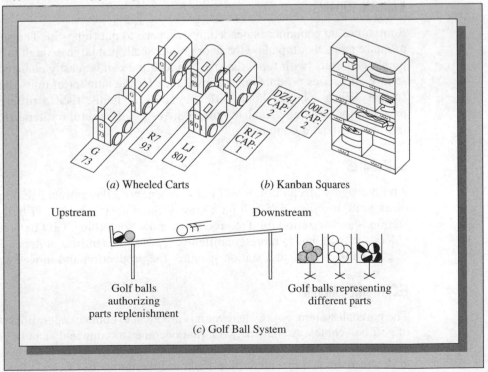

(a) Wheeled Carts   (b) Kanban Squares

Upstream   Downstream

Golf balls
authorizing
parts replenishment

Golf balls representing
different parts

(c) Golf Ball System

FIGURE 8.20
Kanban carts.

across it to show when the number of remaining full carts is low or when replenishment is needed (analogous to a signal kanban). Figure 8.20 shows some kanban carts on a factory floor.

KANBAN SQUARES

Sometimes no container is needed, just a space to put things in. The space might be a square painted or taped on the floor or on a shelf, just large enough to hold a certain number of units (with tape, the size and location can be easily changed). An empty square authorizes production or conveyance for the number of units that will fill the square. When a buffer holds different kinds of items, then a different square is provided for each item. Kanban squares are especially useful for items that are readily movable without a container.

GOLF BALLS

Another signal mechanism is golf balls. Whenever a downstream station needs more of an item, it rolls a golf ball on a gravity chute upstream. A golf ball arriving at a station is authorization for it to produce or move something. Golf balls have different colors and markings to represent different types and quantities of items. The sequence of golf balls arriving at a station specifies the production and move sequence.

ELECTRONIC KANBAN

The golf ball system works wherever it is practical to connect operations with a system of golf ball chutes. A chute network that becomes too unwieldy can be replaced with an *electronic kanban* that uses monitors and keyboards. In the latter system, workers at downstream stations enter on a keyboard the items they need, which then appear on monitors at upstream stations that supply them. The electronic kanban can also be used in conjunction with, or as a replacement for, conventional kinds of pull signals such as cards.

CLOTHESPIN CLIPS

Imagine a rack of shelves between two work stations, say a circuit-board assembly area and a circuit-board test area. The rack has 50 pigeon holes, each hole for a different kind of circuit board, and each hole holding up to four boards.

On the corner of each circuit board is a detachable clothespinlike clip with a 1-inch disk that shows the stock-keeping number of the circuit board. Whenever a worker from the test area withdraws a board from a pigeon hole, she detaches the clip and puts it on a wire strung horizontally across the top of the hole. As boards are withdrawn, clips accumulate on the wires. Looking at the number of clips on the wire by each pigeon hole, a worker in the assembly area can see which boards need to be assembled. A wire with four clips has highest priority, one with three has next priority, and so on. The worker removes the clips from the wire, assembles the type of board specified, attaches a clip to each completed board, and puts the board into the pigeon hole.

MILK RUN

A basic requirement of Kanban production is that there be somewhat continual demand for a product—not necessarily large demand, just continual demand. To fulfill that requirement, the final stage of production must produce a continual stream of final product. For the final stage to produce continually, however, it is not necessary that all the materials feeding into it also be produced continually. As long as the upstream operations produce materials in sufficient quantity and in time to satisfy the requirements of the final stage, they can produce those materials in intermittent batches.

When materials are produced intermittently, a way is needed to ensure the regular transfer of these materials to the final stage. One way is for a material handler to make a periodic "milk run," say once every 2 hours. The handler starts at the final stage, picks up the empty containers for all parts, then drives to the operations that produce those parts. After visiting every operation and exchanging the appropriate empty containers for full ones, the handler delivers the full containers to the final stage and repeats the cycle. Since pickups and deliveries happen on a regularly scheduled basis, and the quantities and types of materials required tend to be somewhat fixed, upstream operations know what they must produce (batch size and frequency of production) in the time available to fill the containers dropped off earlier.

KANBAN SEQUENCE BOARD

Ordinarily, P-kanbans are processed in the sequence in which they arrive or are posted. When several cards arrive at once, or when there is a backlog of cards, there is a risk that some items will not be produced in time and that downstream operations

FIGURE 8.21

Kanban sequence board.

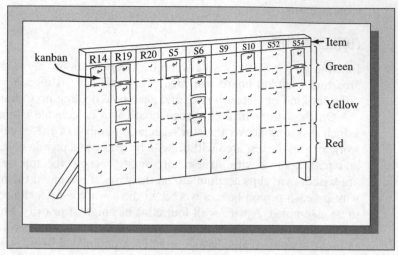

will be idled. To maintain a balanced workload or prevent habitual shortages of some items, production of items that require different cycle times must be carefully sequenced (short cycle times interspersed with long cycle items). One way to enable operators to sequence jobs when several cards accumulate is with a **kanban sequence board.** As cards arrive at a workstation, they are sorted and hung on the board according to type of item. As shown in Figure 8.21, the board is demarcated into regions of importance (green, yellow, red) to represent increasing priority. The cards are hung starting from the top; cards first reaching the red region have priority over those in yellow, which have priority over those in green.

Clearly, the variety of ways to authorize and control inventory in pull production is limited only by the imagination of managers and workers. One further example is the following case in point.

CASE IN POINT: Using Kanban for Batch Production at Strombecker[13]

Strombecker Corporation uses Kanban in the manufacture of toy cap pistols. Parts used in the assembly of the pistols are held in standardized bins, each with an assembly kanban card inside (see Figure 8.22).

When a bin of die-cast parts is depleted, a material handler takes it and the kanban to the die-cast store area where full bins are kept, each with a die-cast kanban inside (see Figure 8.23).

At the store area the handler takes the assembly kanban from the empty bin and places it in a full bin (see Figure 8.24, step *a*). At the same time, he takes the die-cast kanban out of the full bin and places it in a pigeon hole in the lot-making box (step *b*). The handler then takes the full bin to the assembly area (*c*) and leaves the empty bin behind.

FIGURE 8.22

Assembly area showing parts bins.

FIGURE 8.23

Store area: Empty bins, foreground; full bins, background.

The lot-making box, Figure 8.25, is divided into columns, one for each kind of part. Cards are added to pigeon holes in the columns starting at the bottom. When the number of die-cast kanban cards for a part reaches a particular level (Figure 8.24, step *d*), that indicates that a batch of that part should be die-cast. All the cards in the column are removed and taken with an equal number of empty bins to the die-cast area (step *e*). A die-cast machine produces a batch of parts in the quantity as specified by the sum of the die-cast kanbans; this quantity has been

FIGURE 8.24

Kanban procedure.

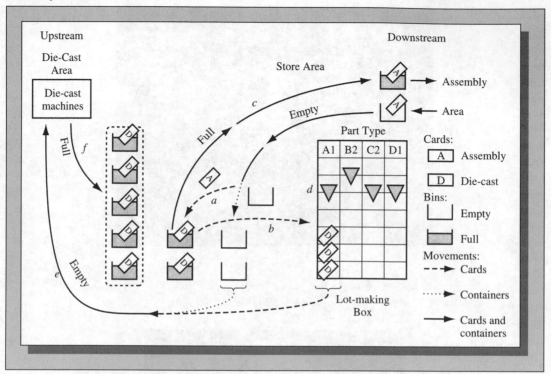

FIGURE 8.25

Lot-making box.

determined in advance as a function of the daily production requirement for each part, the processing and setup time, and the number of different parts to be produced. When die-casting of the batch of parts has been completed, the parts are distributed among the bins, a die-cast kanban card is put into each bin, and the bins are taken back to the store area (step *f*).

TO PULL OR NOT TO PULL

Lest you might have gotten the impression that pull systems are universally preferred over push systems, recall that pull systems need fairly stable, continuous demand. In most pull systems, every kind of material must be held in a buffer, and to justify all those buffers requires that the materials be in somewhat-continuous demand. Also, to keep down the proliferation of buffers, pull production is often confined to a relatively few standardized products. Such production of standardized items on a continuous basis is called **repetitive** production.

For repetitive production, demand does not have to be large, just stable enough so that the final assembly schedule can be smoothed (i.e., have relatively level daily production output). To achieve stability and enable leveled production scheduling, some organizations combine production of different versions of products that were formerly produced separately. Combining production of different products is feasible as long as product differences are add-on features or options and not differences in fundamental design, major components, or production processes. Grouping different products by **product family** is a way to group multiple products for production in a single process. This topic is discussed in the next chapter.

Without stable product demand, the only way to achieve a leveled production schedule is to *stockpile* the finished product. For example, seasonal variation can be accommodated with leveled, repetitive production, but excess output from periods of slack demand must be stockpiled to cover production shortfall during periods of peak demand. Table 8.3 summarizes the requirements for pull production.

WHEN PULL DOES NOT WORK

Referring to Table 8.3, it is clear that even if demand is stable enough so that, conceptually, a leveled production schedule can be developed (discussed in Chapter 16), and if some products can be grouped to get around the limited product variety

---

TABLE 8.3   Pull Production Requirements

1. Continuous, somewhat stable product demand
2. Uniform (level) production plans and schedules
3. Short setup times
4. Limited product variety
5. Continuous flow: Few interruptions from equipment, quality, setup, and other problems

---

requirement, there are other factors that can make pull production impossible or impractical. Robert Hall lists the following as typical.[14]

1. Despite stable demand, the assembly of the final product cannot be executed in a level-enough fashion to provide steady demand for upstream operations. This happens when the assembly involves trials, matching, adjustments, testing, or anything that causes the time for assembly to vary with every unit.

2. Some operations must be started in advance of pull signals. This happens when operations require special, lengthy, or difficult setups which cannot be simplified or significantly shortened and must be scheduled in advance.

3. The product is made in so many options, and the demand for each option is so small or unstable, that it is impractical to carry buffer stocks for all parts everywhere in the process.

4. The high defect level causes too many interruptions to permit continuous flow, and technology is such that the defect level cannot be reduced significantly.

5. Products must be produced as integrated batches throughout the process for reasons of quality control or certification. An example is pharmaceuticals.

BACK TO MRP

Now, although any of the above factors can make implementation of pull production impossible or very difficult, none of them pose a particular problem for a push system like MRP. Besides, MRP readily accommodates products that are nonstandard and have a highly fluctuating or erratic demand. The only requirement for MRP is that the demand can be forecasted far enough in advance to be input into a master schedule. Material requirements planning also does not require much shop-floor worker involvement or the changes in job descriptions and training that go with it.

BOTH SYSTEMS AT ONCE

In any situation where a leveled final assembly schedule *is* feasible, a pull system can be implemented by starting at the final stage and working backward to link the upstream stages into the process. The upstream operations are linked together using pull methods, one stage at a time. Those operations that cannot be linked into the system (because of factors like those listed above) can remain outside of the repetitive process and be treated separately. These outside operations will be treated as job shops that *serve* the repetitive process, but which use traditional push methods for scheduling and control. In other words, two kinds of systems will be used, a pull system for the repetitive portions of the process, and a push system for everything else.

When products can be **modularized** (built as a collection of standardized options and subassemblies, described in Chapter 16), then often the modules can be produced repetitively in a pull system, even though the final assembled product cannot and must be produced with a traditional push system schedule.

Even when a company is able to implement a complete pull production process, say for products it manufactures throughout the year, it still might need a push-oriented system for other products it manufactures only seasonally or on-demand.

Again, two systems, or a mixed system, are needed depending on the products. Many large manufacturers, Canon for example, utilize multiple kinds of production systems (product lines, pull lines, as well as batch-oriented, push lines) whatever best fits the requirements of the product and process. As described in Chapter 18, every pull production system needs some form of traditional system for demand forecasting, and for production, material requirements, and capacity requirements planning, all of which is handily done with MRP-II systems.

GETTING STARTED

In many organizations the initiative to implement pull production starts with midlevel management. To test its feasibility and demonstrate its benefits, pull production is introduced in stages that are limited to the segments of the process that best meet the necessary conditions. Trial and error at each stage enables the application to be fine-tuned and provides the knowledge and experience necessary to expand pull production to greater portions of the process. Many firms are now experimenting with pull production, using it to link only two or three operations in a much larger process.

If the factory experiment is to eventually take hold plantwide, top management must get involved. The changes and investments required to implement pull production on a wide scale are too great for the implementation to succeed without commitment and backing from top management. At least one top manager must serve as the pull production champion.

Often the greatest challenge in implementation is in overcoming cultural barriers. Implementing pull production requires teamwork and moving the locus of control away from centralized staff and toward the shop floor. It requires significant changes in organizational roles, worker responsibilities, job descriptions, and pay systems. These issues are covered in some depth in the discussion on workcell implementation in Chapter 10.

Summary

Ensuring that materials keep moving smoothly through the production process, that the right items get to the right place in the right quantity and at the right times, despite unanticipated problems, is the function of production control. One way to keep materials moving smoothly is to hold enough inventory between stages of the process to buffer against any problems.

Pull production is a way of controlling a process and reacting quickly to changes without relying on inventory. In a pull system, each stage of a process produces exactly what the immediate downstream stage requests; in effect, material is pulled through the process by each stage producing only what is demanded of it from the next stage. This contrasts to push production wherein every stage produces according to a preplanned schedule, then pushes material to the next stage, whether that next stage is ready for it or not.

Production and movement of material through a pull process are contingent on signals coming from downstream. No material is moved downstream, and nothing is produced unless a signal comes from downstream. The most familiar kind of signal system uses cards and is called Kanban. A kanban is a card authorizing production or movement of a standard quantity of material and showing the kind of material needed, its source, and destination.

A pull system reacts immediately to changes or problems anywhere in the process. If a stage faces a problem and ceases to send signals upstream, the upstream stages also cease, at least until the signals resume. A small amount of inventory called a buffer is held between stages to allow downstream demand to be filled immediately while upstream operations work to meet requests for more. The amount held in the buffer is controlled by using a prespecified number of standard containers. The number of containers corresponds to the number of cards (kanbans) deemed adequate for the system to meet demand. Because the number of cards (hence, containers) is regulated, the amount of in-process inventory required for a process to function smoothly can be held to a small quantity.

The rules of pull production are that materials are moved and produced only to meet downstream demand, nothing is moved or produced without a signal (card), nothing defective is moved downstream, and the number of cards (hence inventory) is slowly reduced to expose problems and tighten up the system. By enforcing the last rule, management commits to resolving problems that are the source of waste in the system. The following conditions are necessary for pull production:

· Greater planning and control responsibility at the shop-floor level.

· Motivation to produce only on demand and to keep reducing stock levels.

· Preventive maintenance and setup reduction efforts.

· Leveled production plans.

· Balanced, synchronized operations.

Various kinds of containers and signals are used in pull production. Depending on the item and the need, containers can be small boxes, carts, pallets, or large dollies, and authorization to produce or move items can be signaled using special P-cards, C-cards, or other cards, with computer monitors linking stages of the process, or deduced visually from empty squares or spaces on a shelf or floor—whatever fits the need.

Pull production is not universally better than push production. First, pull production requires repetitive manufacturing, that is, fairly smooth continuous production of somewhat standardized items. Production volume does not have to be large, but it must be somewhat uniform and stable. Products where demand is highly variable and unstable, that require lengthy setups, trials, adjustments, or testing, or where products are uniquely made to customer requirements cannot be produced using pull production. On the other hand, push systems and conventional planning and control systems using MRP can readily accommodate such situations.

Pull production is often used in combination with push production; some processes in the same plant use push, others use pull, depending on the product/demand requirements of the processes. Also, within a given process, some portions can be controlled using a push system, others using pull. For products made from modular components, often the demand for the modules is stable enough that they can be produced using pull, even though demand for the assembled product is unstable and requires push procedures for scheduling and control.

Pull production should be introduced in stages, starting with the last stage of the process and working upstream. Pull production requires commitment and resources from top management, and a shift of most responsibility for production control to worker teams.

Questions

1. Describe the fundamental differences between push production systems and pull production systems. How are they the same?
2. What are the necessary conditions for pull production?
3. Discuss the relationship between pull production and demand stability and variation.
4. Under what situations is pull production inappropriate?
5. Describe the reorder-point system. What is its relation to Kanban?
6. How is pull production more than just a way of controlling inventory?
7. List various ways for authorizing material movement and production in a pull system. How does the proximity of operations determine which of the ways is most appropriate?
8. Explain how some pull systems run without the use of cards.
9. For the following, indicate whether MRP or Kanban would be more effective for production control:
   a. An automobile assembly plant that produces 10 car models.
   b. A shop that produces a large variety of custom-ordered products.
   c. An assembly operation that involves 20,000 part numbers.
   d. An assembly operation that involves 50 part numbers.
   e. An assembly line plant where all parts are outsourced.
10. What is the role of Kanban in process improvement?
11. Four kinds of signal and control mechanisms are (1) kanban cards and general purpose containers, (2) special purpose containers that had only one kind of item, (3) kanban squares, and (4) an automated conveyor system with no containers. Explain which is best for each of the following situations:
    a. Final assembly of VCRs.
    b. Production and finishing of metal castings of common parts that involve casting, tumbling, heat treatment, and machining.
    c. Repetitive production of kitchen and dining room furniture.
    d. Replenishing stock of parts supplying an assembly line.
    e. Producing small batches of replacement parts in a five-operation process.

12. Explain how each of the following works: (a) a two-card pull system and (b) a single-card pull system. Explain when one or the other is necessary. When are the two systems equivalent?

13. Explain the purpose of signal kanbans for production and material movement. When are signal kanbans used?

14. The assembly shop of a manufacturer of large air conditioners for commercial and industrial buildings has numerous units at various stages of completion, most sitting unattended for lack of parts. As parts and subassemblies arrive from other departments, assembly workers install them. Is this a push or pull system? Explain. Suggest how the system might be improved.

Problems

1. Calculate the required number of kanbans for cases X, Y, and Z.

	X	Y	Z
Demand	110 per day	90 per week	25 per hour
Cycle time per kanban	5 hours	1 day	20 minutes
Container size	40 units	10 units	5 units
Safety margin	10%	0%	30%

2. Superseven Corporation uses a two-card kanban production system. Inventory levels are roughly proportional to the number of kanbans. For one part, the average usage rate is 1400 parts per day, container size is 50 parts, and cycle time per batch is 2 hours. Superseven is working to reduce the lead time to 100 minutes. Assuming no safety stock is carried, what effect would this have on average inventory?

3. An assembly line pulls containers of parts from machining centers at a rate of 600 per day. Each container holds 20 parts and typically waits 2 hours at a machining center before it is processed. The setup and processing time for 20 parts is 6 hours. How many containers are needed if the safety margin is 10%?

4. The daily demand for parts from machining workcell JMB to an assembly workcell is 1600 units. The average processing time is 25 seconds per unit. A container spends, on average, 6 hours waiting at JMB before it is processed. Each container holds 250 parts. Currently, 10 containers are being used for the part.

   a. What percent safety margin of stock is being carried?

   b. If you wanted to retain this safety margin, but remove one container, to what value must the waiting time be reduced?

   c. What would the margin be if the demand for parts increased to 1900 with K = 10?

5. The BOM for an assembly is shown below (numbers in parenthesis indicate the quantity of part for each assembly).

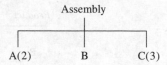

Each 8-hour day the assembly line produces 400 units. Because the assembly line is located in a different area of the plant from the areas where parts A, B, and C are produced, a two-card pull system is used. Information about producing and moving the three parts is shown below (all times in hours):

	A	B	C
Container size	100	50	100
Conveyance:			
Total wait time	1.0	1.5	1.0
Total move time	0.5	0.5	0.5
Production:			
Total wait time	1.0	1.0	0.5
Setup time/container	0.2	0.5	0.5
Processing time/unit	0.008	0.02	0.006

If a safety margin of 20% is to be maintained, how many of each of conveyance and production cards are needed for each of the three kinds of parts? Draw a schematic diagram showing the assembly and parts production areas, and the location of containers and cards.

6. A worker can sort parts at a rate of up to 400 per hour. A material handler arrives every half hour, drops off empty bins and departs with bins of 100 parts. How many kanbans are needed for a safety margin of 20%?

7. For the previous problem, which of the following has the greatest influence on reducing the number of kanbans? (Treat each independently.)
   a. Cutting the material-handler pickup cycle in half.
   b. Doubling the capacity of the bins to 200 parts.
   c. Eliminating the safety margin.

8. A fabrication workcell uses two components, QR1 and QR2, each produced at the rate of 300 per hour. Because the two components are different sizes, they have different-sized containers: the container for QR1 holds 20 units, the container for QR2 holds 30. The operation supplying QR1 takes 15 minutes to fill the container; the operation for QR2 takes 8 minutes to fill the container. Total move and wait time between each operation and the assembly workcell is 10 minutes. How many kanbans are needed between each operation and the workcell? Assume a 10% safety margin.

9. At Fabfour Products, Inc., daily demand forecast for the top 10 products is:

Product	Daily Demand
A	1600
B	1000
C	800
D	600
E	400
F	200
G	100
H	50
I	25
J	25
	4800

The final assembly area produces 600 units per eight-hour workday.

a. Products are produced in batches of 50 units, which is also the container size. In terms of number of batches, what is the daily production schedule for the 10 products?

b. The cycle time for all products is 2 hours per container. Using a 20% safety margin, how many kanbans are needed for the products?

c. If inventory is proportional to the number of kanbans, by what percentage would inventory decrease if the cycle time per 50-unit container was reduced by 1 hour?

d. Assume case (c): What is the benefit of reducing the batch and container sizes to 25 units?

10. The average wait time before starting an order at the machining workcell is 2 hours. It then takes an average 25 minutes to set up the cell for the order. The machine cycle time on each part is 120 seconds. If a container holds 20 parts, management allows a 20% safety margin, and eight containers have been allocated for the part, how much average daily demand can the machining cell handle?

11. Fabfour Products, Inc., receives kits of parts from a supplier. Each kit contains all of the small parts required for an assembly. The kits are boxed in quantities of 50, and boxes are delivered directly to point-of-use racks in the assembly area. Each time a box is opened, a replenishment order is sent to the supplier. The average daily demand is 45 boxes. The lead time on replenishment from the supplier (total order and delivery time) is 10 days. The company likes to hold enough stock for a 20% safety margin. Assuming one kanban card per box, how many cards should there be?

12. Colored wooden blocks used in small-toy assemblies are painted using a tumbling vat and batch sizes of 2000. Six different colored blocks are produced using three vats. A request for additional colored blocks from the assembly area usually waits 3 hours before the paint area begins to process it; it then takes 1.25 hours to clean a vat and prepare it for a different color, 0.25 hour to paint a batch, and 3 hours for the batch to dry and be moved to the assembly area. No blocks are needed at the paint vat while it is being cleaned and readied for a new color. The time between when additional colored blocks are requested from the assembly area and when material handlers move the unpainted blocks from storage to the paint room is 3 hours. Each color of block is

used by the assembly area at the rate of 200 per hour. Standard-sized containers holding 250 blocks are used for both painted and unpainted blocks. Containers of finished painted blocks are stacked for use in the assembly area.

   a. Assuming a 10% safety margin, at what position in the stack of containers should the production signal kanban be placed?

   b. At what position in the stack should the material signal kanban (signal to authorize movement of unpainted blocks to the paint area) be placed?

13. In the previous problem, what is the effect on the kanban positions of reducing the batch size to 1000? Interpret the results. In general, what is the implication when the number of containers in the batch size is fewer than the kanban signal position?

14. The product assembled at operation OpD is made from two subassemblies, each produced in a process that has three operations. The operations within each process are located next to each other, and operation OpD is located next to operations OpC and OpG. The hourly production capacities (fixed hourly production rates) and the fixed arrangement of the operations are shown below. The current demand requires that the output for operation OpD be 75 units per hour. Assume negligible setup and move times and that suppliers are able to fulfill any likely demand rate. The same containers are to be used throughout the process.

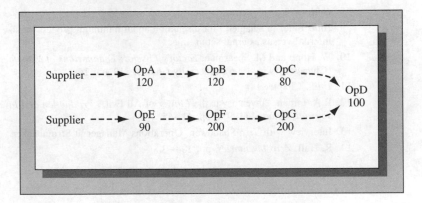

   a. Discuss the size of the container for the overall process.

   b. Discuss the location of stock areas and number of kanbans at each stock area, assuming kanbans are used to link successive operations.

   c. Discuss the location of stock areas and the number of kanbans if a CONWIP system is used. Discuss the relative merits of this approach versus the approach in (*b*).

Endnotes

1. Kanban and the Toyota system are described in T. Ohno, *Toyota Production System—Beyond Management of Large-Scale Production* (Cambridge, MA: Productivity Press, 1988); much the same topical material is also in Y. Monden, *Toyota Production System,* 2nd ed. (Norcross, GA: Institute of Industrial Engineers, 1993).

2. Popularity of the term just-in-time as synonymous with pull production is declining. As discussed earlier in this book, JIT today is more generally seen as a management philosophy that emphasizes continuous improvement and elimination of waste. Pull production is but a JIT technique.

3. Actually, there is a method called "broadcast" that permits portions of a production system to operate on a pull basis without inventory buffers for every kind of material. That system, however, also utilizes production schedules, so it is thus not a pure pull system. Another method, called CONWIP, which also does not require buffers for every kind of material, is discussed later in this chapter (it also is not a pure pull system, though it has most advantages of pull systems).

4. D. Pyke and M. Cohen, "Push and Pull in Manufacturing and Distribution Systems," *Journal of Operations Management* 9, No. 1 (1990), pp. 24–42.

5. Adopted from K. Suzaki, *The New Manufacturing Challenge* (New York: Free Press, 1987), pp. 155–7; Japan Management Association, *Canon Production System* (Cambridge, MA: Productivity Press, 1987), pp.133–7; R. Hall, *Zero Inventories* (Homewood, IL: Dow Jones-Irwin, 1983), p. 53.

6. T. Ohno, "Evolution of the Toyota Production System," *Continuous Improvement in Operations,* (Cambridge, MA: Productivity Press, 1991), p. 172.

7. For further discussion of conveyance and production kanbans, *see* Y. Monden, *Toyota Production System;* H. Steudel and P. Desruelle, *Manufacturing in the Nineties,* (New York: Van Nostrand Reinhold, 1992).

8. *Ibid.*

9. *Ibid.* Refer to Chapter 5 for discussion about minimum process lot size and the ramifications of internal versus external setup times.

10. W. Hopp and M. Spearman, *Factory Physics: Foundations of Manufacturing Management* (Chicago: Irwin, 1996), especially Chapters 10 and 14.

11. *Ibid.,* Chapter 14.

12. R.A. Inman, "Inventory is the *Flower* of All Evil," *Production and Inventory Management Journal* 34, no. 4 (1993), pp. 41–45.

13. Interview with Vern Shadowen, Operations Manager at Strombecker.

14. R. Hall, *Zero Inventories,* pp. 308–9.

CHAPTER
9
FOCUSED FACTORIES AND GROUP TECHNOLOGY

A production process is implemented within a physical facility. The facility consists of machines, workers, and material handling equipment assigned to workstations, workcenters, and functional departments. The kind of process (whether things are produced one at a time, in small batches, or continuously) and the configuration and spatial location of the components of the process (the operations, workers, and machines) have a tremendous effect on production lead time, cost, quality, and flexibility.

Part of the difficulty in designing production processes and facility layouts stems from proliferation of products. As will be discussed, the greater the number of different kinds of products manufactured in a single facility, the more difficult it is to produce each one efficiently. Nonetheless, product proliferation is often driven by competition. A company that can modify or customize its products to meet the needs of existing and future customers has a potential advantage over competitors that cannot. Many manufacturers are able to prosper by producing a large variety of products for many different customers. Though demand for each kind of product is small, the sum is great.

Diversity in products is often not just a matter of choices of colors, add-ons, or gimmicks; it often represents major, fundamental differences between products. Regardless, as a way of holding on to its competitive advantage, a company must be able to quickly switch over and make each product in a diversified line in small batches, or make every one of them at virtually the same time.

At some point, however, diversity in products can strangle a company. Simply, no company can do everything well. The diversity itself must be delimited and managed, and waste associated with producing multiple kinds of products must be kept to a minimum. One solution to the problem of managing diversity is to outsource some products to suppliers—a topic addressed in Chapter 19 on supply chain management. Another is to use **group technology** to identify similarities among different products and to group them accordingly, and then produce each group in a single place with the same workers and equipment, that is, within a **focused factory.**

Both group technology and focused factories are considered in this chapter, starting with their place among various ways of doing work. The concept of a **workcell,** which is a particular kind of focused factory commonly found in pull production systems, is also introduced; the next chapter covers workcells and related issues in depth.

WAYS OF DOING WORK

The common ways of performing manufacturing work are as projects, jobs, batches, and repetitive and continuous operations. As shown in Figure 9.1, the suitableness of a way depends on the volume of the end-item (product or part) being produced and the amount of resources required to produce each unit of end-item.

A **project** is a unique, large-scale work effort directed at one or a few end-items. Each end-item is tailored to fit unique requirements. Large one-of-a-kind systems, structures, or machines such as buildings, dams, highways, ships, and automated manufacturing systems are examples. The work involves numerous diverse, often multifunctional activities, the nature of which varies with each project.

A **job** is a small-volume, somewhat small-scale work effort where the output is one or a few identical items, custom-made to fit an order. A custom-ordered machine fitting, a special-purpose casting, and a handcrafted dining room set are examples of jobs. A job can be considered a small-scale project where the work is performed in a small plant or shop, called a **job shop,** by a group of professionals, craftsmen, or skilled tradespeople.

When the job size involves producing several or many identical end-items, the items are produced in a **batch.** Manufacturers that produce in batches tend to focus on more-standardized (less diverse) products than do pure job shops. By producing larger quantities of fewer kinds of end-items, producers can take advantage of economies resulting from fewer machine changeovers, quantity discounts on procured materials, and greater work proficiency in jobs that are less varied and more familiar.

Repetitive and **continuous** operations produce similar or identical items in high volume. Both kinds of operations are called **flow shops** because material moves through them somewhat smoothly and with few interruptions.

FIGURE 9.1

Ways of doing work by quantity of output and size of process or operation.

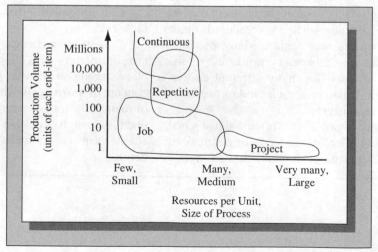

Products made in *repetitive operations* are discrete units such as cars, VCRs, computers, and pens. Equipment in repetitive operations is often designed for single-purpose, high-efficiency operation, and workers are narrowly trained and perform one or a few tasks each.

Products and material made in *continuous operations* actually flow through the process; examples are fluids, minerals, and mixtures such as foodstuffs, paint, steel, paper, coal, and petroleum. Such products are produced in large volume and are sometimes considered commodities in that they are indistinguishable among producers. In a continuous production process the product seldom changes. Production is scheduled and controlled by volume output, not by discrete units. Often, not until after packaging is the product identifiable as discrete units.

Hybrid ways of doing work are also common, such as batch production within continuous or repetitive processes. A variation of the hybrid theme is to produce a batch of one kind of product repetitively, then modify the process to produce a batch of a slightly different product. The batches are usually large and changeovers are infrequent. An example is a repetitive manufacturer of garden tools that in midsummer switches over to produce rakes, then switches in fall to produce snow shovels, then in midwinter to again produce garden tools.

VARIETY/EFFICIENCY TRADE-OFF

When a manufacturer changes its usual method of work from job production to batch production and then to repetitive and continuous production, several things happen: material flow through the plant becomes more continuous, less intermittent, and more steady; work task efficiency increases; and unit time and cost of production decrease. Smoother, steadier flow happens because the number of stops, starts, and changeovers in daily production decreases. In a job shop virtually every end-item requires a setup, whereas in repetitive manufacturing setups happen relatively infrequently, as seldom as a few times a year or every several thousand units. Production efficiency increases because more attention, knowledge, and skill are directed at fewer different kinds of things. As a result, less time per unit is wasted, WIP inventory is smaller, throughput rates are higher, and unit costs are lower.

This does not mean that continuous/repetitive manufacturing is better than job or batch production on all counts. As a company shifts from job production to repetitive production, it also shifts emphasis from product variety to output quantity. Historically at least, it seems that as a company increases its ability to produce things efficiently and in large quantity, it decreases its ability to produce things in large variety. Henry Ford was able to achieve high efficiency with his Model T, but he only produced one kind of car that had few options (the saying was, "Any color you want, as long as it's black.").

Solutions to the problem of achieving both high efficiency *and* variety lie partly in the way products are designed, partly in the way jobs are planned and scheduled, partly in the way operations and equipment are physically arranged in the factory, and partly in the way products are grouped for production. The first two ways, product design, and planning and scheduling, are discussed in Chapters 12 and 16–18, respectively. The other two ways, physical arrangement of factory facilities and grouping different products into families for production purposes, are discussed next.

FACILITIES LAYOUT

The three common types of facility layout are **fixed-position, process,** and **product.**

FIXED-POSITION LAYOUT

In a fixed-position layout, the end-item remains in a fixed or stationary position while it is being produced. Fixed-position layouts are common for end-items that are large and difficult to move (project end-items such as ships, hydroelectric turbines, electrical transformers, and aircraft) and for items custom-produced by a group of craftspeople (racing cars and machine tools). This kind of layout was used by Henry Ford, initially, and other early mass producers. At Ford, each car was assembled at one location, materials were brought to it, and workers walked around it to perform tasks.

As Ford discovered, however, it is often easier to keep the workers and equipment stationary and to move the end-items to them, especially when the end-items are readily movable and production volume is large. Actually, this is true even for large end-items such as aircraft. Bombers mass-produced during WWII were moved to staging areas throughout cavernous assembly plants. At each staging area (in effect, a fixed-position shop) a major portion of work was completed—such as attaching wings to the fuselage—then the airplane was moved to the next staging area for additional work, like attaching engines to the wings.

PROCESS LAYOUT

In a **process layout** similar types of operations (similar equipment and tools, workers with similar skills and expertise) are clustered into functional work areas or **departments,** and each job is routed through the areas according to its routing sequence of operations. Take for example four products with the following given characteristics:

Product	Operations Sequence	Annual Volume
X	J–B–L–T–P	100,000
Y	T–L–P–T	8,000
Z	P–L–B–J	20,000
W	J–L–P	11,000

In a process layout, all the J-type operations would be done in one department, say department J, all the B-types would be done in department B, and so on. Figure 9.2 shows a process layout with departments J, L, P, T, and B, and the resulting routings for the four products. Each department has one or more machines and workers that perform one particular kind of operation such as milling, drilling, painting, printing,

FIGURE 9.2

Process (functional) layout and product routings.

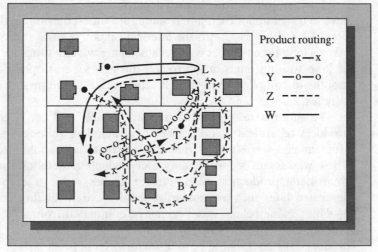

casting, or assembly. The production machines within each area are similar or identical and are considered general purpose in that they can perform work on a variety of different products. Most equipment (including hand tools, drills, mills, presses, and PCs) in machine, wood, and printing shops is general purpose. Job shops, which manufacture items individually or in small batches, use process layouts.

The advantage of process layouts is that they can readily process any product that requires work in any of the departments, regardless of the product's production volume or routing sequence. The fact that annual production among the given four products varies has no bearing on the layout. Production output can be increased or decreased, new products can be added, old ones can be dropped, all without changing the basic departmental layout of the facility. Custom, made-to-order products are simply routed through areas of the plant in the appropriate sequence. Capacity in the plant is increased by adding overtime or machines to each area, as needed. Often, the justification for procuring additional general purpose equipment is that it can be employed on a variety of products, is readily available, and is less costly than more-specialized equipment, which must be custom-designed.

Beware, however, that beneath the simple appearance of a process layout lies potential for much complexity and waste. Consider job routing. If, for example, five products can be produced by any combination of five different operations, there are 5! = 120 possible routings. Of course in an actual factory many of these combinations would be eliminated as illogical routing sequences. Nonetheless, the fact remains that the number of possible routings is large and many of them require moving material over long distances (as is obvious in Figure 9.2). Moving and handling of material is, of course, non-value-added.

Process layouts also require considerable effort for scheduling, routing, sequencing, and tracking of jobs. There is much stop-and-go of work and material movement.

When a job arrives at a work area, it must wait until previous jobs are completed. Jobs waiting throughout a typical plant represent a sizable quantity of WIP inventory.

Further, jobs waiting in each department are for different end-items, so machines have to be set up for each job. If setups are time-consuming, that encourages production of large batches, with the attendant quality, cost, and time drawbacks. If each takes a long time to process, that causes long waiting times for all other jobs. Because of long waiting times, a job routed through several operations can take weeks or months to complete, even though actual value-added processing takes only hours or minutes.

To summarize, process layouts are flexible and can accommodate a variety of products regardless of differences in demand or processing, but they are also inefficient and wasteful in terms of time, material handling, defects, and inventory. These wastes can be mitigated by lean production methods already described, such as small-batch production, small transfer batches, reduced setup times, and by methods described later such as standard operations, tight quality control, and defect foolproofing. Nonetheless, waste cannot be eliminated from a process layout. Unless the product mix consists primarily of small-quantity, custom-designed, or one-of-a-kind products, the goal should be to move *away* from process-type layouts toward product layouts.

PRODUCT LAYOUT

Facilities in a repetitive or continuous processes are arranged in a **product layout.** All the necessary operations for producing a product are arranged in a sequence called a line—a production line, assembly line, or flow line. Product X, for example, requires the sequence of operations J–B–L–T–P, so the product layout for it would consist of equipment and workers at work stations as laid out in Figure 9.3. Plants that produce repetitively or continuously using a product layout are called **flow shops.**

Continuous/repetitive production and product layouts go together. Only one or a few kind of end-items are produced, and they all follow the same routing sequence

FIGURE 9.3

Product layout for product X.

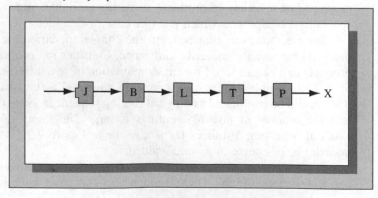

through the line. Work scheduling in a product layout consists of determining the flow rate or cycle time necessary to satisfy demand, then designing the line so it produces at that rate. Since material moves continuously from operation to operation, and since neighboring operations are located adjacently, there is little or no inventory waiting between operations. Throughput time per unit is not much more than the processing time in the line. Material handling consists of transferring items from one operation to the next. The transfer can be automated, or for small, light items, manual. On a fully mechanized **transfer line,** material at each machine is automatically loaded, machined, unloaded, and moved to the next machine.

The big drawback of a product layout is, of course, that it is dedicated to producing just *one* kind of thing. Once the line has been created, that is, once the operations sequence and transfer system have been installed, it can produce only products that follow that one sequence and require all the operations built into it. It is termed *product* layout because it is designed specifically around one kind of product. Though minor variations in the product might be introduced at places throughout the line, they are usually cosmetic and constrained to whatever the sequence of operations and production rate allow.

Product layouts are also constrained in terms of output capacity since the production rate is designed into the layout. To alter the rate, the line must be rebalanced, which means individual operations must be reconfigured to change the rate of material processed through them. The more mechanized the line is, the more time-consuming and costly it is to rebalance it. The process must be stopped and changed over, which can take hours or days, even after setup-reduction efforts. Often the easiest way to increase capacity of the line is to simply run it longer through overtime or additional shifts. To decrease capacity, the line is periodically stopped.

The capital investment in a product layout can be large. To achieve high efficiency and rapid flow rates, lines often use special-purpose machines and transfer systems. The equipment is often custom-made, one-of-kind, so it is expensive to design, fabricate, install, and maintain. Since resequencing and rebalancing the line to accommodate changes in product options and production rates is costly, producers try to keep changes to a minimum. Workers do not see much variety either. Their tasks are often narrowly defined, and since the products seldom change, their minute-to-minute tasks stay the same and can become boring.

Product and process layouts represent two pure types of layouts at opposite ends of a continuum. Just as many plants use different work processes, so they use mixed or hybrid layouts. Some areas of the plant are arranged as process layouts to produce parts and components for other areas of the plant, which are arranged as product layouts that assemble the parts and components into finished products.

VARIETY/VOLUME TRADE-OFF

There is a perplexing dynamic in manufacturing, a variant of the variety/efficiency trade-off discussed earlier: to increase its product appeal and broaden market scope, a producer should strive for agility so as to offer many kinds of products; at the same time, to reduce production waste and increase profits, it should focus on relatively few products and produce them in high volume. The question is, How can a manufacturer achieve high production efficiency without sacrificing product options and variety? Referring to the above taxonomies of types of work and facility layouts, it seems that a choice must be made between variety and volume, and that efficiency will be the byproduct of that choice: high volume, high efficiency; low volume, low efficiency. The problem is, demand for many products is small, so not every product should be produced in high volume. Also, many companies choose to fill their production capacity with a wide variety of small-volume end-items. So, must companies that produce many kinds of things, each in small volume, be content with low efficiency for all of them?

The answer lies in the way production resources are allocated to individual products. In general, we know that for efficient production of discrete units, repetitive production is much better than job-shop production. Therefore, if items can be produced over and over again, and if, at the same time, the production process can accommodate some differences or variety in those items, then efficient production of a variety of products will result.

To achieve repetitive production, it is necessary to focus on a *few kinds* of products at a time. Now, the way we incorporate variety into repetitive production lies in the way we define a *kind* of product; that is, we define each kind of product so it can actually represent *many* products, each that is somewhat different. The point is that we start with a large number of different products, then collapse that number for purposes of production into a much smaller, more manageable number. This is the purpose of **group technology.**

GROUP TECHNOLOGY

Most of the waste in a job-shop environment comes from trying to use a single, all-purpose facility to make end-items that each have unique components, operations, and routing sequences. In most job shops the number and variety of products and parts is large and ever expanding, and in some shops the proliferation of products and parts is epidemic.

Group technology (GT) is grounded on the premise that, given multiple means to achieve the same end, simpler is better. Ceteris paribus, if products can be reduced in number and made more standardized, and if the processes that make those products can also be reduced in number, then production waste will be reduced and efficiency will be increased.

An important feature about GT, however, is that it does not seek to reduce variety in the kinds of products *offered to customers;* that kind of variety is appreciated and retained. Rather, GT seeks to reduce variety in the kinds of products *produced* by the manufacturer. This is achieved by identifying and exploiting the *similarities* between different products, similarities such as physical characteristics, dimensions, geometrical shapes, and materials. Beyond appearance and composition, GT also identifies and exploits similarities in the processes and operations employed to make products. Products that look quite different might require the same or similar operations, and, thus, from a GT perspective might all be the same. Product similarities are identified using coding and classification schemes.

PRODUCT CODING AND CLASSIFICATION SCHEMES

Product coding refers to assigning a multidigit, alphanumeric code to a product. For example, a product might be coded as "6932AQ," where each of the digits and letters represents a feature or attribute about the product like its dimensions, materials, and machining requirements. A code like this can be used in several ways, such as to specify the design categories to which different products belong or to classify the products into groups based upon similarity of manufacturing processes. Three basic schemes are used to code products: hierarchical, chain, and hybrid.[1]

Hierarchical (Monocode) Structure

This code structure is interpreted as an inverted-tree hierarchy. The code for each product is a sequence of digits created by starting at the top or trunk of the tree, then moving downward through whatever branches apply. For example, the code for the part shown on the right in Figure 9.4 is 0011. It was created by moving through the hierarchy, top to bottom, and assigning digits that correspond to the product's dimensional features: the product is cylindrical (0), has L/D ratio < 1 (0), has I/D ratio ≥ 0. 5 (1), and has inside tolerance ≥ 0.0001 (1).

FIGURE 9.4

Hierarchical coding structure for part 0011: Cylindrical machined part, length 1″, diameter 1.25″, inside bore 1″ with 0.0001″ tolerance.

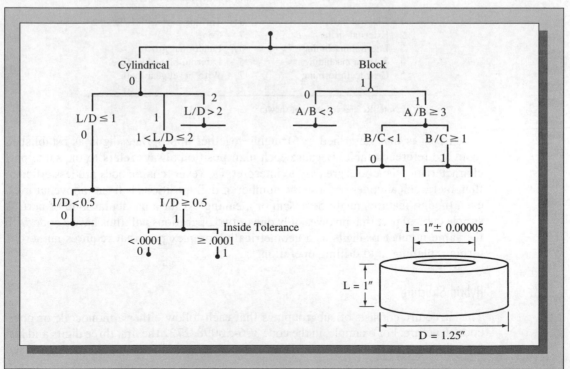

In hierarchical codes, each digit's interpretation depends upon the preceding digit. For example, the second digit, 0, in the code would have a different meaning if the first digit had been 1 instead of 0. The advantage of this structure is that it is compact and assigns only the number of digits necessary to define each part. That is, the number of digits necessary on the inverted tree differs depending on the part being coded. As a result, some parts have seven digits, others only three. However, because of the different possible meanings for each of the digits in a sequence, the code is more difficult to interpret than the next coding scheme.

Chain (Polycode) Structure

In this structure, each digit's position in the sequence always represents the same attribute or feature of a part. Given a five-digit code the first digit would always refer to, for example, the class of the part, the second would refer to the part's external shape, the third would refer to its internal shape, and so on. Each digit has values 0–9 or A–Z, and each value has a particular meaning, which is maintained in a reference table. For example, part code 37357 might be interpreted from the reference table as the following:

Feature/Attribute	
Digit Position	*Interpretation from Reference Table**
1 Class of part	3 = Turning part with L/D > 2
2 External shape	7 = Cone
3 Internal machining	3 = Functional groves
4 Surface machining	5 = External planed surface
5 Gear teeth forming	7 = With bevel gear teeth.

* Note: Reference table not shown.

A part is thus described by stringing together appropriate digits as established from the reference table. Because each digit position always refers to the same part characteristic, the codes are easy to interpret. However, chain codes are less efficient than hierarchical codes because the number of digit positions is fixed (above, at five), even though features might be absent or meaningless for a particular kind of part. A simple cubical part that involves only one or two operations will thus have a code with the same number of digits as a geometrically complex part that requires numerous turning, planing, and drilling operations.

Hybrid Structure

This structure consists of subgroupings that each follow either a monocode or polycode structure. For example, in the code 396-56098-2722 the first three digits and last four digits might be based on a monocode structure, while the middle five are based on a polycode structure. Hybrid codes are versatile because they can be tailored to represent both general attributes of parts as well as process-specific or company-specific features.

PRODUCT FAMILIES AND FOCUSED FACTORIES

Products with similar manufacturing characteristics as identified by GT coding can be grouped together and classified as a **family** of products, parts, or components. All of the items in a product family are generally made from the same material, have similar overall dimensions, and require similar machines, tooling, or routing sequences. Suppose, for example, a seven-digit chain code is used, and the codes for two products U and V are 3020011 and 3120001, respectively. Aside from digits in the second and sixth positions, the codes for the two products are identical. Suppose the first digit represents the kind of material; the second digit, special storage conditions; the third digit, the kind of machining process; the fourth, fifth, and last digits, dimensional aspects of the products; and the sixth digit, a final plating process. Given that both products are made of the same material, use the same machining process, and are almost dimensionally identical, they might be classified as members of a family of products with common materials and production processes.

If sufficient combined demand exists for the products in a family, then a **focused factory** can be set up to exclusively produce that family of products. In one sense, a focused factory is like a product layout: it clusters together the required equipment, tools, and workers to enable production of the product family on a repetitive basis. Unlike product layouts, however, the focused facility is capable of producing *every* item in the family, not just one. Making things in focused factories thus affords efficiencies and economies associated with high-volume production. High volume, however, is achieved by processing different, but similar kinds of items, even though the volume for any one product might be small. The focused factory combines the variety and flexibility of a job shop with the simplicity and efficiency of a flow line.

NOTE ON GT AND PRODUCT DESIGN

Though our interest here is on GT coding for the purpose of classifying products into families, we briefly note GT's role in new product design. Whenever a part is called for in a new product, the designer can access the GT database to see if a part already exists that is similar to the one needed in terms of function and physical features. If so, that part can be used either as-is or with modification. With GT codes, new parts can be designed for interchangeable application in more than one product and to make use of existing processes and operations. The results are fewer unnecessary new and unique parts, more applications for new and existing parts, simpler bills of materials, and simpler production and inventory planning and control.

TO CODE OR NOT TO CODE

The decision about whether to code products, for whatever purpose, is not trivial since the coding process can itself be difficult and expensive. Although coding new products in a new facility is relatively easy because everything is done from scratch, collecting data, assigning codes, and forming families for existing products and facilities can be complex, frustrating, and costly. Just selecting, purchasing, and installing the coding software can be time-consuming and expensive. Some commercial software enables coding for product design, but not for forming part families; some is useful for forming part families based upon physical attributes, though not upon processes or machines, which makes it useless for designing focused factories.

As an alternative to commercial software, the coding and classification procedure can be developed internally. In that case a company starts by reviewing the process route sheets of all parts used, revises the sheets for errors, then assigns in-house codes. Small companies can store part numbers and codes in a personal computer using inexpensive database software and keep any additional information about the parts in a filing cabinet for reference. Although unsophisticated, this kind of system is often sufficient to eliminate redundancies in product design and to identify part families around which focused factories can be formed.

FOCUSED FACTORY[2]

A focused factory is also called a plant within a plant or a *subplant*. Each focused factory is a portion of a plant devoted to making a group of several or numerous somewhat-similar products. Walls, temporary partitions, or lines on the floor serve as boundaries to separate subplants. Each subplant is like an autonomous factory with its own equipment and workers, which can number between 10 and several hundred (around 30 is most common). Often, each subplant also has its own maintenance, purchasing, and engineering support staff on the plant floor or nearby. The staff is small because much of the PM, housekeeping, and simple setups are done by operators and assemblers. Each focused factory also has its own manager or supervisor, depending on its size. A big focused factory has a manager, a small one has a supervisor, and a very small one (three or four workers) has a supervisor that it shares with other small focused factories. To keep management levels to a minimum, the manager of a focused factory ordinarily reports directly to the plant manager.

Most focused factories achieve efficiency through repetitive production of a product family. However, even focused factories that produce in small- and medium-sized batches are somewhat efficient, and certainly much better in terms of cost and quality than job shops. One reason is because the workers and manager in a focused factory are more focused; they have greater direct responsibility for planning, scheduling, and controlling output and for costs and quality. Smaller-sized focused factories (small physical size, small number of workers) tend to be more efficient than larger ones because employees are more directly involved, know the overall process better, are more motivated, and a single supervisor or manager can oversee everything. In small subplants the physical distances are also small, which reduces waste from material handling, communication, and work coordination. It is common that within a subplant, the managers, employees, customers, and vendors work directly with each other.

ON WHAT TO FOCUS

In first writing about the focused factory concept in 1974,[3] Wickham Skinner suggested reorganizing each focused factory around individual products. Today, the organization of a focused factory depends at least as much on the manufacturing processes and operations as it does on products. Although some modern focused factories are devoted to meeting requirements of special customers (such as military, aerospace, or construction contractors), others are devoted to product families and products based on commonality of production processes. Factors of greatest relevance in focused-factory design are the number of individual products or part families to be produced, the routing sequence they follow, and the operations and machines they require.

Focused factories take different forms, three that are shown in Figure 9.5. A **focused flow line** is similar to a product layout, except it can produce all the parts in a part family. It is appropriate when every item in the part family follows the same process sequence and requires about the same processing time on each machine. Variety within product families is achieved by using different but similar parts and components in assemblies, quick changeover machines, and multiskilled workers at each operation. Typically a conveyor, gravity slides, or an automated transport system connects the operations.

A **workcell** has more general application. The workcell on the left in Figure 9.5 can make products that require any of the four operations in the same general sequence. Operations not needed for a product are skipped. The workcell on the right can make products that require any of the five operations, but in any combination or sequence.

A workcell is actually a dedicated job shop with features of a repetitive product layout, but it is capable of economically producing items in small batches, even of size one. Ideally the routings within workcells are unidirectional to allow parts production on a flow-line basis. If the workcell is unidirectional, a conveyor or simple gravity-chute system connects the operations. For omnidirectional flow, the transport system must be more flexible; materials are hand- or cart-carried or are placed on tables in the center of the workcell between successive operations. Machines and workstations in a workcell are usually arranged in a U-shaped pattern so the distances are small and workers can readily move among them.

A **focused workcenter** is similar to a process layout in that machines are clustered into areas by functional type. The difference is that in focused workcenters certain machines in each functional area are dedicated to producing only certain part families. For example, whenever a job for any product in Family 4 is processed, it always goes to machines a, j, m, and v, whereas any job for a product in Family 2 always goes to machines n, t, d, u, and s. This simplifies machine scheduling, saves on setup time, and improves product quality.[4] A focused workcenter arrangement makes sense when each department has multiple machines, when machines are difficult to move or set up, or where product volumes and product mix change so fast that it is impractical to move machines into focused flow lines or workcells.

All of these kinds of focused factories enable better production control and are less wasteful than job shops.

FIGURE 9.5

Some examples of focused-facility layouts.

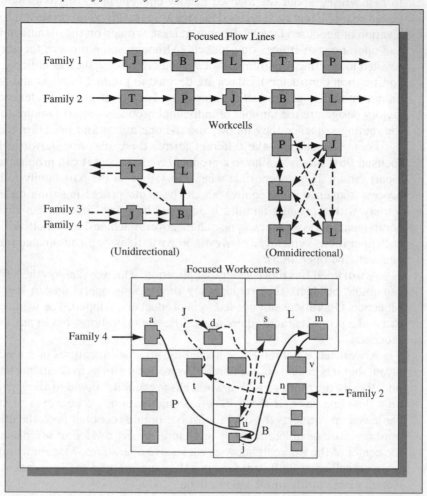

CASE IN POINT: Focused Factories at Iekian Industries

Iekian Industries manufactures two families of compressors, large and small. The small family has three products, S1, S2, and S3; the large family has four products, L1–L4. Demand for the different products varies greatly between them, though for each of them it is somewhat steady. The difference in physical size between the smallest and the largest compressors (S1 and L4) is substantial. Whereas the small compressors can be moved by hand or on small manual carts, the large ones require forklifts or overhead cranes. The manufacturing and assembly equipment also vary with the size of the product; the small compressors require relatively small equipment and the large compressors require large equipment. Aside from some electrical components that are outsourced, the two families have little parts commonality.

Given the differences between the two product families, Iekian reorganized its plant from a process job shop into two focused factories, one for each product family. Additionally, it subdivided the focused factories into focused flow lines based upon commonality of equipment, material handling, and production volume. The principal tasks on each line are main component subassembly, product final assembly, and product checkout. In the focused factory for small compressors, two flow lines were established, one for S1 and one for S2 and S3. Each is a dedicated product line. While the demand for S2 and S3 was too low to justify setting up a line for each, demand for the combination of the two justified dedicating a line to both. The new, focused layout is shown in Figure 9.6.

Using similar rationale, the focused factory for the large compressors was divided into three lines, one each for L1 and L2, one for L3, and one for L4. Demand for L4 is small, so the line is frequently stopped. Since, however, the equipment for making L4 is too large for use on the other compressors, dedicating it to the L4 line does not affect its utilization. Aside from L4, all the product lines produce repetitively.

In addition to the compressor assemblies, Iekian also manufactures most of the major components for the compressors. Component production is done on a batch-repetitive basis. Many of the same machines are used to make components for all of the compressors, regardless of size. Thus, in addition to the two focused factories formed *around products* (one each for the S lines and L lines), four other focused factories were formed *around processes*—one each for welding, plating, pressing, and casting. These focused factories serve as suppliers to the product focused factories. Because the size of metal castings varies from small to very large, and because the castings require a variety of machining operations, the casting focused factory was split into three focused factories, one for small castings, one for large, and one for casting machining.

FIGURE 9.6

Plant layout after reorganization into focused facilities.

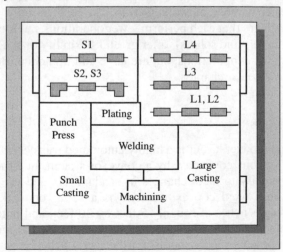

Decisions about which operations should be included in a focused factory depend not only on demand and commonality of products and/or processes, but also on the required or available speed and capacity of the operations. If, for example, a machine can produce parts at a rate of 50 units per hour, but the focused factory it feeds requires parts at a rate of 10 per hour, then the machine produces at a rate five times the requirement. If dedicated to that focused factory, the machine would be utilized only 20% of the time. Now, if no other processes make use of that machine, then low utilization is irrelevant and the machine can be assigned to the focused factory. If, however, the machine is one-of-a-kind and other processes use it, then it should be available for use by other processes and remain outside the focused factory.

A one-of-a-kind machine can be put in a central area, and the focused factories that need it can be located nearby. However, routing parts from multiple processes through one machine always poses scheduling problems, though if the machine has sufficient capacity the problems can be minimized. If, however, the machine becomes a bottleneck, it will be impossible for the focused factories to autonomously schedule and control their work since the bottleneck is outside their control. Such a situation erases much of the advantage of using focused factories. If the capital expense is low relative to the benefits of dedicating machines to focused factories, more machines should be purchased so each focused factory has its own and does not have to route work outside.

MICRODESIGN ISSUES

The guiding principle behind focused factories is simple: form follows function, where function is defined by product-mix and product-volume requirements. Each focused factory should be thought of as a flexible, temporary arrangement that, if necessary, can be changed to meet new requirements. Flexibility in a factory results from flexible workers and flexible, mobile machines. Other things equal, multiskilled workers who can be assigned to different tasks and processes, as needed, offer much more flexibility than a greater number of workers who can each do only one task. Additionally, multiple machines that each perform fewer operations, but are small and can easily be moved (on casters and rollers), offer greater flexibility than a few machines that each can perform many operations, but are large and immobile. Both of these matters are discussed in the next chapter.

Flexible Flow Lines

A traditional product layout is a highly automated transfer line or an assembly line of workers at stations connected by a conveyor system. In either case, the line can be difficult to modify to meet changes in product mix and product volume. A flexible alternative to a fixed conveyor system is a series of work benches. Schonberger suggests using benches of roughly 5 feet by 30 feet, and putting them end to end to form a product line.[5] The benches can be easily moved around, added or deleted, to suit current product requirements. Further, says Schonberger, each bench should be a focused factory, that is, the first bench should be for making parts and components, the next bench for subassemblies, the next for final assembly, and the last benches for testing and packaging.

As shown in Figure 9.7, workers sit on both sides of the benches and are in close contact. Parts are passed between workers and between benches on simple gravity slides. Forming a focused factory at each bench encourages focused problem solving and continuous improvement and simplifies overall line balancing. The amount of WIP at each bench is tightly controlled, either by kanbans (using a CONWIP system for the entire line of benches) or by an amount specified in standard operating procedures, as discussed in Chapter 11.

Flexible U-Lines and S-Lines

Product lines should be curved. For a small assembly or machining process with, say, three to six workstations, the line can be U-shaped, with workers sitting or walking around inside the U. The U-shape minimizes distances between operations and allows a few workers to quickly walk between and operate several machines. The U-shape is common for workcells, as discussed in the next chapter.

For a process that has many workstations, the line should be serpentine or S-shaped. This shape minimizes space requirements and the average distance between workers. Putting people into a smaller space encourages face-to-face interaction and teamwork, and putting materials into a smaller space puts attention on raw-material and in-process inventory as well as on finding ways to minimize them. The relative location of workers, and the actual distances between them, depends on ergonomics and such things as ease of workers reaching for a part and passing it to the next station.[6] Although, in fact, each worker might not be any closer to adjacent workers than on a straight line, on a curved line a worker is closer to all other workers, on average.

FIGURE 9.7

Assembly benches and gravity slides.

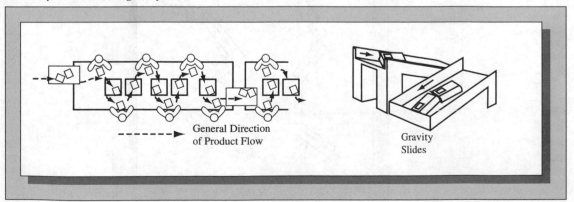

General Direction
of Product Flow

Gravity
Slides

Flexibility in a manual assembly process is achieved by changing the length of the line (adding or deleting benches) and by flexing the line (changing the arc radius of the curves). This is shown in Figure 9.8.[7]

Working Out the Final Layout

The actual relative position of machines and workstations in a focused factory is often determined by trial and error. Workers should have final say in new layout proposals. One way is to put the floor plan on a table in the shop cafeteria. Pieces of paper cut to the shape (footprint) of different machines are located on the plan according to the proposed arrangement. Workers are encouraged to scrutinize the plan, move the pieces of paper around, and try out better arrangements. The author has done this; because workers are often more knowledgeable about the size, weight, shape, and other features of machines than are managers and consultants, they have good arguments about why their plan is better than the one proposed.

Drawings, computer layout analysis, and planning on paper are a good start, but they do not quite give the full picture (you can never tell about roominess or traffic patterns in a plant by looking at blueprints; you have to be *in* the plant, with machines, and walk around). Thus, the next step is to actually move machines and workstations to the proposed location and keep moving them until everyone is satisfied. That is sometimes easier said than done, especially when the machines are big and bulky.

PRODUCT-QUANTITY ANALYSIS

As with other manufacturing decisions, there is no getting around the product-variety/product-volume tradeoff in determining what to produce in a focused factory. For the same reason a manufacturer cannot produce 1000 different things in small volume for

FIGURE 9.8

Flexing an assembly line.

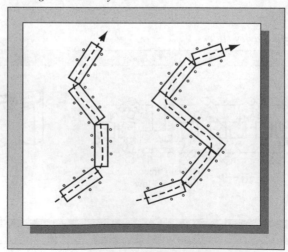

CASE IN POINT: Changing Layout at Hamilton Standard

Hamilton Standard's Windsor Locks plant used a paper doll layout approach for planning facility changes. Since many of the machines are enormous, moving them in trial-and-error fashion is impossible, and workflow analysis on paper is inaccurate. So to analyze alternative layouts, cardboard pieces were cut out with the same floor dimensions as the machines. The pieces were then arranged and rearranged in an empty area of the parking lot until people were satisfied with the layout and walk patterns. The machines were then located within the plant according to the new pattern. Consequently, required floor space was reduced by 75% and required travel distance between machines was reduced by 85%.

the same cost and efficiency as only 10 things in high volume, a manufacturer cannot establish 1000 focused factories.

One principle for establishing focused factories is that the volume of production output of each focused factory must justify the cost of dedicating workers and equipment to producing that output. The decision about what to produce in a focused factory, then, must consider product volume.

As an example, suppose a company makes 800 products, and Pareto analysis indicates that of those, seven account for 49.4% of factory output (see Figure 9.9). If

FIGURE 9.9

Pareto diagram of product volume.

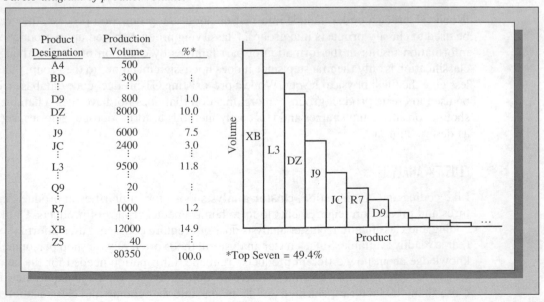

Product Designation	Production Volume	%*
A4	500	
BD	300	⋮
⋮		
D9	800	1.0
DZ	8000	10.0
⋮		⋮
J9	6000	7.5
JC	2400	3.0
⋮		
L3	9500	11.8
⋮		⋮
Q9	20	⋮
⋮		
R7	1000	1.2
⋮		
XB	12000	14.9
Z5	40	⋮
	80350	100.0

*Top Seven = 49.4%

one or a more of these seven products could be produced in one or more focused factories, not only would they be produced more efficiently, but the reduced plant-wide workload and inventory would also improve the scheduling and production of the other 793 products.

While the emphasis is first on the highest-volume products, the volume of one or a few products alone might not be sufficient to justify a dedicated focused factory. In that case emphasis switches to a focused factory that can produce multiple products, and, in particular, products that constitute a product family. This is where the concept of grouping products according to commonality of operations comes into play in forming focused factories.

ESTABLISHING PRODUCT AND MACHINE GROUPS

Forming a focused factory involves two things: (1) forming a cluster or group of products or parts that are similar in terms of processing requirements (the product family) and (2) forming a cluster or group of operations, machines, workers, and tools (the focused factory to produce that product family). From here on the term group will refer to the combination of products *and* the machines that produce them. The ideal situation is where groups are completely independent, which means that each focused factory contains all the operations required to produce a complete product family. In forming focused factories the goal is to maximize the degree of independence of groups, although complete independence between groups is often difficult to achieve.

Two kinds of approaches are used for configuring groups: (1) parts coding and classification and (2) cluster analysis.[8]

CODING AND CLASSIFICATION

When GT product codes include information about the production process, they can be used to classify products into groups. Classifying products based upon production information results in the formation of part families by common processes, though classification is only the first step since it does not assign machines to the group, much less give the final, physical layout. While a pre-existing GT product code database can be used to create product groups, an organization that does not have such a database should consider using simpler and less costly methods to form focused factories, such as described next.

CLUSTER ANALYSIS

Like coding and classification, **cluster analysis** looks for similarities in product features and production requirements to form homogeneous groups of products. Unlike coding and classification, cluster analysis does not require codes and uses information that is readily available. Since cluster analysis methods often rely on shop personnel's knowledge about how different products are made, information needed for the analysis is relatively simple and inexpensive to obtain. Based on their experience in more than 400 factories, Harmon and Peterson state that coding and classification is impractical and unnecessary for establishing focused factories,[9] and they suggest instead starting with information about product routings through operations. One plant where they used this approach was able to determine the product–machine groups to form workcells and specific layouts for the workcells in only a few days. The same plant had earlier employed a consultant who spent 6 months coding and analyzing parts, only to conclude that the parts were too dissimilar for focused factories.

As illustrated next, when the numbers of products and machines are not too large, the analysis can be performed by just *looking* at the process routings.

Example   1:   Group Formation by Visual Process-Routing Analysis

The group formation procedure should begin by focusing on products with the highest volume. Suppose a product-quantity (PQ) analysis gives the results shown previously in Figure 9.9, and the resulting seven largest-volume products are selected for process-routing analysis. Table 9.1 shows the process routings, which are the sequences of machine operations required for each product.

Products with similar operations are clustered together. The example includes only five operations, so it is easy to cluster products according to similar operations and similar sequences. The result, Table 9.2, shows two natural groups: the first includes machines A, B, and C and produces products XB, JC, L3, and R7; the second includes machines D and E and makes products D9, J9, and DZ. Each group is a candidate for a workcell. Except for product D9, the products fall into either of two workcells and could be wholly produced by a single cell. The situation with D9

TABLE 9.1

Product	Volume	Process Routing (Machine Sequence)
XB	12000	A $\longrightarrow$ B $\longrightarrow$ C
L3	9500	C $\longrightarrow$ B $\longrightarrow$ A
DZ	8000	E $\longrightarrow$ D
J9	6000	D $\longrightarrow$ E
JC	2400	A $\longrightarrow$ B $\longrightarrow$ C
R7	1000	C $\longrightarrow$ A
D9	800	C $\longrightarrow$ D $\longrightarrow$ E

TABLE 9.2

Product	Volume	Process Routing (Machine Sequence)	
XB	12000	A $\longrightarrow$ B $\longrightarrow$ C	
JC	2400	A $\longrightarrow$ B $\longrightarrow$ C	
L3	9500	A $\longleftarrow$ B $\longleftarrow$ C	
R7	1000	A $\longleftarrow$ C	
D9	800	C $\longrightarrow$ D $\longrightarrow$ E	
J9	6000	D $\longrightarrow$ E	
DZ	8000	D $\longleftarrow$ E	
		Workcell 1	Workcell 2

is common since products often involve operations which do not entirely fit into only one workcell. Perhaps for D9, operation C could be performed in cell 1 on a batch basis, then the batch could be moved to cell 2 for machining on D and E.

This example considers only the seven largest-volume products, though ordinarily the routing analysis would include as many products as practical. Although products might each have small volume, when grouped into part families their collective volume might justify a focused factory. If, for example, other products could be found requiring only operations C, D, and E, then procuring a C-type machine for use in cell 2 might be justified. These and other considerations for cell formation are discussed later.

Visual methods are practical if the number of products and machines under consideration is somewhat small. When the volume of the few highest-volume products is insufficient to justify a focused factory, then products with successively lower volume in the Pareto ordering are included. Focused factories commonly produce a large number of similar products where the demand for each product is somewhat small.

PRODUCTION FLOW ANALYSIS

Production flow analysis (PFA), popularized by Burbidge in the mid-1970s,[10] is a another methodology for forming groups of part families and machines. The term PFA has also come to refer to many subtechniques for simplifying material flow systems at any level of an organization. Like the visual method, PFA techniques use information about process operations to simultaneously form product and machine groupings; the techniques, however, are more rigorous than the visual method.

One group of such techniques performs *factory flow analysis* that divides a factory into major, largely independent focused factories, where each factory completes all the parts it makes. These techniques also connect focused factories such that products flow in a simple, unidirectional fashion throughout the factory. Another group of PFA techniques performs *group analysis,* which divides each department into groups or workcells that are largely independent and responsible for performing most or all of the operations to make a family of products. Other PFA techniques address other levels of the production system. From here on we will focus on techniques primarily for group analysis and for forming independent workcells.

PFA techniques usually start with product–machine information as represented on a product–process matrix, hereafter termed simply the **process matrix.** Figure 9.10 is the process matrix corresponding to Table 9.2; it shows the machines required for each product, though not the ordering (sequence) that products visit machines. Each column in the process matrix represents a product or part; each row represents a machine or operation. A "1" means that the part visits (is processed by) the machine. In Figure 9.10, product XB visits machines A, B, and C; product D9 visits C, D, and E; product DZ visits D and E; and so on.

Notice in Figure 9.10 that the 1s fall into two dense blocks along the main diagonal. In general, dense blocks of 1s suggest natural groupings of products and machines. The dense blocks in Figure 9.10 suggest the obvious: form one workcell with machines A, B, and C to make products XB, JC, L3, and R7; form the other workcell with the remaining machines to make the remaining products. Only Product

FIGURE 9.10

Process matrix corresponding to Table 9.2.

				Product			
Machine	XB	JC	L3	R7	D9	J9	DZ
A	1	1	1	1			
B	1	1	1				
C	1	1	1	1	1		
D					1	1	1
E					1	1	1

FIGURE 9.11

Initial process matrix.

Initial				Binary Ordering Algorithm				
				Part				
Machine	1	2	3	4	5	6	7	8	9
A					1	1		1	
B					1	1		1	1
C		1		1	1		1		
D	1		1						
E					1	1			
F	1		1	1					
G					1	1	1		1	1
H		1		1			1		

D9 is considered an exceptional product because it requires operations in more than one group. (Machine C could be considered an exceptional machine because it is needed by products in more than one group.) Many of the PFA techniques use the process matrix to form workcells. Following is an example.

Binary Ordering Algorithm

In terms of the process matrix, assignment of products and machines to groups happens by rearranging 1s so they lie in diagonal, dense-block form. The **binary ordering algorithm** (BOA) is a procedure for transforming (as near as possible) any N-column, M-row, binary (0-1) matrix into this form. BOA rearranges rows so that similar rows are adjacent, then does the same for the columns. Consider as an example the process matrix in Figure 9.11 (the term "part" is used instead of "product," though the terms are interchangeable, depending whether the end-item is a component part or completed product).

Example   2:   Binary Ordering Algorithm Procedure

The procedure works as follows:

1. Assign a value to each column k, where the value is 2^{N-k}. In Figure 9.11, $N = 9$, $k = 1, 2, 3, \ldots, 9$. These values are shown at the bottom of the matrix in Figure 9.12.
2. For each row, obtain a sum by adding the 2^{N-k} values wherever a 1 appears in that row. These row sums are shown at the far right in Figure 9.12. For example, for machine A, a 1 appears in columns 5, 6, and 8 (circled in Figure 9.12), so the row sum $= 16 + 8 + 2 = 26$.

FIGURE 9.12

Process matrix: steps 1 and 2.

Machine	1	2	3	4	5	6	7	8	9	Sum
A					①	①		①		㉖
B					1	1		1	1	27
C		1		1	1		1			180
D	1		1							320
E					1	1				24
F	1		1	1						352
G					1	1	1	1	1	59
H		1		1			1			164
2^{N-k}	256	128	64	32	⑯	⑧	4	②	1	

Part (column header spanning columns 1–9)

3. Rearrange rows in decreasing order of row sum—F, D, C, H, etc. Figure 9.13 shows the new row ordering.
4. Assign a value to each row k, where the value is 2^{M-k}. These values are shown on the far right in Figure 9.13; there, $M = 8$ and $k = 1, 2, 3, \ldots, 8$.
5. For each column obtain a sum by adding the 2^{M-k} values wherever a 1 appears in that column. These column sums are shown on the bottom of the matrix in Figure 9.13. For part 1, for example, a 1 appears in rows F and D (circled in Figure 9.13), so the column sum $= 128 + 64 = 192$.
6. Reorder the columns in decreasing order of column sums. The new column ordering is 1, 3, 4, 2, etc. This is shown in Figure 9.14, the final matrix.

FIGURE 9.13

Process matrix: steps 3–5.

Machine	1	2	3	4	5	6	7	8	9	2^{M-k}
				Part						
F	①		1	1						⑫⑧ +
D	①		1							⑥④ =
C		1		1	1		1			32
H		1		1			1			16
G				1	1	1		1	1	8
B					1	1		1	1	4
A					1	1		1		2
E					1	1				1
Sum	⑲②	48	192	184	47	15	48	14	12	

FIGURE 9.14

Final matrix: diagonal, dense-block form.

Machine	1	3	4	2	7	5	6	8	9
				Part					
F	1	1	1						
D	1	1							
C			1	1	1	1			
H			1	1	1				
G			1			1	1	1	1
B						1	1	1	1
A						1	1	1	
E						1	1		

PFA procedures are more efficient than GT coding for forming workcells because they identify product families solely by processing requirements, not by appearance or physical features. PFA techniques are more versatile than the visual method because they permit analysis of larger numbers of products and machines and allow for other considerations such as constraints on group size and machine availability. PFA methods rely on existing information about processes and equipment, and so they can be used to analyze alternative facility layouts with minimal expense.

A drawback of PFA techniques is that they do not guarantee answers that can be implemented. They usually ignore the direction of workflow between machines, so further analysis is needed to achieve unidirectional flow. The results of PFA must be evaluated and usually fudged before a final, acceptable product–machine group emerges. Results may call for duplication of a machine where, in actuality, only one such machine is available. Final machine assignments to workcells do not necessarily furnish high, or even moderate, utilizations of equipment.

DENSE BLOCKS, THEN WHAT?

Three dense blocks are very apparent in Figure 9.14. These indicate three possible (obvious) workcells to which parts and machines could be assigned:

> Cell 1: Machines F and D; parts 1 and 3.
> Cell 2: Machines C and H; parts 2 and 7.
> Cell 3: Machines G, B, A, and E; parts 6, 8, and 9.

Parts 4 and 5 are exceptions: Part 4 straddles all three blocks and part 5 straddles the second and third. There are several possible ways to handle these: (1) redesign part 4 so it does not need machines F and G, and redesign part 5 so it does not need machine C; (2) add machines F and G to the second cell so part 4 can be entirely processed there, and add machine C to the third cell so part 5 can be entirely processed there; (3) combine all three groups into one group; (4) combine any two groups into one group, and add whatever machines are still needed to the remaining group; or (5) route part 4 through all three groups, and part 5 through machine groups 2 and 3. Of course, the viability or feasibility of any of these alternatives is open to question, depending on availability of other machines or capital funds to procure machines.

Demand, sequence of operations, transportation distance and cost, and setups are also factors that the initial assignment ignores. Consider for a moment the assignment shown in Figure 9.15 and the question as to where to put machine C. If demand for part 3 is greater than for part 4, put it in workcell 1. If the cost of transporting part 4 is much greater than part 2, then put C in workcell 2. Suppose the parts routing is A–C–B for part 3, and C–D–E for part 4; then put machine C in workcell 1 so it does not have to backtrack (go from cell 1 to cell 2, then back to cell 1). A 1 in the process matrix indicates only that a machine is used to make product, not how many times it is needed. Suppose the machine sequence for part 3 is A–B–C, and for part 4 it is D–C–E–C. In that case machine C should probably be put into workcell 2, otherwise part 4 would have to backtrack (cell 2 to cell 1, then back to cell 2).

Machine setup time can also influence the product–machine assignment. If the setup procedure is lengthy, then it is desirable to cluster products with machines that require similar or identical setups. The result might be several workcells that contain identical machines, but within each cell the machines are set up to process a particular product group.

FIGURE 9.15

A part–machine grouping.

		Part				
Machine		1	2	3	4	5
Workcell {A		1	1	1		
1 {B		1	1	1		
C					1	1
Workcell {D					1	1
2 {E					1	1

FIGURE 9.16

Process matrix; dense-block form.

	Part								
Machine	1	3	4	2	7	5	6	8	9
F	1	1	1						
D	1	1	1						
C			1	1	1	1			
H			1	1	1				
G			1			1	1	1	1
B						1	1	1	1
A						1	1	1	
E						1	1		

Machines arranged for unidirectional flow, either as focused flow lines or unidirectional workcells (shown in Figure 9.5), give the most efficient processing. Referring to Figure 9.16, a workcell with four sequential operations G–B–A–E could process part 6 efficiently if the part had that sequence, though it could not process part 5 efficiently if that part had the sequence A–B–C–E–G. However, by skipping operation E that same cell could efficiently process part 8 if the part had the sequence G–B–A. In general, the more a focused factory is designed for unidirectional, repetitive production, the more efficiently the items that follow the flow can be processed. As with product layouts, however, the routing sequence restricts the number of products the focused factory is capable of processing. Even within a focused factory, the trade-off between production efficiency and product variety remains.

The factory arrangement finally chosen might consist of a variety of focused-factory configurations. Referring to Figure 9.16 again, suppose analysis of demand, routing sequences, and so on, leads to the following layout (where FF refers to focused factory):

FF1, Focused workcenter: F, D, E.
FF2, Unidirectional workcell: C–H.
FF3, Focused flow line: G–B–A.

With this assignment, some parts will be processed entirely within a single focused factory (parts 8 and 9 in FF3, parts 1 and 3 in FF1, and parts 2 and 7 in FF2), some by being routed through two focused factories (part 4 in FF3 and FF2; part 6 in FF1 and FF3), and one part, 5, by being routed through FF2, FF3, then FF1.

It might appear from the discussion that a large degree of subjectiveness is involved in establishing final product–machine groupings. The degree of subjectiveness is lessened with some PFA techniques (two of which are described in the supplement at the end of the chapter), however all PFA techniques are limited in the scope of things they consider. Subjectiveness can be reduced, but not eliminated. Design of focused factories in plants that have many tens of operations and similar numbers of products is complex and time-consuming, and there are literally millions of possible clustering combinations. For these, computer simulation and what-if analysis should be used to narrow the possibilities and evaluate the trade-offs.

Throughout this chapter the terms operation and machine have been used interchangeably. In many cases, the operation will not involve a machine, either fully or partially, but will be a manual procedure such as filing, inspection, or assembly. The following chapter distinguishes between manual and machine operations in focused factories as well as differences in the design of an assembly workcell (wherein all operations might be manual) and the design of a machining workcell (wherein all operations might be automated). Focused-factory design and implementation go beyond technical matters and involve organizational and human behavior issues; these are also addressed in the next chapter.

ADVANTAGES AND DISADVANTAGES OF FOCUSED FACTORIES

Focused factories offer advantages over job shops and flow shops. Compared to product layouts, focused factories require less capital investment and are significantly more flexible. Compared to the process layouts, focused facilities are significantly less wasteful. According to Steudle and Desruelle, the following results were achieved:[11]

- 70–90% Reductions in lead times and WIP inventories.
- 75–90% Reductions in material handling.
- 20–45% Reductions in required factory floor space.

- 65–80% Reductions of overall machine setup times.
- 50–85% Decreases in quality-related problems.
- Simpler shop-floor control procedures and reduced paperwork.
- Greater worker involvement, productivity, flexibility, and satisfaction.
- Reduced overhead costs (cross-trained workers perform tasks formerly done by support staff).

Similar improvements were reported by Ewaldz:[12]

- 95% Reduction in WIP.
- Reduced response time to customer demand from months to hours.
- Increased ownership of tasks and functions by operators.
- Work imbalances and bottlenecks handled by trained workers.

Improvements at one manufacturer, Stewart, Inc., include:[13]

- 80% Reduction in WIP.
- 60% Reduction in finished goods inventory.
- 86% Reduction in lead times.
- 96% Reduction of late orders.
- 56% Reduction in manufacturing space.

Reductions in lead times, WIP inventory, material handling, and quality problems result largely from the fact that production in focused facilities is more similar to continuous/repetitive production than to process, job shop production. Any well-researched move from a job shop to a product-focused approach will bring such benefits. Required space is reduced because machines are relocated closely together into groups, and where possible, the groups themselves are located closely together. Overall time devoted to setups is reduced because parts in product groups require similar kinds of setups, so both the frequency of setups and the extent of each setup are reduced. Special fixtures and tools can be developed to speed the setup process, and dies and anything else needed can be stored at or near the focused factory. As will be discussed more in the next chapter, workers take on greater responsibility; at minimum, each worker is capable of operating several or all of the machines in the focused factory. Each worker might also be responsible for machine setups, routine machine maintenance, quality control, and job scheduling. This requires considerable training, but the result is less boredom and, possibly, greater satisfaction.

CASE IN POINT: Lockheed Aeronautical Systems

Lockheed Aeronautical Systems' plant in Marietta, Georgia, is structured into 13 focused factories such that each is a manufacturing cell devoted to similarly processed parts such as extrusions, machinings, sheet metal parts, tubing, and composite parts. The focused factories were implemented and refined over a 3-year period. Since completion of the implementation, throughput time for parts has improved by a minimum factor of 2.5. For one part in particular, small extrusions, throughput time fell from 65 days to 11 days, and in-process inventory decreased from 6000 units to 500 units.

CASE IN POINT: Sun Microsystems

Sun Microsystems' plant in Milpitas, California, manufactures desktop computer workstations.[14] When the production became incapable of meeting swings in demand, Sun set up a pilot line in a vacant area of the plant. On the pilot line, called SimplePlant, one worker can assemble a complete workstation in less than 15 minutes. Unlike the original facility, which was a highly automated assembly line, most of the tasks in SimplePlant are manual, including transfer of components and products with inexpensive handcarts.

Morale improved because workers in SimplePlant work together, control the pace of the process, and are involved in all or most of the steps, not just one like before. As a result, idle time and work stoppages were virtually eliminated and productivity increased by 12%. After 3 months, Sun decided to really push it to the limit by requiring SimplePlant to double its output, which it did with no problem. To everyone's amazement, SimplePlant was producing state-of-the-art workstations at high productivity and quality levels, yet with only simple hand-me-down workbenches and carts to transfer parts and products.

Based on the results of the pilot, the factory was restructured into three discrete, identical cells. Whereas the former automated line had to be run at 20–100% capacity to meet changes in demand, the three cells can be run in any combination, each at 100% capacity. Also, the assembly and package areas of each cell have mirror-image sides that can be turned on or off, which allows for six possible levels of production.

One disadvantage of focused factories is the *potential* for low machine utilization since any machine dedicated to a focused factory is delimited in its use. The greater the constraint on how a machine is to be used, the greater the potential is that it will be used less. As shown in the example at the end-of-chapter supplement on the machine utilization approach, product–machine groupings may require the purchase of more machines, even though some of the machines might be utilized very little. But, again, this might be of small consequence if the advantages listed above are realized.

Plants that shift from a process layout to focused factories always lose some flexibility. Sure, they are more flexible than flow line layouts and less wasteful than job shops, but each focused factory's effectiveness depends on it having adequate customer demand for the product group it produces. As that demand decreases or shifts, the focused factory might no longer have sufficient demand to justify its existence. This is an argument for employing multiskilled workers and equipment and machinery that is mobile and can readily be relocated to form new groups.

There is also the issue of deciding which workers to assign to a subplant or workcell, which can become a point of contention with workers, supervisors, and the union. Assigning workers to subplants requires working with the union, adjusting contracts, modifying job descriptions, and telling workers what is going to happen and why.

Despite reports about workers being more happy in workcells, most of them are anecdotal, and one of the few comprehensive studies to research the subject came up with mixed results.[15] In that study, attitudes of cell workers and functional workers were compared in two plants that had been using workcells for over 2 years. While the cell workers showed greater satisfaction about some aspects of their jobs, they showed less satisfaction about others and expressed feelings of greater role conflict, role ambiguity, and less commitment to the company than workers in traditional functional jobs.

From a management perspective, a big disadvantage of focused factories is the considerable effort and expense associated with designing and implementing them. Simply moving equipment into groups is not enough. Workers must be cross-trained and taught to work in teams, individual machine setup times must be reduced, and equipment reliability must be increased. Also, reassigning workers and equipment is disruptive to ongoing operations. Suffice it to say, implementing focused factories is a long-term commitment and a big change to the way many organizations are accustomed to operating.

Summary

Process design and facility layout are the major determinants of a manufacturer's ability to produce a wide variety of products in any volume—high, medium, or low. Job shops accommodate large variety, but they are inherently wasteful. Repetitive operations are significantly better in terms of manufacturing speed and cost, though their use has traditionally been restricted to relatively high-volume production of very similar or identical products. To achieve repetitiveness, however, it is not necessary to repeatedly produce the same product over and over; it is only necessary to repeat the same process. This is true even with products that are physically different or that follow different routing sequences.

Group technology is a way to identify physical, functional, and processing similarities between different products. GT coding is a tool for describing properties of parts and products and for classifying parts and products by commonality of function, appearance, or production. Knowing the physical or functional properties of existing parts enables better utilization of those parts in new products and reduces the proliferation of new part designs. Group technology is also a tool for grouping products according to common production processes.

A focused factory is a portion of a larger factory devoted to a particular kind of product or group of products. The focused factory achieves efficiency by exploiting commonalities among the end-items it produces. In the focused factory, setups and changeovers are reduced because of similarities in products, and workers operate with high proficiency because their attention is directed to fewer things. Waste of handling and transportation is reduced because workers and machines are clustered closely together. Many focused factories are able to operate on a repetitive basis by producing items that share the same process or operations, even though the items are physically different and each have small demand. For these reasons, focused factories are less wasteful than job shops.

The next chapter focuses on one kind of focused factory, the workcell. Workcells have been growing rapidly in popularity and are especially common among JIT manufacturers.

Chapter Supplement

CLUSTERING ALGORITHMS

The dense blocks resulting from the binary ordering algorithm indicate potential machine–product groupings; however, because the algorithm ignores aspects of manufacturing such as product demand, operations sequence, availability of machines, transport cost of the groupings, problems of exceptional machines and products, and many others, the groups are at best provisional, and final decisions about grouping and layout require considerable additional analysis. Many algorithms have been developed to address this need, although they too ignore so many other variables that their results require additional analysis and fudging to arrive at final product–machine arrangements.[16] As examples, two of these algorithms are presented here.

KEY MACHINE APPROACH[17]

It is often necessary or desirable to form groups around certain or **key machines**—machines that are one-of-a-kind, perform special operations, are difficult to relocate, are very expensive, and so on. Heat treating metals is an example: a special furnace is required, the plant usually has only one, and it cannot be relocated. The key machine approach starts by identifying a key machine. Parts that require processing on the key machine are identified, then, in turn, each part is examined to determine all other machines needed to process it. These other machines then become candidates for inclusion in the group with the key machine.

Suppose in the previous example (Figure 9.11, repeated in Figure 9.17) that machine C is the key machine. Referring to row C in Figure 9.17, we see that machine C processes parts 2, 4, 5, and 7. Referring now to the columns for those parts, we see that they are processed by machines H, F, G, E, A, and B (in addition to machine C). These machines all become candidates for assignment to a single cell that includes machine C. Whether we actually want to assign them all to one cell depends on other considerations. In this example, we would end up with a cell that has seven machines, and only one machine, D, is left out. This same cell also would perform all or most of the operations on all nine products.

It is easy to see that if the number of products and/or operations is large, the method can readily lead to formation of large, and possibly impractical, cells. Thus, some way is needed to constrain the number of machines to be admitted into a cell. Suppose only machines that

FIGURE 9.17

Process matrix for key machine case.

Machine	Part 1	2	3	4	5	6	7	8	9
A					1	1		1	
B					1	1		1	1
C		1		1	1		1		
D	1		1						
E					1	1			
F	1		1	1					
G					1	1	1	1	1
H		1		1			1		

have a somewhat high percentage of products in *common* are allowed together in a cell. A way to measure the commonality of products among machines is to use a **similarity coefficient.** One way to compute the similarity coefficient between two machines i and j is

$$S_{ij} = \frac{P_{ij}}{P_i + P_j - P_{ij}},$$

where

P_{ij} = number of parts visiting machines i and j,
P_i = number of parts visiting machine i,
P_j = number of parts visiting machine j.[18]

The similarity coefficients of all machine pairs are represented in a machine–machine matrix such as Table 9.3. Entries in Table 9.3 are derived from information in the process matrix. For example, referring to the process matrix in Figure 9.17, we see that machine A processes three products (5, 6, 8), machine B processes four products (5, 6, 8, 9), but the two machines have only three products in common (5, 6, 8). Thus, the similarity coefficient is

$$S_{AB} = \frac{3}{3 + 4 - 3} = \frac{3}{4}.$$

Since the machine–machine matrix is symmetrical, only entries above the diagonal are shown in Table 9.3.

As the similarity coefficient between two machines approaches 1.0, the maximum, it becomes more desirable to include the machines together in a group. Suppose we use a similarity coefficient between two machines of 0.5 as the minimum criteria for grouping the two together. Again, starting with C as the key machine, we see from Table 9.3 that of the candidate machines (F, H, G, B, A, E), only machine H has a similarity coefficient with C large enough, so only machine H will be grouped with machine C.

TABLE 9.3

Machine	A	B	C	D	E	F	G	H
A	0	3/4	1/6	0	2/3	0	3/5	0
B		0	1/7	0	1/2	0	1	0
C			0	0	1/5	1/6	2/7	3/4
D				0	0	2/3	0	0
E					0	0	2/5	0
F						0	1/7	1/5
G							0	1/8
H								0

Now, to assign the remaining machines to other groups, repeat the process. First, select another key machine; suppose it is machine B. Machine B processes parts 5, 6, 8, and 9, which in turn, require machines C, G, A, and E (besides machine B). Machine C has already been assigned, and of the other four machines, only A, E, and G have similarity coefficients with machine B of 0.5 or greater. Thus, machines B, A, E, and G would constitute another group. The remaining (unassigned) machines are D and F. The similarity coefficient between them is 0.67, so they would be grouped together. Summarizing the results, the groups are as follows:

Group 1: Machines C and H.

Group 2: Machines B, A, E, and G.

Group 3: Machines D and F.

Notice that this grouping is the same as that suggested by the BOA method, Figure 9.14. In general, however, the key machine method will not necessarily give the same groupings as BOA since groupings in the former method depend upon constraints on the key machines (e.g., can key machines be in the same group?), and on the minimum value of the similarity coefficient used to cluster machines.

MACHINE UTILIZATION APPROACH[19]

This approach assigns machines to groups such that the resulting **machine utilizations** are as large as possible, given constraints. A constraint that we will consider is an upper limit to the number of machines in a group. This method will yield a solution with no exceptions (i.e., no products requiring intergroup processing) as long as the number of machines visited by any product does not exceed the upper limit on the size of the group. The feasibility of any solution also depends on the number of each *type* of machine assigned to different groups and whether that number of machines is actually available. This will be discussed later.

The procedure starts with a diagonal, dense-block process matrix but replaces the 1s with **utilization coefficients** (or utilizations, for short). Products and their associated machines are added to a group, one at a time, as long as the machines in the group have adequate remaining utilization (capacity) to accommodate them. If additional capacity is needed, more machines are added. When adding machines (either to provide additional capacity for existing types of machines or to allow for additional types of products to be processed) results in the number of machines in the group exceeding the maximum allowable, then a new group is formed.

FIGURE 9.18

Machine–part utilization coefficients.

Machine	Part 1	3	4	2	7	5	6	8	9	Total	Minimum Machines
F	0.3	0.6	0.3							1.2	2
D	0.2	0.4								0.6	1
C			0.4	0.7	0.3	0.4				1.8	2
H				0.3	0.6	0.1				1.0	1
G			0.4			0.2	0.6	0.5	0.8	2.5	3
B						0.3	0.1	0.2	0.1	0.7	1
A						0.4	0.3	0.1		0.8	1
E							0.6	0.3		0.9	1

The following example illustrates the procedure. Assume first a diagonal, dense-block process matrix, where 1s have been replaced with utilization coefficients. This is shown in Figure 9.18. Below is one way to compute the utilization coefficient for machine m, processing part i:

$$U_{mi} = \frac{C_{mi} + P_{mi}}{A_m},$$

where

C_{mi} = total setup time per period devoted to part i
  = $S_{mi}\,(D_i/Q_i)$,
P_{mi} = total processing time per period for i = $T_{mi}\,D_i$,
S_{mi} = setup time per batch of i,
D_i = demand per period for i,
Q_i = batch size for i,
T_i = per-unit processing (includes loading, unloading)
  time for i,
A_m = time available per period for machine m (allows for interruptions, breakdowns, etc.).

For example, assume

S_{mi} = 0.7 hrs/batch,
D_i = 1000 units/year,
Q_i = 10 units/batch,
T_i = 0.5 hrs/unit,
A_m = 1900 hrs/year,

then

$$C_{mi} = 0.7(1000/10) = 70 \text{ hrs}$$

and

$$P_{mi} = 0.5(1000) = 500 \text{ hrs.}$$

Thus,

$$U_{mi} = \frac{70 + 500}{1900} = 0.3.$$

This is the utilization indicated for machine F, part 1 in Figure 9.18. Figure 9.18 also shows the Total (utilization), which is the row sum—the utilizations for all the parts a machine processes. The last column is the minimum number of machines necessary to achieve the required total (utilization).

Moving left to right through the matrix, assign parts and associated machines to a group. As each additional product is added to a group, the total utilization of each machine in the group is tallied, noting also the remaining utilization. Whenever the remaining utilization for a machine becomes less than that required by the next product under consideration, another machine of that type must be added to the group. If, however, adding a machine to the group

TABLE 9.4

Group	Parts Assigned	Machines Assigned	No. Machines	Remain. Util.
1	1	F, D	2	F, 0.7; D, 0.8.
	3		2	F, 0.1; D, 0.4.
	4	F2*, C, H, G	6 (exceeds max)	
2	4	F2, C, H, G	4	F2, 0.7; C, 0.6; H, 0.7; G, 0.6.
	2	C2*	5	F2, 0.7; C, 0.0; H, 0.1; G, 0.6; C2, 0.9**.
	7		5	F2, 0.7; C, 0.0; H, 0.0; G, 0.6; C2, 0.6.
	5	B, A, E	8 (exceeds max)	
3	5	C3, G2, B, A, E	5	C3, 0.6; G2, 0.8; B, 0.7; A, 0.6; E, 0.4.
	6		5	C3, 0.6; G2, 0.2; B, 0.6; A, 0.3; E, 0.1.
	8	G3*	6 (exceeds max)	
4	8	G3, B2, A2	3	G3, 0.5; B2, 0.8; A2, 0.9.
	9	G4*	4	G3, 0.0; B2, 0.7; A2; 0.9; G4, 0.7**.

*Assign an additional machine of this type because the utilization requirement for this part exceeds the remaining utilization on this type of machine.

**Assume when multiple machines of the same type are assigned to one group, the remaining utilization on one machine is used up before the next machine is employed.

causes the number of machines to exceed the maximum allowable, then a new group must be started. A new group must also be started whenever a product is encountered that has no machines in common with the machines in the current group.

Assume the maximum allowable machines in a group is five. The steps are shown in Table 9.4

The resulting groups are as follows:

Group 1: Machines F and D; parts 1 and 3.
Group 2: Machines F2, C, C2, H, and G; parts 4, 2, and 7.
Group 3: Machines C3, G2, B, A, and E; parts 5 and 6.
Group 4: Machines G3, G4, B2, and A2; parts 8 and 9.

Although this result requires no intergroup movement of parts, it does require a total of 16 machines, many of which have substantial remaining utilization (unused capacity). Eight machines, for example, have remaining utilization of at least 0.6 (F2, G, C2, C3, B, B2, A2, G4). Though utilization figures are based on current demand, which is subject to change, it may be difficult to justify acquiring machines that will be used less than 40% of the time. Since most of the machines in group 4 have large remaining utilizations, we might relax the five-machine limit and combine groups 3 and 4 to see what happens. Starting with group 3 in the above analysis, but relaxing the five-machine constraint, gives

Group	Parts Assigned	Machines Assigned	No. Machines	Remain. Util.
3	5	C3, G2, B, A, E	5	C3, 0.6; G2, 0.8; B, 0.7; A, 0.6; E, 0.4.
	6		5	C3, 0.6; G2, 0.2; B, 0.6; A, 0.3; E, 0.1.
	8	G3	6	C3, 0.6; G2, 0.0; B, 0.4; A, 0.2; E, 0.1; G3, 0.7.
	9	G4	7	C3, 0.6; G2, 0.0; B, 0.3; A, 0.2; E, 0.1; G3, 0.0; G4, 0.9.

Since group 3 now requires seven machines, the total number of machines needed for all three groups is 14. But six machines still have remaining utilizations of at least 0.6 (which is 40% utilization, at best); in many (most?) plants this *might* be insufficient and may turn managers against forming groups.

Although 40% utilization might not seem very high, in general, high utilization for its own sake should not be a goal in forming product groups. Emphasizing machine utilization alone makes no sense, because without sufficient demand it only results in overproduction and inventory buildup. The demand for products keeps changing (as do the products themselves), and equipment utilization should fluctuate up and down, roughly corresponding to these changes. A major benefit of product–family groups is flexibility, and some remaining utilization is essential to accommodate increasing or highly variable demand. Besides, since machine times for future (not yet made) products cannot be known, it is impossible to predict machine utilization requirements for the future. Remaining utilization built into a product group translates into having the capacity when it is needed.

As in product layouts, the machine utilization in a product group will be constrained by the slowest machine (the bottleneck) in the group, so that estimated machine utilizations will be incorrect (and too high) whenever machines are placed in groups with slower machines. According to Harmon and Peterson,[20] however, actual experience in rearranging machines from process layouts into products groups indicates that the effect on individual machine utilization is minimal.

Questions

1. Define, compare, and contrast job operations and repetitive operations.
2. Compare the features, advantages, and disadvantages of product layouts and process layouts.
3. For what manufacturing situations is a process layout appropriate? For what situations is a product layout appropriate?
4. What is a product family?
5. What is a focused factory? Described each of the following kinds of focused factories: focused flow line, workcell, focused workcenter.
6. How does a focused factory combine the features of a product layout and a process layout?
7. What is group technology? What is its purpose? How is it used in product design? How is it used to form product families?
8. Compare and contrast GT polycode, monocode, and hybrid code structures.
9. What are the drawbacks of using GT codes for forming focused factories?
10. What is production flow analysis (PFA)? Why use PFA instead of simple visual techniques?
11. What are the limitations of results from PFA analysis?
12. Discuss the potential advantages and disadvantages of focused factories.

Problems

1. Four components—W, X, Y, and Z—are classified using an eleven-digit code. Each digit of the code refers to a particular production operation, material, or general physical feature of the component. The coding numbers are as follows:

Digit Component	Code Number of Operations				Code Number of Materials				Code Number of Features		
	1	2	3	4	5	6	7	8	9	10	11
W	2	2	2	2	1	1	3	1	1	2	2
X	1	1	2	1	1	2	3	1	1	3	4
Y	2	1	2	2	1	1	3	1	1	1	2
Z	1	2	2	1	2	3	3	2	1	3	2

Cluster components as follows:
   a. According to most-shared operations.
   b. According to most-shared materials.
   c. According to most-shared features.
   d. For focused-factory production. Explain your rationale.

2. Shown below are seven manufactured components and their corresponding production volumes and machine sequences.

Component Part	Volume	Machine Sequence
L7	50,000	A, B, C, D
R6	30,000	S, M
P1	9,000	C, D
O3	10,000	S, M, R
F7	1,000	S, R, A
J4	15,000	B, A, D
H5	1,000	B, D, M

Assume the plant has one of each kind of machine.
   a. Form workcell groupings using the visual method (i.e., determine the machine–component clusters). Discuss the result and how you would handle exceptional parts or machines.
   b. Create the process matrix. Form workcell groupings using the binary ordering algorithm. Discuss the result.

3. Shown below are six manufactured components and their corresponding production volumes and machine sequences.

Component Part	Volume	Machine Sequence
PAC	10,000	Q, S, T
QBB	100	X, Q, S
RCC	100	X, M, Q, S
PDL	1,000	X, M
JGR	5,000	Q, T
CHB	5,000	T

Assume the plant has one of each kind of machine.
   a. Form workcell groupings using the visual method. Discuss the result.
   b. Create the process matrix. Form workcell groupings using the binary ordering algorithm. Discuss the result.
   c. Assume two Q machines, two S machines, and one of every other machine. Discuss the resulting workcell groupings.
   d. Besides the information given above, what other factors would you need to know to determine the appropriate workcell groupings?

4. Ten manufactured products and the corresponding weekly production volumes and machine sequence are shown below.

Products	Volume	Machine Sequence
SA	9,000	A, B, C
SB	8,000	B, C, E
SC	80	E, F
SD	6,600	C, D, E
SE	40	A, B
SF	600	A, E, F
SG	10,000	A, B, D
SH	6,000	D, E, F
SK	1,000	B, C, D
SL	2,100	A, B, D

Assume one of each kind of machine.

a. Form workcell groupings using the visual method (i.e., determine the machine–component groupings). Discuss the result.

b. Create the process matrix. Form workcell groupings using the binary ordering algorithm. Discuss the result.

c. Assume all products require about the same production time per unit on all machines. Suppose each machine has a maximum weekly output capacity of 30,000 units. Does this influence the workcell grouping?

d. Suppose each machine has a maximum weekly output capacity of 20,000 units, and you have a capital budget to acquire at most *three* additional machines. Which machines would you acquire, and how would you allocate them among workcell groupings?

5. Using the products and machines from problem 4, form workcells using the **key machine approach** discussed in the supplement. The key machines are A and E; three machines at most can be in a workcell.

6. Repeat the example in the **machine utilization approach** discussed in the supplement (Figure 9.18), except assume that instead of five machines, a maximum of seven machines is allowed in each workcell group. Compare the result with that in the discussion.

7. Assume the example discussed in the machine utilization approach is for the most-likely demand case. Suppose the maximum-likely demand case increases the demand for part 5 by 50%.

a. Determine what effect this has on the estimated minimum number of machines required.

b. Use the machine utilization approach to determine the new workcell groupings. Assume a maximum of five machines allowed in each group.

Endnotes

1. *See,* for example, H. Opitz, *A Coding System to Describe Workpieces* (New York: Pergamon Press, 1970); and U. Rembold, C. Blume, and R. Dilman, *Computer Integrated Manufacturing Technology Systems* (New York: Marcel Dekker Inc., 1985).

2. Probably the best reference on the subject is R. Harmon and L. Peterson, *Reinventing the Factory* (New York: The Free Press, 1990), pp. 12–35.

3. W. Skinner, "The Focused Factory," *The Harvard Business Review,* May/June 1974, pp. 113–21.

4. Because every machine is unique, using different machines to perform a given operation causes machine-specific variations in the product. When a product family is consistently assigned to the same machines, each machine can be set up and adjusted to make allowances for its uniqueness, which results in reduced variation.

5. R. Schonberger, *World Class Manufacturing: The Next Decade* (New York: The Free Press, 1996), p. 158.

6. D. Alexander, *The Practice and Management of Industrial Ergonomics* (Englewood Cliffs, NJ: Prentice-Hall, 1986); M. Sanders and E. McCormick, *Human Factors in Engineering and Design* (New York: McGraw-Hill, 1987).

7. R. Schonberger, *World Class Manufacturing: The Next Decade,* pp. 159–60.

8. One study of workcell design identified six categories of ways to form workcells: GT coding and classification, clustering methods based on machine or product similarity, visual examination, key machine, production flow analysis, and naturally apparent product lines. The discussion in this chapter is on the most commonly used of these methods. See F. Olorunniwo and G. Udo, "Cell Design Practices in U.S. Manufacturing Firms," *Production and Inventory Management,* 3rd Quarter 1996, pp. 27–33.

9. R. Harmon and L. Peterson, *Reinventing the Factory,* p. 124.

10. J.L. Burbidge, *The Introduction of Group Technology* (New York: John Wiley & Sons, 1975).

11. H.J. Steudel and P. Desruelle, *Manufacturing in the Nineties* (New York: Van Nostrand Reinhold, 1992), pp. 119–23.

12. D. Ewaldz, "Caveats for Cellular Manufacturing," *Tooling and Production* 61, no. 7 (October 1995), p. 9.

13. G. Levasseur, M. Helms, A. Zink, "A Conversion from a Functional to a Cellular Manufacturing Layout at Stewart, Inc.," *Production and Inventory Management* (3rd Quarter 1995), pp. 37–42.

14. K. Laughlin, "Increasing Competitiveness with a Cellular Process," *Industrial Engineering,* April 1995, pp. 30–33.

15. S. Shafer, B. Tepper, J. Meredith, R. Marsh, "Comparing the Effects of Cellular and Functional Manufacturing on Employees' Perceptions and Attitudes," *Journal of Operations Management* 12 (1995), pp. 63–74.

16. For a review of clustering algorithms, *see* G. H. Cheng, A. Kumar, and J. Motwani, "A Comparative Examination of Selected Cellular Manufacturing Clustering Algorithms," *International Journal of Operations Management* 15, no. 12 (1995), pp. 86–97.

17. Details on this and related methods are in A. McAuley, "Machine Grouping for Efficient Production," *Production Engineering* 2 (1972), pp. 53–7; H. Seifoddinin and P. M. Wolfe, "Application of the Similarity Coefficient Method in Group Technology," *IIE Transactions* 18, no. 3 (1986), pp. 271–7; P.H. Waghodekar and S. Sahu, "Machine-Component Cell Formation in Group Technology: MACE," *International Journal of Production Research* 22, no. 6 (1984), pp. 937–48.

18. Another way is $S_{ij} = \max(P_{ij}/P_i, P_{ij}/P_j)$.

19. A. Ballakur and H. J. Steudel, "A Within-Cell Utilization Heuristic for Designing Cellular Manufacturing Systems," *International Journal of Production Research* 25, no. 4 (1987), pp. 639–65.

20. R. Harmon and L. Peterson, *Reinventing the Factory,* p. 134.

10 WORKCELLS AND CELLULAR MANUFACTURING

Focused factories are a common sight in JIT/ TQM manufacturers because they are more efficient than job shops and more flexible than flow shops. They are also common in pull production processes because pull production requires repetitiveness, and, often, focused factories allow for repetitive production, even of low-volume products. The concept of performing all of the necessary operations to make a part, component, subassembly, or finished product in a *workcell* is called **cellular manufacturing.**

Cellular manufacturing and pull production go hand in hand. Often, an entire large-scale pull production process can be created by stringing together many workcells. The workcells produce parts, components, and subassemblies that are assembled into the final product at the last stage of the process. Because each workcell can produce a variety of parts and components, the overall production system is capable of producing a variety of products.

This chapter begins where the last chapter left off—with the assumption that product or part families exist and that the combined volume of products in the family justifies dedicating machines and workers to focused workcells. It looks in depth at cellular manufacturing applications, the design of workcells, and how workcells function individually and as elements of pull production systems. Worker staffing and assignment, equipment availability, and organizational, behavioral, and attitudinal issues of workcell implementation are also addressed.[1]

WORKCELL CONCEPTS

WORKSTATIONS, WORKERS, AND MACHINES

The basic building blocks of a workcell are workstations, machines, workers, and means for holding and transferring items between workstations. Workstations (or **stations**) are the places where operations are performed. In a workcell they are located close together, ideally in the routing sequence for a product or product family. The tasks in a workcell might be performed entirely by workers. Manual assembly of components is an example: the role of workers in such a cell is to perform assembly tasks, inspect items, and transfer them to the next station.

Cell with one worker and six machines.

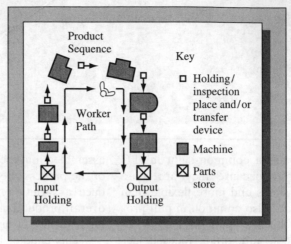

The tasks in a workcell might also be performed by machines at some or all of the workstations. The role of the workers in that case is to set up and monitor the machines, turn machines on and off, load and unload parts, inspect parts, and transfer parts between machines. The functions of loading, unloading, inspecting, and transferring parts might also be automated so that the workcell operates with little human intervention.

Some workcells can be run with as few as one worker. Figure 10.1 shows a workcell with six machines and one worker who walks between them. The machines are arranged in the process routing sequence so that parts can be produced one at a time, continually. Parts are transferred between stations by hand or by using gravity chutes or small carts. The stations are arranged in a U-shaped layout so the worker can move quickly around the cell. Obviously, the worker must know how to operate all the machines and be able to keep everything in the cell running smoothly.

WORKCELL OUTPUT AND NUMBER OF WORKERS

The output rate of a workcell can often be manipulated by changing the number of workers. For example, Figure 10.2 shows two possibilities of the six-machine cell in Figure 10.1, but with two workers. In Figure 10.2(*a*) each worker moves among three machines and has responsibility for half the cell. If the output rate of the cell is a function of the time it takes the workers to do their tasks, then adding a second worker like this will roughly double the production rate of the workcell. This will be explained later. Figure 10.2(*b*) shows another way of adding a second worker, called **rabbit chase,** where both workers move around the cell, one following (or chasing) the other. This, too, will be discussed later.

FIGURE 10.2

Cell with two workers. (a) Divided subcells. (b) Rabbit chase.

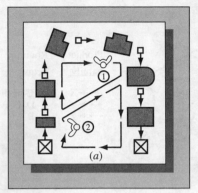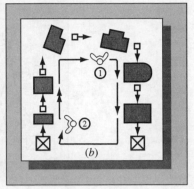

WORKCELL APPLICATIONS

TYPICAL WORKCELL END-ITEMS

Often an entire product can be produced in a single workcell, though such a product is usually somewhat simple in terms of the number of components and operations it requires. It is typically a one- or few-pieced item such as a metal casting on which a series of drilling, boring, and finishing operations is performed, or a somewhat simple assembly of components, such as a PC disk drive.

Workcells can also be used to manufacture products that are more complex and involve numerous operations and component parts, such as stereo CD and cassette players and electronic communications equipment for aircraft and missiles. Producing somewhat complex products in a workcell is practical as long as the skills and abilities of the workers fit the range of tasks required.

Many workers welcome the opportunity to learn and apply a broad range of skills, and larger cells that produce more complex items offer that opportunity.

The physical size of the cell necessary to encompass all of the operations involved is also a determining factor when considering complex end-items. The number of workstations in the cell and the distances between them must be small enough so workers do not get overwhelmed by different tasks and waste excessive time walking among stations. Further, a larger workcell might require more machines, which takes more machines away from non-cell-produced parts and products. Also, in larger cells with more workers, teamwork suffers.[2] For problem solving, work coordination, and cohesiveness, a group size of between five and seven people is optimal. While workcells with 2 to 6 workstations are very common, those with 10 or more workstations are less common, at least as observed by the author. For all these reasons, workcell production of complex components and assemblies in their *entirety* is less common.

Figure 10.3

Cell for producing multiple product families.

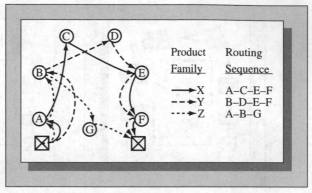

Product Family	Routing Sequence
→X	A–C–E–F
--→Y	B–D–E–F
···→Z	A–B–G

WORKCELLS FOR MULTIPLE PRODUCT FAMILIES

Though a workcell commonly focuses on producing one product family, it can also be designed to produce *multiple* product families when the families require similar operations and sequences. Figure 10.3 shows a workcell wherein three product families all follow the same general routing sequence, though some families skip some operations. To help workers avoid confusion about which machines are used on which families, lights are mounted on the machines. To make a product in the X family, for example, the worker presses a button at the master panel for "X," which illuminates lights on machines A, C, E, and F.

LINKED WORKCELLS AND SUBCELLS

Products that involve numerous assembly steps and that are made from parts that also require numerous machining and assembly steps can also be made in workcells, but by first dividing all the operations into several workcells, then linking the workcells so parts flow from one cell to the next in a coordinated manner.[3] Figure 10.4 shows an example of several workcells (the small U's) linked in sequence to produce families of parts that are used in two subassembly lines and a final, main assembly line.

The workcells can be linked piece by piece with conveyors or mechanical feeders, in which case the material flows somewhat continually between workcells, or they can be linked in small batches with handcarts or forklifts, in which case the flow is intermittent. In the latter case, the material transfer is authorized by kanbans (in a pull system) or by schedules (in a push system).

When the workcells are located immediately adjacent to each other, they perform as if they are subunits of a larger workcell. For example, Figure 10.5 shows two kinds of linked workcell processes: (*a*) a cluster of four clearly distinguishable workcells connected by containers and (*b*) four subcells that function together as one.

FIGURE 10.4

Facility of linked workcells.

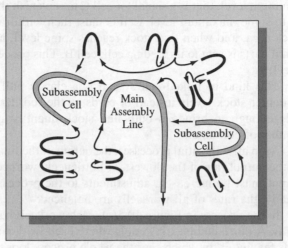

FIGURE 10.5

Linked cell and subcell examples.

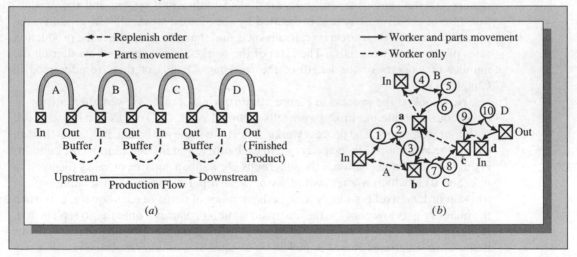

Parts in cluster Figure 10.5(*a*) move between cells in small lots using pull signals. As cell D produces items, it withdraws parts from containers at its inbound stock area. When the parts in the stock area reach a certain level, a replenishment order is sent to the feeding cell, cell C. Some stock of finished parts is held in containers at each cell's outbound stock area, which enables orders from downstream cells to be filled immediately. The stock also serves as a safety stock for minor delays and breakdowns in the process. As containers are withdrawn to replenish the inbound stock at cell D, the outbound buffer stock quantity of cell C is reduced. When it reaches some minimum level, that is a signal for cell C to replenish those items in its outbound stock up to some maximum level. Cell C must then withdraw items from its own inbound stock area, and when that stock reaches some level, a replenishment order for additional parts is sent to its feeding cell, cell B. This procedure repeats at cell B and then at cell A.

This kind of linked-cell system is a classic pull production system (but using container stock levels instead of cards as the reorder function). Each cell produces only enough to bring its outbound stock quantity up to the maximum allowable number of containers.

As in all sequential processes, the output of the final workcell in the chain depends on the output rate of the slowest, or bottleneck, workcell. Thus, whenever the process output must be increased, adjustments to the process start at the slowest workcell. Ideally, the rates of all workcells are balanced.

In the process in Figure 10.5(a), each workcell has only one upstream cell feeding it. A more complex system is where each workcell has multiple upstream workcells feeding it, in which case the whole process looks like a tree diagram, with final assembly at the stem. Moving upstream, each cell branches outward into multiple feeding cells, and they, in turn, branch outward into still more cells. Although the process might appear more complicated than the single-sequence case, the dynamics are the same: the workcells are linked with a pull system and the production rate of the overall system is dictated by the slowest workcell. (In actuality, the production rate of the *system* is set in advance, and that rate determines the production rates of all of the workcells.) The rates of the workcells are adjusted by altering the number of workers or the length of the workday. Details of this are addressed in Chapter 17.

Now look at the process in Figure 10.5(b), which can be viewed alternatively as either four separate but linked workcells (denoted A, B, C, D) or as one big workcell with four subgroups. The process works almost the same as the one in Figure 10.5(a), except the subgroups are located close to each other, and instead of movable containers in the stock areas between the subgroups are kanban squares or racks (denoted **a**, **b**, **c**, and **d**) at which workers withdraw or deposit parts. Rather than sending replenishment orders, workers simply look at the number of items in each square, and when the quantity gets low enough, the upstream station produces a quantity to replenish it. Each subgroup receives inputs from multiple feeding subgroups (subgroup C receives items from subgroups A and B, picked up at squares a and b, respectively; subgroup D receives items from subgroup C and elsewhere, picked up at squares c and d). The production rates of each subgroup are balanced so that both supply and demand rates between subcells are roughly equal.

Aside from the way replenishment orders are placed, and the way materials are held and transported, this arrangement of subgroups operates in the same manner as the linked workcells in Figure 10.5(a). Conceptually and analytically, the two can be treated as identical, except that in the linked-workcell case, Figure 10.5(a), allowance must be made for time delays in communicating replenishment orders and transporting materials between workcell stock areas. In the subgroup case, communication and transportation times are negligible.

All of the workcells in a linked process must produce at a rate that is about the same as the rate required to satisfy demand for the final end-item. If the production schedule for the final end-item specifies one unit every minute, then that is the minimum allowable rate for every workcell in the process. When the required rate is greater than the maximum rate capable for a given workcell, then additional workcells for making the same part must be added to the process. Suppose a workcell is already producing parts at its maximum rate, say one unit per minute, and the process requires that part at an average rate of 1.5 units per minute. It will be necessary to add another workcell to the process with an average production rate of 0.5 unit per minute (or one unit every 2 minutes) such that the two workcells combined can meet the required rate of 1.5.

For pull production, material flowing to and between workcells everywhere in the process must be synchronized and coordinated. Everything discussed in Chapters 5–8 now comes into play. Since delays or shutdowns anywhere will affect the entire process, setup times must be short, equipment cannot break down, and materials ordered from suppliers must arrive on time. The methods of placing orders and transporting materials, the size of containers, and the frequency of transport all require special attention.

Attempts to reduce inventories and to smooth the production flow through small batches in the linked system will not succeed without a corresponding increase in the frequency and reliability of materials transport. Suppose setup times are reduced so that production batches can be cut in half. To cut in half the buffer at the outbound stock area, the frequency of pickups from that area must be doubled. That means that, somehow, the efficiency of material handling must be improved, otherwise costs associated with the frequency of pickups will double. Shortening distances between workcells, eliminating double-handling of materials, and using low-cost chutes or light-weight carts are ways to improve the handling efficiency. Balancing the system is a dynamic procedure. For every change in the final assembly schedule, corresponding changes are required in the production rates of the workcells.

WORKCELL DESIGN

There are two fundamental kinds of workcells, assembly cells and machining cells. In **assembly cells** the work tasks are entirely or mostly manual. Usually, the tasks performed in these cells are difficult or costly to automate, for example, hand assembly or welding and testing of multiple components. Assembly workcells produce components or completed products such as electronics (VCRs, PC keyboards, circuit boards, telephones), furniture (wooden and metal chairs, desks, tables, filing cabinets), toys (wagons, bikes, remote-controlled models), electric motors, hand power tools, small appliances for home and industry, and many other products.

In contrast to assembly cells, in **machining cells** the work tasks are usually simpler, more-easily automated, and largely or entirely performed by machines. The products of machining cells are single-piece items that require no (or little) manual assembly. The workcell process involves a series of machining operations on a piece of metal, wood, plastic, or other material.

Because both kinds of cells produce items piece by piece, cycle time, discussed next, is a crucial design parameter.

BRIEF DIGRESSION: CYCLE TIME CONCEPT

A central concept in workcell facility design is that of **cycle time.** Cycle time is the time between when units are completed in a process.[4] If, for example, the cycle time for a workcell is 10 minutes per unit, that implies that the cell turns out a completed unit *once every 10 minutes*. Expressing production in terms like this—time per unit—is important since it automatically gets people thinking in terms of piece-by-piece product flow.[5] The cycle time concept is thus important in pull production because it implies repetitiveness and smooth, steady flow of material throughout a process.

Cycle time can also be thought of as the inverse of **production rate,** since, for example, saying that a process has a cycle time of 10 minutes is *almost* the same as saying it has a production rate of six products per hour. The difference, again, is that cycle time implies smooth, uniform production one piece at a time whereas production rate does not.

In the design of a production process, we distinguish between the required cycle time and the actual cycle time. **Required cycle time** is the production target of a process or operation. It is determined by the *demand* for the item being produced. If the demand is 80 units per day, that translates into a required cycle time of

$$CT_r = \frac{Time\ Available}{Required\ Demand} = \frac{480\ \text{min/day}}{80\ \text{units/day}} = 6\ \text{min/unit.}$$

To satisfy demand, the workcell or process must be designed so that the actual cycle time does not exceed 6 min/unit. In some literature, required cycle time is referred to as **tackt time**.[6]

Actual cycle time represents the actual production capability of a process or operation. In a workcell, the actual cycle time is determined by physical conditions such as the time to perform manual or automatic operations, to walk around the cell, and so on, as will be discussed shortly.

Production capacity of a facility is a function of actual cycle time. For example, a workcell with an actual cycle time of 10 minutes per unit that operates for 480 minutes a day has a daily production capacity of 48 units.

Establishing and standardizing work in a process such that the actual cycle time is as close as possible to the required cycle time is an important concept in lean production. This is discussed in Chapter 11.

FIGURE 10.6

Assembly cell example.

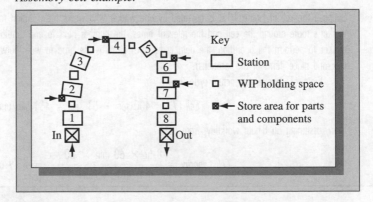

ASSEMBLY WORKCELLS

Figure 10.6 shows an example of an assembly workcell. Depending on the required cycle time, the workcell can be operated by as few as one worker or as many as eight workers.

Figure 10.6 shows WIP holding spaces between stations. When a workcell has more than one worker, every worker has a container or holding space in which to put items just completed.[7] As a way of controlling WIP within the cell, each holding space has room for only one or a few items. When the space is full, no more items can be added, and works stops at the preceding workstation. In effect, items are pulled through the workcell since each workstation only produces enough items to replenish those withdrawn by the succeeding workstation.

The large "X" boxes in Figure 10.6 represent inbound and outbound stock areas for incoming parts and outgoing end-items, respectively. Also shown are four small "x" boxes that represent areas for stocking additional parts and components at their points of use; these areas are replenished using kanbans or schedules, depending on whether the process is a pull or push system.

In an assembly cell, the actual cycle time is entirely a function of the cell **manual time,** which is the time required for workers to perform their tasks and move between workstations. If only one person operates the assembly cell, the actual cycle time, CT_a, is the sum of the operation times at every station and the walk times between them:

$$Cell\ CT_a = \Sigma\ Operation\ Times + \Sigma\ Walk\ Times. \tag{1}$$

Given the actual cycle time, the capacity of the workcell is then

$$Cell\ Capacity = \frac{Time\ Available}{Cell\ CT_a}. \tag{2}$$

This is illustrated next.

Example 1: Workcell CT and Capacity

Suppose the cell in Figure 10.6 is operated by one worker who walks from station to station. Figure 10.7 shows the worker's route around the cell and the relevant times: the number next to each station is the time required for the worker to perform the operation; the number by each arrow is the time to walk between locations (including time to pick and place items at the locations).

From (1) above, the actual cycle time is

$$Cell\ CT_a = 400\ sec + 51\ sec = 451\ sec/unit.$$

Then, assuming an 8-hour workday, from (2),

$$Cell\ Capacity = \frac{8\ hr \times 60\ min \times 60\ sec}{451\ sec/unit} = 63.9\ units/day.$$

With only one worker, the cell's capacity is at its minimum. To increase the capacity of the cell, more workers are added, and the cell is divided among them into subcells. Each worker walks around and tends exclusively to his own subcell. If each subcell were independent of the others, then its cycle time would be determined soley by equation (1). The subcells, however, are not independent; each subcell hands off or picks up material from another. Given that the cycle times (CTs) of the subcells are not all equal, subcells with shorter CTs must wait on the subcells with longer CTs. As a result, the cycle time of the entire workcell is determined by CT of the subcell that takes the longest, or

$$Cell\ CT_a = \max(CT\ of\ each\ subcell). \tag{3}$$

Each time another worker is added to the cell, the cell CT gets smaller. The smallest CT occurs when there is a worker at every station. At that point, workers no longer walk between stations, and cell capacity is at its maximum.

The following example illustrates all these concepts.

Example 2: Reducing Assembly Workcell CT by Adding Workers

Suppose the workcell in Figure 10.7 is divided between two workers, as shown in Figure 10.8: the first worker has stations 1, 7, and 8 (and the inbound and outbound holding spaces); the second worker has stations 2 through 6. Note in Figure 10.8 the addition of holding spaces **a** and **b** as buffers to hold items from each worker until the other worker can get to them.

From equation (1), the sum of the operation and walk times for the first worker is 231 sec/unit; for the second worker it is 238 sec/unit. Thus, from equation (3), the cycle time of the workcell is 238 sec/unit.

The workcell performs like this: After completing operation 1, the first worker drops off an item at holding space **a**, then proceeds to holding space **b** to pick up an item for processing at stations 7 and 8. Although the first worker has a shorter CT than the second worker, she cannot proceed to stations 7 and 8 until an item is dropped off at **b**.

FIGURE 10.7

One-worker assembly cell.

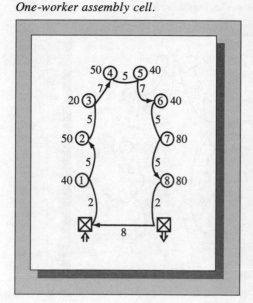

FIGURE 10.8

Two-worker assembly cell.

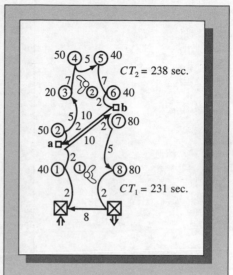

Since an item is dropped off at **b** every 238 seconds, by default, 238 seconds becomes the CT for the first worker, and, thus, the CT_a for the workcell.

As another example, the cell is subdivided among five workers as shown in Figure 10.9. The subdivision was determined by trial and error while attempting to balance the CTs of workers. Notice the addition of holding spaces at four locations (a–d) where the workers interface. Summing the operations and walk times for each worker, the CTs are as follows:

Worker	Subcell Stations	CT (sec)
1	1 and 2	109
2	3 and 4	91
3	5 and 6	101
4	7	90
5	8	90

From equation (3) the cell CT_a is 109 sec/unit; from equation (2) the cell capacity is

$$\frac{8 \text{ hr} \times 60 \text{ min} \times 60 \text{ sec}}{109 \text{ sec/unit}} = 264 \text{ units/day.}$$

Notice that because of the imbalance of CTs among the workers, all workers except the slowest have to wait. Since worker 1 is the slowest, the total idle time for the other four workers is the difference between their CTs and 109 seconds, or $18 + 8 + 19 + 19 = 64$ sec/unit.

FIGURE 10.9

Five-worker assembly cell.

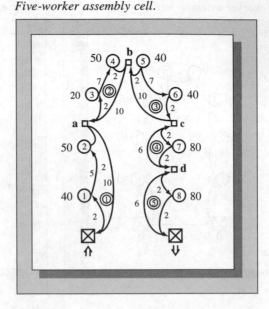

As a final example, suppose every workstation is assigned a worker. Walk times are eliminated, but suppose picking up and placing items at each station takes 4 seconds. The cell CT_a will be the longest workstation time, which is at stations 7 and 8:

$$CT_a = 80 \text{ sec} + 4 \text{ sec} = 84 \text{ sec/unit.}$$

The resulting cell capacity is 342 units/day.

Notice again the amount of worker idle time in this arrangement. Only workers at stations 7 and 8 require the full 84 seconds for each unit, while all the others require considerably less. Station 3, for example, needs only $20 + 4 = 24$ sec/unit; the remaining 60 sec/unit is idle time.

An alternative to adding workers and dividing them among subcells is to add workers using the **rabbit chase** scheme shown in Figure 10.2(*b*). Each worker carries, slides, or carts the workpiece or item from station to station with him. There is no need to balance subcell CTs (since there are no subcells, just one big cell) and no need for special WIP buffer spaces. With rabbit chase, the cycle time of the workcell is thus

$$Cell \ CT_a = \frac{Cell \ CT, \ One \ Worker}{Number \ of \ Workers},$$

where the "Cell CT, one worker" is for the slowest of all the workers. (Rarely do workers perform at exactly the same pace, and in rabbit chase the workers end up having to follow the slowest worker around the cell.) For example, using five workers in rabbit chase as an alternative to the subcell scheme in Figure 10.9, and assuming 451 sec/unit is the CT for the slowest worker,

$$Cell\ CT_a = \frac{451\ sec/unit/worker}{5\ workers} = 90.2\ sec/unit.$$

With rabbit chase there are no inequities since everyone works the same amount of time for each unit produced. One might think that continuously walking around the cell would fatigue workers, and fatigue *is* a problem when the CTs are somewhat short (less than 5 or 10 minutes) and tasks are simple. When CTs are longer and tasks are more challenging, rabbit chase can actually increase worker alertness and productivity over stationary workers doing only one task. The drawback of rabbit chase in such cases is that every worker must be skilled at performing tasks at every station in the workcell.

MACHINING WORKCELLS

Machining workcells differ from assembly workcells in several ways. To begin with, virtually all operations are done by machines, with one or a few machines located at every workstation. These machines are often **automatic, single-cycle** machines that stop after the machining operation has been completed. Additionally stations and machines are connected to one another using a variety of devices called **decouplers** because they allow machines in a sequence to operate somewhat independently. Like a holding space or container between workstations in an assembly cell, each decoupler holds one or a few parts to enable the workcell to continue operations even though subcells or workstations are not perfectly balanced.

Decouplers between operations can serve additional functions:[8]

1. WIP control: The preceding machine is automatically stopped when the number of units in the decoupler reaches the maximum (one or a few parts).

2. Transportation: Decouplers automatically transfer parts from operation to operation; examples include gravity chutes, slides, or mechanical conveyors.

3. Worker freedom of movement: Because of (1) and (2), workers (or robots in an automated cell) can move in any direction around the cell, even counter to the product-flow direction.

4. Automatic inspection: Mechanical or electronic sensors on decouplers perform inspection of critical dimensions as parts move from one operation to the next; in cells that produce multiple kinds of parts, sensors check features of a part to determine to which of several possible downstream machines the part should be routed and to what parameters the next machining operation should be set.

5. Part manipulation: A decoupler reorients the part so it is ready for insertion into the next machine.

6. Leap-frog or skip operations: A decoupler identifies different kinds of parts, allowing downstream operations to be selectively bypassed.

7. Converging or branching: A decoupler enables multiple machines to feed into a single machine or a single machine to branch into multiple machines.

Because little or no assembly work is done in a machining cell, all material used in the cell arrives at the inbound stock area. Upon completion of the machining sequence, the finished parts or products emerge at the outbound stock area.

The actual CT of a machining cell is based upon the CTs of the machines in the cell and on the CTs of workers. Assume that each station in a machining cell has a single-cycle automatic machine, that is, a machine that automatically stops after its operation has been completed. In that case, the **machine CT** is the time *per unit* to set up the machine (unload, change over, and load machine) and for the machine to perform its operation. The **worker CT** is the time for the worker to complete a trip around the cell. Specifically, it is the time for the worker to unload, change over, load, and start every machine (the task times) plus the times for the worker to walk between all the stations:

$$Worker\ CT\ =\ \Sigma\ Task\ Times\ +\ \Sigma\ Walk\ Times. \tag{4}$$

Now, in a one-person machining cell, one of two things will happen as the worker walks around the cell: either the worker arrives at a machine before the machine has finished its operation, or the machine finishes its operation before the worker arrives. Thus, the cell CT for a machining cell, CT_m, depends on whichever takes longer—the worker CT or the CT of the machine in the cell that takes the longest:

$$Cell\ CT,\ One\ Worker\ =\ max(Worker\ CT,\ Longest\ Machine\ CT). \tag{5}$$

Just as with an assembly cell, to decrease the CT of a machining cell, add more workers and divide the cell into subcells. Subcells with shorter CTs must wait on subcells with longer CTs; thus, the cycle time of the entire cell, CT_m, depends on the subcell with the longest CT:

$$CT_m\ =\ max(Subcell\ CT_m s). \tag{6}$$

The following example illustrates this concept.

Example   3:   Reducing Machining Cell CT by Adding Workers

Start with the one-worker machining cell in Figure 10.10. The number between adjacent stations is the worker walk time. Assume the task time (load, unload, start) is 10 seconds per machine per unit. From equation (4),

$$Worker\ CT = 8(10\ sec)\ +\ 51\ sec\ =\ 131\ sec/unit.$$

In Figure 10.10 the number next to each station is the automatic CT—the time for the machine to automatically perform one cycle, then stop. Assume the machine CT is the automatic CT plus 10 seconds setup time per unit. The longest machine CT is at station 7 or 8,

$$Longest\ Machine\ CT\ =\ 70\ sec/unit\ +\ 10\ sec/unit\ =\ 80\ sec/unit.$$

Therefore, from equation (5),

$$CT_m\ =\ max(131,\ 80)\ =\ 131\ sec/unit.$$

FIGURE 10.10

One-worker machining cell.

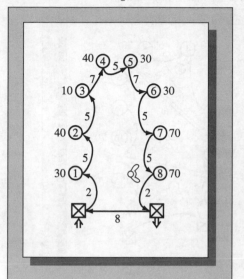

FIGURE 10.11

Two-worker machining cell.

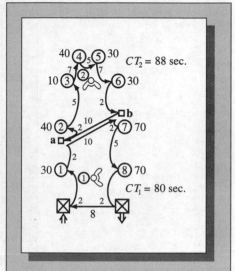

Assuming an 8-hour workday, from equation (2) cell capacity is

$$\frac{8 \text{ hr} \times 60 \text{ min} \times 60 \text{ sec}}{131 \text{ sec/unit}} = 219.8 \text{ units/day.}$$

To decrease the actual CT, suppose we add one more worker and divide the cell as shown in Figure 10.11. From equation (4),

Subcell 1: $CT = 3(10 \text{ sec}) + 31 \text{ sec} = 61 \text{ sec/unit,}$

Subcell 2: $CT = 5(10 \text{ sec}) + 38 \text{ sec} = 88 \text{ sec/unit.}$

Since the longest machine CT is still 80 sec/unit,

$$CT_m = \max(Longest \ Worker \ CT, \ Longest \ Machine \ CT)$$

$$= \max(88, 80) = 88 \text{ sec/unit.}$$

The workcell capacity is now $(8 \times 60 \times 60)/88 = 327$ units/day.

Keep adding workers and eventually the longest worker CT will be less than the longest machine CT. When that happens, the cell CT becomes 80 sec/unit, the longest machine CT. Suppose that the *required* cell CT must be *less than* 80 sec/unit. If the existing workcell grouping must be retained (i.e., the existing product-family and machine combination), then the only way to reduce the cell CT below 80 seconds would be to add a machine at the bottleneck stations.[9]

In the example, an additional machine must be put at stations 7 and 8; the CT at those stations would then effectively be reduced to 40 seconds per unit (80/2). Worker 1 operates machines 8A and 8B on an alternating

FIGURE 10.12

Three-worker machining cell.

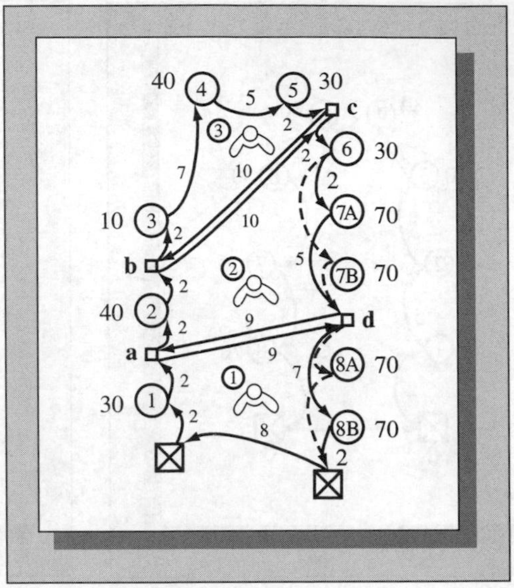

basis, and worker 2 does the same on machines 7A and 7B. So now the theoretical longest machine CT in the cell is 50 sec/unit at stations 2 and 4. Suppose we have three workers, and subdivide the cell as shown in Figure 10.12. In that case,

$$\text{Subcell 1: } CT = 2(10 \text{ sec}) + 30 \text{ sec } = 50 \text{ sec/unit,}$$

$$\text{Subcell 2: } CT = 3(10 \text{ sec}) + 32 \text{ sec } = 62 \text{ sec/unit,}$$

$$\text{Subcell 3: } CT = 3(10 \text{ sec}) + 26 \text{ sec } = 56 \text{ sec/unit.}$$

Since the longest worker CT, 62 sec/unit, exceeds the theoretical longest machine CT, the cell CT becomes 62 sec/unit. The cell capacity becomes 464.5 units/day.

Besides adding workers, cell CT can be reduced by reducing the manual task times. Refer to Figures 10.11 and 10.12; these figures show holding spaces at places where the workers interface. By replacing the holding spaces with decouplers—automated transfer devices (chutes or conveyors)—a second or two could be shaved off the task time at each station. Doing so could reduce the cell CT by many seconds.

One benefit of machining workcells is that as long as the machine CTs are less than worker CTs, the workcell output depends not on machine speed but on the number of workers, which can be easily altered. In the example, the big disparity in machine CTs (20 sec/unit at machine 3 versus 80 sec/unit at machines 7 and 8) would have no effect on cell capacity as long as the cell required CT was less than 80 sec/unit.

WORKCELL CAPACITY

The above examples demonstrated the effect of changing the number of workers on actual cell CT and cell output capacity. In designing workcells, one objective is to determine the number of workers necessary to meet the required CT and, hence, to achieve the desired output capacity. To avoid overproduction, desired output capacity should be based upon demand. However, since demand varies, design alternatives should also be considered. Design issues include not only the number of workers, but also the number of machines in the workcell, procurement of new machines, cross-training of workers, preparation of backup cells, and expansion of existing cells.

To account for changing demand, at least two scenarios should be considered: most likely and maximum likely. As an example of a way to do this, consider the machine utilization approach described in the supplement in the last chapter. That approach involves computing utilization coefficients for every machine based upon an assumed demand. The coefficients are then used to determine groupings of machines and part families. If most-likely demands are used in computing the coefficients then, presumably, the part–machine groupings will be adequate to handle the most-likely demand situation. Now, to assess the adequacy of these same groupings under different conditions, retain the groupings, but change the utilization coefficients. For instance, to determine if a cell can accommodate the maximum-likely demand, recompute the coefficients for each machine using maximum-likely demand, then sum the coefficients for all parts processed on that machine to see if the number of machines in the cell would be sufficient. Example 5 illustrates this procedure.

Example   4:   Machine Utilization Approach for Testing Maximum-Likely Demand

Figure 10.13 is a reproduction of Figure 9.18 in the previous chapter. The dense blocks in the figure indicate that parts 1, 3 and machines F, D are grouped into a cell. The utilization-coefficient total for machines F and D for *only*

FIGURE 10.13

Assignments and utilization coefficients.

Machine	Part 1	3	4	2	7	5	6	8	9	Total	Minimum Machines
F	0.3	0.6	0.3							1.2	2
D	0.2	0.4								0.6	1
C			0.4	0.7	0.3	0.4				1.8	2
H			0.3	0.6	0.1					1.0	1
G			0.4			0.2	0.6	0.5	0.8	2.5	3
B						0.3	0.1	0.2	0.1	0.7	1
A						0.4	0.3	0.1		0.8	1
E						0.6	0.3			0.9	1

Table header: *Machine Assignments Based Upon Utilizations — Part (columns 1, 3, 4, 2, 7, 5, 6, 8, 9)*

parts 1 and 3 are 0.9 and 0.6, respectively. Suppose these coefficients were determined by using most-likely demand. Since both of the utilization-coefficient totals are less than 1, only one machine of each type is required for most-likely demand.

Suppose next that the utilization coefficients are recomputed for machines F and D by using maximum-likely demand for products 1 and 3 and that the resulting utilization-coefficient total for machine D, parts 1 and 3, becomes 0.9, and for machine F it becomes 1.3. This suggests that if demand rises to the maximum-likely level, one machine D would be adequate, but one machine F would be inadequate. It would be prudent, then, to add a second machine F to the cell.

Beside machines, requirements for resources such as workers, tools, decouplers, space to expand, and so on, must also be assessed for different demand scenarios. The same approach is used to plan for demand changes regardless of source, including seasonal variation.

In designing workcells for adequate capacity it is impossible to cover all eventualities since events such as machine breakdowns, material shortages, and erratic demand spikes cannot be predicted. However, two ways to be prepared for most eventualities are (1) backup workcells and (2) planned-in excess utilization. For every product family there should ideally be a backup cell to which work can be off-loaded should the original cell become temporarily overloaded or incapacitated. The backup cell is ordinarily used for other purposes, but can with slight changes readily accommodate another product family. When it is impossible to establish a backup for every cell, then the priority should go to establishing backups for cells for the longest running or bread-and-butter products.

A second way to prepare for unanticipated events is to plan cell work such that normally it falls well within a cell's capacity; in other words, schedule work such that the cell can accommodate current demand *and then some.* Every cell should ordinarily have ample excess capacity on all machines. A cell normally scheduled to run, say, 35 hours a week will have 5 hours excess capacity to accommodate demand spikes or work interruptions; a cell scheduled for 40 hours also has remaining capacity, but only by way of overtime or additional shifts. A cell scheduled for three full shifts, 7 days, has no excess capacity. Scheduling for excess capacity is necessary for backup cells too because unless a backup has excess capacity, it cannot take on additional work from cells it is supposed to be backing up.

COST/CAPACITY TRADE-OFF ANALYSIS

Changing the number of workers alters not only a workcell capacity, but also the unit manufacturing cost of the cell. Particularly if a cell grouping is intended to be long standing, and if cell workers must be newly hired and trained, the unit cost might be a key factor in determining the feasibility of assigning multiple workers to the cell.

Adding workers to a cell increases the cell output rate, but the marginal rate of increase gets smaller with each additional worker. Figure 10.14 illustrates this for the eight-station assembly cell from Example 2. Also, with each additional worker, the direct labor operating cost of the cell increases by the worker's wage. Now, given that with each additional worker the marginal increase in the output gets smaller as the

FIGURE 10.14

Effect of adding workers on cell output.

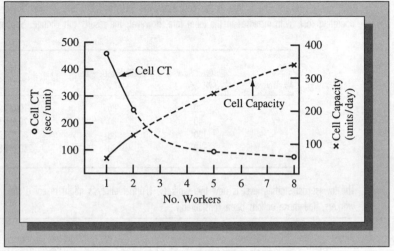

direct operating cost gets larger, at some point the cost will overtake the benefits. The following simple cost analysis shows this.

Example   5:   Cost/Capacity Trade-off Analysis

Consider again the eight-station assembly cell example and the four staffing levels investigated earlier. Reviewing the results,

No. Workers	Cell CT(sec)	Output = 60 sec × 60 min/cell CT (units/hr)
1	451	7.98
2	238	15.13
5	109	33.03
8	84	42.86

Suppose the machine operating cost of the cell is $80/hr, and the labor rate per worker is $10/hr. The total direct labor cost is then $10/hr × number of workers, and total unit manufacturing cost is:

No. Workers	a: Direct Labor Cost $/hr	b: Machine Operating Cost $/hr	Unit Cost = $\frac{(a + b)}{Output}$ ($/unit)
1	10	80	90/7.98 = $11.28
2	20	80	100/15.13 = 6.61
5	50	80	130/33.03 = 3.94
8	80	80	160/42.86 = 3.73

In this case, it is clear that increasing rates of output from additional workers more than offset increasing direct labor costs. In general, if the labor rate is low relative to other cell costs, then it is cost-effective to operate the cells with many workers. This is true in this case since the $10/hr labor rate is much lower than the $80/hr machine operating cost. With increases in the labor rate, however, the results can change. Suppose the labor rate is $20/hr:

No. Workers	a: Direct Labor Cost $/hr	b: Machine Operating Cost $/hr	$Unit\ Cost = \dfrac{(a + b)}{Output}$ ($/unit)
1	20	80	100/7.98 = $12.53
2	40	80	120/15.13 = 7.93
5	100	80	180/33.03 = 5.45
8	160	80	240/42.86 = 5.60

The lowest-cost staffing level is now five workers. (Further analysis might reveal a still lower cost at four or six workers, had those options been considered.)

The point of the example is that to determine staffing levels to achieve lowest unit cost involves weighing the trade-off between increasing direct labor costs and increasing output rate. If the cell CT is constrained by machine time (as in Example 3 where the machining cell CT was constrained to 80 sec/unit), then more machines must be added. The question then is whether increases in cell output from more machines offset the increases in both machine operating costs and direct labor cost.

In situations where cells process many small jobs of different products with frequent changeovers, the number of workers is determined more by the required cell CT (that is, by demand) than by manufacturing costs. This is because the same workers are regularly shifted among different cells in the plant on an as-needed basis. Cross-trained, the workers are assigned to whatever cells need them to meet the CT requirements of immediate jobs. Shifting workers like this among cells takes advantage of worker competencies and gives the company maximum flexibility. The point is, adding or deleting workers at a particular cell represents no net change in the number of employees to the company, so the true manufacturing cost does not increase or decrease. Workers are transferred from one place to another, and in that case, questions about the effect of direct labor cost on unit manufacturing cost are moot. The same is true about the effect of machine cost when the same machines are regularly moved between different cells as needed.

CELLS FOR BATCH SIZE = 1

One advantage of workcells is that they can produce any batch quantity, even a quantity of one, assuming the setup times are sufficiently small. Suppose that a cell forms parts A, B, C, and D in a five-machine process and that demand for the parts from a downstream cell is in one-unit quantities. To conform to the demand the cell must be capable of producing parts in batches of size one. Figure 10.15 shows the cell for making these parts. Between each workstation is a rack large enough to hold one unit of every part of A, B, C, and D. When the downstream cell withdraws a part from

FIGURE 10.15

Example of cell for making one-unit batches.

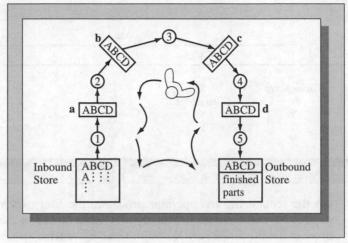

the outbound store area, that is a signal to replenish that part. Suppose a part B is withdrawn from the outbound store. Starting at machine 5, the cell operator takes a part B from holding area **d**, loads the machine and turns it on. She then goes to machine 4, loads a part B from holding area **c**, and turns the machine on. She also goes to machine 3, then machine 2, then machine 1, loading the B parts and turning on the machines. Upon returning to machine 5 she unloads the part and puts it on the outbound store rack. The process is repeated every time a part is withdrawn from the outbound store rack.

The machines are all single cycle, and they might automatically eject the parts to the next holding area at completion of machining. If not, the operator simply unloads the part before loading the next one. Except for the last machine, parts can also be left in the machines until the next time the operator cycles around the cell (the machine becomes the holding area for one part). Perhaps obvious is that the task of changing over between making different parts must be quite simple, ideally a one-touch operation that takes only seconds.

SEQUENTIAL CHANGEOVER TASKS

Regardless of batch size, whenever a workcell must produce a different part or product, machines and fixtures at each station must be changed over. One way to do the changeover is to stop the cell and change everything at once. Another, less disruptive way is to integrate the changeover into the cell's sequence of operations. Instead of shutting down the cell, the changeover is done at only one station each time the operator walks around the cell. Suppose a cell has five machines, is currently making part X, and is to be changed over to make part Y. As shown in Figure 10.16, the changeover can be completed by the operator after five trips around the cell. On the first trip the operator changes over machine 1 from X to Y, then walks around the remainder of the cell to process the last four part Xs on the remaining four machines.

FIGURE 10.16

Sequential changeover of machines.

	Machine				
Cycle	1	2	3	4	5
1	Changeover	X	X	X	X
2	Y	Changeover	X	X	X
3	Y	Y	Changeover	X	X
4	Y	Y	Y	Changeover	X
5	Y	Y	Y	Y	Changeover

On the second trip the operator processes the first part Y on machine 1, walks to machine 2 and changes it from X to Y, then walks to the other three machines to process the last three part Xs. With three more trips around the cell, the changeover from part X to part Y is completed.

Setup-reduction efforts are especially important in workcell operations. So that the entire changeover procedure causes minimal interruption to the process, change-over procedures must involve minimal steps, no trial-and-error adjustment, and result in parts that are defect-free and meet specifications, starting with the first try.

PRODUCTIVITY IMPROVEMENT

Workcell productivity improvement efforts are aimed at accomplishing the required CT with the minimum number of workers. Recognize that the emphasis on improve-ment is decidedly *not* on reducing the cell CT, since reducing the CT below the required CT and without any anticipated increase in demand only results in overpro-duction. Workcell improvement efforts start with the required CT, then seek ways to achieve it with the fewest workers. Suppose, for example, that to meet a required cell CT of 123 sec/unit, the five-worker assignment shown in Figure 10.9 is initially adopted. With this assignment, the actual worker CTs and idle times (assuming workers conform to the 123 sec/unit requirement) are as follows:

Worker	Subcell Stations	Cycle Time (sec)	Idle Time (sec)
1	1 and 2	109	14
2	3 and 4	91	32
3	5 and 6	101	22
4	7	90	33
5	8	90	33
			134

The total worker idle time for the assignment, 134 seconds, is high. In fact, given that it exceeds the required CT of 109 seconds, the theoretical implication is that one less worker is needed than the five currently assigned. To reduce the number of workers, a way must be found to reduce task times and reassign the workers so that most of the idle time falls on just one worker. Suppose through productivity improvement efforts the task times are reduced at some stations, and workers are reassigned such that the following results:

Worker	Subcell Stations	Cycle Time (sec)	Idle Time (sec)
1	1 and 8	120	3
2	2 and 6	120	3
3	3	30	93
4	7	94	29
5	5 and 6	101	12
			140

This assignment might at first seem worse than the initial assignment because total idle time is now 140 seconds. Most of the idle time, however, is with worker 3, so if ways can be found to reduce the task time by 1 second at either station 3 or 7 (currently at 124 seconds, total), then both stations could be combined and handled by worker 4. Worker 3 would be removed from the cell, leaving just four workers. The assumption is that the remaining workers in the cell have the skills necessary to take over tasks for the removed worker.

In practice, the worker chosen to be removed from a cell as the result of productivity improvement should be the one recognized by members of the cell team as being, overall, the most highly skilled worker. There are two reasons for this. First, workers removed from one cell are reassigned to another cell, and the more skilled the worker, the easier it is to reassign her to another cell. Second, the message conveyed to all workers is that reassignment is a reward for good performance, not a penalty for poor performance. Also, this practice of reassignment identifies to everyone the top-performing workers, though it does not expose or handicap average or below-average workers. An example of this is at Allen-Bradley in Milwaukee, where a group of highly experienced and able workers in a volunteer group called the SWAT team accept assignments anywhere in the plant, based on demand.[10]

Most workcells are capable of producing items in at least one product family. Ideally, the operation of the workcell and the number of cell workers should not have to be changed every time the cell switches to producing a different product, assuming no change in the required CT. The objective is to hold the basic cell functioning and number of workers relatively constant; consequently, productivity improvement should include efforts to equalize the task times and machine times for every item in a product family.

QUALITY CONTROL

Workers monitor product quality as pieces move through the cell. No item identified at a station as defective is allowed to proceed to the next station. Sometimes colored lights are located above each station to indicate work status. The lights, called **andons,** are green as long as work is proceeding normally, but are switched to yellow when a worker needs assistance and a possible delay is expected from that station. If the problem is severe and the process must be stopped, the worker switches the light to red, and the entire cell stops until the problem has been resolved. Lights are used particularly where noise or other factors make verbal communication difficult, or where workcell status must be quickly communicated to areas of the plant that provide inputs to the cell or that rely on the cell's outputs—as in a pull production system formed by linked workcells.

WORKERS IN CELLS

STAFFING A WORKCELL

Workcells are responsibility centers where workers have considerable autonomy and perform functions ordinarily done by staff experts, including equipment setup and changeover, equipment maintenance and basic repair, job scheduling, and quality control. Workers sometimes also perform cell-related planning and problem solving, accounting, and ordering of parts from vendors. They even meet with suppliers to resolve issues about incoming parts, and with customers to better understand their requirements and how the cell output is used. Though each cell usually has a stable core of workers and a supervisor or group leader, as described, workers are sometimes rotated between workcells depending on demand requirements.

Though a workcell's cycle time can be adjusted by changing the number of workers, such changes should occur relatively infrequently and only as dictated by changes in the required CT. In assembly plants, the required cell CT is set by requirements of the final-assembly stage.

Decisions about workcell assignments are made by cell supervisors on the shop floor. Determining the number of workers and their assignments to workstations to meet a required CT can be somewhat difficult initially, but it gets easier with practice as supervisors learn what staffing combinations yield the desired cell CTs. Analytical tools such as computer simulation are useful for helping to make staffing decisions. In some plants, staff planners run computer simulation models to formulate recommendations for supervisors; in other plants, the supervisors themselves run the computer simulation models.

SIMULTANEOUS STAFFING OF MULTIPLE CELLS

Workers cross-trained to perform operations in more than one cell can be assigned to operate *more than one cell at one time*. Strictly speaking, what was stated earlier about a cell being operated by as few as one worker is slightly incorrect since a single worker can operate two or more cells located together. To see how this happens look at two possible staffing assignments for cells A–E in Figure 10.17. Assignment (*a*) has seven workers; (*b*) has four. In both the (*a*) and (*b*) assignments, the cells are linked

FIGURE 10.17

Workers with overlapping cell assignments.

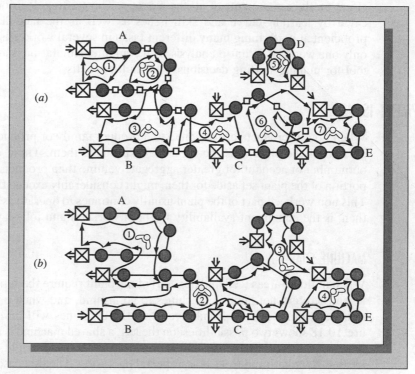

by each worker relying on another worker for parts or materials. Looking at (*b*), worker 1 cycles through cells A and B; worker 2, through cells B and C; worker 3, through cells C and D (with an additional stop at the inbound stock area for station E); and worker 4 through only cell E. Because they are linked, the cells all have the same CT, which is the CT of the worker who takes the longest. Adding workers reduces the overall CT, so in Figure 10.17 the CT for seven workers (*a*) will be less than that for four workers (*b*).

When the required output of the different cells is different, the worker assignment gets more tricky. Cells that require less output (i.e., have longer required CTs) can be visited by workers on every second, third, or more cycles, but that increases the time available for them to perform operations in other cells they visit. This means they have time to do more operations in those cells. As an example, suppose in assignment (*b*) that the output of cell A should be roughly half that of the other cells. Worker 1 might visit cell A only on alternate cycles, but he then will have roughly doubled his available time for doing tasks in cell B. More operations in cell B could be assigned to worker 1, but that would change the assignment for the other worker in cell B, worker 2.

Adjusting worker 2's assignments in cell B affects his assignment in cell C, which affects worker 3, and so on. Any attempt to change the CT in one cell has a ripple effect on the assignments of all the workers. The staffing decision is further complicated by learning-curve and skill issues as well as the fact that workers are less proficient at performing many different tasks in several workcells than fewer tasks in only one workcell. What-if analysis with computer simulation is an almost mandatory tool for making staffing decisions with multiple cells.

EQUIPMENT ISSUES

When not all products are assigned to a product family or production in workcells, a portion of the plant must be set aside to produce them. These odd products might outnumber or account for greater aggregate volume than products in families, and the portion of the plant set aside for them might considerably exceed the workcell portion. This non workcell part of the plant usually continues to operate as a job shop. At issue, then, is the equipment availability for both workcell and job-shop applications.

MACHINE SHARING

When multiple areas (cell and noncell) of the plant require the same kind of machines, when there are not enough machines to go around, and when procurement of additional machines is cost prohibitive, then the machines will have to be shared. Figure 10.18 shows two possibilities: on the left, a shared machine is located between two adjacent cells so that, theoretically, it resides in both; on the right, a shared machine is located elsewhere and treated as a special operation. The first case offers convenience

FIGURE 10.18

Shared machines.

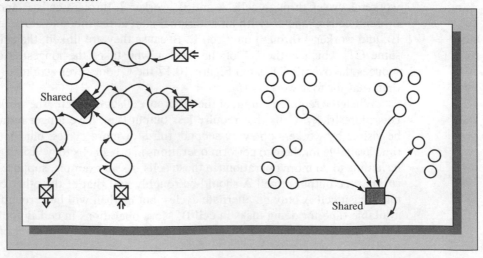

for both cells, but it also interrupts the operations of both. Specifically, a shared machine must be periodically switched over to process jobs from the cells sharing it, and while one job is being processed, jobs from the other cells must wait; this further leads to WIP accumulation and increased lead times—just like in traditional batch processing. The second case has the same drawbacks in addition to requiring greater material handling effort; however, it is the only solution when a machine is immobile and must be shared by many processes.

Sometimes the shared-machine approach is adopted to ensure that a machine will get high usage. If the machine is expensive and has multiple capabilities, shared usage is a way to exploit its capabilities and amortize the cost. These are not good reasons, but they are common reasons. In summary, when cells share machines, the advantages of cellular manufacturing are diminished.

MACHINE ACQUISITION

Criteria for machine acquisition traditionally consider the trade-off between a machine's production rate or multipurpose capability and its cost. For plants with focused factories, traditional acquisition criteria need to be rethought since they can lead to results opposite the intended, such as a multipurpose machine *decreasing* the plant's flexibility, and a special, high-speed machine *increasing* production lead times.

Multipurpose machines can be quickly changed over to do many things or even do several things at once. Such machines have the capability to perform a variety of machining operations on products with a wide range of sizes, shapes, and configurations. Such machines, however, usually cost much more than fewer-purpose machines, so purchasing them leaves less funds to purchase other machines, and that increases the possibility that focused factories will have to share machines. Even when a multipurpose machine can be dedicated exclusively to a single workcell, the tendency is for managers to try to expand the variety of the cell's output and to route products from other workcells or autonomous operations through the machine to take full advantage of its capabilities. The same situation can result from procuring costly high-speed machines: fewer of them can be acquired, so focused factories must share them, jobs have to wait longer, and so on.

The alternative to costly multipurpose or special-order machines is inexpensive, slower, and fewer-purpose machines, but many of them. Every workcell that needs one gets one and can then function autonomously. Although a multipurpose machine offers high flexibility through quick changeover and rapid production rate, all else equal, conventional fewer-purpose machines might provide even greater flexibility when employed in a number of manufacturing cells. Conventional machines are also simpler for workers to operate and less costly to maintain.

Every workcell is eventually changed, either in response to changes in demand or product-family mix or as a result of cell productivity improvements. Plantwide, workcells are in flux; some are being newly created or reconfigured while others are being disbanded. To minimize the time and cost of reconfiguring workcells, machines and workstations should be small, mobile, and have simple utility hookups.

SPECIAL OPERATIONS

Machine and equipment considerations in workcell design extend beyond cost and flexibility. An operation might involve large, heavy machines that need massive foundation supports and special utility hookups; it might involve machines or work areas that are unique and must serve the entire plant (welding areas, paint rooms, heat-treatment rooms); it might require uncommon procedures and isolation from the rest of the plant (for venting toxic fumes or shielding against heat or radiation). Although equipment for operations such as these might not be relocatable to workcells, there are ways to include them as part of a focused-factory or workcell process. One way is to move products back and forth between the special operation and the workcells. Processing at each special operation is done on a batch basis, though the batches are kept small to minimize wait times and WIP inventory.

When most of the products in a product group require the same special operation, then a workcell can be built around that operation (see Figure 10.19). If the special operation requires batching, then inventory is allowed to accumulate just ahead of the operation until the right quantity is built up. If the operation is continuous and not shared by other cells, then items can be routed through as if it were any other operation in the cell.

CELL AUTOMATION

Automation of a cell is often an evolutionary transformation, starting with installation of single-cycle, automatic machines where workers manually load and unload the machines and transfer parts between them. When all manual functions have been automated, the transformation is complete. Figure 10.20 shows a workcell with a centrally located robot that pivots to transfer, reorient, load, and unload parts at any of the stations and in any sequence. The robot and machine operations are automatic and controlled by microcomputers.

FIGURE 10.19

Cells built around special operations.

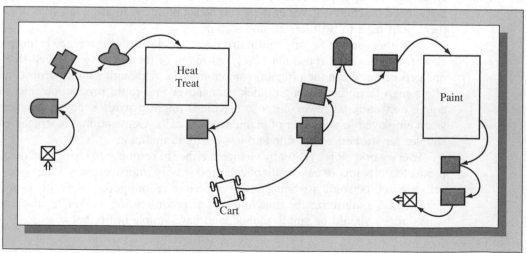

Benefits of automation include low setup time, high output rate, and low process-induced variability in the output. A manufacturing cell, or system of linked cells, that is completely automated by virtue of robots and computer control is called a **flexible manufacturing system (FMS).** Like other, less-automated workcells, an FMS can be an economical way to produce a variety of different products, even if each has only small or moderate demand. Economy is attained by high machine utilization from processing many products that require a similar process. With automation it is possible to achieve very high tolerance standards and low variability. Like manual workcells, FMSs can be linked together. Flow of material into a cell's inbound stock area and out of its outbound stock area (the "X" boxes in previous figures) can be linked by conveyors or automated guided vehicles. The linked FMSs make up a larger FMS, complete with automated machine tools, automated handling equipment, and computers that coordinate work within and between the FMS subsystems. Effective operation of FMSs still requires human operators, who provide important services such as equipment monitoring, quick intervention when operational problems arise (stuck tools, incorrectly positioned parts, an automated guided vehicle going to the wrong place), problem solving and cell improvement, and assisting engineers in the design of parts to be manufactured.[11]

FIGURE 10.20

Robotic cell.

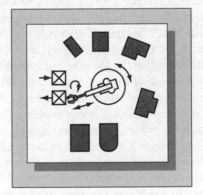

Full automation is expensive. Because "unmanned" cells still require human support, the labor savings is not always as great as expected. FMSs are also inherently somewhat less flexible than cells having greater manual labor content and machines and transfer systems that can be easily relocated and reconfigured. Unlike cross-trained workers, which can be reassigned virtually anywhere to perform a broad range of tasks, robots are limited in the range of tasks they can be programmed to perform. The capital cost for automated systems is much higher than for simpler, manual systems, and the maintenance cost for automated systems is usually higher too. Still, there are many cases where the right combination of product variety and production volume make automation the logical choice. Many cellular manufacturing plants employ a range of cellular processes, from fully manual to fully automated.

IMPLEMENTING CELLULAR MANUFACTURING[12]

This and the previous chapter have largely addressed issues of production technology. While attention to these issues is necessary for successful implementation of cellular manufacturing, it is not sufficient. Like JIT and TQM, focused factories and cellular manufacturing represent more than changes in production technology; they represent a different philosophy about managing and performing work. The following sections put issues associated with implementing cellular manufacturing into three broad categories: planning and control, organization, and attitudes. Many of these issues are interrelated and logically span more than one category.

PLANNING AND CONTROL[13]

Every production process has a system for planning and control. The system anticipates production requirements for materials, labor, and facilities and checks that they are within the capability of the production process. The system performs job routing, workstation loading, detailed scheduling, job sequencing, job dispatching, and tracking of jobs as they move through the system. Although a workcell is a shop-floor phenomenon, its implementation must be integrated with planning and control mechanisms beyond the shop floor. Organizations implementing workcells usually have centralized planning and control systems already in place, so ways have to be found to adapt them to the control procedures of workcells. The common MRP-type planning and control system discussed in the Appendix is an example of such a centralized system. With MRP the focus of attention is on order releases and completion dates for *all* individual components and higher-level assemblies in a product. In contrast, in cellular manufacturing the focus of attention is primarily on completed products, that is, on what goes out of the cell, not on what is happening within it. Unless modified, all of this order-release information from an MRP system about intermediate operations is of no use in cellular manufacturing.

At issue is the primary unit of focus in planning and control. In traditional noncell shops, the machine or the workstation is the unit of focus, and jobs are scheduled and tracked at every machine and station. In workcell shops, the *whole cell* is the unit of focus. All that matters is what goes into the cell and what comes out of it. This change of focus greatly condenses the amount of scheduling and control information generated since material is tracked at only two places—the points where it enters and leaves the cell. Only in workcells where the cell throughput times are very long or where the operating and overhead expenses of machines in the cell vary greatly are individual machines or workstations retained as the unit of focus.

This is not to say that MRP-type planning and control systems are useless for workcell operations. In a survey of 57 companies that implemented cellular manufacturing, 75% had used MRP planning and control systems before implementation. After implementation, 71% *still* used MRP systems, though of these, 33% had also adopted Kanban systems. Only 13% of the companies used Kanban-only systems, and only 31% used MRP-only systems.[14] Because workcells themselves have virtually no planning or forward-looking capability, they depend on a system such as MRP for future planning and order entry. Though cell operators might be responsible for short-term capacity planning and job scheduling, the size and frequency of jobs arriving at the cell is determined elsewhere by the centralized system. The centralized system forecasts demand, accumulates job orders, performs rough-cut capacity planning, and prepares and coordinates master production schedules. To adapt MRP systems for releasing orders to workcells, the product bills of materials must be restructured. The MRP system is then used to send jobs to workcells. Once a job arrives at a workcell, all detailed job sequencing, scheduling, and control are performed by workcell supervisors and operators. These matters are further discussed in Part V.

ORGANIZATIONAL ISSUES

Implementing workcells requires that job roles, responsibilities, and relationships be redefined. The roles of workers are expanded, teamwork is emphasized, and production output and compensation measures are group oriented. Workcell implementation usually involves considerable worker training as well as modification of performance appraisal and pay systems. In fact, implementing workcells affects all areas of human resource management, which, in addition to the areas mentioned, include employee relations and employee selection. As a result, many or most of the human resource policies and practices traditionally applied in shop settings require some alteration.[15]

Roles and Responsibilities

Accompanying cellular manufacturing are changes to the roles of supervisors and staff-support professionals. The most evident change, however, is to the role of the shop-floor worker. To take full advantage of workcell production methods, shop personnel must be empowered. The locus of production-control decision making must be moved from functional support departments to the shop floor. Workers must be made responsible not only for a full range of assembly and machine-operation assignments, but also for performing tasks previously reserved for support staff such as inspection, basic maintenance and repair, job prioritizing, and dispatching.

As workers take on more of these responsibilities, the primary function of staff professionals shifts to supporting the workers. Ostensibly, the purpose of staff groups everywhere is to provide support and expertise, but in workcell operations the support staff is held to that charge. Support happens in the form of training workcell operators, providing on-demand technical guidance, and performing tasks that require high-level expertise. For instance, instead of routine repairs, maintenance staff only do difficult repairs, and spend the rest of the time training workers, analyzing equipment failures, overhauling equipment, and improving maintenance and operation procedures; instead of routine inspection, the quality control staff does company quality audits, certifies suppliers, trains workers in inspection procedures, and does tests and inspections that require specialized skill and knowledge.

Though noncell plant operations still require staff assistance of a traditional nature, more responsibility being transferred to shop-floor workers means less remaining for planners, schedulers, dispatchers, and other support staff. As a result, the size of the support staff can be reduced, as can the accompanying overhead cost. For the remaining support group, however, there will be greater prestige and respect, since the group will have switched from doing tasks that are routine to tasks that are more challenging and require high-level competency.

Cellular manufacturing also affects people not directly involved in production planning, control, or execution. Design engineers, for example, are accustomed to being judged for the number and creativity of the designs they create. Cellular manufacturing and group technology encourage design engineers to find ways to improve product quality while taking maximum advantage of existing parts and manufacturing capabilities.

Incentive Plans

Traditional incentive plans reward workers based on individual performance. The plans are typically based on piece rates, and earnings are a function of the number of units produced.[16] Thus, each worker can maximize her pay by maximizing her output. In workcell operations that require teamwork, however, such plans are usually ineffective because workers who help others have less time to devote to maximizing their own output. For this reason, it will probably be necessary to replace the traditional incentive plan with some form of *group-based* incentive system to maintain productivity and to minimize worker resistance to teamwork.

Two group-based plans are **pay-for-skill** and **gain-sharing.** Both tend to promote behaviors and attitudes important for teamwork. Pay-for-skill plans increase the wages of workers for each new skill they learn.[17] The available skill options depend on worker responsibilities and include machine operation, setup, maintenance, inspection, and so on.

Gain-sharing plans provide team members with bonuses for improvements in team performance as measured against a baseline standard.[18] Whenever the team performs better than the baseline, it accumulates bonus points in a pool. Some plans apportion the bonus pool equally to everyone in the group, others to workers as a percentage of their base salary or number of hours they worked. Measures of team performance include cell output rate, cell defect rate, setup times, equipment effectiveness, cell inventory level, and average worker skill level. Because the measures are based on cell performance as a whole, they motivate teamwork. Performance against baseline is tracked by cell team members, both for gain-sharing and continuous improvement purposes. The team must agree that the baseline standards are reasonable, and if they do not, the baseline can become a sore point with them and ineffective as an incentive.

Whatever compensation plan is adopted, it must not result in workers receiving less pay when they move to workcells. Implementing a pay plan that hurts workers financially will guarantee workcell failure. In fact, it can be argued that workers should justifiably be paid more because workcells require higher skill-level and more responsibility from them.

Time and Rate Standards[19]

A **time standard,** or standard time, is the amount of time required to perform a particular task. Time standards are used for many purposes:

- Computing the quantity of a product that can be produced in a given time period (standard output rate).
- Determining the number of workers or machines needed to meet production demand.
- Distributing work among employees.
- Assessing alternative production approaches.
- Setting production schedules.
- Estimating production costs and setting selling prices.
- Assessing employee performance in wage-incentive plans.

For a team-oriented process, the fundamental unit of measure must be the group. Since existing time standards are usually based upon one person performing a single task, they are relatively useless in cells where workers move among different tasks or perform tasks collectively. Thus, workcell implementation usually involves developing workcell-based standards, most of the information for which must be newly collected.

As examples, look back at the machining cell Example 3 (Figures 10.10–10.12) where the cycle times for three different staffing levels for the cell were determined. Among the reasons that cell CT is so important is that it serves as the cell standard time, which is used for determining other cell standards, such as standard output rates. For instance, from the cell CTs in the cell in Example 3, the standard output rates are determined as follows:

Number of Workers	*Cell CT (sec)*	*Standard Output Rate = (60 sec × 60 min)/Cell CT (units/hr)*
1	131	27.48
2	88	40.91
3	62	58.06

Establishing the cell CT is not necessarily easy. Recall that the cell CT is determined by taking the greater of the longest worker time and the longest machine time:

$$Cell\ CT = \max(Longest\ Worker\ CT, Longest\ Machine\ CT).$$

Both the worker CT and machine CT are themselves standard times. The machine CT is the time for the machine to perform a particular single operation, and this standard time is usually already well-established, and if not, it is easy to measure.

The worker CT is another matter. Worker CT is the time for a worker to walk between machines and perform tasks, but since the time can vary considerably from worker to worker, it can be difficult to ascertain as a standard. One way to get standard worker CT is to use time-motion analysis for each walk and machine-task segment and then to sum the times over all segments along the route of the worker. A better way is use work sampling: observe the actual times of different workers performing a particular walk/machine-task sequence and take the average. The problem with relying on work-sampling data from cell operations is that the data to develop standard times cannot be obtained until *after* the cell is formed, yet standard times are needed to *plan* the cell. In such a chicken-and-egg case, the initial cell standard times might have to be derived from times collected elsewhere from operations considered similar to those in the cell. These initial standards are used to design the cell, then are revised as soon as data from that actual cell can be obtained. A pilot cell, discussed later, is useful for establishing the initial cell standards.

Another tool for developing cell standards *before* a workcell begins operation is computer simulation. Since workcell standards vary depending on factors such as the product, workstation configuration, and number and skill-level of workers in the cell, computer simulation is a good way to establish initial cell standards that best fit a given combination of factors. Simulation also can take into account variability in machine and worker times and show the likely range of expected performance outcomes. Thus, through simulation, standards can be established that have a high likelihood of being met. The standards used in computer simulation models are originally best estimates. As real workcell experience is gained and actual time and performance data are accumulated, the estimates are revised for accuracy and used as standards for later simulation studies. The next chapter gives further details about work standards development.

Time and output standards, once determined, are used to set labor standards. A labor standard is the average labor time required to produce each unit of product. The labor standard for a cell is computed by dividing the standard cell output rate by the number of workers in the cell. For example, using the above standard output rates,

Cell Staffing (No. Workers) /	Standard Output Rate (units/hr) =	Labor Standard (hr/unit)
1	27.48	.0364
2	40.91	.0489
3	58.06	.0517

Labor standards are used for capacity planning, product costing, work scheduling, and deriving gain-sharing baseline measures.

Team Education and Training

Obviously, for workcell teams to be able to perform the expected wide range of tasks, training is essential. In addition to the basics of workcell operation, workers should learn to do machine setup, basic machine upkeep and PM, simple machine repair, product inspection and quality control, and to work as members of a team. They should be trained to operate many or all of the machines in the workcell and possibly in other workcells, too. The best training for machine operation, maintenance, and setup is hands-on experience with assistance from veteran operators and support staff. As workers become proficient, the assistance is phased out. Operation of complicated machines can sometimes be modified to allow workers to master them in a short time.

Like the workers, supervisors should be capable of working in a variety of areas, depending on demand requirements. Rotating supervisors among different work areas improves not only plant staffing flexibility, but human relations also. One plant, for example, had a history of supervisors in different areas constantly arguing over schedules and parts shortages. After being required to exchange jobs, the supervisors stopped bickering because they better appreciated the kinds of problems facing other supervisors.

A record of employee skills (as shown in Figure 10.21) is maintained for workcell staffing assignments and pay-for-skill incentives. Once workers have gained new skills, they should be rotated daily or weekly among the stations within a cell, or in different cells in a focused factory, so they can utilize and improve those skills.

In addition to classroom and shop-floor training, workers learn about workcell concepts and operations by visiting other plants that have implemented workcells. They discuss implementation and operational issues with workers at the site and learn about procedures, mistakes, and how to do things better.

ATTITUDINAL ISSUES

Adopting workcells involves more than a shift to new layouts and procedures; it requires a basic shift to worker empowerment. Many staff people and supervisors will perceive that transfer as a reduction in their power. Power, by whatever means achieved, is not something most people willingly relinquish, and those with the perceived loss will argue against the change.

FIGURE 10.21

Worker skill chart.

Name	Machine and Task Skills							Comments
	M1	M2	M3	M4	M5	Insp'n	SPC	
Bill	1	2	2			2	1	
Jane	2	2		1	2	2	2	Goal: master M4
Wonda				1	1	1		Trainee
Igor	2	2	2	2	1	2	1	Goal: master M5 and SPC
Talia			1	2	2	1		Goal: master M3 and insp'n, basic SPC

Competency levels: 1 = basic (operation); 2 = master;
3 = 2 + preventive maintenance; 4 = 3 + repair maintenance

Shop-Floor Workers

Education and training alone will not modify people's attitudes. Many shop workers who are accustomed to performing narrow tasks will not eagerly welcome the chance to learn and utilize new skills. They will have to be convinced that the changes are an improvement, that their work will be more challenging and less boring, and that their ideas and opinions, not just their physical labor, will be valued. Although there is much anecdotal evidence that workers in cells are more satisfied with their jobs, the evidence is not unequivocal. Many ambitious workers will gladly accept the change, but others, conditioned by years of management disdain, lack of responsibility, etc., will resist it. Union contracts outlining job descriptions and pay rates will have to be rewritten to account for the cross-functional, team-orientation of workcell jobs. Union spokespeople might be skeptical and view workcells as a ploy to squeeze more productivity out of workers.

Supervisors

Supervisors will also be skeptical.[20] Job security is one of their concerns; they wonder whether their role will become redundant and unnecessary once workers are empowered. While management often makes guarantees to hourly workers about their jobs, no comparable guarantees are made to supervisors. Supervisors are also anxious about their job function. They wonder what they're supposed to do and how they will be measured. Again, management often devotes much attention to these issues for hourly workers, but not for supervisors. A third concern is about the amount of added work. Implementing workcells requires additional work for training, coordinating, and problem solving, all for which supervisors might be responsible but for which there may be no additional pay.

Management

Management too may oppose many of the necessary changes in organization structure and responsibility and have to be convinced about the benefits of focused factories and workcells. The employee training, equipment relocation and retooling, and new setup and maintenance procedures associated with workcell implementation require considerable time and some capital outlay. Alone, traditional managerial decision criteria such as short-term payback period, internal rate of return, and high equipment utilization might argue against cells. For managers to understand the benefits of workcells, they must first understand the importance of reduced defects, shortened lead times, reduced inventories, and increased reliability and flexibility of operations. Analysis to justify adopting workcells requires use of multicriteria methods that besides financial costs consider the intangible benefits of quality, flexibility, employee satisfaction, and improved management, as well as the intangible risks (market and technology) of not adopting them.[21]

One reason cellular manufacturing programs fail is because management tries to cut corners.[22] For example, by cutting training costs, companies end up with workers incapable of performing well in workcells. By avoiding team-oriented personnel selection criteria and group social issues, they end up with workcell teams that will never be very effective. By avoiding costly relocation of equipment, they end up with cells formed around pseudo products instead of around actual product families. Like all things in JIT/TQM, cellular manufacturing requires long-term commitment. It cannot be done quickly or cheaply, and it requires the support of management.

Resistance to workcells is certainly not universal, and in many organizations people welcome (even get excited about) implementing workcells and being assigned to work in them. At the McDonnell & Miller plant, a union shop that years ago began using machining and assembly cells, enthusiasm about being assigned to workcells is so high that workers are on a waiting list. Cell workers say they enjoy the added responsibility and variety of the tasks, and the absence of close scrutiny by supervisors. Although the average pay of cell workers is actually slightly less than in other parts of the plant, many employees say they would be willing to accept a small pay decrease to be transferred to a workcell.

GETTING STARTED

Initial planning for workcells should be conducted by a multifunctional steering committee. This committee, comprising representatives from the functional departments, the union, shop-floor workers, machine operators, top management, and possibly a consultant with workcell implementation experience, addresses the issues described above and gains the support of all the affected parties. The committee oversees high-level planning and coordination of all activities, including product-family/machine grouping, layout and equipment changes, space allocation, training, site visits, union contract negotiations, changes in jobs and reporting relationship, modifications to planning and control procedures, and major equipment procurement. An effective steering committee should be able to overcome most problems of workcell implementation.

Besides the steering committee, a core team should be formed for each workcell to handle detailed workcell design and final implementation. The core team should include people from industrial engineering and production management, the supervisor, and workers who will eventually staff the cell. The team is provided financial and technical support from the steering committee and specialists in functional departments. Members of the core team should be selected for demonstrated willingness and ability to work in a team, high-level experience and qualifications, adaptability to change, and acceptance of new ideas. The team should receive team-building and group dynamics training soon after it is formed to help it develop into a cohesive work group.

Many companies start workcell implementation using one or two pilot cells and a product family that accounts for a sizable proportion of the firm's volume.[23] A pilot cell serves many purposes: engineers and workers tinker with it to fine-tune the design; managers collect data to assess its costs and benefits; workers train in it, learn to operate machines, do setups, maintenance, and quality checking; and staff specialists use it to discover ways to reduce setup times and eliminate quality problems. A single pilot cell can usually be implemented in 6 months, though it can take longer. Assuming the cell performs well, the benefits it demonstrates will open the way to additional workcells. When the intent is to establish a series of linked workcells in a pull production process, the conversion to cells usually begins downstream and works backward, starting at the final assembly area and successively converting upstream operations into cells.

Remember, despite the benefits, workcells are not the best way to produce everything. Focused facilities and workcells make sense where there are distinct product families and where the volume of the products in a family is clearly enough to justify devoting facilities and machines solely to it. For low-variety, high-volume products, a product-oriented assembly line is better than a workcell; and for producing numerous dissimilar items, each with small, erratic demand, a job shop is better.

Summary

Cellular manufacturing is manufacturing done in a workcell. A workcell is a group of dissimilar operations formed to produce a product family. Benefits of cellular manufacturing, including high quality and efficiency, result from the workcell's focused nature; workers and equipment are clustered together and dedicated to producing a family of outputs on a repetitive basis. Flexibility is also a benefit since in workcells it is easy to change product volume and the kind of product. The output rate of a workcell is easily modified by changing the number of workers and machines, and a workcell can efficiently produce output for virtually any batch size, even one. It can produce all the items in a product family; some can even produce multiple product families. By linking workcells together, it is possible to produce complex end-items.

Implementing cellular manufacturing requires commitment to many of the principles of JIT and TQM. Setup procedures must be simplified, and machine reliability and commitment to quality must be high. Cellular manufacturing requires empowering workers. Besides performing assembly and machining operations, the workcell team assumes responsibility for most machine changeovers, basic PM and repair, and quality inspection. Sometimes the team also does its own workcell planning, priority decision making, and material purchasing.

Cellular manufacturing greatly simplifies production scheduling and control. Whereas in traditional shops jobs are scheduled and tracked from operation to operation, in cellular manufacturing they are tracked only at the start and the finish of the cell. Although this simplification saves a tremendous amount of non-value-added paperwork and processing, it requires modification of traditional MRP-based planning and control systems for scheduling and tracking at the workcell level.

Since workcell operation is a collective effort of workers and a supervisor, wage and incentive systems must be modified to encourage team-oriented behavior. The roles of support staff change too; as shop-floor workers assume most of the routine tasks formerly performed by staff, the staff assume responsibility for other tasks that take better advantage of their higher-level skill and knowledge base.

Cellular manufacturing is best implemented by starting slowly and with a pilot cell. The pilot cell should be formed such that it has the greatest chance of success.

A product family that has sufficient volume to justify dedicating people and machines to it should be chosen. A steering committee should be formed to handle broad issues such as gaining support from the union and functional departments, providing resources, and coordinating cross-functional activities. A shop-floor core team should also be formed to handle details about pilot workcell design and implementation. Only workers who are open to change, highly qualified, and eager to participate should be selected. The purpose of the pilot is to teach everyone about the way a workcell works, to experiment with setup reduction, PM, and extended worker involvement as well as to demonstrate to everyone the potential benefits of workcells. The pilot cell might require 6 months to 1 year to be up and fully functioning; meanwhile, everyone will be watching to see what happens. Designing for the best chances of success minimizes the time for the pilot to become fully operational. Emphasis on pilot success serves another purpose too: if cellular manufacturing cannot be made to succeed in the pilot, then it will be clear that there is no way it can be made to succeed anywhere in the plant.

Questions

1. In what situations would it make sense for workers to walk around a workcell in a direction opposite the parts flow?

2. Explain the difference between required CT and actual CT?

3. How might increasing the number of workers in a cell result in a longer cell CT?

4. Why is the cost (wage rate and associated costs) of workers in a workcell sometimes irrelevant in determining the number of workers to assign to a workcell?

5. Discuss the drawbacks of not being able to include every machine needed for processing of an item within one workcell.

6. Why should workcell productivity improvement efforts be centered around the required CT? In what situations would the improvement effort focus on reducing the actual cell CT?

7. What are the advantages and difficulties in assigning workers to operate multiple cells simultaneously?

8. For what reasons might a workcell have to share machines or operations with other workcells or operations?

9. Why must schedules that are generated by a traditional MRP system be modified for use by workcells?

10. How are production planning and control simplified by cellular manufacturing?

11. Discuss how cellular manufacturing impacts the role of workers. Why can't workers' traditional role of performing one function be maintained in workcell operations?

12. Why is performance of workers in workcells measured on a group basis?

13. How are time standards set for workcell planning?

14. Discuss the concept of a pilot cell, including what it is, what purposes it serves, and how to set one up.

15. A twelve-station assembly workcell is being formed for a new process. The work at each station requires several complex assembly and inspection subtasks. The difference between the longest and shortest workstation times is 15%. Analysis indicates that to satisfy the required CT, three workers must be assigned to the workcell. Discuss the pros and cons of subdividing the workcell into three subcells versus using rabbit chase.

Problems

1. A workcell is being planned to produce a part to meet a requirement of 420 units/day. What is the required CT of the workcell? Suppose for planning purposes the company uses 7 hours as its normal workday. Should the workcell be designed so that it has an actual CT longer or shorter than the required CT? Explain.

2. A process that produces part A operates for 480 minutes a day. The required daily output for part A is 320 units.
   a. What is the required CT for part A?
   b. If the same process must also produce 130 units per day of part B, what is the average required CT for both products? What is the minimal required daily production capacity of the process?

3. A workcell with two workers is divided into two subcells; one subcell has an actual CT of 323 seconds, the other has a CT of 392 seconds. The workcell must produce a part with a required CT of 410 seconds. What is the required production capacity of the workcell? Does the workcell have adequate capacity?

4. Referring to the cell in the previous question,
   a. If it produces at the required CT, what is the resulting amount of daily idle time of the two workers?
   b. If it produces at the current maximum possible rate, how much will its daily output differ from the required output?

5. Three workers cycle around a cell in rabbit-chase fashion. If they were each working alone, one worker could cycle around the cell (task time + walk time) in 13 minutes, another in 14 minutes, and the other in 15 minutes.
   a. What is the CT and capacity if workers cannot pass each other.
   b. What is the cell CT and daily cell capacity if faster workers can pass slower workers?
   c. In a rabbit-chase workcell, is it possible for faster workers to pass slower workers? Discuss.

6. This chapter distinguished between assembly cells and machining cells. What about cells with *both* assembly operations and automatic machines? Refer to the assembly cell in Figure 10.7:
   a. Suppose the operation at workstation 5 is performed by a single-cycle machine that takes 10 seconds to load and start, but then runs for 30 seconds and stops after completing the operation. What effect does that have on the actual cell CT? What is the new cell CT?
   b. Suppose all the operations are manual assembly with the exception of operations at workstations 7 and 8, which are each performed by single-cycle machines that takes 10 seconds to load and start, then runs for 70 seconds and stops when finished. What is the new cell CT?

c. What can you conclude about the actual CT of workcells where some operations are manual and some are automatic?

7. Use the eight-station assembly cell shown in Figure 10.7 to answer the next several questions. Also, assume the following:

- Task times are as shown in Figure 10.7.
- Holding areas are placed between any subgroups (for example, shown as a, b, c, and so on in Figure 10.9).
- Workers assigned to only one station have zero walk time but require 4 seconds to pick up and place items.
- The walk time between any holding area and the nearest work station is always 2 seconds.
- Station-to-station walk times are as shown in the table below.
- The walk time between any two holding areas is the median of the walk times of the four stations involved. For example, as shown in the boxed area in the table, if one holding area is between stations 2 and 3, and the other is between station 6 and 7, the walk time between them is 10.

From Station	To Station									
	In	1	2	3	4	5	6	7	8	Out
In	0	2	6	7	10	12	11	11	9	8
1	2	0	5	6	7	8	9	10	9	9
2	6	5	0	5	10	10	10	10	9	9
3	7	6	5	0	7	10	10	11	11	12
4	10	7	10	7	0	5	8	10	11	12
5	12	8	10	10	5	0	7	8	9	9
6	11	9	10	10	8	7	0	5	6	7
7	11	10	10	11	10	8	5	0	5	5
8	9	9	9	11	11	9	6	5	0	2
Out	8	9	9	12	12	9	7	5	2	0

a. Divide the cell among four workers so times for them are as close as possible. What are the resulting cell CT and daily capacity?
b. Repeat (a) for six workers. What are the cell CT and capacity?
c. What is the unit manufacturing cost for four workers? Assume machine operating cost is $80 and the labor rate is $20/hr. Given this result and results in the chapter for other numbers of workers, what number of workers gives the lowest unit manufacturing cost?

8. Use the eight-station machining cell shown in Figure 10.10 to answer the following questions. Assume all machines are single-cycle, automatic, and require a 10-second setup time.
a. Divide the cell among four workers so the times among them are as similar as possible. What are the resulting cell CT and daily capacity?

   b. Suggest a way to reduce cell CT to at least 40 sec/unit by subdividing the cell among five workers and adding machines. Indicate the number of workers and their machine assignments; also indicate the number of each kind of machine needed at each workstation. Add 2 seconds of walk time for every machine a worker walks past (i.e., bypasses without stopping).

9. Refer again to the assembly cell in Figure 10.7. Suppose the product of the cell is small and that instead of walking around the cell with just one unit of product, the worker carries a rack that holds six units of the product. As a result, the worker does tasks on six units at a time at each workstation. Assume the walk times are as shown in Figure 10.7. The operation times shown in Figure 10.7 are for assembling one unit. Assume handling of each unit at each workstation takes 3 seconds. What is the average CT per unit in seconds?

10. A four-workstation cell has single-cycle machines to perform all operations. The walk time around the cell is 60 seconds. The times (in seconds) for the machine operating cycles and setup (unload, changeover, load, and start machines) are listed below.

	Machine			
	A	B	C	D
Operating Cycle (sec)	152	173	175	190
Setup (sec)	23	31	52	28

   The cell produces different kinds of parts continuously, one unit at a time.
   a. What is the actual CT?
   b. Assume the cell CT must be reduced to 215 seconds. Discuss where in the cell you would have to make changes to achieve this CT. Discuss alternatives or possible actions for making the changes.

11. For the workcell in the previous problem, assume that parts are produced in 20-unit batches (i.e., 20 of one part are produced in the cell, the machines are changed over, then 20 of the next part are run, etc.). The operating times are the same as shown in the above table, except that setup times apply only when the machines are changed over between batches of parts. Between identical parts, the automatic load–unload time is 2 seconds. What is the actual CT of the workcell?

Endnotes

1. Instead of workcell the simpler term cell is often used. John Burbidge, a major proponent and writer on the topic, avoids using the word cell because, he says, telling shop-floor employees they will be working in cells (as in prison) is likely to be counterproductive! J. L. Burbidge, "Production Flow Analysis for Planning Group Technology," *Journal of Operations Management* 10, no. 1 (January 1991), pp. 5–27.

2. This number is based on numerous small-group research studies; *see* R. Napier and M. Gershenfeld, *Groups: Theory and Experience* (Boston: Houghton Mifflin Co., 1973).

3. The system of coordinated cells may itself be considered a focused factory for the production of a part or product family.

4. The term cycle time is also commonly used to refer to the total throughput time for a product, that is, the sum of the operation times required to make the product. The definition of cycle time chosen for use throughout this book is common in engineering and in the literature on pull production.

5. G. LaPerle, "Letter to the Editor," *Target,* July/August 1995, p. 51.

6. *Ibid.;* Y. Monden, *Toyota Production System* (2nd ed.) (Norcross, GA: Industrial Engineering and Management Press, 1993), pp. 303–4.

7. If there is only one worker, then there is no need for holding places between stations. The worker simply moves the items being worked on from station to station with him.

8. J. T. Black, *The Design of the Factory with a Future* (New York: McGraw-Hill, 1991), pp. 190–4.

9. The feasibility or practicality of adding machines depends on whether additional machines can be relocated from elsewhere in the plant, the impact of relocation on other products, or whether new machines must be purchased. While it is simple to determine where machines should be placed in a cell to reduce the CT, decisions to procure the machines require economic costs/benefit analysis.

10. R. Schonberger, *World Class Manufacturing: The Next Decade* (New York: Free Press, 1996), p. 168.

11. M. J. Maffei and J. Meredith, "Infrastructure and Flexible Manufacturing Technology: Theory Development," *Journal of Operations Management* 13, no. 4 (December 1995), pp. 273–98.

12. Portions of this section are derived from J. T. Black, *The Design of the Factory with a Future,* pp. 88–91; N. L. Hyer and U. Wemmerlov, "Group Technology and Productivity," *Harvard Business Review,* July/August 1984, pp. 140–9; R. Schonberger, *World Class Manufacturing,* pp. 112–14; H. J. Steudel and P. Desruelle, *Manufacturing in the Nineties* (New York: Van Nostrand Reinhold, 1992), pp. 133–7, 155–62; U. Wemmerlov, *Production Planning and Control Procedures for Cellular Manufacturing Systems* (Falls Church, VA: American Production and Inventory Control Society, 1988).

13. U. Wemmerlov, *Production Planning and Control Procedures . . . ,* discusses in detail planning and control issues and considerations in workcell manufacturing.

14. Other kinds of planning and control mechanisms, including reorder-points and bottleneck scheduling, were among the systems studied. *See* F. Olorunniwo, "Changes in Planning and Control Systems with Implementation of Cellular Manufacturing," *Production and Inventory Management* 37, no. 1 (1st Quarter 1996), pp. 65–70.

15. V. Huber and K. Brown, "Human Resource Issues in Cellular Manufacturing: A Socio-Technical Analysis," *Journal of Operations Management* 10, no. 1 (January 1991).

16. For an introduction to traditional, piece-rate incentive plans, *see* D. Miller and J. W. Schmidt, *Industrial Engineering and Operations Research* (New York: John Wiley, 1984).

17. A good discussion of issues and implementation guidelines for pay-for-skill plans is J. D. Orsburn, L. Moran, E. Musselwhite, and J. H. Zenger, *Self-Directed Work Teams* (Homewood, IL: Business One Irwin, 1990), pp. 182–94.

18. *Ibid.,* for discussion of gain-sharing plans.

19. For detailed coverage of time standards and work measurement, see "standard" texts on industrial engineering or motion and time study. *See,* e.g., E. J. Polk, *Methods Analysis and Work Measurement* (New York: McGraw-Hill, 1984).

20. J. Klein, "Why Supervisors Resist Employee Participation," *Harvard Business Review,* September/October 1984, pp. 87–95.

21. D. Dhavale, "A New Book from FAR," *Management Accounting* 77, no. 7 (January 1996), pp. 63–4.

22. I. Winfield and M. Kerrin, "Toyota Motor Manufacturing in Europe: Lessons for Management Development," *Journal of Management Development* 15, no. 4 (April 1996), pp. 49–57.

23. A good discussion of pilot cell implementation is in "Empowerment Pumps Duriron Up," *Tooling and Production,* October 1994, pp. 13–15.

Effective application of focused facilities, work-cells, and pull production is predicated on a large measure of work discipline on the shop floor, discipline established by considering the best way to do work, then monitoring to ensure the work is being done that way. Such is the purpose of **standard operations** and **work standards.**

Standard operations are also fundamental to the process of continuous improvement. What many organizations fail to realize is that without good standards it is difficult or impossible to achieve high production efficiency, to match production output with demand, to keep WIP inventories small, or to improve quality.

The principal focus of this chapter is on the elements of standard operations, including standard times, standard operations routine, and standard in-process inventory. The chapter addresses the issues of how standards are developed, why they are important, and who uses them. Necessary conditions for successful development and application of standard operations, and the place of standard operations in continuous improvement are also considered.

STANDARD OPERATIONS

Standard operations are a group of standards that completely defines all aspects of a task, operation, or process. They are also called **standard operating procedures,** though here the more-abbreviated term standard operations is used to imply the broadest-possible definition of work standards, which goes beyond standards of procedures.

SHOP-FLOOR RELEVANCY

Standard operations define best practice, although what constitutes best practice is a relative thing, depending on the situation. Since no one standard of work can fit all situations, no standard should be considered rigid and unchangeable. Standard operations must be adapted to reflect, for example, changes in product demand, current worker skill and proficiency levels, current equipment, as well as how work is actually performed. As things change on the shop floor, so should the standard operations.

Standard operations are not the same as standards for product requirements or process performance, which are typically developed by engineers and used in product design and quality assurance. Rather, they are the work procedures, sequence of tasks, and times *prescribed for the shop floor* to produce a unit of output.

In JIT plants, production flexibility is achieved through continuous, small adjustments to production capacity, schedules, and priorities based on decisions made on the shop floor. Ideally the facilities are arranged in focused factories and workcells where multiskilled operators each perform multiple functions. Given that, standard operations provide the supervisors and workers the information necessary to determine the appropriate work procedures, routing sequences, and number of workers to staff to meet given product demand and product-mix requirements.

SHOP-FLOOR INVOLVEMENT

Initially, the key people in the development of standard operations are industrial engineers, with a large measure of participation from shop-floor supervisors and workers. Eventually, the goal should be for supervisors and workers to perform the work measurement and standards development, and for engineers to provide only assistance. Supervisors usually have the most current information about the status of everything on the shop floor, and they are often the most knowledgeable about the best way to schedule and use facilities to achieve production goals. When supervisors help determine the standards, they have a better grasp of the standards and can explain them better to workers.

Putting responsibility for standards development and implementation at the shop level can result in standards that are more accurate, up-to-date, and more accepted by workers than those developed by staff personnel (who are sometimes viewed as outsiders). It can also result in process improvements that are overlooked by staff specialists. Maffei and Meredith describe one case, a flexible manufacturing cell, where operators suggested process changes to improve the consistent quality of production output.[1] The engineer in charge of process quality felt that the changes were unnecessary, but when the operators took the initiative and implemented the changes anyway, the scrap rate dropped from over 50% for hard-to-make products to a very small percentage.

Of course, so that supervisors and workers will be capable of developing good standards and applying them to planning, scheduling, and control, first they must be trained in the methods and procedures of operations analysis, time/motion study, and related tools.

BENEFITS

A benefit of putting standards development at the shop-floor level is that whenever changes in operations occur, the standards can be revised immediately. Otherwise, the revision must wait until a staff person gets around to it. Ability to revise standards quickly is especially important in plants where cell configurations and worker assignments are in constant flux. Further, creating up-to-date standards permits staff planners to prepare master schedules that are feasible and that reflect shop-floor status and current capabilities. Standard operations also make it is easier to identify safety hazards and procedures that lead to or permit defects and then to modify them.

In a flexible factory, workers are rotated among jobs and responsibilities, depending on product demand. Posted standard operations, located where workers can easily reference them, enable workers to quickly become familiar with the standards and procedures of their new work assignments. They also make it easy for workers and supervisors to periodically check actual work against the standards, which corrects backsliding and prevents workers from falling into bad habits.

We will consider four aspects of standard operations: cycle time, completion time per unit, standard operations routine, and standard WIP inventory.

CYCLE TIME

The starting point for setting standard operations is to determine the **required cycle time**.[2] That's because the quantity of something to be produced should be based upon a production output goal, and that goal is best stated in terms of the frequency that an item must be produced in the allotted time—the required cycle time (CT). Once the required CT is set, operations are planned so that the timing of production output is as close as possible to that time.

As an example, the last chapter discussed worker staffing levels in cellular manufacturing. Setting the staffing level begins with setting the required CT, and then adjusting the number of workers up or down to make the actual cell CT as close as possible to the required CT. The required CT is

$$CT = \frac{Daily\ Time\ Available}{Required\ Daily\ Quantity} = \frac{T}{Q}.$$

If, for example, 192 units a day must be produced and the available time is 480 minutes, then

$$Required\ CT = \frac{480\ min/day}{192\ units/day} = 2.5\ min/unit,\ or\ 150\ sec/unit.$$

Assuming the process runs continuously throughout the day, it must produce one unit every 150 seconds.

In determining the CT, no allowance should be made for waste in the process. The daily time available should *not* be reduced to allow for equipment breakdowns, idle time, or rework, and the required daily quantity should not be increased to allow for defective items. When the CT includes allowances for waste, as it often does, the sources of waste are never addressed or eliminated. When no allowance is made for sources of waste, attention is drawn to them and they are remedied.

COMPLETION TIME PER UNIT

Another aspect of standard operations is **completion time per unit,** or the average (actual) time required to process one unit. Completion time per unit is determined for every task and operation, even for non-value-added tasks like handling, picking and placing, inspecting, and so on.[3]

To avoid confusion, the terms **task** and **operation** are distinguished as follows: A **task** refers to an elemental unit of work—a simple step or motion; an **operation** refers to a *group of tasks,* such as those usually performed at a workstation. For example, suppose a worker performs six tasks. If the worker does the six tasks in sequence, without interruption or doing any other tasks, then those six tasks combined form an operation.

TIME TO COMPLETE A TASK OR AN OPERATION

To determine the completion time per unit, start by determining the standard **task time,** which is the expected time for an average worker to perform a task at a satisfactory level. The task time must include all manual and machine time involved in the task. Suppose a part is machined at a workstation using a single-cycle, automatic machine that runs for several seconds and then shuts off. As defined in the last chapter, the automatic run time is the **machine time.** Suppose the worker at the workstation also performs several tasks by hand such as unloading and loading the machine, setting the machine, turning it on, and so on. The sum of the times for these tasks is the **manual** or **handling time.**

Determination of the manual time is based upon well-established work measurement techniques.[4] Briefly, it involves measuring with a stopwatch the actual time required for a worker to perform a task. Each task must be measured many times to get an accurate average. In addition, the standard involves a judgment call about the worker's speed, which should include consideration of the skill level of the worker, the amount of effort she is expending, and particular conditions under which she is operating. Supervisors are often familiar with an individual worker's skills, motivation, and work habits, which is another reason for involving them in standards development.

Calculation of the standard time is based upon the actual, observed time for the task, the performance rating of the worker, and any allowance factor for unavoidable delays:

Standard Task Time

$$= (Actual\ Time) \times (Performance\ Rating) \times (Allowance\ Factor).$$

If a worker is thought to be of average skill, then her **performance rating** is 100%. If her skill is higher or lower, then the percent is raised or lowered accordingly. The **allowance factor** takes into account delays that are unavoidable but that are expected as a normal part of the operation and cannot be eliminated. It is important that the allowance factor *not* account for delays that can be eliminated (sources of waste) and *not* be used as a fudge factor to allow for *potential* (unexpected) delays. Ordinarily, the worker being measured for the standard should be selected for being average in terms of speed and performance, and only when such a worker is not available will it be necessary to adjust the time with a performance rating. The worker performance rating is assessed by the worker's supervisor prior to time study.

For a newly created task, there will be a **learning curve** effect, even for an average worker. Not until a worker gains proficiency in a task will she be able to perform at the normal level. For a newly designed task (one for which no worker has reached normal ability), the standard task time will have to be periodically remeasured to account for the worker's increasing proficiency.

Suppose a time study indicates that it takes a worker 23 seconds on average to perform a task. The supervisor, who feels that the worker in the time study is a little less proficient (less capable or less experienced) than other workers, sets the performance rating of the worker at 90%. The supervisor estimates that unavoidable interruptions from upstream stations will cause the station of the task being studied to be idle about 20% of the time. As a result, the standard time of the task is

Standard Task Time

$$= 23 \text{ sec} \times 0.90 \times 1.20 = 24.84, \text{ or } 25 \text{ seconds.}$$

Standard task times are used to determine production capacity and work schedules. Because not every worker will perform according to the standard, workers sometimes end up producing too much or too little in the scheduled time. A Kanban system will prevent overproduction, even if workers perform better than the standard, but shortages can occur if workers consistently produce below the standard. If the latter happens, the standard time should be revised upward so that production schedules will be realistic, and a short-term improvement plan should be implemented to improve workers' performance. An alternative is to retain the existing standard and bring in workers who are able to meet it. So, as much as possible, the standard times must accurately account for the realities of the shop floor, including workers' abilities. When several workers are rotated to do one task, then the task time must be adjusted to represent the weighted average time of all the workers.

COMPLETION TIME PER UNIT

The **completion time per unit** is the time to process one unit. It might be, though not necessarily, the same as the standard task time. For example, referring to Figure 11.1, suppose that for the third task the inspect portion of the task is done only on every other part. If a part is inspected, the task time is 7 seconds; if a part is not inspected, the time is 3 seconds. Thus, the completion time per unit is the average time for two units:

$$\frac{3 \text{ sec} + 7 \text{ sec}}{2} = 5 \text{ sec/unit.}$$

The six tasks in Figure 11.1 make up a simple operation on the machined part shown. In the figure, standard task times are listed in the Act column, and completion times per unit are listed in the CTU column. Assuming the full operation comprises only the six tasks, and those tasks are performed in the sequence listed, then the completion time per unit for the operation is the sum of the completion time per unit for all the tasks, 40 seconds.

Tasks and completion times per unit for a machined-part operation.

Part R2D2-block	Part (description or drawing)			
Station 4, BZ				
Operation 1 A: 225/insp				

Task	Description	Procedure	Act	CTU	Notes
1	Press eject	Check mill 225 autoselect switch: rotation stopped; machine is off.	1	1	
2	Turn autoselect to 0	Check part has ejected.	1	1	
3	Pick up part or Pick up part, Inspect part	Pick up part from rack. Drop part into right chute or slip part through sleeve (every second part only), then drop part into right chute.	3 7	5	
4	Insert part	Pick up part from left chute. Place part into mill slot. Ensure part is notch-side down. Ensure part rests snugly in slot.	2	2	
5	Press start button	Check that autoselect switch is rotating.	1	1	
6	Autocycle	Mill 225 autorun for one cycle, then stop.	30	30	
			CTU Total	40	

PRODUCTION CAPACITY

Accurate completion time per unit is important because it is the basis for estimating **production capacity,** the number of units that can be produced in the available production time. Production capacity can be computed for every level of work—an individual task, an operation or workstation, a production process, or even an entire plant. In the case of batch production, accurate information about the process **lot size** and the process **setup time** is also necessary.

One way to compute production capacity, N, for an operation is

$$N = \frac{T}{C + m},$$

where

C = completion time per unit,
m = setup time per unit,
T = total operation time.

Using the operation in Figure 11.1 as an example, if parts at this operation are produced in batches of 300, if each batch requires a setup time of 3 minutes, and if the total operating time per day is 480 minutes, then

$$m = \frac{180 \text{ sec}}{300 \text{ units}} = 0.6 \text{ seconds/unit,}$$

$$N = \frac{480 \text{ min/day}}{[(40 + 0.6)/60] \text{ min}} = 709.4 \text{ units/day.}$$

STANDARD OPERATIONS ROUTINE

Once the completion time per unit has been determined for every task (or operation, depending on the level of analysis), the next step is to determine the sequence in which the tasks will be performed. This sequence is called the **standard operations routine,** or **SOR.** At the task level, the SOR gives the required sequence in which a worker must perform the tasks in a given operation. At the operation level, the SOR is the sequence in which a worker performs a series of operations.

KINDS OF SORS

There are three kinds of SORs, one for each generic kind of work routine.[5]

SOR for a Single Repeated Operation

This SOR gives the prescribed sequence in which a group of tasks is to be performed again and again. If, for instance, the worker in the above example had to perform the operations in Figure 11.1 in the sequence as listed, then that sequence would be the SOR for that operation. If the tasks listed in Figure 11.1 could be performed in some other sequence and still give the same results, then these other sequences would also be considered before a final, prescribed SOR sequence is selected.

SOR for Multiple, Repeated Operations

This SOR gives the prescribed sequence in which *several* operations are to be performed on a repeating basis. If a worker runs several machines or performs several operations at multiple workstations, as in a workcell, then the SOR will show the sequence in which the worker is to visit the workstations. An example is shown later.

SOR for Multiple, Nonrepeated Operations

This SOR gives a sequence of operations or tasks that vary throughout the day, but that, combined, are the same every day. For example, suppose a worker operates a

Figure 11.2

SOR sheet for a single, repeated operation. Total CT = 40 sec.

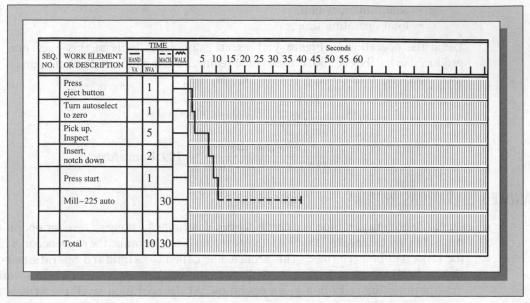

machine and is responsible for setting up and starting the machine, periodically loading batches of parts into it, periodically sampling and inspecting the parts, periodically recalibrating the machine, and then stopping the machine, cleaning it, and doing simple PM. The SOR would give the sequence and approximate times throughout the day when each of these tasks and operations is to be performed.

SOR SHEET

One way to determine the SOR is with the **SOR sheet.** Figure 11.2 shows the general appearance of an SOR sheet for a *single,* repeated operation based on the information from Figure 11.1. The times in Figure 11.2 correspond to the completion times in Figure 11.1. In general, a solid line moving downward through the time grid on an SOR sheet represents the time a worker spends doing the manual tasks; a dashed line represents the run time of the machine after the worker turns it on.

Example 1 illustrates how an SOR sheet is created for *multiple,* repeated operations.

Example   1:   SOR for Multiple, Repeated Operations

Eight operations are performed in a workcell that uses single-cycle, automatic machines. Each machine automatically stops when processing for a part has been completed. Assume the eight operations are arranged in the workcell

Figure 11.3

Location of operations: one per workstation.

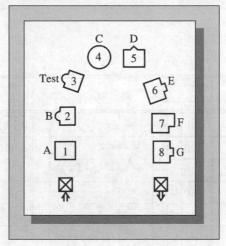

Table 11-1

Order of Operation	Descrpn of Operation	Handling Time (sec)	Machine Time (sec)	Completion Time/Unit (sec)
1	A: 225/insp	10	30	40
2	B : 26/909	10	40	50
3	Test 1 : A/B	10	10	20
4	C: R9/223/ ZZ6/422	10	40	50
5	D: L28/899	10	30	40
6	E: 225/R76	10	30	40
7	F: R9/890/44 67/LPT Test 2: F	10	70	80
8	G: HU356/3 46P/567 Test 3 : G	10	70	80

shown in Figure 11.3. All of the manual (hand) times, machine times, and completion times per unit for the operations are shown in Table 11.1. For each operation the times are standard times as developed from a time study of tasks for the operation. As a case in point, the times for operation 1 in Table 11.1 are based on the times shown in Figure 11.2.

The procedure for creating the SOR now follows.

a. The SOR for any group of operations must be designed such that each work cycle will be completed within the required CT. First, then, determine the required CT and draw it on the SOR sheet. Assume the required CT here is 150 seconds. This is shown at the vertical line marked (1) on the SOR sheet in Figure 11.4.

FIGURE 11.4

SOR sheet for multiple, repeated operations. Total CT = 131 seconds.

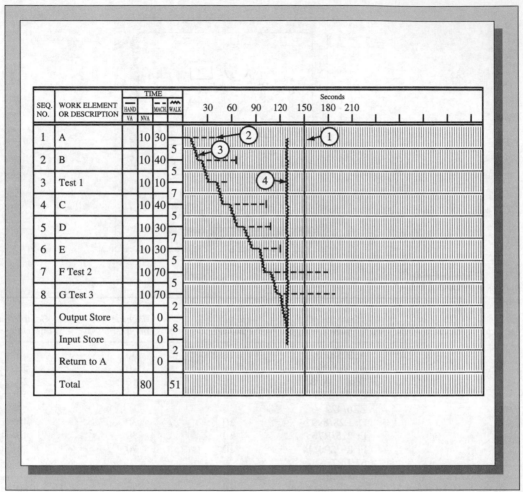

b. Determine the approximate number of workers and the range of operations that each worker will be able to perform within the required CT. The range (the number and kinds of operations that a worker is assigned) is determined by the worker CT, which is the time required for the worker to walk among the operations and perform the manual tasks. The worker CT cannot exceed the required CT. If the worker CT exceeds the required CT, then the worker has too many operations to perform in the available time, and some of them must be reassigned to other workers.

Likewise, the completion time per unit at each of the operations cannot exceed the required CT. If it does, some way must be found to reduce it. Perhaps the manual time can be shortened, some of the manual tasks can be automated or eliminated, or the entire operation can be replicated (thereby effectively cutting the completion time per unit in half). Simply speeding up a machine is usually not an option because machines operate at prescribed speeds with limits, and increasing the speed accelerates machine deterioration and contributes to defects.

As Table 11.1 shows, the completion time for any one of the eight operations is well below the required CT of 150 seconds. As the table also suggests, the sum of the manual times for the eight operations is 80 seconds, which indicates that as long as the total walk time between the eight operations in succession is less than $150 - 80 = 70$ seconds, the worker will be able to perform all eight operations. The theoretical way of verifying this is to divide the sum of the manual times for the operations by the required CT. In this case the resulting ratio is $80/150 = 0.533$. The ratio, being less than 1, suggests that one worker is needed.

c. Draw on the SOR sheet the completion time per unit for the first operation that the worker performs. On Figure 11.4, this is shown as the dashed line marked (2) on the grid part of the sheet. The solid portion of the line represents the manual time of the first operation, while the dashed portion represents the machine time. The combined length of the solid and dashed portions represents the completion time per unit at that operation.

d. Whenever a worker must walk between operations, the walk times are also represented on the SOR sheet. To show the walk time, draw a wavy line from the ending of the manual portion of the first operation to the time when the next operation is to begin. Suppose in the example the walk time is 5 seconds. The wavy line marked (3) on the SOR sheet, going from the end of the first operation to the beginning of the second operation, represents 5 seconds walk time. (Note in contrast that the SOR sheet in Figure 11.2 has no wavy lines. That is because the operation involves tasks the worker can perform while standing or sitting at one workstation.)

e. The previous steps, (c) and (d), are repeated for all operations. The result is shown in Figure 11.4 as the combined manual task and walk times, represented by the line running diagonally down the page, and the machine processing times, represented by dashed lines. In the actual workcell, the procedure would be as follows: the worker would walk around the cell, stopping at every machine; at each machine he would unload one part, load another part, then set the machine and turn it on; he would then walk to the next machine, carrying the part from the last machine with him, and repeat the procedure.

f. If the worker must walk from the last operation in the routing sequence back to the initial operation to resume the routine (that is, walk around the cell again), then this is also shown as a wavy line. In Figure 11.4 this is shown as the wavy line marked (4).

g. If the worker arrives back at the initial operation at or before the required CT (line (1)), then the operations routine sequence is verified as feasible. In the example, the worker arrives at the initial operation at 131 seconds. Thus, the actual CT is 131 seconds.

h. After the SOR has been developed, the supervisor performs the SOR sequence to ensure that the in-practice CT conforms with the actual (theoretical) CT on the SOR sheet. If it does, and if the supervisor feels comfortable with the operations sequence and procedure, then the SOR is retained and taught to workers.

OPERATIONS ROUTINE AND PROCESS ROUTING SEQUENCE

Part of establishing the SOR is establishing the sequence in which workers will perform tasks and operations. In the above example, the SOR followed the same sequence as the process routing sequence; in general, however, the two do not have to be the same. To avoid confusion, we distinguish the **SOR** as the order in which the worker performs a sequence of operations and the **process routing sequence** as the order in which operations must be performed to make a part or product, that is, the route a product must follow from workstation to workstation.

A worker in a cell might walk from station to station in a route that is *opposite* the route followed by the product. This is shown in Figure 11.5. Alternatively, the cell

FIGURE 11.5

Operations routing sequence counter to process routing sequence.

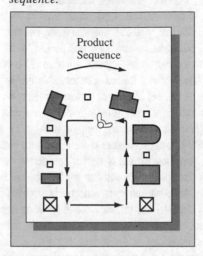

might be divided among several workers, each performing a subset of cell operations, and in that case the SOR for each worker would be different from (and only a portion of) the routing sequence of the product. For example, the cell shown in Figure 11.3 might be split between two workers, one at workstations 1, 2, 7, 8, the other at 3, 4, 5, 6. In neither case would the worker SOR be identical to the processing sequence of 1, 2, 3, . . . , 8. While routing workers through operations in a sequence other than the processing sequence might be necessary, it is more difficult to determine whether the resulting worker CT conforms to the required CT.

IDLE TIME

In Example 1, Figure 11.4, the worker has $150 - 131 = 19$ seconds of time remaining at the end of each cycle. The question arises as to what should be done with this time. In general, considerable difference between actual CT and required CT means one thing: opportunity or mandate for improvement. If the actual CT is *less than* the required CT, that suggests a *potential* for reducing the number of workers (assuming more than one worker is assigned to the process) or for giving existing workers additional tasks (possibly for another product and even in another cell, as discussed in the previous chapter). Any operations can be added to the SOR sequence as long as the resulting additional handling and walk times do not exceed the remaining time, in the example, 19 seconds.

Now, if the actual CT *exceeds* the required CT, that means improvement is *mandatory* if the output is to meet demand. The initial improvement might be to simply increase the number of workers to sufficiently reduce the actual CT.

STANDARD QUANTITY OF WIP

The standard quantity of work in process (WIP) is the minimum in-process inventory necessary for the process to function. It consists solely of the items being processed at each operation and any items held between operations. Ordinarily it is the minimum quantity of material necessary to achieve smooth flow of work, although that quantity will vary depending on the type of machine or workstation layout and the SOR. For example, if the SOR sequence is the same as the process routing sequence, then it might not be necessary to hold any items between operations. In that case, the standard WIP quantity will be the same as the number of operations. In the machining cell example in Figure 11.3, one part will be held at each machine; since the SOR sequence is the same as the processing sequence, the worker can transfer a part from one operation to the next as he walks between machines. No additional parts are necessary, so the standard WIP would be eight parts.

If, however, the SOR sequence is the *opposite* of the process routing sequence, then to avoid backtracking at each machine at least one piece must be held between every pair of machines. (That way, each time the worker unloads a part from a machine, he can put it into the holding area on the *right* of the machine, then take a part from the holding area on the *left* and load it into the machine.) In the machining cell in Figure 11.3, this would increase the standard WIP to 15 units, not counting stock at the input and output storage areas.

Usually there are additional considerations that factor into the size of the standard WIP. When multiple workers cycle through different parts of a process, even when they follow the same general direction as the process routing sequence, some units must be held at the places in the process where workers hand off items to each other (an example is given later). It might also be necessary to accumulate some quantity of items to, say, perform quality checking, allow time for machine temperature to cool down or heat up, or perform an operation in which batching of items is necessary.

The reason for specifying the standard WIP quantity is to keep WIP to the minimum required for effective operation. Any observer can easily refer to the standard WIP quantity as posted, look at the quantity actually on hand, and determine if there is a big discrepancy. If there is a discrepancy, then questions arise as to what is wrong and what needs to be done to correct it. This is another example of visual management.

STANDARD OPERATIONS SHEET

Information about the completion time per unit, the SOR, and standard WIP are combined and displayed in one place—on the **standard operations sheet (SOS),** or standard worksheet. The SOS as originated at Toyota contains the required CT, the SOR, standard quantity WIP, the actual CT, as well as diagrams indicating at which locations in the process to check for quality and pay attention to safety.[6] Figure 11.6 shows the SOS sheet for the one-worker operation in Figures 11.1 and 11.2. Another example of an SOS, representing a two-worker operation, is shown in Figure 11.10. Details about this figure are explained later.

SOS sheets should be displayed at each operation and at each sequence of operations (such as a workcell) so workers can readily refer to them. The SOS sheet is an

FIGURE 11.6

SOS sheet for one operation.

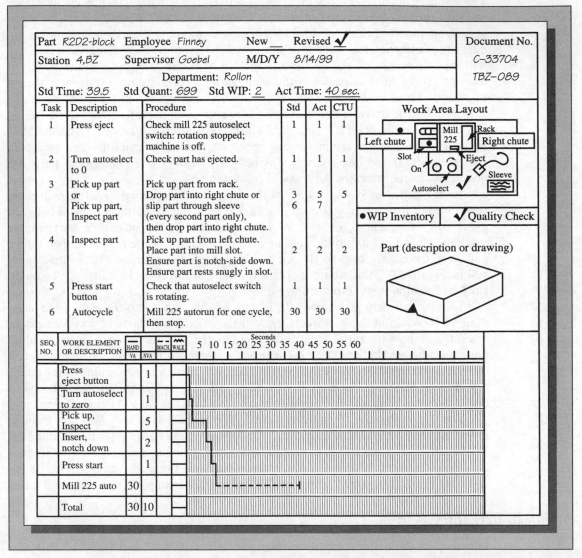

important tool for three areas of visual management:

1. It serves as a guide to inform each worker about the SOR, completion times, and other important aspects of the operation.
2. It helps the supervisor assess whether the operations are being done according to standards.
3. It serves as a tool to evaluate performance and improvement.

The SOS sheet is always dated to indicate when the last revision occurred.

IMPROVEMENT TOOL

The SOS should be revised regularly, since, says Monden, standard operations "are always imperfect and operations improvements are always required in a process."[7] Standard operations should never be considered fixed. They must be adapted to reflect changing demand, worker skills, etc., and ongoing improvements in the process. Even after they have been adapted to the situation, they should be continually scrutinized for places where the process can be tightened up to improve efficiency, reduce cost, and improve quality.

Example 2 is an illustration of how the SOR is adjusted to fit a new situation.

Example   2:   Adjusting SOR to Meet Increased Demand

Suppose increased demand for the item produced in our eight-operation machining cell mandates that the 150-second required CT be reduced to 95 seconds. Clearly, the standard operations must be changed. Assuming that the completion times per unit cannot be reduced, then it will be necessary to add more workers. Suppose we add one more worker. Either we can cycle both workers through all the operations in a rabbit-chase fashion, or we can split responsibility for the operations between the two workers. Suppose because of the required skills, it is more practical to split the cells between the workers. Figure 11.7 shows the range of operations for each worker and the sequence the workers will follow. It also shows the locations of two in-process holding areas, **a** and **b**, places where the workers hand off parts to each other. As mentioned, such holding areas are necessary whenever there is more than one worker and when their CTs differ.

Figure 11.8 shows the SOR sheet for worker 1. The worker CT is 88 seconds, which falls within the required CT of 95 seconds.

Figure 11.9 shows the SOR sheet for worker 2. Two cycles of work are shown to illustrate the point that, although the worker might be capable of completing a work cycle in only 61 seconds (shown for cycle 1), because

FIGURE 11.7

Range of operations assignments for two workers.

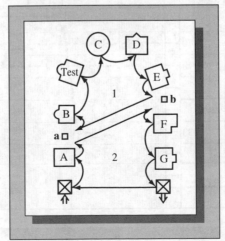

FIGURE 11.8

SOR sheet for worker 1. Total CT = 88 seconds.

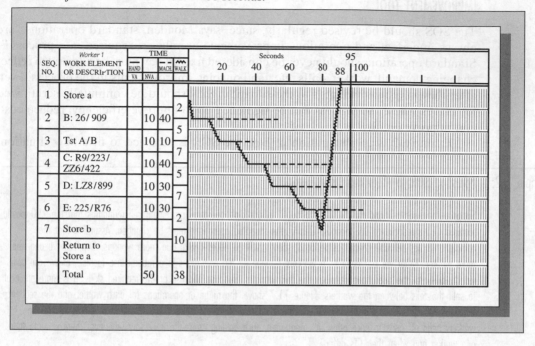

FIGURE 11.9

SOR sheet for worker 2. Total worker CT = 61 seconds, which is less than the 80-second CTs at operations 2 and 3; therefore, CT = 80 seconds.

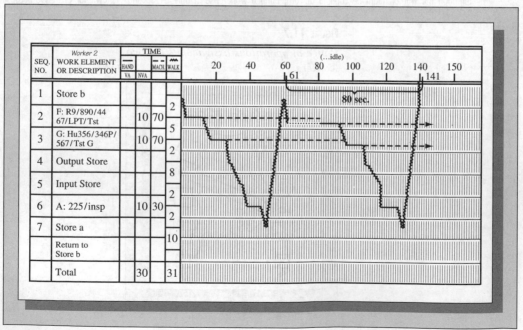

some operations take as long as 80 seconds, the worker is forced to accept a CT of 80 seconds (shown for cycle 2). Since the completion times per unit at operations 2 and 3 are each 80 seconds, the worker has to wait at operation 2 for 19 seconds until the machine has finished.

Finally, the SOS sheet for the eight-operation, two-worker cell is shown in Figure 11.10. To create this sheet the SOR sheets for the two workers must be made compatible. The CT for worker 1 is 88 seconds, so the CT for worker 2 must also be 88 seconds. Because of the discrepancy in the CTs for the two workers, worker 2 will have to wait about 8 seconds each cycle at store area **b** to receive a part from worker 1.

FIGURE 11.10

SOS sheet for two-worker cell.

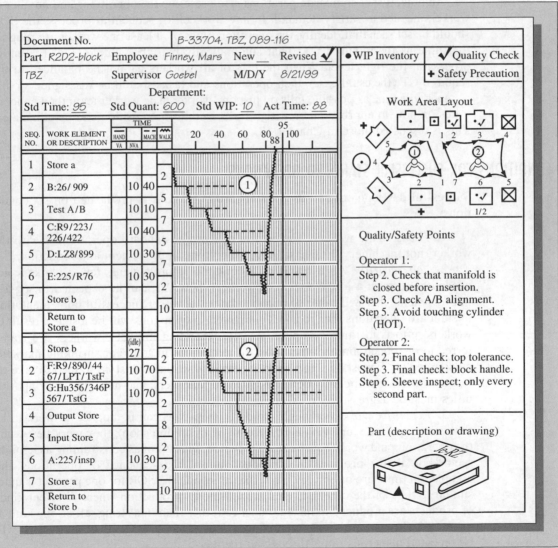

The SOS sheet in Figure 11.10 prescribes procedures that result in an 88-second worker CT. Since the required CT is 95 seconds, each worker will be idle for 7 seconds every cycle. (For worker 2, the 7 seconds is in addition to the 8 seconds she is already idle from waiting on worker 1.) Although it is unlikely that this is enough time to introduce other operations into the cell, the idle time might be used to make improvements of other forms, such as inserting tasks that would reduce defects, increase safety, or increase the reliability of the machines. Additionally, if the cell is not linked into a pull system, the two workers could run the cell at the 88-second CT, in which case they would fill the daily requirement before the day ends. They could then use the remainder of the day for problem solving, equipment PM, and so on.

An objective of standard operations is to prescribe the operations and number of workers needed to satisfy demand. In any workcell or sequential process, the SOR should be set such that, ideally, the operation times of at least one worker are roughly the same as the required CT. That automatically puts the actual CT of the entire process at the right level. When the CTs of all workers cannot be balanced to the required CT (the usual case), then operations and tasks should be reassigned so that as much idle time as possible falls on just one worker. The worker team then concentrates on how to improve and reassign tasks so that that position can be eliminated. This is discussed more in Chapter 17.

CONDITIONS FOR SUCCESSFUL STANDARD OPERATIONS[8]

Successful development and use of standard operations is predicated on six conditions:

1. *Focus on the worker.* The central concern in standard operations is with the worker, not machinery. Emphasis is on labor-time improvement and reduction.

2. *Job security.* As a result of labor-time improvement, fewer workers are needed to perform a job. No team of workers, however, can be expected to suggest improvements that will cause someone to be out of work. Successful implementation of standard operations thus requires guarantees that no jobs will be lost as a result of workers' efforts to improve operations. In expanding markets, workers are transferred to or rotated among other jobs. To retain jobs in stable or shrinking markets, outsourced work must be returned to the factory, workers must be trained to take on responsibilities traditionally done by staff and managers, and new business opportunities must be aggressively pursued.

3. *Repetitive work.* Although standard operations can be applied to work tasks that are unique for every job (as in the case of a pure job shop), they work best when the operations and work sequences are repeated. This is not as constraining as it might seem. For all the products in a product family, the sequence of operations and completion times are often very much the same, and the SOR for one product is quite similar to that for the others. Even in mixed-model production where different kinds of products are produced in mixed sequence rather than in a string, all of one kind at once, and where several SORs are followed depending on the product, every SOR will be repeated numerous times throughout the day.

4. *Level production*. Revising the number of operators, sequences of work, and groupings of operations every day is not practical, so the production schedule must be held level for some period of time.

5. *Multiskilled operators*. Workers must be able to operate different machines within a workcell and, ideally, in other workcells and areas of the plant so they can be rotated weekly or daily, as needed to meet demand requirements for all products.

6. *Team effort*. Standard operations are established by a team consisting of a supervisor, workers, or operators. The team is trained to do analysis for standard operations. Collectively, team members agree on the task sequences, number of workers, and worker assignments. Shops where jobs are rigidly classified and based on seniority will not be able to implement standard operations. Where union contracts are involved, the contracts must be renegotiated. Most unions, however, are now aware of the importance of standard operations (as well as the importance of expanded work roles in pull production and cellular manufacturing) and are willing to work through the implementation issues with management.

Summary

Standard operations are the work procedures, sequence of tasks, and times prescribed for production of a unit of output. They are developed in large measure by suitably trained shop-floor supervisors and workers, with assistance from planners and engineers. Putting responsibility for standards development at the shop-floor level results in standards that are more accurate, current, and accepted by workers.

The main elements of standard operations are the standard completion time per unit, standard operations routine, and standard WIP. The completion time per unit is the average time required to complete a task or an operation (group of tasks). A group of operations combined in a particular, prescribed sequence is the standard operations routine (SOR). The standard WIP is the minimum in-process inventory necessary for a process to function effectively. All information about completion times per unit, the operations routine, and standard WIP is summarized on a standard operations sheet (SOS). The SOS is prominently displayed so workers at each operation and workcell can readily refer to it.

Standard operations serve vital functions in competitive manufacturing. They are essential for communicating and training standard times and procedures, and they provide planners and schedulers with accurate, up-to-date information about cycle times and operations capacity. With standard operations, production plans and master schedules are more realistic and likely to meet production goals. For the most part, however, standard operations are a shop-floor tool. Workers and supervisors use them for their own capacity planning, work scheduling, production control, and work method improvement. They provide an important contribution in efforts to put planning and control responsibility back on the shop floor. Along with setup-time reduction and equipment PM, standard operations are a prerequisite for pull production, cellular manufacturing, and, more generally, for agile, lost-cost, high-quality manufacturing.

Questions

1. Define standard operations. What are the four key components or aspects of standard operations? Explain each.

2. Why should supervisors be involved in developing standard operations? What are the reasons for putting development of standard operations at the shop-floor level?

3. Discuss the use of standard operations for each of the following: planning, control, worker training, improvement.

4. Explain the difference between **standard task time per unit** and **completion time per unit**.

5. How is workcell production capacity as described in the last chapter consistent with production capacity as defined in this chapter?

6. What does the **standard operations routine** (SOR) show?

7. Why are standard operations never considered permanent?

8. Discuss the contents of the **standard operations sheet** (SOS).

9. Discuss how SOR could be used for setup analysis and reduction.

Problems

1. A time study indicates that a worker takes 430 seconds to perform an operation. The worker is known to be quite skilled, and the supervisor estimates before the timing that her performance will be about 10% better than average. During a normal 7-hour workday, anticipated delays from various sources are estimated to be about 20 minutes of downtime on the operation.
   a. What is the standard task time for the operation? What is the average completion time per unit?
   b. If this operation is performed once every third item, and the standard task time for each of the other two items is 380 seconds, what is the average completion time per unit?

2. Operations are performed on eight machines as follows:
   1. Face: lathe #609
   2. Drill-Tap: machine #501
   3. Drill: machine #101
   4. Tap: machine #301
   5. Drill: machine #102
   6. Tap: machine #302
   7. Drill: machine #103
   8. Tap: machine #303

   The times for the operations are shown on the SOR sheet in Figure 11.11
   a. Reproduce a copy of Figure 11.11. On the copy draw in all of the times as illustrated in Figure 11.4; determine the actual cycle time.
   b. The lathe #609 is a large, but somewhat movable machine. The drill-tap machine #501 is very large, and cannot be moved. All of the other drill machines and tap machines are somewhat small and mobile. Sketch the layout of the machines in a workcell such that one worker could easily move between them in the 2−5 seconds

FIGURE 11.11

SOR sheet for problem 2.

SEQ. NO.	WORK ELEMENT OR DESCRIPTION	HAND VA	NVA	MACH.	WALK	TIME SCALE
1	Face		17	50		
					3	
2	Drill & Tap	29				
					3	
3	Drill 1/4" NPT		12	13		
					2	
4	Tap 1/4" NPT		12	13		
					2	
5	Drill 2 Holes 3/4" NPT		10	23		
					2	
6	Tap 2 Holes "		10	23		
					2	
7	Drill 2 Holes 3/4" NPT		13	23		
					2	
8	Tap 2 "		13	23		
					5	

(TIME SCALE: 10 30 50 70 90 110 130 150 170)

allotted. Show the worker's path and the locations of stock areas for incoming and outgoing material.

3. Refer to Table 11.1. Assume machines at all eight operations have been replaced with machines that have completion times per unit of 45 seconds (including 10 seconds for setup and handling). Assume also that demand for the product has increased such that the resulting required cycle time is reduced from 95 seconds to only 49 seconds. The machine at operation B is more than twice the size of the other machines, which are somewhat small, mobile, and can be located about 2 seconds apart (walk time). Determine the number of workers required, and discuss the necessary changes to the SOS sheet in Figure 11.10. Make your own assumptions about walk times.

Endnotes

1. M.J. Maffei and J. Meredith, "Infrastructure and Flexible Manufacturing Technology: Theory Development," *Journal of Operations Management* 13, no. 4 (December 1995), pp. 273–98.

2. In some texts, especially those written in Japan, the term tackt time is used instead of required CT.

3. See, for example, E. Polk, *Methods Analysis and Work Measurement* (New York: McGraw-Hill, 1984).

4. Work measurement techniques are described in, for example, R.M. Barnes, *Motion and Time Study* (7th ed.) (New York: John Wiley, 1980); B.W. Niebel, *Motion and Time Study* (6th ed.) (Homewood, IL: Richard D. Irwin, 1988); and E. Polk, *Methods Analysis and Work Measurement*.

5. These three types are used by Canon Corporation and are described in Japan Management Association, *Canon Production System* (Cambridge, MA: Productivity Press, 1987), pp. 153–60. Other variations are possible, depending on the nature of the work.

6. For other examples, *see* Y. Monden, *Toyota Production System* (2nd ed.) (Norcross, VA: Industrial Engineering and Management Press, 1993), p. 157; and K. Suzaki, *The New Manufacturing Challenge* (New York, The Free Press, 1987), p. 139.

7. Y. Monden, *Toyota Production System*, p. 158.

8. See D. Edwards, R. Edgell, and C. Richa, "Standard Operations—the Key to Continuous Improvement in a Just-in-Time Manufacturing System," *Production and Inventory Management,* 3rd Quarter 1993, pp. 7–13.

QUALITY PRODUCTS, QUALITY PROCESSES

Think for a moment about the methods covered in the preceding chapters—improving setups and equipment, reducing inventories and linking operations using pull production, organizing facilities into focused factories and workcells, and standardizing operations. These methods increase competitiveness by enabling a company to be more flexible and produce things in less time and with less waste.

Customers always consider the cost, availability, and delivery of a product, but, of course, they also look at quality. If they are confident that the quality of something is good, often they are willing to pay a little more or wait a little longer for it. The Japanese demonstrated to the world that quality itself can be a fierce competitive weapon, and also that such quality must originate at the source, which begins by getting the product requirements and design right, and then maintaining those requirements throughout the manufacturing process. This is the concept of quality at the source, and the meaning of quality built into the product.

Quality products begin with product specifications based upon what customers say they want and need. Capturing the essence of what customers really want—the voice of the customer—and translating it into a design faithful to those wants is the first step in producing a

quality product. But the design must account for many things besides what the customer wants; it must consider the realities of the manufacturing process; the skills, equipment, technology, and resource capabilities of the manufacturer; the availability of purchased materials and parts; and the development and manufacturing costs of the product. All of this is the realm of **quality of design.** To develop a high-quality, low-cost product, and do it in less time than the competition requires early, simultaneous attention to a plethora of issues affecting people in engineering, marketing, sales, finance, manufacturing, customer service, and purchasing, as well as suppliers and the customers themselves. Early and continued involvement of all these parties is necessary for designing a product that meets both the requirements of the customer and the capabilities of the producer.

Besides quality of design, there must be **quality of conformance:** the product *as produced* must meet the design requirements. The foundation of quality of conformance is **statistical quality control.** The two major categories of methods in statistical quality control are **acceptance sampling (AS)** and **statistical process (SPC) control.** For many decades AS was the traditional approach to quality control. However, when Japanese producers adopted the concept of statistical quality control, they chose SPC and rejected AS. Everyone learned SPC, and workers on the shop floor used it as a tool to prevent problems and continuously reduce process variation. Today, modern TQM organizations everywhere use SPC in that same way. Nonetheless, there are a few places where SPC cannot be used or where organizations are just beginning to implement statistical methods. In these cases, AS methods are still useful, at least in the short run.

By their very nature, statistical methods rely on samples, and with samples comes the risk of missing something or making incorrect judgments. Sole reliance on statistical methods can only improve a process just so much; to get a process down to zero defects requires going to the sources of defects and eliminating them. This is the concept of **pokayoke,** which is the Japanese term for mistake proofing or foolproofing.

Quality of design, acceptance sampling, statistical process control, and pokayoke are the subjects of the chapters in Part III:

QUALITY OF DESIGN

> Here and elsewhere we shall not obtain the best insight into things until we actually see them grow from the beginning.
> *Aristotle*

> I find it as impossible to know the parts without knowing the whole, as to know the whole without knowing the parts.
> *Blaise Pascal*

> He has exceeded my expectations and done even better.
> *Yogi Berra*

A quality product cannot be manufactured unless there is first a quality design.[1] To paraphrase John Rydz:

> No single discipline—not automation, robotics, not even advanced technology—will play as large a role in determining the success or failure of manufacturing in the future as product design. The customer's perception of the product, the cost to manufacture the product, the selling price to the customer, the cost to service the product, the profit to the company, the materials used in the product, the manufacturing process ultimately used to make the product, and the shop-floor experiences of workers all have their roots in how well the engineer designed the product for manufacture.[2]

This chapter deals with the philosophy and methodology for **quality of design.** Quality of design is the concept of, to use Taguchi's phrase, designing quality *into* a product. US manufacturers have always been known for their engineering competency and innovative ideas, though the same cannot be said about their attentiveness to customer requirements or ability to translate designs into products of the highest quality.[3] For US companies, improving quality of design is not so much a matter of changing technology as it is of changing the design *process*. They must figure out how to structure the design process so as to account for all the knowledge and information necessary to make good product-design decisions and incorporate that into the design of the final product. In large part, the answer is to use a cross-functional team during the design process and to provide the team with tools that guarantee effective intercommunication and problem solving. The focus of this chapter is on cross-functional design approaches, and on three important tools for design quality: quality function deployment, design for manufacture and assembly, and robust design.

CONCURRENT ENGINEERING

THE DESIGN PROCESS

The relationship between product design and product manufacturing is undergoing dramatic changes. Traditionally, the two functional areas of design and manufacturing had relatively little interaction, and their relationship was serial: Engineers in the product design group would design the product, then "throw the design over the wall" to the manufacturing group, which then had to figure out how to make the product. The

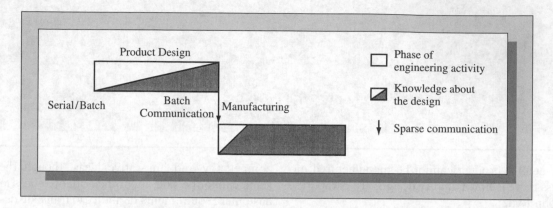

manufacturing group was pretty much out of the design loop and had to wait until the design group had fully or substantially completed its work before seeing what the new product looked like.

As shown in Figure 12.1, the process is analogous to batch production wherein no material is passed to the next stage until the entire batch is completed at the previous stage. Accumulating knowledge relevant to the product is assumed to be the sole function of the design group. Major decisions about product configuration, materials, and the buildup of parts and components are made solely by design engineers. Manufacturing simply inherits the design, and when it does, it must virtually start from scratch to determine how to make the product. Historically, the design group is segregated from the manufacturing group, not just by walls and physical distance (the two functions might reside in different buildings, states, or countries), but by different and divergent attitudes and perspectives. Manufacturing does not participate in the design either because it is not invited to participate or because it is too busy dealing with daily problems in the plant. Paradoxically, the less the manufacturing group contributes to product design decisions, the more design-related product problems it will later face in the factory, which further prevents it from contributing to future product designs.

People in all functional areas have a stake in product design. Says Dan Whitney, the designer asks "What good is it if the design doesn't work?" the salesperson asks "What good is it if it doesn't sell?" the finance person asks "What good is it if it isn't profitable?" and the manufacturing person asks "What good is it if we can't make it."[5] The term **concurrent engineering** (also called simultaneous engineering and integrated engineering) refers to the integrated, combined effort of product designers and producers to ensure that all these questions get asked, then get answered to the mutual satisfaction of everyone.[6] Manufacturing companies now realize that to reduce quality problems and production costs, designers and producers have to work together from the earliest stages of product design (see Figure 12.2).

The term concurrent engineering somewhat misses the point because issues regarding sales, marketing, purchasing, finance, and quality, not just engineering, must all be addressed from the start. In typical usage, however, the term concurrent

FIGURE 12.2

Concurrent interaction between design and manufacturing groups in product development.[7]

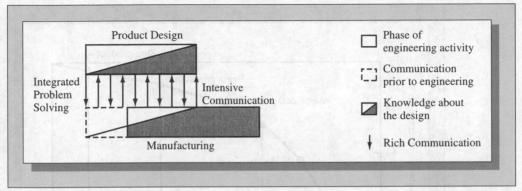

engineering connotes simultaneous, early attention to all these issues, especially to those concerning the codesign of a product and its manufacturing process.

LIFE-CYCLE COSTS AND ENGINEERING CHANGES

Initial product design decisions have dramatic impact on the product's development schedule and life-cycle cost. The process of product design nominally consists of several distinct, though overlapping, stages, including product conceptual formulation, preliminary design and analysis, and detailed design.[8] During these stages, decisions are made that will determine the product's **life-cycle costs,** which include the cost of materials, production, distribution, and operation of the product for as long as it continues to be manufactured and in use. Mistakes in early design decisions become solidified. As Figure 12.3 shows, the later problems or mistakes in design are discovered, the more costly and difficult it is to rectify them. Studies suggest that somewhere around 80% of a product's life-cycle cost is determined in the conceptual and design stages of a product, well before the product is manufactured. This means that whatever the product ends up costing, 80% of that cost is based upon choices made in the early stages of product design.[9] Unless important decisions affecting the manufacturing process are made correctly at the start, the consequences can be grave. Besides high production costs, the consequences include a protracted product-development cycle, delayed product launch, and poor product quality. By integrating manufacturing process issues into product design, necessary design changes and product rework can be eliminated or reduced, and the design and development processes substantially shortened.

In the typical serial product-development process, sometimes no one besides the design group sees any portion of the design until the entire design has been completed. Smith and Reinertsen recount one product that had over 600 new and unique parts, for which three-fourths of the drawings were released into manufacturing in a single day! The project could be tracked just by observing the huge pile of drawings moving from desk to desk as manufacturing engineers tried to figure out how to make the

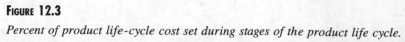

FIGURE 12.3

Percent of product life-cycle cost set during stages of the product life cycle.

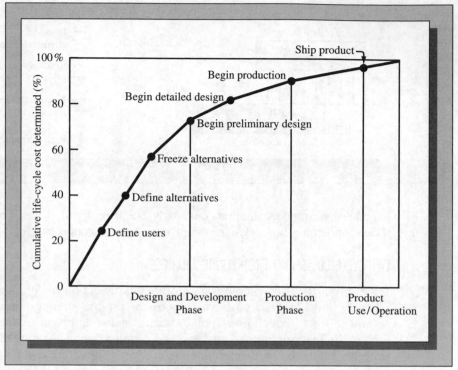

parts, and buyers tried to find suppliers from which to procure materials and components for the parts.[10]

In a process like that, every time the manufacturing group discovers features of
the design that will be difficult to produce in the factory, or the purchasing group
discovers parts or materials specified on the design that will be difficult or costly to
obtain, the design must be sent back for modification. This design–redesign process,
which involves multiple iterations and numerous **engineering change orders,** can be
lengthy, and the result may still be far from good.

The impact of using serial design versus concurrent engineering design on design
changes is shown in Figure 12.4. Company 2, which uses the serial approach, experiences a surge of change orders after the design is passed to the manufacturing group,
which has less than 6 months to get ready for production. At the time production
is scheduled to begin, there is still a huge number of changes to be processed, and this
number surges again after the product moves into production. At a later time (beyond
Figure 12.4), there will be other waves of change orders in response to complaints
from customers and suppliers. In contrast is Company 1, which started integrating
process-design with product-design decisions 2 years before scheduled production. By
the time production occurs, most bugs have been worked out of the design, and the
remaining changes are few.

Figure 12.4

Impact of integrating concurrent product–process design on the number and timing of required changes.[11]

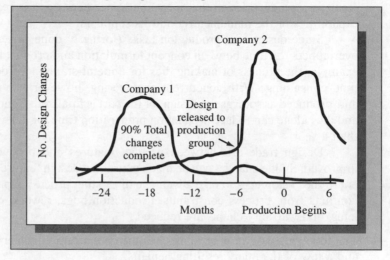

WHAT CONCURRENT ENGINEERING TEAMS DO[12]

Concurrent engineering teams face a wide range of responsibilities. Their major charges are to

1. Determine the overall character of the product, its design, and method of manufacture.
2. Perform product functional analysis so that design decisions are made with full knowledge of how the product is supposed to work. Functional analysis results in a list of product priorities so that everyone on the team will be working toward the same goals.
3. Conduct studies to determine how to improve producibility and usability of the product, without impairing either.
4. Design a process for product assembly and production control, and design the parts of the product to be compatible with the assembly process.
5. Design the manufacturing process for the product, taking into account the methods and capabilities of workers and suppliers (existing skills, processes, and capabilities) as well as production strategies (for example, reduce lot sizes, minimize the setups).

BENEFITS OF CONCURRENT ENGINEERING

The benefits of concurrent engineering can be summarized as follows:

· Concurrent engineering combines the interests of engineers, planners, buyers, marketeers, customers, and suppliers from the start so that customer requirements and production and procurement issues are identified early. Concurrent engineering emphasizes early and complete understanding of customer requirements and priorities and translating the requirements into product features and production processes. The result is a product design that meets customer needs and is realistic in terms of the capabilities of the manufacturer and its suppliers.

· Since design and production tasks (formerly done in serial fashion) are now overlapped, the time between concept formulation and product launch is reduced. For example, the process of making dies for a metal-stamping process is expensive and time-consuming. With concurrent engineering, however, the dies can be designed and produced as soon as the design for the part is finalized. Concurrent design of parts and dies alone can reduce production preparation time for a new automobile by more than a year.

· Design trade-offs between product features and production capabilities are improved. Subtle changes can be made in product design features—changes transparent to the customer—to take advantage of existing process capabilities and eliminate conflicts from process constraints. Production bugs, rework, customer usage problems, and warranty claims are reduced.

The following case in point illustrates the concurrent engineering process at Boeing and a few of the many resulting benefits.

CASE IN POINT: Design—Build Teams at Boeing[13]

Says Alan Mulally, leader of the Boeing 777 aircraft development program:

> When you're creating something, you have to recognize that it's the *interaction* that will allow everybody to come to the fundamental understanding of what it's supposed to do, and how it's going to be made. And I think we should always be striving to have an environment that allows those interactions to happen, and not have things be separate and sequential in the process.

It used to be at Boeing that the factory was on the bottom floor, and the engineering group was on the top. Whenever there was a problem in the factory, the engineers just walked downstairs to look at it. Today there are over 10,000 people at Boeing, and interaction like that is hard to achieve. Like other major manufacturing corporations, Boeing's engineering, manufacturing, planning, and finance units had evolved into semiautonomous enclaves, and each had a strong us-versus-them attitude.

To overcome that attitude and promote functional interaction in the 777 program, Boeing implemented the concept of the design–build team, or DBT. A DBT is a team with representatives from all involved functional units, as well as the customer airlines and major suppliers.

The DBT concept emerged from the simple question, How do we make a better airplane? The answer, Boeing managers realized, was not just a matter of knowing about aircraft design, but of knowing about things like aircraft manufacture, operation, and maintenance. To capture knowledge about such things, Boeing developed the DBT concept wherein customers and manufacturers could meet with engineers to listen to each other and try to incorporate each other's objectives into the design—the first time.

Responsibility for the airplane was assigned to DBTs based on a physical breakdown of the major components and subcomponents of the airplane. For example, the wing was divided into major subareas like wing leading edge and trailing edge, and each of these was broken down into specific components like inboard flap, outboard flap, and ailerons, and the responsibility for each component was handed to a DBT. Each DBT numbered 10–20 members and was run like a little company. Though initially Boeing planned on 80–100 DBTs to do the job, eventually over 250 were needed. Every DBT met twice a week for a couple of hours. Each meeting was orchestrated by a team leader, followed a preset agenda, and conformed to a regimen of taking notes, making decisions, assigning responsibilities, and following up actions. Having so many new people sit in on design meetings—people from airlines, finance, production, and quality—was a totally new concept at Boeing, but since there were *so many* new people at these meetings, no one stood out.

Most every component in an airplane interacts with numerous other components, so most participants in the program belonged to multiple DBTs. One, the representative for manufacturing, belonged to 27 DBTs. He had responsibility for telling engineers what would happen when their elegant designs met with the realities of metal, manufacturing processes, and assembly line and maintenance workers, and he made many suggestions so the airplane would be manufactured properly. One suggestion concerned the cover on the strut faring that holds the engine to the wing. Inside the faring there is a lot of electrical and hydraulic equipment that requires access for maintenance. Engineers didn't notice that the faring cover was too small and that removal of components from inside for repair would require removal of the entire faring. But the manufacturing representative did, and he suggested a bigger door on *both* sides of the faring. The new design allows greatly improved access and simpler removal of equipment with little effort and delay.

CONCURRENT ENGINEERING TEAM ORGANIZATION

Concurrent engineering is implemented through cross-functional teams. Each concurrent engineering team must have maximal control over making product-design decisions and should be organized to facilitate intercommunication and commitment to the design effort. The following conditions affect the performance of concurrent engineering teams:[14]

· *Autonomy.* Once members are placed on a concurrent engineering team, they should be relieved of other unrelated obligations and give full commitment to the concurrent engineering effort.

· *Full time, full duration.* Ideally, concurrent engineering team members should have continuous input and be party to all decisions throughout the entire product-development process. That's what concurrent means.

· *Colocation.* When the team works together and shares an office, communication is continuous and spontaneous. Formal meetings and reviews that might ordinarily occur over weeks or months are replaced by numerous informal chats happening in a matter of days.

· *Small size.* A team must be small enough to allow good communication and encourage team commitment, yet large enough to include representatives from all the affected functional areas (and perhaps customers and suppliers, too). Research shows that about 6 people is an optimal team size, though as many as 10–12 can be effective. If more than that are needed, smaller subteams can be formed, coordinated by a concurrent engineering core team or steering group.

Versatile members. Though each concurrent engineering team member is a specialist in some area (design engineering, manufacturing, marketing, purchasing), she should be willing to assume a wide range of responsibilities and obligations. Concurrent engineering members must be can-do folks willing to visit customers and suppliers, work on CAD/CAM, do modeling, do light assembly work, or whatever needs to be done.

Involvement in concurrent engineering requires more than just getting people together at meetings. Product designers wander through the factory to get an appreciation of how their designs are manufactured and what features of the design make it hard to manufacture. At the same time, they explain to production engineers and assembly workers why a design feature is important and must be retained. General Motors requires that its design engineers actually spend 1 full day every 3 months assembling the portion of the car they helped design.

Because concurrent engineering requires doing so many more things at once than serial product development, the amount of information exchanged during the process and the complexity of issues to be dealt with simultaneously increase greatly. Relying solely on traditional formal and informal means of communication makes it difficult for people in different functions to see things from a similar perspective and to reach consensus. To help improve information sharing and interactive decision making, concurrent engineering teams often rely heavily on information technology, such as CAD/CAM and interactive design databases. In addition, they use formal, structured techniques, developed so people from different functional areas have a common framework and language with which to communicate with each other, formulate goals, identify problems, and reach solutions. Prominent among these techniques are the three described in the following sections: quality function deployment, design for manufacture and assembly, and robust design methods.

QUALITY FUNCTION DEPLOYMENT[15]

Two problems facing quality-conscious companies are how to determine what really matters to customers, and how to translate what matters into requirements that are meaningful to and can be acted upon by designers and producers. **Quality function deployment (QFD)** is a planning, communication, and documentation technique that resolves those problems. It is a structured process for translating customer values into specific product or service characteristics and for specifying the processes and systems to produce that product or service. QFD is a process that starts with defining the voice of the customer in the earliest stage of product conception. It then integrates that voice throughout the design and manufacturing stages in such a way that the resulting product will better meet customer needs and be delivered in less time and at lower cost than possible with traditional product development methods.

QFD was developed by Mitsubishi's Kobe Shipyards in 1972, and it was adopted by Toyota in 1978 and many other Japanese companies soon afterward. In the US, QFD was first adopted by Ford in 1983 to counter Toyota. QFD has since been adopted by numerous US companies including General Motors, Procter & Gamble, AT&T, Digital Equipment, Omark Industries, Hewlett-Packard, and Chrysler.

HOUSE OF QUALITY

The utility of QFD is that it requires a company to clearly articulate the means by which it will achieve customer requirements. It relates customer or market needs to high-level internal technical design requirements using a planning matrix called the **house of quality.** The basic structure of the house of quality is shown in Figure 12.5:

FIGURE 12.5

Structure of the house of quality.

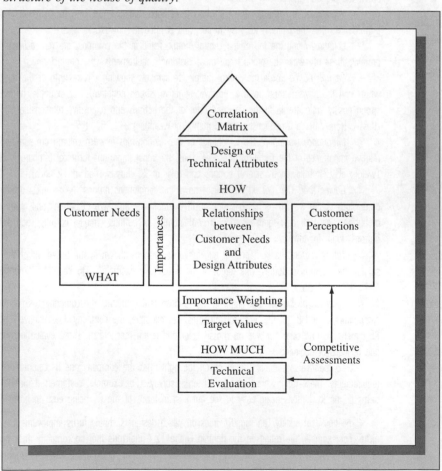

· Listed on the left side of the matrix is what the customer needs or requires.

· Listed along the top of the matrix are the design attributes or technical requirements of the product; these are how the product can meet customer requirements.

· Shown in additional sections on the top, right, and bottom sides are correlations among the requirements, comparisons to competitors, technical assessments, and target values.

Features of the house of quality are explained in Example 1.

Example   1:   House of Quality for a TV Remote Control

Figure 12.6 is a portion of the house-of-quality matrix used by engineers to improve the design for an existing television remote control (RC). The house is interpreted as follows:

· *Rows:* Listed left of the central matrix are *customer* requirements; these are what customers think is important about the product (the product *whats*).

· *Importance to customer:* The six whats have been rank ordered 1–6 by customer preference; multifunction buttons are rated the highest; RC easy to see/find is rated the lowest.

· *Columns:* Along the top of the central matrix, listed in the columns, are the *technical* attributes of the product; these are ways the product can meet customer requirements (the product *hows*).

· *Central matrix:* Inside the central matrix are symbols showing the strength of the relationship between the whats and the hows (strong positive, positive, negative, strong negative). For example, buttons easy to see has a strong positive relationship to the size and color of the buttons and a positive relationship to the size of the RC chassis. Note that each relationship has a numerical weighting — 1, 3, or 9.

· *Importance weighting:* The weightings of the relationships in each column are summed to determine the relative importance of the technical attributes. Thus, the most important technical attribute is dimensions of the RC (weight of 22), followed by size of buttons and color of RC chassis (tied at 12 each).

· *Gabled roof:* The roof on the house shows the correlations among the technical attributes. For example, dimensions of the RC chassis has a strong positive correlation with size of buttons and number of buttons, while size of buttons has a strong negative correlation with number of buttons (smaller buttons, room for more buttons; larger buttons, room for fewer).

· *Target values:* The numerical or qualitative descriptions shown in the basement of the house are design targets set for the technical attributes. One target of the design, for example, is to keep the dimensions of the RC within $6 \times 18 \times 2$ cm.

· *Technical evaluation:* The graph in the subbasement compares the company (us) against two of its competitors, A and B, on the technical attributes. For example, the company does relatively poorly on the attributes of RC dimensions and color but well on chassis color and return mechanism. These evaluations are based on test results and opinions of engineers.

· *Competitive evaluation:* The graph on the right rates the company and its competitors in terms of customer requirements. These ratings are based on customer surveys. For example, customers think the company does worst in terms of the RC buttons being easy to see but best in terms of the RC being easy to hold.

The house of quality can suggest areas on which designers should focus improvement efforts to gain a market niche. For example, the rating on the right in Figure 12.6 indicates that no company does particularly well in terms of buttons easy to see despite the fact that customers rank that requirement second in importance. A requirement that customers rank high, yet on which they rank all companies low, suggests a design feature that could be exploited to

FIGURE 12.6

House of quality for television RC.

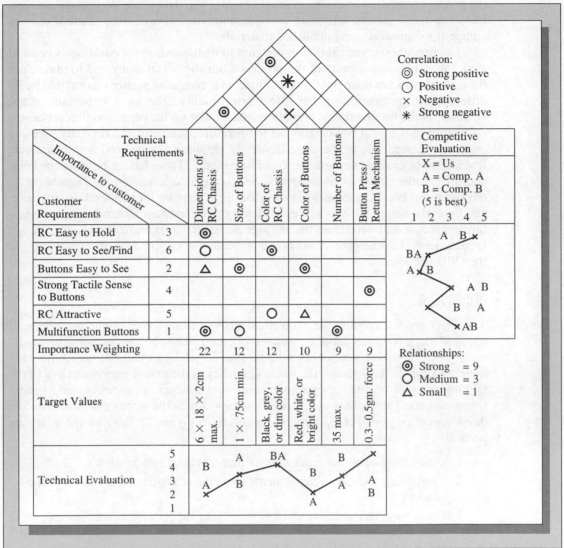

help improve a company's competitive standing. The company making the RC, for example, might try to improve the visibility of the buttons by increasing the size of buttons and/or using bright colors.

The house provides a systematic way to organize and analyze data for comparing the hows with the whats, and prevents things from being overlooked. It tells where and where not to concentrate investment in time and money. It is important to note that the results of QFD are only as good as the data that go into the house. The competitive evaluations require at minimum two perspectives: customers, to say how the product compares to the competition, and engineers and technicians, to say how, objectively, the product compares on technical requirements. The data come from many sources, including focus groups, telephone and questionnaire surveys, experimental tests of competitors' products, and published materials.

The important consideration in design is to distinguish in the customer's point of view the critical few aspects of the product from the trivial many and to make sure the critical ones are done right. For example, in a computer printer there might be 30 different design dimensions that affect print quality. The most important factor, however, is the fusion process of melting black toner on the page, and that process is a function of the right combination of temperature, pressure, and time. By focusing on time, pressure, and temperature the design emphasis is narrowed to the relatively few factors of greatest importance to performance.[16] These factors become the engineering parameters for which designers seek the right values using the Taguchi methods discussed later. Once the nominal values have been set for temperature, pressure, and time, the design analysis moves to identify the important factors in the manufacturing process and determine the settings necessary to achieve the product design requirements. In other words, the house of quality is just the first of several steps in the QFD process.

QFD PROCESS

The QFD process requires far more than filling in the house-of-quality matrix. It requires that a company adopt a customer-oriented philosophy and a cross-functional teamwork orientation where each internal functional area treats the next as its customer. As Figure 12.7 shows, the house of quality is the first of many matrices in the QFD process of translating customer needs into product requirements and system specifications. The number of matrices corresponds to the number of phases in the development process. For example, the matrices in Figure 12.7 are for the following phases:

1. Converting customer requirements into technical requirements.
2. Converting technical requirements into characteristics of key parts of the product.
3. Converting characteristics of key parts into the process to manufacture these parts.
4. Converting characteristics of the manufacturing process into detailed production procedures and control methods.

The purpose of the matrices is to show clearly and concisely the data needed to make decisions about product definition, design, production, and delivery. With the matrices, information needs become obvious, attention to detail is increased, and communication among members of design teams everywhere is improved.

The QFD process strengthens cross-functional participation in product development. It ties together the interests of marketing, engineering, and production while maintaining focus on the voice of the customer. By integrating departmental activities

FIGURE 12.7

QFD process and relationships between matrices.

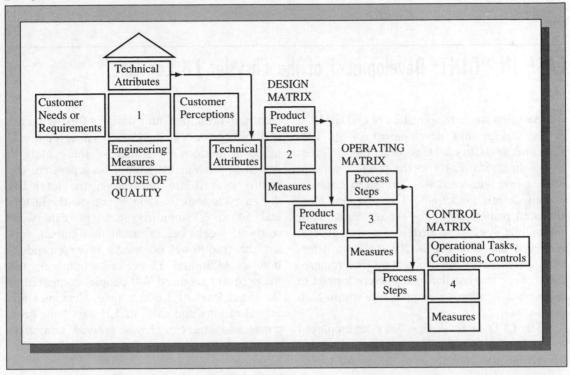

through common task requirements, the process minimizes deviations between customer wants and the final product. To paraphrase Cole, use of the matrices and the mandate that they be completed ensures that different departments work together to match up customer wants and needs with engineering specifications. The matrices require that data be collected such that the fit between any two functional areas can be measured. When the fit is not right, the two areas must keep working together until it is.[17]

The effectiveness of QFD depends on the product and its components having attributes that are quantifiable and easily tied to a few design parameters. QFD is applicable not only for new-product development, but for improvement of existing products, services, and processes. In fact, it is more effective on existing products than on new products because customers have an actual product instead of a concept to relate to and consider.

Although the QFD process takes longer to produce an initial design, the time to produce the *final* design is less, largely because the process improves communication and decision making, which results in less redesign and fewer engineering change orders after the product goes into production and to the customer.

The QFD process bears a strong resemblance to the **policy deployment** process described on Chapter 4. That is no coincidence. Both processes serve as a way to deploy a quality-related message such that every area of the organization can translate, interpret, and redefine that message into terms upon which it is able to act.

CASE IN POINT: Development of the Chrysler LH Car Line[18]

Chrysler first started application of QFD in 1986 in the design and development of its LH-platform cars (Chrysler Concorde, Eagle Vision, Dodge Intrepid). Early in the product concept stage a program team was formed to establish overall design guidelines. The program team allocated responsibility for the different major automobile systems to different design groups, and each group set up a QFD team to determine system-level requirements. Once requirements were set, smaller groups were formed to focus on designing the components within each system.

The QFD methodology Chrysler employed was part of a broader concurrent engineering effort that also made use of design-for-manu-

facturing principles and design-of-experiments methods (both described next). Though individual contributions from each of these tools to design improvements cannot be separated, the results overall are impressive: the total LH design cycle took 36 months, versus the historical 54 to 62 months; prototype cars were ready 95 weeks before production launch, versus the traditional 60 weeks (giving production an additional 35 weeks to prepare); and the program required 740 people, compared to the usual level of 1,600 people. Customer approval ratings and sales of LH cars have been good, and the cars have received numerous awards and magazine citations for design excellence.

DESIGN FOR MANUFACTURE AND ASSEMBLY

When designing a product it is easy to overlook or misjudge the realities of manufacturing. When that happens, the result is a design that is frustrating and irritating to manufacturing and sales personnel. The practice of ensuring that the realities of manufacturing are incorporated into the product design is called **design for manufacture and assembly** or **DFMA**.[19] DFMA considers features about a product's design that will simplify its manufacture and assembly, and, usually, also simplify the design of the manufacturing process, reduce direct and indirect manufacturing costs, and improve manufacturing quality.

Translating a concept into a manufactured product involves numerous considerations; such as

- Materials to use (metals, plastics, ceramics, organic materials).
- Material forming and shaping procedures (extruding, stamping, pressing, casting, forging, molding).

- Machining processes (milling, drilling, reaming, broaching, sawing, grinding).
- Machine and tool changeover procedures.
- Material handling.
- Quality control.

DFMA includes methodologies and tools to make sure such considerations are incorporated into the product design. Much of DFMA involves reference to design guidelines and use of computer-aided tools. Probably the most widely used guidelines and software for DFMA are those developed by Geoffrey Boothroyd and Peter Dewhurst.[20] Included in DFMA methodology are design axioms and guidelines for **design for manufacture** (DFM) and **design for assembly** (DFA). In the following sections we consider design axioms, specific DFM and DFA guidelines, and broader issues of manufacturing-focused product design.

DESIGN AXIOMS

Product design starts with defining customer requirements and product functional requirements. The redundant requirements are eliminated, and the incompatible ones are reconciled. The requirements are then rank ordered by importance, and design axioms are applied to each requirement. **Design axioms** are principles of design practice. Some axioms pertain to target markets and target costs, some to product quality requirements, and some to engineering and manufacturing principles.

One axiom, for example, is to design the product so that it meets the quality and cost requirements of a specific market or customer base. This axiom is intended to keep designers focused on product designs that will achieve high customer acceptance, yet not entail exotic solutions or innovations that will be too costly to manufacture. Such an axiom also justifies having marketing, sales, and customer representatives on the design team.

Design axioms also reinforce principles of good engineering design; examples are: avoid putting holes too close to the bend on a metal component, specify hole sizes that correspond to standard drill sizes, avoid sharp edges, and avoid abrupt discontinuities in stressed areas. Figure 12.8 shows an example of two designs. The one on the right incorporates design axioms for maximizing strength and reducing points of stress concentration; the one on the left does not. Design axioms cover many, though by no means all, aspects of product design. They tend to apply to design of particular components and do not consider trade-offs or relationships in the design of multiple, interrelated components.

DFM GUIDELINES

DFM guidelines are rules of design intended to improve product manufacturability by increasing the product designer's awareness of manufacturing issues. For example, in

FIGURE 12.8

Product design without (left) and with (right) consideration of design axioms.

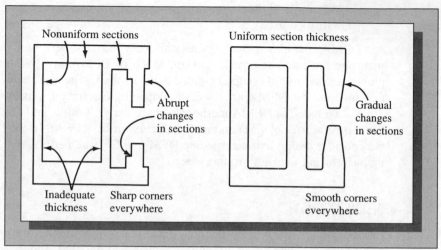

designing the Proprinter, IBM subscribed to the following guidelines:

Minimize number of parts	Design for minimal handling
Eliminate adjustments	Minimize subassemblies
Avoid separate fasteners	Develop modular designs
Use standard parts	Design for robustness
Eliminate need for special jigs and tools	Design parts for many uses
Design for efficient, adequate testing	
Design for efficient, adequate parts replacement	

The Proprinter, considered a benchmark for good product design, had 65% fewer parts and could be assembled 90% faster than its Japanese competitor product.

To show the broad impact of DFM guidelines on manufacturing cost, time, and quality, consider the first five listed above.

Minimize Number of Parts.   This guideline has perhaps the greatest impact on manufacturing cost, quality, and time of all DFM guidelines. Fewer parts translate into fewer suppliers (hence, lower supplier-related costs), simpler bills of materials (hence, lower costs of parts accounting, handling, and control), fewer assembly steps (hence fewer workstations and lower direct cost and manufacturing overhead), easier assembly (hence fewer assembly mistakes), and higher product reliability (hence less maintenance, fewer breakdowns, and reduced maintenance and warranty expenses).

In theory, a separate part is necessary only when (1) the part needs to move relative to the rest of the assembly, (2) the part must be made of a material different from the rest of the assembly, or (3) the part must be separate for reasons of assembly access, replacement, or repair.

Example   2:   Minimum Parts Determination

The top of Figure 12.9 shows a product assembly diagram and nine parts (ignoring any fasteners, which if included could easily double the parts counts). Below the diagram is a table for determining which of the parts could be combined based upon the three conditions stated above. The analysis shows that the product can be done with four parts instead of nine.

FIGURE **12.9**

Product assembly diagram and minimum parts analysis.

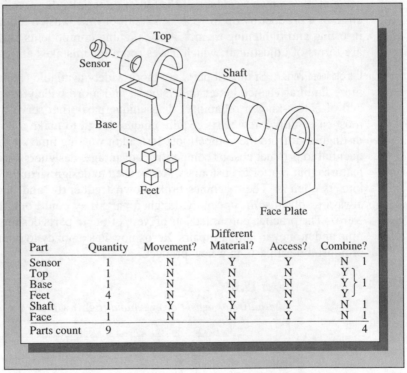

Part	Quantity	Movement?	Different Material?	Access?	Combine?	
Sensor	1	N	Y	Y	N	1
Top	1	N	N	N	Y	
Base	1	N	N	N	Y }	1
Feet	4	N	N	N	Y	
Shaft	1	Y	Y	Y	N	1
Face	1	N	N	Y	N	1
Parts count	9					4

Any part that does not qualify as a theoretical separate part should be integrated with another part. As the third condition above suggests, however, minimizing the number of parts requires prudence and foresight about later production, operation, and upkeep of the product throughout its life cycle. For example, because of clearance that might be needed to attach additional parts during the manufacturing process, or to access parts for removal and repair, sometimes an assembly consisting of several smaller components is preferable to a single, larger component. Suggestions and comments from assembly line workers, customer operators, and product repair workers help designers know to what extent DFM guidelines can be followed or must be modified.

Eliminate Adjustments.   As explained in Chapter 6, any process that involves adjustments takes longer than a process without adjustments. In addition, because an adjustment allows for latitude in results, error rates and defects are higher in processes with adjustment steps. Thus, removing adjustment steps from manufacturing reduces production lead time and defects and makes it easier to eventually automate the process.

Eliminate Screws and Other Fasteners.   A design with fewer fasteners has fewer parts. Figure 12.10 shows a one-piece design replacement for a design with nine parts, six of which are fasteners and washers. Even when fasteners cost just pennies apiece and account for a tiny percentage of the bill of materials, they can increase the assembly costs of a product by up to 75% as a result of time wasted aligning components and inserting and tightening them.[21] Also, aligning components and tightening fasteners are forms of adjustment, which leaves room for mistakes and defects.

Use Standard Parts.   Standard parts are more widely available (hence easier to procure), more familiar (hence better understood), and more widely used (hence, less costly, and of better-known reliability) than unique parts that serve the same function. In most cases only a few parts require unique design to make a product innovative and distinguish it from the competition. Instead of wasting time on parts that are inconsequential to product cost or competitive advantage, designers should focus on product features that matter to customers. Xerox used to design virtually every part that went into its copiers. The machines broke down frequently, and because repairs almost always involved some specially designed part, they could only be procured through Xerox. The practice consumed lots of Xerox time in parts design, and lots of customer time and money in copier repairs. Xerox now has a policy to minimize the percentage of nonstandard parts in a new product.

FIGURE 12.10

Alternative designs, (left) *with and* (right) *without fasteners.*

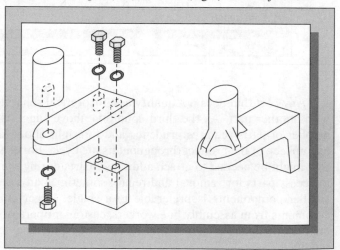

Eliminate the Need for Special Jigs and Tools. A jig is a fixture to hold an item securely while it is being machined or assembled. If every item needs a special jig, then each time a new item is to be worked on, the jig must be changed. Changing from one jig to another accounts for much of the time and cost of production setup. Obviously, setup time can be reduced if different items are designed to use the same jigs in production or not to use any jigs at all.

In summary, DFM guidelines put boundaries on design requirements to keep them within the capability of the manufacturing process. When designers follow the guidelines, they increase the likelihood that the product can be produced to satisfy the time, cost, and quality requirements.

DFA PRINCIPLES

Design for assembly methodology is similar to DFM, except it focuses explicitly on simplifying product assembly. DFA includes guidelines and procedures for minimizing the number of parts to be assembled, assessing procedures to assemble the parts, and determining the best sequence of assembly. Considerations for determining the best assembly sequence include ensuring

- That parts can be easily mated.
- Easy access to components for quality control tests.
- Easy access to fasteners or points for maintenance.
- That parts needing lubrication or maintenance later are not hidden and are easily accessible.
- That parts can be added with minimal turning or reorientation of the product.
- That as parts are added, the combination of them does not deform, move out of tolerance, scrape against, or hit other components.
- There is sufficient space for hands, tools, robotic grippers, and so on, to perform assembly tasks.

From a DFA perspective, it should be apparent that the lowest material cost in a product does not necessarily equate to the lowest product cost. For example, although usage of low-cost, standard fasteners is one way to achieve material savings, especially when the product requires many fasteners, DFA considerations might suggest a fastener that is shaped differently and is slightly more expensive but is easier to install, allows robot insertion, and speeds up production enough to offset the cost.

Since even for a modestly sized product there might be many tens of steps and hundreds of possible assembly sequences, computers are the standard tool for DFA analysis. Boothroyd and Dewhurst have compiled a computerized list of generic shapes, along with the procedures and the estimated times to assemble them.[22] The software includes guidelines for minimizing the number of assembly steps, minimizing the number of reorientations of parts during the assembly, and determining whether assembly should be manual or automated. Designers, by looking at the assembly

CASE IN POINT: DFMA at Halmar Ribicon[23]

A 1996 survey of 250 midsize manufacturers indicated that 64% were using concurrent engineering in product–process design. One of them, Halmar Ribicon, used DFMA to redesign the drives for its 15–30 hp AC motors. Engineers consulted with the assembly line staff for opinions about components, materials, and assembly steps in current products. They also asked external parts suppliers for critiques and suggestions about design concepts for new products. Thanks to concurrent engineering and DFMA, Halmar

Ribicon's new line of drives is less expensive and easier to manufacture. For the new drives, the parts count was reduced from 137 to 50 (64%); screw connections, from 168 to 95 (43%); control wires, from 54 to 14 (73%); and power wires were eliminated. This has resulted in reductions in assembly labor from 13.4 hours to 3.5 hours (74%); test time, from 3.9 hours to 2.0 hours (49%); and production cost, from $2500 per unit to $1500 (40%).

procedure as they incorporate a shape into a design, are able to determine the most practical and least time-consuming assembly procedure for the shape.

With computer-aided DFA and CAD engineering programs, designers can fashion three-dimensional models of components on a computer screen, determine whether the components will fit together properly without interference, and analyze the assembly of components for overall performance and durability. IBM used this kind of software to design the Proprinter. Boeing used a very sophisticated computer system for the design of most components and systems for its 777.

The design team must be familiar with the production process, equipment, and facilities, as well as the process capabilities of both the prime manufacturer and its parts suppliers. Process capabilities include the ability of workers to learn, acquire, or adapt to new methods and processes; of equipment to perform or be adapted to a variety of procedures or methods; and of the process to deliver output within design specifications (such as measured by the process capability index, C_{pk}, described in the next chapter). Holding the design team accountable for designs that conform to the capability of the process ensures that they will weigh capability matters during the design process.

FULLY EXPLOITING DFMA

Although DFM and DFA guidelines can dramatically reduce manufacturing costs and improve production quality, abiding *solely* by them can be detrimental. Take for example the guideline to minimize the number of parts, and suppose one large part is proposed to replace several smaller ones. The larger part might, in fact, be more difficult to install during assembly than the smaller parts, which would increase assembly costs. Also, if designing the larger part takes longer than designing the smaller parts, the product launch date could be delayed, which would defer sales revenues and possibly destroy any first-to-market advantage. Another example is illustrated in Example 3.

Example   3:   Lifetime Analysis of Design Alternatives

Consider two design alternatives for the buttons on the television RC from Example 1. As shown in Figure 12.11, design A uses plastic buttons inserted on top of a formed rubber pad and design B uses buttons formed into the pad, with a small metal ball impregnated inside.

FIGURE 12.11

Design alternatives for button mechanism on television RC.

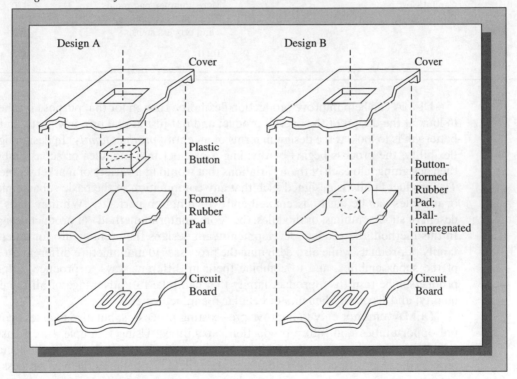

The effect of shifting from design A to design B on manufacturing performance as measured in lifetime costs is shown in Table 12.1. Costs like those in the table can be estimated using activity-based costing procedures, described in Chapter 20. The implication of the analysis is that a shift from design A to design B will increase the lifetime cost by $365,000. Although design B is simpler and offers advantages of reduced labor, cycle time, and process costs, the high cost associated with its development, capital equipment, and materials outweighs the advantage.

TABLE 12-1 Impact of Design Alternatives on Lifetime Cost

	(current) Design A: Plastic Buttons and Formed Rubber Pad	(proposed) Design B: Formed Rubber Pad with Metal Inserts	($1000) Lifetime Cost Differential of Shift from Design A to Design B
Labor Cost	Current assembly is 50% automated	Simpler to assemble; can automate 100%	−320
Material Cost	Inexpensive	Pad more costly; eliminate plastic buttons	290
Development Time	None	Design new pad mold and mold process	640
Production CT	Simpler assembly	Reduce assembly time by 8 sec/unit	−75
Capital Cost		More complex pad molds	420
Process Cost		Fewer parts, suppliers, and process steps	−590
		Total	365

DFMA can help improve production flexibility, though for that purpose it is better to look at the design of the overall product and not just at one or a few parts. In fact, better yet is to look at the design in terms of an entire *product family*. In designing for flexibility, the process begins by dividing a product into modules or subassemblies, then designing into each of them variations that would fit a variety of market segments. The product family is designed such that any combination of the basic subassemblies or modules can be easily assembled and will function perfectly. Whitney calls this design of subassemblies, or modules, the "combinatorial method" of product design.[24] In this method, the product development team designs the architecture for an entire family of products while also designing the processes to manufacture different models of the subassemblies, and to combine them in different ways to produce different products. The result is a product family that can take full advantage of all the cost, quality, and flexibility benefits of cellular manufacturing.

DFMA aims not only to improve pre-existing processes, but also to assess potential opportunities and future production capabilities. Using Example 3 as a case in point, the design team might decide to proceed with design B despite the associated process development cost of $640,000 (Table 12.1) if it believes the new process has potential applications beyond the product under immediate consideration.

Another aim of DFMA is to clarify relationships between features of product design and manufacturing so that decisions about products can improve manufacturing performance. For example, Figure 12.12 shows two QFD-type matrices for a television RC. The first matrix (design) links attributes of the product design with those of the process design; the second (operating performance) links attributes of process design with manufacturing performance criteria. The connection between the two matrices is that in the first matrix, process design attributes are in the columns, whereas in the second matrix, they are in the rows.

FIGURE 12.12

Matrices for investigating relationships between product attributes and manufacturing system features.

Design Matrix

Process Design Attributes

Product Design Attributes	Material Handling	Complexity of Forming Process	Complexity of Ball-Insertion Process	Difficulty of Assembly Operation
Size of Ball	✕		○	
Centeredness of Ball			◎	
Pad Resilience		○	✕	✕

Relationships:
◎ Strong Positive
○ Positive
✕ Negative
✴ Strong Negative

Operating Performance Matrix

Manufacturing Performance Criteria

Process Design Attributes	Labor Cost	Material Cost	Process Cost	Process Flexibility	Quality Control	Lead Time
Importance	10	5	10	25	30	20
Material Handling		○				
Complexity of Forming Process	○		○	✕		○
Complexity of Ball-Insertion Process			◎	✴	✴	
Difficulty of Assembly Operation			○			

The symbols in the matrices represent the direction and strength of relationships. For example, the design matrix shows a strong positive relationship between the centeredness of the ball in a button, and the complexity of the step of inserting the ball into the button. It also shows a weak negative relationship between the resilience of the pad material and the difficulty of performing the assembly procedure. Although qualitative relationships are shown, engineers might be able to determine more precise, quantitative measures.

Now, by knowing relationships like these, engineers can manipulate both the product and process design attributes to assess the impact on manufacturing performance. Alternatively, the design team can *start* with manufacturing performance goals and work backwards to derive details of the product and process design. For example, the operating performance matrix in Figure 12.12 indicates that quality control and process flexibility are very important. The matrix also suggests that both quality and flexibility can be improved by reducing the complexity of the ball-insertion process. The design matrix, however, suggests that to reduce the complexity of the insertion process, the product design must allow for a ball that is smaller in size and somewhat off-centered inside the button. If using a smaller ball and allowing some off-centeredness do not detract from the product's ability to meet customer requirements, then incorporating them in the product design specification will improve manufacturing performance but not harm product functionality.

TAGUCHI METHODS[25]

Every product feature or characteristic has a nominal, or target, value. Any deviation from that target results in higher costs to the consumer and producer, which is what Genichi Taguchi calls the "loss to society". The goal, says Taguchi, should be a never-ending effort to reduce variability and to hit the target. Taguchi developed the foundation for his quality philosophy during the 1950s and 1960s as manager of the electronics communication laboratory at Nippon Telephone & Telegraph Company. In 1966 he was awarded the Deming prize for this philosophy (the first of four Deming awards he would receive).

Taguchi's philosophy is centered on three concepts for improving quality of design: robust design, design of experiments, and the quality loss function.

ROBUST DESIGN

One measure of a product's quality is its ability to maintain consistent performance over a range of conditions, regardless of variations in the way it is manufactured and used. This is called **robust design.** The robust design concept can improve product quality without increasing product manufacturing costs.

TAGUCHI APPROACH TO DESIGN

The Taguchi approach to design differs from the traditional engineering design process. In the latter, principles of science and technology are invoked to arrive at a product design configuration and to set nominal values for product parameters. For our purposes, a **parameter** is any product or process variable that is directly or indirectly relevant to product performance. Examples include product physical dimensions, types of materials used, and operational settings on equipment to manufacture the product. The testing exposes the product or model to a variety of real-life situations to assess the product's functionality, durability, and reliability.

In the traditional design process, a prototype or model of the product is made based on the design configuration and initial design parameter settings. Tests are performed and, depending on the test results, the design parameter settings are varied. This design–test procedure is repeated until the desired performance is achieved. The procedure tends to be somewhat unsystematic and completely ignores the impact of the manufacturing process on product performance.

Taguchi's design approach, in contrast, emphasizes systematic testing of different parameter values to determine the combination of values that *minimize performance variation*. The goal of the approach is, through experimentation, to determine the parameter values that will make product performance the least sensitive to variations in user and manufacturing conditions. Unlike the traditional two-stage, design–test approach, Taguchi's methodology has three stages:

1. *System design.* Technology, science, and experience are used to develop the initial system design. This stage might utilize a technique such as QFD to identify and map the relationships between variables for customer needs, design configuration, and parameters important to product and process performance. For example, the design of a printed circuit board would include consideration not only of variables in the circuit board itself, but also of variables in the design of the process that will *assemble* the boards, which would include all the steps in the assembly process and the machines needed to perform axial insertion, surface-mount parts placement, flow soldering, and so on.

2. *Parameter design.* Nominal values are set for parameters in the system. Taguchi says the values should be selected so as to minimize the influence of noise factors in the environment on output performance. **Noise** refers to factors that are uncontrollable (or uncontrolled), but which influence performance. The nominal settings for parameters should be chosen so as to make the product the least sensitive (most robust) to noise.

During parameter design, Taguchi advocates use of systematic experiments and **design-of-experiment** methods. Experiments should not be confused here with tests in the traditional design–test process. Whereas the latter involves exposing a product with semifixed design parameters to a series of tests to assess performance, the former involves *purposely varying* the parameters in a systematic fashion to investigate the effect on performance. In the circuit-board assembly process, parameter design would entail looking at different possible locations to put components on the board, different possible numbers and types of assembly machines for producing the board, and the influence of those possibilities on the quality of the final assembled board.

3. *Tolerance design.* **Tolerance** is the amount of deviation from a target value as allowed in the design. For example, specifying the value of 8.52 ± 0.01 cm on a design indicates that the target is 8.52 cm, but anything in the range 8.51–8.53 cm is acceptable. According to Taguchi, however, the closer to the target value, the better (tolerances notwithstanding) so the tolerance should be selectively reduced so as to minimize the loss of deviating from a target value. Tolerance design starts with determining the relative effect that different parameters have on the variability of performance. Those parameters that have a great effect are designed with narrower tolerances; those that have little or no effect are designed with wider tolerances. In the circuit-board assembly design process, this step would involve determining the locations of components and the machine settings that most influence product quality,

putting tight tolerance limits on them, and then establishing procedures for keeping the assembly process within the tolerance limits.

PLANNED EXPERIMENTATION

The purpose of experimentation in parameter design is to identify particular combinations of parameters that optimize design criteria and performance. This is much different from simple testing wherein many units of a product are subjected to field conditions for the purpose of determining life expectancy, durability, etc., and wherein a failure to meet requirements leads to a new cycle of redesign and retest.

With planned experimentation, the purpose is to discover how changing design parameters and configurations can lead to improved quality and productivity. With this approach, design parameters and even major aspects of the design configuration are based upon experimental results.

Example   4:   Experiment to Determine the Effect of Parameter Settings on Product Performance

As shown in Figure 12.13, when a force is applied to the part at points F and G, the part deflects by an amount ϵ as measured in degrees. Since this angular distortion affects the performance of the part, designers would like to learn how to minimize it. An experiment is designed to study the influence of changing two parameters on deflection: parameter **a** (thickness) and parameter **b** (radius of curvature). Suppose that to keep weight and cost to a minimum, values for parameters **a** and **b** should be as small as possible.

FIGURE 12.13

*Parameters (**a**, **b**) and performance measure (ϵ) on a part.*

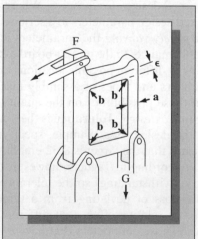

An initial experiment is run on four possible designs to assess what influence varying the parameters has on deflection. Note that testing many more parameter settings would be desirable, but only four are described here to keep the presentation simple. The results are shown in Table 12.2. The experiment suggests that manipulating

TABLE 12-2

Design	Parameter *a* Setting (mm)	Parameter *b* Setting (mm)	Deflection (degrees)
1	50	10	.011
2	50	15	.014
3	80	10	.020
4	80	15	.021

parameter **a** from 50 to 80 mm has much greater influence on the magnitude of the deflection than does manipulating parameter **b** from 10 to 15 mm.

Suppose next that 80 trials are run, 20 for each of the four possible designs. The results, plotted in Figure 12.14, reveal something not previously known: although manipulating parameter **b** has little effect on the average (nominal) deflection, it has a large effect on the *variation* in the deflection from trial to trial. Together, the experiments show that to decrease the deflection level, parameter **a** should be set to the smaller value, and to minimize the deflection *variation*, parameter **b** should be set to the larger value.

FIGURE 12.14

Results of 20 trials for each design.

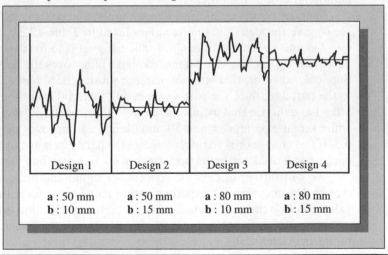

The average output of a process is called the process **signal**, and the variation in output is referred to as **noise**. In Example 4, the signal (average angular distortion) is controlled by adjusting parameter **a**, while the noise is controlled by adjusting parameter **b**.

Both aspects of performance are expressed together as the **signal-to-noise ratio:**

$$S/N = Average/Standard\ Deviation.$$

TABLE 12-3   Signal to Noise Results

Design	Parameters a	b	Signal (average)	Noise (standard deviation)	S/N
1	50	10	0.010	0.005	2.0
2	50	15	0.011	0.002	5.5
3	80	10	0.020	0.005	4.0
4	80	15	0.021	0.003	7.0

Taguchi suggests using the S/N ratio to assess experimental results. He also suggests setting parameter values in product designs so as to improve the S/N ratio. In general, the S/N ratio can be improved in two ways: for a given noise level, by improving the signal (increasing or decreasing it, depending on the desired effect); or for a given signal level, by decreasing the noise. While US and European engineers typically focus on increasing the signal as a way to improve performance, Taguchi argues that often it is better to decrease the noise instead. Design methods for increasing the signal usually involve more or better resources and materials, redundant systems, or increased attention to inspection and control, all which also increase the cost of a process. In contrast, often the noise can be decreased for little or no additional cost to the process.

Suppose results of 20 trials on each of the four designs in the experiment (Example 4) give the signal and noise values listed in Table 12.3.

Assume we start with design 1, and the goal is to maximize S/N. Increasing just parameter **a** (thickness) to 80 mm (design 3) improves the S/N ratio from 2.0 to 4.0. Suppose, however, that such an increase substantially raises the amount of material in the part and, thus, the part's weight and material cost—both undesirable. On the other hand, notice that by just increasing parameter **b** (radius) from 10 mm to 15 mm while keeping parameter **a** at 50 mm (design 2) improves the S/N ratio from 2.0 to 5.5. If this change only slightly increases the part's weight and cost, then just changing parameter **b** results in better performance *for less cost* than just changing parameter **a**.

We will further discuss the concepts of signal and noise later. The point here is that by learning through experimentation about the effects that different parameter values have on the performance mean (signal) and variation (noise), parameter values can be set so as to optimize trade-offs between performance criteria and manufacturing/operating costs.

DESIGN OF EXPERIMENTS

Perhaps obvious is that when studying a process or product, attention is focused on those factors which, when allowed to vary, cause the performance to vary. The experiment must be designed such that the relative roles that factors play in governing performance can be understood. As the example above showed, some factors influence average performance, others influence the variation in performance. In addition, among the factors that influence performance, some can be controlled by the designer but others cannot. A good experimental design affords the opportunity to learn about the relationships between *all* key factors and output performance, even those factors over which the designer has no control. In particular, the experimental design should permit:

- Understanding the average, individual effects of changing any of the factors alone.
- Understanding the joint effects, or independency, of changing two or more of the factors.
- Replication so the effect of experimental error can be determined.

Suppose we want to measure the effects of the following factors (individually and in concert) on automobile fuel economy as measured in miles per gallon (MPG): carburetor type, engine displacement, transmission, tire pressure, and driving speed. If we choose to look at only two levels or alternatives for each factor, we would use a **two-level factorial design.** The factors and the alternatives for each are as follows:

Factor	Level 1	Level 2
Carburetor model	Type A	Type B
Engine displacement (liter)	2.8	3.4
Transmission (drives)	2-wheel	4-wheel
Tire pressure (psi)	22	28
Driving speed (mph)	45	55

To determine the right levels of all four factors to achieve lowest MPG would require a total of $2^5 = 32$ tests. For design engineers, however, determining the right levels for *all* of the factors would be somewhat pointless since under actual driving conditions they cannot control three of the factors—transmission-drive setting, tire pressure, and speed—all which vary according to the discretion of the driver. Factors like these are considered *environmental* conditions because in everyday usage of the product, the designer has no control over them. Nonetheless, the factors are important to the designer because changes in them *do* influence MPG performance. As such, these factors still need to be understood and taken into account when designing the product. Experiments should thus be structured so as to account for all factors known to significantly influence performance, whether or not the factors are controllable.

Controllable and uncontrollable factors have the following relationship to the noise and signal factors discussed earlier:

1. **Signal factors** are factors that are adjusted by product *operators* to achieve certain performance (for example, a driver setting a dashboard switch to shift the transmission to either two-wheel drive or four-wheel drive).

2. **Control factors** are design parameters on the product and production process set by product–process *designers* (for example, an engineer specifying the carburetor type and engine displacement on the automobile, and specifying settings on manufacturing equipment). Selecting the nominal values for these factors is the role of parameter design.

Signal factors and control factors are both considered controllable to the extent that they are preset or specified by the design configuration and parameter settings.

3. **Noise factors** are factors that influence performance, but that are uncontrollable (road terrain, weather, elevation), or that, *in principle,* are controllable, but because of difficulty, expense, or impracticality are better considered as uncontrollable for design purposes (tire pressure or driving speed).

DOE AND DFMA FOR PROCESS IMPROVEMENT

As suggested above, sometimes factors that *could* be controlled by designers are treated as noise factors for purposes of manufacturing efficacy and economic advantage. In a manufacturing process there are so many factors influencing the production output that it is impractical or impossible to try to control all of them. Through experiments, however, factors that should be controlled can be distinguished from those that should be treated as noise and left uncontrolled. Also, on the controlled factors, the settings or levels to minimize the variability effects of noise factors can be determined. Such was the case in Example 4, where it was determined that increasing the value of parameter **b** would decrease the amount of variability. In other words, by setting parameter **b**, the control factor, variation from uncontrollable factors (whatever they are) can be minimized. Following is an example of how to determine which process factors to use as control factors in a manufacturing process.

Example   5:   Experiment to Determine Machine Settings

In an injection-molding process, the control factors that influence the shrinkage of a product part include

Mold cavity finish
Holding time
Holding pressure
Screw speed
Mold nozzle temperature
Raw material moisture content
Water temperature for cooling mold

Not all of them, however, can be controlled to the same degree and for the same expense since they involve work functions done by different people. For example, mold cavity finish is controlled by the mold designer and moldmaker; screw speed, by the molding machine operator; moisture content, by the raw material supplier; and water temperature, by the plant custodian.

Each factor can be treated as a control or a noise factor, depending on the chosen perspective and objective. For example, moisture content of material can be treated as a control factor by designers imposing tighter specifications on the material supplier; alternatively, it could be treated as a noise factor, in which case the specifications are not tightened. If tightening the specifications increases the cost of the material, then it might be better to treat moisture content as noise and look for ways to mitigate the influence of moisture on part shrinkage by focusing on other factors that are easier and cheaper to control. Similarly, it might be impractical to alter plant water temperature to suit the requirements of injection-molded parts (that is, to try to control it), in which case it would be better to treat temperature as a noise factor, and focus instead on determining parameter settings for the part, the die, and the molding-machine operation so that the influence of water temperature on part shrinkage will be minimal. Given that perspective, experiments will be performed in which moisture content and water temperature are treated as uncontrollable (noise) factors, and the other five factors are treated as controllable (design parameters).

The objective of the experiments is to determine the settings for the five design parameters that minimize parts shrinkage. It is noted, however, that while the two noise factors will be uncontrolled during normal operations, for the experiments they *will* be controlled.

Suppose that each of the five control and two noise factors are tested at two levels or settings each (rough vs. smooth finish, long vs. short time, high vs. low pressure, high vs. low moisture content, high vs. low temperature, and so on). The result is a two-level factorial design that requires $2^7 = 128$ trials.

ORTHOGONAL ARRAYS

Only the factors believed "most likely" to have large effects are included in an experimental design. When the number of factors (seven in the above example) and/or the number of choices or levels for each (only two, above) is large, the number of trials required in the experiment to test all combinations can be enormous. Part of Taguchi's design-of-experiments approach includes the use of **orthogonal arrays,** which are short-cut methods that enable uniform measurement of interaction effects in a more efficient manner than full-factorial experimental designs. An example of a Taguchi orthogonal array for a two-level, seven-factor experiment is shown in Figure 12.15. Each row represents a trial, and each column the setting for a factor. In trial 1 every factor is set to the first level, in trial 2 the last four factors are set to the second level, and so on. The settings specified for the trials in the array enable a large amount of information to be gained with relatively few trial runs. This experiment requires only 8 runs, whereas a two-level full-factorial experiment of seven factors would require 128 runs. Development of orthogonal arrays is beyond our scope, and the reader is referred to the texts by DeVor, *et al.* and Phadke cited at the end of this chapter for thorough coverage.

FIGURE 12.15

Orthogonal array for a two-level, seven-factor experiment.

Trial	Column						
No.	1	2	3	4	5	6	7
1	1	1	1	1	1	1	1
2	1	1	1	2	2	2	2
3	1	2	2	1	1	2	2
4	1	2	2	2	2	1	1
5	2	1	2	1	2	1	2
6	2	1	2	2	1	2	1
7	2	2	1	1	2	2	1
8	2	2	1	2	1	1	2

QUALITY LOSS

As part of the design process, engineers specify the tolerance or the range in dimensions or performance within which aspects of a product must fall. As long as the product stays within the upper and lower tolerance limits, it is considered acceptable. As Taguchi asserts, however, not all acceptable items are of the same quality since there can be much difference between barely meeting a tolerance limit and hitting the target value, which (usually) is located at the midpoint between the upper and lower tolerance limits. The target value is considered optimal, so hitting it results in maximal quality, while missing it results in lesser quality.

In general, the farther an item is from its target value, the lower the quality of the item. Taguchi expressed this concept with the **quality loss function,** a mathematical function that quantifies the amount of quality loss or benefit forgone to the manufacturer or customer as the consequence of a product deviating from the target. Quality loss is expressed as a function of the deviation squared,

$$Loss = f(\text{Deviation})^2,$$

where deviation is the difference between the target value and the actual value. The loss concept has implications for setting the tolerance range on parameters in product and process designs and for controlling quality in manufacturing processes. More will be said about the loss function and its implication for manufacturing process control in Chapter 14.

CRITICISM OF TAGUCHI

Though many companies claim success using Taguchi's experimental methods, critics claim that most of these companies did not have a prior history of good experimental design practice, and, as such, were bound to see improvements just because they began to experiment—whether they used Taguchi methods or not. Some of Taguchi's design-of-experiment and data analysis methods have been criticized for not adequately dealing with potential interactions, for sometimes leading to inefficient experiments, and for producing spurious results.[26] However, because Taguchi's orthogonal arrays greatly reduce the number of required trials and make experimentation less daunting, many more companies are now doing product and process experimentation than before and that in itself is a good thing. Presumably, as these companies become more experienced with experimentation, they will better understand the limitations of orthogonal arrays and adopt compensating methods.

Regardless of the criticisms about Taguchi, all of which focus rather narrowly on technical matters, his quality-of-design philosophy remains sound. Taguchi's ideas about the role of engineering design in product quality, the use of manipulating control factors to reduce variation from noise factors, performance improvement using the S/N ratio, and the concepts of robust design, parameter design, and quality loss function are all significant contributions to product quality and continuous process improvement.

Summary

A quality product starts with a quality design—a design that both fulfills customer requirements and meets production capabilities. Design decisions made early during product conception affect the cost and time of product development as well as the cost of manufacture, assembly, and quality.

Concurrent engineering is an integrated team approach to the product-development process that addresses important customer, manufacturing, financial, and marketing issues early in product conception. The benefits of concurrent engineering include more efficient trade-offs between product design and production capabilities as well as better achievement of marketing, financial, and production goals. Concurrent engineering generates a great deal of information and requires joint decision making, so new methodologies are needed to help manage that information and guarantee its effective usage. One such methodology, QFD, determines the voice of the customer, then makes sure that voice gets integrated everywhere in the design process and shows up in the finished product. QFD utilizes a series of matrices to ensure that the contribution of every functional area fits the requirements of other functional areas and is traceable back to original customer needs and design attributes as articulated in the house-of-quality matrix.

DFMA is a methodology that facilitates product and process codesign by keeping product designers aware of the manufacturing and assembly ramifications of product design. DFMA can be applied to the design of individual products, to the design of product families, and to assessing the impact of product designs on utilization and flexibility of production facilities.

One measure of a product's quality is its ability to perform as specified under differing usage or manufacturing conditions. Taguchi advocates design-of-experiment methods in the design process for determining factors that most influence product performance and for setting values for design parameters that make the product robust and insensitive to many of these factors. Experimental methods are used to determine which manufacturing factors affect process variability and which factors should be controlled to reduce variability and costs.

The emphasis in quality of design is on *setting* the right requirements, although it should be obvious that simply having the right requirements is not sufficient to guarantee a high-quality product or service. Also necessary is a system or process for tracking and controlling the manufacturing process, its inputs, throughput, and outputs to ensure that the requirements are *executed* on a continuous basis and without exception. This is the matter of **quality of conformance,** which refers to a process's ability to produce outputs in conformance with established requirements. In the next three chapters we discuss methods to achieve quality of conformance, in particular, ways for monitoring the production process and its outputs so that product design requirements are continuously maintained. Not until a product has quality of design (incorporates the needs of customers in its design targets) and is produced with quality of conformance (virtually hits the design targets) can it truly be said that it is a quality product.

Questions

1. Explain how the **serial approach** to product design increases the cost and length of time to develop new products and contributes to higher costs and quality problems for manufactured items.

2. What parties should or might be included in a **concurrent engineering** team? What are the contributions of each? How does their inclusion in the team improve (*a*) the product development process and (*b*) the resulting, final product?

3. What do you think are some of the major difficulties in changing from a serial to a concurrent design approach?

4. Briefly, define the purpose of QFD.

5. In QFD, what is the source of customer needs or requirements that appear in the house of quality?

6. How do you think that the QFD process can be used as part of concurrent engineering?

7. In 10 words or less, define the purposes of and distinguish between DFM and DFA.

8. Discuss the relationship between DFMA principles and ultimate product cost and quality.

9. What does it mean for a design to be robust?

10. What is the connection between
    a. DFMA and concurrent engineering?
    b. DFMA and QFD?
    c. DFMA and design of experiments?

11. Rico Corporation has a policy that requires its product design engineer to spend 1 day a month working in the plant to become familiar with production processes. Still, by most customer surveys Rico products are assessed as only average. How can that happen?

12. One practice in improving quality of design of products assembled from procured parts is to let suppliers have a greater hand in designing the parts they produce. Suppose a manufacturer decides to reduce the specifications of parts it sends to suppliers to the minimum necessary and give maximal flexibility to the supplier for the overall part design. What are the potential advantages and disadvantages of allowing the supplier latitude in design? How might the manufacturer ensure that the design of the parts is exactly what it had in mind?

13. These days CAD computer software enables designers to check whether their parts, as designed, will be easy to combine with other parts, will allow sufficient clearance for other parts, will not interfere with the placement of other parts, and so on. In the absence of software, what other ways are there to determine these things?

14. What is the difference between Taguchi's experimental designs and traditional experimental designs? What is the criticism of Taguchi's designs?

15. Contrast the traditional design engineering process with the Taguchi design process. Why, during the design process, is experimentation more useful than testing?

16. Where in the Taguchi process does planned experimentation take place? What is the purpose of planned experimentation in the Taguchi design process?

17. Where in the Taguchi design process does the concept of the loss function occur?

18. Why is planned experimentation preferable to one-variable-at-a-time experimentation?

Problems

1. Review issues of *Consumer Reports* or product- or life-style focused magazines (*PC World, Stereo Review, Golf World*) for articles evaluating competing brands of products. Note the measures that they used regarding quality, customer satisfaction, and so on. Which provide information useful for QFD? What are the limitations of the information in allowing consumers to make a good assessment of the products? What additional information would be needed to complete a house of quality?

2. Think about or use whatever consumer research material is available to you to define customer needs or requirements for the following:
   a. A "good" college course.
   b. Toaster (or other home appliance of your choosing).
   c. Cellular telephone.
   d. Coffee mug for your car.

   For each, define a corresponding set of physical or technical characteristics. Using the format of Figure 12.16, construct a house-of-quality matrix and show the relationship between the technical characteristics and customer requirements. Use the matrix in each case to design or suggest what the ideal product or service would be like or look like.

Figure 12.16

QFD matrix for problem 2.

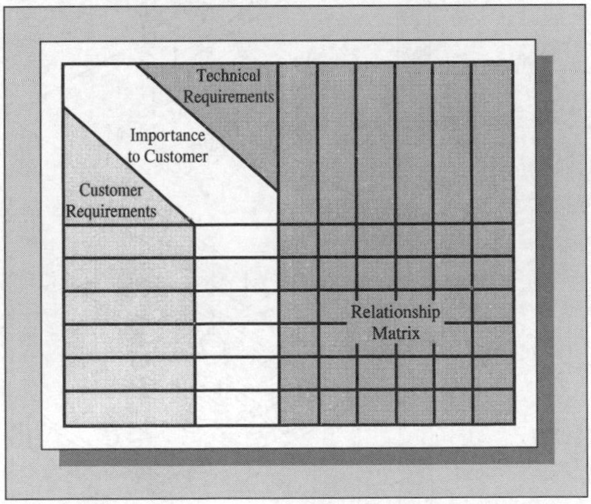

3. For each product or service from problem 2, find two, real competing products or services and assess them according to the characteristics and requirements you defined.

4. Find some products you have recently purchased and comment on whether you think they were designed with manufacturing and assembly in mind.

5. You have received a contract to design modular, prefabricated housing structures that can be constructed by snapping together, say, a few hundred parts. Discuss the DFM and DFA principles that would serve as the most important guidelines in your design.

6. Figure 12.17 is the design for a garage door opener remote control (RC). The RC is assembled by arranging the parts as shown, inserting and tightening two screws (h), and affixing the visor clip into the preformed holes on the base. The battery for the unit (not shown) goes between the two contacts (e). To replace the battery, the two screws and base part (f) must be removed.

The company that assembles the RC also makes the plastic parts a, b, and f. All other parts are outsourced: parts c, e, and g are metal and produced by the same supplier; part d, the board, is produced by another suppler. The metal parts are produced by simple cutting and bending operations. Parts c and e use the same type of metal, but are of slightly different gauges.

Suggest possible design improvements based upon the DFM and DFA guidelines listed in the chapter. Look at the overall design, as well as the design of outsourced parts. Include any assumptions in your analysis. Discuss in what ways your design suggestions would improve upon the existing design.

Figure 12.17

Garage door opener RC (problem 6).

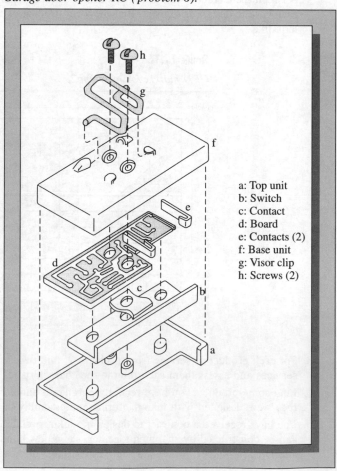

a: Top unit
b: Switch
c: Contact
d: Board
e: Contacts (2)
f: Base unit
g: Visor clip
h: Screws (2)

7. Suppose you must evaluate possible differences in performance between two comparably priced copier machines. Develop an experimental plan to determine whether there are differences in the copiers. Discuss what things you must take into consideration in designing the comparative experiment.

8. Two kinds of machines are being assessed for capability to maintain tolerances. Ten parts produced on machine X and seven parts produced on machine Y are randomly selected from parts produced on the machines over the last week. The amount of deviation, in millimeters, from the nominal value for the parts is

    Machine X: 113, 102, 110, 119, 124, 116, 120, 115, 100, 128
    Machine Y: 109, 94, 118, 86, 102, 92, 120

    a. What analysis would you propose for the data?
    b. What would you like to know in addition to the data above?

Endnotes

1. Maybe there is, but it would be strictly fortuitous.
2. John Rydz, *Commonsense Manufacturing* (New York: Harper & Row, 1990), p. 177.
3. It *used* to be (prior to the 1970s) that US-manufactured products were perceived high in quality and in ability to meet customer needs, but that perception was due in large part to the relative lack of quality products made elsewhere with which to compare them. By today's standards, many of those same products would be perceived as poorly made and lacking in attention to important customer requirements.
4. Adapted from S. Wheelwright and K. Clark, *Revolutionizing Product Development* (New York: The Free Press, 1992), p. 178.
5. D. Whitney, "Manufacturing by Design," *Harvard Business Review,* July/August 1988, pp. 83–91.
6. B. Prasad, *Concurrent Engineering Fundamentals: Integrated Product and Process Organization* (Englewood Cliffs, NJ: Prentice-Hall, 1996); C.S. Syan and U. Menon, *Concurrent Engineering: Concepts, Implementation, and Practice* (London: Chapman and Hall, 1994).
7. Adapted from S. Wheelwright and K. Clark, *Revolutionizing Product Development,* p. 178.
8. J. Nicholas, *Managing Business and Engineering Projects* (Englewood Cliffs, NJ: Prentice-Hall, 1990), Chapters 5 and 6.
9. P. Smith and D. Reinertsen, *Developing Products in Half the Time* (New York: Van Nostrand Reinhold, 1991), pp. 224–5.
10. Ibid., p. 231.
11. Adapted from L.P. Sullivan, "Quality Function Deployment," *Quality Progress,* June 1986.
12. D. Whitney, "Manufacturing by Design," p. 85.
13. Portions adopted from K. Sabbagh, *Twenty-First Century Jet: The Making and Marketing of the Boeing 777* (New York: Scribner, 1996).
14. Adopted from J. Nicholas, "Concurrent Engineering: Overcoming Obstacles to Teamwork," *Production and Inventory Management Journal* 35, no. 3 (3rd Quarter 1994), pp. 18–22.
15. Sources for this section include G. Bounds, L. Yorks, M. Adams, G. Ranney, *Beyond Total Quality Management* (New York: McGraw-Hill, 1994), pp. 275–82; R. Fortuna, "Quality of Design," in Ernst & Young Quality Improvement Group, *Total Quality: An Executive's Guide for*

the 1990s, Chapter 8 (Homewood, IL: Dow-Jones Irwin, 1990); J. Hauser and D. Clausing, "The House of Quality," *Harvard Business Review,* May/June 1988, pp. 63–73.

16. For another example of quality of design in computer printers, *see* T. Survant, "Changing the Way We Think Is Key to Successful New Products," *Target* 11, no. 2 (March/April 1995), pp. 9–15.

17. R.E. Cole, "Large-Scale Change and the Quality Revolution," *Large-Scale Organizational Change* (San Francisco: Jossey-Bass, 1989), pp. 241–2.

18. A. Lockamy and A. Khurana, "Quality Function Deployment: A Case Study," *Production and Inventory Management Journal* 36, no. 2 (2nd Quarter 1995), pp. 56–59.

19. A more generic form of "design for" is called **design for X,** where X can stand for cost, simplicity, producibility, environment, or whatever else should matter to the designer. *See* S. Pugh, *Total Design: Integrated Methods for Successful Product Engineering* (Menlo Park: Addison-Wesley, 1991).

20. G. Boothroyd and P. Dewhurst, *Design for Assembly* (Wakefield, RI: Boothroyd-Dewhurst, Inc., 1987).

21. O. Port, "The Best-Engineered Part Is No Part at All," *Business Week,* May 8, 1989, p. 150.

22. G. Boothroyd and P. Dewhurst, *Design for Assembly*.

23. From J. Ingalls, "How Design Teams Use DFM/A to Lower Costs and Speed Products to Market," *Target* 12, no. 1 (Jan/Feb/March 1996), pp. 13–19.

24. D. Whitney, "Manufacturing by Design," p. 87.

25. Portions of this section are adapted from R. DeVor, T.H. Chang, J. Sutherland, *Statistical Quality Design and Control* (New York: MacMillan, 1992) and M. Phadke, *Quality Engineering Using Robust Design* (Englewood Cliffs, NJ: Prentice-Hall, 1989). *See also* G. Taguchi and D. Clausing, "Robust Quality," *Harvard Business Review,* January/February 1990, pp. 65–76.

26. For example, D. Montgomery, *Introduction to Statistical Quality Control* (2nd ed.) (New York: John Wiley & Sons, 1991), pp. 534–43.

CHAPTER 13 QUALITY INSPECTION AND STATISTICAL SAMPLING

Inspection, the first topic of this chapter, refers to the process of making systematic observations and comparing them to quality requirements or standards. For obvious reasons, inspection is fundamental to TQM. Quality-of-design efforts establish the necessary requirements and specifications on products, but without inspection there is no way of knowing whether the manufacturing process is meeting the requirements. This chapter introduces principles of inspection, the concept of inspection accuracy, and the role of inspection in quality management and control.

The other main topic of this chapter is statistical acceptance sampling. It is called acceptance sampling because, based on an inference about the batch made from the sample, the batch is either accepted or not accepted. The practice of acceptance sampling in some ways violates TQM philosophy because it assumes that a certain level of defects is acceptable and also because it is intended to discover defects that have already occurred, not to discover ways to prevent defects from occurring in the first place. Thus, the practice of acceptance sampling alone will never allow a company to achieve very high-level quality in its products. As the chapter explains, however, acceptance sampling can play a limited role in aspects of a quality-control program and is often used as a stepping stone to more effective quality control procedures. The focus of discussion in this chapter is on acceptance sampling for assessing the percentage of defective items in discrete batches, though it also reviews other procedures and applications of acceptance sampling, as well as the drawbacks.

ROLE OF INSPECTION

Inspection is a major element of TQM and an inherent part of the quality process. Even when inspection is not performed as a formal part of the production process, it happens anyway, by (as Deming says) the "inspector of last resort"—the final customer.

In past times the sole purpose of inspection was to weed out defects. In some organizations that is still the case. Batches of incoming parts and materials, and finished products are routinely inspected and bad items are separated from the good, or the entire batch is returned, reworked, or scrapped. Inspectors make periodic rounds in the plant to check in-process items, again for the purpose of weeding out defective items.

While this role potentially increases the quality of the product going to the final customer, it does nothing to alter *overall product quality*. This is because this kind of inspection does nothing to improve the *process*. Suppose an inspector finds that 1 in 10 products is defective and to handle the problem management assigns an additional inspector. The quality of the product sent to the final customer will likely improve since two inspectors can find more defects than one; the overall product quality, however, will not have been improved one iota since nothing was done to change the production process. The percentage of defective items produced, which is inherent to the number of defects introduced before and during production, remains the same. Besides, the cost of the process will have increased because two inspectors cost more than one. The role of inspection in TQM organizations is different: it is not to weed out defects, but to provide information about sources of defects and to eliminate those sources.

Whenever there is a quality problem, the magnitude of its impact (greater cost and waste, poorer service) is proportionate to how long it takes to discover and resolve the problem. In batch production, a mistake in setting up a machine that is not discovered until later affects every item in the batch. If discovered very early, only one or a few items will have been affected. If discovered many operations later, however, much or all of the work performed on every item in the batch will have been wasted, and every item will have to be scrapped or reworked. If the batch makes its way out of the plant and to the customer, the amount of waste increases again because of costs associated with warranties, returns, replacements, and loss of reputation, customers, and market share. To prevent all this, the role of inspection should be to monitor the process and to provide immediate feedback to workers and suppliers so they can make adjustments to the process before any defects occur.

CONFORMANCE TO SPECIFICATION AND FITNESS FOR USE

All inspection involves a judgment as to whether a unit or batch of a part, product, or service is acceptable. The judgment entails deciding the extent to which the item inspected is in **conformance** with some set requirement, standard, or limit. In this chapter we consider inspection for determining whether something is in conformance with product requirements. Recall from the previous chapter that requirements of performance and features of a product are defined in terms of a **target** or **nominal value** and a **tolerance,** where the tolerance is the permissible range of variation from the target.

When an item does not meet all the requirements, it is, by definition, judged as **nonconforming.** The terms defects, mistakes, nonstandard, and problems refer to any kind of nonconformity. For an item judged as nonconforming, an additional judgment arises: Is it still **fit for use?** Sometimes the magnitude of the nonconformity is severe, and the item must be reworked or discarded. Other times, the nonconformity is less severe and the item is still fit for use, though in ways or by customers other than originally intended. Factory seconds or irregulars are examples; they often end up with discount distributors or outlets and are offered at reduced prices. Regardless of the ultimate disposition of items, information about any nonconformity must be communicated upstream so that the producers can try to identify the source of the nonconformity and prevent it from recurring.

To achieve zero defects and world-class quality, a manufacturer must emphasize *conformance* to specifications, not simple fitness for use. When nonconforming items are deemed fit for use and are shipped, workers and inspectors get the impression that conformance to specifications is not really important and that even defective items can be acceptable. To prevent that kind of attitude from taking hold, workers and managers must know the distinction between complete conformance and simple fitness for use and must recognize the consequences of the two in terms of markets and profits. If the goal is 100% conformance, then the reaction to every nonconformance (even those classified as fit for use) must be the same: identify the source of the nonconformity and fix it. (In TQM operations, even conformance to requirements is not good enough; the goal is to exceed the requirements. But that is another issue and is addressed in the next chapter.)

ASPECTS OF INSPECTION

Inspection itself adds no value and is wasteful, so the ideal is not to have to do it at all. Paradoxically, one goal of quality inspection is to do it now so that, ultimately, it might not ever again have to be done. Although inspection can never be totally eliminated (even defect free processes require inspection to ensure they stay that way), through attention to quality of design and quality of inputs, both the frequency of inspection and the places in the process that require inspection can be reduced while the quality of the output is increased.

Throughout this and the next chapter we refer to different aspects of inspection. Following is a brief definition of terms used and of different ways of performing inspection.

1. *Inspection process*
   a. **Internal inspection:** Inspection conducted as part of the operation or work process (e.g., an assembler noting how well parts fit together).
   b. **External inspection:** Inspection conducted separate from the operation (e.g., an inspector measuring parts for tolerance fit).

2. *Inspection measurement*
   a. **Sensory inspection:** Inspection by human senses, including touch, vision, hearing, taste, smell, or perception (e.g., looking for scratches on lenses, general perception of the quality of room service in a hotel).
   b. **Physical inspection:** Inspection with instruments or devices (e.g., calipers, lasers, scales, thermometers, pressure sensors).

3. *Population inspected*
   a. **100% Inspection:** Inspection of every item or unit in the population (where *population* refers to a particular lot or batch of items or items produced by a particular process). This is also called *screening*.
   b. **Sample inspection:** Inspection of a fraction or subset of the population; the result is used to make an inference about the entire population.

4. *Inspection judgment*
   a. **Subjective inspection:** Inspection and conclusions made by the person who also did the work; also called *self-inspection.*
   b. **Objective inspection:** Inspection performed by someone other than the person who did the work. It includes *automated* inspection (mechanical devices) and *successive* inspection (inspection by downstream workers).
5. *Quality characteristics inspected*
   a. **Variables inspection:** Inspection of a feature that is represented and measured with a continuous numbering system or scale (e.g., physical dimensions, and features such as weight, pressure, and temperature).
   b. **Attributes inspection:** Inspection of a feature that falls into a simple classification scheme (e.g., conforming or nonconforming, defective or nondefective, poor/average/good, high or low).

As an example of these terms, consider an inspection on item X that is a subjective, external, sample, physical, and variables inspection. This implies that

· The inspector is the same person who worked on X.
· She inspects an item of X *after* she works on it.
· She inspects only a subset of all of the items on which she worked.
· She inspects each item with a measurement device.
· The device provides a numerical result using some scale.

INSPECTION LOCATIONS

The usual locations or places where an inspection is performed can be generalized as follows:

1. *Input inspection:* Inspection of inputs—such as parts and materials from suppliers—performed at the beginning of a process. This is also called *incoming inspection.* The purpose of input inspection is to prevent defective items from entering the process.
2. *Process inspection:* Inspection of items as they move between various stages of the process. The most common locations to perform process inspection are
   a. *Immediately after the setup* of an operation but *prior to the production* run, with the purpose of discovering and remedying setup mistakes before they can affect an entire batch.
   b. *Before moving* an item or batch from one operation (especially an operation prone to producing defects) to the next, with the purpose of precluding additional work on items that are already defective.
   c. *Before* performing an operation that hides defects or is irreversible, with the purpose of discovering defects while they are still discernable and can be readily fixed.
   d. *During* the actual running of the operation, with the purpose of tracking the operation, making sure it stays in control, and quickly rectifying any changes.

3. *Final inspection:* Inspection of finished goods at the completion of the process but prior to delivery to finished goods stores or the customer. The intent of final inspection is to discover defects that all of the above inspections might have missed.

Wherever inspection is performed, the overriding objective should not be to simply weed out defects or nonconformities but to identify the sources of defects as quickly as possible and take remedial action.

To ensure that inspection reveals nonconformities, inspection procedures must provide high-accuracy results.

INSPECTION ACCURACY

Inspection accuracy is the degree to which an inspection procedure provides correct results, either in terms of saying something about the status or state of affairs of the item inspected or of leading to conclusions about the item's conformance or nonconformance. The reason for choosing a particular procedure and location for inspection should be to attain the highest accuracy possible given product requirements and constraints on time, cost, and other resources.

As an example of the concept of accuracy, suppose 10 inspectors all examine an item using the same inspection procedure, and 6 conclude that the item is in conformance, while the other 4 conclude it is not. Clearly, the procedure does not give very accurate results since it leads to so much variation in conclusions. An improved procedure would give a unanimous judgment, or, say, 9 out of 10 in agreement. As another example, suppose five successive measurements are made of the thickness of the same metal plate, yielding the following, in centimeters:

$$0.013 \quad 0.012 \quad 0.014 \quad 0.010 \quad 0.011.$$

No two are alike. Now, while it might not be possible for inspection to achieve perfect accuracy (all results the same and all identical to the true or reference value), the accuracy must be high enough to enable inspectors to draw correct conclusions.

Inspection accuracy depends on the thoroughness of the inspection system and the degree of error introduced by people and instruments while doing the inspection measurement. Human error is a big source of inaccuracy when the inspection task is repetitive and boring. Even when it is not, errors occur because of inadvertent mistakes, inspection techniques that are mistake prone, and inspection procedures that involve judgment.

Steps to increase accuracy include improving inspection techniques to mistake proof them and improving inspection practices and judgments through better inspection training and definition of requirements. The requirements themselves (the specification of what constitutes conformity) must be clear and unambiguous. Requirements definition is sometimes improved through use of photographs and physical samples. Inspectors at a clothing manufacturer, for example, use cloth swatches to show the permissible shades of color. Colors fade, so the swatches themselves must be checked and replaced.

BIAS AND PRECISION

Two aspects of inspection accuracy are bias and precision.

Bias is the systematic tendency for an inspection technique to yield results that differ in one direction (larger or smaller) from the accepted (true) reference value. Bias is caused by a measurement instrument being out of calibration or improperly used or by an inspector or method that is predisposed to inflate or deflate the results.

Precision refers to the extent to which an inspection technique yields similar results when the inspection is repeated on the same item. If multiple inspections of the same item give similar results, then the method is precise; if they vary widely, the method is imprecise. Imprecision is also caused by worn or improperly used instruments or by methods or procedures that allow or encourage variability between measured results.

High accuracy means *both* high precision and low bias. Figure 13.1 shows the four possible bias–precision combinations. The desired combination is number 1. All inspection methods result in *some* bias and imprecision, and in each case the acceptable level of bias and imprecision must be determined. Ways to measure accuracy are described next. Methods for determining the required accuracy and for controlling and reducing measurement errors are provided in statistical quality control books.[1]

FIGURE 13.1

Precision–bias relationship to accuracy.

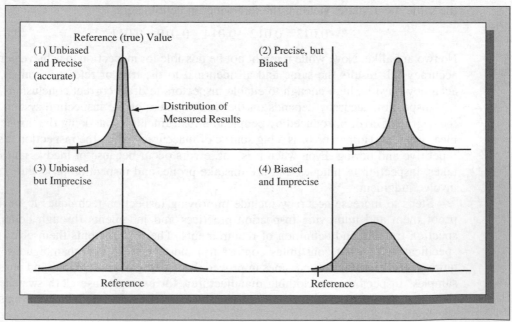

Bias Measure

A measure of bias is the **average error,** which is the average difference between inspection results and a prespecified reference value:

Average Error = (Average Measurement) − (Reference Value).

For example, suppose the thickness of a metal plate, which is *known* to be (has a reference value of) 0.011 cm, is measured five times, and the results, in centimeters, are 0.013, 0.012, 0.014, 0.010, 0.011. The average of the five results is 0.012, so

Average Error = 0.012 − 0.011 = 0.001 cm.

Thus, the inspection procedure gives measured results that are, on average, 0.001 cm too large.

It is important to note that in determining the average error, the number of inspections, n, must be large enough to conclude that the inspection process is stable. Although the above example used $n = 5$ to simplify the presentation, in practice such an n would be too small to provide results that could be trusted. As a rule of thumb, the number of inspections should be at least 20, though more is better.[2]

Precision Measure

Precision is measured by the variability or spread among the inspection results: the smaller the variability, the greater the precision. One gauge of precision is the **standard deviation,** s. Standard deviation is a measure of the amount by which individual results vary from the average of all the results. If the variability in inspection results is assumed to conform to a normal distribution, then about 67% of the inspection results will lie within one standard deviation of the average value; about 95% will lie within two standard deviations; and over 99% will lie within three standard deviations. This is shown in Figure 13.2.

FIGURE 13.2

Areas under normal distribution.

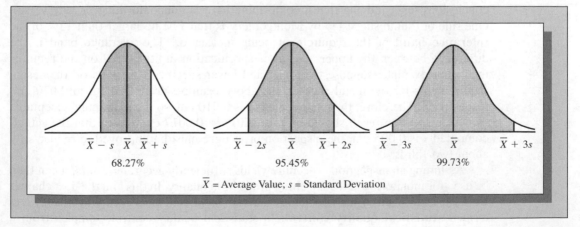

$\overline{X} - s$ $\overline{X}$ $\overline{X} + s$ $\overline{X} - 2s$ $\overline{X}$ $\overline{X} + 2s$ $\overline{X} - 3s$ $\overline{X}$ $\overline{X} + 3s$

68.27%   95.45%   99.73%

$\overline{X}$ = Average Value; s = Standard Deviation

To compute the standard deviation using inspection results, start with the **mean squared error (MSE),**

$$MSE = \frac{\Sigma \ (Average \ Result \ - \ Individual \ Result)^2}{n - 1}.$$

In the example, the average of the five inspections is 0.012 cm. The differences between this average and the five individual results are

$$-0.001 \quad 0 \quad -0.002 \quad 0.002 \quad 0.001.$$

Squaring these gives

$$0.00001 \quad 0 \quad 0.00004 \quad 0.00004 \quad 0.00001.$$

Their sum is 0.00010. Therefore,

$$MSE = 0.00010/4 = 0.000025.$$

Now, by definition, the standard deviation is the square root of the MSE,

$$s = \sqrt{MSE},$$

so

$$s = \sqrt{0.000025} = 0.005.$$

We can thus conclude that repeated measurements with the same inspection procedure would yield results in which, referring to Figure 13.2, 67% fall within 0.005 cm of the mean of 0.012 cm, 95% fall within 0.010 cm, and over 99% fall within 0.015 cm.

REQUIRED ACCURACY

The allowable degree of inspection bias and imprecision in a given situation is dictated by the requirements placed on the process or item being inspected. The requirements must be considered, lest the inspection technique yield results leading to the wrong conclusions (e.g., judging that a conforming item is nonconforming or vice versa). One rule of thumb suggested by Montgomery is that s be no larger than 17% of the **tolerance band** of the requirement being measured.[3] The tolerance band is the difference between the upper and lower specification limits placed on the requirement. For example, suppose the upper and lower specification limits on the design requirements for the metal sheet in the above example are 0.010 cm to 0.020 cm, respectively. Therefore, the tolerance band is 0.010 cm, so the maximum acceptable s of the inspection result should be $0.17(0.01) = 0.0017$ cm. Given that the actual, computed s is 0.005 cm, the inspection procedure must be improved to reduce s by about two-thirds.

Assuming an inspection procedure yields sufficiently accurate results, it can then be used for monitoring and controlling production quality. In this and the next chapter we look at inspection methodologies derived from statistical sampling theory and termed **statistical quality control.** In statistical quality control, samples from a population are inspected for the purpose of making statistical inferences about the total population. The two main approaches in statistical quality control are **acceptance sampling** and **statistical process control (SPC).** Acceptance sampling is discussed in the following section; SPC is discussed in the next chapter.

ACCEPTANCE SAMPLING[4]

Acceptance sampling (AS) is the process of determining the acceptability of a quantity of items based upon inspection of a sample of the items. AS is commonly used for items obtained or produced in discrete lots, such as a shipment of items received from a supplier or a quantity of items made in a production batch. AS can, however, also be used to monitor the acceptability of items which do not fall into natural lots, such as items produced continuously on a production line.

As an example of how AS works, suppose the acceptance standard used by a hot dog vendor is that 98% of the buns in each shipment from the supplier must be obviously fresh, which he judges using the criterion of soft to the touch. Each morning when he receives a batch of buns from the bakery, he picks a few packages at random, squeezes them, then decides to accept or reject the entire shipment. As another example, a padlock manufacturer tests the brittleness of samples from a batch of lock casings after they have been heat treated. If some of the casings fail, then a few more are tested. If these all pass, then the entire batch of casings is accepted, but if a certain number of these fail, then every remaining casing is tested so the failed ones can be sorted out.

Although the intent of sampling is to provide information leading to an accept or reject decision, the decision is often not that simple. Rejecting a batch can be costly and problematic (what does the hot dog vendor use for buns if the shipment is returned?) and, as a result, a reject decision might be followed by actions other than simply rejecting the batch. Typical alternatives include inspecting additional samples, accepting the batch but paying a lower price for it, or screening. When the batch is supplied by a supplier, the terms of acceptance and return costs are arranged contractually in advance.

PROS AND CONS OF AS

Acceptance sampling might be necessary when

- The cost of inspection is very high relative to the consequences of accepting a defective item.
- The inspection is destructive (items are destroyed in the process of being inspected).
- The inspection procedure is tedious and screening is likely to result in low inspection accuracy.
- The process is not stable and SPC techniques as discussed in the next chapter do not apply.

When inspection is costly or very difficult to perform, or when the repercussion of a few defects going undetected is small, then AS makes economic and practical sense. When the inspection requires destroying an item to determine its acceptability, AS also makes sense, since, in lieu of sampling, the entire batch would have to be destroyed to judge its acceptability! When the quantity involved is very large, and when the fatigue and monotony of inspecting every item would lead to mistakes, AS might make sense then, too. In most of these cases, however, the reason for doing AS is the same: economy. Simply, it is less costly to inspect a few items than all items.

The drawback with AS is that it cannot guarantee that the sample items chosen for inspection are accurate representations of the larger batch. As a result, there is always some risk in AS of drawing the wrong conclusion, and that is one reason against using AS. In addition, and a more damning reason, is that the practice of AS provides little information about the sources of problems leading to nonconformities. What information it does provide is too late. The lock manufacturer described above, for example, discovers problems with the heat treating process only *after* it has produced an entire batch. Because AS happens after the fact, some, much, or all of the batch might have to be reworked or scrapped. Although rejecting an entire batch *is* strong incentive to find what caused the problem, AS itself will provide little information about the cause.

Nonetheless, AS can serve a role (albeit a limited role) in continuous improvement through periodic auditing of batches to ensure that inputs (components, raw materials) and outputs (items produced in lots) do not contain more than a certain prescribed level of defectives. Some examples of this are given later.

ECONOMICS OF AS

When items are produced in a batch, and when the production process is stable and the output is uniform, only then should the first and last items in the batch be inspected. If the two are conforming, then everything in between is assumed to be conforming also. If inherent uniformity cannot be guaranteed throughout the process, then additional items must be sampled to assess the state of the process between start and finish.

Economic analysis can be used to determine whether to do zero inspection, 100 percent inspection, or sample inspection (i.e., AS). The analysis considers the trade-off of the cost of defectives and the cost of inspection. Suppose the process is stable, and that

D = cost of a defective (nonconforming) item being missed,
I = cost of inspecting an item,
N = total batch size,
p = actual percentage of defective (nonconforming) items.

With no inspection the total inspection cost is zero, but the total defective cost will be NpD. With 100 percent inspection the total inspection cost is NI, but then the total defective cost is then zero. Given that the break-even point is $NpD = NI$, define the break-even proportion defective as $p_b = NI/ND = I/D$. Thus, when

$p < p_b$, it is more economical to use sampling or no inspection.

$p \geq p_b$, it is more economical to screen (100 percent inspection).

For example, suppose $D = \$15$ per unit and $I = \$0.30$ per unit. Then $p_b = I/D = 0.30/15 = 0.02$. Thus, when the average quality of a batch of this item is thought to be worse than 2%, screening is more economical than sampling; but when the average quality is better than 2%, no inspection is necessary.

It should be noted, however, that this kind of analysis assumes complete stability in the process. When the quality is known to vary from batch to batch, or when the process is unstable, then sampling is *necessary,* even when p is close to p_b or somewhat better on average. It is common in batch production for the average output to vary somewhat from batch to batch owing to slight differences in machine setups, materials, and operators.

Given that a decision has been made to assess quality by using samples, then the size of the sample, n, must be determined. The size of the sample to be used depends on the percentage of defective items anticipated in the process and on the level of risk considered tolerable for drawing an incorrect conclusion. We consider the matter of risk next, then explain its relation to the sample size.

RISK OF SAMPLING ERROR

Any judgment about a population based upon a sample can be wrong since seldom does the composition of the sample exactly replicate the parent population. Although the sample is the basis for judging whether to accept or reject a batch, the percentage of nonconforming items in the sample will usually be slightly larger or smaller than in the total population. Such is the risk of sampling.

Types of Risk

Two types of risks are associated with sampling:

- Mistakenly rejecting a good batch. This is called a **type I error,** and the probability of this error is called **alpha** (α).
- Mistakenly accepting a bad batch. This is called a **type II error,** and probability of this error is called **beta** (β).

Alpha is also called the **producer's risk,** and beta is also called the **consumer's risk.** For example, the risk of the hot dog vendor mistakenly rejecting a fresh (acceptable) batch is the producer's (the baker's), risk, while the risk of the vendor mistakenly accepting a stale (unacceptable) batch is the consumer's (the vendor's) risk. These terms and associated probabilities are summarized in Table 13.1.

The level of both risks is a function of the sample size: the larger the sample size, the smaller the risks. With a 100% sample size, assuming perfect inspection accuracy,

TABLE 13-1

	Batch Quality (in fact)	
Decision	*Acceptable*	*Unacceptable*
Accept batch	Correct decision $1 - \alpha$	Type II error β (consumer's risk)
Do not accept batch	Type I error α (producer's risk)	Correct decision $1 - \beta$

the risk is zero; with a tiny sample size, the risk is high. The point is, when the inspection procedure involves sampling, the first step is to decide what level of risk (i.e., probability of an incorrect judgment) is considered tolerable. Based on that, it is then possible to determine the size of the sample that will yield that level of risk.

Acceptable Quality: AQL and LTPD

An objective in using acceptance sampling is that good batches have a high probability of being accepted, and bad batches have a low probability. With that objective in mind, we define the following quality levels:

· **Acceptable quality level** or **AQL.** This is the maximum allowable percentage of defective (nonconforming) items in a batch for it to be considered definitely good.

· **Lot tolerance percent defective** or **LTPD.** This is the percentage of defective items necessary in a batch for it to be considered definitely bad. (LTPD is always higher than AQL.)

For example, if we set AQL = 2% and LTPD = 8%, then a sample with an average of 2% or fewer defective items will indicate that we should accept the batch, whereas a sample with an average of 8% or more defective items will indicate that we should not accept the batch.

Different samples from the same batch or process will not all show the same percentage of defective items. Even if the actual average of defective items in the entire batch is exactly the AQL, different samples will show defective levels larger or smaller than the AQL. That is the nature of sampling. The range between the AQL and the LTPD takes this variability into account, but sets a maximum level of defective items in the sample (LTPD) above which a batch should *definitely not* be accepted.

The relationship between the α and β risks, and the AQL and the LTPD, is shown in Figure 13.3. On the figure, the terms are interpreted as follows:

· The probability of accepting a batch (P_a) with AQL percentage of defective items (a definitely good batch) = $1 - \alpha$.

· The probability of accepting a batch (P_a) with LTPD percentage of defective items (a definitely bad batch) = β.

FIGURE 13.3

Relationship among α, AQL, β, LTPD, and the OC curve.

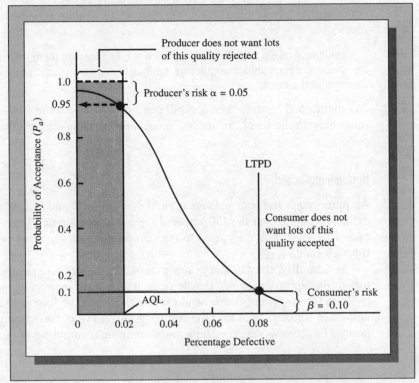

Figure 13.3 shows AQL = 2%, α = 5%, and LTPD = 8%, β = 10%. These two combinations for probability of acceptance and percentage of defective items form two points. The curve connecting the two points on the figure is called the operating characteristics (OC) curve.

The OC Curve

In general, the relationship between the probability of accepting a batch and the actual percentage of defective items in the batch is represented by the **operating characteristics curve,** or **OC curve.** The OC curve shows the probability P_a that a batch with a specified (though unknown) percentage of defective items will be accepted when a sample of given size is used. The OC curve in Figure 13.3 is an example. The dotted line indicates that if a batch were actually to contain 2% defective items, a sample (of some specified size n) would lead to accepting the batch 95% of the time.

The interpretation of the OC curve in Figure 13.3 is that inspection of a sample of some size n will lead to acceptance of a bad batch (8% defective or worse) 10% of the time, and acceptance of a good batch (2% percent defective or less) 95% (100% − 5%) of the time. We will refer back to Figure 13.3 momentarily.

SAMPLING PLANS

The procedure for doing AS involves a **sampling plan.** The simplest kind of sampling plan consists of two parameters, a sample size n and an acceptance value c. The plan says:

> randomly take n sample items from a batch and inspect them; if c or fewer of the sample items are nonconforming, accept the batch; if more than c are nonconforming, do not accept the batch.

(As mentioned before, "not accept" can mean to reject the batch, screen every item remaining in the batch, or defer the decision pending the results of additional sampling.)

Determining n and c

As mentioned, the four parameters [AQL, $(1 - \alpha)$] and [LTPD, β] on Figure 13.3 define two points on the OC curve. In general, the shape of the OC curve is determined by the relative location to the two points and whatever will enable it to pass through them.

In actuality, the OC curve represents a cumulative hypergeometric distribution (or similar approximation), the shape of which is a function of the parameters n and c. Once the two points have been established from the four parameters, values for n and c are selected such that the resulting OC curve passes through (or nearby) both points. In other words, the steps in determining a sampling plan are as follows:

1. Set the four parameters (α, β, AQL, LTPD), hence defining the two points.
2. Find values of n and c such that the resulting curve fits the points.

Detailed computation of the hypergeometric distribution is unnecessary since the values for n and c are available in published standard tables.[5] Although the OC curve for values of n and c from the tables might not exactly pass through the two specified points, it will be close. The following example illustrates one of many procedures for using the standard tables to determine n and c for a sampling plan.

Example   1:   Procedure to Determine n and c for a Sampling Plan

The procedure is as follows:

1. Set the LTPD and AQL. Suppose LTPD = 5% and AQL = 2%.

2. Compute the ratio of LTPD/AQL. The ratio = 2.5.

3. Refer to Table 13.2 and find the entry in column (2) equal to or slightly larger than this ratio. The closest entry in the table is the last one, 2.50.

4. Refer to the corresponding entry in column (1) of the table. The entry is $c = 10$.

TABLE 13-2   Parameters to Define Attributes Sampling Plans ($\alpha = .05$, $\beta = .10$)

(1) *c*	*(2)* *LTPD/AQL*	*(3)* *(AQL)n_α*
0	45.10	.051
1	10.96	.355
2	6.50	.818
3	4.89	1.366
4	4.06	1.970
5	3.55	2.613
6	3.21	3.285
7	2.96	3.981
8	2.77	4.695
9	2.62	5.425
10	2.50	6.169

5. Refer to the corresponding entry in column (3), and divide the entry by the AQL to get the sample size, *n*. The entry in column (3) is 6.169 and AQL = 0.02, so 6.169/0.02 = 308.

The resulting sample plan says to inspect 308 items and accept the batch if the number of defective items is 10 or fewer.

When the AQL and the LTPD are set close together, then the resulting OC curve will be very steep. The corresponding *n* will be large, sometimes so large that the sample size is nearly 100%. To reduce the sample size, the values of the AQL and the LTPD must be set farther apart. In Example 1, suppose that the computed sample size of 308 is deemed too large to be practical. Instead of LTPD = 5% and AQL = 2%, select values that are farther apart, say LTPD = 6% and AQL = 1%. The procedure explained in the example will then give *n* = 82 and *c* = 2.

Although it is a simple matter to adjust the LTPD and the AQL to derive a smaller sample size, obviously small sample size should not, in itself, be the goal. In general, the smaller the sample size, the greater the probability that a batch with an unacceptably high percentage of defective items will be accepted. The converse holds for larger sample sizes. As the sample size is *increased* for a given acceptance number *c*, the OC curve becomes steeper, which means the sample inspection becomes more discriminatory and the risk of accepting a bad batch is reduced. This can be seen by comparing curves 2, 3, and 4 in Figure 13.4. Similarly, when the value of the acceptance number *c* is decreased for a given sample size *n*, the curve gets steeper, which means better protection against accepting a bad batch. This also is shown in Figure 13.4 (compare curves 1 and 2). In summary, the risk associated with any sampling plan depends on

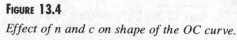

FIGURE 13.4

Effect of n and c on shape of the OC curve.

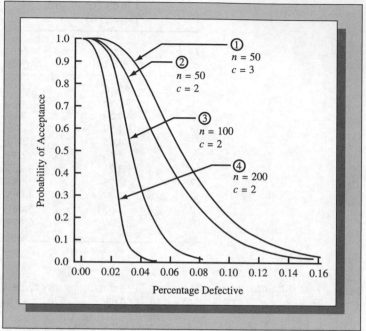

the sizes of n and c: the larger the n and the smaller the c, the lower the risk. Values for n and c should not be selected arbitrarily, but according to the desired level of risk as defined by the AQL and the LTPD.

The values in Table 13.2 assume $\alpha = 5\%$, $\beta = 10\%$, and a fairly large batch size. When the batch size is not large, the values for n and c derived from the table will actually yield more accurate sampling judgments, so the risks of error, α and β, will be less than 5% and 10%, respectively. As an example, had the total batch size (population) in the preceding example numbered 82 items or fewer, then α and β would both have been reduced to zero because 82 was the sample size, and the inspection would have been 100%.

AVERAGE OUTGOING QUALITY

The OC curve is but one way to gauge the effectiveness of a sampling plan. Another measure is the resulting **average outgoing quality (AOQ)** of batches after they have been inspected. Assume that rejected batches are *screened,* which means all the items in them are inspected and nonconforming items are sorted out and replaced with conforming items. Thus, batches that were initially rejected and then screened will have *no* defective items. The batches that were originally accepted, however, will still contain defective items. Now, if the accepted batches are combined with the batches that were rejected and screened afterward, then the AOQ is the *average percentage defective* of the combined batches.

The AOQ depends on p, the actual proportion of defective items in a batch (prior to inspection), as well as the characteristics of the sampling plan.

For very large batches,

$$AOQ = pP_a(p),$$

where

p = percentage defective in the batch,
$P_a(p)$ = probability of accepting a batch with p percentage defective.

For smaller batches,

$$AOQ = \frac{pP_a(p)(N - n)}{N},$$

where

N = batch size,
n = sample size.

The value of $P_a(p)$ is determined for corresponding values of p from the OC curve, which, of course, depends on a given sampling plan defined by n and c. In Figure 13.3, for example, when $p = 0.08$, $P_a(p) = 0.10$.

An example of how the AOQ changes with varying levels of p is shown in Figure 13.5. At $p = 0$, AOQ = 0, and as would be expected, as p increases, so does

FIGURE 13.5

AOQ as a function of percentage defective.

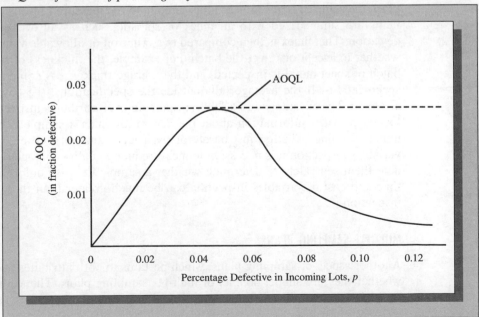

the average percentage defective (AOQ) of the outgoing batches. As the percentage of defective items in the batches increases so does the proportion of the bad batches that are discovered and rejected (the greater the number of defective items, the more likely they will be discovered). These batches are then screened such that no defective items from them will be passed along. As the proportion of batches rejected continues to increase (which happens as the percentage of defective items in the batches continues to increase), the percentage of defective items passed along decreases because ever-greater numbers of batches are subjected to screening.

Of interest is the peak of the curve, the worst possible average outgoing quality. This, called the **average outgoing quality limit** or **AOQL,** represents the maximum percentage of defective items, on average, that will be passed along from the inspection process.

Each sampling plan (*n* and *c* combination) yields different probabilities of acceptance, so each has a different AOQ curve. By comparing the AOQ curves for different plans, a sampling plan can be selected to achieve a desired AOQL.

VARIABLES SAMPLING PLANS

Whenever an inspection procedure gives results that are categorized or fall into simple classifications (unacceptable vs. acceptable, defective vs. nondefective, etc.), it is called **attributes inspection.** The hot dog vendor judges buns as either fresh or stale; the lock manufacturer judges casings as OK or too brittle. The sampling plan in such cases, and the one described in Example 1, is called an **attributes sampling plan** because inspections result in the item being classified as either defective or nondefective.

Another form of inspection is **variables inspection.** In a **variables sampling plan,** the sampled items are each measured, and the measured results of the sampled items are summarized with an index or statistic, such as an average or standard deviation. That index is then compared to a criterion or allowable value to determine whether to accept or reject the batch. For example, the thickness of samples from a batch of sheet metal is inspected, and the average thickness is compared to product specifications. If the average falls outside the specifications, the batch will not be accepted. The advantage of variables inspection over attributes inspection is that the former provides information about the *degree* to which a sample is conforming or nonconforming (whether just barely or by a large amount). Often, however, with variables inspection it is necessary to measure many quality characteristics and evaluate them separately to determine whether a sample item is conforming. Thus, the time and cost of variables inspection can be much greater than those for attributes inspection.

MULTIPLE SAMPLING PLANS

Another aspect of sampling plans, which pertains to both attributes and variables, is whether they are single, double, or multiple sampling plans. The sampling plan described earlier is called a **single sampling plan** because it prescribes a single random sample of size n to make a judgment. With a **double sampling plan,** an initial sample is taken, and based upon the sample a decision is made to accept or not to accept, *providing* that the acceptance criterion is either clearly met or not met. If the decision is unclear, then a second sample is taken, and the results of the two samples are combined to reach a decision.

Example   2:   Application of Double Sampling[6]

The variables in a double sampling plan are defined as follows:

n_1 = size of first sample,

c_1 = acceptance number of first sample (maximum number defective to allow acceptance based on first sample),

n_2 = size of second sample,

c_2 = acceptance number of first and second samples combined (maximum number defective to allow acceptance based on both samples).

Suppose the double sampling plan specifies $n_1 = 36$, $c_1 = 0$, $n_2 = 59$, and $c_2 = 3$. Then the plan would be interpreted as follows:

1.   Select a sample of size 36.

2.   If the sample has zero defective units, accept the batch.

3.   If the sample has more than three defective units, reject the batch.

4.   If the sample has one, two, or three defective units, select another sample, this time of size 59.

5.   If the number of combined defective units in the first and second samples is three or fewer, accept the batch.

6.   If the number of combined defective units in both samples exceeds three, reject the batch.

   Multiple sampling plans do more of the same. Three, four, or more successive samples might be taken before making a decision to reject or accept a batch. With each sample, the result is compared to an upper and lower value to determine whether to reject, accept, or sample again. The plan specifies the maximum number of sampling steps and opportunities to make a decision, after which the batch is automatically rejected. The advantage of double and multiple sampling plans is that, given equivalent probability of accepting a lot of specified quality, the average size of each sample is less than with single sampling plans, so the average number of items that must be inspected to reach a decision is less. Producers (suppliers) prefer double and multiple plans because they are given two (or more) chances for acceptance. The disadvantage of double and multiple sampling plans is that they are more time-consuming and costly to administer than single sampling plans.

AS FOR CONTINUOUS PRODUCTION PROCESSES

So far, all the discussion of AS has focused on sampling plans employed for acceptance of items produced in discrete batches. AS sampling procedures also exist for items continuously produced. The goal of **sampling plans for continuous production** is to monitor the average quality level of items produced over the long run. The plans involve alternating between screening and sampling inspection as defined by two parameters, i and f, where

> i = the number of successive items inspected (screened) that must be conforming before switching to sampling.
>
> f = proportion of successive items to sample.

When i successive items are found to conform, the inspection switches to sampling. For example, say $i = 54$ and $f = 1/4$. That means inspect all items, and when 54 items in succession are found to conform, then begin random inspection of only one out of every four units produced thereafter. Whenever a defective unit is found, reinstate screening.

A policy value, S, specifies the maximum number of consecutive units screened, at which point it will be necessary to take action, such as suspending production or deliveries and determining the source of the defects.

PUBLISHED TABLES

Values of parameters n and c for single and multiple sampling plans and for f and i for sampling continuous processes are published in standard tables included in textbooks on statistical quality control, such as those included in the references.[7] The most popular tables are **mil std** (military standard) and **Dodge-Romig.** The mil-std tables were developed during WWII and have since been revised and become the most widely used acceptance sampling procedures in the world. The civilian version of mil std is called ANSI/ASQC Z1.4 and is quite similar to the military standard. The **mil-std-105** tables include sampling plans and OC curves for single, double, and multiple sampling of batches; **mil-std-1235** tables are for continuous sampling. The mil-std tables include provision for normal, tightened, or reduced levels of inspection; tightened levels are applied when recent quality has deteriorated and reduced levels are applied when recent quality has been very good. The mil-std tables create a sampling plan based upon a desired AQL and are applied in a way similar to that of Table 13.2 in Example 1. Since several possible sampling plans are given for each AQL level, the one selected depends on the batch size and desired level of inspection.

The Dodge-Romig tables give two types of sampling plans—one for LTPD protection, the other to provide a specified AOQL. The LTPD protection of Dodge-Romig plans is preferred to AQL-oriented plans (mil std) for critical parts, such as electronics components. The LTPD sampling plans are designed so that the probability of acceptance for a desired LTPD is 0.1% (0.001). The Dodge-Romig plans assume that rejected lots will be subject to screening, which must be the case otherwise the AOQL concept would be meaningless.

AD HOC PLANS

Sometimes people think statistical acceptance plans are unnecessary and that simple ad hoc plans are just as good. An example of an ad hoc plan is to arbitrarily decide to inspect 5% of the items in a batch, and reject the batch if one unit is defective. A second example is to inspect one item, and if it is defective, to inspect another, and if that is defective too, to reject the batch. Ad hoc plans do not take into account the risks of accepting bad batches, rejecting good batches, or, for that matter, what constitutes a good batch or a bad batch. The risks associated with ad hoc plans are often very high. For example, the plan in the second example gives a 75% probability of accepting a batch that is 50% defective![8] So if you must do AS, use a statistical-based plan.

AS: ROAD TO TOTAL QUALITY AND WORLD CLASS?

Acceptance sampling is a way to, post facto, assess the quality of a batch or process. It is not a way to control a process. Because of the nature of sampling, even when batches are identical, some will be accepted while others are rejected. Since AS appraises what has already been done, not what is being done, TQM organizations do not rely on it much. They do not use AS for incoming inspection because they do not *do* incoming inspection. Instead, they rely on their suppliers to guarantee zero defects and to keep their processes stable. Neither do they use AS for monitoring production processes, even when they produce in batch quantities, because to them judging the disposition of a batch *postprocess* is too late. They want information about operations in-process, not afterward, so they can fix problems and defects while they are still small and insignificant. AS is not much good for any of this.

Besides, for organizations striving to eliminate defects, the concept of AQL is a concession to less-than-perfect quality, a compromise that sets the level of defects that is allowable. Some Japanese suppliers are puzzled at the AQL concept, since they are more accustomed to providing 100% quality (AQL = 0). The following is a case in point:

> Apparently [IBM] decided to have some parts manufactured in Japan as a trial project. In the specifications, they set out the limit of defective parts that would be acceptable at 3 units per 10,000. When the delivery came in, there was an accompanying letter. "We Japanese have a hard time understanding North American business practices. But the 3 defective parts per 10,000 have been included and wrapped separately. Hope this pleases.[9]

Also, as organizations set higher quality goals (lower AQLs), the practice of AS becomes increasingly more impractical because it requires such large sample sizes. For tiny AQL levels, the sample sizes could, theoretically, exceed the size of the batch. For example, an AQL of 0.001 requires samples of magnitude 1000; an AQL of 0.0001, samples of magnitude 10,000. Companies that have reached TQM status no longer think in terms of percentage defects. Instead, they think in terms of defective parts per million (ppm). Even a firm that has reduced its average defect rate to 1% is

CASE IN POINT: AS for Continuous Improvement at NASA[10]

A review of items received from suppliers at NASA Langley Research Center indicated that over 10% were defective. To address the problem, the center set out to develop a sampling inspection program that would not only reduce the defect rate, but serve as a means to keep reducing it.

The existing incoming inspecting process used a traditional sampling plan with acceptance of a batch predicated on meeting an acceptance value, c. The acceptance value c was often greater than zero, and the center's management realized this was inconsistent with their quality goal of zero defects. The existing process also involved significant costs. For batches that failed the initial inspection, the current plan called for additional inspection, screening, or both, the additional effort and cost for which fell entirely on the center's receiving group.

A new acceptance program called zero acceptance was developed. The new program put full responsibility for quality on the suppliers and motivated continuous quality improvement. The major features of the new program included the following practices:

1. Only incoming batches with zero defects in the sample will be accepted ($c = 0$).

2. When a defect is identified in a sample, the batch will be returned to the supplier. The supplier will assume full responsibility for assuring that all items returned to the center meet specifications. A supplier that has three batches returned will be removed from the vendor list.

Though technically not capable of guaranteeing zero defects, a sampling plan with $c = 0$ does provide superior defect protection and require fewer inspections than do plans with $c > 0$. For a given percentage defective in a batch, a plan with $c = 0$ always has a lower probability of acceptance than a plan with $c > 0$. As an example, refer to Figure 13.6, which compares the mil-std-105 and zero-acceptance OC curves for one case, AQL = 2.5% and lot sizes between 91 and 150 units. The probability of acceptance for any lot percentage defective is always less for the zero-acceptance plan than for the mil-std plan. For instance, for a lot with 10% defective items, the chance of acceptance with the standard plan is 40%, but is 31% with the zero plan. This means that the zero-acceptance plan is more discriminating.

Further, as shown in Table 13.3, the zero-acceptance plan uses smaller samples sizes. Using, for example, a lot size between 501 and 1200, the standard plan calls for a sample size of $n = 80$ whereas the zero-acceptance plan calls for $n = 19$. In fact, the actual average sample size with zero acceptance is usually *much* less than for standard plans since for $c = 0$ the inspection stops as soon as even one defect is encountered, which is usually well before the full sample is inspected.

NASA Langley Center implemented the new sampling plan and notified suppliers that batches failing to meet the zero-defect standard would be returned. The center offered consultation and site visits to assist suppliers in improving their quality programs.

In the first year of the program, the average incoming percent defect rate was cut roughly in half, and management expected that the rate would drop somewhat further. With so much less required for inspection, the receiving group now has more time for pinpointing quality problems and working with suppliers. In many cases, suppliers have been able to improve their internal processes and to suggest to NASA substitutions for items of better quality at equal or lower prices.

FIGURE 13.6

OC curves for zero acceptance and mil std 105.[11]

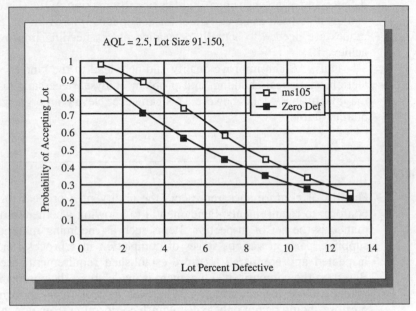

TABLE 13-3   Sample Size Comparison, AQL = 2.5[12]

| | Mil Std 105 Plan | | Zero-Defect Plan | |
Lot Size	Sample Size	Accept/ Reject	Sample Size	Accept/ Reject
2–8	5	0/1	5	0/1
9–15	5	0/1	5	0/1
16–25	5	0/1	5	0/1
26–50	5	0/1	5	0/1
51–90	20	1/2	7	0/1
91–150	20	1/2	11	0/1
151–280	32	1/2	13	0/1
281–500	50	2/3	16	0/1
501–1200	80	5/6	19	0/1
1,201–3,200	125	7/8	23	0/1
3,201–10,000	200	10/11	29	0/1

not doing all that well: 1% is the equivalent of 10,000 defective ppm. TQM companies are accustomed to working at defect levels of 100, 50, or even 10 ppm. One hundred ppm translates into a defective percentage rate of 0.0001, for which it would be ludicrous to apply AS.

Yet there are places for AS in organizations aspiring to world-class quality status, such as when inspection is destructive, until suppliers accept responsibility for zero defects, and as an occasional audit device. By making AQLs successively smaller, AS can even be used as an early tool for continuous improvement, although other techniques are needed to actually determine places needing improvement and ways to achieve it.

Thus, AS can improve quality and help lead to the kind of systematic data collection, statistical thinking, and problem analysis necessary to advance quality in manufacturing. Alone, however, AS can never elevate an organization to world-class quality status.

Summary

Quality of conformance represents the ability of a process to produce items that conform to requirements. Fundamental to knowing whether something is in conformance is the act of inspection. Items such as incoming materials received from a supplier, parts at various stages of completion in a process, or finished goods are inspected and compared to a pre-established requirement, specification, or limit. Based on the comparison, a judgment is made about the conformance or nonconformance of the inspected items. Wherever inspection is performed, the overriding purpose should be not only to distinguish conforming from nonconforming items, but also to identify sources of nonconformance so quick remedial action can be taken.

The validity of inspection depends in part on the accuracy of the inspection procedures, sensors, and measuring devices. The degree of accuracy required in an inspection depends on the process and product requirements: the narrower or tighter the requirements, the greater the accuracy necessary to check those requirements.

Inspection to monitor quality using samples and statistical theory is called statistical quality control. One form of statistical quality control, acceptance sampling, is used to determine the *acceptability* of a quantity of items based upon inspection of a sample. Acceptance sampling is implemented by using a sampling plan. Because statistical procedures rely on samples to make inferences about a larger population, there is always some risk of drawing incorrect conclusions about the population. Thus, part of choosing a sampling plan is to specify the level of acceptable risk in using the plan. For a specified level of risk, the basic sampling plan consists of two parameters, the sample size (number of items to inspect), and the maximum allowable number defective for accepting the batch (acceptance number). When the allowable number of defective items is exceeded, the alternatives are to reject the entire batch, inspect all of the remainder of the batch, or take another sample. Acceptance sampling can be done with multiple, successive samples, and on items produced continuously as well as in batches. Sampling plans for specified risk levels and batch sizes appear in published tables, the most common being mil std 105 and Dodge-Romig.

Acceptance sampling is applicable where inspection involves destructive testing, the mandated level of quality is not very high, and as an interim measure until more effective quality control procedures can be implemented. Today, world-class organizations demand exceedingly high levels of quality measured in terms of number of defective parts per million. Acceptance sampling is inadequate for such high quality standards because it would require sample sizes of extreme size. Beyond that, acceptance sampling runs counter to modern manufacturing practices and JIT/TQM philosophy, which is to build in quality, eliminate waste, and continuously improve. Since acceptance sampling happens *after* a batch has been received or produced, any items found defective must be reworked or scrapped, and the sources of defects are often difficult to determine after the fact.

In contrast, statistical process control (SPC) focuses on the process producing the items and seeks to identify potential defect-producing problems and resolve them before damage can occur. As a result, SPC allows for a much higher level of quality control than does acceptance sampling. SPC, the subject of the next chapter, along with source inspection and pokayoke, the subjects of Chapter 15, are the bread-and-butter quality-of-conformance tools for world-class manufacturers.

Questions

1. What role does inspection play in TQM? How does the role of inspection differ from what it was in the past?

2. Explain the terms target (or nominal) value and tolerance.

3. Distinguish between conformance and fitness for use.

4. What is the difference between sensory inspection and physical inspection? Give examples of both.

5. What is the difference between variables inspection and attributes inspection? Give examples of both.

6. Consider the following measurements:

discoloration of part	scratch on glass
tensile strength of part	part missing from component
diameter of O-ring	weight of an assembly
brittleness of O-ring	loose fastener
error in order entry	ft-lbs of torque on fastener

   Are they attributes or variables? Explain. Discuss which can be either or both.

7. Discuss the difference between measurement precision and measurement bias.

8. What is the purpose of acceptance sampling? List some cases where acceptance sampling is necessary. What are the significant drawbacks of relying on acceptance sampling for ensuring conformity to requirements and as a basis for continuous improvement?

9. Distinguish between a type I error and a type II error. What do the probabilities α and β signify?

10. Define the meaning of AQL and LTPD. Give an example using both.

11. Explain the trade-off on the OC curve between sample size n and the difference between AQL and LTPD.

12. Define sampling plan.

13. Explain the concept of AOQL.

14. Suppose the AQL for a product is 0.001%. For acceptance sampling of batches of this product, what magnitude of sample size is required? Why does this kind of acceptance sampling make little sense?

Problems

1. A circuit board costs $0.75 per unit to inspect, though the cost of replacing a defective board after it is installed in a computer is $75.
   a. What is the break-even probability? Interpret what this means in this case.
   b. Currently, screening reveals an average of five defective boards out of every batch of 1,000 units. If each computer contains two of these boards, how much is the manufacturer saving or losing per computer with the current inspection practice?

2. An instrument measures the diameter of a part as 9.7456 cm. A study of the instrument reveals the following:

   Accuracy: −0.0035 cm (instrument reads this amount low)

   Precision: 0.0015 cm (one standard deviation)

   What can you say about the true value of the 9.7456-cm diameter just measured?

3. A rod is measured by an inspector 10 times using two micrometers, X and Y. The results in centimeters follow:

Measurement	Model X	Model Y
1	8.7437	8.7441
2	8.7438	8.7441
3	8.7440	8.7442
4	8.7437	8.7440
5	8.7439	8.7441
6	8.7438	8.7442
7	8.7437	8.7442
8	8.7436	8.7441
9	8.7438	8.7440
10	8.7437	8.7440

The true rod diameter is given as 8.7440 cm. Calculate the accuracy and precision of each of the instruments. Suppose the tolerance band specified for the rod is 0.0005 cm. Comment on the adequacy of the two instruments.

4. Rico Industries produces thousands of units of a part each day. The maximum acceptable defective level for the part is 2%, and no more than 5% defective can be tolerated. Assuming $\alpha = .05$ and $\beta = .10$, determine the sampling plan (n and c).

FIGURE **13.7**

OC curve for problem 8.

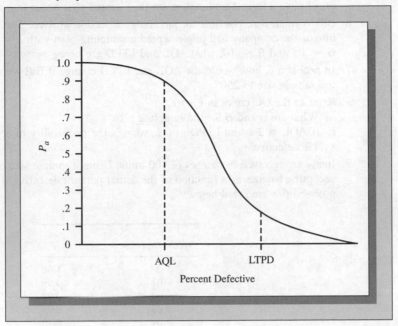

FIGURE **13.8**

OC curve for problem 10.

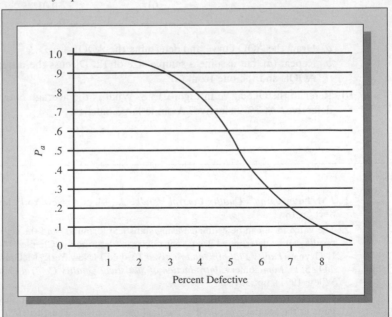

5. Rico Industries has decided to tighten its quality standards for parts, with the AQL being 1% and LTPD being 3%. Assuming $\alpha = .05$ and $\beta = .10$, what is the sampling plan? Give a logical explanation for the changes that occur in n and c from problem 1.

6. Bill Wyman is responsible for incoming inspection at Rico. The manager who preceded him at the company had implemented a sampling plan with $n = 199$ and $c = 7$. If $\alpha = .05$ and $\beta = .10$, what AQL and LTPD are being assumed here?

7. In problem 6, how would the AQL and LTPD change if Bill were willing to increase the sample size to 250?

8. Refer to the OC curve in Figure 13.7.
   a. What are α and β for the sampling plan?
   b. If AQL = 2% and LTPD = 6%, what is the probability of accepting a batch that is 4% defective?

9. Items are received in batches of 100 units. Using a sample size of 9, the probability of accepting batches as a function of the actual percent defective is determined. The probabilities are listed below.

Percent Defective	P_a
.00	1.00
.01	0.99
.02	0.97
.03	0.95
.04	0.70
.05	0.38
.06	0.12
.07	0.06
.01	0.01

   a. Draw the AOQ curve and determine the AOQL.
   b. Repeat (a), but assume a sample size of 12. Discuss the difference between this AOQL and the one from (a).

10. Refer to the OC curve in Figure 13.8. What is the average outgoing quality at 2% defective? At 7% defective? Assume large batches.

Endnotes

1. J.M. Juran, *Juran's Quality Control Handbook* (4th ed.) (New York: McGraw-Hill, 1988), Section 18.

2. The value for n can be estimated using statistical formulas, and the stability of the measurement results can be determined using control charts (described in Chapter 14). *See*, e.g., J. Juran and F. Gryna, *Quality Planning and Analysis* (3rd ed.) (New York: McGraw-Hill, 1993), pp. 213, 444–5; D. Montgomery, *Introduction of Statistical Quality Control* (2nd ed.) (New York: John Wiley, 1991), pp. 391–3.

3. Based on the assumption that a measurement device should be calibrated in units one-tenth as large as the accuracy required of the final measurement. Thus, $6s/(USL\text{-}LSL) \leq 0.1$, or

$s \leq 0.167$ (*USL-LSL*), where s is the standard deviation, and *USL* and *LSL* are the upper and lower specification limits, respectively. *See* D. Montgomery, *Introduction to Statistical Quality Control.*

4. For in-depth discussion of statistical acceptance sampling, *see* J. Banks, *Principles of Quality Control* (New York: John Wiley, 1989); E. Grant and R. Leavenworth, *Statistical Quality Control* (6th ed.) (New York: McGraw-Hill, 1988); D. Montgomery, *Introduction to Statistical Quality Control.*

5. When the batch size is large, at least 10 times the size of the sample, then the curve can be determined using a binomial distribution, or, in cases where the proportion defective is small (typical in product AS), it can be approximated using the simpler Poisson distribution.

6. *See* E. Grant and R. Leavenworth, *Statistical Quality Control*, pp. 409–13 for discussion and analysis of this example.

7. *See*, for example, J. Banks, *Principles of Quality Control* and D. Montgomery, *Introduction to Statistical Quality Control.*

8. $P_a = P$ (Accept First) $+ P$ (Reject First, accept second)
   $= 0.50 + 0.50(0.50) = 0.75.$
   If the batch were 70% defective, there would still be a 51% chance of acceptance $(0.30 + 0.70(0.30) = 0.51).$

9. H. Gitlow and S. Gitlow, *The Deming Guide to Quality and Competitive Position* (Englewood Cliffs, NJ: Prentice-Hall, 1987), p. 32.

10. P. Kauffman and C. Cockrell, "Strategic Management of Receipt Inspection," *Production and Inventory Management Journal* 37, no. 3 (1996), pp. 47–51.

11. Ibid. This figure originally appeared as Figure 2 on p. 49. Reprinted with permission of APICS, The Educational Society for Resource Management, Falls Church, VA.

12. Ibid. This table originally appeared as Table 1 on p. 49. Reprinted with permission of APICS, The Educational Society for Resource Management, Falls Church, VA.

STATISTICAL PROCESS CONTROL

Every manufacturing process produces output that is variable in some way, though as long as the variability remains small, it is inconsequential to quality. Statistical process control is a way to monitor a process to determine when the variability *is* consequential, that is, when the process has changed from an expected performance level to a different, potentially harmful level. Methods of statistical process control, or SPC, are used not only for tracking and control, but also for assessing the capability of a process. Given design specifications for a product, a production process is capable only if a very high proportion of the output lies within the specifications. If the process is not capable, then SPC provides a way to set improvement targets and to monitor improvement progress. This chapter considers all of these matters, as well as particular SPC methods, SPC implementation, and the role of SPC in continuous process improvement.

VARIATION IN PROCESSES

It is a fact that every process, natural or humanmade, is variable. Nothing happens exactly the same again and again. Celestial bodies wobble in their orbits, subatomic particles behave with uncertainty, and, in between, outputs from human production and service operations are in constant flux. The changes in production output from one unit to the next might be very small, but when measured with sufficient accuracy they are always evident. This continuous variation in output has two basic causes: common causes and special causes.

COMMON CAUSES

Common causes of variation are small, random forces that act continuously on a process. Celestial bodies wobble because of slight changes in external gravitational fields and in internal forces (plate tectonics, volcanic eruptions) that subtly influence mass and momentum. Outputs of human manufacturing processes vary because of small fluctuations in operating environment (temperature, humidity, barometric pressure), small equipment vibrations, small variations in the materials used, and so on. When a process varies in such a way that, over time, it becomes predictable, then the causes of the variation are referred to as **common, chance, or system** causes. Such causes of variation are fundamental or endemic to the process.

Consider a process that manufactures metal shafts. Although each shaft has a slightly different length, when a large number of shafts are taken together the lengths are seen to fall nicely into a frequency distribution with a fixed mean and standard deviation. Suppose, for example, that the lengths of many shafts are measured, and the accumulated results lie in a normal distribution with a mean of $\mu = 8.520$ cm and a standard deviation of $\sigma = 0.00775$ cm. Now, if the causes of the variation are common causes, then the lengths of shafts produced in the future will *continue* to fall in this same distribution. In that case, we can accurately predict the likelihood that any shaft will be of a given length. In general, as long as the outputs of a process lie within the expected amount of variation, variation that results from common causes, then the process is said to be **in statistical control** or, simply, in control.

SPECIAL CAUSES

Special causes of variation produce differences in output that are abnormal and cannot be predicted. These causes are extraneous to the process and disrupt or interfere with the routine operation and normal dynamics of the process. Special causes are also called **assignable causes** because the variation they produce is out of the ordinary and can often be traced back to them. For example, a special cause of planetary wobble is a collision of the planet with a large asteroid. The collision would cause a big deviation from the planet's normal wobble and perhaps even send the planet into another orbit. The collision is a special event, not part of the usual system of forces acting on the planet. Such an event happens infrequently, and it is not possible to accurately predict its precise effect. Noting the abnormal wobble, however, astronomers can tell that something special happened to cause it.

In a manufacturing process, examples of special causes of variation in output include a machine wearing out or drifting out of calibration, an inferior batch of raw materials used in the product, a poorly trained operator, an incorrect work method, or a rapid change in plant temperature. Any of these would cause special variation in the process output, variation that could not have been predicted and that, unless rectified, could harm the quality of the output of the process.

Suppose in the shaft example that the machine that regulates shaft length begins running erratically and produces shafts with lengths that are slightly longer on average than before. The fact that the process has changed fundamentally, that is, that the shaft lengths are no longer represented by the statistical distribution determined earlier ($\mu = 8.520$ cm and $\sigma = 0.00775$ cm), symbolizes that the process has been affected by a special cause. Whenever a process is judged to have been influenced by a special cause, the process is said to be **out of control.**

TAKING ACTION

In manufacturing it is important to be able to distinguish whether a process is in control or out of control because each requires **taking different action.** For variation that appears to stem solely from common causes (situation in control), usually no immediate action is required (this statement is qualified and will be elaborated on later in the discussion of process capability). However, for variation that appears to have come from a special cause (situation out of control), immediate action is necessary to determine what happened (find the assignable cause) and to rectify the situation.

For example, if variation in shaft lengths is determined to have occurred because of common causes, then the process need not be stopped because the variation is as expected and the process is predictable. If, however, the variation is suspected to have come from a special cause, then the process must be stopped, the possible special cause found, and the process restored.

STATISTICAL PROCESS CONTROL

With **statistical process control (SPC)** methods and periodic process inspection, we can determine whether a process is staying in control or is potentially moving out of control at a given point in time.

It is important to note here a big difference between the purposes of SPC and **acceptance sampling,** discussed in Chapter 13. Whereas acceptance sampling seeks to determine the acceptability or conformance of outputs, in SPC no such judgment is made about the *goodness* or fitness of a process or its outputs. That is a separate issue. In fact, only *after* a process or output has been deemed good (how that is done is addressed later) does SPC have a role. Given that we have a good process, we then use SPC as a tool to monitor the process and make sure it does not change. In the shaft example, recall that the process $\mu = 8.520$ cm and $\sigma = 0.00775$ cm. If we decide to employ SPC, the tacit *assumption* is that this process is desirable and should be retained. We then track the process with SPC to make sure that the mean and standard deviation do not change.

Having made the assumption that the existing process is good and should be retained, we can implement the SPC procedure as follows:

1. Periodically select from the process a sample of items, inspect them, and note the result.
2. Because of common or special causes, the results of every sample will vary. Determine whether the cause of the variation is common or special.
3. Take action depending on what was determined in (2).

This procedure is enacted through the use of **control charts.**

CONTROL CHARTS

Suppose we employ SPC to monitor the length of metal shafts from the above example. Assume the parameters of the process output have been determined, $\mu = 8.520$ cm and $\sigma = 0.00775$ cm, and that these parameters have been judged to be acceptable. The SPC procedure will then be used to monitor the process for any special changes. As long as there are no special changes, the process is in control.

COLLECTING DATA AND PLOTTING POINTS

Perform step (1) of the SPC procedure by periodically taking samples. Suppose we use a sample size of five and sample every 0.5 hour (how often and how much should be sampled are discussed later). Measure the shafts and compute the mean length. Suppose the shafts in one sample have the following lengths, in centimeters:

8.526   8.511   8.528   8.518   8.513

The mean length of the sample (total divided by 5) is 8.519 cm. Suppose we repeat this procedure several times.

Table 14.1 shows the results for six samples. Figure 14.1 shows the plotted sample means; the process mean is also shown for reference (assume the process mean, $\mu = 8.520$ cm, as determined earlier). As expected, the points vary.

Every time we measure a sample of shafts and record the mean length on the chart, we make a judgment as to whether the process is still in control or has moved out of control. This is step (2).

TABLE 14-1   Results from Six Samples

Sample*	X (Measured Results)					Mean
1	8.526	8.511	8.528	8.518	8.513	8.519
2	8.521	8.515	8.513	8.520	8.517	8.517
3	8.512	8.529	8.521	8.522	8.525	8.522
4	8.522	8.516	8.521	8.523	8.519	8.520
5	8.523	8.517	8.525	8.524	8.520	8.522
6	8.511	8.518	8.513	8.516	8.517	8.515

*Samples contain five shafts and are taken 30 minutes apart.

FIGURE 14.1

Average (Mean) shaft lengths from Table 14.1.

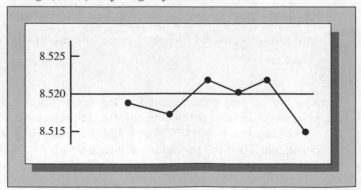

FIGURE 14.2

Out-of-control situations: (a) change in process mean; (b) change in process standard deviation.

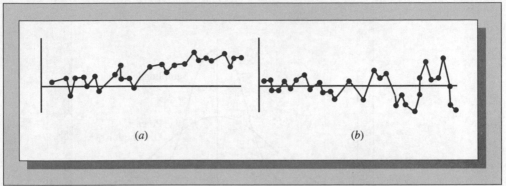

(a)   (b)

Given that we expect the average lengths to vary from sample to sample, we must determine whether the amount of variation is normal (from common causes) or abnormal (from a special cause). To this end, assuming we know the population mean shaft length (8.520 cm), we can draw logical conclusions just by comparing individual sample means, or a string of sample means, to that mean.

If the causes of variation are common, then the sequence of points on the chart should appear random. Whenever a sequence shows an apparent upward or downward trend, lies predominantly above or below the process mean, or shows an increase or decrease in variation, that suggests possible nonrandom behavior and a special cause. Figure 14.2 shows two examples, a sequence with an upward trend (*a*), suggesting that the process mean is drifting, and a sequence with increasing dispersion (*b*), suggesting the process standard deviation is increasing. Although the process in (*b*) appears random, it is nonrandom in the sense that the standard deviation is systematically increasing. Both (*a*) and (*b*) indicate fundamental changes in the process distribution and a special cause. Detailed rules for determining whether a sequence of points is random and constitutes in-control behavior are given later.

Another way to determine whether a process is in control is to compare the result with the process mean each time a sample is taken; the closer the result is to the process mean, the more likely it is that the cause of the variation was common, not special. Look, for example, at samples 5 and 6 in Table 14.1. If we assume that both samples were drawn from the same process ($\mu = 8.520$ cm, $\sigma = 0.00775$ cm), then we can compute the probability that each would come from that process. To show how we do that, we need to first consider the sampling distribution.

Sampling Distribution

In SPC, practically everything we know about a process is based upon samples. Unless we sample 100%, we never see the actual process distribution. In our example, what we know about the process is what we see from samples of size five, and it is the mean of each sample, not the values of the individual five shafts, that we use to track the process.[1] Therefore, to determine the probability with which observed samples

FIGURE 14.3

Process distribution and sample distribution.

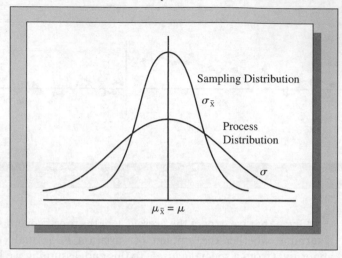

having certain means should occur, we rely not on the process distribution, but on the **sampling distribution of the mean.** The sampling distribution is what we see as a result of taking samples repeatedly. The following, illustrated in Figure 14.3, characterize the sampling distribution of the mean:[2]

- It is a normal distribution.
- It has a mean of $\mu_{\bar{X}} = \mu$, where μ is the mean of the process.
- It has a standard deviation of $\sigma_{\bar{X}} = \sigma\sqrt{n}$, where σ is the process standard deviation and n is the sample size.

From here on we refer to $\mu_{\bar{X}}$ and $\sigma_{\bar{X}}$ instead of μ and σ. Returning to the example, $\mu = 8.520$ and $\sigma = 0.00775$; therefore,

$$\mu_{\bar{X}} = 8.520 \qquad \text{and} \qquad \sigma_{\bar{X}} = \frac{0.00775}{\sqrt{5}} = 0.00347.$$

Given that the sampling distribution is normal, we can compute the probability that a sample mean of a given size or larger would occur in a distribution with parameters $\mu_{\bar{X}}$ and $\sigma_{\bar{X}}$ using the formula $z = (X - \mu_{\bar{X}})/\sigma_{\bar{X}}$.[3] Going back to the sample means for samples 5 and 6, 8.522 and 8.515, respectively, we can compute the probability that each came from the presumed process:

$$z = \frac{8.522 - 8.520}{0.00347} = 0.576 \quad \text{for the first sample.}$$

Similarly,

$$z = -1.441 \quad \text{for the second sample.}$$

Using the standard table of z-statistics, Table 14.2,

$$P(z \geq 0.576) = 0.50 - 0.2177 = 0.2823,$$

$$P(z \leq 1.441) = 0.50 - 0.4253 = 0.0747.$$

TABLE 14-2   Areas under the Normal Curve, 0 to z

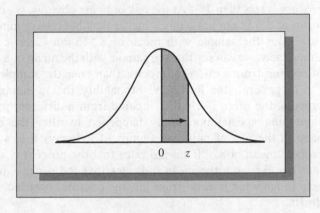

z		.00	.01	.02	.03	.04	.05	.06	.07	.08	.09
0.0	. . . . .	.0000	.0040	.0080	.0120	.0160	.0199	.0239	.0279	.0319	.0339
0.1	. . . . .	.0398	.0438	.0478	.0517	.0557	.0596	.0636	.0675	.0714	.0753
0.2	. . . . .	.0793	.0832	.0871	.0910	.0948	.0987	.1026	.1064	.1103	.1141
0.3	. . . . .	.1179	.1217	.1255	.1293	.1331	.1368	.1406	.1443	.1480	.1517
0.4	. . . . .	.1554	.1591	.1628	.1664	.1700	.1736	.1772	.1808	.1844	.1879
0.5	. . . . .	.1915	.1950	.1985	.2019	.2054	.2088	.2123	.2157	.2190	.2224
0.6	. . . . .	.2257	.2291	.2324	.2357	.2389	.2422	.2454	.2486	.2517	.2549
0.7	. . . . .	.2580	.2611	.2642	.2673	.2703	.2734	.2764	.2794	.2823	.2852
0.8	. . . . .	.2881	.2910	.2939	.2967	.2995	.3023	.3051	.3078	.3106	.3133
0.9	. . . . .	.3159	.3186	.3212	.3238	.3264	.3289	.3315	.3340	.3365	.3389
1.0	. . . . .	.3413	.3438	.3461	.3485	.3508	.3531	.3554	.3577	.3599	.3621
1.1	. . . . .	.3643	.3665	.3686	.3708	.3729	.3749	.3770	.3790	.3810	.3830
1.2	. . . . .	.3849	.3869	.3888	.3907	.3925	.3944	.3962	.3980	.3997	.4015
1.3	. . . . .	.4032	.4049	.4066	.4082	.4099	.4115	.4131	.4147	.4162	.4177
1.4	. . . . .	.4192	.4207	.4222	.4236	.4251	.4265	.4279	.4292	.4306	.4319
1.5	. . . . .	.4332	.4345	.4357	.4370	.4382	.4394	.4406	.4418	.4429	.4441
1.6	. . . . .	.4452	.4463	.4474	.4484	.4495	.4505	.4515	.4525	.4535	.4545
1.7	. . . . .	.4554	.4564	.4573	.4582	.4591	.4599	.4608	.4616	.1625	.4633
1.8	. . . . .	.4641	.4649	.4656	.4664	.4671	.4678	.4686	.4693	.4699	.4706
1.9	. . . . .	.4713	.4719	.4726	.4732	.4738	.4744	.4750	.4756	.4761	.4767
2.0	. . . . .	.4772	.4778	.4783	.4788	.4793	.4798	.4803	.4808	.4812	.4817
2.1	. . . . .	.4821	.4826	.4830	.4834	.4838	.4842	.4846	.4850	.4854	.4857
2.2	. . . . .	.4861	.4864	.4868	.4871	.4875	.4878	.4881	.4884	.4887	.4890
2.3	. . . . .	.4893	.4896	.4898	.4901	.4904	.4906	.4909	.4911	.4913	.4916
2.4	. . . . .	.4918	.4920	.4922	.4925	.4927	.4929	.4931	.4932	.4934	.4936
2.5	. . . . .	.4938	.4940	.4941	.4943	.4945	.4946	.4948	.4949	.4951	.4952
2.6	. . . . .	.4953	.4955	.4956	.4957	.4959	.4960	.4961	.4962	.4963	.4964
2.7	. . . . .	.4965	.4966	.4967	.4968	.4969	.4970	.4971	.4972	.4973	.4974
2.8	. . . . .	.4974	.4975	.4976	.4977	.4977	.4978	.4979	.4979	.4980	.4981
2.9	. . . . .	.4981	.4982	.4982	.4983	.4984	.4984	.4985	.4985	.4986	.4986
3.0	. . . . .	.4987	.4987	.4987	.4988	.4988	.4989	.4989	.4989	.4990	.4990

Thus, the probability that a mean of 8.522 or larger came from the presumed process is about 28%, and the probability that a mean of 8.515 or smaller came from the same process is less than 1%. At the risk of being obvious, we can say that the sample with mean of 8.522 cm has a much higher likelihood of coming from the original process than does the sample with mean of 8.515 cm (28% compared to less than 1%). Conversely, we can say that the sample with the mean of 8.515 has a greater likelihood of coming from a different process than does the sample with mean 8.522.

In general, the lower the probability that a sample came from the original process, the more likely that it came from a different process, which is to say that something special potentially happened to alter the original process. Referring back to the plot of points in Figure 14.1, it says that a point that lies close to the process mean of 8.520 cm indicates that the process is still in control, whereas one that lies far from the mean indicates that the process might be out of control. To help judge what is close from far, the control chart includes criteria called **control limits.**

CONTROL LIMITS

A sample result that is judged far from the process mean is one that, statistically, has a very small chance of occurring in a process with specified parameters. That is to say, the sample result could have occurred from common causes, though the probability is very small, and more likely the result was caused by something special. As a gauge of what constitutes too far, the control chart has two limits, an **upper control limit (UCL)** and a **lower control limit (LCL).** A point lying on or outside of these limits indicates that a process is possibly out of control.

Position of Upper and Lower Limits

The UCL and LCL are located equidistant from the process mean, the **center line (CL)** on the chart. This is illustrated in Figure 14.4. The limits are positioned far enough away from the center line so that the probability of a point lying outside of them for the given process is very small. This is the same as saying that a point lying so far from the center line is unlikely to have originated from common causes. Figure 14.5 demonstrates this concept. The original distribution (*a*) is the one being monitored. The control limits have been set such that only a small percentage of sample points from this distribution would ever fall outside the limits (shaded area). The figure also shows what would happen if the process were to change in any of three possible ways; a change in the mean (*b*), a change in the standard deviation (*c*), and a change in both the mean and the standard deviation (*d*). Note in cases (*b*), (*c*), and (*d*) the relatively large proportion of points that would lie outside the original control limits (shaded areas).

Suppose we position the control limits so that only 5% of the sampled means from a given process will fall on or outside those limits. Given such a small percentage,

FIGURE 14.4

Position of limits on a control chart.

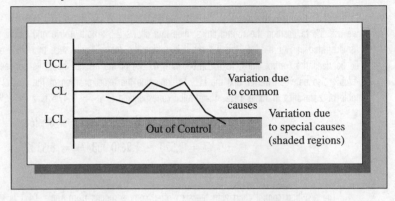

FIGURE 14.5

Proportion of out-of-control points for different process distributions.

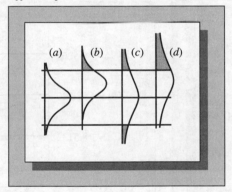

a point that lies outside those limits is likely to represent an out-of-control situation and warrant an investigation.

The limits are positioned with the formulae

$$UCL = \mu_{\overline{X}} + z\sigma_{\overline{X}},$$

$$LCL = \mu_{\overline{X}} - z\sigma_{\overline{X}},$$

$$CL = \mu_{\overline{X}}.$$

This kind of chart is called a **means control chart** because it is used for the purpose of monitoring the average, or mean, of a process. Given this chart, we periodically draw samples, compute the mean, and plot it. Any mean that falls on or outside the limits is regarded as a potential out-of-control situation and should be investigated.

Example   1:   Constructing a Means Control Chart

In the shaft example, assume that the sampling parameters of $\mu_{\bar{x}} = 8.520$ and $\sigma_{\bar{x}} = 0.00347$ are known. If we use 5% to position the control limits, then that allows 2.5% both above and below the UCL and LCL, respectively. As illustrated in Figure 14.6, this will result in setting the control limits such that 95% of the sample results should lie between the control limits. As a consequence, 47.5% of the results should lie between the CL and the UCL, and 47.5% also between the CL and the LCL. To determine the exact position of the control limits, refer to the standard table of z-statistics in Table 14.2. The z-value corresponding to $p = 0.475$ is $z = 1.96$. Therefore,

$$UCL = 8.520 + 1.96(0.00347) = 8.5268,$$

$$LCL = 8.520 - 1.96(0.00347) = 8.5132,$$

$$CL = 8.520.$$

The resulting control chart with the six plotted sample means from Table 14.1 is shown in Figure 14.7.

FIGURE 14.6

Location of control limits.

FIGURE 14.7

Means control chart.

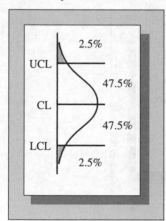

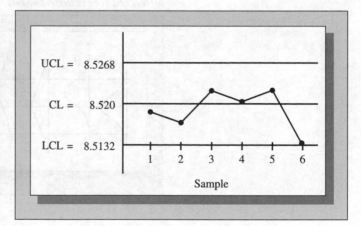

Risks of Error

Of course there is a hitch. Although points lying on or outside the control limits will in most cases correctly indicate an out-of-control situation, occasionally they will indicate the wrong thing. Go back to the example where the control limits were set using a 5% probability: this means that given that the presumed process has not changed, 5% of the sample means can be *expected* to lie outside the limits. In other words, there is a 5% chance that the process will be judged out of control when actually it is not. And, when that happens, the process will be stopped and the search will begin for an assignable cause even though *none exists*. The paradox is that when a process is mistakenly deemed out of control, a mistaken cause might be found and fixed, which would then actually alter the process and really put it out of control.

As with acceptance sampling, there are thus risks in SPC of making wrong decisions. Concluding that a process is out of control when, in fact, it is in control is a **type I error.** The probability of a type I error is **alpha,** α. In the example, α was chosen to be 5%. Split equally, this is represented by $\alpha/2 = 2.5\%$ in Figure 14.6.

Since the probability of a type I error is α, and since the size of α is a matter of choice, why not simply make α (and, hence, the risk of a type I error) much smaller (say, 0.001% instead of 5%)? The reason is that as α is made smaller, the control limits are moved farther away from the CL. Moving the limits outward certainly reduces the risk of mistakenly assuming a situation is out of control, but it creates another problem—that of not being able to accurately judge when a process is *actually* out of control. The farther out the limits are placed, the greater the likelihood they will accommodate points from an abnormal deviation and allow an out-of-control situation to go undetected. This leads to the error of concluding that a process is in control when actually it has moved out of control, a **type II error.** As α is reduced, the risk of a type II error is made larger. The terms are summarized in Table 14.3.

Because of the trade-off between type I and type II errors, common practice is to set the control limits at *three sigmas* ($\mu_{\overline{X}} \pm 3\sigma_{\overline{X}}$), which corresponds to an α of 0.026%.[4] Control charts may additionally include one- and two-sigma limits (z is 1 and 2, resp.,) for use with rules to help detect nonrandom behavior. Within a sequence of points, even when none fall outside the control limits, the process is considered out of control if the sequence of points is nonrandom. For determining nonrandom behavior, the control chart is divided into six zones, each zone one $\sigma_{\overline{X}}$ wide, shown in Figure 14.8. A process is considered out of control for any of the following five situations:

Situations Out of Control
1. A point lies outside the control limits.
2. Any two of three consecutive points fall in the same A zone.
3. Four out of five consecutive points fall in the same B zone.
4. Eight or more consecutive points lie on the same side of the CL.
5. Eight or more consecutive points move continuously in the same direction, either upward or downward.

From here on, our examples will focus on control charts with three-sigma limits only.

TABLE 14-3   Errors in Process Control

	Process (in fact)	
Conclusion	*In Control*	*Out of Control*
In control	Correct conclusion	Type II error
Out of control	Type I error	Correct conclusion

FIGURE **14.8**

The A, B, and C zones for a control chart.

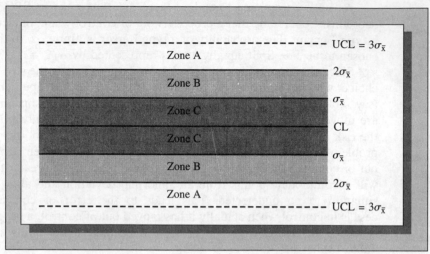

There are actually several different kinds of control charts, each used to monitor something different about a process. To determine the control limits for the means control chart described above, the parameters μ and σ for the actual process must be known. Unless the process is long running and unusually stable, the actual parameters will ordinarily not be known. In that case, control charts must be constructed with the use of *estimated parameters*. Among different kinds of control charts constructed from estimated parameters, four will be discussed: **X-bar charts, R-charts, p-charts,** and **c-charts.**

X-BAR CHARTS

Although every process has a target value, only rarely will outputs of the process ever hit that value, no matter how good the process. In the shaft example, the target length is, say 8.520 cm, however because of common-cause variation, seldom will a particular shaft ever be of length *exactly* 8.520 cm. Thus we settle for a process that *on average* produces outputs of a particular value (e.g., shafts of a particular length); in fact, because of difficulties or costs associated with setting up a process, the particular value we settle for might not (probably won't) even be exactly the same as the target value.[5]

Stated another way, since any given process produces variable outputs, we must settle for a process that furnishes outputs that, *on average,* approximate some pre-specified, sought-after value. To monitor the average we use an **X-bar chart.** The purpose of an X-bar chart is to make sure a process remains centered, that the average of the process is hitting the prespecified, sought-after value. (If process parameters μ and σ are known, we could use instead the means control chart discussed before. We are, however, presuming now that those parameters are unknown.)

Like the means control chart, the X-bar chart has a center line and control limits. As long as the sample means are random and fall within the control limits on the X-bar chart, the process is considered centered and the variation is attributed to common causes. Should the sample means take on a nonrandom pattern or move beyond the control limits, then a special cause is presumed, and the mean is assumed to have shifted.

On the X-bar chart,

$$UCL = \bar{\bar{X}} + 3\sigma_{\bar{X}}$$

$$LCL = \bar{\bar{X}} - 3\sigma_{\bar{X}}$$

$$CL = \bar{\bar{X}},$$

where

$\bar{\bar{X}} = \Sigma\, \bar{X}_i/m$, the average mean for all the samples, $i = 1, \ldots, m$,
$\bar{X}_i$ = average mean for sample i, $\Sigma\, X/n$,
$\sigma_{\bar{X}} = \sigma/\sqrt{n}$,
 n = sample size,
 m = number of samples.

Since the population standard deviation often cannot be determined, an estimate for σ is used:

$$\sigma = \bar{R}/d_2,$$

where

$\bar{R} = \Sigma\, R_i/m$, the average range for all the samples, $i = 1, \ldots, m$,
R_i = range for sample i (difference between largest and smallest values in sample i),
d_2 = a factor to convert average range into the estimated population standard deviation.

Values for d_2 for sample size n are found in standard tables such as Table 14.4. Therefore,

$$UCL = \bar{\bar{X}} + 3\bar{R}/d_2, \qquad (1)$$

$$LCL = \bar{\bar{X}} - 3\bar{R}/d_2.$$

The above formulae give three-sigma ($z = 3$) limits, and it should be apparent how they would be modified to get one- or two-sigma limits.[6] The formulae for three-sigma limits can be simplified with the substitution $A_2 = 3/d_2$:

$$UCL = \bar{\bar{X}} + A_2\bar{R}, \qquad (2)$$

$$LCL = \bar{\bar{X}} - A_2\bar{R},$$

where values of A_2 for sample size n are given in Table 14.4.

TABLE 14-4   Control Chart Constants

Number of Observations in Subgroup/Sample, n	$d_2 = \dfrac{\overline{R}}{\sigma}$	$d_3 = \dfrac{\sigma_R}{\sigma}$	A_2	D_3	D_4
2	1.128	0.8525	1.880	0	3.267
3	1.693	0.8884	1.023	0	2.575
4	2.059	0.8798	0.729	0	2.282
5	2.326	0.8641	0.577	0	2.114
6	2.534	0.8480	0.483	0	2.004
7	2.704	0.8332	0.419	0.076	1.924
8	2.847	0.8198	0.373	0.136	1.864
9	2.970	0.8078	0.337	0.184	1.816
10	3.078	0.7971	0.308	0.223	1.777
15	3.472	0.7562	0.223	0.348	1.652
20	3.735	0.7287	0.180	0.414	1.586

Constructing the X-Bar Chart

Constructing the $\overline{X}$-chart from sample data involves the following steps:

Step 1. Determine the number of samples, m, and the size of each, n, to collect. Considerations for setting n and m are discussed later; for now suffice it to say that n and m are determined by the cost and time of sampling and the degree of sensitivity desired in the sample results.

Step 2. Take m samples, each of size n.

Step 3. Compute the estimated process parameters, the center line, and the control limits; check to see that the limits are acceptable (what constitutes acceptable is addressed later). When the acceptable limits have been determined, put them on the control charts.

Example   2:   Constructing an X-Bar Chart

Suppose we construct a chart to monitor the average length of metal shafts as mentioned earlier.

Step 1. Assume the chart will be based upon the results of $m = 30$ samples, each of size $n = 5$.

Step 2. On 30 occasions (say, once a day for 30 days) measure the lengths of five shafts. The results of the sampling process are shown in Table 14.5 (actual values are shown only for four of the 30 samples). Each row gives the measured results of one sample, the sample mean $\overline{X}_i$ and the sample range R_i, where

$\overline{X}_i$ = the mean of sample $i = \Sigma\, X/n$,
R_i = the range of sample $i = X_{max} - X_{min}$ (difference between the largest and smallest values in sample i).

For instance, for sample 1 ($i = 1$),

$$\overline{X}_1 = (8.521 + 8.516 + 8.511 + 8.519 + 8.514)/5 = 8.516,$$

$$R_1 = 8.521 - 8.511 = 0.010.$$

TABLE 14-5   Results of 30 Samples

Sample (i)	X (measured results)					$\overline{X}_i$	R_i
1	8.521	8.516	8.511	8.519	8.514	8.516	0.010
2	8.522	8.516	8.521	8.513	8.519	8.518	0.009
⋮	⋮	⋮	⋮	⋮	⋮	⋮	⋮
14	8.502	8.500	8.501	8.502	8.515	8.504	0.015
⋮	⋮	⋮	⋮	⋮	⋮	⋮	⋮
23	8.518	8.526	8.501	8.491	8.524	8.512	0.035
⋮	⋮	⋮	⋮	⋮	⋮	⋮	⋮
30	⋯	⋯	⋯	⋯	⋯	⋯	⋯
					$\Sigma\ \overline{X}_i = 255.450$		$\Sigma\ R_i = 0.462$

Step 3. Compute the center line and control limits. From Table 14.5, $\Sigma_i\ \overline{X} = 255.450$ and $\Sigma\ R_i = 0.462$, so

$$\overline{\overline{X}} = 255.450/30 = 8.515,$$

$$\overline{R} = 0.462/30 = 0.0154.$$

From equation (2) and Table 14.4,

$$UCL = \overline{\overline{X}} + A_2\overline{R} = 8.515 + 0.577(0.0154) = 8.5239,$$

$$LCL = \overline{\overline{X}} - A_2\overline{R} = 8.515 - 0.577(0.0154) = 8.5061.$$

R-CHARTS

Because of common causes, there is always variation in a process and, hence, in the sampling results. That variation, and the size of it, are important. Although some variation around the target value is expected, only a *certain amount* is expected for a process with prespecified parameters. Any amount of variation other than the expected is noteworthy. Figure 14.9 shows the distributions of two processes: both produce outputs with identical means, μ, though the variabilities of the two are clearly quite different. Given that the means of both distributions match the target value, process 1 would generally be preferred over process 2 because a greater proportion of its output lies closer to the target value. Conversely, a greater proportion of the output of process 2 lies farther away from the target value. (The shaded areas represent the proportion of each process that falls outside the region of acceptable deviation.) For just that reasoning, processes that have smaller variability are, in general, more desirable than those with larger variability. So, once an acceptable deviation level has been set for a process, then the process variability itself should be monitored to make sure it does not change. Just as the process mean is influenced by common causes and special causes, so too is process variability. Variability that results from common causes is expected and tolerated, but if the variability shifts because of a special cause (i.e., the process variability moves out of control), then the cause needs to be identified and rectified. It is common practice to monitor the variability of a

Figure 14.9

Distribution of outputs for two processes.

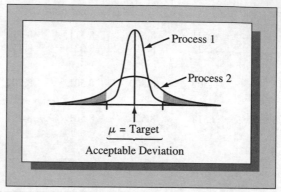

process with an **R-chart,** or range chart. Like other kinds of control charts, it has a center line and control limits for detecting nonrandom behavior or possible shifts in a process.

For the R-chart, the CL is $\bar{R}$ and

$$UCL = \bar{R} + 3\sigma_R,$$
$$LCL = \bar{R} - 3\sigma_R,$$

where

$$\sigma_R = \bar{R}d_3/d_2$$

and d_3 is obtained for sample size n in Table 14.4. Therefore,

$$UCL = \bar{R} + 3(\bar{R}d_3/d_2) = \bar{R}(1 + 3d_3/d_2), \tag{3}$$
$$LCL = \bar{R} - 3(\bar{R}d_3/d_2) = \bar{R}(1 - 3d_3/d_2).$$

The above formulae give the three-sigma ($z = 3$) control limits, though they are easily modified to get one- and two-sigma limits, if desired.

The equations in (3) are simplified by replacing the bracketed term in the UCL equation with D_4 and the bracketed term in the LCL equation with D_3; both factors are listed for values of sample size n in Table 14.4. Thus, the control limits are

$$UCL = \bar{R}D_4, \tag{4}$$
$$LCL = \bar{R}D_3.$$

Example   3:   Constructing the R-Chart

As you might expect, given that both the $\bar{X}$- and R-charts use the same data, steps for constructing them are much the same. Referring to Example 2, $\bar{R} = 0.0154$. In Table 14.4 for $n = 5$, $D_3 = 0$ and $D_4 = 2.114$. Thus, using formula (4) for the R-chart,

$$UCL = 0.0154(2.114) = 0.0326,$$
$$LCL = 0.0154(0.0) = 0.$$

ACCEPTABLE CONTROL LIMITS

One additional consideration before actually using the computed X-bar and R control limits is to decide *whether the limits are acceptable*. To be acceptable, all of the individual means and ranges, $\overline{X}_i$ and R_i, must lie within their respective control limits. If an $\overline{X}_i$ or an R_i lies outside its respective control limits, the sample for it must be investigated for a possible special cause. If a special cause is found, then the sample cannot be considered representative of the true process and must be discarded.[7] Upon discarding the sample, new control limits are computed, and the remaining samples are checked against them. The procedure is repeated until all the remaining values of $\overline{X}_i$ and R_i lie within the most recently computed limits.

Since the control limits for the X-bar chart are based upon the average range $\overline{R}$, start by looking at the R-values first. Once acceptable control limits have been established for the R-chart, use the remaining samples to compute the X-bar control limits, then check to ensure that all the $\overline{X}$s fall within these limits. The samples for any outlying $\overline{X}$s are discarded, and new limits are computed for both the $\overline{X}$- and R-charts. If too many samples are discarded, the process is probably unstable and needs adjustment.

Example   4:   Determining Acceptable Control Limits

Returning to Table 14.5, note that $R_{23} = 0.035$ exceeds the range UCL of 0.0326 (Example 3). Suppose upon investigation, it is discovered that bar stock for that day was obtained from a different source and that the metal was slightly softer than the usual metal. The sample is therefore discarded. After dropping sample 23, the new ΣR is $0.462 - 0.035 = 0.427$. For the 29 remaining samples, the new $\overline{R}$ is $0.427/29 = 0.0147$. Therefore,

$$UCL = 0.0147(2.114) = 0.0310,$$

$$LCL = 0.$$

Suppose R_i of all remaining 29 samples lie within the above computed limits. Now we can move our attention to the $\overline{X}$-chart.

Compute the center line and control limits for the remaining samples. Dropping $\overline{X}_{23}$, the new $\Sigma \overline{X}_i = 255.450 - 8.512 = 246.938$. Therefore, for the remaining 29 samples,

$$\overline{\overline{X}} = 246.938/29 = 8.515.$$

For $n = 5$ in Table 14.4, $A_2 = 0.577$; using formula (2),

$$UCL = 8.515 + 0.577(0.0147) = 8.523,$$

$$LCL = 8.515 - 0.577(0.0147) = 8.506.$$

As before we need to ask, Are all remaining values of $\overline{X}_i$ within these limits? Since $\overline{X}_{14} = 8.504$, we must investigate it. Suppose we determine that the sample was taken following a brief shutdown due to a power failure and that the equipment had likely not yet resumed its normal operating temperature. Being a special cause, we discard the sample from the data. Tossing out that sample means tossing out *both* the R and $\overline{X}$ associated with it, and so new limits must be computed for *both* the R- and the $\overline{X}$-charts. Tossing out sample 14, the new totals are

$$\Sigma R = 0.427 - 0.015 = 0.412, \quad \text{so} \quad \overline{R} = 0.412/28 = 0.0147,$$

$$\Sigma \overline{X} = 246.938 - 8.504 = 238.434, \quad \text{so} \quad \overline{\overline{X}} = 238.434/28 = 8.5155;$$

FIGURE 14.10

$\overline{X}$- and R-Charts with results of 21 subsequent samples.

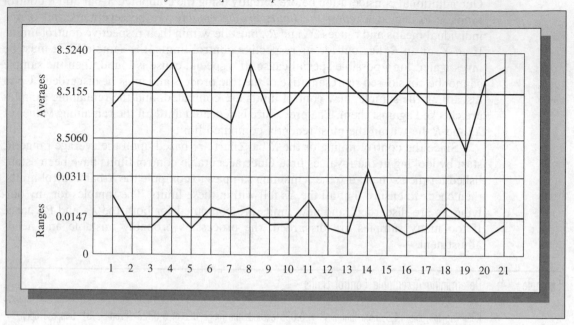

the new limits for the R-chart are

$$UCL = 0.0311,$$

$$LCL = 0.$$

Repeating the procedure, check that R_i for the remaining 28 samples all lie within the limits; suppose they do, then the limits on R are acceptable. Having arrived at acceptable limits for $\overline{R}$, we now return to the $\overline{X}$-chart. The value for $\overline{R}$ from the R-chart, 0.0147, is used to compute the new X-bar control limits:

$$UCL = 8.5155 + 0.577(0.0147) = 8.5240,$$

$$LCL = 8.5155 - 0.577(0.0147) = 8.5070.$$

Once again, check that $\overline{X}_i$ for the remaining 28 samples all lie within the X-bar limits. Suppose they do. Given that all remaining R_i and $\overline{X}_i$ lie within their respective limits, we now accept these as the *final* limits and draw them on the control charts.[8] Figure 14.10 shows the resulting control charts. Plotted points on Figure 14.10 represent hypothetical results from 21 samples taken at a later time.

USE OF CONTROL CHARTS

Once limits for the R- and $\overline{X}$-charts have been determined, the limits are held fixed for use thereafter to track the process. The final values for $\overline{\overline{X}}$ and $\overline{R}$ determined in the charting procedure (in Example 4, 8.5155 and 0.0147, respectively) become the estimated parameters for the process. As long as subsequent sample results lie within the control limits, the process is presumed to conform to those parameters.

Ordinarily both the R-chart and the X-bar chart are employed together and displayed in one place, as in Figure 14.10. Both the mean and the standard deviation of a process are important, and an out-of-control indication on either chart suggests that at least one of those process parameters has changed, and that the process is out-of-control and should be investigated.

Use of the charts involves periodically taking a new sample, computing the mean and range, and plotting them on the charts. Returning to the previous example, five metal shafts are randomly sampled each day, their lengths are measured, and the resulting average $\overline{X}$ and range R are plotted. The process is assumed in control as long as the plotted values on both charts lie within the limits and appear to be random (using the five rules listed earlier). Whenever points appear nonrandom or lie on or outside of limits, the process is stopped to search for a special cause.

In Figure 14.10, for example, points lie outside the limits on the $\overline{X}$- and R-charts on days 19 and 14, respectively. Presumably, on both days the process was stopped and possible assignable causes were investigated.

It should be noted that on R-charts with LCL $>$ 0, a point falling below the LCL (indicating a possible decrease in process variability) still requires that the process be stopped and a special cause sought. Even an apparently advantageous change should be investigated to assess the economic impact or feasibility of permanently incorporating it into (or removing it from) the process.

When and When Not to Change Control Limits

Once a control chart has been constructed for a process, newly sampled data are used only to assess the state of the process; the new data are not used to change the control limits. Students newly introduced to control charts sometimes think that each new sample point should be combined with prior sample points to determine new control limits. It should not. The control limits are changed only when the process (a) has been intentionally changed or (b) is thought to have changed inadvertently: the latter case is an out-of-control situation as suggested by the location of a sample point on the control chart. *Anytime* anything is done that might alter the process, Steps 2 and 3 in Example 2 (take m samples, compute the parameters and the control limits) must be repeated to see whether the estimated parameters $\overline{\overline{X}}$ and $\overline{R}$ (or $\overline{p}$ and $\overline{c}$, discussed next) were altered, and if they were, to reconstruct the control charts to reflect the changes. If the limits must be changed, then the three-step process is initiated anew to determine the new limits. This applies to all control charts, including the ones discussed next.

ATTRIBUTES CONTROL CHARTS: P-CHARTS AND C-CHARTS

The control charts discussed so far—means, X-bar, and R-charts—are used to monitor characteristics that are measurable, that is, characteristics that are represented in terms of a continuous numbering scale. Physical characteristics such as dimensions (inches or centimeters), weight (pounds or grams), temperature (degrees), pressure, and speed are examples of features that can be monitored with such charts. These charts are referred to as **variables** control charts.

When a characteristic is monitored not by measuring it, but rather by classifying it or by tallying it, then an **attributes** control chart is used. Inspecting items for, say, apparent flaws, irregularities, or inconsistencies, counting the frequency of such occurrences, and/or categorizing the items as acceptable or defective are examples of uses for an attributes control chart. We will consider two kinds of attributes charts: the p-chart and the c-chart.

P-Charts

A **p-chart** or proportion chart is used to monitor the *proportion* of items in a process that fall into a certain category. For example, if a specific proportion of a process output is *expected* to be defective, a p-chart would be used to monitor the proportion to make sure it does not change. A p-chart is used like the $\overline{X}$- and R-charts, except it tracks $\overline{p}$, the fraction of items that fall in a category out of n items sampled.

The steps for constructing and using a p-chart are similar to those described for constructing variables control charts:

Step 1. Select the sample size n and the number of samples m for collecting data for the chart.

Step 2. On m occasions take samples of n items, and count the number of items judged as defective. For each sample i, if the number of defective items is d_i, then the corresponding fraction defective is $p_i = d_i/n$.

Step 3. On the p-chart, the CL is $\overline{p}$, and the limits are

$$UCL = \overline{p} + z \sqrt{\frac{\overline{p}(1 - \overline{p})}{n}},$$

$$LCL = \overline{p} - z \sqrt{\frac{\overline{p}(1 - \overline{p})}{n}},$$

where

$\overline{p} = \Sigma \ p_i/m = $ fraction defective of all samples taken, $i = 1, \ldots, m$
$p_i = \Sigma \ d_i/n = $ fraction defective in the ith sample,
$z = $ number of standard deviations, usually three.

When the computed value for the LCL is negative, set it to zero since it is physically impossible to have a negative fraction defective.

Example   5:   Setting Control Limits for a p-Chart

Step 1. Suppose $n = 50$ and $m = 25$.

Step 2. On 25 different occasions (for example, every hour for 25 hours) select samples of 50 items each, and count the number of items judged as defective. Partial results of the sample data are shown in Table 14.6. Each row represents a sample and includes the number of items judged as defective, d_i, and the fraction defective, $p_i = d_i/n$.

TABLE 14-6   Defective Items in Samples

Sample i*	No. Defective Units, d_i	Fraction Defective, $p_i = d_i/n$
1	2	0.04
2	0	0
3	6	0.12
4	1	0.02
⋮	⋮	⋮
25	2	0.04
		$\Sigma\ p_i = 1.02$

*Each sample is of size $n = 50$.

Step 3: From Table 14.6, $\Sigma\ p_i = 1.02$, so $\bar{p} = 1.02/25 = 0.041$. Using three-sigma limits, the values on the p-chart are

$$UCL = 0.041 + 3\sqrt{\frac{0.041(1 - 0.041)}{50}} = 0.1251,$$

$$LCL = 0.041 - 3\sqrt{\frac{0.041(1 - 0.041)}{\sqrt{50}}} = -0.0431 = 0.$$

Similar to the procedure for constructing other control charts, all the values of p_i used to determine the control limits must lie within the limits. If not, outliers are investigated for special causes; if special causes are found, outliers are discarded and values for $\bar{p}$ and the limits are recomputed. Assuming in the above example that p_i for the original 25 samples all lie within the initial computed limits, we would have a p-chart that looks like Figure 14.11, which shows the control limits and hypothetical sampling results for some future 31-day period.

FIGURE 14.11

P-Chart and results from 31 subsequent samples.

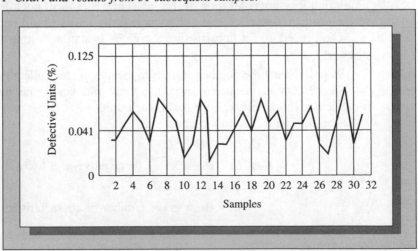

To use the p-chart, periodically take new samples, compute and plot $\bar{p}$, and interpret the meaning. Suppose the sampling frequency is once every hour and the sample size is 50: each hour randomly select 50 items, tally the number of defective units, and plot the resulting p-value. The process is assumed in–control as long as p-values remain within the control limits and show a random pattern. Points beyond the limits suggest an out-of-control situation.[9]

Suppose the LCL is a nonzero value, say 0.002, and suppose a sample produces a point that falls on or below it, say at 0.001. This, seemingly, is a good thing (after all, the defect rate is apparently dropping), so, you might ask, should the process be stopped and a special cause sought? The answer is yes because if something has caused the defect rate to drop, then the cause should be identified to make sure it has not also caused negative consequences such as increasing the cost of the process. Also, if there are no negative consequences, then identifying the cause might allow it to be incorporated as a permanent part of the process.

The limits on the p-chart are held constant as long as the process is presumed to remain unchanged. As with the other charts, anytime something is done to alter the process, Steps 1–3 in Example 5 must be repeated to determine new values for $\bar{p}$ and new control limits.

C-Charts

A **c-chart** is used to monitor the number of times a characteristic (such as a defect) occurs in a single unit. A *unit* is whatever is being inspected, such as a single part, a single product, a batch of products, or even a physical space or region. A c-chart could be used to monitor, for example, the number of defects or imperfections observed on each product coming off an assembly line, the number of accidents occurring in a factory, or the number of things missed or poorly handled by the custodial staff in a hotel room. An excess of the characteristic being counted does not necessarily render a unit defective, per se, or worthless, though the fewer of the observed characteristics, the better. For example, while a few scratches observed on the casing of an electric motor or a few spots of dirt on the rug of a hotel room will not affect the performance of the product, fewer scratches or spots (ideally none) would be preferred.

The procedure for constructing a c-chart is similar to that for the other charts discussed:

Step 1: Select the number of units to sample, m, for collecting data for the chart.

Step 2: On m occasions inspect a unit and count the number of times, c, a particular characteristic appears on each unit.

Step 3: The limits on a c-chart are:

$$UCL = \bar{c} + z\sqrt{\bar{c}}$$
$$LCL = \bar{c} - z\sqrt{\bar{c}} \quad \text{(if negative, use LCL=0)}$$
$$CL = \bar{c}$$

$\bar{c}$ = the average number of characteristics

$$= \frac{\text{total number of events observed}}{\text{number of units inspected}}$$

Example   6:   Setting Control Limits for a c-Chart

Suppose the shaft referred to in the previous examples is made of polished glass, and inspection of each shaft involves noting any imperfections (cracks, scratches, or bubbles) in the glass. To construct a control chart, 20 shafts, each produced one hour apart, are randomly inspected and the number of imperfections, c, on each is recorded. The results are listed in Table 14.7.

Thus, $\bar{c} = 102/20 = 5.1$, and the standard error is $\sqrt{5.1} = 2.258$. If $z = 3$,

$$UCL = 5.1 + 3(2.258) = 11.874$$

$$LCL = 5.1 - 3(2.258) = -1.674 \text{ (use 0)}$$

The computed limits contain all the sample values (Table 14.7), so they can be used on the control chart without modification. The resulting control chart is shown in Figure 14.12. Also shown are the values for 21 samples taken at later times, all in control.

TABLE 14-7   Imperfection Found on Shafts

Shaft No.	Imperfections, c	Shaft No.	Imperfections, c
1	3	11	6
2	5	12	8
3	4	13	5
4	2	14	4
5	7	15	7
6	5	16	2
7	9	17	4
8	6	18	5
9	3	19	7
10	4	20	6
			102

FIGURE 14.12

C-chart and results of 21 subsequent samples.

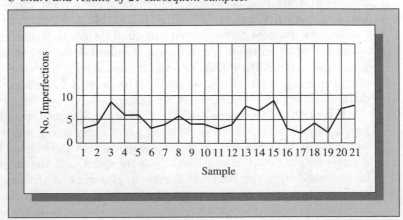

Pros and Cons

Organizations first introduced to SPC often start with attributes control charts such as p-charts or c-charts, then move up to variables control charts. Attributes control charts are somewhat easier and, sometimes, less costly to use. For example, inspection of an automobile crankshaft (a rather complicated item) requires gauging at several places on the crankshaft, and a defect or other nonconformity noted *anyplace* on the crankshaft will result in the crankshaft being classified as defective. Thus, only one chart is needed to track the fraction defective of all crankshafts produced.

It should be apparent, however, that this approach is only of limited value for identifying and resolving special causes of defects. On crankshafts, simply knowing the percentage defective is not of much use because, among other things, it is necessary to know *where* on the crankshaft defects are occurring. Maintaining several variables control charts to reflect the several places inspected on each crankshaft is more costly, but makes it easier to zero in on special causes. Also, attributes charts track defects or other nonconformities that have already occurred, whereas variables charts enable you to track processes and *anticipate*, as well as resolve, special causes before they lead to defects.

Similar to the reasons they restrict use of acceptance sampling, world-class organizations restrict use of attributes charts because, to them, it is an acknowledgment that some nonzero level of defects or nonconformities exists. Still, for some manufacturing processes that are rather complicated, and for services where the range of things to inspect can seem limitless, it is virtually impossible to reduce nonconformity rates to less than a small percentage. Attributes charting helps ensure that the nonconformities are not on the increase, although other tools are needed to detect their causes and suggest ways to improve the process.

As a review, Table 14.8 lists the five types of control charts described, and their features.

BRIEF DIGRESSION ON PROCESS STABILITY

A control chart is used to pinpoint occurrences of special causes of variation in a process in which *only* common causes of variation are *expected*. Such a process is in **statistical control** and, by definition, is a **stable** process.

A stable process conforms to a particular distribution that can be described with estimated parameters for the mean and standard deviation. In contrast, an unstable process is erratic; the effects of special causes on it are so great that it does not conform to any particular distribution. The process is constantly changing, so, by definition, the process parameters are changing too.

For example, the process of hand-fashioning an item would constitute a stable process if the same skilled worker fashioned every item, and if the only source of variability in the work was the variability inherent to any manual labor. The worker's average output could be described by some mean, and the output variability could be described by some standard deviation. However, if the same item were hand-fashioned by a random, nonrepeating sequence of different workers, each with different skill levels, then the process would not be stable. With the introduction of each

TABLE 14-8   Review of Control Charts

	Purpose	*Control Limits*
For Variables:		
Means chart	To monitor process central tendency based on actual process mean	$UCL = \mu_{\bar{x}} + z\sigma_{\bar{x}}$, $LCL = \mu_{\bar{x}} - z\sigma_{\bar{x}}$
X-bar chart	To monitor process central tendency based on estimated process mean	$UCL = \bar{X} + A_2\bar{R}$, $UCL = \bar{X} - A_2\bar{R}$
R-chart	To monitor process variability based on estimated process range	$UCL = \bar{R}D_4$, $LCL = \bar{R}D_3$
For Attributes:		
P-chart	To monitor proportion or fraction of process in a category	$UCL = \bar{p} + z\sqrt{\dfrac{\bar{p}(1-\bar{p})}{n}}$, $LCL = \bar{p} - z\sqrt{\dfrac{\bar{p}(1-\bar{p})}{n}}$
C-chart	To monitor count, or number of occurrences	$UCL = \bar{c} + z\sqrt{\bar{c}}$, $LCL = \bar{c} - z\sqrt{\bar{c}}$

new worker, in effect each being a special cause, the process would change such that no one, true process would ever exist; as a result, the overall estimated process mean and standard deviation could not be determined. Since constructing control charts requires knowing the estimated process parameters, it is not possible to develop a final control chart for a process that is not stable.

Consider the three-step procedure described for constructing a control chart. Assuming that the control limits are eventually set, the process is presumed stable and is represented by the final estimated parameters, $\bar{\bar{X}}$, $\bar{R}$, $\bar{p}$, $\bar{c}$, or others.

Now, the same procedure for determining whether a process is stable can be used as a way to help *stabilize* a process. Anytime in Step 3 a sample lies on or beyond the computed limits, the sample is investigated for a special cause, and if a special cause is found, it is corrected. Standard tools of process analysis and improvement discussed in Chapter 2 such as tally sheets, process diagrams, Pareto analysis, and fishbone diagrams are used to identify special causes. As additional special causes of variation are identified and eliminated from the process, the process moves toward becoming more stable. Once all special causes have been eliminated, all sample points will lie inside the control limits, and the process can be considered stable.

ESTIMATED PARAMETERS

The values $\bar{\bar{X}}$, $\bar{R}$, $\bar{p}$, and $\bar{c}$ are estimated values of process parameters as computed from sampling data. These estimates are used to construct control charts because the actual parameters of a process, μ and σ, p or c are usually unknown.

In the metal shaft example the estimated process mean was computed to be $\overline{\overline{X}} = 8.5155$ cm. Suppose the ideal, target mean (specified as a design requirement) for the same process is 8.520 cm. Even so 8.5155 and not 8.520 is used as the CL on the X-bar chart because the control chart monitors an *existing*, real process. The values used on the control chart must be representative of that process, and since $\overline{\overline{X}}$ is based upon data from the process, it best represents the process mean. The value 8.520 is only a target value and not the actual process mean, so it makes no sense to use it on the control chart. Using target values for a process is probably one of the most widespread mistakes in constructing control charts.

Now, there is another, related issue, that must also be addressed in the use of control charts: given that we have computed a particular estimated value for $\overline{\overline{X}}$, $\overline{R}$ or other parameter, *should* we use control charts to track them? To repeat what was stated earlier in the chapter, control charts are used to monitor a process, but the presumption is that the process is *desirable* and *needs monitoring*. If a process is *not* desirable, then it does not need to be monitored, it needs to be fixed! Only after a process is at the point where it is considered acceptable or desirable should control charts be constructed to monitor it.

In the example we computed $\overline{\overline{X}} = 8.5155$ cm, then used that value to construct an X-bar chart. The implicit assumption was that someone judged $\overline{\overline{X}} = 8.5155$ as close enough to the target value of 8.520 cm to regard the process as acceptable and worth tracking. Had 8.5155 cm been judged unacceptable, then the *process itself would have had to have been modified,* perhaps repeatedly, to move the estimated $\overline{\overline{X}}$ closer to the target value. What is considered as close enough for values of $\overline{\overline{X}}$ and $\overline{R}$, or other parameters, for a given process is the role of process capability analysis, discussed later.

SAMPLING ISSUES

Four important issues for constructing and using control charts are sampling basis, sample size, sampling frequency, and the initial number of samples for computing trial limits.

Sampling Basis

The sampling basis is the way outputs are grouped for sampling so as to maximize the chances of exposing special causes of variation. To identify special causes, it is necessary that sampled items be *homogenous*, that is, all be representative of the same, identical process. When items are completely homogenous, then any variation between them can be attributed solely to common causes, that is, causes inherent to the process. A **rational subgroup** (or rational sample) is a sample that meets this requirement. Suppose, for example, a process involves two workers doing the same thing. One sampling basis would be to combine the output of the two workers into a single pool, then sample from that pool; another basis would be to sample from each worker separately. If the difference between the actual output of the two workers is *in*significant, then sampling from a single pool constitutes rational sampling since the

FIGURE 14.13

Consecutive sampling and resulting control charts.

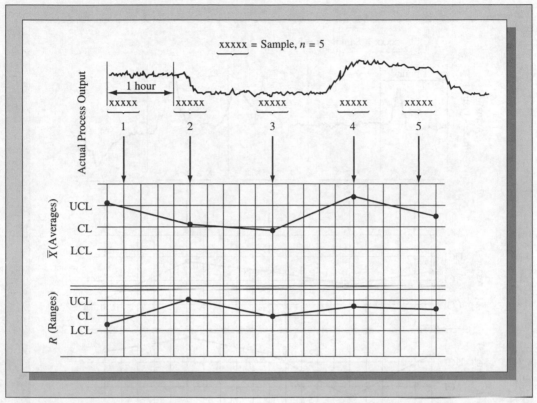

pool is homogenous. If, however, the output of the two workers differs, then it is more appropriate to sample from each worker separately, that is, from two sample pools.[10]

One common basis for rational sampling in continuous production is the time-order of production, and one way to implement that approach is to use a procedure called **consecutive** sampling. In that procedure, a sample of items produced at about the same time (say, all within a 10-minute period) is periodically taken throughout the day (say, once an hour, every hour). Figure 14.13 illustrates this procedure, showing the actual process output, as well as what would be observed using sampling and control charts. The sampling procedure in Figure 14.13 is to inspect the first five units produced at the beginning of every hour. As illustrated, with this procedure the X-bar chart is able to detect shifts in the process mean that are abrupt and sustained.

Another time-ordered way to sample is called **distributed** sampling. In that procedure, the composition of each sample is chosen so as to be representative of the entire sampling interval. One way to do this sampling would be to inspect items at uniformly spaced times throughout the interval. Figure 14.14 illustrates this, showing the actual process output and what would be observed by sampling and control charts.

FIGURE 14.14

Distributed sampling and resulting control charts.

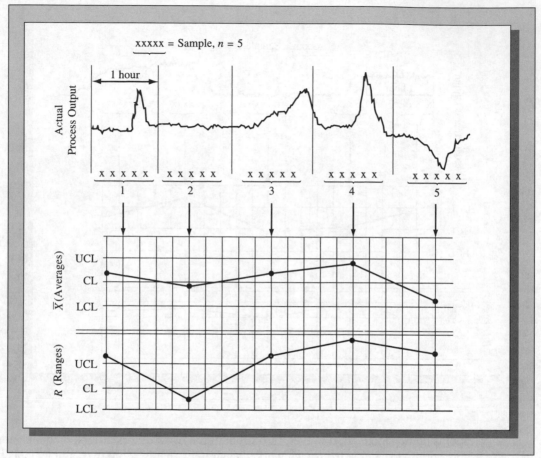

The sampling procedure in Figure 14.14 is to inspect five items uniformly throughout each 1-hour interval. (Alternatively, items produced every hour would be batched, and a random sample of five would be inspected.) The distributed sampling procedure is effective for detecting shifts in process means that are short lived or gradual. For instance, the R-chart in Figure 14.14 reveals spikes in intervals 1, 4, and 5, and a trend in period 3. Had consecutive sampling been used instead, neither the R-chart nor the X-bar chart would have revealed the shifts in the actual process shown in Figure 14.14.

Although time-ordered sampling is a good way to reveal special causes that come and go with time, it does not reveal the many other special causes that are not time related. If, for example, a consecutive sample is formed by, say, combining the last few items produced in one work shift with the first few items from the next shift, differences between the shifts might initially go undetected, especially if only one sample is taken each day.

As another example, suppose three machines perform the same operation, say cutting metal bar stock to produce shafts, all presumably of the same length. After cutting, shafts from the machines are combined and sent to the next operation, prior to which they are randomly sampled and the results of which are plotted on control charts. Now, mixing items together like this for sampling makes it very difficult to identify when and where improvements are needed. If the X-bar and R-charts were constructed using shafts mixed from all the machines, they would represent a process distribution of all the machines combined. As a result, any problems with an individual machine would be difficult to track.

As a final example, suppose two holes are drilled simultaneously on a bar, one at each end, both supposedly with the same diameters. Periodically the diameters of both holes are measured, and the results are combined. The problem this presents for controlling the hole diameters is the same as in the other examples. The sampling procedure assumes that since the two holes are on the same bar, combined they represent a single process; in fact, if the holes are drilled by different machines, they represent different processes.

The concept of rational subgrouping applies not just to machines and work shifts, but to anything that potentially differentiates processes—work centers, operators, batches of raw materials, operating conditions, and so on. Before going ahead with SPC, you need a good understanding of the potential special causes in a process and how to detect them. You also need a firm grasp of how to create rational samples. A good reference is Grant and Leavenworth.[11]

Sample Size n

The sample size, n, is a critical sampling design issue because it dictates not only the cost of sampling, but also the ability of a sample to detect special causes of variation. Obviously, as sample size increases, so does the sampling cost; someone (or something, if sampling is automated) must do the sampling and record the result, and that effort (strictly speaking) is non-value-added. Also, large sample sizes are often undesirable because they are less likely to reveal special-cause variations (abrupt, short-term process shifts will not be detected from a large sample taken over a long period). The most common sample size for variables control charts is five because that size is economical, is easy to use in computation, is small enough to be subject to mainly common causes of variation, and is large enough to meet the requirement for sample means to fall in a normal distribution.

Another consideration for choosing sample size is the degree of sensitivity necessary for a control chart to signal significant changes. By definition, a control chart identifies possible significant changes having occurred whenever a sample falls on or beyond control limits. But the limits are a function of the size of n. With a larger n, the control limits are *closer* to the center line (in Table 14.4, A_2 gets smaller as n increases) so the chart identifies smaller process shifts as significant. For example, with a sample size of 12, a variables control chart will detect process changes on the order of just one process standard deviation. When the sample size is smaller, say five, the control limits are farther out, so the chart only detects process changes on the order of two or more standard deviations.

For attributes control charts the sample sizes are usually much larger than for variables charts; for a p-chart a sample size of five would likely be worthless. In sampling for attributes control charts, the sample size must be large enough for at least one nonconformity to be detected, so if $\bar{p}$ (the nonconformity rate) is small, then n must be large. Suppose we want to monitor a process for $\bar{p} = 0.01$; we then need at least 100 items to be able to *detect* 1% nonconforming, though because of sampling error even 100 is not adequate. A rule of thumb for using p-charts is that both $n\bar{p}$ and $n(1 - \bar{p})$ should equal at least five.[12] If $\bar{p} = 0.01$, then $n \geq 5/p = 5/0.01 = 500$, and $n \geq 5/(1 - \bar{p}) = 5/0.99 = 5.05$, so the sample size must be at least 500.[13] Such a large sample size might not only be costly but, unless the process has a very high throughput rate, also preclude rapid feedback on developing problems.

Sampling Frequency

The ideal way to sample is to take somewhat large samples (n of 10 or 20) on a frequent basis, though, again, economic constraints might require either smaller samples taken at shorter intervals, or larger samples taken at longer intervals. But the frequency of sampling should also depend on the nature of the process, particularly on the likelihood of special causes occurring or of the process becoming unstable. Somewhat erratic processes need to be sampled more frequently so that places needing improvement can be identified quickly. Frequent sampling also reduces the time between when a process shift occurs, is identified, and is corrected. Generally, the frequency of sampling should be increased as the opportunity for special causes in a process increases. A process involving, for example, rotation of machine operators, frequent insertion of new batches of raw materials, or even fluctuations in ambient temperature or pressure, should be sampled often enough to catch irregularities that could emanate from these events.

Often, the immediate cost of doing sampling is given too much weight in decisions about sample size and sample frequency. Devor, et al. write:

> What is often not recognized is that the real waste of money due to sampling arises when samples are collected too infrequently, since the information/value content of the data is so low. [There is evidence that] many companies waste large amounts of money by sampling so infrequently that the resulting charts have no value.[14]

Initial Number of Samples *m*

In constructing control charts the number of points lying within the final control limits (out of the initial *m* samples taken) must be large enough to ensure that the points accurately represent the process. This leads to the matter of determining the size of *m*, the number of initial samples to be taken. Ideally the number of points remaining inside the final control limits should be large, which would require that the initial number of samples be even larger since those samples falling beyond computed limits will be discarded. As a practical matter, a rule of thumb is that to be somewhat certain a process is stable, at least 20 samples should remain *within* the final control limits. Therefore, given that some or several initial samples will have to be discarded, the initial number of samples, *m*, must exceed 20. Thirty or 40 samples are a good start, though a larger number is still better. Regardless of the initial number of samples taken, if, after discarding samples, fewer than 20 remain, then more samples must be collected.

PROCESS CAPABILITY

After a process has been determined to be stable (remaining samples all lie within control limits), the process parameters can be used to estimate the **process capability.** The process capability is, roughly, how capable the process is of producing output that conforms to certain requirements.

People sometimes confuse the notions of a process being in control and a process being capable. The two notions, illustrated in Figure 14.15, are very different. A process is in control as long as it follows a pattern of behavior as predicted by process parameters. On the control chart, a process is in control as long as sampled points stay within control limits and exhibit random variation. In contrast, a process is capable as long as it meets certain requirements, which is to say, as long as it falls within **specification limits.** *Control limits and specification limits are not the same thing.* Control limits are computed as a mathematical function of the estimated mean and range, while specification limits, or specs, are set by product designers according to, presumably, customer requirements or expectations. To get control limits, you need to take samples from the process; to get spec limits, you need to talk to customers or refer to the product design specifications. The two kinds of limits serve different purposes and are usually set by different people, so it is entirely possible for a process to be well in control, yet be miserably incapable (the reverse is also possible, though rare in practice).

CAPABILITY INDEX

Process capability is determined by comparing the natural variability of a process (or product or service) to customer or engineering specifications. The capability is

FIGURE 14.15

Control limits and specification limits.

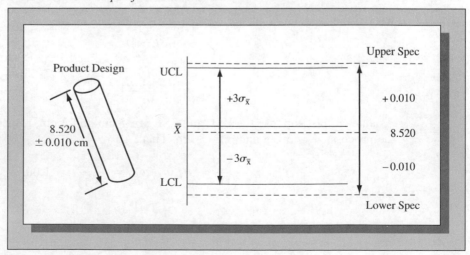

quantified with a measure called a **process capability index,** C_p, the ratio of the spec width to the natural tolerance of the process, where

- **Spec width** is the difference between upper and lower specification limits, that is, USL − LSL.
- **Natural tolerance** is defined as 6σ, where σ is the process standard deviation, usually as estimated from the R-chart.

In numerical terms, the process capability index is expressed as

$$C_p = \frac{USL - LSL}{6\sigma}.$$

Suppose the spec width is 6 cm and the process $\sigma = 1$ cm; then, $C_p = 6/6(1) = 1$. Technically, $C_p = 1$ means that the process is capable because virtually the entire process distribution lies within the specs. This is illustrated in Figure 14.16(*a*). In terms of world-class requirements, however, $C_p = 1$ is not nearly good enough. The natural tolerance of the process (defined as 6σ for a normal distribution) includes only 99.74% of the process distribution, which leaves 0.26% outside the specs (in nonconformance), hardly world class. It is much better when a higher percentage falls within specs. Suppose $\sigma = 0.5$ cm, then $C_p = 2$. As shown in Figure 14.16(*b*), this process is nestled so tightly within the specs that only a tiny proportion of it ever falls outside. The opposite, poor capability, happens when C_p is small. Suppose $\sigma = 2$ cm, then $C_p = 0.5$. As shown in Figure 14.16(*c*), the natural tolerance leads the process to spill well beyond the specs such that much of the output is nonconforming. In fact, when $C_p = 0.5$, only about 87% of the process is in conformance. For starters, a good C_p to strive for is 1.33.

Correct application of C_p presumes that the process mean is located at the target value, that is, the process is squarely centered between the upper and lower spec limits. If the process is not centered, then the following indexes apply instead:

$$C_{pk} = \min(C_{pu}, C_{pl}),$$

where

$$C_{pu} = \frac{USL - \mu}{3\sigma},$$

$$C_{pl} = \frac{\mu - LSL}{3\sigma}.$$

As an example, suppose the USL and LSL are 7 cm and 2 cm, respectively, and for the process, $\mu = 5$ cm and $\sigma = 1$ cm. Then,

$$C_{pu} = \frac{7 - 5}{3(1)} = .67, \qquad C_{pl} = \frac{5 - 2}{3(1)} = 1.00,$$

so

$$C_{pk} = 0.67.$$

FIGURE 14.16

C_p-values for various process standard deviations.

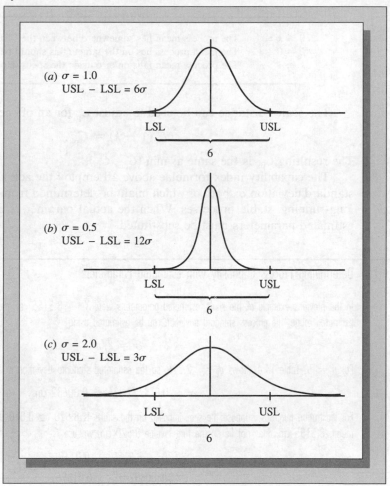

(a) $\sigma = 1.0$
USL − LSL = 6σ

LSL   USL

6

(b) $\sigma = 0.5$
USL − LSL = 12σ

LSL   USL

6

(c) $\sigma = 2.0$
USL − LSL = 3σ

LSL   USL

6

Beyond Specs

The above capability indexes put emphasis on the proportion of a process that lies within specs, which is a somewhat out-of-place emphasis in the thinking of TQM organizations. More important to them than just simply *meeting* specs is *hitting or coming as close as possible* to the *target value* and doing it as often as possible. Closeness to hitting a target value is measured by the **scaled distance k:**

$$k = \frac{2\,|\mu - \text{target}|}{USL - LSL}$$

where the target is midway between the USL and the LSL. Roughly, k can be interpreted as follows:

$0 \leq k \leq 1$	The process mean lies somewhere between the USL and the LSL.
$k = 0$	The mean process lies on the target (this should be the goal).
$k \geq 1$	The process mean falls on or outside the specs (a pathetic process).

The scaled distance can be used to adjust C_p for an off-center process using

$$C_p(1 - k) = C_{pk}.$$

The resulting C_{pk} is the same as min (C_{pu}, C_{pl}).

The capability index formulae above all employ the actual process mean μ and standard deviation σ, both of which might be determined from large sample sizes for long-running, stable processes. When the actual parameters cannot be determined, estimated parameters must be substituted.

Example 7: Determining Process Capability with Estimated Parameters

In the previous example of the shaft, estimated parameters were $\overline{\overline{X}} = 8.5155$ cm and $\overline{R} = 0.0147$ cm. From the estimated range, the process standard deviation can be estimated using

$$\sigma = \overline{R}/d_2.$$

For $n = 5$, Table 14.4 shows $d_2 = 2.326$, so the estimated standard deviation is

$$\sigma = 0.0147/2.326 = 0.00632 \text{ cm.}$$

For illustration purposes, suppose the spec imposed on the shafts is 8.520 ± 0.010 cm. Since the estimated process mean, 8.5155 cm, does not lie on the target value 8.520 cm, we use C_{pk}:

$$C_{pu} = \frac{8.530 - 8.5155}{3(0.00632)} = \frac{0.0145}{0.01896} = 0.76,$$

$$C_{pl} = \frac{8.5155 - 8.510}{3(0.00632)} = \frac{0.0055}{0.01896} = 0.29,$$

so

$$C_{pk} = .29.$$

Alternatively, compute C_p and adjust it for an off-center process:

$$C_p = \frac{8.530 - 8.510}{6(0.00632)} = 0.527, \qquad k = \frac{2|8.5155 - 8.520|}{0.020} = 0.45$$

so

$$C_{pk} = (1 - .45).527 = 0.29.$$

(Notice that the capability of this process is very poor, primarily because of the relatively large process variation. In previous examples we determined the limits for charts to help control this process. Were this a real process, we would not bother to try to control it until we had first improved it by substantially reducing σ.)

Process Capability for Process Improvement

Although process capability cannot be accurately assessed unless a process is stable, a preliminary process capability analysis can be performed to determine, for given specs, the final process parameters (mean and standard deviation) necessary to make the process capable. Given, say, a goal of $C_{pk} = 1.67$, a process improvement team can determine the values of process parameters $\bar{X}$ and $\bar{R}$ to shoot for, and then use the control-charting procedure described above to stabilize the process around these values.

Clearly, larger C_{pk}'s (and C_p's) are preferred over smaller ones, so C_{pk} can be used as an existing standard or future goal. Process capability applies to any level or aspect of a process, including inputs, outputs, individual operations, and pieces of equipment, so it can be used, for instance, as a contract requirement for equipment or parts purchases, for determining maintenance or replacement needs, or as a criterion in continuous improvement efforts.[15] As an example, suppose the spec width is 5 inches and the existing process is centered with a σ of 1.11 inch. The existing C_p is $[5/6(1.11)] = 0.75$, certainly not very good. Management might set improvement goals for this process in terms of C_p, say to increase it to 1.0 within 6 months, then to 1.5 within 1 year, and then to 2.0 within 2 years. Assuming the same spec width, achieving those goals requires that σ be first reduced to

$$\sigma = (USL - LSL)/6(C_p) = 5/6(1) = 0.833 \text{ inch,}$$

then to 0.555 inch, and finally to 0.417 inch.

Notice, the process is improved by reducing σ, which, recall, is the variability in the process arising solely from common causes. Earlier the statement was made, with qualification, that if process variation stems solely from common causes then no immediate action is necessary. The qualification is that no action is necessary, *providing* the process is capable enough. If the process is not capable enough, then it is necessary to identify the sources of *common* causes and to reduce their effect on variability. Common-cause variation is inherent to a process or system, and isolating and treating its sources is often an expensive and difficult proposition. To improve process capability, only a few other alternatives exist: (a) widen the spec limits or (b) screen to eliminate all out-of-spec items. The latter alternative might be feasible, at least in the short run and until the process variability can be brought into line, but the former has it all backwards, unless the specs were originally set well inside the customer requirements.

HOW MUCH VARIATION REDUCTION IS GOOD ENOUGH?

Recall in the shaft example that the target value was 8.520 cm and the spec limits were 8.510 cm and 8.530 cm. A zero-defects advocate would say, as long as a shaft meets the specs, that is good enough. While at one time such thinking might have

FIGURE 14.17

Quality loss for deviating from the target.

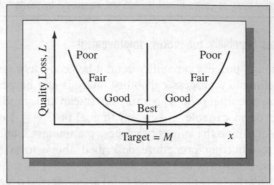

enabled an organization to be competitive, that is no longer the case. In world-class competition, meeting specs is not good enough; continuous improvement is the name of the game and here that translates into forever trying to get closer to the target.

Taguchi Loss Function

Continuous improvement in this context can be expressed in terms of the Taguchi **loss function** mentioned in Chapter 12.[16] The loss refers to costs incurred or profits forgone by deviating from a target value. Presumably the target value was set for good reasons (economics, performance, whatever) and any deviation from the target is suboptimal. Taguchi says the amount of loss is a direct function of the degree of deviation from the target value, and for that reason alone it is important to reduce variability. Also given that rationale, the minimum loss occurs at the target value. This is illustrated in Figure 14.17.

For instance, suppose the shaft from the running example is to be fit between two supports on a frame. To simplify the example, suppose the supports are exactly 8.530 cm apart. Assume the shaft should rotate freely, and a small amount of lubricant is to be applied at places where the shaft meets the supports. Some amount of play between the shaft and the supports is necessary to contain the lubricant; the ideal play is 0.005 cm at each support (half the difference of the distance between supports and the shaft target value, 8.530 − 8.520 cm). With too little play there is insufficient room for lubricant and the shaft occasionally binds; with too much play, the shaft wobbles and wears out sooner. Either situation prompts customer complaints. Assume the loss is the cost of these complaints plus increased manufacturing costs. The loss, as a function of the deviation from target, is often expressed by the quadratic equation[17]

$$L = k(deviation)^2 = k(x - M)^2,$$

where

M = target value,
x = actual value,
k = loss constant.

Suppose the average cost of a customer complaint (costs of warranty to the manufacturer, customer inconvenience, and the eventual loss of some repeat customers) is $100. Given that the tolerance on the shaft is ± 0.01 cm, the loss constant is thus

$$k = \$100/(0.01)^2 = \$1,000,000.$$

This loss assumes that if a shaft deviates exactly by the tolerance amount of ± 0.01 cm, the loss is $100 per unit. Notice that if the length deviates by just ± 0.005 cm, an amount well within the tolerance, the estimated loss is

$$1,000,000(0.005)^2 = \$25 \text{ per unit.}$$

The implication of being content with just meeting specs is further illustrated by the following case.

CASE IN POINT: Quality Loss of TVs Manufactured at Two Plants

The impact of meeting specs versus exceeding specs is seen in a well-known comparison of TVs produced at two Sony plants, one in Japan and one in America. The color density of every TV shipped by the American plant met the specs, while at the Japanese plant some did not. Nonetheless, Sony discovered that customers were more satisfied with, and warranty claims were much less for, TVs produced in the Japanese plant. A comparison of the color density distributions of TVs from the two plants showed that a much higher proportion of Japanese-produced TVs fell closer to the color density target value than did American-produced TVs (see Figure 14.18): at the American plant, $\sigma^2 = 8.33$, while at the Japanese plant, $\sigma^2 = 2.78$. Sony estimated the loss constant k to be 0.16, so the average loss per TV was

$$L(\text{American}) = 0.16(8.33) = \$1.33,$$
$$L(\text{Japanese}) = 0.16(2.78) = \$0.44.$$

In other words, although all units from the American plant met the specs and some units from the Japanese plant did not, the average loss for an American TV was still $0.89 more than for a Japanese TV.

FIGURE 14.18

Comparison of color density of TVs.

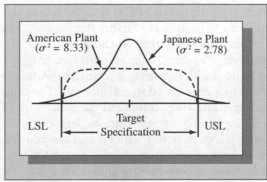

Going back to the question as to how much variation reduction is good enough, the loss function indicates "the more reduction, the better." The loss function also exposes limitations of focusing exclusively on process capability. Improved process capability is achieved by a combination of centering the process and reducing the variation, though in any case the raison d'etre of process capability is to raise the likelihood of meeting specs. Process capability assumes that falling *anywhere* within specs is equally OK, that is, falling on a spec limit is just as good as hitting the target. The chosen spec limits are themselves assumed good, and once set, they forever are the criteria against which process capability is measured.

The loss function, however, points out that, generally, narrower specs are better than wider specs; that is, the loss from specs set closer to the target is less than the loss from specs set farther away. Further, according to Taguchi, manufacturers should not be content with existing specs; they should forever work to make them tighter. And in world-class competition, that is what is happening; not only is variation being reduced to increase process capability, but the requirements themselves are being tightened. Shifting attention to the loss function is actually a move to the next level beyond SPC, to improvement not only of processes to satisfy existing design requirements, but to improvement of the design requirements as well.

SPC IN PRACTICE

WHERE AND WHERE NOT TO USE SPC

SPC can be applied virtually everywhere in operations—to products and services as well as to the processes that render them. Ordinarily it is used to monitor measures of an output or end result, characteristics of a product or service such as thickness of a contact lens or customer satisfaction rating of restaurant service. It can also be used to keep tabs on aspects of the process itself, for example setup times, supplier delivery and customer shipment delays, production lead times, worker tardiness, or anything else that is measurable and consequential. Control charting and monitoring ensure that a process remains stable. Monitoring, say, the number of mistakes on documents such as contracts, proposals, or blueprints enables discovery not only of when mistakes are on the rise, but also when the system for identifying mistakes is getting lax.

One restriction on the use of SPC is that the size of the population must be large enough for sampling to determine whether the population is stable. When the size is too small to employ sampling, then tracking and control decisions must instead be based upon screening. To detect process shifts that might result in nonconformities, a tool that can be used with screening is a **run diagram.** A run diagram looks similar to a control chart, though it has no statistical basis. The center line is usually the target value, and the upper and lower limits are the spec limits. To use a run diagram you inspect and plot *every* unit, monitor the pattern of points, and make a judgment. For example, a sequence of points with an upward or downward trend could suggest that a process is gradually shifting, so the process might be stopped and adjusted before any units move outside specifications. However, the judgment is completely subjective.

PRECONTROL

Assuming a process is stable and highly capable (as determined by SPC methods), another method, called **precontrol,** can then be used to monitor for changes that might result in nonconformities. While control charts monitor for shifts in a process that are statistically significant, precontrol *only* monitors for shifts that affect the number of nonconformities. Precontrol uses limits derived from the product specs.

There are many precontrol schemes; Figure 14.19 shows an example of one kind of precontrol chart. This chart is divided into three regions: an inner green region on either side of the target value that equals 50% of the total spec width and, on either side of that region, a yellow region that takes up the remaining 50% of the spec width (or 25% on either side of each green region); everything outside the specs is considered in the red region.[18]

To qualify a process for precontrol, initially every unit is inspected and adjustments are made to the process until *five consecutive units* fall inside the green region. At that point the process is considered OK (stable and conforming), and thereafter only two units are inspected at random times. The process is considered still OK as long as both inspected units are green, or one is green and one is yellow. However, should both units be yellow, or either be red, then the process is stopped for adjustment. After the adjustment, every unit is inspected until five consecutive greens occur, then random inspection resumes. The process does not actually require plotting points, nor even the existence of a precontrol chart; just compare the results of sample measurements to limits for the green and yellow regions, and do whatever the rules specify.

Most processes require periodic adjustment to remain within specifications, and six pairs of measurements between adjustments are considered adequate to ensure that a process stays within specs.[19] If, for example, a process ordinarily needs adjustment once an 8-hour day, a pair of measurements should be made about every 80 minutes.

Precontrol is based on the concept of **narrow-limit gauging,** which is to use tightened limits for inspection procedures as a way of reducing the risk of accepting

FIGURE 14.19

Precontrol limits.

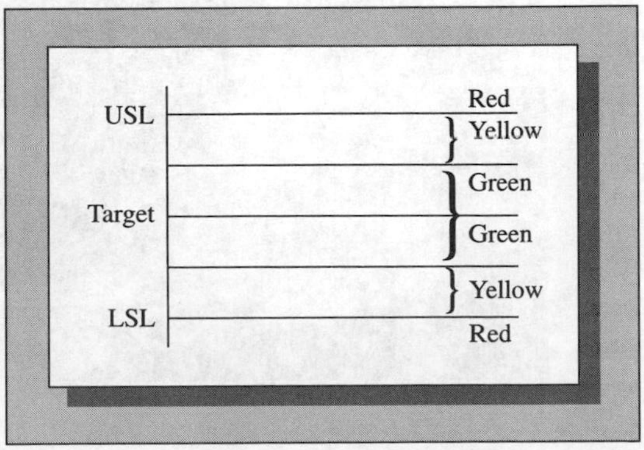

nonconforming products. Although precontrol is easy to perform, it applies only to processes that are stable, nearly centered on the target, and have a natural tolerance width (6-sigma) that is somewhat less than the spec width. Some authors argue that precontrol is effective only for processes with a capability index much greater than 1, even as much as 2 or 3.[20] Like process capability, precontrol solely emphasizes meeting specs and gives no value to being well inside them.

WHOSE RESPONSIBILITY IS SPC?

SPC in many organizations is done solely by experts in departments charged with assuring quality. Since knowledge of statistical concepts and construction and application of control charts are considered beyond the comprehension of the average worker, only professional inspectors are allowed to construct charts and take samples. Since process adjustments and improvements are considered technical matters, only quality engineers are allowed to diagnose and remedy special causes. Other people, the line workers, operators, and assemblers might collect samples and plot them, but interpretation of results and follow-up action are always left to others.

In TQM organizations, SPC is done by the experts too, however the acknowledged experts there are the operators and the workers. This is the concept of **on-line quality.** The line workers don't just take samples, they use the samples with control charts to determine when a process appears out of control, and then decide what to do about it—sometimes only halting production and calling in a supervisor, other times making an on-the-spot diagnosis and fixing a problem (Figure 14.20).

Giving workers responsibility for SPC makes sense for reasons of time and experience. Early warning and rapid feedback are the crux of process control, and there

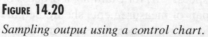

FIGURE 14.20

Sampling output using a control chart.

is no faster monitoring/corrective system than when workers do the diagnosing and fixing themselves. Often, an experienced worker can see and remedy a problem as well as a staff professional and can do it in less time than it would take just to call in a professional.

Although trusting workers with most of the responsibility for SPC changes the roles of former inspectors and other quality-assurance professionals, it does not diminish the importance of those roles. In place of inspection, the quality professionals take on responsibility for backing up and assisting the workers. They teach SPC and inspection methods, and develop sampling and inspection techniques. They even continue to perform some inspections and tests, but only the ones that are unique, technically complex, and require special expertise. They perform quality audits, both in-house and of suppliers, rate the process capability of suppliers, and certify suppliers. They also re-emphasize and reinforce the importance of following SPC procedures to workers, who sometimes, for lack of understanding, backslide while trying to do their best. At one company, workers decided it would be more efficient to inspect samples of four items instead of five, the number upon which the control charts were based. They had no idea that using the wrong sample size invalidated the control limits.

The following case in point is the experience of another company.

CASE IN POINT: SPC Empowerment at McDonnell & Miller[21]

In one area of the McDonnell & Miller plant, workers have full responsibility for SPC sampling and charting of their stage of the process. At another stage of the process, workers were discovering problems with part tolerances, even though the place where those problems originated—the stage monitored by workers using SPC—never once reported an out-of-control condition. When asked, the workers keeping the charts admitted that if a sample result fell outside the control limits, they simply plotted it inside the limits because, they said, it was too disruptive to shut down the process. Besides, they exclaimed, since points only *occasionally* fall outside the limits, what harm would there be to keeping the process running? Though the workers had attended an SPC seminar, appar-

ently all they understood were the mechanics about constructing control charts, sampling and inspection, and plotting results, not the purpose behind SPC.

The supervisor explained the need for accurate reporting and shutting down the process to investigate causes for out-of-control points. Though the workers now know why they should report out-of-control points, the question is, Will they? Who knows. To them, stopping the process is a hassle, and unless they completely understand the impact of not stopping it on product quality, customer satisfaction, company competitiveness, or their job security, it is possible they will continue to misrepresent results, at least sometimes.

Employees might be motivated to do the best they can, but what they see as best is relative to their understanding of why certain things must be done. When employees attend a 2–4-hour seminar on SPC, which is standard for training workers new skills sets, the best that can be hoped for is that they come away with *some* understanding of the seminar's content. Since the portions of the seminar absorbed and the depth of understanding will vary, employees' ability to apply what they learned will vary too (this of course applies not just to frontline workers, but also to managers and staffers).

Workers first introduced to SPC are often puzzled about its purpose. Although they might be accustomed to dealing with specs and be able to distinguish conforming items from nonconforming items, they find statistical control concepts sometimes confusing. For example, confusing specs with control limits, they might question what to do when a process moves outside control limits, but stays within specs. Such questions lead to confusion about, and possible resistance to, the purpose of SPC. It is best to address such questions before they are actually ever raised by using recurring SPC training sessions, on-the-job assistance, and establishing company policy on quality issues. For these reasons, empowering workers with SPC will take a while to succeed.

THE SPC/DOE CONNECTION

Design-of-experiment (DOE) methods can be useful in SPC. An important part of process control is diagnosing sources of variation. To get to the root cause, it might be necessary to experiment—to purposely change certain factors in hopes of observing changes in the way the process responds. Sometimes the problem is a large degree of random variation: the process is stable, but the variation is too great. High process variation can originate from a large number of factors (numerous common causes). Without an organized analysis approach such as that offered by DOE, attempts to identify the relevant factors can be time-consuming and costly and won't contribute much to new understanding.

Conversely, SPC can be used as a tool in DOE for ensuring that processes are stable and reducing process variation before experiments begin. Although process stability (that is, statistical control) is not a prerequisite for drawing conclusions from an experiment, a stable process is more sensitive to changes. The quieter the process, the easier it is through experimentation to observe the effects of small changes in process parameters. Also, actions taken as the result of knowledge gained from experiments are more likely to yield the anticipated results when the process is stable.

SPC CAVEATS

SPC addresses only the production–delivery piece of the overall total quality scheme. Two other pieces also have to be in place, one before SPC, the other afterward; otherwise, in the long run, SPC is worthless. First there must be a design effort that ensures that products or services, as designed, fulfill or exceed customer expectations. This effort, the subject of Chapter 12, provides the spec *targets* to which production–delivery seeks conformance.

At the other end is full-service follow-up on products and services; this provides (1) necessary support so customers can maximally benefit from products and services already obtained and (2) information about existing and future customer requirements and competitors' best products and best practices for use as input for redesigns and new designs.

SPC cannot always quickly catch an out-of-control condition, nor can screening. A few out-of-control situations and possible resulting nonconformities still get by, if only because of inspection errors. These will be discovered at later stages of the process or eventually by the final customer. Regardless of when a problem is first discovered, the best way to prevent it from happening again is to identify the cause and inform the source or producer. Every organization should have a rapid-feedback system that connects every stage of the process (including suppliers and final customers), and that points out defects, complaints, and out-of-control conditions to the stages that can rectify them. General Electric, when it redesigned a dishwasher, thoroughly surveyed the first thousand purchasers, then used the results to improve both the product design and the manufacturing process.

Summary

Statistical process control is a method for tracking, identifying, and controlling process changes. Assuming that a process starts out doing what it is supposed to, then as long as there is no fundamental change the process is considered suitable and in-control. One difficulty with determining whether a process is doing the same thing or has fundamentally changed is that all processes exhibit variation due to common causes and special causes. Variation from common causes represents variation inherent to the process, and such variation represents no fundamental change. Variation from special causes, however, is not inherent to the process, and its occurrence represents a change in the process, an out-of-control situation.

Since process variation is ongoing and expected, a way is needed to distinguish whether a given measured variation is due to common or special causes—whether the process is in control or out of control. With SPC, samples from the process are periodically inspected, and the results are plotted on control charts. A control chart has upper and lower control limits, and as long as the results stay within the limits and appear random, the process is assumed to be in control. Results that fall outside the limits or appear nonrandom suggest an out-of-control situation, in which case the process is stopped and a special cause is sought. If a special cause is found, it is remedied and a new control chart is constructed. Like all statistical sampling procedures, use of control charts involves risks of concluding that a process is in control when it is not, or that a process is out-of-control, when in fact it is in control. Control-chart design requires consideration of the acceptable level of risk.

Control charts are used to monitor different process parameters. For variables-type inspection, the means chart and X-bar chart are ways to monitor the mean or central tendency of a process, and the R-chart is a way to monitor variation about the mean. For attributes-type inspection, p-charts monitor the proportion of items in a category and c-charts monitor the count, or number of occurrences of a characteristic in a sample.

Before a control chart is used to monitor a process, the process must first be stable, otherwise the process mean, range, standard deviation, or other parameters cannot be determined. The procedure for constructing a control chart is one way to determine whether a process is stable and, if not, what must be done to make it stable.

A manufacturing process is capable when a very high proportion of the output meets product specifications. Capability and process stability and control are separate issues, so a process can be stable and in control, yet fail miserably at meeting product specifications. SPC procedures are used to assess process capability and to guide efforts to improve that capability.

Process capability, per se, provides no motivation to improve a process beyond meeting product specifications, although the Taguchi loss function, another capability concept, does. This function quantifies the cost of not hitting the target specification. It goes beyond process capability and drives home the importance of hitting the target, not just coming close.

SPC is applicable to any process that runs long enough to be stabilized and from which samples can be periodically inspected. For short-running processes, alternative control approaches include run diagrams and precontrol charts.

In JIT/TQM organizations, most control charting and process monitoring is done by the workers. A purpose of control charting is to spot problems and quickly fix them. The most effective way to do that is to incorporate sampling and charting activities into the work process. By giving workers SPC training and responsibility, a process can be continuously monitored and emerging problems can be identified and resolved before they harm output quality.

Companies diligent at SPC and that practice quality of design can achieve a very high level of quality. Nonetheless, there are limitations to what even SPC and design can achieve, so to meet even higher quality standards requires further measures. These measures, which include self-checking and successive checking, source inspection, and pokayoke, are the topics of the next chapter.

Questions

1. Describe the difference between common causes of variation in a process and special causes of variation. Give specific examples of both not mentioned in this chapter.

2. For dinner you order a pizza from a place that you have ordered pizza from numerous times. The measure of the pizza is how well you think it tastes. What are some common causes of variation in the result? What are some special, assignable causes?

3. What is the meaning of a process being in statistical control?

4. What does it mean for a process to be stable?

5. For what purposes are control charts used?

6. What happens to the variation of the sampling distribution as the sample size is increased?

7. Explain the following concepts described in this chapter: sampling basis, sample size, and sampling frequency. Discuss how each affects the validity of sampling results.

8. Explain the purpose of the following: $\overline{X}$-charts, R-charts, p-charts, c-charts. Give examples of processes where each is appropriate.

9. Suppose you sample a process and determine that the estimated mean is not the same as the target mean. What should you do?

10. Suppose you sample a process, create control limits, toss out sample values that lie outside the limits, recompute the limits, etc., and you are left with 10 samples. What might you conclude? What should you do?

11. What is the difference between the natural tolerance of a process and the specification tolerance (spec width)?

12. What do C_p and C_{pk} mean? How are they different?

13. Interpret each of the following:

$$C_p = 0.5, 1.0, 1.33; C_{pk} = 1.0, -1.0.$$

14. What logical conclusion is drawn from Taguchi's loss function? How does the loss function concept differ from the traditional focus on conformance to specs?

15. Comment on the following statement: Suppose the output of a process is uniformly distributed but lies entirely inside the specs; since all units meet the specs, there is no need to improve the process.

16. When are control charts not practical or feasible? What are the alternatives to control charts?

17. Discuss the pros and cons of employees performing SPC (data collection, charting results, follow-up).

18. If workers take over responsibility for sampling inspection and control charting, what happens to the role of the traditional inspector and the quality control department?

19. Why might a process that is *not* in statistical control be a good candidate for experimentation?

Problems

1. The data below are $\overline{X}$-and R-values for 25 samples, size $n = 5$, taken from a process that produces gaskets.

Time	Sample	$\overline{X}$	R	Time	Sample	$\overline{X}$	R
8:00 AM	1	2.93	0.24	12:20 PM	14	2.92	0.11
8:20	2	2.79	0.07	12:40	15	2.91	0.20
8:40	3	2.95	0.15	1:00	16	2.92	0.11
9:00	4	2.92	0.25	1:20	17	2.90	0.27
9:20	5	2.90	0.19	1:40	18	3.00	0.09
9:40	6	2.95	0.21	2:00	19	2.91	0.25
10:00	7	2.91	0.22	2:20	20	2.90	0.25
10:20	8	2.90	0.22	2:40	21	2.87	0.22
10:40	9	2.89	0.20	3:00	22	2.92	0.13
11:00	10	2.93	0.21	3:20	23	2.86	0.21
11:20	11	2.87	0.27	3:40	24	2.40	0.22
11:40	12	2.88	0.24	4:00	25	2.86	0.17
12:00	13	2.95	0.19				

Set up $\overline{X}$- and R-charts for the process. If necessary, assume outliers have assignable causes and recompute the control limits. Does the process appear to be in statistical control?

2. A glass producer examines its production output for cracked glasses. The size of each sample is 24. The results for 20 consecutive days follow:

Day	No. Cracked or Broken	Day	No. Cracked or Broken
1	1	11	3
2	6	12	11
3	9	13	6
4	7	14	2
5	3	15	4
6	4	16	3
7	10	17	3
8	2	18	5
9	4	19	6
10	5	20	4

Set up a p-chart to monitor the process. If necessary revise the limits. Does the process seem to be in control?

3. Fifty parts are inspected each day over 25 working days, and the number with defects are recorded in the table below. Construct a p-chart. If points lie outside the limits, assume an assignable cause, and revise the chart.

Day	No. Defective	Day	No. Defective	Day	No. Defective
1	3	10	3	18	8
2	2	11	0	19	1
3	0	12	1	20	3
4	3	13	2	21	3
5	0	14	4	22	7
6	2	15	4	23	0
7	0	16	1	24	2
8	1	17	0	25	1
9	2				

4. Assembly of a certain product requires the use of many fasteners. Workers spend much time aligning the holes for the fasteners on parts to be assembled. The supervisor believes that the number of cases where holes do not properly align is on the rise, though assembly workers feel that the number of alignment problems is staying about the same. The workers keep track of alignment errors on 30 products. The results are shown below.

Product	Alignment Errors	Product	Alignment Errors	Product	Alignment Errors
1	5	11	2	21	5
2	3	12	3	22	9
3	1	13	4	23	2
4	5	14	7	24	4
5	2	15	5	25	3
6	4	16	3	26	5
7	1	17	2	27	6
8	3	18	11	28	4
9	4	19	3	29	5
10	5	20	5	30	3

   a. Construct a c-chart.

   b. Is the number of alignment errors stable?

   c. Is there any indication that the number of errors is on the increase?

5. Control charts for $\overline{X}$ and R are maintained for an important quality characteristic. The sample size is $n = 8$. After 25 samples we find that

$$\sum_{i=1}^{25} \overline{X}_i = 105.80, \qquad \sum_{i=1}^{25} R_i = 2.64.$$

Set up $\overline{X}$- and R-charts and calculate the estimated standard deviation. For outliers, assume assignable causes, and recompute.

6. Thirty samples of size $n = 4$ are taken from a production process every hour. A quality characteristic is measured, and $\overline{X}$ and R are computed for each sample. After 30 samples have been analyzed, we have the following results:

$$\sum_{i=1}^{30} \overline{X}_i = 720, \qquad \sum_{i=1}^{30} R_i = 12.$$

   a. Find the control limits for the $\overline{X}$- and R-charts.

   b. Assume the process is stable, regardless of what you may have found in (*a*). Find the standard deviation.

   c. If specs are set at 24 ± 0.25, estimate the fraction of the process output that is nonconforming.

7. Fifteen samples of size $n = 3$ are taken from a process with the following results:

				$\overline{X}$	R
1	96.2	89.1	80	88.4	16.2
2	66.3	136.9	83.3	95.5	70.6
3	58.4	97.4	81.9	79.2	39
4	95.3	82	130.4	102.6	48.4
5	115.3	92.7	90.6	99.6	24.7
6	86.1	71.8	86.9	81.6	15.1
7	106	70	76.1	84.1	36

(Continued)

				$\bar{X}$	R
8	61.8	107.9	65.2	78.3	46.1
9	78.9	57.2	67.7	67.9	21.7
10	97.4	79.5	47.1	71.3	50.3
11	148.2	128	129.6	135.3	20.2
12	153.1	105.6	131.6	130	47.7
13	105.9	116.4	127.9	116.8	22
14	98.3	106.7	117.7	107.6	19.4
15	137	143.2	123	134.4	20.2

    a. Compute the limits for $\bar{X}$- and R-charts. Assume assignable causes for outliers. Recompute if necessary. Use

$$\sum_{i=1}^{15} \bar{X}_i = 1473, \qquad \sum_{i=1}^{15} R_i = 498.$$

    b. Assume the process is stable. Compute the standard deviation, C_p and C_{pk}.

    c. Assume the specs are set at 90 ± 10. Estimate the proportion of the process that conforms to the specs.

  8. A manufacturing process is producing an important piece for a door lock mechanism. After 20 samples of size $n = 5$, the results are as follows:

$$\sum_{i=1}^{20} \bar{X}_i = 9.69, \qquad \sum_{i=1}^{20} R_i = 0.228.$$

    Assume the process is in statistical control. The specs are set at 0.48 ± 0.025 cm. Calculate C_p and C_{pk}.

  9. Assume a process is in statistical control. Specs are set at 0.34 ± 0.015. Twenty-five samples of size $n = 4$ are drawn with the following results:

$$\sum_{i=1}^{25} \bar{X}_i = 8.58, \qquad \sum_{i=1}^{25} R_i = 0.643.$$

    Calculate C_p and C_{pk}.

10. The output of a process is normally distributed and has a mean of 55.25 and a standard deviation of 1.50. The spec on the item is 55.25 ± 3.25.

    a. Compute the capability indexes C_p and C_{pk} and interpret their meaning.

    b. Suppose the mean is 50.25. Recompute the indexes; interpret their meaning.

    c. How much would the standard deviation have to be decreased for the process in part (*b*) to have a C_{pk} of 2.0?

11. A process has upper and lower specs of 45.5 and 43.5, respectively. The customer requires a minimum C_{pk} of 2.0. What must the process mean and standard deviation be, assuming the process is normally distributed?

12. A drilling process results in bore holes that are normally distributed. The spec for the bore is 1.585 ± 0.007 cm. Eight samples of five parts are measured, as shown in the following table. What are the upper and lower capability indexes C_{PU} and C_{PL}? What percentage of the process output will be outside the specs?

			Sample				
1	*2*	*3*	*4*	*5*	*6*	*7*	*8*
1.567	1.584	1.583	1.585	1.586	1.590	1.588	1.584
1.576	1.597	1.598	1.575	1.587	1.587	1.582	1.586
1.586	1.588	1.587	1.582	1.586	1.588	1.587	1.582
1.574	1.583	1.589	1.583	1.582	1.585	1.586	1.590
1.590	1.594	1.590	1.588	1.584	1.567	1.584	1.583

13. The spec for a part is 3.550 ± 0.010 inch. The cost of reworking a part outside the spec is $5. What is the Taguchi loss function?

14. A motor is designed for an output of 5000 ± 50 rpm. Failure to meet this requirement is estimated to cost $500.
    a. What is the *k*-value for the Taguchi loss function?
    b. If the process meets the nominal (target) value with a standard deviation of 30 rpm, what is the expected loss per motor?

15. A shaft and hole are designed so that the clearance between them is $3.000 \pm .002$ mm. The loss due to not meeting the spec is $8. Twenty-five assemblies are randomly checked for clearance, with the following results:

2.999	3.001	3.001	3.000	2.998
3.000	3.002	3.000	3.000	2.999
3.000	3.001	2.998	2.999	3.000
3.000	3.001	3.000	2.999	3.001
3.001	3.000	3.000	3.002	3.000

    a. What is the *k*-value for the Taguchi loss function?
    b. What is the expected loss from this process?

16. In production of a machined part, any part that exceeds a width by ± 10 cm is unacceptable and results in a loss of $600. The manufacturer estimates that this tolerance can be guaranteed by adding a procedure that will cost $2.00 per unit.
    a. What is the Taguchi loss function?
    b. If the nominal value is 100 cm, at what tolerance should the part be manufactured?

17. A manufacturer of vessels for holding gas under high pressure monitors the thickness of the vessel walls by measuring the thickness of a sample at four locations and calculating the average. Five averages are considered a rational subgroup, and a subgroup is inspected every day.
    a. After 25 days of inspection,

$$\Sigma \bar{X} = 15.5, \qquad \Sigma R = 2.35.$$

    Determine the control limits for $\bar{X}$ and *R*-charts.
    b. Each data point is the average of the wall thickness measured at four locations on a vessel. Based on the discussion in the chapter on rational subgroups, what might be a weakness of this procedure?

Endnotes

1. We use sample means, not individual values, because there is less variability to means than to the values used to compute them. When sampling, every time we inspect the process, we look at multiple items. Looking at multiple items instead of only one gives a more accurate representation of the process. The larger the sample size, the more accurate the representation.

2. The Central Limit Theorem tells us this.

3. On a continuous distribution, the probability that a sample lies on a point is zero. Thus, to find a probability that a sample would be a particular value, we must instead compute the probability that it be of a particular value *or greater;* this computation provides the *area* under the normal curve starting from that point and outward.

4. It is common practice in the US. Elsewhere in the world, it is also common practice to start with a desired value for α, then to choose the corresponding z-value.

5. Although, for example, the target value is 8.520 cm, we might settle on, say, 8.5155 cm as the average shaft length for the process. It might be economically infeasible to adjust the process to get any closer to 8.520, or, perhaps 8.5155 average length is deemed good enough to satisfy the customer. More about this later.

6. Besides the three-sigma limit criterion, there are other statistical tests commonly used in control charts to indicate that a process may be out of control involving one- and two-sigma limits, as described before in application of Figure 14.8. *See* J. Banks, *Principles of Quality Control* (New York: John Wiley), p. 141; and D.C. Montgomery, *Introduction to Statistical Quality Control* (2nd ed.) (John Wiley, 1991), p. 117.

7. Once in a while no special (assignable) cause will be found, in which case the sample is presumed to have originated from common causes and is, therefore, retained for the computation. Remember, the sampling distribution is normal, so occasional outliers are to be expected.

8. It is worth repeating that if, in the course of the above procedure, too many samples are discarded, the process is possibly unstable and in need of adjustment. Following adjustments, the procedure is repeated again, starting from scratch with m new samples.

9. Other statistical rules, as remarked on earlier and in note 6 above, might also be used to judge potential out-of-control behavior.

10. Successful application of the concept of rational sampling is essential to SPC. An excellent discussion is provided by E. Grant and R. Leavenworth, *Statistical Quality Control* (6th ed.) (New York: McGraw-Hill, 1988), pp. 154–76.

11. *Ibid.*

12. The classification of something into one of two possible categories follows a binomial distribution, though to simplify construction of the p-chart that distribution is *approximated* using a normal distribution. That approximation, theoretically, requires that both np and $n(1 - p)$ be greater than 5.

13. The sample size n for an attributes control chart must be large enough so there is a high probability of detecting at least one nonconformity. For the computational details, *see* D.C. Montgomery, *Introduction to Statistical Quality Control,* pp. 160–2.

14. R. DeVor, T.H. Chang, and J. Sutherland, *Statistical Quality Design and Control,* (New York: Macmillan, 1992), p. 200.

15. Motorola promotes "six-sigma" to imply a C_p of 2.0; thus, the goal is to develop manufacturing processes where one must go six standard deviations above or below the mean before encountering a spec limit. When specs are set at $\pm 6\sigma$, shifts as large as $\pm 1.5\sigma$ result in only 3.4 ppm (parts per million) falling outside the specs.

16. Critics charge that Taguchi's ideas are not original. Regardless, what is original is the way he packaged the ideas into a total philosophy encompassing both managerial and engineering design criteria. See Chapter 12.

17. This loss formula applies when the target value is fixed. In cases where the target value is as large as possible (e.g., tensile strength), the formula is $L = k(x)^2$; when the desired target value is as small as possible (e.g., static interference), $L = k(1/x)^2$.

18. This is but one way of setting precontrol limits; another is described by R. Schonberger in *World Class Manufacturing: The Lessons of Simplicity Applied* (New York: The Free Press, 1986), pp. 132–4.

19. J.M. Juran and F. Gryna, *Quality Planning and Analysis* (3rd ed.) (New York: McGraw-Hill, 1993) pp. 391–2.

20. *See* D. Montgomery, *Introduction to Statistical Quality Control,* pp. 332–4.

21. Conversation with Avi Soni, Manager of Manufacturing, ITT McDonnell & Miller.

15 SYSTEMS FOR ELIMINATING DEFECTS

The man [or woman] who makes no mistakes does not usually make anything.

Bishop W.C. Magee

It is the nature of man [and woman] to err, but only the fool perseveres in error.

Cicero

This chapter represents the next step in a logical progression of quality of conformance methods, a progression that starts with tools for discovering and weeding out defects, moves to ways that signal emerging problems before they affect quality, and ends with methods for eliminating the very sources of defects.

The key to all quality of conformance methods for discovering and eliminating defects is inspection procedures that give accurate and timely information about causes of defects. SPC is one such informative kind of inspection system: whenever a problem is detected, the stage of the process where the problem likely originated is identified so the cause can be diagnosed and corrective action taken. There are, however, other kinds of inspection systems that do the same thing and, argues Shigeo Shingo,[1] the prominent Japanese production expert, if the goal is to **eliminate defects,** these other kinds, *not SPC alone,* must be employed.

The four concepts for eliminating defects discussed in this chapter are complete inspection, source inspection, pokayoke, and jidoka. Though listed here separately, the concepts overlap considerably, and a single method or procedure might simultaneously incorporate all of them. These concepts are part of the total quality management toolkit, and they are applied in concert with the SPC and quality-of-design tools discussed in previous chapters. It takes all of them, not one or two alone, to elevate quality to the level mandated by world-class competition.

SPC LIMITATIONS

There is no worker, machine, or process that does not, on rare occasion, do something incorrectly. Given the random nature of errors or mistakes in production systems, there is the probability that a defect will occur at sometime other than during sampling. Since SPC relies on sampling, it can miss occasional defects from sources that are ephemeral. Even when shifts occur in process parameters and are detected by sampling, the time lag between when the process shift occurs and is first detected allows time for a substantial quantity of items to be affected and for the cause of the shift to disappear. Further, to achieve very small defect levels using SPC, it is necessary to employ variables inspection. Yet there are cases where variables inspection is inappropriate and where defects can be detected only through human sensory inspection or automated inspection of attributes.

Besides limitations from sampling, there are situations where SPC is simply not practical or feasible, for example, when items are produced only in small batch quantities or in quantities too small to establish guaranteed process stability, and in processes where *no* defects or process shifting is allowable. This chapter discusses forms of inspection systems and related measures applicable when SPC alone is inadequate or cannot be employed, or where the goal is not to just reduce defects, but to eliminate them.

100% INSPECTION (SCREENING)

As mentioned, the two fundamental drawbacks of SPC are that it relies on sampling and that it allows a sometimes substantial delay between when a problem originates and is corrected. So, to minimize the chance of overlooking defects or of missing random problems that have fleeting causes, it is necessary to do 100% inspection.[2] Additionally, to minimize the time lag between when a problem is identified and remedied, it is necessary to combine inspection, analysis, and corrective action with the original work task. To this end, wherever feasible, responsibility for these duties should be given to the people actually doing the work. This is accomplished via self-checks and successive checks.

SELF-CHECKS AND SUCCESSIVE CHECKS

Self-Checks

After a worker performs a task, he checks the result. If he detects a problem and if the solution is within his capability, he immediately fixes it. Self-check inspection and correction are the most rapid of informative inspection systems. Potentially, however, self-check objectivity and accuracy can be poor if workers are biased in judging their own workmanship or if they forget to inspect things. One way to increase inspection objectivity and reduce oversights is with successive checks.

Successive Checks

With this method, the next worker in the process inspects the previous worker's output. In Figure 15.1, worker B checks worker A's output, worker C checks worker B's output, and so on. Whenever a worker detects a problem that originated upstream, he passes the item back to the previous worker, who is then responsible for correcting the problem and doing whatever is necessary to prevent it from recurring. For exceptionally important items there can be double checking: both worker B and worker C check the output of worker A.

If it is impossible for the worker at the immediate successive stage of a process to perform the inspection, then the worker at the next-nearest subsequent operation does it instead. Whenever inspection calls for particular knowledge, skill, or judgment, an additional **specialized check** is introduced wherein a worker with the requisite skill or knowledge also does checking. After each day's work, the special inspector meets

FIGURE 15.1

Self-checks and successive checks.

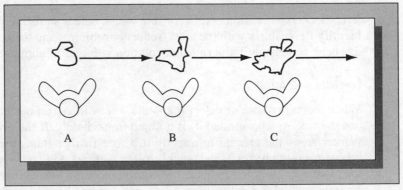

with the worker whose output she inspected and any workers doing successive checks to discuss the results. The purpose of the discussion is to point out defects or problems the workers missed and, eventually, to transfer inspection skills from the special inspector to the workers.

Despite the potential for lower objectivity, self-checks, conducted properly, can be more effective than successive checks. Quick feedback is essential to achieving zero defects because unless identified immediately, problem sources vanish, only to reappear and cause difficulties later on. Self-checks permit *immediate* problem identification and response. Also, given that most people prefer to find their own mistakes over having others find them, self-checks do not garner worker animosity or resistance.

In the same vein, successive checks are more effective than are checks performed by supervisors or staff inspectors. Successive checks result in somewhat-quick feedback about quality problems, though beyond that, workers tend to be more accepting of mistakes pointed out by their colleagues than by managers and staff members. An immediate colleague can point out a particular mistake made only moments earlier, whereas a supervisor or inspector will more likely speak in generalities about something that happened possibly hours or days before.

REQUIREMENTS FOR SELF-CHECKING AND SUCCESSIVE CHECKING

Some minimal requirements for effective screening with self-check and/or successive checks include setting appropriate check targets, enabling quick feedback and action, and management showing consideration and providing support to workers.

Check Targets

Requiring workers to check too many things on every item is counterproductive. They either forget to check them all, or they get sloppy with whatever they do check. Only two or three check targets should be inspected by each worker. Features that are critical in terms of safety, performance, appearance, and so on, or are subject to frequent problems should always be checked. Other features should be checked based upon statistics maintained on defect occurrences as identified by the worker, successive checkers, or customers. Every few weeks defect statistics should be reviewed to identify the features with the most frequent problems, and these should be considered as check targets until a permanent solution is found to eliminate them.

Feedback and Action

Whenever a problem or defect is spotted, the worker responsible for the problem (if not the worker who spotted it) is notified immediately. If the problem is chronic, the worker stops the process to remedy it before further items are affected. When the problem cannot be remedied quickly, other workers and staff specialists are called in for assistance. Colored lights called **andons** located at each workstation, and **status boards** located centrally above a line or a workcell for everyone to see, are used to signal each workstation's status and/or need for assistance. For example, a green light (or light off) means "situation normal"; yellow means "working to resolve a problem"; red means "difficult problem, send help." Yellow and red usually suggest a temporary stoppage of work at the workstation; if the process is synchronized, then every station stops. Problems in manufacturing processes often stem from inappropriate procedures and inadequate worker training, and with andons it is easy to identify the stages where workers need training, procedures need changing, and so on.

Consideration and Support for Workers

Workers are obviously at the core of self-checks and successive checks, so there is no way this process will work without worker dedication. There are several important interrelated points here:

1. Workers must know (and management must ensure) that the inspection process is not used as a tool to evaluate them. If they think the purpose of inspection is to gather data to evaluate them, the workers will collectively undermine the process by overlooking problems. Some human error is inevitable and is expected; the purpose of self-checks and successive inspection is to identify places where inadvertent or procedural errors occur and to improve procedures to reduce errors.

2. Workers must be given a time allowance to improve quality. They must be given extra time during the production day to permit line stoppages and interim problem corrections, as well as at the end of the day or week to discuss problem causes and solutions. Providing workers this additional time is one way management shows commitment to finding long-term solutions to quality problems.

3. In most operations, workers have relatively little control over major factors that influence quality, so simply giving them additional responsibility is not enough. Joseph Juran distinguishes between worker-controllable and management-controllable situations. In terms of preventing or discovering and eliminating defects,

· A worker-controllable situation is one where workers are provided with
(1) knowledge about what they are supposed to do, (2) knowledge about

what they are actually doing, and (3) a process that is *capable* of meeting specifications.

· If any of these three conditions is missing, the situation is management-controllable.

Juran estimates that about 80% of defects are management-controllable regardless of industry, that is, situations where, simply, workers do not have adequate knowledge or an adequate process to do quality work.[3] Competent inspection and problem solving by workers is predicated on their being well trained in the tools of inspection, data collection, and problem solving. Besides training, management must provide whatever technical resources are necessary to make the process capable (e.g., redefining specifications or altering the process). Worker effort alone is often insufficient to improve process capability.

4. Pre-existing quantity-oriented quotas and piece rates must be eliminated before workers can be expected to take seriously any responsibility for self-checking and successive checking.[4] Workers paid according to production quotas or piece rates will overlook defects because they are, in effect, being paid to overlook whatever reduces their volume of output.

AUTOMATION

Although it is often believed that automated inspection is better than human inspection, in general, it is not. When 100% manual inspection is employed using self-checks and/or successive checks, the rate of error detection can be almost as good as with automated devices. Only in places where it is very difficult or physically impossible for humans to do an inspection, when the unit cycle times are very short, and when the inspection accuracy must be very high is automated inspection necessary or more effective. Generally, however, the overriding advantage of automation is not accuracy or reliability of measurement, but cost. Replacing manual inspections with automated inspections tends to reduce inspection costs in the long run, especially when items are produced in very large volumes and have a large number of inspection targets.

CYCLE TIME

The typical contention about using self-checks and/or successive checks, especially with screening, is increased cycle time. Shingo argues that, although the cycle time increases initially (workers need additional time to perform inspections and remedy problems on the spot), the increase is often small (sometimes only 10%) and, eventually, drops to only a few percent or less. As the inspection procedures become more familiar, workers integrate them into their pre-existing tasks. As defects are spotted and problem sources are eliminated, the frequency of work stoppage decreases. Even when the ultimate cycle time does not return to the pre-existing value, the overall average production lead time is reduced since final inspection and rework are virtually eliminated. In processes where the cycle times are very short and where inspection time would have a significant impact, then less than 100% inspection, say, every second, fifth, or tenth item, can be done instead. As mentioned, automated inspection is also a consideration.

PURSUIT OF PERFECTION: LIMITS OF INSPECTION

Screening with self-checks and successive checks can improve quality levels beyond sampling inspection by increasing both the comprehensiveness of screening and the speed of feedback; however, even it cannot achieve perfection. Recall the discussion of inspection accuracy in Chapter 13. Just as inadvertent mistakes exist in any production task, so they exist in inspection. Inadvertent inspection mistakes are inevitable, and no amount of measurement calibration, inspection experience, or training can eliminate them. Even in cases where the reliability and consistency (degree of error variation) of inspection can be improved by automation, *some* inaccuracy will still be present.

The accumulated effect of small inaccuracies in inspection can be significant, even when the process defect rate (rate prior to inspection) is already small. For example, suppose an operation with an average defect rate of 0.25% (.0025) employs 100% inspection with both self-checking and successive checking. Further, suppose the self-checks and successive checks are each 95% effective at finding defects. At the operation itself, where a 0.25% defect rate translates into 2500 defective ppm, the self-check will identify 95% of them, or 2,375 ppm. Thus, 125 defective ppm will remain undetected and go to the next operation. At the next operation, the successive check will identify 95% of the undetected defects, or 119 ppm more. Thus, 6 defective ppm will remain undetected—an overall defect rate of 0.00007%.

Although a defective rate of 6 ppm might seem inconsequential, consider that a typical product comprises numerous components assembled at many stages and that the cumulative effect of defects in every component on the final product is exponential. In the example, suppose the final product consists of 100 components, each of which has a final defect rate of only 6 ppm. Since each part is 999,994 ppm good, the overall effect on the final assembled product of 100 parts is 0.999994^{100} or 0.9994002, the equivalent of 999,400 ppm of final product with no defective parts. This leaves 600 ppm that contain defective components. Had the product comprised 1000 components of similar quality, the overall good yield would be only 0.999994^{1000} or 0.994018, which results in 5982 ppm of final product with defective components. These examples illustrate the extreme difficulty and virtual impossibility of achieving zero defects, even when using 100% inspection and double-checking items that were pretty good to start with!

SOURCE INSPECTION AND POKAYOKE

Shingo asserts that since traditional inspection is aimed at finding problems in *outputs* (parts, materials, products), any conclusions drawn from such inspection will serve to remedy defects or restore process parameters, but not to *prevent* the defects or process changes in the first place. As a result, Shingo reasons, given that every defect or process change has a cause or source, the only way to achieve zero defects is to discover the conditions that give rise to defects or process changes and eliminate them. This is what Shingo refers to as **source inspection.**

Most often, defects occur because of the following situations:

1. Inappropriate work processes or operating procedures (e.g., unsuitable heat-treatment temperature, incorrect assembly or machining procedure).
2. Excessive variation in operations (e.g., excessive play or wobble in a machine) resulting in machine wear, vibration, out-of-adjustment operation, or lack of specificity in procedures.
3. Damaged or defective raw materials.
4. Inadvertent errors by workers or machines (e.g., an occasional random oversight by assembly workers or a machine occasionally jamming because of dirt buildup).

In general, the first three of these problematic situations can be resolved, respectively, by

1. Improving work processes and procedures and using standard operation routines.
2. Exercising good housekeeping, preventive maintenance, constant monitoring of equipment, and using standard operation routines.
3. Working with suppliers to ensure no defective materials ever enter the process.

Nevertheless, even with perfect procedures, perfect equipment, and perfect raw materials, defects will occur because of situation 4, *inadvertent* errors. Screening will catch most defects from inadvertent error, but some defects will still get by.

Before discussing the solution to the problem of defects from inadvertent errors, consider the following five examples of situations where no amount of worker training or vigilance would eliminate defects.

Example 1.   A worker in an assembly workcell spot welds frames at eight locations. The cell produces three different kinds of frames; the three frames all require eight welds, but the welds are in slightly different places for each frame. The problem is that sometimes the worker misses a weld.

Example 2.   Five similar but different products move along the same assembly line (in a mixed-model assembly process). The different models require different fittings that workers select from bins and attach to the products as they move by. Occasionally workers select and attach the wrong fittings to a product.

Example 3.   Small batches of items arrive at a paint department, and each batch is painted the color specified by a code number on a kanban ticket attached to the batch. Sometimes the wrong paint is selected, and the entire batch is painted the wrong color.

Example 4.   Metal panels are formed by inserting rectangular sheets into a stamping press. Occasionally the worker inserts the sheet upside down.

Example 5.   A worker installs three switches on a control panel, and for each switch she must first insert a spring. Sometimes she forgets to insert the spring. Without the spring, a switch will not work.

SOURCE INSPECTION

In all of the above examples subsequent inspection of the part or product will likely reveal the defects, although no amount of inspection will ever prevent the defects from occurring again. Since complete inspection will ultimately reveal most of the defects, the concern here is more with the waste incurred by the defects than with the fact that they occurred in the first place. In Example 4, the defective metal sheets will have to be scrapped, and in all the other examples the defective parts will have to be disassembled or reworked.

One commonality in the above examples is that in each case the *source* of the defects is known. That being the case, these sources can be monitored and eventually eliminated. Eliminating the source of a defect is equivalent to eliminating the opportunity for the defect to ever occur again. This is the principle of **source inspection.**

FIGURE 15.2

Example 1: Pokayoke to ensure correct number of welds.

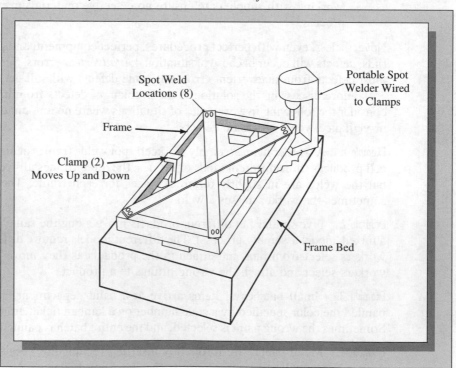

Shingo refers to schemes or devices used in source inspection as **pokayoke,** a Japanese term that is roughly equivalent to error proofing or mistake proofing. The following gives examples of pokayoke solutions for eliminating mistakes and defects in the five examples.

Example 1. Each time a frame is welded, it is first placed on a frame bed where two clamps automatically drop over it (see Figure 15.2). The spot welder is attached to a counter, which in turn is attached to the clamps. Only after the number of spot welds reaches eight will the clamps release. No frame with fewer than eight welds can be released from the frame bed.

Example 2. Attached to the side of each product is a large card with a bar code. Just before the product arrives at the station where the fittings are to be attached, a scanner reads the card and automatically turns on lights on all bins containing parts for just that product (see Figure 15.3). The normal time required for a worker to withdraw and attach parts to each product is 40 seconds. Every bin has a motion sensor, and unless parts have been withdrawn from all the appropriate bins within 30 seconds, lights flash at the bins where parts have yet to be withdrawn. A buzzer sounds and the line stops until the parts are withdrawn.

FIGURE 15.3

Example 2: Pokayoke to ensure correct parts selection.

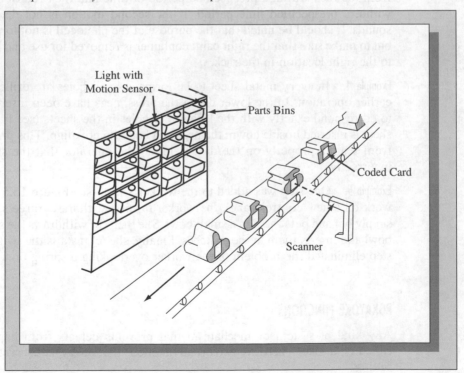

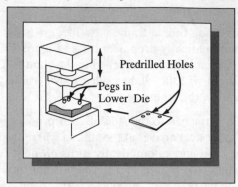

FIGURE 15.4

Example 4: Pokayoke to ensure proper placement of sheet in press.

Example 3.   Similar to Example 2, attached to each container of items to be painted is a kanban card that specifies the paint color. The worker inserts the card into a card reader, which activates a light by a paint container located on a large rack. In addition, a photocell by each paint container monitors for two motions: removal of the container from the rack within a prespecified period of time and then return of the container within a prespecified time period. If the second motion is not detected, a buzzer sounds. It should be noted that the purpose of the photocell is not to pace the worker but to make sure that the right paint container is removed for use and then is returned to the right location in the rack.

Example 4.   In every metal sheet to be formed, small holes are drilled as part of an earlier operation. In the lower die of the press, pegs have been inserted at locations to correspond exactly with the location of holes in the sheets (see Figure 15.4). If a sheet is inserted upside down, the pegs and holes do not align. This prevents the sheet from seating properly on the die, a clue to the operator that the sheet is inserted incorrectly.

Example 5.   One step was added to the worker's task (see Figure 15.5): upon starting work on a new control panel, the worker (a) first withdraws three springs from the supply bin and puts them in a small bowl. She then (b) withdraws the springs from the bowl and inserts them in the switches. Finally, she (c) installs the switches. This little step eliminated the problem of the worker overlooking a spring on a switch.

POKAYOKE FUNCTIONS

Any kind of system or mechanism that prevents defects from happening can be called pokayoke. There are two broad functions that pokayokes serve: regulatory and setting.

Figure 15.5

Example 5: Pokayoke to eliminate missing springs.

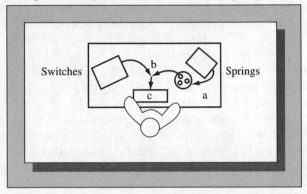

Regulatory Pokayokes

These are devices that either *control* a process or give *warning* about it. A *control pokayoke* is a device that shuts down an operation whenever it detects an abnormality, thereby preventing defects in a succession of items. An example is a sensor on a drill press that detects erratic motion or breakage of a drill bit and automatically stops the machine. Example 1 is a form of control pokayoke: as long as fewer than eight welds have been made (an abnormality), the clamp prevents a frame from being released and moved to the next stage of the process. The line-stop in Example 2 is also a control pokayoke.

A *warning pokayoke* is a device-activated light or buzzer that only signals an abnormality. The photocell activated buzzer in Example 3 is a warning pokayoke. In a continuous production process, warning pokayokes are less effective at eliminating defects than control pokayokes since they allow the abnormality to continue until someone heeds the warning and shuts off the process.

Setting Pokayokes

These are devices that check for or ensure proper *settings* or *counts* in a process. These pokayokes apply anywhere positioning or orientation is important. Placement of pegs in the lower die in Example 4 is a form of setting pokayoke; it guarantees that a sheet is properly placed into the press. The device in Example 1 is a count pokayoke; it guarantees that no less than eight spot welds are made on each frame. Example 5 is another count pokayoke; it helps ensure that the worker will always insert a spring in a switch before installing the switch on the panel.

Many pokayokes use automatic switches attached to electronic counters, proximity and photoelectric sensors, motion and vibration sensors, and pressure and temperature sensors; other pokayokes, however, are but simple fixtures or procedures that require nothing automated or electronic (Examples 4 and 5 above).

The pokayokes in all the above examples are intended to prevent inadvertent human mistakes. Pokayokes can also be attached to machines to prevent even fully automated processes from deviating. For example, a piece of equipment that must stay within certain operating parameters (temperature, pressure, rpm's, etc.) can be monitored so that the process stops if the required limits on parameters are exceeded.

The concept of pokayoking can be applied anywhere that mistakes can happen (which means, literally, everywhere!). Applications also include pokayokes installed on equipment to prevent mistakes in equipment *changeovers* and setups and in periodic equipment *preventive maintenance* procedures.

Most pokayoke solutions are somewhat simple in concept, easy to implement, and inexpensive. Shingo, in what is perhaps the best reference on the subject, details numerous examples of pokayoke solutions, most which use devices or materials that cost only a few hundred dollars or less.[5] Inexpensive pokayoke devices such as bins with lights and motion sensors are now commercially available.

The following example further demonstrates the range of pokayoke applications.

CASE IN POINT: Pokayoke at a Military Retail Supply Operation[6]

The US Army retail supply system connects all military units with storage depots that stock repair parts. Part of that system, the supply support activity (SSA) at Fort Carson, Colorado, maintains a stock of repair parts for equipment used at the base. SSA orders, tracks, and controls the parts.

SSA faced many problems caused by inadvertent errors caused by both customers and SSA operators:

· Customers sent orders for parts via diskette or automatic file transfer. Frequently they used the wrong diskette or diskettes that were not even formatted and, as a result, the information provided was wrong or nonexistent. Customers were not informed by SSA about these errors until weeks later.

· Customers sometimes placed an order that contained outdated or erroneous information, so the SSA system could not process the order.

· Customers often did not pick up parts when they arrived, which caused a shortage of storage space at SSA and problems with inventory control.

· SSA performed batch processing daily, weekly, and monthly. The processing required operators to perform a series of intricate procedures to compile and send information to suppliers. The procedures resulted in many inadvertent errors that prevented the system from processing order requisitions. The system never flagged operators about errors, and subsequently it would be impossible to determine who had made an error. Ill will grew between operators and customers over who was to blame for order errors.

· Part-number information for arriving parts was occasionally entered incorrectly into the SSA system. The system would ignore the mistake and take no further action. In effect, the order was lost: the customer did not receive the item, the supplier did not get paid, and ultimately the item had to be reordered.

SSA has since adopted several pokayoke procedures to cover errors at all stages of customer ordering, batch processing, and order receipt. To solve batch-processing errors, operators are now forced to perform procedures properly, promptly, and sequentially. Operators are given strict guidance and a warning list. A computer program checks inputs and does not allow an operator to continue processing data until the right procedural sequence is followed.

A bar-code reader ensures accurate processing of incoming parts. All incoming parts have bar-code labels that are read upon receipt at SSA. A bar-code printing system has also been installed to prepare labels for inventory parts tracking and locating all items held in stock.

Customers are now required to load the current parts catalog onto their local computer systems before placing orders on diskette. This prevents outdated or erroneous information about orders from ever being placed on diskette. Customers are also required to pick up any ordered parts that have arrived prior to placing new orders.

The following results have been realized:

· Monthly adjustments to dollar amount of inventory holdings dropped from $3000 to $250.

· Inventory accuracy (percentage of items in the correct inventory location) went from 65% to 98%.

· Percent of receipts with some kind of error dropped from 90% to 0%.

· Batch processing errors dropped from 15 to 20 per month to 0.

· Errors in information from customers dropped from 22% to 0.

· The average request processing time (difference between date when a supplier receives a request and the original date on the request) fell from 12.5 days to 1.6 days.

The main cost for the pokayokes was the time and effort to isolate the problems and determine appropriate foolproofing devices. The investment was less than $1000.

POKAYOKE IDEAS

Many pokayoke ideas originate with shop and line workers, particularly ideas for how they can eliminate their own mistakes. To implement these ideas requires assistance from supervisors, engineers, maintenance staff, machinists, toolmakers, and so on. They team up with the workers to share concepts, refine ideas, consider alternative ways to implement the ideas, and, where technology is involved, to analyze and work out the details. The McDonnell & Miller case in point (next page) is an example of workers, team leaders, and supervisors teaming up for a pokayoke idea.

Of course, other people who help the workers implement pokayoke ideas have pokayoke ideas of their own that might or might not be related to the workers' ideas. Pokayoke ideas can come from everywhere, and everyone must be encouraged to "think pokayoke." To this end, for example, product designers should think of ways to build features into products or components that will preclude the possibility of workers making mistakes in assembling them. Product engineers can design parts to have subtle differences that would be transparent to the customer but would prevent assembly workers from ever confusing the parts. Toolmakers, machinists, and process engineers can design equipment, fixtures, procedures, and entire systems such that human mistakes are virtually impossible or such that abnormalities in worker or equipment functioning are quickly detected and the process stopped before the output is affected. Many of these pokayoke ideas should be addressed early, while design issues are being resolved in product development. As argued in Chapter 12 such

CASE IN POINT: Error-Proofing at McDonnell & Miller[7]

The following notice was posted on the shop bulletin board:

Recently a letter from a customer alerted us to a problem that existed in our diverter valve assembly. The customer had received an order of our diverter valves that contained a unit that was incomplete in its assembly.

The Focused Factory No. 4 team found that an operator had inadvertently forgotten to include a spring and thermostat in the unit's body. Upon investigation, it was found that it was quite easy for an operator to forget these parts.

A team was formed to address the problem and find a solution. Mr. Amaro, the group leader in the diverter area, drew up a plan to install a limit switch to the holding fixture that would not allow the operator to remove the valve body from the fixture if any of the internal components were missing.

The focused factory supervisor and team leader listened to Mr. Amaro's idea and agreed that the switch would work. The approval to go ahead was given, and within 1 week the fixture was retrofitted with the limit switch. The cost for this work was minimal.

Tests were performed by the operators. The results were excellent. The limit switch can sense the weight (or lack of weight) of the spring and thermostat. If any parts are missing in the body, the switch will not let the operator remove the assembly from the fixture. This feature assures us that no incomplete assembly will leave the work area and be sent to our customers.

Due to the action taken by Mr. Amaro, research will begin to see if this idea can be adapted to other areas of the plant.

issues are best dealt with by a cross-functional team engaged in concurrent engineering of the product and process designs.

Shingo advises striving for the simplest, most efficient, and most economical monitoring and control systems. To this end, minor adjustments in operations and procedures should be considered before costly automated inspection and control systems are installed.

Improvements should not be put off because of the desire to do further analysis (paralysis from analysis). Simple solutions to reduce quality problems should be implemented immediately as stopgaps until more effective and robust measures are found and implemented. Ideally, these on-line quality (Taguchi's term) efforts support off-line quality (quality-of-design) efforts by feeding back data about process control problems to concurrent engineering design teams.[8]

Many kinds of complex operational systems, including aircraft, ships, nuclear power plants, and missile defense systems, have foolproofing devices and backup systems to prevent catastrophic consequences from human error or system failure. In concept, these are forms of pokayoke. The designers, operators, and managers of these systems anticipate possible mistakes that could result in a system failure, then incorporate into the systems features that preclude those mistakes from occurring.

CONTINUOUS IMPROVEMENT

The concept of pokayoke includes never-ending improvement: not only can the pokayoke for a particular application be improved (made simpler, more reliable, more cost-effective), but new pokayokes must continually be developed for new processes, new applications, and new circumstances. In Example 4, the pegs in the lower die preclude mistakes, but only for one kind of stamped part; for other parts made with other dies, other solutions are needed to prevent the metal sheets from being inserted the wrong way.

In some of the examples above the pokayokes themselves introduce the possibility of error: In Examples 2 and 3, coded cards on each product or batch indicate the right parts or paint color, but there is nothing to prevent the wrong card from being attached to the product or batch. The counter on the spot welder in Example 1 ensures that every frame gets eight welds; however, if a seven-weld frame were added to the product mix a way would have to be found to ensure that the frame got seven welds and that it did not get confused with the eight-weld frames. In all of these cases, what is needed is a *metapokayoke,* a device or procedure that will prevent mistakes in the application of the pokayoke itself!

In a particular production system, whether existing or conceptual, it is seldom necessary to muse about where problems or defects might originate. Experience and accumulated data from workers performing self-checks and successive checks, statistics on defects, customer complaints, and warranty claims provide information about defects that can be traced to the defect-producing sources. What is necessary, however, is that good data be collected about products and processes and that the data be used to refine existing products and processes and to design new ones. The data will indicate where existing systems need changes to eliminate defects and will guide designers of new products and processes to minimize defects. Nonetheless, even a new, so-called foolproof system will never be completely foolproof. Any operational system must be monitored, and the resulting data used to determine what needs changing, either in terms of fundamental design modification or by simple pokayoking.

Every process can be continually improved by adding pokayokes, but eventually, as the process itself is modified, the pokayokes become outmoded or inappropriate and must be replaced by new or different ones. As part of continuous process improvement, the process of improving pokayokes must be continuous too.

JIDOKA

A concept related to pokayoke and source inspection is **jidoka,** a Japanese term that in one sense refers to automation in the usual way, but in another sense refers to automatic control of defects. Automatic control, however, refers to the fact that the process has a mechanism incorporated in it such that it will not be allowed to proceed if a defect or abnormality is detected. This automatic shutdown of a process in the event of a problem is also called **autonomation,** and the concept applies to manual processes as well as automated ones.

AUTONOMATION

One form of autonomation is line-stop, which, as mentioned, refers to worker responsibility for stopping a process when a problem is discovered. Line-stop should also occur when a worker is unable to complete a task in the required cycle time. For example, if the required cycle time is 15 minutes and a worker needs 15.5 minutes, then the process will be held up 30 seconds while the worker finishes. This is an example of a manual form of autonomation. A situation like this requires analysis and improvement of the task, as well as a change in procedures and times on the standard operation routine. Autonomation can also be incorporated into an automated, mechanical process. An example of mechanical autonomation is a sensor on a machine that stops the machine whenever (a) it has completed one machining cycle, (b) the number of parts between the machine and the next machine (intermachine buffer) reaches a maximum, or (c) the machine's performance begins to change.

Managers often resist giving manual line-stop responsibility to workers because it interrupts production schedules, increases cycle times, and idles facilities. Of course, line-stop responsibility *should* cause interruptions, especially initially, otherwise there will be no indication that quality problems are being identified and resolved. As problems are eliminated and fewer remain that necessitate stopping the line, the frequency of interruptions should drop to near zero. Eventually there should be considerable improvement in quality, both because workers become more vigilant and because they do not want to be responsible for stopping the line. As sources of defects are eliminated, so are scrap and rework at the end of the process.

The importance of stopping a process in a manually controlled system to correct a defect or to take the time to do it right even if it exceeds the required cycle time must be impressed on workers, who, often, are hesitant to slow production or draw attention to themselves. However, as Monden points out, even when workers are motivated to conform to the line-stop concept, mechanical means might be required to assist them. For example, at Toyota workers walk next to a moving assembly line for a certain distance within which they are expected to be able to complete their tasks. If the worker walks farther than the expected distance, he steps on a mat that stops the line. The same line has a hand drill connected to a rail running next to the line. A worker using the drill to put lug nuts on wheels walks next to the line, but if the drill connection passes a certain point on the rail, the line stops.[9]

ANDONS

Andon lights, described earlier, are an important part of autonomation. It is not enough to give workers responsibility for line-stop; there must also be a mechanism to inform everyone in the process of the source of the line-stop and the nature of the problem. For example, besides a defect problem, the line can be stopped because of a machine problem, a shortage of material, a required setup, or because the required amount has been produced. When everyone knows the workstation origin and source of the line-stop, they can then take appropriate action—continue working, stop working and go to the workstation needing assistance, or stop working and wait for instructions.

Summary

There is no worker, machine, system, or process that does not on rare occasion perform incorrectly, and, given the random, fleeting nature of these performance lapses, no amount of statistical sampling will detect them. In addition, many human-caused errors are inadvertent, that is, mistakes that no amount of training or diligence can prevent. To preclude these and other sources of rare quality problems, measures beyond SPC must be employed. One measure is 100% inspection (screening), which will usually detect the random, rare defect missed by sampling inspection. Screening also provides immediate feedback so the source of the defect can be found and remedied. In assembly and other tasks that are often performed manually, such inspection should be built into the task so that each worker is his own inspector. In cases where an occasional inspection error allows some defects to go undetected, then successive checks and special checks can also be instituted.

At some point, however, even all that checking is not enough to prevent some (albeit a very tiny percentage) of the defective units from getting through. Shingo asserts that to achieve zero defects it is necessary to monitor the *sources* of defects and then to eliminate them. This is the concept of **source inspection.** According to Shingo, sources of defects are abnormalities in materials, machines, and procedures, so if *those* sources are screened, then inspection of outputs is unnecessary. In effect, via source inspection a defect can be stopped at its source before it occurs. This includes, for example, monitoring equipment operation so equipment will shut down when it starts to perform abnormally.

Many defects are the result of human mistakes in procedures, such as a worker occasionally overlooking a step or doing it incorrectly. The solution is to identify how the step affords opportunity for error and to alter the step or incorporate other steps that will preclude that opportunity. Pokayoke, or mistake-proofing, involves adding steps or simple manual or automated checking mechanisms to eliminate inadvertent errors. Pokayoke devices and procedures are also used to shut down an operation to prevent an impending error or warn about abnormalities that could lead to errors. Most pokayoke ideas are relatively simple, inexpensive to implement, and come from worker suggestions.

An important part of ensuring 100% quality is to prohibit any defect discovered from progressing further in the process. This is the concept of jidoka. Either the defect is fixed immediately, or the defective item is set aside for later analysis or rework. Process-related problems are quickly resolved by workers as soon as they are discovered, if possible; otherwise, workers have authority to stop the process or production line, which is the concept of autonomation or line-stop. Autonomation also refers to electronic or automated sensing systems that stop the process upon detecting a defect or operational abnormality. Workers throughout the plant are kept apprised of the status of each machine and the overall process by lights on every machine (andons) and overhead lighted displays (status boards).

Pokayokes for mistake-proofing are especially important in JIT/TQM factories where no defects are tolerated and in pull production systems where inventories are small and a problem anywhere can soon halt the entire process. It should be obvious, however, that the quality-enhancing benefits from source inspection and pokayoke are realizable in all production and service processes, not just in pull systems or even manufacturing.

Questions

1. Why is it not possible to eliminate defects by solely using SPC?
2. In self-checks and successive checks, what happens when a worker spots a defect?
3. Why do managers resist giving line-stop responsibility to workers?
4. Before workers can be expected to take on the responsibility and authority associated with self-checks and successive checks, what assurances and resources must they have?
5. In generic terms, what are the typical sources of defects? Give examples of each.
6. In 10 words or less, what is the principle of source inspection?
7. Of the different possible sources of defects, what sources does pokayoke address?
8. Describe the difference between control pokayoke, warning pokayoke, and setting pokayoke. Give an example where you might apply each in your work or daily experience (allow yourself freedom to be creative on this).
9. Word-processing software contains many kinds of pokayokes. Where?
10. What is jidoka? What is autonomation? Describe the relationship between jidoka and autonomation.

Problems

1. A product is made of an assembly of 10 parts, each produced at a different workcell. The average defect rate of the parts before inspection in each cell is 5%. Before leaving the cell, every part passes through a two-stage inspection process, each stage of which identifies 95% of the remaining defects. No identified defects are allowed to proceed without being corrected.
   - *a.* What is the defect rate of parts following the inspections? What is this rate expressed as ppm?
   - *b.* Suppose a defect in any of the 10 parts results in a defective assembled product. What is the defect rate of assembled products in ppm?
   - *c.* If a mistake occurs while assembling 1 in every 1000 products (assuming the assembly uses the 10 parts described above), what then is the defect rate in ppm?
   - *d.* Assume the maximum acceptable defect rate is 250 ppm. Assuming no change in the quality of the 10 parts used in assembly, what must the mistake rate during assembly be reduced to?

2. Boxed-Goods, Inc., packages replacement-parts kits. The company packages 10 different kinds of kits. Each kit has between 4 and 8 different kinds of parts, and the total parts count for a kit is between 20 and 55. As an example, a kit with 1 part J, 9 part K's, 3 part L's, 14 part P's, and 7 part R's would have a total parts count of 34, and would comprise five different kinds of parts. Parts range in size from an average

1 inch on a side to 4 inches on a side. Kits are hand-packaged in batches according to customer order. A typical order is for 10,000 kits. The packaging rate is a function of kit-size: roughly 1.5 sec/part, plus 20 seconds; thus, for example, a 20-piece kit takes 50 seconds.

The problem facing Boxed-Goods is that occasionally a worker makes a mistake resulting in an incorrect parts count or wrong kind of part in a kit. Suggest at least two pokayoke procedures that might eliminate the parts-count problem, the wrong-part problem, or both at once. State any assumptions about the parts necessary for the procedures to work. Discuss the pros and cons of each procedure in terms of time, cost, quality, and flexibility.

Endnotes

1. Much of the material in this chapter is adapted from S. Shingo, *Zero Quality Control: Source Inspection and the Pokayoke System* (Cambridge, MA: Productivity Press, 1986).

2. Inspection accuracy is seldom perfect, so even screening will not find every defect. Still, assuming high accuracy in the inspection, the percentage of defects missed will be less than with random inspection.

3. For discussion of the concept of self-control *see* J.M. Juran and F. Gryna, *Quality Planning and Analysis* (3rd ed.) (New York: McGraw-Hill, 1993), pp. 348–60.

4. This is precisely the message of the eleventh of Deming's 14 Points: eliminate numerical quotas. In a quota system such as piecework, people are paid for the number of units they produce, whether or not they are defective. *See* M. Walton, *The Deming Management Method* (New York: Perigee Books, 1986).

5. S. Shingo, *Zero Quality Control*.

6. T. Snell and J.B. Atwater, "Using Poka-Yoke Concepts to Improve a Military Retail Supply System," *Production and Inventory* 37, no. 4 (1996), pp. 44–49.

7. Courtesy of Avi Soni, Manager of Manufacturing Engineering, ITT McDonnell & Miller.

8. C. Dyer, p. 73, *in* G. Taguchi and D. Clausing, "Robust Quality," *Harvard Business Review*, January/February, 1990, pp. 65–76.

9. Y. Monden, *Toyota Production System* (2nd ed.) (Norcross, GA: Industrial Engineering Press, 1993), pp. 227–9.

PART IV SIMPLIFIED PRODUCTION PLANNING AND CONTROL SYSTEMS

Previous parts of this book addressed JIT/TQM concepts, methodologies, and tools for continuous improvement, waste reduction, and total quality as applied to manufacturing. This part focuses on how the JIT and lean-production concepts and techniques of Part II fit within the broader context of manufacturing planning and control.

A recurring topic is pull production, introduced in Chapter 8. A quick look at the key features of pull production—kanban cards and containers—tells a great deal about pull production's purpose, which is to authorize and control work on the shop floor. Certainly, pull production is also a tool for continuous improvement, but that improvement happens through pull production achieving ever-better control over aspects of factory work.

Control implies the existence of standards, goals, or plans to which system performance is compared and upon which corrective action is taken. No control technique can be fully understood without reference to the broader system that it is supposed to control, and that is also true of pull production. In this part of the book we

take a big step back and look at the broader production system, a system that besides physically producing the product also forecasts demand, accumulates customer orders, and translates forecasts and orders into broad plans, detailed plans, daily schedules, and authorizations to procure materials and execute work that, ultimately, lead to the final product. After looking at techniques for planning and scheduling work and for balancing and synchronizing stages of the production process, we look at a broad framework that integrates these techniques with pull production and JIT techniques discussed earlier. We then again take a step forward to look more closely at what is necessary to adapt MRP-based production planning and control systems to pull production.

The chapters in this part of the book are

Chapter 16 : Scheduling for Smooth Flow
Chapter 17 : Synchronizing and Balancing Processes
Chapter 18 : Planning and Control in Pull Production

SCHEDULING FOR SMOOTH FLOW

In the perfect manufacturing environment, every operation would be quickly and easily adjusted to fit market demand changes, no matter how erratic or great, with minimal effect on labor levels and expenses. Everyone would be content—customers, workers, managers. Of course, that environment does not exist. To prepare for increases in demand, manufacturers must produce in excess of current demand and build up inventories or must maintain excess labor and equipment capacity and be ready to elevate production on short notice. To handle short-term demand changes, they shuffle job priorities. Although this gets jobs with high priority out on time, it disrupts production flow, puts the system in chaos, and clogs it with in-process inventory. Costs in terms of inventory storage and financing, lead times, personnel hiring, overtime, and added shifts are high. Even plants that have a high degree of inherent production flexibility from, for example, variable-length workdays and flexible production methods such as group technology, workcells, short setup times, and cross-trained workers, find the experience of meeting production swings disruptive and costly. It is thus not surprising that they try to minimize fluctuations in planned production levels and to freeze production schedules once they are set.

A characteristic of an efficient production system is that jobs and materials flow smoothly through the system, most production lead time is value-added processing, and jobs hardly ever wait. Since production schedules dictate the frequency and level of changes in products and output volumes, smooth production flow is largely a matter of production scheduling.

This chapter discusses ways to prepare production plans, master production schedules, and final-assembly schedules that meet customer demand, yet minimize production disruptions and changes in production capacity. One way to do this is to use **production leveling** techniques to hold the frequency and size of changes in production schedules to a minimum.

The chapter also describes how final assembly schedules are prepared in pull production systems. Pull production requires somewhat uniform demand, and, as such, the concepts of production leveling and pull production scheduling are related. In addition, the chapter discusses the broader topic of production scheduling in three manufacturing environments: make-to-stock, make-to-order, and assemble-to-order. Ways to minimize costs and problems associated with scheduling disruptions in nonpull production and make-to-order systems are also discussed.

Some of the topics covered in this chapter and the next two chapters involve concepts about which the reader is presumed already familiar, including bills of materials, master production scheduling, and MRP-based planning and scheduling. If you are not familiar with these concepts, or need a refresher, read the Appendix before continuing.

PRODUCTION LEVELING

Plants that make a variety of different products typically use batch production. The frequent changeovers between different products and varisized batches result in variation in the daily workload of every department and workcenter. Figure 16.1, for example, shows the production schedule for three products, A, B, and C. Each shaded block represents one or more work shifts scheduled for producing a batch of one product. The schedule shows large variation in two ways—in the size of the production runs (batch size) and in the frequency of production runs (batch interval). If other products besides A, B, and C must also be produced, they will have to be scheduled somewhere in between the batches shown in Figure 16.1, so the schedules for them will also exhibit large variation in terms of batch size and interval.

Variation in scheduled batch size and batch interval partly results from management's attempts to match production levels with demand. Demand levels vary because of sales fluctuations, promotional schemes, end-of-month quotas, and so on, and management adjusts the sizes and intervals of production batches to compensate. Variation in scheduled production also stems from variability inherent to the production process. Even when production is scheduled using fixed time periods (the schedule in Figure 16.1 uses half-shift minimal time blocks), the output quantity in any specified time period will vary due to material shortages, worker absenteeism, and equipment problems. These factors reduce output below expectations, and the shortfall must be filled in subsequent time blocks (other shifts or overtime). Conversely, output sometimes exceeds the planned amount, and production in subsequent time blocks must be reduced.

LEVELING PRODUCTION WITH BUFFER STOCKS

Any variation in scheduled production for a finished product has a ripple effect on the production and delivery schedules of every upstream operation and supplier. A common way for the upstream stages of the production/distribution chain to absorb that variation is to carry buffer stocks of raw and in-process material. Buffer stocks provide some degree of certainty, and during periods of slack demand they keep materials flowing and workcenters productive. Managers and supervisors are sometimes

FIGURE 16.1

Production schedule for products A, B, and C.

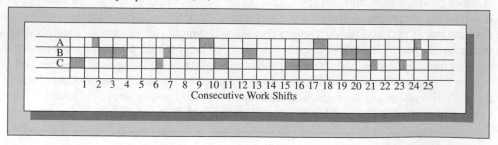

evaluated on personnel and equipment utilization, so they try to maintain a backlog of work to preclude idle time or underutilized resources. Thus, in-process buffer stocks and work backlogs are one tactic for leveling production.

There are of course drawbacks to the tactic. Recall discussions from earlier chapters of the consequences of high inventories, then consider the vast quantity of inventory that accumulates plantwide when an organization relies on buffer stocks to level production. Though removing uncertainty and variation in production output is desirable, the question is, Does it have to come at such great expense?

The answer is no. Another, sometimes better way to minimize variation is simply to **level the production schedule,** that is, to establish a master production schedule (MPS) where every product is produced on a regular basis and in a fixed batch size. A level production schedule provides the same benefits as WIP buffer stocks without the drawbacks.

LEVELING PRODUCTION WITH UNIFORM SCHEDULES

With a uniform, **level production schedule,** the same quantity is made in each production run for a product, and the production runs occur at regularly scheduled intervals. In other words, the batch size and batch interval for a given product are constant. Figure 16.2 shows two uniform, level schedules for products A, B and C. For each product, the same quantity is produced in each batch, and the production runs are evenly placed. With a level schedule, every upstream operation follows a pattern that specifies how much and when to produce for every product. This pattern introduces an element of routine into the daily work of every workcenter, and routine is easier to handle than change.

FIGURE 16.2

Two uniform, level schedules. Note that for each schedule the batch size and batch interval for each product stay constant.

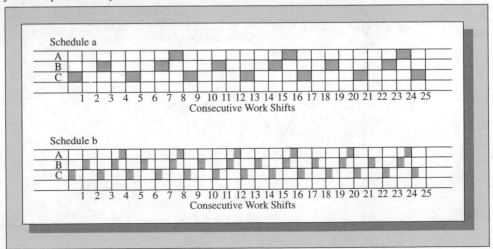

The smaller the batch size and the interval, the leveler the schedule and the smoother the flow of materials plantwide. In Figure 16.2, for example, schedule b is leveler than schedule a; in general, schedule b would result in smoother flow of material, which means smaller backlogs, less WIP inventory, and shorter lead times than schedule a.

Besides the time, cost, and quality benefits of smaller WIP, level schedules give supervisors and workers more time to focus on the *work at hand*. With fewer distractions from changing workloads, and fewer problems from work expediting and slowdowns, workers have more time to identify areas of the process that need improvement, and to develop solutions and implement them.

REQUIREMENTS FOR LEVELING PRODUCTION SCHEDULES

For production leveling to be practical, three requirements, or conditions, must be met. The first requirement pertains to product demand, something over which a company might or might not be able to control. The other two are things a company can and must do.

Continuous, Stable Demand

To maintain a level production schedule in the presence of a fluctuating demand curve, *some* quantity of finished product must be held as buffer stock. This buffer stock protects the entire production/distribution process from product demand variability, and allows upstream stages to operate on a somewhat level basis. This is illustrated in Figure 16.3.

FIGURE 16.3

Effect of level schedules and finished goods buffer on upstream operations and suppliers.

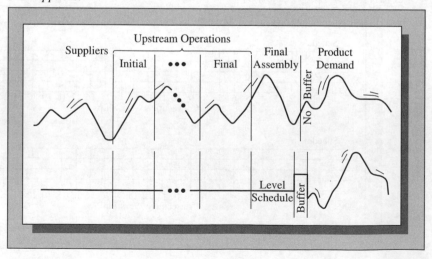

Now, keeping a buffer stock of finished product is practical only if demand is somewhat continuous; it is not practical with sporadic demand, since the buffer stock can sit there for a long time, possibly indefinitely. As a practical matter, demand does not have to be large, and a few units a week, every week, might be enough. When demand is continuous, then the higher cost of carrying some finished goods inventory is offset by the lower costs of carrying smaller WIP inventories everywhere else.

Of course, recommending inventory anywhere is a contradiction to JIT principles. To keep that inventory small, the company must *manage* the *demand* so as to minimize variation. One way to do that is to segregate customers into tiers:[1]

- First tier: high volume, common processes (no special setups or operations).
- Second tier: substantial volume and much process commonality.
- Third tier: low volume, sporadic orders, little process commonality.

The first two tiers represent the best or bread-and-butter customer accounts; the last tier represents the low profit margin and harder-to-satisfy accounts. Often, the first two tiers account for 20–40% of the total customers, but 70–90% of sales. It is often possible to work with first-tier customers and even second-tier customers to circumvent abrupt changes in demand. These customers inform the manufacturer of anticipated needs far enough in advance so that it is unnecessary to carry finished goods stock to service them. Production schedules for these customers are gradually raised or lowered to meet demand.

During peak demand periods, the focus should be on satisfying first-tier and second-tier customers, and possibly even turning down orders from third-tier customers. During slow periods, orders from third-tier customers are accepted because production schedules have ample excess capacity and the orders are not disruptive.

Short Setup Times

The time to change over a process from one product to another must be short. As discussed in Chapter 6, lengthy changeovers consume too much of the workday and leave relatively less time for actual production. Ceteris paribus, they also mandate larger batch sizes (e.g., see schedule a in Figure 16.2), which reduces the allowable degree of production leveling. The ideal changeover operation is a one-touch procedure that takes only a few minutes, although changeovers as long as 30–60 minutes might also be practical, depending on the number of products, length of workday, and demand.

Production = Demand

The frequency of production runs and the size of batches in leveled production should roughly correspond to the average actual demand for the product. This means that the batch sizes and intervals between production runs should be based upon product demand, and not something arbitrary, like a daily work shift or half-shift. The goal of each production run should be to achieve the scheduled output quantity, *not* to maximize output.

In addition, the scheduled production quantity (batch size) should be periodically readjusted to match the average level of demand over a specified time period. The more often the demand level shifts, the more often the production schedule must be readjusted. This will be discussed later.

The demand figure used to plan production levels for future periods is typically based on a forecast. When the goal is to level the production of a number of different products, the forecast should be for the **aggregate** demand for those products (demand for a product group or product family); it should not be for the demand of each product. This is an important point. A forecast for aggregate demand is more accurate because the numbers in the aggregate forecast are larger than for individual product forecasts, and patterns for large numbers are inherently more stable than patterns for small numbers.[2] In this context, more stable means more predictable. Also, estimates for individual products are always high or low, though in the aggregate the high estimates and low estimates cancel each other out, giving better accuracy.

LEVELING FOCUS

In organizations that produce a variety of products, the focus should be on leveling the schedules for the highest-volume products. This goes back to what was said before about tier-one and -two customers. A company that produces 60 different product groups wherein, say, five customers account for 50% of the production volume can dramatically reduce WIP levels and lead times plantwide just by leveling the production schedules for those five. Even when most of the other products continue to be scheduled and produced in the usual erratic fashion, leveling the schedules of the few highest-volume ones will substantially reduce workload variation and uncertainty for most workcenters. P-Q analysis, described in Chapter 9, is useful for assessing which product groups have the highest volumes and for which schedules should be leveled.

LEVELING THE MASTER SCHEDULE

The way to *force* level production on a product is to level the MPS. The concept of leveling implies selecting a quantity of production output and producing that same quantity on a periodic basis. Leveling production, a common topic in classical aggregate planning,[3] is reviewed here as a precursor to the techniques described later. We start with the simplest case, leveling the production schedule for a product group, then look at leveling production schedules for multiple products simultaneously.

Leveling One Product Group

One consideration in choosing the level of production is the time period over which that level is to be maintained. Although it is desirable to keep the production level fixed for as long as possible, it is evident that demand changes will preclude maintaining any one level indefinitely. Occasionally the level must be changed. Whether the change is every 3 months, every month, or sooner depends upon the anticipated demand pattern. The solid line in Figure 16.4 represents the anticipated demand pattern over a 2-year period. Demand variation appears to be seasonal and the overall trend, downward. The dotted line represents the planned uniform level of production.

FIGURE 16.4

Level production over a 2-year period.

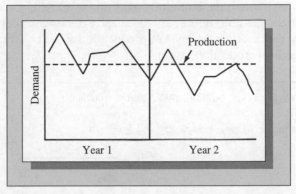

FIGURE 16.5

Level production in the first year only.

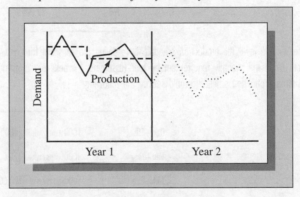

Leveling production over a 2-year period like this is inappropriate for at least three reasons. First, since the level of production during year 1 is less than average demand, an initial stock of inventory must be available to meet demand, and the inventory investment for the first year would likely be high. Second, the production level throughout most of year 2 exceeds demand; this plus the fact that demand appears to be declining, will likely result in a large stock of inventory remaining at the end of the second year. Reason three is that any demand forecast becomes more unreliable with time, so planning the first year's production based largely on the second year's demand is chancy.

The plan in Figure 16.5 considers just the first year (the second year shown only for reference), and sets production at two levels that, together, more closely fit the demand pattern than the one level in Figure 16.4. Closer fit means lower cost from inventory necessary to meet the initial demand peak, and from inventory buildups during slack periods.

It should be noted, and is clear from the example, that the level of production chosen cannot simply be the average demand over some time horizon. The level chosen must account for pre-existing stock and be able to satisfy periods of peak demand.

Although the intent of production leveling is to keep production uniform for as long as possible, if forecasted demand exhibits considerable variation between seasons or months, then the level of production should be adjusted seasonally or monthly, as needed (production = demand); see Example 1.

Example   1:   Level Production Schedule with Seasonal Variation

Demand for the seasons is forecasted as follows:

Winter	12,000
Spring	48,000
Summer	60,000
Fall	42,000

One way to level the production schedule is to divide the seasonal forecasts by three to get monthly requirements, then divide the monthly requirement by four (assuming 4 weeks per month) to get weekly requirements. The resulting production schedule would specify the following:

Dec.–Feb.	1000 units/wk	(4000/mo)
Mar.–May	4000 units/wk	(16,000/mo)
June–Aug.	5000 units/wk	(20,000/mo)
Sept.–Nov.	3500 units/wk	(14,000/mo)

To avoid extremes (going from 1000 to 4000 and from 5000 to 3500) the schedule could be modified to 3500 per week in the first and third quarters, though that would involve carrying inventory from the first to the third quarter.

Leveling Multiple Products

Next consider leveling the production schedule for several products at once. Though we are now looking at multiple products, the procedure is similar to leveling one product group. For each product, we seek to produce about the same amount every period. The size of the period can be a month, week, or day, though the smaller the period, the smoother (more level) the production schedule. For example, if the plan indicates that 4000 units of a product must be produced every month, then one approach would be to produce all 4000 in the first week of the month. Though the *monthly* schedule looks level, the *weekly* schedule would look choppy because in each month it specifies one week on (making the product) and three weeks off (not making it), a pattern that is repeated over and over. Had the plan specified instead 200 units a day (assuming 20 days/month), then production would be uniform throughout the month.

Example   2:   Leveling Production of Three Products

Assume the production requirements for 1 month are

Product A	4000
Product B	2000
Product C	1000

Other products are made too, but A, B, and C are the highest-volume ones.

Schedule *a* in Figure 16.6 shows one possible MPS for the products. Although the production schedule looks somewhat level (it remains at 2000 units for 3 weeks and changes only once, to 1000, during the month), it is not. Because of the large size of the batches (2000 or 1000), production involves correspondingly large batches of components and subassemblies, which imposes large week-to-week variation in the workloads of upstream operations that supply parts. Products A, B, and C are different, and equal quantities of them do not imply equal production times, types and quantities of components, or any other measure of resources and capacity required to produce them.

Now, if changeover times throughout the production system are long, then schedule *a* might be the only feasible schedule. If, however, the changeover times are small, then possibly some amount of every product could be produced *every week*. This is shown in schedule *b* in Figure 16.6. Since in schedule *b* the same amount of each

FIGURE 16.6

Three MPS alternatives

	Week 1	Week 2	Week 3	Week 4
a	2000A	2000A	2000B	1000C
b	1000A	1000A	1000A	1000A
	500B	500B	500B	500B
	250C	250C	250C	250C
	Day 1	Day 2	Day 3	etc.
c	200A	200A	200A	200A
	100B	100B	100B	100B
	50C	50C	50C	50C

product is produced every week, the requirements imposed on upstream operations will be the same, week by week. At least for production of parts and components going in to products A, B, and C, the schedules for upstream operations will be uniform and entirely predictable. Uniformity translates into a weekly routine, which means simplified weekly work planning and scheduling for upstream operations.

Even better than a weekly level schedule is a daily level schedule. If changeovers can be reduced to one-touch procedures, then the same amount of every product could be produced *every day*, as shown in schedule c. With this schedule, every upstream operation every day produces the same volume of every kind of part for the three products.

In a **daily level schedule,** the production volume for each product is set at 1/20 the monthly requirement (assuming 20 working days/month). If the monthly demand for a product is 4000 units, then the daily level would be 200 units. If the demand variation *within* the month is large, then half-month demands can be used instead, and the daily production level for each half-month can be set at 1/10 of the half-month amount.

To take this a step further, suppose demand fluctuates significantly from day to day. Does that mean that the scheduled production level should also fluctuate day to day? The answer is both no and yes. No, because a production schedule that changes every day is obviously not level. It lacks daily routine and requires that every upstream operation carry buffer stock or readjust its capacity (setups, inputs, outputs) to meet fluctuating workloads. This is a common predicament, but one which level production seeks to avoid. On the other hand, yes, but *only* if the daily change in production level represents a relatively small adjustment to a base schedule that is somewhat level. The allowable degree of adjustment will depend on how much variation upstream operations are capable of absorbing on short notice. Toyota, for example, uses a level 10-day production schedule as a base, but adjusts it daily to incorporate the most-recent customer order information. That daily adjustment, however, is limited to ±10% of the base scheduled amount. Still, even with such a small adjustment limit, this procedure provides enough flexibility to vary day-to-day production by as much as 23%.

LEVEL SCHEDULES: A COOPERATIVE EFFORT

Preparing level production schedules is not something a few planners do occasionally and behind closed doors. Schedules are constantly refined as new, more accurate demand information becomes available.

Practical, feasible scheduling requires involvement from people in sales, marketing, engineering, production, and finance. The production level selected must be able to satisfy actual, firm customer orders and projected demand requirements yet do so with existing capacity and minimal buffer stock. Thus, planning the production level must take into account production's ability to adjust capacity, as well as sales' ability to provide quick order information and accurate sales forecasts.

The marketing department must coordinate promotional schemes with manufacturing to ensure that production output can keep up with anticipated sales increases. Marketing must be sensitive to the goal of production leveling and avoid

CASE IN POINT: Level Production at an Electronics Plant

Park[4] performed a simulation study for a large Korean electronics manufacturer to answer management's question as to whether level production would be good for the company. He investigated the effect of level production on various sublines and suppliers. Figure 16.7 is an example of one month's demand imposed on a supplier when the electronics firm used traditional nonlevel production schedules. Though daily demand averaged about 9000 parts, because it fluctuated between 12,500 and 5000 parts, the supplier had to operate at a capacity of 11,000. Even with that, it was necessary for the supplier to preproduce several days in advance and carry 3 days inventory to meet days with peak demand. Similar fluctuations were experienced by many of the firm's 200 vendors. Within the manufacturer's own plant, sublines carried 3 days average inventory, plus an additional day of inventory as a safety stock, to handle schedule fluctuations.

Figure 16.8 shows the demand for the same supplier assuming the electronics firm switched to level production (the half-load days are Saturdays). With level demand, the supplier no longer has to preproduce. Prior to leveling, the supplier required 1 week to fill orders; after leveling, 3 days. On the sublines in the plant, the inventory level dropped by 50%. The leveling had no effect on the amount of finished goods inventory.

FIGURE 16.7

Supplier demand before level production.[5]

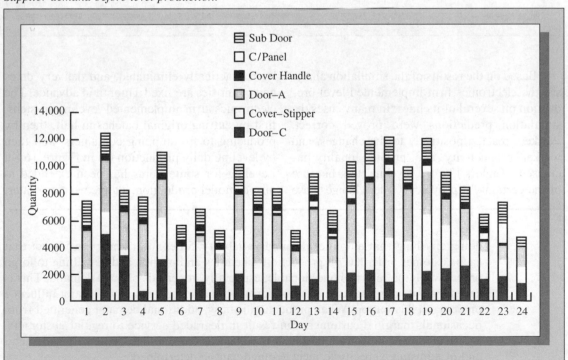

Figure 16.8

Supplier demand with level production.[6]

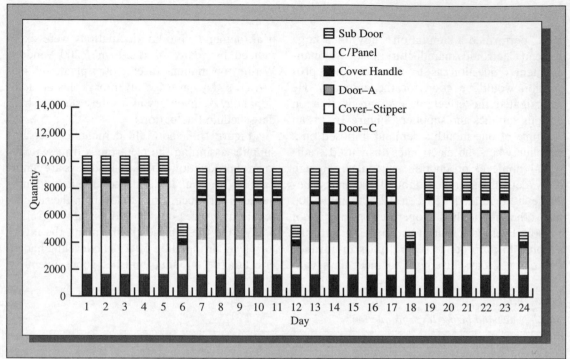

Based on the results of the simulation analysis, the electronics firm implemented level production on several of its lines. In many cases the simulation predictions were proved correct. Workers reacted positively to the changes, and worker productivity and product quality increased. Vendors like the leveling, too, because of the certainty it provides. Order changes have been practically eliminated, and delivery dates and quantities are fixed a month in advance. The electronics firm implemented leveling in steps, first by cutting original batches in half, then by producing to fill shipping containers, and then by leveling daily production (as in Figure 16.8). Leveling for some items has been extended to mixed-model production, a topic we cover later.

doing anything that amplifies demand variability. Sales must know the impact that each customer order has on production schedules and profits, and be willing to forgo orders when the return is questionable, especially in periods of peak demand. This is an important point, because sales and promotional efforts can have a major influence on demand fluctuation. When production is busy, additional demand generated from occasional, marginal customers can result in degraded service to regular customers. By having finance involved, the dollar ramifications of stimulating or quelling demand and of adjusting capacity to meet demand can be determined.

Achieving level production also requires that the parts and components of different products be somewhat interchangeable. For effective production of multiple products in uniform small batches, design engineers must be mindful of the effect their designs have on production processes and changeovers. Among other matters, DFMA efforts must consider the effect of product design on production leveling.

LEVEL SCHEDULING IN PULL PRODUCTION

Production leveling can be applied in any production environment that meets the requirements listed before. For pull production systems, however, production leveling is itself the requirement. Pull production systems function well only when demand for materials at every stage is smooth and steady. For that kind of demand, production schedules must be level.

MIXED-MODEL PRODUCTION

Final-Assembly Schedule

Unlike a push production system, which requires a schedule for every operation, a pull production system utilizes only *one* schedule, a schedule for the last stage of the process. As shown in Figure 16.9, each operation in pull production produces in response to an order from downstream. Since orders move upstream, the process is initiated by orders that come from the final operation. Whatever orders the final operation must meet, so must the operations upstream. The final operation is often an assembly station—the place where all the components and subassemblies produced upstream are finally put together. Thus, the schedule or order list at the final operation is referred to as the **final-assembly schedule,** or **FAS.**

FIGURE 16.9

Process initiated by orders from final operation.

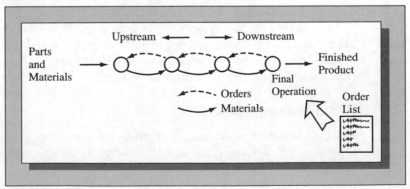

Heijunka: Mixed-Model Production

A pull system that produces multiple kinds of products requires a uniform production schedule for every one of them. Ideally every product has its own final-assembly station and that station produces according to its own FAS. But usually it is not cost-effective or feasible for every product to have its own separate line or final-assembly station, especially when the number of products is large and demand for each is relatively small. In the usual case, several different products will be assembled at the *same* production line or final-assembly station.[7] Production of multiple kinds of products on a repetitive basis, in a mixed fashion (some As, some Bs, and so on), and at a single line or station is referred to as **mixed-model production** (MMP) or mixed-model assembly. The Japanese term for MMP is **heijunka,** which at Toyota refers to "distributing the production of different [product types] evenly over the course of a day, a week, or a month."[8]

In heijunka or MMP, batch production of different products is avoided; instead, products are interspersed and produced in a mixed sequence. Mixing different products in sequence like this results in smooth, steady demand for the upstream operations that supply components and materials.

Batch Size

As stated above, the mixing of different products in MMP is done in systematic fashion to *avoid batching* of consecutive products. For example, going back to Figure 16.2, if products A, B, and C are produced in the same final-assembly area, the schedules represent a *form* of MMP because production of the three products is mixed. The schedules, however, are a very crude form of MMP because they result in production of somewhat large batches (in Figure 16.2, each production run in schedule *a* extends for an entire shift and in schedule *b* half a shift) with somewhat long intervals between batches. For each batch of product, the required materials and component parts must be produced in advance by upstream operations, and when the batch is large, the materials that go into it are usually produced in large batches also.[9] In general, large-batch production at final assembly imposes large-batch production on immediate upstream stages, which impose large-batch production on earlier stages, and so on. The irregularities resulting from large batches such as in Figure 16.2 might be more than a pull production system can handle.[10]

In a pull production system, working with small WIP is the modus operandi.[11] Given that the size of the batches at final assembly somewhat dictates the size of batches throughout the production process, then to keep WIP small everywhere, the batch size at final assembly must also be small.

MMP and Production Smoothing

Producing in mixed, small batches smooths the demand requirements everywhere in the process. This is shown in Figure 16.10 using the three schedules from Figure 16.6. Product A is highlighted to illustrate how reducing the size of the production batch results in a smoother production schedule. Smoothing the production schedule results

FIGURE 16.10

Effect of smaller batches on production smoothing.

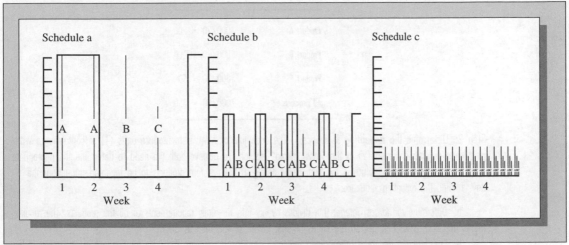

in a smoother flow of orders going upstream and, hence, a smoother flow of materials going downstream, everywhere in the process.

THE MMP SCHEDULE

Theoretically, maximal smoothing is achieved by scheduling production at final assembly in batches of size one. A batch of size one means that, ideally, one unit of A is produced, then a unit of B, a unit of C, and so on, and the resulting production sequence is ABCABC . . . This repeating sequence is called an **MMP schedule.** In pull production, this MMP schedule is the FAS. The sequence tells workers at final assembly what they must produce and in what order. This is the only schedule required in pull production.

Now, looking more closely at the MMP schedule, if it specified ABCABC . . . , then the result would be units of A, B, and C produced in *equal* quantities. If the demand for the three products is different, as would be expected, then the schedule has to be modified so that the different products will be produced in the desired quantities. The frequency that a product appears on the MMP schedule should be proportionate to the demand for that product. The following example gives a procedure for determining the MMP schedule that will yield the desired quantity of each product.

Example   3:   Establishing an MMP Schedule

Monthly demand for products A, B, and C is 4000, 2000, and 1000 units, respectively. Assume the products involve similar components, technology, and processing steps, and thus can all be assembled at the same final-assembly stage. There are three steps to setting the MMP schedule.

Step 1: Determine the Daily Production Requirements.   Assuming 20 working days per month, the daily production requirements are as follows:

Product A	$4000/20 = 200$
Product B	$2000/20 = 100$
Product C	$1000/20 = 50$
All products	$7000/20 = 350$

Step 2: Determine the *Repeating Sequence*.   The dual goal of MMP is to produce units (1) in conformance with production requirements and (2) in the "most mixed" fashion. To achieve both we need to determine the appropriate MMP **repeating sequence**, which is the particular ordering of the different products to be repeated throughout the day. To find the repeating sequence:

a. Determine *the largest integer* that divides evenly into the daily requirements of all the products. The requirements are 200, 100, and 50, so the largest integer divisor of the three is 50.

b. Calculate *the minimum ratio* among the three products by dividing the daily requirement of each product by the integer divisor. For the integer 50, the ratio is $4:2:1$. The sum of the ratio numbers is 7, so each repeating sequence will have 7 units: 4 product As, 2 product Bs, 1 product C. Note that this sequence must be *repeated* 50 times a day to produce the required amounts for every product.

Step 3: Determine the *Product Ordering* within the Repeating Sequence.   One possible ordering is AAAABBC. This ordering satisfies the ratio requirement of 4 As, 2 Bs, 1 C, but is still somewhat choppy since it batches all the As and all the Bs together. A less choppy (more-mixed) sequence would be AABABAC. This is probably the most-mixed ordering possible for this example.

Assuming this ordering is adopted, the production process would repeat the sequence AABABAC 50 times a day. The only other information necessary to round out the FAS is to specify the cycle time (CT). If the work day is 8 hours, then, on average, the unit CT must be $8/350 = 0.02285$ hours, or about 82.3 sec/unit. The matter of applying this CT to synchronize the process is described in the next chapter.

Maximally mixed ordering gives the smoothest flow, though for other purposes maximal mixing might not be best. If, to continue the same example, the unit CT is very short and the changeover times between products are somewhat long, then the ordering AAAABBC might be preferred over AABABAC because it requires fewer changeovers from product A to product B, then to product C, and so on. Or, if the products are packaged two to a container, then AAAAAAAABBBBCC (repeated 25 times) might be better because items could then be packaged as soon as they are made (in AABABAC units have to wait: production of successive B units is interrupted by an A unit, and C units can be packaged only in alternate sequences).

Seldom is the demand in nice round numbers as in the example, so the procedure for determining the minimum ratio usually requires ad hoc adjustments. For example, if the daily demand for product A were 213, that figure might first be rounded to 200 so a repeating sequence could be easily determined. The remaining units (13 here) would be added to (or deleted from, if rounding were upward) the schedule at the start of the day, at the finish of the day, or uniformly throughout. When the number of different product models is very large, finding the most-mixed MMP sequence is more difficult, and in that case manufacturers use computational computer algorithms to develop the daily sequence.[12]

REQUIREMENTS FOR MMP

The minimal requirements for MMP are the same as those for level production schedules: somewhat continuous demand, small setup times, and demand-driven production. As with level production schedules, trying to implement MMP when demand is discontinuous or one-time is impossible or impractical. Maximal mixing in MMP can require almost continual equipment changeover, so setups must be simple, one-touch, and time-minuscule. MMP schedules are demand driven, but the demand is a composite of incoming customer orders and level production schedules. Details of this are explained in Chapter 18.

Mixed-model production has three additional requirements, all familiar elements of JIT: flexible workers, total quality assurance, and small-lot deliveries of materials.

Flexible Workers

Workers must be cross-trained and equipment adaptable to work on every model in the MMP sequence. Ideally, besides being able to perform a variety of tasks at a given workstation, workers should be able to perform tasks at any of multiple workstations. That way a bottleneck anywhere caused by a quality problem, too-high CTs, or insufficient capacity can be tackled by shifting workers between operations.

Effective Quality Assurance

Moving workers between operations increases flexibility, but it can also increase quality problems since workers must remember many different tasks and operations. Pokayoking, source inspection, and line-stop are thus essential to preventing workers from skipping steps, taking incorrect steps, or using wrong parts. At the Toyota assembly plant in Georgetown, Kentucky, use of autonomation and worker line-stop causes an average of 1,700 shutdowns per shift. The attitude of management is that the 6% production downtime is well worth it because of all the problems being discovered.[13]

Small-Lot Material Supply

Since MMP involves producing a variety of products or models all at once, variety in the materials used is also large. To minimize the amount of in-process inventory and confusion about which parts go into which models, materials must be synchronized to arrive at the final-assembly stage in the exact quantities and at the exact times needed. The process of synchronizing upstream parts production with final MMP assembly is described in the next chapter.

ADVANTAGES OF MMP

MMP has all the advantages of level production schedules, including low variation in production schedules, low WIP inventory, reduced lead times, and ability to meet demand with lower average production capacity. Other advantages of MMP are discussed in the following sections.

Elimination of Losses Due to Line Changeover

On a traditional assembly line, the entire line is shut down for changeover between production models, and the shutdown can take days or weeks depending on the extent of differences between models. With MMP an entire line is rarely shut down for changeover. Unless the changeover is for a new product that requires substantial process retooling, the line continues to function during changeovers, which occur almost continually. Of course, elimination of changeover downtime is predicated on one-touch changeovers at every step of the process.

Process Improvement

Workers rotating through a variety of tasks and operations in MMP are more attentive to problems and motivated to eliminate them than are workers assigned to only one model. In large production runs where, say, one model is produced monthly between changeovers, process problems tend to be patched and then forgotten; months later when the model is run again, the problems recur, and workers must again learn the process and patch the problems. In MMP, a problem that is not fixed appears over and over, which motivates workers to find a permanent solution.

Balanced Work Loads[14]

MMP on an assembly line results in even allocation of work throughout. In the usual single-model line, tasks at different stations require different times, say 40 seconds, 45 seconds, and 55 seconds on a three-station line operating at a 60-second CT. Not only do workers with long task times find this inequitable and aggravating, but workers at stations with short task times have no incentive to rotate to the other stations or to contribute to finding ways to reduce the process CT. With MMP and rotating assignments, the workloads among stations are more balanced, and workers have no vested interest in the task times at any one station.

Fewer Losses from Material Shortages

In the event of a material shortage in MMP, only particular models that require that material are affected. Work continues on all other models, and more of those models are produced until the material arrives. When the shortage ends, production of the interrupted models resumes and is temporarily increased until the deficit is filled.

PRODUCTION PLANNING AND SCHEDULING UNDER DIFFERENT CIRCUMSTANCES

The fewer the number of final products and the larger, more stable the demand for each, the simpler it is to do production planning and scheduling, including for MMP. Conversely, the greater the number of products and the smaller, less stable the demand, the more difficult it is.

One way companies prepare plans and schedules to accommodate different product-variety and product-volume combinations is to modify their definition of an **end-item** to whatever works best. In general, an end-item is whatever item a company prepares plans and schedules to produce. It is the item that appears in the MPS and at the top-level (0-level) of the bill of materials. Beyond this general definition, however, what a company chooses to use as an end-item can vary depending on the complexity and volume of the product and on the production philosophy to which the company subscribes.

PRODUCTION PHILOSOPHY

Consider the three most common production philosophies: make-to-stock, assemble-to-order, and make-to-order.

Make-to-Stock

Make-to-stock (MTS) companies make products in anticipation of demand. Usually these products go into finished goods stock before being withdrawn to fill customer orders. Relatively few products (say, less than 100) are produced, though they are produced in large volume, and each product typically contains a large number of components. In MTS companies, the end-item is a *finished product* or a group of products that are identical except for minor features. Televisions are an example. The MRP system, if one is used, maintains a separate bill of materials (BOM) for each end-item and creates a separate MPS for every product. Since products are made in advance of actual orders, the quantities in production schedules are based on forecasts.

Assemble-to-Order

Assemble-to-order (ATO) companies produce subassemblies according to forecasts, then combine the subassemblies in unique combinations as requested by customers. A large variety of different products can be produced by combining different combinations of relatively few kinds of subassemblies. Computers and automobiles are examples. In ATO companies, the end-item is the *option* for a kind of *subassembly*. For example, say a company makes golf carts by assembling engines, drive trains, and chassis, and the drive-train and chassis subassemblies each come in different models or options—the chassis come in medium and stretched versions and the drive trains come in standard and heavy duty. The focus of the MPS is on the production of subassembly options, not the final product, golf carts, and these subassembly

ptions are produced in advance of customer orders. Similarly, the BOMs maintained
y the MRP system are for subassembly options, not for final products. The use of
ptions, also called modules, in production scheduling is explained later.

Make-to-Order

Make-to-order (MTO) companies produce products in response to actual customer
orders, so they carry little finished goods inventory. They can produce many kinds of
products (many hundreds) each in small quantity by using different combinations of
relatively few kinds of components. Pharmaceuticals are an example. Because of the
large number of potential products and possible small demand for each, it is impossible to forecast demand for products. Also, it is impractical to maintain the BOM for
every product. (In a related philosophy, *engineer-to-order* products are not only
produced but are designed to meet requirements of particular customers. Before the
customer order, the product does not exist, hence, neither does the BOM.)

If the number of products is not too large, say less than 100, then all products can
be included in the MPS. To prepare a master schedule solely from customer orders,
there must be a backlog of orders. From this backlog, orders are chosen and inserted
into the schedule according to order priorities and production capacity constraints.[15]

When the number of products is large, it is difficult to handle all of them on the
master schedule. In that case, the end-item in the master schedule can represent a
group of products such as a *product family*. Requirements for parts and components
for each product within the group are derived from percentages of the anticipated mix
of products within the group. This procedure is discussed later.

The three production philosophies represent three fundamental types of product
structures, as shown in Figure 16.11: few products, each potentially consisting of
many kinds of parts; many products, each made from a different combination of subassembly options, and where each subassembly, itself, might consist of many parts;
and many products, each consisting of different combinations of relatively few kinds
of parts. In general, items at the narrowest part of each product structure should be

FIGURE 16.11

*Different kinds of product structures and levels at which master-production scheduling
is performed.*

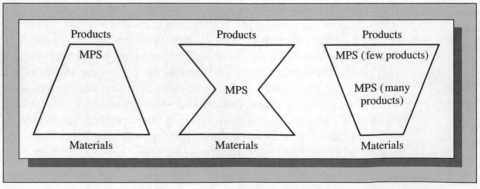

the items upon which requirements planning (in MRP) and master production scheduling are based. This is because the narrowest part of the structure represents the point of greatest commonality among all products, and items at that level are the simplest to plan and schedule.

Production planning and scheduling for MTS and ATO usually focus on items at the top and middle of the product structures, respectively. For MTS, master scheduling focuses at any level of the structure depending on the number of final products, though for simplicity it should be on items somewhat low in the structure— materials, parts, and subassemblies of relatively common items.

FINAL ASSEMBLY VERSUS MASTER PRODUCTION SCHEDULING

It is important to distinguish between scheduling for MPS and scheduling for final assembly. The difference is one of immediacy: whereas the MPS often portrays anticipated orders or forecasted demand, the FAS usually portrays actual orders. While the former drives material procurement and preparation to do work, the latter drives the actual execution of work. Paraphrasing Mather:[16]

> Think of the master schedule as the means for bringing raw materials and purchased items to the plant and processing them. The final assembly or finishing schedule now takes over and converts the items and materials into finished goods. The analogy is a relay race. Here, the baton is passed from the master schedule to the final-assembly schedule. The objective is to make the final-assembly schedule responsive to market conditions while at the same time keeping the master schedule stable.

The MPS must look far enough into the future so that material and capacity requirements can be anticipated, ordered, and on hand when needed. As a result, production and procurement lead times are the determining factor in setting the time horizon for the MPS. In contrast, the time horizon for the FAS must cover only the time between when all components or subassemblies become available for production of an item and when the production of the item is completed.

When the number of kinds of final products is very small (for example, aircraft), the FAS *is* the MPS. In such cases, no product is made without an existing product order, and actual customer orders drive the MPS.

In MTS companies, the MPS drives the FAS, that is, final assembly happens in anticipation of demand. Even then, however, the FAS must take into account existing (actual) orders and most-recent changes in anticipated demand. If current demand falls off substantially, or if inventories reach the maximum desired levels, then production should be stopped.

When the number of final products is very large, the MPS focuses on subassemblies or options, not on individual products. The FAS specifies the particular products to be made through various combinations of subassemblies and components, while the MPS assures that those components and subassemblies will be available to final assembly in sufficient quantities to meet the FAS.

The remainder of the chapter discusses particulars for smoothing production schedules (FAS or MPS, whichever is appropriate) under each of the three manufacturing philosophies.

MTS: UNIFORM-LOAD PRODUCTION SCHEDULE

Products that have large, stable demand can be readily scheduled using MMP as described earlier. However, even products that have small demand can be scheduled with MMP, providing that the demand is somewhat continuous. For example, suppose P-Q analysis is used to single out from hundreds of products the 11 with the highest volume. One way to level the production schedule is to produce some of the top four products *every day*, some of the next three products every *week*, and all of the last four products *every* month, once a month.

Example   4:   Creating a Uniform Production Schedule

Figure 16.12 shows the monthly demand and production breakdown for the 11 products. According to the figure, it should be possible to satisfy demand for all 11 products with a daily average production rate of 475 units. Therefore, in creating the daily production schedule, the goal should be to maintain an average of 475 units/day.

FIGURE 16.12

Demand volume and scheduled production volume.

Product	Monthly Volume	Daily Production	Weekly Production	Monthly Production
A	4000	200		
B	2000	100		
C	1000	50		
D	760	38		
E	540		135	
F	500		125	
G	300		75	
H	150			150
I	100			100
J	80			80
K	70			70
	9500	388	355	400

Average daily production = 9500/20 = 475.

One possible production schedule for the 11 products is shown in Figure 16.13. Daily production in that schedule varies from a high of 495 to a low of 445. The largest day-to-day variation is in weeks 3 and 4 when production goes from 485 in day 3 to 445 in day 4. This amount of variation (40/445 = 0.089, about 9%) is small, and the process should have no trouble adjusting to it. In actuality the lowest production rate of 445 per day would never happen because many other products besides the 11 listed must also be produced, and production of them would be scheduled during periods of low production activity — days 4 and 5 during weeks 3 and 4.

FIGURE 16.13

Level daily production schedule.

		**Production Schedule**
	colspan="5"	**Week 1 (days)**	colspan="3"	**Week 2**	colspan="3"	**Week 3**	colspan="3"	**Week 4**
Product	1	2	3	4	5	*	4	5	*	4	5	*	4	5
A	210	210	210	190	180									
B	150	150	50	50	100									
C	60	60	60	60	10									
D	60	60	60	20	20		same			same			same	
E			135											
F				125										
G					75									
H				50	100									
I							25	75						
J											80			
K														70
	480	480	485	495	485	*	470	460	*	445	455	*	445	445

* Note. Production schedule for days 1–3 remains the same every week.

The identical MMP schedule is used on days 1 and 2 to produce products A–D, and a different schedule is used on day 3 to include product E. Once the MMP schedules for these 3 days have been set, they remain the same week after week. For days 4 and 5, different MMP schedules are used on different weeks to accommodate products F–K. Unless the overall level or mix of demand changes, once set, all of these MMP schedules will remain about the same, month after month.

The MMP schedule represents *anticipated* production, and the actual daily FAS schedule will differ somewhat to reflect recent demand changes and actual customer orders received.

ASSEMBLE-TO-ORDER

When a company makes a large number of different products (1000s, 10,000s, or 100,000s of combinations of styles, options, features), it is impossible to anticipate demand, plan production, or to maintain a detailed BOM for each of them. A way to deal with the problem of too much variety is to sidestep it and instead deal with something for which there is much less variety.

Modular Bills

In ATO practice, a BOM is maintained for each subassembly option or component option but not for individual final products. The BOM for such an option is called a **modular bill** of materials.

FIGURE 16.14

Modular bill showing options available for product family X. Each box represents a module.

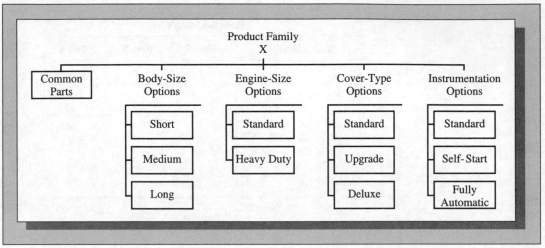

Figure 16.14 shows the modular bill for product family X, where product family X represents all possible variations of a product. Each column represents a major subassembly (body-shell size, engine size, and so on) and shows the available options. Together, different combinations of options yield a possible 54 variations (3 bodies × 2 engines × 3 covers × 3 instrumentations) of product X. Since, ordinarily, the BOM for a product shows the particular, or unique, combination of subassemblies used in the product, 54 product BOMs would be required to show the same information expressed in Figure 16.14.

As Figure 16.14 indicates, a modular bill shows all the possible options, but not particular combinations of them. Each box in the figure is a **module** and represents an option. Since there are 11 options (3 bodies, 2 engines, 3 covers, 3 instrumentations), product X can be fully represented by 11 BOMs, one for each option. (In Figure 16.14 there are 12 BOMs; the additional one represents common parts, or parts used in *all* versions of product family X). In a modular bill, the options are elevated to level 0 status in the tree structure, and the BOM for final products (products in family X), does not exist.

Since many final-product variations result from different combinations of options of relatively few subassemblies, the demand for each option is always larger than the demand for each variety of final product. As a result, it is easier to estimate demand for modules than it is for particular products. Although demand for the products in which subassemblies are used might be erratic and unstable, the requirements for the subassemblies themselves, when aggregated over all products in which they are used, is often stable and predictable.

In Figure 16.14, for example, there are 54 possible kinds of products, but only two sizes of engines. The demand for *each* of the 54 products might be small and hard to predict; however, the aggregate demand for *all* 54 kinds of products will, obviously, be larger and thus easier to predict. Once this aggregate demand is forecasted, the requirement for a kind of engine is determined by multiplying the forecast by the percentage expected to require that engine (the percentage is usually derived from the percentage of past sales having that engine). This is explained later.

The use of modular bills presumes that the BOMs are structured in terms of the modules from which final products are made. In many cases, however, pre-existing BOMs are for final products, not for modules. The next section discusses how to create modular BOMs from a group of BOMs for final products.

Modularization Procedure[17]

To restructure the BOMs for a group of product models into modules, first look at the level 1 components in the BOMs for the product models to determine which components are common to all models and which are unique to only certain ones. Then, cluster the components into the categories they have in common. Some components will not be assignable to categories, in which case the level 2 components should be investigated for commonalities.

Example 5:   Modularization of Products

Consider a product that comes in the following variations:

Body size: big, small
Clutch torque-speed: high, medium, low

There are thus six possible variations or models for the product. Suppose the level 1 BOM for each of them is as shown in Figure 16.15. The level 1 components share the following categories:

Common to all models: J, S
Big models: L, Z
Small models: K, W
High-speed models: C, O, R2
Medium-speed models: B, N, R3
Low-speed models: A, M, R4

The remaining components (D1, D2, E1, E2, and so on) are unique to each model. Now, to determine whether these components can be modularized, look at the level 2 BOM and observe the parts breakdown of each component. Suppose the level 2 breakdowns are as shown in Figure 16.16. Next, refer back to the original categories (common, big, small, high, medium, and low) to see whether it is possible to classify the level 2 components into the same categories. As it turns out, it is possible, with the following results (level 2 components in **bold**):

Common: J, S, **H3**
Big: L, Z, **C4**
Small: K, W, **C5**
High: C, O, R2, **C1, G5**
Medium: B, N, R3, **C2, G3**
Low: A, M, R4, **C3, G4**

FIGURE 16.15

Components in level 1 BOMs for six product models.

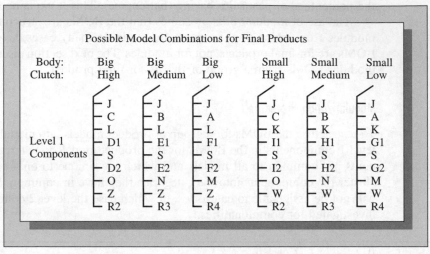

FIGURE 16.16

Level 2 BOM.

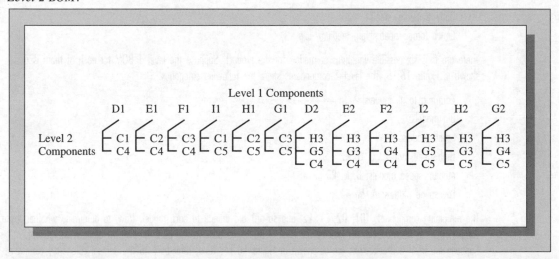

Thus, the six final-product BOMs can be replaced by six modular bills: common, big, small, high, medium, and low. In this example, the number of modular bills is the same as the number of product models, six, though as explained, when the number of possible product models is very large, the number of modular BOMs will be much smaller.

Usually, a module is a subassembly that is produced and temporarily held in stock until a customer order arrives that calls for its use in a product. The production lead time required to assemble modules into a final product is one determinant of the level of the item chosen for modularization. If the time to combine modules into a final product exceeds the customer-expected lead time, then the level of the subassembly in the module might have to be raised from a simple subassembly to an assembled group of modules, or a major subassembly. As a rule, it takes longer to assemble many simple subassemblies than a few major subassemblies (groups of already-combined simple subassemblies). Thus, the acceptable lead time at final assembly is an important criterion for choosing the appropriate level of subassembly to call an end-item module.

Example   6:   Impact of Lead Time on Choice of Module as an End-Item

Product J is made of four modules—S1, S2, S3, and S4—temporarily held in stock until an order is received. During final assembly, S1 is combined with S2, S3 is combined with S4, and the two combinations are themselves combined into the final product. Suppose it takes 1 day to do the S1–S2 and S3–S4 assemblies and another day to assemble the final combination. Thus, the total assembly lead time is 2 days.

Suppose the standard industry lead time is only 1 day. It is possible to reduce the lead time on product J to 1 day by stocking just two modules, M1 (major subassembly of S1 and S2) and M2 (major subassembly of S3 and S4) since, that way, when an order arrives, only M1 and M2 need to be combined.

Of course, by using higher-level subassemblies as modules, a greater number of different modules must be held to be able to handle the same degree of variety in the final product. Suppose in the example that S1, S2, S3, and S4 each come in four versions, and that any version of a module can be combined with any version of any other module. By holding 16 kinds $(4 + 4 + 4 + 4)$ of modules, it is possible to produce $4 \times 4 \times 4 \times 4 = 256$ final product models. However, to be able to offer the same number of product models from just *two* modules of major subassemblies, M1 and M2, it would be necessary to carry 32 kinds of modules (16 for each major subassembly). Using higher-level modules as a strategy to reduce lead times will thus increase the quantity of inventory and also the cost of each item in inventory since major subassemblies are worth more (higher value-added) than simpler subassemblies.

Planning Bills

Modular bills elevate lower-level items in the BOM to level 0 (end-item) status, and eliminate the need for the former (final product) level 0 item. In the example for product X, each subassembly module is considered an end-item in itself.

When the number of possible final products is very large, a type of modular bill called a **planning bill** is used for production scheduling. Planning bills greatly simplify production scheduling and improve the ability of production schedules based on forecasts to satisfy actual customer demand. As a case in point, in the example for product X in Figure 16.13 there are 54 product variations. Whereas it is probably difficult to accurately anticipate demand for each of the 54 possible variations, it is relatively easy to forecast the percentages of products that will involve different options from sales records and conversations with major customers. These percentages are precisely what a planning bill provides. The planning bill does not specify the exact amount of each product to produce, but it does specify the amount of materials and subassemblies needed to fill actual orders in MTO or ATO factories. Following is an example.

Example 7: Production Planning Using Planning Bills

Figure 16.14 illustrated the modular bill concept. Suppose past sales of products in product family X are evaluated for customer preference, and the relative percentages for options in the family are as shown in Figure 16.17.

Suppose for the upcoming month, forecasted demand for all product models is 2000 units. A level production schedule is used, and the MPS specifies a daily rate of 100 units. The schedule, however, does not specify the exact mix of the 54 models since that will not be known until customer orders are compiled and the FAS is prepared.

Without knowing the actual orders for individual product models, the planning bill makes it possible to go ahead and estimate the average number of each type of component that will likely be needed. Assume an MRP system orders materials using weekly time buckets, 4 weeks per month. Based on the planning bills in Figure 16.17 and assuming a 5-day workweek, the weekly requirements for the module will be [percentage × 5 days × daily rate], or

CP 500	BL	100	ES	150	CS	100	IS	100
	BM	150	EHD	350	CU	250	ISS	250
	BS	250			CD	150	IFA	150

These numbers represent the quantities of each option that will be made available to final assembly each week to meet anticipated demand for all varieties of the product.

To illustrate how planning for modules is tied to MMP, suppose the same company (that produces the 54 models) also produces the body shells (BL, BM, BS) and the instrumentation packages (IS, ISS, IFA) on two separate pull production lines. For each line, the FAS can be expressed in terms of a daily MMP sequence:

Body shells: Sequence of two BLs, three BMs, and five BSs (e.g., BS–BM–BS–BL–BS–BM–BS–BM–BS–BL) repeated 10 times a day, 5 days a week.

Instrumentation packages: Sequence of two ISs, five ISSs, and three IFAs (e.g., ISS–IFA–ISS–IS–ISS–IFA–ISS–IFA–ISS–IS) repeated 10 times a day, 5 days a week.

FIGURE 16.17

Planning bills showing percentage breakdowns. Each box represents a module.

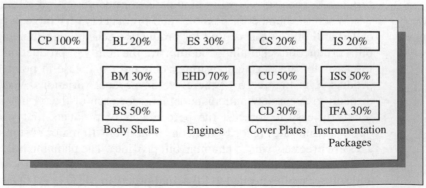

The MMP sequences for body shells and instrumentation packages also determine the requirements for parts and components that are produced by upstream workcells.

As with assembly of the final product, the FASs for body shells and instrumentation packages are modified daily to reflect actual customer orders as received. Benetton, the Italian clothing manufacturer, does a twist on this, producing 25% of its output undyed, then coloring it at the last minute based on current sales data. The other 75% of output is produced with color according to a sales forecast.

The percentages in the planning bills must be periodically checked and adjusted to reflect the most recent product order mix. Since actual requirements for final assembly will likely vary from the amounts estimated by the planning bill, safety stock for some items might be necessary. It is OK to carry an excess of inexpensive parts but not so for expensive parts, so close tabs must be kept on the latter. To avoid stockout of items controlled by kanban, kanban links should be established with upstream operations and suppliers (i.e., material supply links with guaranteed short production lead times for items produced in-house and short purchasing lead times for vendor-supplied items).

Alternative to Planning Bills

An alternative to planning bills is to forecast demand for each option directly. Using time series of the historical requirements for each option and taking into account anticipated changes in trends, the requirement for each option is forecasted separately. Whether this gives a more accurate requirements forecast than planning-bills percentages is an open question; the answer is to try both methods, and pick the one that gives the best results.

Role of Concurrent Engineering

Simplified production planning and scheduling follows the principle "plan for the few, but produce for the many." Helping production conform to this principle is yet another area where concurrent engineering plays an important role.

Example   8:   Simplified Planning through Simplified Design

A manufacturer produces 10 kinds of electrical motors. For each kind of motor, it also produces a mount and cover. Each cover has an access hole, and to accommodate customers' different requirements the hole comes in eight sizes. Therefore, the total number of combinations of covers and hole sizes is 80. Besides these covers, the material requirements include the 10 sizes of motors and 10 sizes of mounts.

Now, suppose the design team redesigns the motor mount such that one mount size can be used with any motor size without loss of functionality. Also, suppose with only one mount size, there need be only one cover size. The material requirements are now 10 sizes of motors, one size of mount, and eight covers (one for each hole size). Note that there are still 80 possible final combinations (10 motors, eight possible hole sizes in each cover).

As a further simplification, a team of product and manufacturing engineers determines that the hole in the cover can be drilled at the time of final assembly according to the customer order. The hole size is thus specified on the FAS, and now the number of possible different covers is reduced to one.

Simplifying products to simplify planning takes the combined effort of people in marketing, engineering, production, and purchasing. Marketing determines from customers the kinds of options they want, then discusses with engineering ways to design the product to meet the range of wants. Marketing, production, and engineering discuss ways to achieve the wants through possible combinations of options, then zero in on the combinations that will simplify planning and scheduling, minimize production costs and lead times, and be feasible given constraints of production costs, capabilities, and lead times. The end result is something more pleasing to both customers and producers. At one time, General Motors' midsize cars were produced in 1,900,000 combinations. The corporation is working to reduce that to 1,000 combinations by 1997–98.[18]

MAKE-TO-ORDER

When demand is sporadic or every order is somewhat unique (the true job shop), then level production is impossible. If, however, product demand is uniform and somewhat continuous, then level production is possible.

Suppose demand is continuous, but is also highly variable. The only way to level production in that case is to maintain a backlog of orders. Given a sufficient backlog, then the production process has a pool of orders from which to continuously draw at a uniform rate. Of course, any backlog increases the time that customers must wait, though that wait also depends on how long orders are held before being released to production and how long setup and production take. Thus, even with a backlog, lead times can be shortened if (1) marketing sends to production only confirmed orders (orders from paying customers) and (2) production minimizes the time to execute the orders (minimizes times for setups, workers reassignments, routing, and so on).

Scheduling with Backlogs

Briefly the procedure is as follows. Upon receipt of an order, marketing enters the order into the backlog. In about a week, marketing confirms the order and, at that time, gives production notice of all confirmed orders in the backlog. About a week later, the list of confirmed orders is transferred to production; at that time, production starts fitting the orders into the production schedule for, say, 2 weeks later. Given a 2-week lead time and backlog, it might be possible for production to prepare a somewhat level production schedule.

The total lead time in this example (time between orders being first received and being filled) is 3–4 weeks. The size of the time buckets (time blocks for each stage of order receipt, order confirmation, order transmittal to production, and so on) is assumed to be 1 week and that contributes to longer lead times. With experience, the size of the time buckets at different stages should be reduced, which will reduce the time customers have to wait.

Minimizing Scheduling Problems

The worst case for production scheduling is when the number of products is large and volume for each is low or one-of-a-kind. In this case, level production schedules and pull production are impossible. Nonetheless, the goal is still to reduce waste, and that is done in the following ways:[19]

1. *Simplify the BOMs.* Reduce the number of levels in the BOMs to a minimum; this will reduce the number of parts to be managed, the numbers of transactions to be processed, and the time and cost of processing.

2. *Use group technology and standard parts.* Design products so that almost anything a customer would want could be achieved by assembly of similar or identical components. For procured components and parts, stick with standard items that are less expensive to procure and stock and that can readily be procured on short notice. At the same time, try to keep WIP inventory to a minimum, and use simple visual controls to track inventory.

3. *Make only what is needed.* Do not use estimated lead times to anticipate what will be needed, and do not keep backlogs of work just to keep everyone busy. A simple form of visual kanban can be used to signal when a workcenter should produce more to meet demand at downstream workstations. When a workcenter becomes a bottleneck, workers at upstream workcenters should stop and provide help to relieve the bottleneck. Items that must be produced in advance should be produced in small batches on a regular basis, say four times a year or once every month. The latter procedure is a crude start toward repetitive production.

4. *Produce in lot sizes that are small and easy to count.* Produce large jobs in small batches and use small transfer batches (for an order of 100 units, process and move it along in batches of 10 at a time). This is done to avoid waiting at every operation until the entirety of a large batch is produced, which increases WIP inventories and lead times everywhere in the plant.

5. *Use simple visual control systems.* Replace sophisticated, remote tracking systems with visual systems. Described elsewhere in this book, they include production schedules posted where everyone can see them; signals such as andons and status boards to display production status (normal or malfunction); production procedures and standard operations charts; and charts of goals versus performance (production, quality, worker skill proficiency). Other visual means to facilitate production control include kanban cards, standard-sized containers to limit inventory, and shop-floor layouts that allow people to *see* things important to their jobs (the status of upstream and downstream workcenters, equipment functioning, stock levels, etc.).

6. *Do not overload the shop or particular operations.* Overloading the shop floor increases WIP and lead times everywhere. Keep the workload at an amount that the shop *can* handle. If downstream operations experience problems, then upstream operations should slow down or stop. Keep the amount of rework at each operation below a prespecified limit; if the limit is reached, stop the operation until the rework is completed.

7. *Use days or hours for planning lead times.* Products that are custom-made, one-of-a-kind, or that have erratic demand cannot be effectively produced using pull production, and traditional means for planning and scheduling as provided by MRP

systems are more appropriate. Although long lead times and high WIP inventory are hallmarks of MRP systems, both can be reduced if the procurement and process run times used in scheduling accurately reflect reality. Wherever possible, the MRP system should be modified to use daily, or even hourly lead times, and the times should be continuously checked and frequently updated. Following is an example of detailed work scheduling in a push system using short time buckets.

Example   9:   Scheduling in a Push System

Alpha Company makes customized furniture for corporations, churches, temples, and museums. Each batch of furniture is made according to customer requirements. Orders originate mostly from architects and interior decorators. Rarely is a design used by more than one customer, so every job is unique. Both the frequency and the size of job orders is highly erratic.

    Suppose an order is received to make 10 units of a kind of a wooden table. The table is an assembly of a top, four legs, and support pieces for the legs. The top and support pieces must be cut and sanded; the legs must be cut, milled, and sanded. After the top, legs, and supports are assembled, the table is given a coat of primer, then four coats of paint. The steps of the process (represented by the product **bill of activities**) and the lead time at each step are shown in Figure 16.18.

FIGURE 16.18

Bill of activities for table manufacture. Lead times (shown in parentheses) are for producing 10 tables.

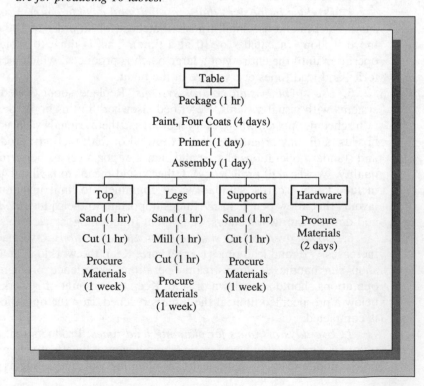

To minimize the production lead time, each component (legs, supports, and tops) is scheduled separately at each of the operations (cutting, sanding, etc.). For example, cutting the legs, cutting the top, and cutting the supports are considered three jobs, and each job is scheduled separately. (This contrasts lumping all the components together and scheduling them as one cutting job.[20])

The scheduling process begins by assigning a due date for shipment to the customer. This is the time by which the last operation, package, must be completed; if the shipment occurs midday, then it would be possible to schedule packaging for early the same day. Moving down the bill in Figure 16.18, the next operation is paint, which is scheduled to start 4 days earlier. The procedure of scheduling the start of an activity by going backwards from the time when the activity must be completed is called **backscheduling.** This procedure is repeated for the next activity, primer, and for all remaining activities.

When the schedule shows more than one job at an operation, a decision must be made as to which job gets priority. For example, the top, legs, and supports must all be sanded, so a decision must be made about which goes first, which second, and which last.

Figure 16.19 shows the resulting backschedule for manufacturing the 10 tables. The dotted lines in the figure represent waiting times, for example, in the sand operation the legs must wait until the tops are sanded, and the supports must wait until the legs are sanded.

The total lead time for the entire 10-table order is the length of the longest lead-time branch on the backschedule. In Figure 16.19 this is the supports branch, the length of which, starting with procurement and ending with packaging, is

$$5 \text{ days}(1 \text{ wk}) + 5 \text{ hrs} + 6 \text{ days} + 1 \text{ hr} = 11 \text{ days} + 6 \text{ hrs}.$$

Assuming that batches of components for the tables must wait no longer than the times shown in Figure 16.19, the order should be completed within 12 days.

Figure 16.19

Backschedule for table manufacture. Lead times are not shown to scale.

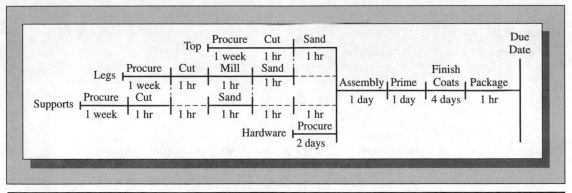

With an MRP system capable of scheduling in daily or hourly time buckets, production lead times can be held to a minimum. Of course, a concomitant requirement is that shop-floor operations are tightly controlled so the lead times are, in fact, the same as assumed by the MRP system and that the system is immediately updated to reflect any changes in lead times. Small time-bucket planning combined with small-batch production minimizes the time wasted from jobs waiting.

HYBRID SYSTEMS

Some companies handle high product variety by using a combination of ATO and MTO production activities. Each kind of product is assembled on an order-by-order basis and involves common modules and subassemblies, as well as unique, one-of-a-kind components. The modules are produced in repetitive fashion using pull production methods and MMP schedules; the unique components are produced order-by-order and are backscheduled. In these hybrid cases, daily scheduling of workcells and isolated workstations is done by a combination of kanban cards for the repetitive pull jobs and MRP-generated orders for the one-of-a-kind push jobs.[21] Following is an example.

Example   10: Hybrid Scheduling Process

Beta Company makes furniture for several national department store chains. Although the models and styles produced for the chains are different, the main components for all of them are similar. Thus, the aggregate demand for components for all of the products is somewhat stable and predictable.

Since Beta Company, unlike Alpha Company in the previous example, makes products from different combinations of identical components and since each component has stable demand, the components can be produced repetitively using level schedules and pull production, even though the final-product assemblies cannot. The final-product assemblies, as well as any operations that are unique to particular orders, are scheduled with an MRP-type backscheduling system.

Among the company's products are tables. The company makes tables in different dimensions, woods, and finishes, though the feature that most distinguishes a table is the table *top:* each top is made to customer requirements. Otherwise, every table the company produces uses the same hardware, leg supports, and one of three styles of legs—A, B, or C.

FIGURE 16.20

Hybrid system: pull and backscheduling.

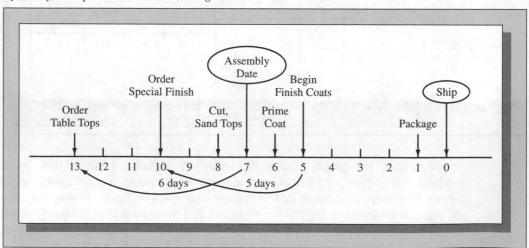

Demand for legs for all tables produced is large and somewhat stable, so legs can be produced using a pull system—either in small batches of A, B, or C, or in an MMP sequence, whichever works best. Thus, whenever the company receives an order to produce a particular kind of table, only the tops must be backscheduled. The backschedule includes lead times for procuring the tops and for every operation performed on them. If additional steps must be performed on the tables after assembly, then those steps must be backscheduled also.

Suppose 10 tables are ordered and suppose the lead time for procuring, cutting, and sanding the 10 tops is 6 days. Thus, the tops must be ordered 6 days prior to table assembly. Further, suppose after the tables are assembled they are to receive one primer coat and four paint coats, and then be packaged. If the coating operations are specific to the customer order, then they also must be backscheduled. If the paint is special and not carried in stock, then the paint procurement must be backscheduled too. Say we allow the following lead times: 5 days to procure paint, 5 days to apply primer and four paint coats, and 1 day to package the tables. Based on those lead times, the production schedule will be as shown in Figure 16.20.

The legs, supports, and hardware will arrive at the assembly station 7 days before the shipping date; these materials will have arrived there using kanban cards or other pull signals. The assembly date, 7 days before the shipping date, has been set to allow 1 day for assembly, 6 days for applying the primer and paint coatings, and 1 day for packaging. The overall lead time is thus 13 days.

Summary

Variation in production schedules contributes to longer production lead times and higher costs, shortages, overages, and defect rates. Conversely, smooth, level production—producing items at a uniform rate and in small batches—minimizes uncertainty, reduces costs, improves capacity utilization, and yields better product quality and customer service. In many companies the Pareto principle dominates demand: relatively few products account for the highest volume. These products are the primary focus for production leveling. In level production the ideal case is to produce some of every item every hour, though for low-volume items the alternative is to produce some of the item every day or some every few days or weeks.

Achieving level production is a cross-functional effort since imbalances between demand and production often result when marketing, distribution, and production work independently and at cross-purposes. A multifunctional planning team with members from marketing, sales, finance, production, and other areas coordinates decisions and information about product launch, promotion strategies, customers' demands, and planned levels of production.

Level production is a prerequisite for pull production. Pull production requires somewhat uniform demand, which is achieved through a level production schedule for the final stage of the process. Since items are pulled through the process, if the schedule at the final stage is level, demand everywhere upstream will be level too. When a number of different items is produced in the same process, uniform demand is achieved by intermixing products. This is called mixed-model production (MMP) and refers to the mixed sequencing of different items as they move through the process. The more uniformly that items are intermixed in the sequence, the more uniform the demand for materials everywhere in the process. Mixed-model production requires flexible operations, cross-trained workers, strong emphasis on quality assurance, and small-lot delivery of incoming materials. In addition to the time, cost, and quality benefits of level production, MMP reduces losses from line changeovers and material shortages and enhances process improvement.

Level and mixed-model production strategies are easily implemented in make-to-stock operations where demand is stable and predictable. They can also be implemented in make-to-assemble situations for production of subassembly options (modules), though usually not for the final products in which the options are used. Demand for options or modules tends to be more stable than demand for the differentiated products comprising them, so the modules can be produced at a relatively uniform rate and then combined into final products to satisfy last-minute customer orders. The ability to modularize products requires forethought about simplicity and commonality of parts in product design.

The most difficult production planning and scheduling situation is make-to-order where product variety is high and demand for each product is sporadic or one-time. In that situation the Pareto principle is applied to determine which, if any, products could be made-to-stock or made-to-assemble, for which cases production leveling and mixed-model strategies can be used. For products that must be custom-made on an order-by-order basis, the emphasis must be on achieving high-quality, good service and low cost by ways discussed elsewhere in this book, including producing in small lots, avoiding overproduction, simplifying product design, using visual shop-floor tracking systems, and employing accurate lead-time information.

Questions

1. What are the major sources of variability in production schedules?
2. In 10 words or less define level production.
3. Why level production? What advantages are offered over nonlevel production?
4. Discuss the requirements for level production schedules.
5. Suppose a monthly production schedule shows that 1000 product Ws, 2000 product Ys, and 1500 product Zs are to be produced every week. Since the same quantity of each product is produced every week, is this an example of level production? If it is, why? If not, why not, and what must be done to make it level?
6. What is the contribution of sales, marketing, and product engineering to level production?
7. Explain how mixed-model production (MMP) maximizes production leveling.
8. Referring to the products in question 5, what would the sequence of products be if an MMP procedure were used?
9. In a pull production system, what is the relationship between the amount of WIP required between upstream stages of the process and the amount of leveling in the production schedule?
10. For what reasons would a sequence other than the maximally mixed MMP sequence be employed?

11. Describe the following three production philosophies: make-to-stock, make-to-order, assemble-to-order. In each case, where is the end-item for production planning purposes?

12. Contrast the relative roles of the final-assembly schedule (FAS) and the master production schedule.

13. Describe how a bill of materials and a modular bill of materials differ. How is each used? Why use one instead of the other?

14. Explain the pros and cons of holding in stock higher-level subassemblies (*assemblies* of subassemblies) versus lower-level subassemblies (subassemblies or modules).

15. Explain what a planning bill is. How is it used?

16. Discuss how concurrent engineering efforts ultimately affect production scheduling procedures.

17. What are some rules for reducing waste and improving quality and service in make-to-order production environments?

18. Give some examples of companies or situations that would use a combination of pull production with mixed-model FASs and MRP-generated push schedules.

Problems

1. Forecasted annual demand for a product line is given below. Assume a minimum batch size of 50 and a 250-day work year.

Product	Forecast
A	150,000
B	75,000
C	50,000
D	37,500
E	25,000
F	7,500
G	2,500
H	1,250
I	1,250

a. Develop a level production schedule for the line assuming minimal product batches and no time required for changeover.

b. The line produces at a rate of 160 units/hr. Is the current 7-hour workday adequate to produce the quantity in the level schedule? If not, to what time must the workday be modified?

c. The company wants to produce the daily batches in a mixed-model sequence. Suggest such a sequence.

2. The LAN's End company produces peripheral devices for computer networks. Among its products are three styles of modems: LEB, LEM, and LEX. The FAS, which is fixed

4 weeks in advance of production, specifies producing one LEB, four LEMs, and six LEXs every 20 minutes throughout the day in a 7-hour workday.

  a. What is the daily total production for each of the three products?

  b. By trying to maintain a 7-hour workday, the company finds that on average it falls short by 11 units/day. What is the problem? What are some alternatives to resolve it?

3. The LAN's End line assembles three kinds of switching boxes: SBA, SBN, and SBX. Demand for SBA is half that for SBN, but is the same as that for SBX. Assembly of SBA takes 6 minutes; assembly of SBN and SBX, 2 minutes each.

  a. Develop a mixed-model sequence for the three products. How often does it repeat every 420-minute workday, and what is the daily production for each kind of box?

  b. Repeat (*a*), except suppose that demand for SBA is three-fourths that for SBN, and that demand for SBX is one-fourth that for SBN.

4. What is the mixed-model repeating sequence for meeting a daily production requirement of 48 model As, 24 model Bs, 12 model Cs, 36 model Ds, and 24 models Es?

5. A product comes in three models, J, K, L, and the demand for each relative to the total is 10%, 30%, and 60%, respectively. What is the mixed-model repeating sequence?

6. A schedule calls for producing 40 As, 20 Bs, and 30 Cs. Process time is 5 minutes per A, 8 minutes per B, and 10 minutes per C.

  a. Develop the mixed-model repeating sequence. Assuming 60 seconds changeover between products, how long will the scheduled production take?

  b. Assume no more than 700 minutes a day is available to produce these products. Suggest a way to reduce the required production time to meet this constraint.

7. Following is a level 1 breakdown of the parts for four models of a product:

	Commercial		**Military**	
	Standard(CS)	*Deluxe (CD)*	*Standard (MS)*	*Deluxe (MD)*
Small parts	CP	CP	CP	CP
Body shell	BSS	BSM	BSL	BSL
Engine size	ESS	ESHD	ESHD	ESHD
Cover type	CTS	CTD	CTU	CTU
Instrumentation	IS	IFA	IS	IFA

  a. Modularize the components. How many planning bills are required? Can the components be completely modularized?

  b. Suppose the level 2 breakdown for the three body-shell components shows:

Subassembly	Parts
BSS	F, SS, BF
BSM	F, SM, BF
BSL	F, SL, BF, J

  Revise the planning bills from (a).

  c. Suppose on average total demand for all models is expected to be about 2000 units/mo. Further, based on historical sales, the following sales breakdown is expected: CS, 40%; CD, 20%; MS, 30%; MD, 10%. What is the percentage breakdown of commercial and military products, and standard and deluxe products? What is the monthly demand for each?

  d. Assume the percentage breakdown given in (c) and that production is leveled to 100 products/day. From the planning bills, determine the daily material requirements for all components.

8. Juarez, Inc., manufactures telephone/answering-machines in the following configurations:

Options	No. Choices
Colors	6
Cord/cordless	2
Memory capability	3
Features switch	2
Tone select	2
Volume select	2

  a. If there is a BOM for each possible configuration, how many BOMs are required for all configurations?

  b. If modularization is possible, what number of BOMs is required?

  c. The Juarez company sells 10,000 phones/wk. Considering only choices of tone select and volume select, the breakdown is as follows:

Tone select (T)	30%
No tone select (NT)	70%
Volume select (V)	60%
No volume select (NV)	40%

  What number of each possible choice should the company plan to produce? Can you determine the number of each possible combination (e.g., both T *and* V)?

9. To simplify the items at level 1 of a product BOM, Julia Megan & Company has started putting small, loose parts for its products in kits. For four of the products, the number and kind of small parts is very similar; in particular,

Part	Product A	Product B	Product C	Product D
Nut 2403	6	6	7	5
Washer 7403	6	6	7	5
Bolt 6403	6	6	7	5
Nut 2614	3	3	4	2
Bolt 6614	3	3	4	2
O-ring 4320	1	2	2	1
Belt 2118	2	2	1	1
Seal 18J	1	1	1	0

One kit is to be used for all four products (on the product BOMs, the part numbers above will be replaced by a single number, that of the kit). List the contents of the kit.

10. The figure below shows the level 1 BOMs for different options offered in a product. Can the components be completely modularized? List the planning bills of the components that can be modularized.

Options				Products			
Chasis	St	St	St	St	Del	Del	Del	Del
Motor	Big	Big	Sma	Sma	Big	Big	Sma	Sma
Carriage	Hi	Lo	Hi	Lo	Hi	Lo	Hi	Lo
Components, level 1 BOM	L	L	L	L	M	M	M	M
	J	J	K	K	J	J	K	K
	C	D	C	D	C	D	C	D
	I	I	I	I	I	I	I	I
	A	A	A	A	B	B	B	B
	N	O	P	Q	N	O	P	Q
	G	G	H	H	G	G	H	H
	E	F	E	F	E	F	E	F

11. For the above problem, suppose the level 2 breakdown shows the following:

Component	N	O	P	Q
Parts, level 2 BOM	R	R	S	S
	T	U	T	U
	W	V	V	V
	V		W	

Is it now possible to completely modularize the parts and components for the products in problem 10? List the planning bills.

12. Zemco Dynamics, Inc., makes tables with the following options:

Top size: small, medium, large

Top material: cherry, maple, oak, Corian

Legs: spindle, ornate, Corinthian

Leaves (offered on medium and large only): 0, 1, or 2

a. Assume legs and leaves are matched to the tables by material and size (e.g., a large table with a cherry top will be matched with large cherry legs and large cherry leaves). What is the number of possible configurations of tables?

b. If complete modularization were possible, how many planning bills would be needed? List them.

c. Suppose, historically, annual demand has been for 12,000 tables with the following percentage breakdown for options:

Size		Material		Legs	
Small	30%	Cherry	20%	Spindle	50%
Medium	50	Maple	30	Ornate	30
Large	20	Oak	40	Corinthian	20
		Corian	10		

Oak Leaves		
	Large	Medium
none	30%	20%
1	60	50
2	10	30

Assume uniform production throughout the year. For any month, can you determine the number of large oak tables produced?

d. Suppose 80 large oak tables must be produced. Can you determine the number of spindle legs and the total number of leaves needed for these tables? If you can, give the answer. If you cannot, discuss why.

Endnotes

1. R. Schonberger, *World-Class Manufacturing: The Next Decade* (New York: The Free Press, 1996), pp. 147–50.

2. This principle is called the law of large numbers.

3. See, for example, N. Gaither, *Production and Operations Management* (6th ed.) (Fort Worth: Dryden Press, 1994), Chapter 9; R. Chase and N. Aquilano, *Production and Operations Management* (7th ed.) (Chicago: Irwin, 1995), pp. 529–31.

4. P. Park, "Uniform Plan Loading Through Level Production," *Production and Inventory Management,* 2nd Quarter 1993, pp. 12–17.

5. *Ibid.,* this figure originally appeared as Figure 1 on p. 13; reprinted with permission from APICS, the Educational Society for Resource Management, Falls Church, VA.

6. *Ibid.,* this figure originally appeared as Figure 3 on p. 14; reprinted with permission from APICS, the Educational Society for Resource Management, Falls Church, VA.

7. The concept of mixed-model production is frequently used in continuous and repetitive processes such as manufacture of automobiles and electronics. The concept also applies, however, to production of small batches of products in a family in focused job shops and production workcells.

8. *The Toyota Production System* (Toyota City, Japan: TMC International Public Affairs Division and Operations Management Consulting Division, 1992), p. 2.

9. Actually, stages feeding into final assembly *could* produce materials in smaller batches *if* they could guarantee that a sufficient number of the smaller batches would arrive at final assembly in time for the large-batch production. However, the scheduling and coordination of production and delivery of varisized batches at different stages of the process—all to ensure that an adequate amount of materials is on hand for batch production at later stages—is rather cumbersome, particularly when production involves batches of different kinds of products (requiring different kinds of input materials). As a result, it is common to schedule production of batches of roughly equivalent size at all stages throughout the process.

10. Pull production with large-batch final assembly is possible, but it requires building large stocks of material at each stage of the process, possibly too large to make sense. The large stocks of materials negate one reason for pull production, which is to keep stock low and reveal problems in the system.

11. Again, a pull system *will work* with large stocks, though, given the emphasis in pull production on reducing the size of stocks as much as possible, it makes little sense to *try* to use pull production while also maintaining big inventories.

12. Monden, for example, describes a rather sophisticated method used by Toyota for mixing assembly of automobiles that have a large variety of product features and options. The method results in maximal smoothing of the final assembly sequence. *See* Y. Monden, *Toyota Production System* (2nd ed.) (Norcross, GA: Industrial Engineering and Management Press, 1993), especially Chapter 17 and Appendix 2; for another method, *see* T. Vollmann, W. Berry, D.C. Whybark, *Manufacturing Planning and Control Systems* (New York: Irwin/McGraw-Hill, 1997), pp. 484–7.

13. B.J. Coleman and M.R. Vaghefi, "Heijunka (?): A Key to The Toyota Production System," *Production and Inventory Management,* 4th Quarter 1994, pp. 31–5.

14. *Ibid.*

15. R. Hall, *Zero Inventories* (Homewood, IL: Dow-Jones Irwin, 1983), pp. 69–72.

16. H. Mather, *Competitive Manufacturing* (Englewood Cliffs, NJ: Prentice-Hall, 1988), pp. 86–7.

17. S. Narasimhan, D. McLeavey, P. Billington, *Production Planning and Inventory Control* (2nd ed.) (Englewood Cliffs, NJ: Prentice-Hall, 1995), pp. 313–23.

18. R. Schonberger, *World-Class Manufacturing: The Next Decade,* p. 119.

19. *See* R. Hall, *Attaining Manufacturing Excellence* (Burr Ridge, IL: Irwin, 1987), pp. 208–9; R. Schonberger, *World-Class Manufacturing,* pp. 106–8.

20. Why scheduling three jobs results in shorter lead time than scheduling one job should be obvious: when scheduled separately the three jobs can each be processed separately (legs, top, supports), then moved on to the next step (cutting, milling, sanding, whatever); when scheduled as one job, enough time must be allowed for *all* the components (legs, top, supports) to be processed.

21. For discussion of hybrid shop-floor control systems, *see* B. Williams, *Manufacturing for Survival* (Reading, MA: Addison-Wesley, 1995), pp. 281–6.

Uniform flow is an important aspect of pull production. To achieve uniform flow, the master production schedule must be leveled, and the size of discrete batches produced for final assembly must be small. A uniform flow of mixed orders moving upstream from the final stage will result in a correspondingly uniform flow of materials moving downstream. But uniform flow at the rate necessary to meet requirements of the final stage takes more than level master production schedules and mixed-model assembly schedules. Although these schedules establish the necessary production level, material requirements, and production sequence, there remains the matter of production **timing.**

In pull production, the rate of production of every stage must correspond to the rate of assembly. In mixed-model production (MMP), all materials should move through the process in a uniform fashion and arrive at the final stage at the time and in the quantity and sequence specified by the final assembly schedule (FAS). Aligning the production rates and sequences of all upstream workcenters so that materials arrive at the rate needed at the final stage, called **synchronization,** is a subject of this chapter.

To achieve smooth flow and uniform production rates, the capacity of every operation must be adjusted such that, on average, all of them are capable of processing materials at the required rate. Achieving smooth, uniform flow by equalizing the capacity and/or workload of all stages is called **balancing** and is the other main subject of this chapter.

SYNCHRONIZATION

In make-to-stock (MTS) processes and portions of assemble-to-order (ATO) processes that manufacture products on a repetitive basis, the production process should be synchronized such that every upstream operation produces at the *rate* required to satisfy demand. In a pull system, that rate is set by the FAS. To visualize a synchronized process, imagine a conveyor system that moves material continuously from one operation to the next. The speed of the conveyor system is set according to the demand rate of the final product. To enable the entire system to meet demand without interruption or WIP inventory buildup, *every* operation along the conveyor must produce at about the same rate—the rate at which the conveyor system is moving. Such is a synchronized process.

In general, however, it is not necessary to link operations by a conveyor or other rigid means for the process to be synchronized. To enable somewhat synchronous flow of materials between successive workstations, it is only necessary that the rate of production and transfer of items at upstream stations roughly match the rate of demand for these items at downstream stations. Extending this concept, the flow of materials throughout the entire process is synchronized by setting the rate of production of *every* operation (and the rate of transfer of materials between operations) equal to the rate of demand at the final stage of the process. That demand rate is, in turn, determined by the production schedule at final assembly.

SYNCHRONIZED CYCLE TIMES

In a pull system, synchronization is achieved by setting the *cycle times* (CTs) at every upstream operation according to the CT at final assembly. As mentioned, in a pull system only the last stage of the process has a daily schedule. If production is to involve repetitive manufacture of multiple, similar products, the daily schedule will be a MMP schedule. This MMP schedule is used to determine the CTs of all products, and these product CTs are used to derive the maximum CTs of every upstream operation that supplies parts for the products. Briefly, an operation is synchronized to the overall process by setting its CT as a multiple of the required product CT. The following example illustrates this concept.

Example   1:   Setting CTs to Synchronize the Process

Suppose the daily requirements for three products are

Product A	200 units
Product B	100 units
Product C	50 units
All Products	350 units

Assuming 420 min/day for production, the required product CTs are

Product A	$420/200 = 2.1$ min (60 sec/min) $= 126$ sec
Product B	$420/100 = 252$ sec
Product C	$420/50 = 504$ sec
All Products	$420/350 = 72$ sec

In words, the final assembly station must complete a product A every 126 seconds, a product B every 252 seconds, and a product C every 504 seconds. Overall, the final assembly station will complete a product every 72 seconds on average. This 72-second CT is the **drumbeat** of the process.

Consider for a moment just product A. To synchronize production of this product, every upstream operation that supplies parts for it must produce and transport a part once every 126 seconds, on average. If two of a kind of part are needed for each product A, then the operations making the part must produce and transport one part every 63 seconds, on average. The same rationale applies to parts and materials produced for products B and C.

Suppose the process for manufacturing the three products consists of five major subprocesses, described below and shown in Figure 17.1.

Subprocess I.   This is the final assembly line for products A, B, and C. Assume the FAS specifies an MMP sequence of AABABAC, repeated 50 times, and one product every 72 seconds, on average. As Figure 17.2 shows, with this sequence and a 72-second average CT, the required CTs for all three products are indeed achieved.

Subprocess II.   This subprocess continuously produces a part that is used in *all* three products. Since 350 units of this part must be produced each day, the CT for every operation in this subprocess must be the same as the CT at final assembly, 72 seconds.

Subprocess III.   This subprocess continuously produces a part that is used only for *product A*; thus, it must produce 200 units of this part per day. The CT of every operation in this subprocess must be, at most, the same as the CT of product A at final assembly, 126 seconds.

Subprocess IV.   This subprocess produces in alternate batches a part for *product B* and a part for *product C*. Suppose the size of the batches is 10 units, the same as a standard container. Also assume that production of each batch is preceded by a changeover (from a batch of parts for B, to a batch of parts for C, and vice versa) that has an internal setup time of 10 minutes.

FIGURE 17.1

Final assembly and subprocesses for producing products A, B, and C.

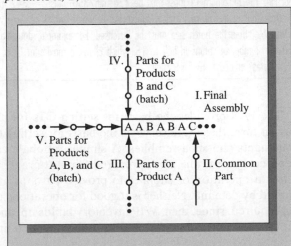

Figure 17.2

Correspondence between 72-second interval and product CTs.

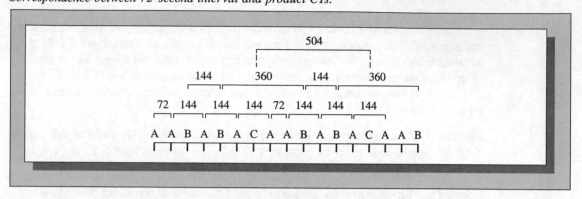

Each day subprocess IV must produce 100 parts for product B and 50 parts for product C. Since the batch size is 10, the corresponding mixed-model batch sequence will be BCBBCBBCBBCBCBB (where each B and C represents a batch of 10). Thus, the daily number of average setups is 10.

The time consumed by 10 setups is 100 minutes, which leaves $420 - 100 = 320$ min/day for production. Thus, the CT for every operation in this subprocess must be, at most,

$$(320 \text{ min})/150 \text{ units} = 2.133 \text{ min, or } 128 \text{ sec.}$$

Subprocess V. This subprocess alternately produces parts for product A, product B, and product C. Determining the CT is done the same way as for subprocess IV. Daily, this subprocess must produce 200 parts for product A, 100 parts for product B, and 50 parts for product C. Assuming again a batch size of 10 units, the corresponding batch sequence will be identical to the sequence shown in Figure 17.2, except in this subprocess each A, B, and C represents a *batch* of 10 units. Thus the sequence AABABAC must be repeated five times a day. Since there are six changeovers between batches of different parts in a single mixed-model sequence (AA, B, A, B, A, C), there are 30 setups a day. With 10 min/setup and a 420-minute workday, $420 - (30 \times 10) = 120$ minutes remain for production. The maximum CT must thus be 120 min/350 units $= .342$ minutes $= 20.5$ seconds.

Note that in this process and in subprocess IV where setups are involved, if the required CTs are too small to be attainable, then the batch size must be increased. For example, doubling the batch size to 20 units at subprocess V cuts the number of setups in half to 15, which allows a maximum CT of $[420 - (15 \times 10)]/350 = .771$ minutes, or about 46.2 sec/unit.

The FAS provides the basis for setting CTs for all components and subassemblies; in turn, these CTs serve as the basis for setting CTs of parts that feed into the components and subassemblies. A similar rationale can be continued back through the process and to the parts procured from external suppliers. It is of no use for an upstream operation or supplier to provide parts at a rate slower than, on average, required by demand. Neither is it good for operations to produce at rates much faster than required, since, then, WIP inventory builds up, and operations must periodically shut down to allow time for final assembly to catch up.

After product CTs have been set, the operations at all upstream processes are structured to produce roughly at those times. If the operations include linked work-cells, as described in Chapter 10, the actual CT of each cell is adjusted by assigning workers and refining tasks such that it does not exceed the required product CTs. Further, these CTs are posted on the standard operating routines (described in Chapter 11) and become the goal toward which process improvement is directed.

Given all the bother to establish product CTs and synchronize the process around them, the MMP and final assembly schedules must be held somewhat frozen for at least a few weeks. Substantial changes in CTs are permitted only with advance notice. This is the topic of the next chapter.

THE ESSENCE OF CYCLE TIME

The concept of CT in synchronous production does not mean exactly the same thing as *production rate,* even though, mathematically, one is the inverse of the other. For example, a process with a CT of 60 seconds has a theoretical production rate of $\frac{1}{60}$ unit/sec, which is the same as 1 unit per min or **60 units per hour.**

Yet even if every operation were to produce at the *rate* of 60 units/hr, the process would not necessarily be synchronized. In a *synchronized* process, a required CT of 60 seconds means one thing: one unit of a finished product (or part or component) will be produced *every* 60 seconds, *uniformly, throughout the day.* In contrast, a production rate of 60 units/hr can mean many things, including 120 units/hr produced once every 2 hours, 480 units/hr produced once every 8 hours, and so on. Any of these ways results in an *average* production rate of 60 units/hr, yet unless all operations in the process are coordinated, there will sometimes be WIP buildups and shortages between stages of the process. However, when every operation produces according to the same required CT, materials flow smoothly, and there are minimal WIP buildups and no material shortages along the way.

BOTTLENECK SCHEDULING

An assumption in synchronizing a process around the FAS is that all operations have adequate capacity to meet that schedule, otherwise the process would not be able to keep up with the required pace. In essence, this is like saying that if there is a bottleneck in the process, then it is at the final-assembly stage. In a process that is somewhat long-running and stable, it is possible to adjust capacity everywhere such that, in fact, all operations are able to meet the requirements of final assembly with only minimal adjustment.

In many other cases, however, the product mixes and volumes keep changing, and as a consequence bottlenecks appear at places other than at final assembly. In such cases, the FAS can no longer be the determinant of what flows through the system, nor can it set the pace; the bottleneck, wherever it is, sets the pace. Scheduling a process based upon the bottleneck constraint is called **bottleneck scheduling.**

PRINCIPLES

Much of the current awareness about and principles of practice for managing a process from the bottleneck are based on the pioneering work of Eliyahu Goldratt.[1] Given that the bottleneck constrains process throughput, efforts to increase throughput must start at the bottleneck. To increase bottleneck throughput, the setup time must be reduced or the size of the process batch must be increased. To minimize the lead time when the process batch is large, the transfer batches from the bottleneck should be small.

Synchronizing a production process by managing the bottleneck involves the following principles.

Throughput Pace

Given that the throughput of a process is restricted to whatever the process bottleneck can handle, it makes sense to set the pace of the process according to the capacity of the bottleneck. This is similar to the manner in which FAS sets the drumbeat when the process everywhere has sufficient capacity.

Buffer Stock

Goldratt says that an hour lost at the bottleneck is an hour lost everywhere in the system. To ensure that the bottleneck is never without work, a buffer of jobs should be maintained ahead of it. If upstream operations are interrupted, the buffer will permit the bottleneck operation to continue working. The buffer is established by releasing jobs into the process so that they arrive at the bottleneck operation ahead of when that operation is expected to be ready to process them.

Process Scheduling

It does not make sense to release more jobs into the system than can be processed through the bottleneck since the excess jobs will queue up as WIP inventory. Thus, the timing of jobs released into the process should be predicated on the bottleneck's capacity to process those jobs. The jobs should be released upon receipt of order signals from the bottleneck. In essence, this is the same as starting at the bottleneck and pulling jobs into and through the system by a logistical rope in the form of schedules or kanbans.

Drum–Buffer–Rope

The concepts of (1) setting the drumbeat for the process based on the bottleneck, (2) establishing buffer stock ahead of the bottleneck, and (3) pulling material into the process from the bottleneck are illustrated in Figure 17.3. Application of these principles together is referred to as the **drum–buffer–rope** system, or **DBR.** In Figure 17.3, jobs are pulled through lines A and B upon release of orders (or a

FIGURE 17.3

Drum–buffer–rope system.

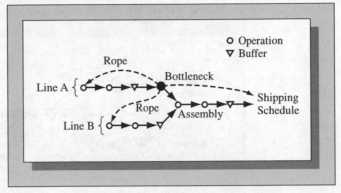

schedule derived) from the bottleneck. Operations downstream from the bottleneck are faster than the bottleneck, so they do not need a schedule.

In addition to the buffer before the bottleneck, Figure 17.3 shows two other buffers, one before assembly to ensure that interruptions in line B will not interrupt the assembly process and one before shipping to ensure the integrity of the shipping schedule. The shipping schedule for a job is based upon the time the job is expected to leave the bottleneck plus the time it will take to move through the remainder of the process. For details about locating and sizing buffers, as well as setting schedules based on the bottleneck, see the references in the endnotes.

Any operation can become a bottleneck. If a large batch is released to an operation in a short time, the operation will not be able to handle it. The easiest ways to locate a bottleneck are to look for an operation that consistently has jobs waiting and to ask shop workers.

Increasing process throughput starts with improving the bottleneck, though as soon as the bottleneck is improved enough, a new bottleneck will form at another operation (what was formerly the next-slowest operation). If the process can be re-engineered to change the location of the bottleneck, the bottleneck should be placed as close as possible to the start of the process. That is because in a sequence of inter-dependent operations, earlier operations are less influenced by variability in other operations and hence are easier to control.

PULL FROM BOTTLENECK[2]

The rope in DBR can be a kanban card issued from the bottleneck operation to the first stage of the process. When material must enter the process at multiple places, shown as A and B in Figure 17.3, cards must be sent to all of them. This procedure works well in processes where the bottleneck is stable and where the times through the process routing are constant.

FIGURE 17.4

Routing for three processes and the signal system connecting them to the bottleneck.

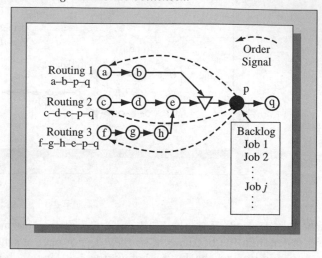

In plants where the process consists of multiple possible routings and a common bottleneck, it is possible to synchronize operations by using a CONWIP system. This is illustrated in Figure 17.4 where three processes, represented by routings 1, 2, and 3, pass through the same bottleneck operation.

In the CONWIP system described in Chapter 8, an order is released into the process every time a completed job departs from the process. The problem with that kind of CONWIP system is that an interruption at any operation in the process can halt the bottleneck operation, even if the interruption happens downstream from the bottleneck. (Since an interruption prevents a job from being completed, it prevents orders for new jobs from being released; hence, eventually, the bottleneck will run out of work.) However, by modifying the CONWIP system to connect the *bottleneck* operation (not the final operation) with the first operation in the process, orders are released into the process such that the bottleneck will never run short. In Figure 17.4, the bottleneck is connected to each of the three product routings with a Kanban or other form of signal system.

To schedule from a bottleneck, a backlog of job orders is maintained at the bottleneck. Periodically, a job order from this backlog is released to the start of the process with a kanban or other signal. The kanban specifies the routing sequence, quantity, and other pertinent information. The key factor here is *timing* of the order release so that the job will arrive at the bottleneck at the right time (analogous to synchronizing the arrival of parts at final assembly). The time when a given job order *j* should be released depends on

· The time when the bottleneck operation will be ready for the job. For job *j*, this is the time when the bottleneck operation will have completed all *j* − 1 jobs scheduled ahead of it. Suppose that each job takes time *b* to process through the bottleneck. Thus, the bottleneck will be ready to process job j after time $\Sigma\ b_i$, where $i = 1, \ldots, j - 1$.

· The amount of time the job will take to reach the bottleneck. This is the sum of the times on the routing for the job to get to the bottleneck, or the before-bottleneck lead time. This time should be relatively constant for a given routing since the wait times at operations in the routing (which are not bottlenecks) should be minimal. Call the lead time for job j, L_j.

· The amount of time the job should arrive at the bottleneck *before* the bottleneck is expected to be ready to process it. This is the *buffer time,* and its size depends on how much protection is desired to keep the bottleneck from running out of work. Call this buffer time W.

Suppose the bottleneck has $j - 1$ jobs on a backlog list. That means that the bottleneck will be ready to process job j after it has processed the $j - 1$ jobs, which will be at time $\Sigma\ b_i$, $i = 1, \ldots, j - 1$. Since job j will take time L_j to arrive at the bottleneck, and we would like it to arrive W time units early, the order for job j should be released only when

$$L_j + W \le \sum b_i.$$

Following this rule will ensure a constant backlog of job orders in the bottleneck buffer and allow no more jobs in the system than the bottleneck has capacity to handle.

Example 2:   Scheduling from a Bottleneck

Refer to the Figure 17.4. Assume the routing lead times *up to* the bottleneck and the process times at the bottleneck, in hours, are as follows:

Routing	Routing Lead Time up to Bottleneck (L)	Process Time at Bottleneck (b)
1	4	1
2	2	1
3	2	2

Table 17.1 shows the order list (backlog) for 16 jobs and for each job, the routing, and L and b times. Assume that the desired buffer time at the bottleneck (W) is 1 hour.

Figure 17.5 shows the results of a hand simulation to illustrate the release of job orders from the bottleneck and the subsequent processing of the jobs.

Assume that the first three jobs have already been released and are scheduled for the bottleneck operation as shown. Since the sum of the bottleneck times for jobs 1, 2, and 3 is 3 hours and this time equals $L + W$ for job 4, the order for job 4 can be released ($L_4 + W \le \Sigma\ b_i$ for $i = 1, 2, 3$). Thus, job 4 is shown as release 1. Assume this happens at time 0. The wavy line represents the lead time for the job to arrive at the bottleneck, 2 hours. The dashed line is the time the job waits before it can be processed by the bottleneck, 1 hour. The solid line represents processing time at the bottleneck, 2 hours.

TABLE 17-1   Order Backlog

Job	Routing	L	L + W	b
1	2	4	5	1
2	1	3	4	1
3	1	3	4	1
4	3	2	3	2
5	2	4	5	1
6	3	2	3	2
7	3	2	3	2
8	1	3	4	1
9	2	4	5	1
10	3	2	3	2
11	2	4	5	1
12	1	3	4	1
13	3	2	3	2
14	3	2	3	2
15	1	3	4	1
16	3	2	3	2

FIGURE 17.5

Schedule of order releases from bottleneck.

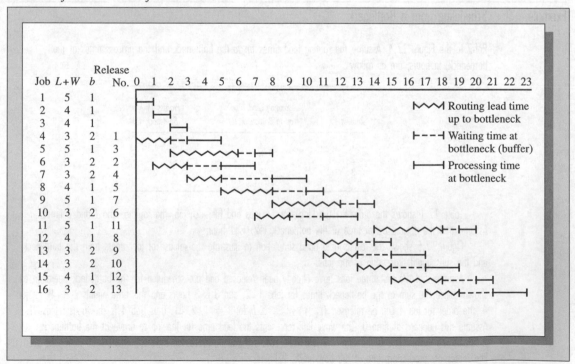

At hour 1, job 1 is completed at the bottleneck. At that time the bottleneck has 4 hours of work scheduled for jobs 2, 3, and 4. For job 5, $L + W = 5$, and since this is *greater* than the time scheduled on the bottleneck, job 5 should not be released at that time.

For job 6, $L + W = 3$; since this is less than the bottleneck times for jobs 2, 3, and 4, job 6 can be released (release 2).

At hour 2, job 2 is completed at the bottleneck. The bottleneck has 5 hours of time scheduled for jobs 3, 4, and 6. Since this equals $L + W$ for job 5, job 5 can now be released (release 3).

At hour 3, job 3 is completed at the bottleneck. At that time, 5 hours are scheduled at the bottleneck for jobs 4–6. Since $L + W$ for job 7 is 3 hours, job 7 can be scheduled next.

The procedure continues for the remaining jobs.

All 16 jobs are processed through the bottleneck in 23 hours. Ignoring the first three jobs, the average buffer (wait) time for jobs at the bottleneck is 22 hr/13 jobs = 1.69 hours.

Notice that (like the mixed-model scheduling discussed earlier) this "scheduling" procedure involves no set schedules, but rather a sequence of job-order releases. That is OK, though, because orders are released when operations are ready, which is not necessarily the case when schedules are used. Schedules tend to become more inaccurate with time and hence less dependable.

Example 4 is for a somewhat simple case where each product is created from one single routing. When a process involves simultaneous scheduling of parts through multiple routings and a common bottleneck, and the parts must be coordinated to arrive *together* at a final assembly station, then the order release procedure is a little more complicated. It is, however, readily doable using a CONWIP system that links the final assembly stage with the starting points of all routings for parts that comprise the assembly. Details of this procedure are discussed in Hopp and Spearman.[3]

BALANCING

Once the CTs in a synchronized process have been set, the production capacity of all work centers must be adjusted to conform to those CTs. The adjustment can involve, for example, increasing capacity at bottleneck operations, decreasing capacity at nonbottlenecks, or reconfiguring tasks at workstations so they require less time or more time.

Balancing refers to the procedure of adjusting the times at work centers to conform as much as possible to the required CT. A **balanced process** is one where the actual cycle times at every stage are equal. Strictly speaking, the goal of achieving a completely balanced process is appropriate only in processes that are **paced,** that is, where material moves on a conveyor or chain at a constant speed past workstations. Such is the case of product layouts and mixed-model assembly lines. In other processes that are more similar to job shops and where many products and routings are involved, the goal of a balanced process is inappropriate. Seeking to balance a process around one product or routing in such cases makes it more difficult to adapt the operations to accommodate many routings and products.

In this section, the focus is primarily on balancing tasks in paced production lines, though the procedures discussed pertain to any coordinated sequence of operations, including cellular layouts. The procedures balance workstation times by manipulating assignments of tasks and workers/machines to workstations.

LINE BALANCING

As an introduction to the concept of balancing, consider first a simple example from traditional line balancing. **Line balancing** refers to assigning tasks (elemental units of work) to a workstation or operations sequence such that

1. The CT of the combined sequence of workstations satisfies the required CT (product CTs, as described before).
2. The tasks are assigned in the right order.
3. The assignment is as efficient as possible.

The first point states that the output of the sequence of workstations is adequate to meet demand. For that to happen, the CT of the slowest workstation in the line (the bottleneck) must not exceed the required CT.

The second point states that the assignment of tasks to workstations meets precedence requirements. Whenever a number of tasks are to be performed, there is a logical sequence or ordering that must be followed. Certain tasks take precedence over others, so they must be done before the others can be started.

The third point states that the resultant number of workstations or operations in the line is the minimum possible given the required CT and precedence relationships.

The example below illustrates a simple line-balancing procedure.

Example   3:   Simple Line Balancing Using the Longest Operation Time Rule

Suppose the assembly procedure for a product involves the following seven tasks:

Task	Time (min)
1	0.7
2	0.5
3	0.4
4	0.6
5	0.5
6	0.8
7	0.3
Total =	3.8

The total time of 3.8 minutes is the **work content** or actual work time necessary to make 1 unit of product.

Figure 17.6

Precedence diagram for seven assembly tasks.

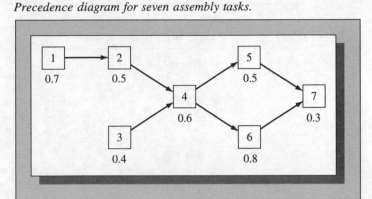

Suppose demand for the product is 420 units/day. The product is produced on an assembly line that operates 7 hr/day (420 minutes), so the required CT is

$$Required\ CT = \frac{Operating\ Time}{Demand} = \frac{420\ min/day}{420\ units/day} = 1\ min/unit.$$

Suppose the seven tasks must be performed according to the relationships shown in Figure 17.6, called the **precedence diagram.** The figure, which can be interpreted by looking at it backwards, says that before task 7 can be performed, both tasks 5 and 6 must be completed; before tasks 5 and 6 can each be performed, task 4 must be completed; before task 4 is performed, both tasks 2 and 3 must be completed; before task 2 is performed, task 1 must be completed.

Now, to assign the tasks to a sequence of workstations on an assembly line, look at the precedence diagram to see which tasks can be assigned to the first workstation. For this purpose, look at the diagram starting on the left. Figure 17.6 indicates that either task 1 or task 3 can be assigned; the question is, Which? There are different ways to decide between tasks when there is a tie. One way is to select the task that requires the **longest operating time** yet does not exceed the time available at the workstation. Therefore, assign task 1 to station 1. Task 1 takes 0.7 minutes, which is $1.0 - 0.7 = 0.3$ minutes less than the required CT. Thus, 0.3 minutes remain available at station 1.

Next we can assign tasks 2 or 3. Since both exceed the available time at station 1, the next assignment must be to station 2. Pick task 2 because it takes longer than task 3. This leaves $1.0 - 0.5 = 0.5$ minutes available at station 2.

The next task to be assigned must be task 3, because the precedence diagram indicates that tasks 3 and 2 must *both* precede task 4. Task 3 requires 0.4 minutes, which fits into the available time at station 2. With both tasks 2 and 3 assigned, station 2 has 0.1 minute available.

Task 4 comes next. The time of 0.6 minutes exceeds the available time at station 2, so the task must be assigned to station 3. This leaves $1.0 - 0.6 = 0.4$ minutes available.

The procedure continues in this fashion until all remaining tasks have been assigned. The assignment procedure results are summarized in Table 17.2. The resulting line will have five workstations as shown in Figure 17.7.

In general, the efficiency of a sequence of stations is determined by

$$Efficiency = \frac{Work\ Content}{(No.\ Workstations) \times (Required\ CT)}.$$

TABLE 17-2   Procedure of Assigning Tasks to Stations

Station	Time Available (min)	Tasks Eligible	Will Fit	Assign (time in min.)
1	1.0	1, 3	1, 2	1 (0.7)
	0.3	2, 3	None	—
2	1.0	2, 3	2, 3	2 (0.5)
	0.5	3	3	3 (0.4)
	0.1	4	None	—
3	1.0	4	4	4 (0.6)
	0.6	5, 6	None	—
4	1.0	5, 6	5, 6	6 (0.8)
	0.2	5	None	—
5	1.0	5	5	5 (0.5)
	0.5	7	7	7 (0.3)

FIGURE 17.7

Resulting task assignment to five workstations.

Workstation	1	2	3	4	5
Tasks Assigned	1	2, 3	4	6	5, 7
Task Time	0.7	0.5, 0.4	0.6	0.8	0.5, 0.3
Required CT	1.0	1.0	1.0	1.0	1.0
Idle Time	0.3	0.1	0.4	0.2	0.2

The efficiency for the line in Figure 17.7 is

$$\frac{3.8}{(5 \times 1.00)} = 0.733, \text{ or } 73.3\%.$$

For high efficiency, as many tasks as possible must be packed into each workstation within the constraint of the required CT and restrictions of precedence relationships. For this example, the efficiency is the feasible maximum.

A line that achieves the required output and is as efficient as possible is considered a balanced line. There are many heuristic and optimal-seeking methods for assigning tasks to stations on a line, though they are beyond the scope of our discussion.[4] Our interest is in assigning tasks to an assembly line, workcell, or routing sequence for MMP.

BALANCING FOR MMP

The individual task times used for traditional line balancing are determined for the *particular product* being produced. In Example 3 the task times are for such a product. In MMP, however, *more* than one product is being produced, and for each product the time for a given task might be different. Unlike traditional line balancing, which considers production of only one product, MMP balancing must consider simultaneous production of multiple different products.

In general, MMP balancing requires assigning tasks to a sequence of workstations such that

1. The CT for each product at each workstation satisfies the required product CT.
2. The assignment for all products is as efficient as possible.

One way to assign tasks to workstations in MMP such that the line produces according to the required CTs for all the products is to use the **weighted average time rule.** The weighted average time is the amount of time, on average, required at a workstation to perform tasks. So that every workstation in MMP can produce the required amount of every product, this rule states that the weighted average time at each workstation cannot exceed the required CT for all product models.

The weighted average time can be written as

$$\sum\sum q_j t_{ij},$$

where

q_j = the proportion of product j in the MMP repeating sequence
  $(j = 1, 2, \ldots, P)$,
  = (production of product j)/(production of all products).
t_{ij} = the time to perform task i on product j, where i is a task assigned to the workstation.

The weighted average rule can be expressed as

$$\sum\sum q_j t_{ij} \leq Required\ CT,$$

where

required CT = (Available Production Time)/(Production Quantity of All Products).

The following example illustrates this concept.

Example   4:   Assigning Tasks Using the Weighted Average Rule

Suppose products A, B, and C are to be assembled on a line. The assembly of each product requires doing four tasks, but the time required for each task varies by product. Table 17.3 shows task times t_{ij}, where $i = 1, 2, 3, 4$;

j = A, B, C. Suppose daily demands for products A, B, and C are 240, 120, and 60, respectively. The total demand is 420.

TABLE 17-3   Task Times in Minutes, t_{ij}

	Product *i*		
Task *i*	*A*	*B*	*C*
1	0.7	0.6	0.5
2	0.6	0.5	0.6
3	0.5	0.4	0.4
4	0.6	0.6	0.7
Work content	2.2	2.1	2.1

To find an assignment, first determine the product proportions $q_i = D_i/\Sigma\, D$. Since $\Sigma\, D = 420$, the proportions are

$$q_A = 240/420 = 0.571, \qquad q_B = 120/420 = 0.286, \qquad q_C = 60/420 = 0.143.$$

Next, determine the required CT for all products, where

$$Required\ CT = (Available\ Production\ Time)/\Sigma\, D.$$

Assume available time is 420 minutes; then,

Product	D (daily)	Required CT (min)
A	240	1.75
B	120	3.5
C	60	7.0
All products	420	1.0

The "all products" cycle of 1 minute represents the *required CT* of the overall process; it specifies that one product will be produced every minute, on average.

Suppose, as a trial, we consider a line similar to that in Figure 17.7, but to simplify the problem, look only at the *first three* workstations. To conform to the weighted average rule, the weighted average task time $\Sigma\Sigma\ q_i t_{ij}$ at each workstation must not exceed the required CT. The weighted average task times at the three workstations are shown in Table 17.4. As defined earlier, these times indicate the time required on average for each workstation to process the multiple kinds of products. To illustrate, assume that the MMP repeating sequence is AABABAC. Figure 17.8 shows the actual task times at each workstation to process the products in one repeating sequence. Note that the average of the times at a workstation in Figure 17.8 is the same as the weighted average task time in Table 17.4.

TABLE 17-4   Weighted Average Times Computation

Workstation	Tasks (i)	Weighted Average Times (min)			
1	1	$0.571(0.7) + 0.286(0.6)$		$+ 0.143(0.5)$	$= 0.643$
2	2, 3	$0.571(0.6 + 0.5) + 0.286(0.5 + 0.4)$	$+ 0.143(0.6 + 0.4)$		$= 1.029$
3	4	$0.571(0.6) + 0.286(0.6)$		$+ 0.143(0.7)$	$= 0.614$

FIGURE 17.8

Workstation average times for three products.

Workstation	1	2	3
Task	1	2 + 3	4
A	0.7	1.1	0.6
A	0.7	1.1	0.6
B	0.6	0.9	0.6
A	0.7	1.1	0.6
B	0.6	0.9	0.6
A	0.7	1.1	0.6
C	0.5	1.0	0.7
Sum	4.5	7.2	4.3
Average	0.643	1.029	0.614

This particular assignment does not conform to the weighted average task time rule since the weighted time at the bottleneck (1.029 minutes at workstation 2) exceeds the required CT of 1 minute. It will thus be necessary to try other assignments, for example combining tasks 1 and 2 at workstation 1 or tasks 3 and 4 at workstation 3, but they too would result in weighted average times too large. If we insist on the assignment in Figure 17.8, then we *must reduce the weighted average time at the bottleneck.*

Focusing on workstation 2, the times for tasks 2 and 3 among products A, B, and C must be reduced such that the weighted average time becomes 1 minute or less. For example, (and you can verify this) shaving 3 seconds (0.05 minute) off task 2 *or* task 3 for just *product A* will bring the weighted average time at workstation 2 down to 1 minute.

With the weighted average principle, balancing in MMP is achieved by pairing tasks of more time-consuming and less time-consuming products together. Thus, it is OK if the task times at a workstation for one product exceed the required CT, *as long as* that product can be paired with other products that have smaller task times, such that the resultant weighted average time of all tasks does not exceed the required CT. Of course, the pairing is not arbitrary but depends on q_i, which depends on the product demand.

OTHER WAYS TO ACHIEVE BALANCE

The assignment of tasks to workstations to achieve balance can be done in different ways. In addition to the general approach described above, there are two alternatives: dynamic balance and parallel lines.

Dynamic Balance

In the example in the previous section, the balance is **constant** since workstations always perform the same tasks, regardless of the product. That is, for example, workstation 1 performs task 1 on *every* product, workstation 2 does tasks 2 and 3 on *every* product, and so on. Another way to achieve balance is to *change* the balance, depending on the product. The balance is **dynamic,** referring to the fact that the mix of tasks can be *changed* with each product. For example, a workstation might perform, say, task 1 on product A, but then do tasks 1 *and* 2 on products B and C. Assuming there are no technical or skill constraints (and that workers are able to keep track of the changing tasks), dynamic balance is another way to conform to the weighted average rule.

Parallel Line

When task times for different products vary considerably, or when the task times cannot be reduced so that the weighted average time satisfies the required CT, then another way to meet the required CT is to split the line into two or more parallel lines. That is, at workstations on the line where the weighted average task time is too large, simply add a parallel workstation.

Example   5:   Balancing with a Parallel Line

Refer back to the line in the previous example. Suppose the task times at workstations 1 and 3 are the same, but at workstation 2 the times are now

Product A	1.3 min
Product B	0.9 min
Product C	1.0 min

Assuming the same product proportions q_i as in the previous example, the weighted average time at workstation 2 is then

$$0.571(1.3) + 0.286(0.9) + 0.143(1.0) = 1.143 \text{ min.}$$

FIGURE 17.9

Parallel lines for lengthy tasks.

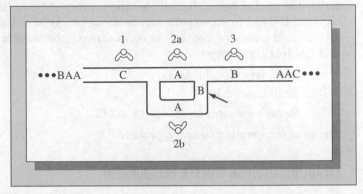

This time exceeds the required CT of 1 minute. Now, if some tasks could not be reassigned to other workstations, then a second workstation might be added in parallel to workstation 2, as shown in Figure 17.9. With these parallel workstations, whenever a part arrives, it goes to either workstation 2a or 2b, depending on whichever is available first. After the part is completed at workstation 2a or 2b, it rejoins the main line.

In general, the effect of having two parallel workstations at a stage of the line is to cut the total task time at that stage of the line in half (if task time at each workstation were 1.143 minutes, then the effective task time at that stage of the process would be $1.143/2 = 0.572$ minutes). In actuality, the average task time from parallel lines in MMP will be somewhat larger than the mathematical average because a part leaving either parallel workstation will sometimes have to wait until after a part leaves from the other workstation in order to *retain the original MMP sequence*. In Figure 17.9, for example, the arrow points to a part B that has been completed at workstation 2b but which cannot immediately reenter the main line because doing so would change the original MMP sequence of AABABAC. Part B must wait there until *after* part A at workstation 2a has been completed and moved to workstation 3.

BALANCING FOR SYNCHRONOUS FLOW

The previous discussion of balancing focused on a particular line, such as a final assembly line. If other areas of the plant feed parts into the line, and if these areas are focused factories or workcells *dedicated* to these parts, then, ideally, the *entire process* (parts production and final assembly) should be balanced. This involves balancing tasks at all upstream operations feeding into final assembly as well as tasks on the final assembly line. To achieve balance, the task groupings at every operation, work-cell, and machining department must be adjusted so the resulting weighted average task time at each of them is as close as possible to the required CT. This is done by adding or subtracting tasks at operations, moving workers between tasks and operations, and by adjusting the time to perform work tasks.

In synchronous production, every operation should produce just enough to satisfy downstream demand. If a Kanban system is employed, the demand is signaled by cards. The goal of workcells and operations everywhere in the process is to match the required CT and to do so with minimum waste. As Monden explains, the balancing process is a matter of continuous improvement and worker reallocation,[5] a process that involves three steps:

1. Eliminate wasteful tasks.
2. Reallocate tasks.
3. Reduce the workforce; return to (1).

The next section illustrates the process.

BALANCING THROUGH WORKER REASSIGNMENT

Suppose the required CT for a workcell is 1 minute, and tasks and workers in the cell are being assigned to meet that CT. Suppose the initial assignment results in five workers at five workstations, with the workstation times shown in Figure 17.10. Workers A, B, and D are the bottlenecks of the cell since they require the longest time. Since that time, 0.9 minute, is less than the required CT, the cell output is adequate. However, because at every workstation the task times are lower than the required CT, every workstation must be idled occasionally so the cell does not produce in excess of the required output. This idle time is represented by the shaded areas in Figure 17.10.

The time shown for each worker is comprised of the times for several separate tasks that can (theoretically) be modified or shifted between workstations. Suppose by a combination of eliminating wasteful motions and reallocating tasks, the tasks can

FIGURE 17.10

Initial worker assignment.

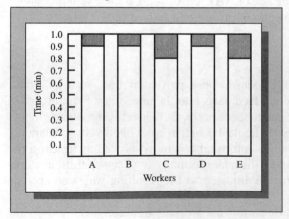

FIGURE 17.11

Possible alternate worker assignment.

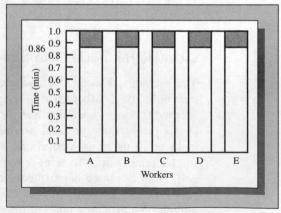

be rebalanced so that every worker takes 0.86 minutes, as shown in Figure 17.11. This might seem to be an improvement because everyone now takes the same amount of time (the cell is perfectly balanced); however it is not, because the improvement cannot be realized. In fact, given that the cell CT must be held to 1 minute, the percent idle time in the cell is unchanged by this so-called improvement.

Since one goal of balancing is to achieve the required CT with the greatest efficiency (i.e., minimum waste), a better solution would be something like the assignment shown in Figure 17.12. There, the tasks have been shifted so that four workers each have 1 minute of work, while the fifth worker has 0.3 minute. Although the cell idle time is still the same, the assignment is better because now all effort can be focused on improving tasks such that, ultimately, worker E's tasks can be reallocated among workers A–D, and worker E can then be transferred out of the cell. The cell can then operate at full capacity with only four workers.

Balancing operations plantwide is a continuous process. Changes in required CTs and delays or shutdowns at individual operations are constant threats to synchronous production. As countermeasures, plants rely on[6]

- Visual signal systems (andons, charts) to keep workers informed about problems at all stages of the process.
- Multiskilled operators, flexible operations, and short changeover times to enable quick adaptation to changes in product demand and product mix.
- Less than full-capacity scheduling to allow for delays or unanticipated demand changes.

Workcells usually have some capability to adapt to changes in CT without stopping work (i.e., without reshuffling workers or tasks). In pull production systems,

FIGURE 17.12

Preferred worker assignment.

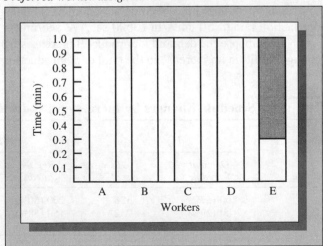

the adaptability is usually within ±10% of the nominal CT. As long as production schedules (rate of production and mix of products) do not change greatly, no capacity planning is necessary for operations to adjust to changing CTs.

MAINTAINING SYNCHRONIZATION

In a synchronized process, whenever the final production schedule is changed, so must the CTs of upstream operations. Changes are inevitable, although maintaining level final production schedules reduces the frequency and magnitude of the changes. If the change in schedule represents but a small daily or weekly adjustment to a level baseline schedule, then a simple way for upstream operations to keep pace is to lengthen or shorten the workday. This is far simpler than having every operation readjust to new product CTs, which requires shifting worker assignments, changing machine configurations, and so on.

It should be evident that a delay or interruption anywhere in a synchronized process has potential to desynchronize the entire process. For that reason **andon** lights located at each operation (or a **status board** located centrally over the entire process) are used to display the status of operations. When a light for an operation flashes red, supervisors and adjacent workers rush over to resolve the problem. In a truly synchronized process, a red light at one operation is a signal for *every* operation to stop. Only after the problem has been resolved (green light) can all operations resume, and they all resume simultaneously.

ADAPTING TO SCHEDULE CHANGES

A major consideration in setting production schedules is the ability of the shop floor to meet the volumes specified by the required CT.

Returning to our three-product example, suppose daily production has been proceeding according to the schedule shown in Table 17.5, column 1. On average, a product is produced at a rate of 1 every 72 seconds, so 72 seconds is the CT to which upstream operations have become accustomed. This CT corresponds to an average production rate of 50 units/hr (3600 sec/[72 sec/unit]).

Now, suppose the demand for product B increases from 100 to 150 units/day. This change results in an increase in the total daily production requirement from 350 units

TABLE 17-5   Schedule Changes by Increasing Production Time

	(1)		(2)		(3)
Product	Original Schedule	CT (sec)	Revised Schedule	CT (sec)	% Change in CT
A	200 (57%)	126	200 (50%)	144	14.3
B	100 (29%)	252	150 (38%)	192	−23.8
C	50 (14%)	504	50 (12%)	576	14.3
All	350 (100%)	72	400 (100%)	72	0

to 400 units (column 2). There are two ways the production process can meet this increase: increase the production workday or decrease the CT (increase the production rate). In general, altering either production workday or production rate, or some combination, is the way production processes adjust to changes in demand.

ALTER THE PRODUCTION WORKDAY

Altering production requires lengthening the production workday. Since going from 350 units to 400 units represents an increase of 14.3% in the required output, the workday must be increased by (0.143 × 7 hours) 1 hour. Instead of 7 hours, the workday will be 8 hours.

In addition, the MMP repeating sequence must be changed to reflect the increase in the demand for product B. Using the procedure described in the preceding chapter, the sequence before the change is AABABAC; to reflect the required increase in B, the sequence must now include *three* Bs with four As and one C. Suppose the sequence ABABABAC is adopted. Repeating this sequence 50 times a day will meet the requirement for every product.

Notice from column 3 that although the CTs for each product change somewhat, the overall CT (all products) remains the same. Although every operation will have to adjust its production rates for the different products by the percentages shown in column 3, the changes might not be too difficult since the CT percentage decrease for product B is offset by CT increases for products A and C. Overall, the hourly capacity of the process will remain unchanged.

ALTER THE PRODUCTION RATE

Suppose that the current 7-hour workday is to be maintained, in which case to meet the product B demand increase it will be necessary to increase the overall production rate. In the example, going from 350 units/day to 400 units will require that the process CT be reduced from 72 seconds to 63 seconds (420 minutes/400 units). The average production output rate must be increased from 50 units/hr to over 57.14 units/hr (400 units/7 hours).

As shown in Table 17.6, columns 2 and 3, the increased production rate will require a significant decrease in CT for product B (33%), which in the short run will

---

TABLE 17-6   Schedule Changes by Adjusting Only CTs

	(1)		(2)		(3)
Product	Original Schedule	CT (sec)	Revised Schedule	CT (sec)	% Change in CT
A	200 (57%)	126	200 (50%)	126	0.0%
B	100 (29%)	252	150 (38%)	168	−33.3%
C	50 (14%)	504	50 (12%)	504	0.0
	350 (100%)	72	400 (100%)	63	−12.5

probably be difficult to achieve because there is no compensating increase in the CT for products A or C (output of B must be increased with no decrease in output for A and C). Unless every operation that provides parts for product B can find ways to decrease the CT by 33% (without affecting the CTs for parts for A and C), the process will not be able to adjust to the change in demand. In that case, the first alternative (increase the length of the workday) must be adopted, at least until ways are found to reduce the CTs for product B.

IN PRACTICE: ADJUSTING TO SCHEDULE CHANGES

There is of course a third way to meet changing product demand and product mix: alter *both* the length of the workday and the product CTs. Initially, the workday length would be increased; then, as ways are found to reduce the CTs, the workday can be decreased, eventually back to normal.

In pull production operations, supervisors and worker teams on the shop floor assume much of the responsibility for deciding how they will meet CT requirements. Management does the long-term macro capacity planning (rough-cut capacity planning), but the daily details are left to the shop floor. Management determines the overall CT requirements for a process by setting the MMP schedule and the length of workday, but then the shop floor must determine how to balance tasks and workers to achieve that CT.

Since, it is often difficult for operations to adjust to large changes in CTs, even with flexible equipment and multiskilled or temporary workers, large changes in production requirements are ordinarily not attempted in successive months, much less in successive weeks. Rather, the overall average production rate is set, and small adjustments are made to the rate on a daily or weekly basis. Though the overall average CT might be changed monthly or more frequently, operations on the floor are given adequate time to plan for the changes. Also, through rough-cut capacity planning, management knows what degree of schedule change the shop floor is capable of absorbing. It then proposes schedule changes far enough in advance so the shop floor has adequate time to adjust. The exact procedure is the topic of the next chapter.

The simplest way to adjust output in the short run is to alter the length of the workday (say, between 7 and 10 hours).[7] During periods of slow demand, the length of the day is shortened, and remaining time is used for problem solving and preventive maintenance. This is simplest only in terms of adjusting output to meet demand, for it is anything but simple from the point of view of workers, many of whom rely on regular work hours for scheduling transportation to and from work, child daycare, and so on. Any considered changes in the workday should take into account potential worker hardships and allow workers adequate time to make personal arrangements.

Adding shifts is another way to adjust the workday. For example, Prince Castle, Incorporated, mentioned in Chapter 3, ordinarily runs a full day shift plus two reduced night shifts with skeleton crews. The skeleton crews on the second and third shifts can be brought up to full force on short notice with temporary help during periods of unusually high or spiked demand.

Summary

There is a saying that timing is everything, and although in pull production it's not *quite* everything, it is still very important. Ideally, materials move through the production process in a smooth, uniform fashion. The schedule of the final stage of the process determines the rate at which materials from upstream are consumed, and hence the rate at which they should move downstream. Everywhere in the process materials should be produced and moved at the same rate. The CT of products going out the end of the process (determined by the rate of demand) should theoretically determine the CT of materials coming from upstream. The procedure of setting the CTs of all upstream operations to meet the CT of the final operation is called synchronization.

The concept of CT rather than production rate is used in pull production because it implies regularity, uniformity, and periodicity in output—a leveled, uniform flow—whereas production rate implies a quantity produced within some period of time without regard to the uniformity.

The pace of a process is determined by the slowest operation, the bottleneck. When the bottleneck capacity is less than demand, the release of jobs into a system should be predicated on the capability of the bottleneck to process those jobs. In a production system that utilizes the drum–buffer–rope concept, the bottleneck sets the pace of production everywhere in the process, a buffer of work protects the bottleneck from upstream interruptions, and jobs are released into the system based on a schedule or work backlog at the bottleneck. A form of Kanban linking the bottleneck with the start of a process can be used to signal the release of new jobs into the process.

Related to synchronization and CT is the topic of balancing. In a balanced process, every stage has about the same work content, and the work content time is equivalent to the required CT. When the times to perform tasks at different workstations in a process are different, the process is unbalanced, which implies that some workers do more work than others. Since process output must be constrained to the required CT, workers whose tasks take less time will be idle during part of every cycle. In MMP, balancing is based upon the weighted average task times for the product models in the mixed-model sequence.

The process of balancing is ongoing and as such is another aspect of continuous improvement. Once tasks have been assigned to workstations, supervisors and workers scrutinize them for waste and improvement opportunities, then rebalance the tasks such that most of the idle time in the process is on one or a few workers. Eventually, as tasks continue to be reassigned, all the work content is shifted to some workers and away from others, who will then be reassigned elsewhere and whose workstations will be eliminated.

Two ways to meet changing demand requirements are to alter the length of the production workday and to alter the rate of the production process. The latter is inherently more difficult since it involves changing the required CT, and, potentially, rebalancing tasks for all operations in the process. Thus, altering the length of the workday is the favored method, at least in the short run, and modern union contracts often specify a range of times, say, 7 to 10 hours, as a normal workday. Such changes, however, can cause hardship for workers, and thus should be somewhat infrequent and follow advance notice. Long-term shifts in demand can initially be handled by changes in the workday or by overtime; through continuous improvement, the CTs should be adjusted so that, eventually, the workday length can be brought back to normal.

Questions

1. Explain the concept of synchronization in a process. What is necessary for a sequence of operations to be synchronized?
2. How is a process synchronized when the completion times per unit of the operations in a process are different?
3. Explain (a) the relationship between production rate and cycle time and (b) their interpretation in synchronous production.
4. Regarding the production capacity of all operations in a process, what is necessary to base the CT of those operations on the required CT at final assembly?
5. Explain the meaning of the terms drum, buffer, and rope.
6. In bottleneck scheduling, why is it desirable to maintain a buffer of work ahead of the bottleneck?
7. Why doesn't the CONWIP system described in Chapter 8 protect the bottleneck from interruptions that occur *downstream* from the bottleneck?
8. What does it mean for the workstations in a process to be balanced?
9. Discuss the meaning of the term line balancing as it applies to an MMP process.
10. Comment on the following: A process has eight workstations in sequence; the workstation with the greatest work content takes 94 seconds; therefore the CT for the entire process should be set to 94 seconds per unit.
11. Discuss ways to reduce the effects of disruptions in a synchronized process.
12. Discuss the ramifications (relative pros and cons, ease or difficulty) of adapting production to schedule changes by (a) altering the length of the workday and (b) altering the production rate.

Problems

1. At Feebo Company, components U, V, W, and X are assembled in a cell in daily quantities of 70, 140, 280, and 35, respectively.
    a. Assuming a 480-minute workday, what is the average overall component CT of the cell?
    b. What is the MMP sequence?
2. Assume the level 1 BOM breakdown of parts for the components in problem 1 are as follows (parenthesis indicates number of this part needed):

	U	V	W	X
Parts	B	A	A	C
Level 1	D	D	B	E
BOM	F	G	E	G(2)
	H(2)	H(2)	F	H
			H	

These parts come from the following places: parts H and E are supplied by a vendor and the other parts are produced in the Feebo plant—parts A and D on another line, parts B and F in one cell, and parts C and G in another cell.

- a. What is the MMP sequence for the line that produces parts A and D? What is the required average CT of the line?
- b. The cell that produces B and F does each in batches of 50. Changeover time between batches is 3 minutes. What must the CT be at the cell for it to satisfy demand for parts going into components U and W?
- c. The cell that produces parts C and G does it in mixed-model fashion. What is the MMP sequence? What is the required average CT?
- d. The supplier delivers parts H and E directly to their points of use in the plant at 8 a.m. and noon. How many of each part, on average, should be in each delivery?

3. Refer to Example 2.
   - a. Repeat the example, but assume (i) a buffer time of $W = 0$ and that the first three jobs are already released and scheduled, and (ii) a buffer time of $W = 2$ and that the first four jobs are already released and scheduled.
   - b. Suppose *after* Jobs 6, 9, and 12 are released, each of them requires 2 hours additional time to reach the bottleneck (in effect, L is increased by 2 hours for each). Repeat the hand simulation for $W = 0$, $W = 1$, and $W = 2$, and in each case note the effect of these delays on the completion time of all jobs, average wait time at the bottleneck, and idle time of the bottleneck operation. Compare and comment on the results.

4. Average daily demand for a product is 95 units. A production workcell has four workstations and runs 400 min/day. The time to complete tasks at the four workstations is 210, 180, 205, and 160 seconds, respectively. Discuss the goal and general strategy for balancing tasks in this process.

5. Figure 17.13 is the precedence diagram for an assembly process. Table 17.7 shows the task time in minutes t_{ij} for $i = $ a, b, c, . . . , h; $j = $ X, Y, Z. Suppose the daily demand is 30 units for X, 15 units for Y, 60 units for Z. Assume a 480-minute workday.
   - a. What is the required CT for X, Y, Z, and overall?
   - b. Compute the weighted average task time for each task.
   - c. Using the weighted average task times and the precedence diagram, assign tasks to a line using the longest operating time rule.
   - d. What is the efficiency of the line?
   - e. What is the potential maximum CT of this line? What would be the daily output of the line at this CT for each of the three products?

FIGURE 17.13

Precedence diagram for problem 5.

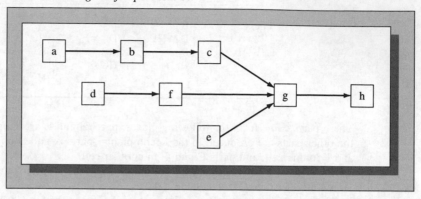

TABLE 17-7   Task Time in Minutes, t_{ij}

	Product j		
Task i	X	Y	Z
a	2	3	2
b	1	2	1
c	3	3	3
d	2	1	4
e	3	2	2
f	4	2	1
g	1	2	1
h	2	2	2

f. If you wanted to increase the output of the line beyond the maximum determined in part *e*, at what workstation would you have to direct your improvement effort? If you were to direct all of your improvement effort at this workstation, what would be the most improvement that you could make (i.e., further improvement at this workstation would not increase the output of the line)?

Endnotes

1. E.M. Goldratt and J. Cox, *The Goal* (Croton-on-Hudson, NY: North River Press, 1984); *see also* E.M. Goldratt and R.E. Fox, *The Race* (Croton-on-Hudson, NY: North River Press, 1986); M.M. Umble and M.L. Srikanth, *Synchronous Manufacturing* (Cincinnati, OH: South-Western Publishing, 1990).

2. Adapted from W. Hopp and M. Spearman, *Factory Physics: Foundations of Manufacturing Management* (Chicago: Irwin, 1996), pp. 444–7.

3. *Ibid.,* pp. 478–83.

4. *See,* for example, R. Askin and C. Standridge, *Modeling and Analysis of Manufacturing Systems* (New York: John Wiley, 1993), Chapter 2. An excellent reference on the topic of sequencing and balancing, including evaluation of some common line balancing methods, is E. Buffa and J. Miller, *Production-Inventory Systems: Planning and Control* (3rd ed.) (Homewood, IL: Richard D. Irwin, 1979), Chapter 9.

5. Y. Monden, *Toyota Production System* (2nd ed.) (Norcross, VA: Industrial Engineering and Management Press, 1993), pp. 179–83.

6. J.T. Black, *The Design of the Factory with a Future* (New York: McGraw-Hill, 1991), p. 152.

7. R. Hall, *Zero Inventories* (Homewood, IL: Dow Jones-Irwin, 1983), pp. 62–3.

PLANNING AND CONTROL IN PULL PRODUCTION

This chapter describes a framework for preparation and execution of the pull production plans and schedules described in previous chapters. The framework is a simplified version of the Toyota production system. Toyota originated pull production and has the longest experience with all aspects of it; as a result, Toyota has become the standard for integrated planning, scheduling, and control in pull production.[1] But the Toyota system is complicated, largely because Toyota is a huge corporation that produces a wide variety of products for millions of customers worldwide. Its planning process must deal with information from a vast network of dealerships, suppliers, and production facilities worldwide. The discussion here avoids the complicating details of the Toyota system and focuses on those aspects of most relevance to other industries.

Today most large and medium US companies use MRP II systems for production planning and control. Thus, in adopting pull production they are not starting with a clean slate, but have pre-existing procedures for planning, scheduling, and controlling production. As explained in the Appendix, some functions of MRP systems remain the same even with pull production, in particular, functions for demand management, rough-cut capacity planning, master scheduling, and aspects of requirements planning. Other functions of MRP systems, however, especially for detailed scheduling, shop-floor control, and inventory update are unnecessary or must be modified for pull production. This chapter addresses these differences and the changes necessary to make MRP-based systems compatible with pull production.

THE WHOLE ENCHILADA

Production planning, scheduling, and execution in pull production are conducted within a **production planning and control** (PPC) system divided into centralized and decentralized components. We start with an overview of the framework and of the two main divisions, shown in Figure 18.1.

CENTRALIZED SYSTEM

The **centralized** part of the system comprises staff personnel and systems that perform order-entry, demand forecasting, rough-cut capacity planning, master

FIGURE 18.1

Planning and control framework for pull systems.

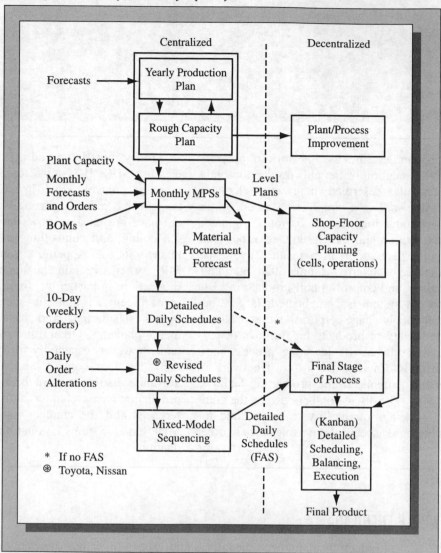

production scheduling, and MRP. The role of this part of the PPC system is to accumulate demand information and formulate production plans and schedules. In a multiplant company, it divides demand information into product categories and prepares master schedules for every plant. It develops medium-range demand forecasts for several months in the future and accumulates short-range and current demand figures for firm customer orders. This demand information is continuously compared to existing and potential production capacity to determine the best level of production, that is, the level that meets demand and is within or near the capability of existing plant capacity and inventories. Most of this forecasting and capacity planning is performed by MRP II systems in traditional ways as explained in the Appendix.

Preparation of level master production schedules (MPSs) begins months in advance of actual production. As the MPSs are finalized, production departments, workcenters, and suppliers are apprised of anticipated changes in production levels and material requirements.

Besides creating forecasts, rough capacity plans, and master schedules, the centralized part of the system also prepares and issues the daily production schedules for the final stage, or the final assembly schedule (FAS). As described earlier, this is the only schedule needed to determine CTs and material requirements for the process.

The centralized system creates daily schedules by incorporating the most recent customer order information into the level schedule. Although recent order information is essential to providing good customer service, it creates variation in daily production requirements. Since a pull system requires a somewhat level daily schedule, the centralized system has a dual goal: to incorporate recent customer orders yet to keep day-to-day production variation to a minimum.

DECENTRALIZED SYSTEM

The role of the **decentralized** part of the system is to oblige the production requirements specified in the MPSs and daily schedules. Because the decentralized part is comprised of departmental managers, shop-floor supervisors, and teams of workers, it is primarily a shop-floor based system. Plant and department managers receive MPS pre-plans from the central system, which they use to determine how to produce products in the mix and volume specified by the plans. If a plan is difficult or impossible to meet, the centralized system is notified and the plan revised.

With the exception of the final stage of the process, every department and workcell is responsible for its own daily scheduling and execution of work. In a synchronized pull system, daily scheduling is largely a matter of each operation or workcell responding to orders from downstream. Most decisions about execution and control are made by supervisors and worker teams. When a job is produced in a batch size that exceeds one container or when multiple kanbans arrive at once, the decision about the batch size or the job priority of the kanban is often made by the supervisor at the operation. Necessary schedule changes resulting from equipment breakdowns, material shortages, and other disruptions are also handled by the supervisors and worker teams.

Though responsibility for planning, scheduling, and execution of work is split between the centralized and decentralized systems, the two systems work together. In setting production levels the centralized system takes into account the production capacity of the shop floor. The shop floor sends the centralized system frequent, updated information about production rates, setup times, equipment reliability, and so on. The centralized system specifies what the shop floor will do but far enough in advance so the plan can be modified if the shop says it cannot do it. Execution and control of the production quantities specified in the MPSs and daily schedules are left almost entirely to the decentralized part of the system.

In the traditional MRP-based PPC system, everything from long-range planning to detailed capacity planning, scheduling, and control is done by the centralized system. But in any business, it is a given that things change and that no plan or schedule will remain completely valid for very long. One drawback with centralized planning, scheduling, and control is that it is almost impossible to quickly revise plans and schedules to account for all the work and priority changes and interruptions happening everywhere in the plant. By the time information gets to the system and schedules are revised, the information and, hence, the schedules are obsolete. Because of this, most traditional PPC systems end up having a decentralized part, which, de facto, does much of the *real* detailed work scheduling and control. This decentralized part consists of workers and supervisors on the shop floor who constantly struggle to overcome shortfalls in the schedules they are supposed to follow. Their actions, however, are informal, sometimes spontaneous and ad hoc, and often not totally effective.

In a pull production system, the role that shop-floor supervisors and worker teams play in PPC is *formalized*. Supervisors and worker teams are trained to be competent to schedule and control work to meet requirements as set by level MPSs. Since it is impossible for a centralized system to get up-to-the-minute reports on everything, it makes sense to decentralize as much of the detailed planning and control as possible (this applies to any production process, pull system or not).

Having said that, we now say this: most pull production systems still rely on MRP-type systems for aspects of production planning and scheduling. After all, MRP II systems do many things, and some of them (forecasting, rough-cut capacity planning, master scheduling, material requirements planning and ordering) must continue to be done even in pull production.

We now look more closely at major components within the centralized system and the decentralized system.

CENTRALIZED PLANNING AND CONTROL SYSTEM

The centralized system anticipates demand, then sets in motion the actions for procurement, organization, and utilization of resources necessary to meet demand. The three main functions of the centralized system are monthly planning of the MPS, daily scheduling of the final production stage, and materials forecasting and procurement.

MONTHLY PLANNING

The centralized system prepares monthly demand forecasts for each product, product group, or other end-items, and then creates the MPSs for each. Figure 18.2 illustrates this process.

FIGURE 18.2

Monthly planning process.

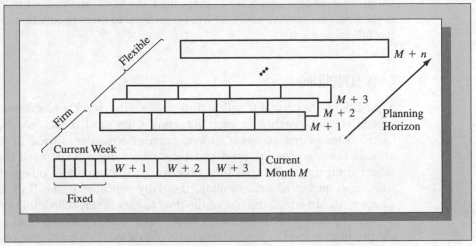

Planning MPSs for Future Periods

Each month the demand over some planning horizon is estimated. If, say, the length of the planning horizon is 3 months, then the demand for the current month and each of the next 2 months is estimated.[2] Master production schedules are then prepared for each of the months, taking into account forecasts, pre-existing production capacity, inventory levels, and known customer orders. The MPSs are leveled as described in Chapter 16.

The tentative MPSs for 2 or 3 months or more into the future ($M + 2$, $M + 3$, etc. in Figure 18.2) are the basis for estimating production capacity requirements. Because no actions or commitments for those schedules will have as yet been made, the schedules are flexible and can be easily revised. However, as shown in Figure 18.2, the MPSs prepared for the current and next month are considered firm or fixed because actions for them have already been taken. Once purchase orders for raw materials have been sent out, additional workers have been assigned or hired, and contracts for outsourced items have been set, the commitment to follow through on an MPS increases, and the schedule becomes somewhat fixed.

MPSs for Shop-Floor Planning

Tentative MPSs for future months are circulated at a predetermined time (usually around the middle of the month) to managers and supervisors of production departments and production lines. From the tentative MPSs and the number of predicted working days in the month, the required average daily production level for a product can be determined. For planning like this, an MRP II system is a useful tool.

Given the average daily production level for every product, the production department can estimate the number of workers needed, equipment requirements, and the length of workdays necessary to meet the level MPS. By midmonth every operation in the process is able to estimate what it must do to meet production requirements for the following month.

DAILY SCHEDULING

The MPS for the current month is broken down into weekly schedules, then into daily schedules, incorporating at each breakdown the most recent information on forecasted demand and customer orders. Such information is used first to develop an average daily production level and then eventually a final, fixed daily production schedule for the final stage of the process (final assembly or otherwise). If the final stage does mixed-model assembly, the daily schedule is the FAS as described in Chapter 16.[3] In effect, the size of the *time bucket* in this scheduling system is 1 day.

Incorporating the most recent order information into the final schedule causes the production level to vary somewhat day-to-day. As a consequence, all operations experience some variation from the planned baseline amount. But since each operation produces only what is authorized from downstream, the entire system readily adapts: slightly high demand at the final stage results in a slight increase in the rate of demand signals sent upstream; slightly lower demand results in a slight decrease in the signals. As mentioned, a pull system can readily absorb a variation of about ±10% from the baseline amount without needing to change the number of cards or containers in use.

Integrating Recent Demand Information

The process of refining daily plans to reflect the most recent order information is illustrated in Figure 18.3. Every week the centralized system receives customer order information for a 10-day period.[4] This order information includes firm customer orders and the most recent sales forecasts from sources such as dealers, sales people, and distributors. The total demand for three successive 10-day orders (i.e., 30 days demand) must fall within the planned production volume of the level production schedule for the month. If it exceeds the planned volume and cannot be accommodated by overtime, then the excess demand must be included in the production schedule for the following month. If it is apparent that demand is on the rise and will continue to exceed current capacity levels, then the overall planned capacity level is ratcheted up.

The central system receives the 10-day demand information at least *1 week* prior to the 2-week time block that the information represents. For example, customer orders to be filled in the first 10 days of May should be received 1 week prior to that, or by April 24. Note that although the system requires 10-day order information a week before production, much of the information might still be forecasted, leaving room to insert actual orders that arrive later. As a consequence, the time between

FIGURE 18.3

Daily planning process.

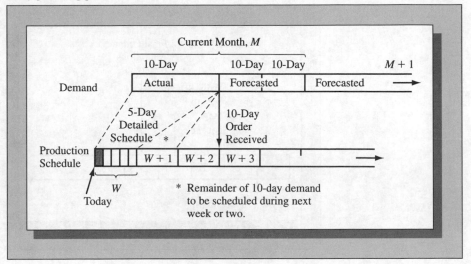

the arrival of a customer order and production to fill that order is often as little as 4–10 days. This is explained in the next section.

Having the 10-day demand for all products allows time to sort out and sequence products so the final production schedule for the first week will closely fit the baseline level of the current MPS. The system then uses this information to estimate the daily production rate for each product or end-item. Out of 10 days demand, only 5 days can be satisfied in the first week (5 working days) of production. The remaining orders from the 10 day plan are then scheduled for production in the following week or, at the latest, within the week after that.[5]

Daily Order Alterations

At companies like Toyota and Nissan, the centralized system performs one additional step in setting the daily production schedules. Besides information on 10-day demand, the system incorporates information received *every day* from sales sources about order *alterations*. Alterations include new orders, canceled orders, and other changes to orders affecting the most recent 10-day period. The daily schedule as originally prepared using 10-day demand figures is then updated to account for these alterations. The updated version becomes the final daily production schedule. Of course, finalization of that daily schedule happens a few days or more in advance of the day the schedule will be used. How far in advance of the production day it is finalized depends on lead times for materials procurement and manufacturing setup.

At Toyota the daily final assembly schedule is prepared *4 days* in advance of the production day (shown in Figure 18.4). While setting the final daily schedule, the

FIGURE 18.4

Incorporating daily demand into daily schedules.

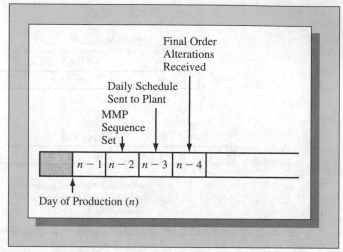

system also sets the requirements for all materials, parts, and assemblies for the day of production, 4 days later. Three days before production, the centralized system transmits the finalized daily schedule to the plant. Two days before production, the plant determines the MMP sequence for the schedule. On the day of production, the MMP sequence is displayed at the final stage of the process, where it is executed. Assuming that the production lead time for final assembly is 1 day, then products coming off the assembly line on any given day will reflect customer order information received as little as 4 days earlier.

For large products like automobiles, major components such as engines and transmissions are each assembled on their own production lines. Each of these lines also has a level daily production schedule and MMP sequence, which is derived from the daily FAS for the automobile assembly line.

Some manufacturers allow salespeople access to the daily production schedule. Since some of the models produced in the MMP sequence are for forecasted demand (not firm orders), these are available for immediate sale. The salesperson can inform customers about these models (the ones available for quick delivery) and also how long they will have to wait for other models not on the current daily schedule.

MATERIAL PROCUREMENT FORECAST

The quantity of materials and parts for all products is estimated from the monthly MPS and the bill of materials (BOM). For each product or other end-item, requirements for procured parts and components are determined using the same logical procedure as employed in MRP systems.[6] At the start of each month, information about the anticipated daily material requirements for that month is sent to suppliers. Forecasted material requirements for the following month or two are also sent to allow the suppliers time to adjust to changes in requirement levels.

Kanban Supplier Link

Many pull production companies have direct **Kanban links** to their suppliers. Supplier Kanban systems, described in Chapter 19, work very much like internal pull systems, except the upstream operations to which replenishment orders and empty containers are sent are external suppliers. Since a level MPS will result in material requirements that are also somewhat level, suppliers can expect the requirements (quantity and frequency of orders) to remain about the same over a given period of time. Although the actual daily requirements might be somewhat variable (just as the MMP sequence and daily production schedule are somewhat variable), the variation, if kept small, can readily be absorbed by the supplier Kanban system. If the variation is anticipated to exceed what the supplier Kanban system can absorb, then the parameters of the supplier Kanban system (delivery CT, number of supplier kanbans, frequency of deliveries, and number of units per container) are revised. Daily production schedules, which are set a week in advance (at Toyota, 4 days), are used to determine daily material requirements. Every week the parameters of the supplier Kanban system are reviewed and adjusted as necessary to reflect demand for the upcoming week.

MRP Supplier Link

Not all pull production manufacturers use Kanban for daily procurement of materials. At Nissan, for example, daily ordering of materials is done by a centralized MRP system that uses *daily* time buckets. The order process combines the finalized daily production schedule for *4 days later* with the BOMs for the products that will be assembled. To meet daily requirements, suppliers make eight deliveries each day. Eighty percent of supplied parts are ordered in this way. For common, standardized parts, orders are placed less frequently, typically about every 2 weeks using the 10-day order information. For specialized parts for low-volume products, orders are placed only monthly.

THE DECENTRALIZED PLANNING AND CONTROL SYSTEM

The most significant difference between pull systems and traditional push systems is that in the former the functions of detailed planning, scheduling, and control are decentralized, while in the latter they are centralized. In pull production, shop-floor supervisors and worker teams assume much of the responsibility for detailed capacity planning, scheduling, and work control. In many instances, they also handle procurement of purchased materials.

DETAILED CAPACITY PLANNING

Initial Capacity Planning

Each month the production output of workcells and independent workstations might have to be altered to meet changes in the monthly MPS. This requires production capacity flexibility, which is achieved through adjustable work hours, flexible work-cells and machine configurations, short changeover times, cross-trained workers, and so on.

If the capacity of workcells or stages of a process cannot be increased to meet the level specified by the MPS and if an eventual shortage cannot be made up through overtime, inventory, or outsourcing, then the capacity of that workcell or stage, not the original MPS, is the process bottleneck and dictates the output rate for the entire process. If that rate is less than the level specified in the MPS, and assuming there are no other means by which to reach the level of the MPS, then the MPS must be revised downward.

The worker team at each cell or department has its own personal computer for performing capacity planning, quality analysis, inventory control, and reporting. Information about the MPS and BOMs is retrieved from the centralized PPC system. Information about current capacity and inventory is sent to the centralized system.

Capacity Fine-Tuning

Even after the MPS and the production capacity of every operation have been mutually adjusted to a feasible level, adjustments continue as more recent information becomes available. The initial MPSs, the preplans prepared 1 or 2 months in advance, provide only forecasts and rough estimates of demand, so any plans for the workcells and departments to meet those schedules are considered provisional. As late as 1 or 2 weeks before production is to begin, the plans for workcells and departments might have to be revised again to incorporate the most recent demand information.

Even as production is executed according to the FAS, workers continue to fine-tune each operation. Through experience and continuous review of SORs (described in Chapter 11) shop teams learn ways to alter the work procedures, number of kan-bans, number and assignment of workers, etc., to achieve a better balance between available work capacity and required CTs.

SHOP-FLOOR CONTROL

In traditional companies the sole purpose of collecting data about the shop floor is to provide the centralized PPC system with information for accounting and planning. But as Steudel and Desruelle point out, that must change if a company wants to achieve global competitive status. The purpose of gathering data about the shop floor must include providing shop-floor people with information for scheduling and controlling work.[7]

Visual Management, Again

In JIT companies, much of the information that worker teams rely on for daily scheduling and control is generated and displayed by the **visual-management system,** visual because people know the status of the system and how much and when to produce simply by looking at kanban cards and containers in the workplace. With a visual system it is not necessary to look hard or look far to see what needs to be done. Other elements of visual management described in this book include information post-its (posted measures about quality, throughput, setup times, machine performance); andons signaling the status of a process, workcell, or machine; posted schedules, quality procedures and control charts; posted SORs; and pokayoke procedures and devices for signaling and preventing defects. Visual management simplifies the tracking of jobs and system status and pinpoints areas on the shop floor having problems or needing improvement.

Role of Worker Teams

Part of the role of worker teams in the decentralized control system is to track performance measures such as production rates, CTs, production lead times, setup times, product quality, and equipment availability and effectiveness. Daily, hourly, and by event, workers update charts about defects, breakdowns, setups, etc. Supervisors prepare summaries of this information and send it (say, via PC network) to the centralized system, which uses it for updating estimates of production capacity levels and setting MPSs and daily production schedules. Up-to-date information from the shop floor keeps the centralized planning staff in touch with reality and helps ensure that MPSs and daily schedules are realistic.

ADAPTING MRP-BASED PPC SYSTEMS TO PULL PRODUCTION

Adapting an MRP-based production system to pull production requires fundamental changes to shop-floor control procedures and to aspects of the centralized PPC system. Assuming that the product demand and the production process meet the requirements of pull production as described in Chapter 8, a company can begin the transition to pull production by addressing the changes described in this section.

SIMPLIFIED BOMS

A primary goal of JIT companies is to manufacture products with the least amount of waste. Associated with this goal is the principle of simplification: accomplish the same ends, but in a less complex, more basic way and with fewer steps. In manufacturing that translates into producing products that have fewer parts and using processes that require fewer steps.

In reducing the number of steps in a process, non-value-added steps such as storage are eliminated first. In pull production, WIP levels are progressively reduced, sometimes to the point where the WIP becomes nonexistent. Eliminating a place where inventory is stored is tantamount to eliminating a place where material must be tracked and scheduled. Pull production can thus simplify a manufacturing process just by eliminating steps that involve administrative procedures, even if no processing steps are eliminated.

Since upstream stages of pull systems do not require detailed work schedules, the centralized PPC system (MRP or otherwise) does not need to process and generate lists of requirements for all stages of the process. The centralized system needs to prepare only a detailed schedule for the final stage of the process and order releases for procured materials for outside, non-Kanban-linked suppliers. In a pull production system, an MRP II system has much less work to do than in a push system.

Software developers have created add-on modules for adapting MRP II computer systems to pull production. These systems assume (or mandate) that BOM structures are expressed in the simplest terms possible and that the places in the process requiring scheduling and tracking are minimized. One of the first things a company must do when converting from push production to pull production is to simplify the BOM for each end-item.

The typical MRP system uses the BOM in many ways. Besides the materials and parts that must be procured, the BOM identifies manufacturing and assembly operations that must be scheduled and monitored. For example, the BOM in Figure 18.5 shows that item R consists of items S and Y, both which must be individually manufactured and then combined. In traditional push manufacturing, the MRP system maintains inventory records for every item at every stage of the production process for purposes of tracking inventory levels and production status. In reference to the BOM in Figure 18.5, inventory records are thus maintained for the finished product (the top level, item R), all raw materials and purchased parts (bottom level, items T, V, D, C), and all WIP (the nodes at intermediate levels, items S and Y)—a total of seven records.

Each record corresponds to a place somewhere in the plant (a shop-floor location, a stock room, etc.) where raw materials, WIP, or finished products are stocked. For

FIGURE 18.5

BOM structure: three levels, seven records.

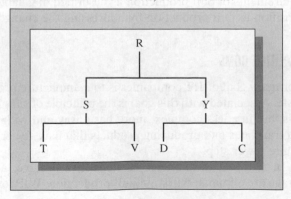

plants that deal with numerous jobs simultaneously, this record-keeping is considered necessary so jobs do not get lost or mixed up. Although record-keeping is often necessary for legal purposes and financial reporting, most record-keeping is wasteful and unnecessary.

It should be obvious that the greater the number of levels and branches in the BOM, the greater the number of records the MRP system must maintain. The greater the number or records, the higher the record-keeping cost, and the more difficult it is to keep the records current for purposes of scheduling and control. Conversely, the fewer the records, the lower the record-keeping cost, and the easier it is to maintain record accuracy.

Since a pull production system controls work and materials throughout the process by delimiting the number of containers, any other form of control mechanism at stages other than at the final one is unnecessary. This is equivalent to saying that, for purposes of scheduling and control, all records at intermediate levels of the BOM are unnecessary. Eliminating these records is referred to as **flattening the BOM.** Once flattened, a BOM has only two levels, one for the end-item and one for the low-level parts that go into it.

Flat BOMs

An MRP system ordinarily maintains records for every location where material is stocked. If instead of being held in stock, a material is moved directly from one stage of a process to the next, or if it is held relatively briefly at a stage and in a small quantity (as in pull production), then there is no need to keep track of it at that stage. Lack of need to keep track of an item corresponds to removing the item from the BOM and to removing the inventory record for it from the MRP system. Hence, by just smoothing production flow and eliminating places where items are stored, the BOM can be flattened, even though the number of component parts in the product and the stages in the process remain the same. (This assumes continuous or repetitive material flow, accompanied by shop-floor visual management.)

Cellular manufacturing (the topic of Chapter 10) also leads to flattening of BOMs. Material in a cell moves directly from one workstation to the next and is held so briefly between stations that it need not be tracked. Thus, whether a product is made in a workcell instead of a job shop (where it is held as WIP inventory between every stage of the process) or in a process where stages are linked by a repetitive pull system, the BOM structure for it can be flattened.

Example 1: Flattening the BOM with Cellular Manufacturing

Suppose product X is ordinarily produced in a job shop and requires nine separate production steps. After each step, it is held in inventory until it can be processed by the next step. The process is represented by the 10-level BOM shown in Figure 18.6. The lowest level in the BOM represents raw material inputs for the first step, and successively higher levels represent WIP and raw material inputs for subsequent steps. Every letter in Figure 18.6 represents a record of

FIGURE 18.6

BOM structure for nine-step process.

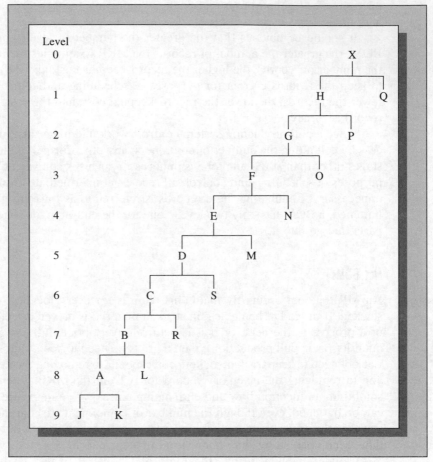

items held in stock; hence, the MRP system maintains 19 records for this product. Every movement of materials into or out of stock represents a transaction and a stock record that must be updated.

Suppose now that the first two steps in Figure 18.6 (combining parts J and K, then combining A and L) are done in one workcell, the next three steps (combining B and R, then C and S, then D and M) are done in another workcell, and the last four steps (combining E and N, F and O, G and P, H and Q) are done in a third workcell. Inventory control rule-of-thumb says that as long as material keeps moving, it is not necessary to track it; the material need be accounted for only at places in the process where it is detained. In a workcell, material generally flows continuously from one workstation to the next, so tracking within the cell is unnecessary. The only places in a workcell where material is held are at the cell's input and output stock areas. Thus, the BOM for a product produced in a workcell can have as few as two levels.

FIGURE 18.7

Flattened BOMs for nine-step process with three workcells (original BOM in Figure 18.6).

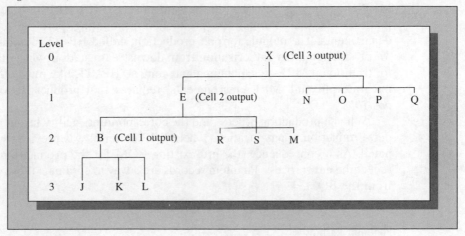

FIGURE 18.8

Flattened BOM for nine-step process all in one workcell.

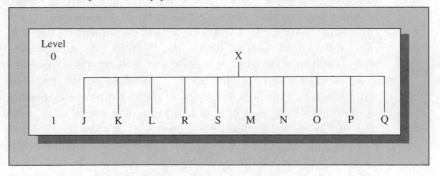

In the present case, where the process has been converted into three workcells, the BOM can be collapsed from 10 levels to just 4 levels, shown in Figure 18.7:

· Level 3 represents stocks of material going into cell 1.
· Level 2 represents stocks of material going into cell 2, including item B, the output of cell 1.
· Level 1 represents stocks of material going into cell 1, including item E, the output of cell 2.
· Level 0 is the stock of output from cell 3, end-item X.

As another example, suppose *all nine steps* are performed by just one cell. The BOM would then be reduced to just two levels, shown in Figure 18.8.

Among several commercial PPC software systems developed for integrating pull production into traditional MRP systems is one by Hewlett-Packard (HP). The system is one of nine modules that make up the Hewlett-Packard MRP II system.[8] Like typical MRP II systems as described in the Appendix, the HP MRP II system allows information to be shared among the production, accounting, purchasing, and marketing departments. The module for pull production, called HP-JIT, combines information for production upon authorization from downstream stations with other information for traditional MRP-style planning and control. HP-JIT, like most other systems that integrate pull and MRP environments, requires that product BOMs be *as flat as possible.*

When a production process and the corresponding facility layout are modified for pull production, many locations where WIP material was previously held are eliminated. As a consequence, the pre-existing BOM for the product must be altered to reflect the new process. Phantom records are a way to eliminate those once-held items from the BOM.

Phantom Records

Suppose a plant is converting a portion of its production process from a job shop to pull production or cellular manufacturing. The pre-existing BOMs of the end-items manufactured in the process can be flattened by removing records for items at intermediate stages within the process or workcell. An alternative, however, to physically removing the records is to transform them into **phantom records.** A phantom record represents a material that never actually goes into storage, but is in a momentary transitional state (a component or subassembly) and is en route to the next stage of the process. By using phantom records, the BOM for an end-item can be simplified without altering the *basic structure* of the BOM or of the inventory data files. This is desirable when the cost of restructuring a data file is large, when the current BOM structure is needed for accounting purposes, or when intermediate items in the structure are used for purposes besides end-item production and must be tracked. In those cases, a phantom record is simply substituted in the existing BOM structure for a pre-existing record. The phantom record retains the location of the original record in the BOM structure and can be ignored, if desired; if tracking and accounting information are needed, the record can be activated and accessed.

Example   2:   Simplified BOM Using Phantom Records

Suppose the nine-steps process described in the previous example is to be performed by a sequence of three workcells. Figure 18.9 shows how the BOM from Figure 18.6 would look if this change were made and if phantom records were inserted in the BOM wherever material was once, but will no longer be, held in stock. Actually, the phantom records represent materials between workstations *within* a workcell. Since the items flow somewhat continuously, they do not need to be tracked, and, given that they are listed as phantoms in the BOM, no transactions (additions or withdrawals) are posted against them. Essentially, the phantom records are ignored by the MRP

FIGURE 18.9

BOM using phantom records (letters with asterisks) for nine-step process performed in three workcells.

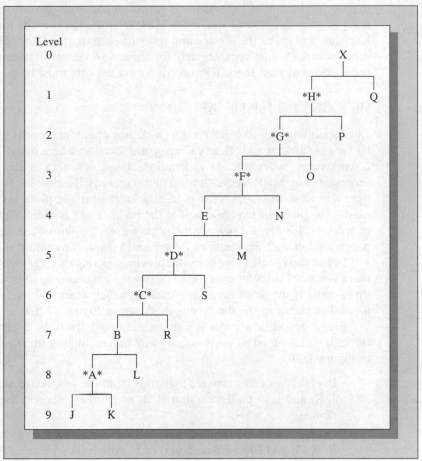

scheduling system (notice, if you delete the phantom records in the structure in Figure 18.9, you get a structure identical to that in Figure 18.7). Since the phantom records are not intended to represent steps in the process, the lead times for them are considered zero. If however, it becomes necessary to track these intermediate items, the phantom records for them are simply activated.

Phantom records are also used for another purpose: to represent items that *are* held in stock *for purposes other than production.* That is, phantom records can represent items that are produced at a stage of the process but which are then separated out and not used in the end-item. For example, some quantity of a component produced in a process might be siphoned off (diverted from the rest of the process) for the purpose of keeping a reserve for service parts or for testing and marketing. The phantom record for this component enables inventory of this component to be monitored, controlled, and maintained apart from inventory of the identical component used in production of the end-item. Although phantom records for these service and test parts are not treated like other MRP records, the records for parts at the lower levels used to make the service and test parts *are* treated like other MRP records. In other words, the net requirements for these lower-level parts must be planned and transactions against the MRP records for these parts must be posted.

STOCK AREAS AND POINT-OF-USE

Corresponding to each MRP record (including phantom records for items momentarily held in stock) is a **stock area,** a physical location where material is held for use by a workcenter, workcell, or workstation. The stock area is the place where items represented by MRP records and phantom records are located. To minimize handling time and cost, the stock area is ideally located at the place where the material is used—the **point of use.** Material at the point of use is ordinarily within close reach of workers. Ideally, a stock record exists for each point-of-use such that if the same part is used in multiple locations throughout a plant, the amount at each can be known.

In the three-cell process in the previous examples (represented in Figure 18.7) there is a stock area for every kind of raw material and for the output of each of the three cells. If the stock areas are located at their points of use, then they would be located at places in the three cells as shown in Figure 18.10.

Every production process can be conceptualized as a series of stock areas through which material moves on its way to becoming a finished product. Referring to Figure 18.10:

- In cell 1, workers remove materials from the respective stock areas for items J, K, and L to produce a unit of B, which they place in the stock area for item B.
- In cell 2, workers remove materials from the respective stock areas for items B, R, S, and M to create a unit of E, which they place in the stock area for item E.
- In cell 3, workers follow a similar process to produce a unit of item X.

In a pull production system each stock area is the location for a production card (P-kanban) or the destination for a withdrawal card (C-kanban). In fact, anywhere there is a **kanban mailbox** or equivalent for posting cards is usually a stock area for keeping containers and material.

Although, ideally, the stock areas are located at points of use, that might be impractical when the number of materials used at a workstation is large. The next-best alternative then is to keep some of the material in a reserve stock location as near as possible to the point of use and for workers or material handlers to retrieve the material as needed. Another alternative is to keep the incoming material in the receiving area. The receiving area serves as a staging area and can itself be treated as a stock area with firm limits on all quantities held.

FIGURE 18.10

Three-cell process showing point-of-use stock areas.

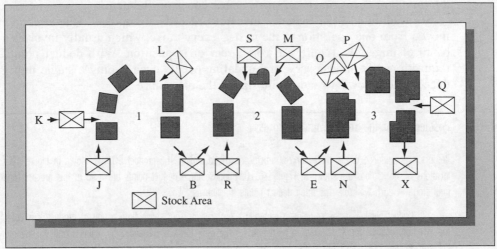

Companies first implementing pull production often have much inventory and cannot locate it all at the point of use. Eventually, as they gain experience with pull production and reduce inventory, however, they will be able to store most if not all materials at the point of use; in addition, deliveries from external suppliers can be made directly to those areas to eliminate the need for storerooms and warehousing. This last point is described in Chapter 19, Managing the Supply Chain.

POSTDEDUCT AND DEDUCT LISTS[9]

Even in pull production it is necessary to keep track of the quantity of completed end-items and procured parts and raw materials that need replenishment. In some PPC systems this updating of stock records is done through a procedure called **post-deduct** or **backflushing.** For every completed end-item, the quantity on the MPS (or final schedule) is decreased by a unit, and the on-hand inventory balance of all parts going into the end-item is reduced by the amounts used. When a new container of material is first accessed or when the quantity of material reaches a minimum level, a replenishment transaction is initiated either electronically by a purchasing module or by a shop worker or supervisor phoning or faxing the supplier. Either way, the transaction might also involve determining the replenishment quantity, adding that quantity to the stock area record (assuming short lead time on delivery), and notifying accounts payable. Such a transaction is called a **purchasing kanban** or **blanket transaction.**

The postdeduct procedure occurs everywhere in the process designated as a **deduct point.** At each deduct point, the inventory records to be updated are specified on a **deduct list.** As items move past a deduct point, the inventory records of items on the list are automatically updated. Often, data-entry terminals or scanners are used by workers at deduct points to simplify data entry to the record-keeping system. As items pass the deduct point, a worker keys in the item code and quantity of units on a terminal or scans magnetic strips or bar codes on the items.

In traditional MRP systems, inventory records are updated whenever items are moved from one operation to the next.[10] Every move, which usually involves a large batch of materials, requires a work order or requisition. With deduct points work requisitions are unnecessary, and updating occurs even if only a single unit is produced. The following example illustrates the procedure.

Example   3:   Postdeduct for the Three-Workcell Process

Product X is produced in the three-workcell process described earlier. The product BOM is shown in Figure 18.7; locations of stock areas are shown in Figure 18.10. Suppose three deduct points are used in this process, one at the final stage of each workcell. The three deduct points function as follows:

1. Deduct point 1 is the completion of product X at cell 3. Thus, each time a unit of product X is completed, the inventory balance for X is increased by a unit (or the MPS for X is decreased by a unit), and the inventory balances for all parts going into X are decreased. The parts whose inventories will be decreased are specified on the deduct list, which, for product X are items E, N, O, P, and Q. (The deduct-list items are indicated as level 1 in Figure 18.7.)

2. Deduct point 2 is the completion of subassembly E. Whenever a unit of E is completed, the inventory balance in the record for E is increased by one unit, and the inventory balances in records for B, R, S, and M are decreased (level 2 items in Figure 18.7).

3. Deduct point 3 is the completion of item B. For each increase in a unit of B, the balances for J, K, and L are decreased (level 3, Figure 18.7).

Sometimes only one deduct point is needed—at the end of the entire process. Upon completion of an end-item, one unit is subtracted from the MPS and the on-hand inventory balances of all parts for the end-item deduct list are reduced by the number of parts used in the end-item. This procedure is called **superflush.** Referring to Figure 18.7 and the three-cell example, each completion of end-item X would be accompanied by a reduction in the balances of items J, K, L, R, S, M, N, O, P, and Q all at once. There would be no transactions for items B and E.

With only one deduct point, however, inventory balances are less accurate because of the time lag between when items are withdrawn from a stock area and when the same items pass from the final stage of production within the completed end-item. In the interim, before they reach the deduct point and before the postdeduct procedure, inventory records will not reflect that the items have been removed. When the CTs are small and the schedules are level, errors in the records will be minimal. When, however, the CTs are long, using only one deduct point at the end of the process can result in significant inaccuracy in inventory records since material consumed at various stages of the process will not be accounted for until much later. In such cases it is necessary to use several deduct points located at various places throughout the process.

In the postdeduct procedure, system software scans the end-item BOM, starting at the top level. The software logic moves through the BOM, bypassing phantom records until it encounters nonphantom, "real" records. It then updates those records. Thus, decisions about whether intermediate stages of a process should be represented by phantom records on the BOM are partly dictated by the throughput rate of the process and the level of inventory accuracy desired. If the throughput rate is fast, phantom records can be used at all intermediate levels of the BOM. If the rate is slow, some real records should be left at intermediate levels to correspond to places in the process where the postdeduct procedure should be performed.

RATE-BASED MASTER SCHEDULES

Traditional MRP systems generate weekly schedules for every operation, though, as mentioned, for pull production these schedules must be converted into daily schedules for the end-item. The conversion starts with the assumption that the MPS is somewhat level. As discussed in Chapter 16, this means that with, say, a monthly planning time horizon, the forecasted demand for the month could be met by producing at a uniform level throughout the month. If a traditional MRP-generated MPS with weekly time buckets is used, the production quantity specified would be about the same for every week.

To convert the MPS into the equivalent of daily time buckets, monthly production volume is translated into a **daily production rate,** which is the rate that will be maintained throughout the month (or whatever time period the MPS covers). Then, instead of issuing authorization orders for each day of production, the MRP will issue only a single authorization order on the day the daily production rate is to commence. No further authorization is issued until the rate is changed. Example 4 shows how the daily production rate is determined.

Example   4:   Daily Production Rate

Refer to Figure 18.11. Row 3 (anticipated demand for the month) is the sum of row 1 (sales projections and promised deliveries) and row 2 (production shortages from prior months).

FIGURE 18.11

Determination of daily production rate.

Row	April	May	June	July
1. Forecast	3900	4100	3800	3700
2. Backlog	90*	0	0	16
3. Anticipated demand	3990	4100	3800	3716
4. Working days	20	23	22	21
5. x Production rate	200	178	172	177
6. Production	4000	4094	3784	3717
7. On hand	0	10	4	0
8. Available units	4000	4104	3788	3717
9. Ending units	10	4	(16)	1

*Shortage for months prior to April.

To determine the daily production rate (row 5), divide the anticipated demand by the number of working days (row 4) and round the result up or down. Available units (row 8) are the number of units produced (production rate × number of working days) plus any stock on hand (row 7). Units left over in any month (ending units, row 9) become the on-hand stock for the following month; negative ending units (shortage) become a backlog for the next month (row 2).

The example presumes a monthly time frame for the MPS. The general procedure for setting the production rate would be identical for shorter time frames of, say, 10 days, as described in Chapter 16.

The production rates are converted into CTs, as described in Chapter 17, and the shop floor is apprised in advance of estimated CTs so workcenters can plan for changes to achieve the necessary capacity and balance. Once the production rate has been set, it can be altered on a daily basis, as described earlier, to accommodate the most-recent orders.

IMPLEMENTING PULL PRODUCTION WITH MRP PPC

Implementing pull production involves changes to both the centralized system and the decentralized, shop-floor system. Many of the changes, including add-on features for making an MRP II computer system compatible with pull production, have been addressed in this chapter; other changes involving planning and scheduling philosophy and practice were covered in preceding chapters. At the shop-floor level, the necessary changes are very broad in scope and encompass almost every aspect of production and quality control addressed in Parts II and III of this book. All told the extent of the change necessary to implement pull production might appear overwhelming. For that reason it must be done in a carefully planned, systematic fashion.

Implementating pull production should begin with a pilot project for a product and production process where the known difficulties are few and where success is most likely. As discussed in Chapters 3 and 8, implementating JIT philosophy and methodologies, including pull production, requires the support of top management, high-level coordination of a steering committee, and the dedicated effort of a committed, enthusiastic shop-floor team. Ideally, the pilot product and process should be relatively autonomous from other processes in the plant. Operations that must work on products outside the pilot project should be avoided. Implementation must consider housekeeping, layout, process routing, setup reduction, equipment reliability and PM, process capability, quality control, and training, in addition to the planning and control topics of this chapter. Personnel in engineering, maintenance, quality assurance, planning, and other support areas must work with the shop-floor team and learn (from then on) how to coordinate their efforts. Many of the problems, issues, and steps in implementing pull production are similar to those for implementing cellular manufacturing as covered in Chapter 10.

Some or significant progress toward setup reduction, equipment PM, quality checking, inventory reduction, and workplace organization must occur before pull production procedures are introduced. Suppliers too must be involved in implementation because pull production requires frequent, small-batch deliveries of high-quality materials. Such commitment from suppliers often requires their participation in setting delivery schedules, defect levels, and even product specifications. These topics are covered in the next chapter.

Besides all of this is the matter of transforming the centralized MRP PPC system and associated shop-floor procedures to enable pull production.[11] The following steps summarize this transformation.

Step 1: Create a Logical Flow; Improve Material Handling

Use of stockrooms should be discontinued and all stock should be located on the shop floor near points of use. When that is not possible, as much stock as possible should be located at points of use and the rest should be kept in an overflow stockroom.

All areas of the shop floor should be linked with a material handling system, either an automated system or a team of special material handlers. The handling system replaces the MRP procedure of extracting inventory from the stockroom.

Information in the MRP system should be revised to show the new locations of all materials. MRP systems often do not indicate the physical location of stock, so when the same material is located at multiple points of use, a way must be devised to keep track of it (either modify the MRP system or adopt a scheme that keeps one record but accounts for multiple stock points).[12]

At this stage the MRP system continues to schedule and release production orders as before. Meanwhile, efforts progress to improve setup and machine-tooling times, machine operations, preventive maintenance, and product quality control. With enough improvements, it is possible to begin producing in smaller batch sizes and to reduce stock levels.

The overall production process is adjusted so the final stage is able to produce at a uniform rate and follow a level schedule. If several models are to be produced, then the length of production runs for each must be reduced to eventually allow for MMP. Start with daily runs (one model per shift), then twice-daily runs, then hourly runs, etc., striving for the goal of single-unit model production.

The layout of the process, including process routing, material traffic flows, and space requirements should be rationalized: Does the routing flow make sense? Does the location of machines, facilities, tools, equipment, and stock areas make sense? Revise the routing and layout to minimize waste (time, inventory, processing, waiting, etc.).

Once the process is able to produce in small batches and follow a somewhat level schedule, the next step can begin.

Step 2: Introduce the Pull System

Given that setup times, product quality, and equipment reliability are sufficiently improved, a pull system using containers, cards, deduct points, and so on, as described in this chapter and Chapter 8, can be phased in. Usually it is easiest to phase in a pull system stage-by-stage, starting at the last stage of the process and working backward. After the container size is determined, the number of cards can be estimated, and stock areas and signal methods (e.g., kanban mailboxes) can be set up. The initial trial will usually reveal problems with setups, quality, and work layout, which need to be resolved (the rocks, or problems, covered by inventory described in Chapter 3). These are handled by keeping extra stock everywhere, though as the problems are resolved, extra stock is no longer needed.

Pull production cannot handle defective components and materials. If the defect rate is high, the defective items must first be sorted out. Says Hall, rule of thumb is that the defect rate should be less than 1% and almost never higher than 3%.[13] The goal is zero defects, but companies first adopting pull production rarely have the maintenance, setup, pokayoke, product design, and other procedures in place to achieve near-zero defect rates. Eventually, however, through quality of design and conformance programs, they should be able to reduce defect rates to well below 1%.

At this stage the MRP system is still used for authorizing workorders and for placing orders from suppliers. The BOMs are flattened (usually by coding the intermediate level items as phantoms) and the system no longer does detailed capacity requirements planning or issuing of detailed schedules to individual operations.

Step 3: Create a New Layout

Once the pull system for a product family or mixed-model group has been balanced and demand has been deemed large and somewhat stable, a new layout—a flow line or linked workcells—can be created. As stock areas are reduced in size or eliminated, operations can be moved closer together.

The role of the centralized MRP II system continues to be transformed; by the end of this stage the sole functions of the system will be to (1) accumulate forecasts and customer-order information for generating MPSs, (2) release daily production rates (FAS or other daily production schedule) to the final stage of the process, (3) generate and release orders for materials to external suppliers that are not Kanban-linked, and (4) update the remaining inventory records in the BOM through the postdeduct procedure.

Step 4: Continuously Improve Processes

Everything is expanded on, including improvements to setups, operations, maintenance, workcell layouts, and application of pull production to processes where it is appropriate. With time and experience, the pull system can be expanded to larger portions of the pilot process, then to additional products and processes.

Summary

Production planning and control in pull production are handled jointly by centralized and decentralized systems. The functions of forecasting, order entry, rough-cut capacity planning, master scheduling, and requirements planning are performed by a centralized staff in much the same way as in traditional MRP-based PPC systems. Based on demand forecasts and current orders, the centralized system develops monthly MPSs. These are shared with suppliers and with departments and workcells on the shop floor so each can plan ahead to meet the schedules. Preplans are sent out months in advance, though the actual daily schedules might incorporate order information received as late as a week before production.

In pull production, much of the short- and near-term planning and virtually all of the shop-floor control is handled at the factory level. Though the centralized system prepares the level MPSs, shop-floor teams and supervisors determine staffing levels and worker assignments. The only daily schedule prepared by the centralized system is the schedule for the final operation. Everywhere else production happens according to cards and the visual management system. As a result, shop-floor operations perform largely on their own, and, consequently, they are largely self-regulating. This eliminates much of the need for centralized tracking and control systems, which are often ineffective anyway. Materials procurement from suppliers can still be done using an MRP batch-ordering system, though another way is to link suppliers directly to the shop floor with kanbans; this, in effect, extends the pull process beyond the factory.

Companies with MRP II PPC systems can adapt the systems to pull production by modifying product BOMs and inventory records in the computer database, altering the inventory update procedure, and switching from batch-oriented to rate-based MPSs. Since material moves somewhat rapidly through a pull production process, the only places where material is considered stored are places where it enters or leaves the process. WIP, because it is small and transitory, often does not need to be tracked. As a result, the BOM in pull production can be flattened, sometimes to include only two levels: raw material and final product.

A simple way of updating inventories while reducing the number of transactions is to use postdeduct or backflushing: upon completion of a product, the inventory balances of all parts in the product are reduced by the number of parts used in the product. To eliminate double handling and inventory transactions, material is held only in stock areas next to the place where it will be used, the point of use.

Successful implementation of pull production involves matters beyond the shop floor, beyond the PPC system, and even beyond the company. Suppliers too must subscribe to JIT/TQM philosophy and become partners in the production process. Accounting practices and performance measures must be revised to support pull production and to encourage waste reduction, continuous improvement, and competitiveness. These are the topics of the remaining part of this book.

Questions

1. Explain the procedure of preparing tentative production plans for pull production. Describe what happens as these plans become more firm and, eventually, fixed. Discuss the purposes of longer-range flexible plans versus shorter-range firm plans. What role does MRP II serve in all of this?

2. Explain the procedure for setting daily schedules based upon initial production plans and incoming customer orders.

3. What is the purpose of sharing tentative production plans and schedules with suppliers?

4. For the following kinds of procurement systems, discuss applications and relative advantages and disadvantages of each:
   a. Supplier Kanban links.
   b. MRP systems for daily (or more frequent) order releases.
   c. MRP systems for less-than-daily order releases.

5. Discuss the relationship between master production scheduling and shop-floor capacity planning. What role does the agility of the shop floor have in this relationship? How is such agility achieved?

6. Describe the purpose of the visual-management system in shop-floor control. Review the ways that such visual management is achieved.

7. What effect does pull production have on product BOMs? Why do products in pull production need fewer-level BOMs than the same products produced in an MRP-type push system?

8. Explain the purpose of phantom records.

9. Explain the concept of postdeduct (backflushing). What is a deduct point? What is a deduct list?

10. Explain the difference between typical MPS and a rate-based production schedule. Why in a pull production system is one preferable over the other?

Problems

1. Shown below is the BOM for a large motor assembly.

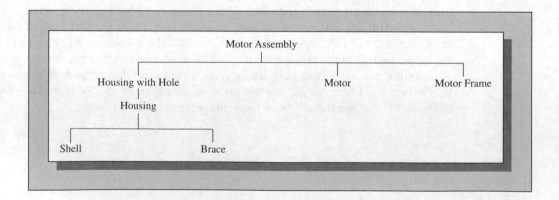

An MRP system is used to schedule each step. Currently for motor assemblies the lot size is 100 units, the lead time is 1 week, and 80 motors/wk are assembled. There are currently 110 units in stock. The MRP record for the motor assembly is as follows:

	Week					
	0	*1*	*2*	*3*	*4*	*5*
Gross Requirement (GR)		80	80	80	80	80
Scheduled Receipts (SR)						
On Hand (OH)	110	110	30	50	70	90
Net Requirement (NR)			50	30	10	
Planned Order Release (POR)		100	100	100		

Assembly of the housing and drilling of the hole in the housing are done in two separate areas of the plant. The final motor assembly is done in a third area. It is proposed that the brace and shell assembly, drilling the hole, and final assembly of finished motors all be done in a single workcell.

a. What would the BOM reflecting this change look like?

b. Assuming now lot-for-lot production, LT = 0, what would the above MRP record look like? Use the same tabular format as above. If the motor housing with hole were phantomed, where in the BOM would the phantom be located?

c. What would the MRP record for the brace look like? Assume a lot size of 30, 80 on hand, and lead time of 1 week.

2. At Gornigs Corporation, pull production with visual shop-floor control and small containers is being implemented for two products, ARM and CARM. Below are the BOMs for the products under the existing push production system:

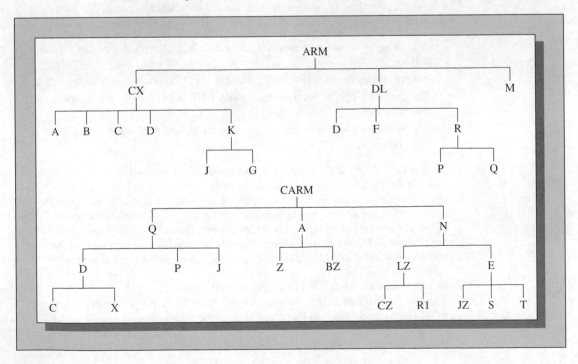

    a. Assuming that both products will be produced repetitively with short CTs, explain how the material should be tracked through the system.

    b. Reduce the BOMs to reflect the tracking system you proposed in (*a*).

    c. For spare parts, the DL component in the ARM product must be produced in excess of the amount required for ARM. Describe how this should be handled by the material tracking system and what effect it would have on the BOM you created for the ARM in part (*b*), above.

3. Below is the BOM for product X.

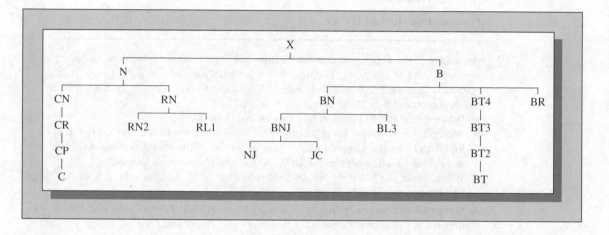

The plant is converting to cellular manufacturing, with stock areas in different cells linked with pull signals. The switch to cells will affect the following operations:

    · All operations to convert item C into items CN will be performed in machining cell 1.

    · All operations to convert item BT into BT4 will be done in machining cell 2.

    · The assembly operations that create parts BNJ and BN will all be done in assembly cell 3.

    · The assembly operations that create parts B, N, and final product X will all be done in assembly cell 4.

    a. Draw a flow diagram illustrating the movement of materials and evolution of the items in the BOM as they go through the cells.

    b. Draw a diagram illustrating the floor plan of the new cellular system. Show the location of the four cells, the operations in each cell (use intermediate levels on the BOM as surrogate operations), all places where inbound and outbound stocks of material are held, and places where materials are transferred from one cell to another. The cells should be arranged so as to minimize intercell distances for transferring material.

    c. Draw the new BOM to reflect the cellular/pull process.

    d. Suppose the original BOM structure is to be retained. Show where in the original BOM phantom bills should be placed to give the effect of a flattened BOM.

4. The July rate-based MPS and the demand for August are as follows:

Row	July	Aug.
1. Forecast	3700	4000
2. Backlog	16	20
3. Anticipated demand	3716	4020
4. Working days	21	20
5. x Production rate	177	?
6. Production	3717	?
7. On hand	0	4001
8. Available units	3717	?
9. Ending units	1	?

Determine the production rate for August and complete the MPS.

5. The December rate-based MPS and the demand for January are as follows:

Row	Dec.	Jan.
1. Forecast	15600	12400
2. Backlog	990	0
3. Anticipated demand	16590	12400
4. Working days	15	21
5. x Production rate	1026	?
6. Production	15390	?
7. On hand	1200	0
8. Available units	16590	?
9. Ending units	0	?

Determine the production rate for January and complete the MPS.

6. Suppose the demand forecast for February is 17,000 units and 860 units are on backorder.

a. Assuming 19 8-hour working days in February, what daily production rate is required?

b. What is the required CT of the process? Assume 480 min/day.

c. The bottleneck operation in the process is a manual assembly procedure that takes 2 minutes. How many workers should be assigned to that operation?

d. By what amount would the workday length have to be increased, starting on the sixth working day, then held the same for the remainder of the month, such that at month's end there would be no backorders? Company policy is to give shop workers 10 working days notice before increasing the length of the workday. Given the 10-day policy, can they implement this change?

e. Suppose that actual new customer commitments (excluding backorders) as of February 1 indicate for the month a daily demand of 850 units for the first 7 days, then 940 units for the next 7 days, then 1100 units for the remaining 5 days. To retain the existing process CT, by how much must the current 8-hour working day be increased to meet demand for the remainder of the month? Assume the same 10-day policy stated above, and that the change will not go into effect until the eleventh working day, but then will stay the same for the duration of the month. Assume no backorders remaining at the end of the month.

Endnotes

1. The most widely referenced material is T. Ohno, *Toyota Production System: Beyond Large-Scale Manufacturing* (Cambridge, MA: Productivity Press, 1988); and Y. Monden, *Toyota Production System: An Integrated Approach to Just-in-Time* (2nd ed.) (Norcross, GA: Industrial Engineering and Management Press, 1993). Many other authors have described in general terms a process for smoothing production schedules and for integrating schedules into a pull production system; it is clear, however, that the model they use is the Toyota process as described by Ohno and Monden.

2. The length of the planning horizon depends on the anticipated month-to-month demand variation. For products with relatively little demand variation, a 2-month horizon might be sufficient; for products with wide demand swings throughout the year, the horizon should be at least 6 months. This reflects the fact that the greater the anticipated changes, the longer it potentially takes the production system to adjust to them. But there is a paradox here: the farther into the future you look, the less reliable your forecast and, thus, the harder it is for you to plan. Hence, as you plan farther into the future, be cognizant of the fact that your plans will have to be revised, perhaps repeatedly, by the time they are executed. This is simply acknowledging the reality of forecasting and planning.

3. If a CONWIP system as described in Chapter 8 is used, the schedule is really an order list sent to the first stage of the process. Orders from the list are processed in sequence upon kanban authorization received from the last stage.

4. The number of days used by Toyota and Nissan is 10. The longer the time is between when customers place orders and when the orders are registered in the order entry system and the more erratic the anticipated customer demand is, the greater the number of days required in the planning period (say, 20 or 30 days instead of 10). However, the problem with increasing the number of days is that relatively fewer actual orders from later days will be included. Thus, in a 30-day order period, there might be few actual orders for the last 10 or 20 days of that period; so as not to underestimate production requirements for those days, it will be necessary to pad the orders with forecasts of anticipated orders.

5. Notice that this system presumes the presence of a large backorder. If a large backorder cannot be accumulated over a 10-day period, then (1) the number of days must be extended (as suggested in note 4, above) or (2) a make-to-stock philosophy must be adopted. Of course, the more you extend the number of days (option 1), the more of the planning horizon you must base on forecasts (again, note 4 above), hence, the more you will make-to-stock. Option 1 becomes option 2, de facto.

6. In fact, as described later, the material requirements estimate might be made in MRP fashion by the centralized system.

7. H. Steudel and P. Desruelle, *Manufacturing in the Nineties: How to Become a Lean, Mean, and World-Class Competitor* (New York: Van Nostrand Reinhold, 1992), p. 301. This book is a good reference on aspects of pull production, especially capacity planning and detailed cell planning, scheduling, and control; see pp. 261–311.

8. Besides JIT, the modules include materials management, sales order management, production management, production cost management, purchasing, accounts payable, accounts receivable, and general ledger.

9. For further discussion of postdeduct and other procedures for inventory accounting and replenishment, *see* W. Sandras, *Just-in-Time: Making It Happen* (Essex Junction, VT: Oliver Wight Publications, 1989), pp. 198–208.

10. Actually, updating may occur only at discrete times, such as when the MRP system software is run.

11. From S.D. Flapper, G.J. Miltenburg, and J. Winjgaard, "Embedding JIT into MRP," *International Journal of Production Research* 29, no. 2 (1991), pp. 329–41; R. Hall, *Zero Inventories* (Homewood, IL: Dow Jones-Irwin, 1983), pp. 271–84; W. Sandras, *Just-in-Time: Making It Happen*, pp. 195–212; B. Williams, *Competitive Manufacturing* (Reading MA: Addison-Wesley, 1996), pp. 282–4.

12. *See* W. Sandras, *Just-in-Time: Making It Happen,* pp. 198–200.

13. R. Hall, *Zero Inventories,* p. 275.

PART V BEYOND THE PRODUCTION SYSTEM

The production system is that part of a manufacturing organization that transforms raw materials, parts, and components into finished products. The subject of most of this book has been JIT/TQM within that system. We now turn to JIT/TQM issues that lie physically and conceptually beyond the production system.

As with any physical system or philosophy, success of a JIT/TQM production system depends upon the support and license the system gets from the other systems with which it interacts and from the larger suprasystem of which it is a part. Successful JIT/TQM manufacturing calls for new roles, attitudes, and practices in virtually all organizational functions, not just manufacturing. The interdependency between manufacturing and sales, marketing, and product engineering has already been discussed; Part V covers the important roles that purchasing and accounting play in JIT/TQM.

In JIT/TQM manufacturing, product design, development, and manufacture are viewed as a single process. Matters relating to speed, quality, and cost are addressed from the top down. Emphasis is on identifying and improving the process elements that add value and eliminating the others. That process perspective extends beyond the factory walls to include suppliers. An organization trying to succeed at JIT and TQM will have a difficult time unless it sees suppliers

as forward elements of its process and as partners in its bid to gain competitive market advantage. Because suppliers are viewed as elements of the greater process, concepts like customer–supplier partnerships, and supply–chain management are especially important in JIT/TQM.

Accounting, too, has a role in JIT/TQM. Methods of cost accounting are used to accumulate cost figures that drive decisions about what to produce and how to produce; these decisions obviously impact manufacturing. JIT/TQM drives decisions about the same things, but unless the method of cost accounting incorporates measures of waste reduction and process improvement, only the costs of JIT/TQM will be noted; the benefits will be ignored. Traditional cost-accounting methods give no respect to JIT/TQM, and they frequently lead to product decisions that are detrimental to manufacturing performance. Fortunately for modern manufacturers, new cost-accounting methods under the moniker activity-based costing are coming into popular usage.

Manufacturers competing in the global economy are familiar with the concept of **world-class manufacturing.** A company wanting to achieve world-class status must adopt a world-class worldview, a philosophy that, if not identical to, at least substantially overlaps with JIT/TQM philosophy. For that worldview to take root and grow, the organization must also adopt and utilize performance measures that reinforce behavior consistent with JIT/TQM philosophy.

A manufacturer striving for competitive advantage must publicly state its goals to customers, suppliers, and employees, adopt criteria that represent those goals, and install procedures to monitor the criteria and report progress. Criteria that are consistent with the world-class worldview and with JIT/TQM philosophy are called enlightened measures. The system for monitoring and reporting on these measures goes beyond traditional tracking and reporting systems and provides decision-making information to every organizational level. Enlightened measures are visible indicators of concepts and techniques described throughout this book. A quick pass through them thus serves as a review of the topics of this book and of everything important in JIT/TQM.

The chapters in Part V are as follows:

I am he as you are he as you are me, and we are all together.   *The Beatles*

All organizations rely on suppliers for inputs, and an estimated 60–70% of the final cost of manufactured items is from purchased materials, components, and services.[1] Manufacturers depend on a network of suppliers not only for materials, but also for tools and machines, spare parts, and services that keep the machines and processes functioning.

The performance of the overall customer–supplier network, called the **supply chain,** affects the competitive advantage of every company. Each company is constrained by the other companies, even when it comes to improvement efforts. Potential cost and lead-time savings and quality improvements at a company can be easily outweighed by the cost, lead time, and defect increases of its suppliers and distributors.

JIT/TQM acknowledges the importance of the supply chain to competitive advantage. The philosophies of both JIT and TQM stipulate that improvement efforts must not be confined to a company, but must be extended to its suppliers and distributors. Extending improvement beyond a company requires that managers take a new look at the costs and tradeoffs of working with suppliers, and that customer and supplier companies adopt new ways of working together.

This chapter covers a range of topics related to supply-chain management: new customer–supplier relationships, the changing role of the purchasing function, and application of JIT concepts throughout the supply chain. The chapter ventures into the territory of **logistics management,** which is managing the movement of materials from suppliers to customers and at distribution points between them. Logistics management is undergoing a revolution of sorts, partly because of the growing numbers of customers that are becoming JIT/TQM companies, and, consequently, the growing quality and service requirements being imposed on suppliers and third-party carriers.

RELYING ON SUPPLIERS

There is an upside and a downside to relying on suppliers for parts, products, and services. While, potentially, a manufacturer has something to gain by outsourcing production of parts and components to suppliers, it also has something to lose.

DOWNSIDE

Purchased materials are a major source of variability in the cost, quality, and delivery of finished products. They account for 50% of the quality problems in manufactured items and as much as 75% of warranty claims.[2] Defective materials increase manufacturing costs, and cause production delays and late deliveries. Defective incoming materials must be weeded out and sent back, and processes that need those materials are interrupted. Quality-caused problems are exacerbated in pull production where there is no stock to protect against shortages.

To account for any one supplier's inability to meet requirements, firms rely on several suppliers for each material, part, or service needed. If one supplier is unable to meet time, quality, quantity, or cost requirements, they go to another. But relying on multiple suppliers is problematic too: multiple suppliers are a burden to manage, and rather than increase quality and reduce delivery variability, multiple suppliers can actually worsen it. For example, since it is usually impractical and costly to segregate parts by supplier, it is hard to determine which supplier produced defective materials or parts. By the time the supplier is identified, it is often too late to determine the cause of defects.

In the past, companies often felt that the best way to control quality and delivery variability was to vertically integrate, that is, to make parts and components themselves and eliminate reliance on suppliers. An extreme case was Ford Motor Company and its monstrous River Rouge plant. In the 1950s, it was producing virtually 100% of a car's parts, even the steel and glass for those parts.

Sometimes vertical integration is a solution, though rarely the complete solution, particularly when the quantity and variety of the required kinds of materials and parts are great. Few companies are able to muster the level of expertise and control necessary to effectively produce *every* kind of part they need. As a company increases the breadth of things it produces, it diminishes its ability to produce all of them well.

UPSIDE

The fact is, smaller, specialized companies can often produce parts and components better and cheaper than huge, vertically integrated corporations. A manufacturer that needs a large variety of different parts (cars being the extreme) can often do better by *not* making the parts and instead relying on suppliers. Relying on suppliers, or **out-sourcing,** for parts and services offers a variety of benefits.[3]

Cost

To produce every kind of item requires significant investment in facilities and expertise. A specialized supplier of an item already has the resources, and usually it is already doing research and development to improve the item and the way it is produced. Because a supplier often has several customers for a given item, it can attain economies in production scale beyond what any one customer could achieve by producing just for itself.

Flexibility

Every time a company changes its product mix, it must redeploy, increase, or divest internal production resources, and that takes more time and effort than simply changing requirements for suppliers. Similarly, whenever demand changes, resources for internally made parts must be reshuffled and rescheduled, which is more difficult than simply ordering more or fewer parts from suppliers.

Quality

The greater the number of different parts and components that a manufacturer makes, the more thinly spread are its resources for improving each of the parts, especially when the parts require different technologies. The manufacturer has limited time and resources available to devote to improving every item it produces. Conversely, a supplier that specializes in a few items can proportionately devote more resources to improving each of them. Suppliers also have expertise about the materials and processes for making the best product.

Expertise

Through experience, a supplier understands a particular product or process much better than its customers. Specialized expertise takes years of focused attention to develop. Whereas the customer must develop the expertise from scratch, that expertise is available immediately from the supplier. Being specialized includes keeping abreast of new technology; by using a specialized supplier, the customer can take immediate advantage of that technology.

Core Competency

Core competency refers to a company's *raison d'être*. Usually it is what a company's customers most recognize about it. For example, automobile makers are recognized for just that—making automobiles. Making automobiles, however, is not the same as making the thousands of parts that go into them. An automaker must have strong core competency in areas closely related to making autos, including design and assembly of the overall auto, and design and manufacture of major systems such as engine/fuel, suspension, electrical, frame, and body. Much less important, however, is that it have competency to design and produce the numerous parts and components that go into those systems. Such things are better left to suppliers with core competencies in those things. By entrusting the design and production of parts and components to suppliers, a company is able to take advantage of suppliers's competencies and be free to concentrate its own resources on further developing critical skills and capabilities for its own areas of competency.

Many companies are now going through a "deintegration" or outsourcing phase and are sending greater portions of the value-added work in their products to suppliers. The US Big-Three automakers have been working hard at this. Though GM still produces around 70% of its own parts, Ford is down to about 50%, and Chrysler to only 30%.[4]

Underlying all the above benefits is the matter of focus. Just as manufacturers do a better job of producing product families by using focused factories, they usually get better parts by procuring them from suppliers that are themselves focused. A predominant issue, then, in choosing between what to make and what to buy (the make–buy decision), is determining on what the company should focus (its core competency).

Not understanding the concept of core competency can be damaging, especially when a company mistakenly outsources its *own* core competency. At one time US manufacturers of TVs outsourced only minor parts and components, then major components like picture tubes and receivers, then finally the entire TV. With time the suppliers were able to also take over product development, marketing, and distribution, and effectively put the companies they had once supplied out of business. In effect, when a company outsources its core competency, it risks outsourcing its future. A manufacturer should thus restrict outsourcing to things not directly tied to its core competency.

But outsourcing alone is not necessarily the way to better, faster, and cheaper products. There is still the potential downside of outsourcing—those problems with quality and delivery variability that keep product costs up and quality and service levels down. To eliminate the downside and maximize the upside, management must begin by taking a new look at the way customers and suppliers relate to each other. Part of this new way is the supply-chain management concept.

SUPPLY-CHAIN MANAGEMENT

THE PHYSICAL SUPPLY CHAIN

The **supply chain** is a multitiered system of suppliers through which information and materials flow, ultimately reaching the final manufacturing customer (illustrated in Figure 19.1). Suppliers that provide materials and information directly to the final manufacturing customer are called first-tier suppliers. Each first-tier supplier is itself a customer supplied by companies from the next lower tier. Timely, right-quantity and high-quality deliveries to customers at every tier depend on the performance of suppliers at the tiers below them. Consequently, the only way a company anywhere in the chain can meet its schedule, quality, and quantity requirements is for suppliers at every lower tier to meet their requirements also. (The concept is analogous to the MRP process for determining parts requirements at every level of the BOM such that the requirements of the end-item can be met.) Such is the thrust of **supply-chain management:** coordinating the activities of suppliers to meet the requirements of customers above them in the supply chain.

FIGURE 19.1

The supply chain.

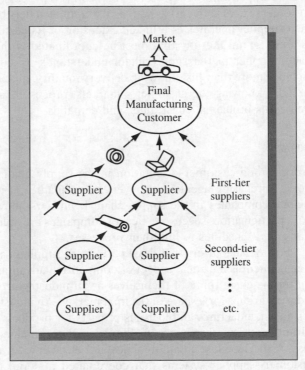

MANAGEMENT PHILOSOPHY

The supply-chain management philosophy is as follows:[5]

- The entire supply chain is a single, integrated entity.
- The cost, quality, and delivery requirements of the manufacturing customer are objectives shared by every company in the chain.
- Inventory is the last resort for resolving supply-and-demand imbalances between the tiers.

The philosophy is supported by three fundamental features of supply-chain management: process orientation, customer orientation, and teamwork.

Process Orientation

Inside a factory, production methods such as cellular manufacturing and pull production leverage the fact that it is linked processes, not isolated functions, that create value in products and services. Supply-chain management moves this concept beyond the factory to processes in companies at the next lower tier, then on down to the lowest tier in the supply chain.

Customer Orientation

Every company knows its location in the linked process, and that includes knowing its customers (tiers above it) as well as its suppliers (tiers below it). Since, conceptually, each supplier operates as a linked extension of its customer's processes, it is treated as an **external factory** that must be coordinated with the factory of the customer. Each supplier in the supply chain understands its customers. This understanding includes more than just knowing delivery, quality, quantity, and cost requirements; it includes knowing the customer's markets, processes, and organizational culture as well as its problems, constraints, and demands.

Teamwork

Process- and customer-orientation in the supply chain are achieved through teamwork. Purchasing agents and buyers in companies at one tier belong to teams that include companies in the supply chain from tiers above and below them. Through team participation, successive tiers of companies are able to develop compatible goals, plans, and schedules to link their processes.

For manufacturers that draw parts from suppliers at multiple tiers, supply-chain management is a critical aspect of competitive advantage. Knowing this, companies within the chain think of themselves as an industry group that competes with other industry groups for a share of the final market. An industry group that coordinates the design, manufacture, and logistics of parts for products in the final market has a big advantage over industry groups that are not coordinated. The early competitive success of the Japanese in automobiles and electronics was largely influenced by tight customer–supplier systems that coordinated material design and manufacture and controlled financing. In the Japanese system, called *Keiretsu,* big customers exercise considerable control over their suppliers, but they are also sensitive to their suppliers's needs and provide for them. Many of the principles of supply-chain management practiced in the West are based on the customer–supplier working relationships observed in Japan.

NEW CUSTOMER–SUPPLIER RELATIONSHIPS

JIT/TQM philosophy recognizes that to acquire the best purchased items, it is often necessary to work *with* suppliers to make them the best. Working with suppliers means many things, but it especially means joint problem solving, practicing quality-at-the-source, and exchanging information.[6]

JOINT PROBLEM SOLVING

Joint problem solving takes many forms. Suppliers and customers participate in product design and concurrent engineering, setup reduction and total preventive maintenance, and implementation of cellular manufacturing and pull systems. Companies solicit from suppliers comments and suggestions about the final product and sometimes give them considerable leeway in parts design by providing only functional requirements, then entrusting them with the entire detailed design and manufacture of the part (for example, the requirements might only specify the dimensions of the part and that it shouldn't warp or discolor after repeated use). To reciprocate, the customer works with the supplier to help the supplier resolve cost or quality problems and find better ways to meet the requirements.

QUALITY-AT-THE-SOURCE

Quality-at-the-source begins with quality-at-the-supplier. When suppliers guarantee 100% quality, the customer can eliminate inspection of arriving materials. Incoming materials can be moved directly to points of use, and buffer inventory to cover defects can be minimized. High quality requires high process capability, and the customer helps its supplier achieve high capability by sharing its own experience and expertise (assuming it has already achieved its own high capability). As described later, companies continue to work with only the few suppliers who are able to continuously meet tough requirements.

INFORMATION SHARING

Companies and their suppliers mutually exchange information about long-range plans, production schedules, design changes, and problems. A company gives its suppliers advance notice about changes in product mix and product demand so the suppliers have time to adjust. Suppliers give advance notice about quality or delivery problems so the customers can help them find solutions and develop contingencies.

For companies and their suppliers to embrace these practices requires nothing short of a fundamental change in the way they customarily relate to each other. It requires moving from an adversarial-type relationship to a more trusting, partnership-type relationship.

OUT WITH THE OLD, IN WITH THE NEW

The traditional customer–supplier relationship is *not* one of loyalty and trust. In fact, the traditional single most important criterion for choosing a supplier is price. To get the best price, companies play suppliers against each other. Additionally, to keep prices low, multiple suppliers are used for each kind of procured part. If a supplier cannot meet delivery, quality, or price requirements, the customer company merely switches to a different supplier.

Although this approach does keep parts prices down, it serves to increase the costs of inventory, purchasing, and inspection, and results in frequent shifting between suppliers. Suppliers who are squeezed for the lowest price feel no obligation to provide anything beyond the absolute minimum quality, delivery, or service, and certainly no obligation to *improve* the quality and delivery of existing parts and services. Stunted improvement of parts will eventually stunt the improvement potential of the final product.

During the 1970s and 1980s, entire US and European industries accustomed to this manner of customer–supplier dealings began to experience declining market share in competition against industry groups from Asia where relationships are much different. In Asian industry groups it is customary for companies throughout the entire supply chain to work together as partners for the greater good of the whole. Differences between this **partnership** form of relationship and the traditional, adversarial relationship, listed in Figure 19.2, are discussed in the following sections.

FIGURE 19.2

Customer–supplier relationships.

	TRADITIONAL	PARTNERSHIP
Purchase Criteria	Lowest bid	Competency, ability, capacity, and willingness to work with customer to improve price, quality, and delivery.
Design Source	Customer	Customer and supplier
Number of Suppliers	Several for each item	One or a few for each item or commodity group
Customer Business Volume per Supplier	Limited: multiple suppliers share business	High: one or few suppliers get all of the business
Type of Agreement	Purchase order; contracts to meet immediate requirements	Contract plus agreement about working relationship
Terms of Agreement: **Duration**	Short-term, or as needed by customer	Long-term, multiple years
Price/Cost	Lowest bid, inefficiencies, and waste keep prices/costs high	Negotiated price/cost savings from supplier improvements shared with customer
Quality	Variable; customer relies on incoming inspection	High; quality at the source; supplier uses SPC, TQM, etc.
Shipping: Frequency/ Size/Location	Infrequent/large/dock or stockroom	Frequent/small/point-of-use
Order Mechanism	Mail or phone	FAX, phone, EDI, or kanban
Customer–Supplier Interaction	Formal information exchange, limited to customer requirements; no teamwork; supplier service limited to minimal requirements	Frequent formal and informal exchange of plans, schedules, problems, ideas; teamwork and mutual commitment based on trust; cooperation to resolve problems and improve supplier's products and processes

Purchase Criteria

In a partnership price matters, but other criteria matter too, sometimes more than price. Even when a supplier does not have the lowest price, it can be selected if it meets other criteria that will reduce the customer's *overall* costs. These criteria include, for example, competency and expertise, production capacity and flexibility, ability to fulfill quality and delivery requirements, and willful acceptance of the need to improve and, sometimes, to adopt JIT/TQM programs and techniques.

Design Source

A major aspect of continuous product improvement is improvement of product components and parts. The traditional relationship stunts such improvement; for example, because parts are designed by the customer, the supplier merely has to produce them to spec. It does not matter whether the design is poor and the parts are difficult to produce or whether the supplier has ideas about ways to, say, reduce the cost or complexity of the parts or increase their durability, reliability, or appearance. In the traditional relationship, the customer is not interested in the supplier's ideas.

In a partnership, the supplier is recognized for competency in design as well as manufacture. The customer develops the requirements and specifications (specs), then expects the supplier to do all or much of the design for the part. Suppliers are included in concurrent engineering to capture their ideas during early product development. A case in point is the Ford Taurus, where the major body components, lights, carpeting, and plastic parts are designed by suppliers. Many of the designs are quite innovative, with attention to detail never seen before on Ford cars. Ford selects suppliers as much for their advice as for their ability to make high-quality parts. One carpet supplier pointed out that Ford was using five different colors of carpet in the trunk, although color did not matter to most customers and 7% on carpet cost could be saved by using one color.[7] Chrysler sought the advice of suppliers even in the design of its new corporate headquarters.

Number of Suppliers and Customer Business Volume

Traditional purchasing practice is to use multiple sources for every kind of part needed. The practice stems largely from distrust and inability of any one supplier to provide parts in the specified time, quality, and quantity; as mentioned, it also keeps prices low through supplier competition.

Multisourcing, however, prevents any one supplier from getting the lion's share of customer business, which prevents it from realizing savings in economies of scale, some of which might be passed to the customer. Further, it inspires low supplier confidence about long-run, sustained business with the customer, which discourages the supplier from doing anything to improve equipment, processes, or technology that might benefit the customer. In addition, suppliers to companies using multiple sources tend to provide parts that can serve the needs of all of them, rather than specialized parts that would serve particular needs better. Although the parts are suitable for a broad range of customers, they are not as good as if the supplier had focused on the needs of just one customer.

Another problem with multisourcing is that it increases the overall variability in quality. As Figure 19.3 shows, even when the variability in quality of parts from each supplier is small (dashed lines), variability of the parts from all suppliers (heavy line) can be large. This concept also applies to variability of other things such as delivery schedules, delivery quantities, and supplier responsiveness.

Further, as mentioned earlier, when a customer discovers a nonconforming or defective part it is difficult to pinpoint from which supplier the part came. Finally, the greater the number of suppliers, the harder it is to improve quality of conformance. A company with many suppliers for a part becomes preoccupied with the part's conformance to spec. As discussed in Chapter 14, however, simple conformance to spec is often not enough; the emphasis should be on reducing process variability and tightening specs. When it is already difficult to enforce conformance to specs, improvement within specs will be unlikely.

In a partnership the number of suppliers is reduced until only the best few remain; the goal, ultimately, is to reduce the number to a single or **sole source,** the one supplier recognized as being most capable of supplying a particular part. To guard against interruptions in deliveries, two or more suppliers with similar capabilities can be retained. Each of these is considered as a **single source** in that, under normal conditions, one supplier provides, say, parts A, B, and C and the other provides parts D, E, and F; both, however, have similar capability, in which case business can be shifted entirely to one supplier if the other has an emergency. Honda in France does this by ordinarily using one supplier for right tail lights and another for left tail lights.[8] Companies that make the same products at multiple plants also use single sourcing wherein each plant has but one supplier for a part, but the supplier is different for every plant.

FIGURE 19.3

Variability from multiple suppliers.

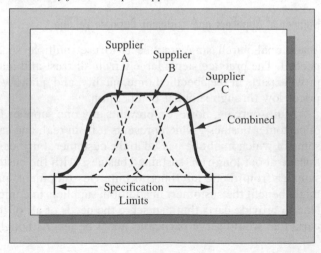

Since it is likely that workers in the plant of one supplier are in the same union as workers in the plant of the two or three alternate suppliers, a strike will shut down all of them. When a strike is imminent, there is still the old standby: build inventory.

Sometimes multisourcing is necessary because there is no single reliable supplier. The goal then is similar to inventory reduction: start with what you have, and keep trying to reduce it.

Both customers and suppliers benefit from single-supplier relationships. The supplier gets *all* of the customer's business, and that is an incentive for the supplier to work harder to retain that business. If the agreement is a long-term contract, the supplier has the incentive to invest in technology and processes to make parts so good as to virtually guarantee contract renewal.

A customer that gives all its business to one supplier can require more of the supplier in terms of product quality and service. Of course, the supplier, once having established a reputation for quality and service, can then demand more in terms of the customer's sharing of information about proposed changes in design, requirements, or business volume. But few of the demands are absolute; instead, the parties work together to accommodate each other. A supplier that takes advantage of its power as a sole supplier by trying to increase prices to increase profits is not a partner, and when the customer realizes this it will seek another supplier and terminate the relationship.

Type of Agreement

Traditional purchase agreements are short-term, apply only to a single order, and are limited to definition of price, specs, quantity, and delivery date. For each purchase, a list of suppliers is reviewed, one is chosen, and the order is sent. To keep suppliers on the list on their toes, orders are rotated among them. The practice is continued even with **blanket purchase orders,** which arc agreements that cover purchases for an extended period of time, by holding similar agreements simultaneously with multiple suppliers.

One way that partnership agreements differ from traditional contracts is that the customer and the supplier mutually agree on aspects of the relationship. The agreement is separate from a procurement contract for a particular commodity. It lays down ground rules the parties must follow, mutual expectations, considerations, and duties as part of the relationship. The agreement can be far-reaching in scope; for example, it might state that the supplier agrees to continuously improve its quality, service, and productivity and reduce inventories and delays. The overall expected long-term quantity to be procured might be indicated, though the exact amount is usually unspecified pending market demand. Expectations regarding price, quality, and delivery are also covered, though broadly since the emphasis of the agreement is on working relationships, not conditions for particular orders.

Terms of Agreement

The major differences between partnership agreements and traditional contracts are in the time-period covered and expectations about product pricing, quality, deliveries, and order placing.

Duration.   Partnership agreements are long-term. Unlike procurement for a one-time order, a partnership agreement extends for at least 1 year. One year is actually too short because it is not enough time for parties to develop the relationship and bend to accommodate each other's needs. Agreements of 3–5 years are becoming common.

Price/Cost.   Prices are negotiated. Savings achieved in the supplier's operations are shared with the customer. A proposed price increase by the supplier is not accepted without explanation. Schonberger[9] mentions the case about a Polaroid supplier that asked for a price increase to cover higher-cost materials. Polaroid buyers went to the supplier's plant and were able to find ways to reduce the supplier's process cost to offset the higher material cost.

Quality.   Partnerships practice quality-at-the-source. The supplier guarantees 100% quality, which obviates the need for incoming inspection by the customer. The customer assists the supplier in the pursuit of quality and improvement: it sends its own quality experts to develop, certify, and coach the supplier in quality methods, it furnishes training (PDCA and SPC, for example), and it provides technology (pokayoke devices, automatic inspection and control equipment). Motorola's suppliers participate in a series of Motorola-run courses on topics such as basic problem solving, DFMA, JIT, and Motorola's own Six Sigma and Total Customer Satisfaction programs for TQM.

Shipping.   Although the traditional practice of shipping infrequently and in batches to fill a truck keeps unit shipping costs to a minimum, it results in higher inventory holding costs for the customer. In a partnership, the supplier makes frequent, small shipments to conform to the customer's immediate needs. In theory, a pull production plant should be supplied on-demand with small shipments from suppliers as an extension of the pull process.

To reduce material-handling time and cost, customers redesign their receiving areas with multiple docks so incoming material can be quickly moved to the points of use. In many cases, supplier drivers are authorized to unload their shipments onto carts and move them to the points of use.

Even for a nonpull production customer, frequent deliveries in small quantities are good because they reduce variability in delivery times, incoming inventory, and the need to carry safety stock. For example, the variability in shipping time for a supplier that promises two deliveries, one between 10 AM and 12 noon and another between 3 PM and 5 PM, will be much less than the variability for a supplier that promises one shipment between 10 AM and 5 PM. Hewlett-Packard stipulates that suppliers should meet a daily delivery window; if they miss the window more than three times a year, they risk losing the contract.

So that small, frequent deliveries will be economical, the supplier is expected to adjust aspects of its operations, such as to use smaller vehicles, locate a plant closer to the customer, or schedule deliveries along multisupplier/multicustomer routes (milk runs). These concepts are discussed later.

Ordering and Vendor-Managed Inventory.   Much of the ordering for materials is performed by the people who actually use, transport, or produce the materials. Sometimes assigned team members on the factory floor place orders via fax and phone directly from workcenters and workcells. Often, however, the supplier is expected to keep track of the customer's on-hand quantity and to determine the amount to ship on each delivery. This concept of the supplier being responsible for managing customer inventory is called, appropriately, **vendor-managed inventory.** Empty Kanban containers are one mechanism for order placing: when the driver arrives with a shipment, he checks for empty containers, which he is authorized to replenish on the next delivery. At a higher level, called **electronic data interchange (EDI),** supplier and customer computers are electronically linked to enable direct ordering, billing, and even funds transfer for payment between them. The supplier can determine at any time the customer's most recent sales and demand projections and know exactly how much to deliver.

Customer–Supplier Interaction

The partnership fosters interaction between people at all levels of the customer and supplier organizations. Supervisors, shop workers and managers in the customer plant are encouraged to meet their counterparts in the supplier plant. The concept of people dealing with people is exploited to diminish the mindset of one company dealing with another company. When customer and supplier organizations see each other's company in terms of the people who work there, they become more sensitive and responsive to each other's ideas, needs, and constraints. A delivery driver who makes daily trips to the point of use in a plant becomes a potential source for suggestions about ways the supplier might improve its service or ways the customer might take better advantage of that service.

Likewise, when shop-floor workers from the customer company meet their counterparts at the supplier company each group develops an understanding about the other group's needs, which helps them determine ways to better produce and use the parts.

Sometimes a supplier will devote a focused factory entirely to one customer, and workers and managers therein deal exclusively with workers and managers in the section of the customer plant that they supply. The supplier's process is a direct extension of the customer's process, and the people in the two processes work together directly to coordinate schedules and deliveries. When the customer business is large enough in terms of shipments, volume, and commitment, the supplier might locate a small plant near the customer. This is a common practice for high-volume suppliers in the automobile and aerospace industries. The ultimate relationship is when the supplier locates *inside* the customer plant and produces components or subassemblies for immediate use. Such a concept is now underway on a large scale in a Volkswagen truckmaking plant in Brazil.

The following case illustrates some of the above points.

CASE IN POINT: Supplier Partnerships at Xerox[10]

In 1991, Xerox's North American operation began an initiative with suppliers of sheet-metal parts that was focused on improving parts quality and delivery performance and reducing parts costs through better utilization of supplier assets. Sheet-metal parts represent about 6000 part numbers and an annual cost of $100 million. The cost of a part depends heavily on the overhead burden allocated to it, and in many cases overhead is 40–60% of the total cost. One of the Xerox's goals was to increase its suppliers's business so overhead costs could be spread over a higher volume and unit costs could be reduced. Higher volume would come from increased business from both Xerox and other customers. Xerox prefers that its share of a supplier's business not exceed 50% and, ideally, be in the 30–40% range.

Xerox had 40 sheet-metal suppliers. As a first step, it formed a team with the task of cutting that number to 10. To decide which 10, the team obtained data from all the suppliers on labor and overhead costs, parts quality, management attitude, delivery performance, and technical capability. It rank-ordered the suppliers, then met with the top 10 to discuss their willingness to participate in a partnership program. As part of the program, Xerox would increase its business to the suppliers, but the suppliers would be responsible for increasing their *non-Xerox* business, both to reduce dependency on Xerox and to increase the volume over which to spread overhead costs. Two of the suppliers declined, so Xerox invited suppliers 11 and 12, both which accepted. The remaining 30 firms were phased out as older Xerox products that used their parts were dropped.

Another feature of the program is that Xerox provide suppliers with improvement tools ranging from simple check sheets to PC activity-based costing software. It runs seminars for the suppliers on topics ranging from leadership to benchmarking and routinely visits the supplier plants. Xerox also sets performance goals for the suppliers; the following goals are typical:

- Guarantee fewer than 300 ppm (defective parts per million).
- Reduce average annual price by 5%.
- Deliver newly ordered products within 7 weeks.
- Meet JIT delivery schedules.
- Participate in continuous improvement programs.
- Use standardized containers for materials shipped.

Each year Xerox evaluates supplier performance against best practices and adjusts the goals to meet the best-practice levels of its competitors in the marketplace.

IT DOESN'T COME EASY

Some manufacturing executives think that establishing partnerships is the hardest part of JIT/TQM. Although some suppliers readily embrace the idea and some actually start out far ahead of the customer in terms of understanding its merits, others reject it out of distrust and resistance to outsiders meddling with their business. As Robert Hall says,

The relationship between the companies must be built with people-to-people bridges at several points—line management, engineering, quality organization, and it is a long developmental journey to this state of thinking if companies are just emerging from order-at-time haggling and expediting.[11]

Richard Dauch, former Executive VP of Manufacturing for Chrysler said that his own experience in forming new supplier relationships was not all milk and honey:[12]

> There was strong resistance . . . We instituted a system of chargebacks for vendor failures to reinforce our recommendations, proposals, requests, and requirements. We did meticulous cost studies to calculate the total expense to Chrysler when a vendor failed to perform [and contributed to such things as] line stoppages, handling, . . . inventory holding costs, record keeping, sorting, reworking, unpacking, repacking . . . We grabbed the supplier's attention by subtracting these costs from submitted invoices. Once we had their attention, we got action!

Given the long tradition of adversity between customers and suppliers, it is not surprising that many companies need convincing about the value of partnerships. One party cannot force another into a partnership—although, as Dauch implies, big companies can exert pressure on their suppliers. But they have always been able to do that. The difference to a supplier in a partnership is that, although they still get pressured, they end up with a bigger share of the customer's business.

Suppliers must be willing to develop methods and procedures to meet customer requirements, and the customer must be willing to assist suppliers and bend requirements occasionally until the suppliers can meet them. As Hall states, "The bottom line to [a partnership is] an appreciation that suppliers and their manufacturing customer are not really in competition with each other. The real competition is for the customer who uses the end-item produced."[13]

SMALL-CUSTOMER/BIG-SUPPLIER PARTNERSHIP[14]

Not every manufacturer is a Toyota or Chrysler and has suppliers lining up to form partnerships. Small companies with relatively little market power are likely to hear suppliers say, "This is what we do. Take it or leave it." Placed in that situation, how does a company motivate a supplier to team up with it and make frequent, small deliveries of reasonably priced, defectfree items?

Part of the answer, it appears, is to use multiple sources, which is contrary to recommended partnership practice. In a survey of 70 small manufacturers that use JIT philosophy, 77% had no intention of reducing the number of suppliers in the next 3 years.[15] Being small customers, they felt, competitive bidding is still the best way for them to achieve good quality, delivery and price. These companies feared that single sourcing and high dependency on one supplier would reduce their power in negotiating with each supplier.

There are, however, two strategies that small companies can use to increase the chances that their big-company suppliers will meet JIT/TQM requirements. First, they can use suppliers that advocate and practice JIT/TQM or are industry or ISO-9000 certified. A supplier that is itself practicing JIT will be more sensitive and responsive to a customer that is trying to do the same. Even if a company does not practice JIT, if it is ISO-9000 or industry certified, it is more likely to be capable of meeting a customer's quality requirements than one that is not. Of course, ISO certification is no guarantee, and every company must be evaluated individually. A big supplier that is certified might be unwilling to enter into a full-scale partnership with a small customer, though it might agree to a limited partnership. The second strategy is for the small company to maintain long-standing relationships with all of its suppliers. Many big companies sustain themselves by serving a multitude of small customers, and they value customers that give them regular business, even though the business is small. A long-standing relationship allows the customer more opportunity to learn about the supplier's strengths and weaknesses, to get to know the supplier's representatives, and, through the representatives, to coax the supplier a little to adopt ways that improve its responsiveness to the customer's needs.

SUPPLIER SELECTION

Suppliers are selected based upon two broad measures: product design and manufacturing process. The supplier provides the customer with a design, model, or prototype of the item it proposes to make, and the customer tests this design to determine if it meets requirements. For the supplier to be selected, however, passing design tests is usually not enough since the design or prototype alone says nothing about the supplier's capability to produce the product. As a result, the supplier selection process usually puts heavy weight on the supplier's process capability. Since it is easier to improve a product design than to revamp a company's manufacturing process or service philosophy, a supplier with an inferior design but a superior process will be selected over a supplier with a better product design but a poorer process.

CERTIFICATION

The procedure for assessing a supplier's capability to meet criteria of delivery, quality, cost, and flexibility is called **certification.** The emphasis in certification is on processes and existing or proposed programs for continuous improvement, variation and waste reduction, and implementation of JIT/TQM methodology. Ford designates suppliers as Q1 to indicate they are certified. A supplier that has been certified is put on the company's short list of suppliers. Buyers and managers using the list have the assurance that suppliers will provide incoming parts that do not need inspection and service that meet minimal standards.

Certification by Customer[16]

A customer team comprising members from purchasing, manufacturing, engineering, and accounting decides certification status. The team reviews a supplier's past performance on the same or similar products using information from buyer's organizations, industry and trade groups, and consumer groups. It also surveys the supplier's technological and process competency, and managerial and financial strengths and weaknesses using, at one extreme, a simple questionnaire, or, at the other, a team visit to the supplier's site.

As an example, a producer of medical devices used the following questions on a survey sent to potential suppliers:[17]

· Have you received the product requirements and do you agree that they can be fully met?
· Are your final inspection results documented?
· Do you agree to provide the purchaser advance notice about production problems, schedule changes, or product design changes?
· Describe the air-filtration system you use.
· What protective garments do your employees wear to reduce contamination?

The most comprehensive form of survey is when the team visits the supplier's plant, observes processes and procedures, reviews documentation, and interviews workers and managers. Depending on the product and industry, the team might look at the following specifics:[18]

· *Management:* philosophy; organizational structure; commitment to TQM, continuous improvement, and JIT.
· *Product design:* design organization; design systems used; merit of specs; use of modern techniques and change control methods; developmental and testing laboratories.
· *Manufacturing:* physical facilities; preventive maintenance/machine availability; special processes; process capability and flexibility; production capacity; lot identification and traceability; systems for production planning and scheduling; setup times; transfer distances; lead time and inventory reduction techniques; shop-floor control; and employee skills and attitudes.
· *Quality assurance:* organizational structure; quality assurance personnel; quality planning; methods of quality analysis and corrective action; disposition of nonconforming items; training, motivation, and involvement of workers; control over subcontractors and suppliers.
· *Data management:* facilities, procedures, effective usage of reports.
· *Performance results:* performance levels attained, prestigious customers, prestigious suppliers and subcontractors; reputation among existing customers.

The on-site survey should be comprehensive enough to enable a conclusion about the supplier's competency to meet *product* requirements. Surveys that focus exclusively on organizational structure, documentation, and procedures are inadequate.

Upon completion of the survey, the team reports to a management group its findings about the supplier's strengths and weaknesses, effectiveness and need for assistance, and whether or not the supplier should be certified.

Certification by Industry Standard or Award

Assessment for certification can be time-consuming and burdensome to a supplier, especially to one that is being surveyed by multiple customers using multiple assessment criteria. A supplier trying to comply with a dozen customer surveys can get bogged down as can the customer who is surveying a dozen suppliers (administering all those surveys is red tape and enormous waste). An alternative is for the customer to rely on industry certification standards such as ISO 9000.

With standardized criteria, the assessment is performed by a third party, not a customer, and all suppliers meeting the assessment criteria appear on a published list. Rather than assessing and certifying each supplier, a company accepts the assessment criteria of the ISO registrars, Malcolm Baldrige National Quality Award examiners, etc., and chooses suppliers only from those that have been certified or received an award. The benefits of standardized quality criteria such as ISO is that suppliers are not subject to multiple assessments based on different, sometimes conflicting criteria, and customers do not have to devote as much time scrutinizing each supplier.

EVALUATION

Companies periodically evaluate their suppliers and provide them with feedback about performance, problems, opportunities, and areas needing improvement. The evaluations are done quarterly, monthly, or sooner if the supplier has problems. The evaluations rate a supplier with respect to minimal customer requirements or against other suppliers. Evaluations that use quantitative ratings are the best because they specify customer expectations in ways that are easily communicated and measurable. Following is an example.

Example   1:   Supplier Evaluation Scheme

A supplier is assessed for three criteria: quality, delivery, and service. The maximum rating for quality is 100 and points are subtracted when a supplier fails to meet minimal requirements. Fifty points each are assigned for on-time delivery and service, with points taken off for deviations from requirements. Thus, there are 200 total possible points for rating the supplier.

If the total drops below, say, 160, the supplier must allow the customer to perform an on-site evaluation audit. If the supplier plant is far away or overseas, the audit is contracted out to a consultant.

Periodic evaluation provides a performance record that clearly shows upward or downward trends. Performance that is mediocre and not improving (say 130 on the scale in the example) is justification to terminate the relationship. Such decertification implies that the supplier is discontinued as a source until it makes certain improvements.

Suppliers that score well on supplier evaluations are sometimes given special recognition and awards. Top-rated suppliers are awarded trophies, and their managers and workers are given parties or luncheons. Some corporations take out full-page advertisements in newspapers acknowledging their best suppliers.

Suppliers rated as superior (through evaluation by prominent customers or in third-party reviews) do not have to wait for new customers to come around. Being certified has marketable value, and certified suppliers seeking more business often solicit potential customers by advertising the areas in which they are strong, admitting to areas where they are weak, and promising to keep improving in both places.

PURCHASING

In many manufacturing companies the only function that deals with suppliers is **purchasing.** Traditionally, the role of this function has been to process and send to suppliers purchase orders and requisitions, reconcile information about incoming items, locate new suppliers, solicit and evaluate bids, and prepare contracts. The role has included dealing with problems and complaints about unmet needs from internal and external customers of procured materials. Buyers on the purchasing staff are sometimes specialized to handle procurement of a particular commodity, component, finished good, or service and deal with suppliers in particular technologies or industries. In general the more advanced, complex, or technically sophisticated a product and its components, the more important it is for buyers to have specialized expertise.

Whereas buyers used to operate independently of other functional areas, today they often participate as members of concurrent engineering and new-product design teams. Buyers know about materials and components, their sources and costs, and can provide engineers with comments and suggestions about ways to improve product quality and manufacturability. Participation in concurrent engineering is one of many ways the purchasing role is changing.

CHANGING ROLE[19]

The procurement process begins when a product is conceptually broken down into its constituent parts. Suppliers for the parts are identified and contracted based on their ability to meet the requirements, quantities, and delivery times. These days, an MRP II system performs and reports the parts breakdown, which a scheduler uses to place detailed orders with suppliers that have already been contracted with by a buyer.

In JIT systems, routine ordering and receipt of parts is often done by team leaders or supervisors on the shop floor. Sometimes the ordering is automatic, a function of the Kanban system that connects the customer's production area with the supplier's production area. Workers intervene only to place orders on an exception basis.

Clearly, with the advent of MRP II and JIT systems much of the responsibility for actual material ordering and receipt has shifted from the purchasing area to manufacturing. Nonetheless, the role of the purchasing function is expanding as companies put more energy into concurrent engineering and supply-chain management and expect purchasing to be active in both. The primary role of purchasing in these companies lies in three areas: specifying requirements, selecting suppliers, and managing supplier relationships.

REQUIREMENTS SPECIFICATION

Purchasing participates with engineering and design in creating specs for new products. There are two kinds of specs:

- Product-related: physical, performance, or other requirements placed on deliverables (end-items being procured).
- Process/delivery-related: requirements placed on production processes and quality control procedures used by the supplier.

The first kind of requirement applies to all procured items. It states what the customer wants. The second kind is more unusual and depends on the customer's need to exert control over the supplier's processes to insure that product-related specs are met. It specifies how the supplier will meet the product requirements. Process and delivery specs are common in the manufacture of products such as pharmaceuticals, sophisticated electromechanical systems, or any item where the performance or effectiveness of the item is difficult to specify or measure.

SUPPLIER ASSESSMENT, SELECTION, AND CONTRACTING

Purchasing communicates to suppliers the product specs, and selects candidate suppliers. For specific contracts, purchasing negotiates the terms for pricing, return policies, warranties, delivery conditions, and penalties for failure to meet quantity, quality, and delivery terms.

For companies seeking partnerships, purchasing seeks suppliers willing to work with the company, then assists in final selection of the suppliers. Purchasing sometimes also assists a supplier in developing capabilities it currently does not possess. This happens when the customer (1) needs an item that is not currently produced by any supplier; (2) wants a supplier that is more reliable, convenient, or less costly than the current supplier; or (3) wants to reduce its reliance on an existing supplier.

MANAGING SUPPLIER RELATIONSHIPS

Purchasing serves as the primary information conduit between the customer and the supplier. It ensures that the supplier understands the customer's production and scheduling procedures, procurement policies, and quantity and delivery expectations. It coordinates production plans and schedules between the customer and the supplier.

Purchasing also develops the quality and delivery goals for the supplier and helps the supplier develop plans for meeting those goals. The goals are based partly on the supplier's ability to meet them and partly on the customer's own internal level of achievement and expectations. A company should not set goals for suppliers that it cannot itself achieve.

Although purchasing's first responsibility is to the customer (the company to which it belongs), it also has responsibility to the supplier. When a supplier has a valid complaint about, for example, the customer making frequent changes to product designs or order schedules—changes that affect the supplier's ability to meet customer needs—purchasing will often represent the supplier and argue its case. One of the US Big-Three automakers used to send a supplier 6-weeks advance notice on its production requirements, in detail, but the advance notice was useless because the actual schedule was changed daily. The supplier never knew for sure what it had to produce until the schedule arrived at 6 AM each day. Purchasing presented the problem to the customer's production managers, who worked out a procedure to reduce the fluctuation in the daily schedules.[20]

Given purchasing's key role in managing supplier relationships, a company that intends to start building supplier partnerships must begin by changing the attitudes of purchasing managers, agents, and buyers about suppliers and their own understanding of the role of purchasing in the company. Agents and buyers must be trained to work with suppliers as coaches and team players. Hall says that every supplier is different, and learning to be a coach for a supplier is like learning to be a consultant.[21] Of course, the onus of change lies not just with purchasing, but with everyone else who will be dealing with suppliers, namely, engineers, production supervisors, quality inspectors, and traffic managers.

JIT IN THE SUPPLY CHAIN

Whether applied to the distribution of final end-products or the transport and handling of raw materials and parts between tiers, application of JIT methodologies reduce waste and improve service and quality everywhere. Customer–supplier partnerships spread the use of these methodologies to companies at every tier of the chain and improve performance of the entire industry group.

The usual transport/distribution process includes numerous steps, most of which, as shown in Figure 19.4(*a*) are non-value-added and unnecessary. If the transport part of the process involves multiple carriers or rerouting and redistribution at intermediate places between the supplier and customer, it too will have numerous wasteful steps. One function of JIT is to eliminate these steps so the process looks more like Figure 19.4(*b*). This section illustrates JIT methods for making such improvements.

FIGURE 19.4

Waste at the supplier/customer interface.

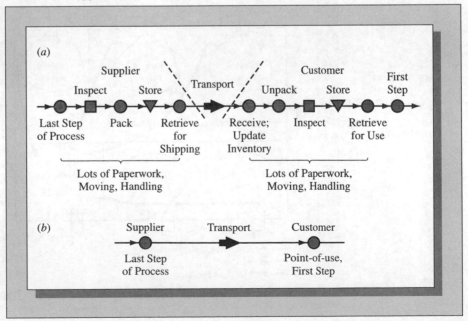

FACILITIES LAYOUT

Materials shipping, handling, and receiving are big sources of waste in supply chains. Materials sit idle and require double handling because of poor layout in receiving and shipping areas. Such waste can be reduced by replacing the usual single set of docks with multiple docks at the start and end of every process.

Figure 19.5 shows the layout of a large plant for an appliance manufacturer. The plant is divided into focused factories that each produce a family of appliances. The plant has few walls to obstruct the movement of materials; equipment and point-of-use storage areas can be easily relocated, as needed. Each focused factory has it own receiving and shipping docks located at the front and back ends of the process. Materials unique to each product family arrive at one dock, and shipments of finished appliances depart from the other. Common materials arrive at the central receiving dock in small containers and are moved by handcart to points-of-use. Finished products to be shipped in mixed-product groups are routed to the general distribution center where they are grouped by customer order and loaded onto trucks. Incoming deliveries of parts and materials and outgoing shipments of finished products are made in small, frequent amounts. Except in the distribution center, there is little inventory in the plant.

FIGURE 19.5

Plant layout organized for minimal waste in shipping, receiving, and handling.

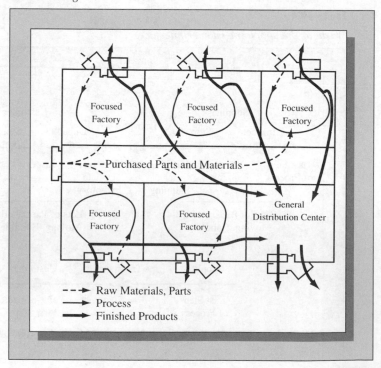

FIGURE 19.6

Truck delivery near point-of-use.[22]

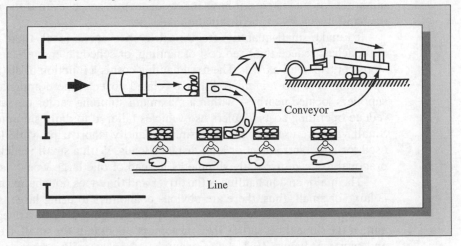

The time and cost of storage and handling can also be further reduced by having delivery trucks drive *into* the plant and to points of use. The example in Figure 19.6 shows items being off-loaded from a truck onto a mobile gravity conveyor chute, on which they slide directly to small storage areas next to the assembly line where they are needed.

TEAMWORK

It used to be that a truck driver would drive a truck, then stand around waiting while dock workers loaded and unloaded the truck and dispatchers prepared freight bills. That is now changing at some companies where drivers are responsible for preparing freight bills and helping load and unload items (depending on the item). At Con-Way Central Express, drivers are responsible for calling customers in advance about weights and destinations of daily pickups. The company holds a Saturday breakfast four times a year for drivers to meet and voice ideas and opinions.[23]

Docks and distribution centers are frequently scenes of confusion and sources of waste and costly errors. Trailers newly loaded are mistakenly unloaded, are loaded with the wrong contents, are sent to the wrong destinations, or sit ready to roll but waiting on paperwork. The confusion often stems from dispatchers, schedulers, dock workers, and drivers working autonomously and not as a team. Like the shop floor, docks and distribution centers can benefit from teamwork and workers sharing opinions and ideas about problems.

TRANSPORTATION SETUP REDUCTION AND SMALL-BATCH SHIPPING

The cost of fuel, tolls, and a driver's wages is roughly the same for a given route whether a vehicle is fully loaded or partially loaded, so full-load shipments are preferred over partial loads because the per-unit hauling cost is less. Thus, analogous to lengthy equipment setups and large batch sizes, it would seem that shipping large quantities on an infrequent basis makes economic sense, even if the resulting greater on-hand inventory at the destination does not.

To make small-quantity, frequent deliveries economical, there are two general approaches: reduce the fixed cost of hauling, or schedule enough customers/supplier stops per trip to fill a truck. The fixed hauling cost is a function of distance and vehicle operating cost. To minimize distance-related costs, some companies only contract suppliers located nearby—within a maximum shipping radius of, say, 100 miles. To reduce operating costs, haulers use vehicles tailored to daily shipping requirements. Small vans are used for multiple small-quantity, short trips while large trailers are used for large, infrequent or long-distance loads. With a small vehicle it can be more practical to make five daily shipments instead of one large weekly shipment.

The major cost in hauling is the driver and that does not change much if the truck is large or small; thus, there are obvious economies to using large trucks and filling them up, especially for long routes. Companies employ several strategies to fill trucks and, at the same time, satisfy their customers's demands for small, frequent deliveries and pickups. Figure 19.7 shows examples of these **milk runs**, or routes for daily deliveries:

· In (*a*), the supplier fills a truck, which then makes deliveries to multiple customers.

· In (*b*), the truck is filled from a cluster or string of multiple suppliers for delivery to a cluster or string of one or more customers.

· In (*c*), the truck is filled from a cluster of suppliers for delivery to a remote, common customer.

· In (*d*), a truck going *to* the customer meets a truck coming back *from* the customer at the halfway point, where drivers switch trucks and return back home. This approach, which can be incorporated into (*b*) and (*c*), is good for long-distance routes because drivers do not have to spend nights away from home.

Customers that receive multiple daily shipments from many suppliers can also direct the shipments into a hub for freight consolidation. The GM/Toyota NUMMI plant in Fremont, California (maker of Geo Prizm and Toyota Corolla) directs shipments from Midwest suppliers to a rail hub in Chicago for daily drop-off. The drop-offs are consolidated for shipment by train and arrive in Fremont 70 hours later.[24]

When trucks or rail cars from multiple suppliers make deliveries to multiple customers, items must be loaded in a sequence such that they can be unloaded at each destination without wasting time shuffling items to access the right ones. One approach is to load items so a path remains to the back of the truck or to items that must be unloaded first. Another is to use trucks with canvas or roll-up sides so items can be loaded and unloaded in any sequence. The same sequencing consideration applies to mixed-items for delivery to a single customer. For example, seats delivered to an automaker should be arranged so they can be unloaded (using a system like in Figure 19.6) in a sequence (color, fabric, etc.) that matches the mixed-model sequence on the assembly line of cars in which they will be installed.

FIGURE 19.7

Configurations of daily milk runs.

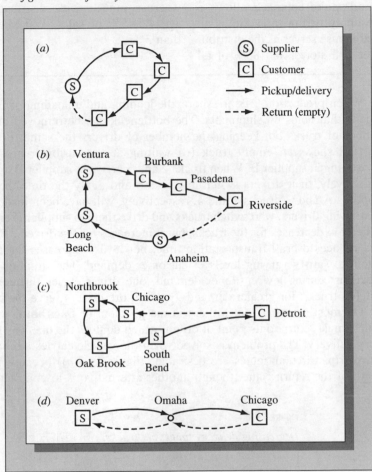

CASE IN POINT: JIT Distribution at Wal-Mart[25]

Wal-Mart's application of cross-docking and hub-and-spoke distribution are examples of supply-chain waste cutting.

With **cross-docking,** a concept developed by Wal-Mart, goods are continuously delivered from suppliers to Wal-Mart warehouses where they are picked, repackaged, and dispatched to individual stores. The warehouses use laser-guided conveyor systems that read bar codes on incoming goods and direct them to trucks going to the right destinations. On average, goods spend no more than 48 hours at a warehouse—the time it takes to move them through the process from one loading dock to another.

Wal-Mart warehouses are strategically located to serve stores within a 150–300 mile radius. This **hub-and-spoke** approach allows a single truck to resupply two or three stores on each trip. Each warehouse serves as the distribution hub for about 175 stores, and 85% of all Wal-Mart goods are routed through this hub-and-spoke system. The process is very effective: whereas industrywide distribution costs average 4.5–5% of sales, Wal-Mart's cost is less than 3%.

When production CTs are short, the loading and unloading of trucks is the bottleneck that holds up shipments. The bottleneck can be removed by increasing the number of trucks but keeping the number of drivers the same. For example, Figure 19.8 shows an empty truck (6) waiting at the customer and a loaded truck (3) waiting at supplier B. When trucks 2 and 5 arrive at supplier B and the customer, respectively, their drivers switch to trucks 6 and 3. By the time these trucks get to suppliers A and C, trucks 1 and 4, respectively, will have been loaded and ready for the arriving drivers, who switch trucks and drive them to supplier B and the customer. Utilization decreases for the trucks, but it increases for the drivers. The approach not only reduces overall transportation time, but it also increases the flexibility of the system to satisfy varying levels of customer demand. The situation is analogous to workcells: during low customer demand, one driver cycles through the route and switches trucks; for greater demand, two or more drivers serve the route.

On most shipping routes there is the problem of **backhaul,** which is that the vehicle must return to its point of origin, which doubles the one-way time and cost of every delivery. The problem is solved when the vehicle carries a billable load on the return trip. Circular routes are desirable (Figure 19.7(*a*)) because they reduce the length of the return route, though another alternative is to contract customers that

FIGURE 19.8

Decreasing delivery times: six trucks, two drivers.[26]

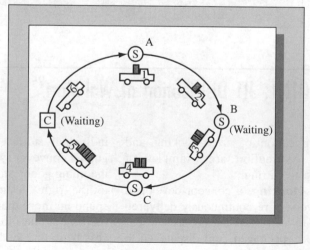

need goods shipped to destinations along the return route. Since trucks returning from JIT customers must carry empty kanban containers, the containers should be "nestable" or collapsible to allow room for goods to be delivered on the way back.

While it is common for large customers to maintain their own fleets of vehicles for making daily deliveries and pickups, the capital equipment costs and logistical complexity of JIT networks (examples in Figure 19.7) often mandate that shipments be contracted out to experienced carriers that have pre-existing shipping/distribution networks. As in choosing suppliers, carriers should be selected on the basis of their ability to meet requirements and become certified. Also like suppliers, the number of carriers should be kept to the minimum so that each gets a larger share of the business and gives better service in return.

PREVENTIVE MAINTENANCE

The role of preventive maintenance and total productive maintenance in the supply chain is to eliminate breakdowns of vehicles (trucks, forklifts, rail equipment) during operation, increase vehicular safety, and tailor vehicles for better service (quicker loading and unloading, better loading organization, quicker freight processing, and quicker repairs). Many TPM concepts from the factory floor also apply to transportation, such as prescheduling as much preventive and predictive maintenance as possible during nonwork hours; training drivers to improve their driving skills and to enable them to perform basic vehicular inspection, simple maintenance tasks, and basic roadside repairs; and improving the design of truck beds, doors, and lift gates based on suggestions from drivers, customers, and suppliers.

KANBAN

The Kanban procedure can readily be extended to external suppliers. Whenever the customer empties a container of parts, that container and the attached kanban become an order signal to the supplier. Empty containers picked up by a driver during each daily delivery are taken back to the supplier, filled, and delivered to the customer on the return trip. The supplement at the end of this chapter gives one procedure for determining the number of kanbans in a supplier-linked pull system.

When the travel time between customer and supplier is long (more than a day or so), an electronic Kanban system can be used. When a container is emptied, the customer faxes the kanban or scans a UPC bar code on the card and transmits information to the supplier about what is needed, how much, and when. Electronic kanbans are especially appropriate for high-volume, repetitive-use items.

Harmon and Peterson give an example of a supply chain connecting an auto assembly plant and four tiers of suppliers: seat assembler, seat-cover manufacturer, fabric mill, and thread supplier. Between the seat-cover manufacturer and the fabric mill is a supplier-linked Kanban process, illustrated in Figure 19.9.

> [The] seat-cover plant starts the [Kanban] process by taking a roll of fabric from focused factory storage for cutting and sewing [1] . . . the bar coded [kanban] on the roll is read [2] . . . this information is accumulated daily and transmitted to the fabric supplier [3],

Figure 19.9

Electronic Kanban system for replenishment orders.[27]

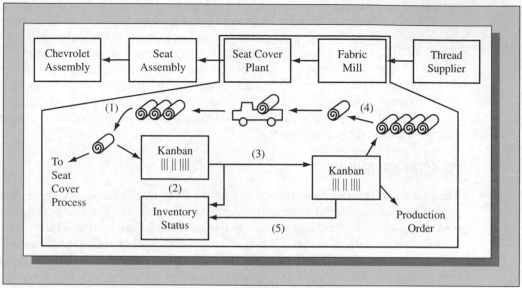

where the information is used to withdraw the required number of rolls from storage for shipment [4]. The [kanbans] on the outbound rolls are read . . . and are transmitted to [the seat-cover plant] to update its inventory status [5].[28]

Information from the kanbans on outbound rolls also signals the supplier about rolls withdrawn from its outbound stock that must be replenished. The fabric suppliers are located at a 30-hour drive from the seat-cover plant. Before Kanban, shipments were made weekly and, thus, the average inventory at the seat-cover plant was half the weekly demand. With electronic Kanban, the requirements updates and deliveries are made daily, so the average inventory is one-half the *daily* demand.

The size and shape of Kanban shipping containers are jointly determined by the customer and supplier to facilitate ease of use, handling, storage, and shipment. The containers are usually small (the guideline being no more than one-tenth the daily demand) for easy handling and standardized in size and shape so they can be used for many different kinds of parts. If the containers are partitioned, then counting the parts in a container is trivial, and the total quantity in a shipment can be determined just by looking at the number of containers. Figure 19.10 shows an example of Kanban containers for incoming material arranged for visual inspection. The particular stock area shown is completely managed by suppliers. Upside-down containers signal authorization for replenishment.

Before suppliers are able to convert their own operations into small-batch, quick-response production, they must, in effect, carry in finished goods stock what was formerly in their customer's raw materials inventory. Though this might appear as a

FIGURE 19.10

*Vendor-managed stock area arranged for simple visual
assessment of on-hand inventory.*

bad thing from the supplier's point of view, from a JIT supply-chain point of view it
is not so bad for a number of reasons, described by Schonberger:[29]

· Transportation costs and return costs are avoided when orders are canceled.

· Materials need not be warehoused by the customer but can be delivered
  directly to the point of use as needed.

· Goods are less likely to be damaged at the supplier's warehouse than when
  sitting on the shop floor prior to use.

· The cost to the supplier holding the stock is an incentive for the supplier to
  develop its own JIT system for reducing inventories.

· The amount the supplier must carry will be small if the customer keeps
  order schedules stable and gives the supplier adequate advance notice about
  changes. This point is elaborated upon next.

COMMUNICATION AND SCHEDULING

Supplier production schedules are driven by a customer's monthly, weekly, or less-
frequent orders. A supplier that values a customer's business and does not want to risk
running short must maintain a stock of finished goods to absorb fluctuations in customer orders. The greater the fluctuations, the more stock the supplier must carry. In
a JIT environment, unless the supplier knows customer demand in advance or can
count on somewhat uniform demand in the short run, it will have to carry even more
inventory. This, however, is not what you call good supply-chain management: the
supplier is not being treated as a partner and the system still has inventory waste, only
it is at a different place (at the supplier).

To enable the supplier to meet customer demand without relying on inventory requires three things: (1) the customer sharing its plans and schedules, (2) production leveling, and (3) point-to-point communication.

Share Plans: Maintain Uniform Schedules

Pull production in a factory requires that operations and cells be notified in advance of the anticipated production level and product mix so they have time to adjust to the required level of capacity. After that, the schedule is held somewhat uniform. Daily fluctuations occur, but every attempt is made to minimize them.

Extending the pull process beyond the factory, the same protocol should apply to scheduling orders for suppliers. The customer notifies the supplier of the estimated mix and volume of orders 1–2 months in advance, depending on the lead time for the supplier to acquire materials and adjust its own capacity. This advance notice enables the supplier to start doing whatever is necessary to meet the requirements—add workers or hours, transfer workers, cut back or build inventory. Once the customer commits to a monthly requirement, it sends orders that are somewhat uniform and coincide with the supplier's own uniform production schedule. There is, in fact, an interesting dynamic here: if the customer does not at first level its order pattern (if its orders remain erratic), then the production and delivery pattern of the supplier will be erratic, too, and that will make it more difficult for the customer to level its production—a circular process. As Hall says:

> If the supplier—one of many—does not deliver or if its material is unusable, either the customer process stops completely or a schedule change goes out to many other suppliers to try to keep everything running. In this chicken-or-egg situation, a uniform load schedule comes first. Without it, there is no pattern to work against, however poor the actual performance to schedule might be.[30]

Point-to-Point Communication

The customer generates and sends to its suppliers monthly forecasts, plans, and anticipated level daily schedules from its centralized planning system. Variations from level daily orders, however, as well as quality complaints, emergent production problems, or suggestions for improvements are handled locally. Workers or supervisors at an operation or workcell in the customer's plant deal directly with workers in the cell or operation that supplies them. Direct communication avoids layers of bureaucracy that typically obfuscate information and extend lead times.

One way to facilitate communication between the customer and the supplier organizations is to link their respective planning and control computer systems. Direct-link EDI enables each party to access portions of the other's system, which eliminates delay in sharing schedule updates.

Milliken and Company, the textile and chemical manufacturer, synchronizes everyone in the supply chain, starting with bar-code point-of-sale information from retailers. By using point-of-sale data from sample retailers to schedule production, the lead time between a retailer store ordering fabric and receiving it has been reduced from 18 weeks to 5 weeks. Wal-Mart has its own version of this kind of system, called

FIGURE 19.11

Production requirements as passed tier to tier.[31]

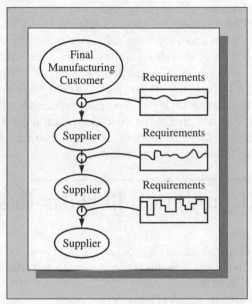

Retail Link, an EDI system that connects stores, warehouses, and suppliers and processes all purchase orders, changes, and confirmations. Retail Link is a proprietary system that enables any Wal-Mart supplier to determine at any time, 24 hours a day, the number of its products being sold. Retail Link eliminates much of the guess work for suppliers in planning for production quantities and cuts days off delivery lead times.

Point-to-point communication not only reduces information time lags but information distortion also. Updates in forecasts and plans for the final customer (top tier) are communicated *directly* to suppliers at every tier of the chain, which can then begin to make immediate adjustment for them. The alternative, the usual stepwise, tier-to-tier downward communication, results in a progressive worsening of distortion in supplier requirements, as shown in Figure 19.11. Even when the schedule at the top level is relatively uniform, just one tier later it becomes choppy, and two tiers down, very choppy.

According to Harmon and Peterson, the following factors in the supply chain amplify this distortion:[32]

- Safety stocks.
- Lead-time allowances in excess of actual process time.
- Inaccuracies in inventory and requirements records and transactions.
- Lot sizing.
- Effects of scrap and rework.
- Planning/scheduling systems with large time buckets (weekly).

They describe a GM division that was able to largely eliminate supply-chain scheduling distortion by adopting daily scheduling time buckets and electronic Kanban between some tiers in the supply chain.[33] Because direct communication between the top of the chain and all suppliers eliminates most of the planning uncertainty for suppliers, it obviates the need for them to rely on safety stocks and safety lead times, which reduces costs and speeds up deliveries everywhere in the system.

Electronic communication, however, does little to facilitate local-level, person-to-person contact. For that purpose, less sophisticated and less expensive technologies (FAX and telephone) are adequate. In fact, relying solely on EDI and not establishing direct links at lower levels can be an expensive mistake. Technology alone is not the answer. Partnerships require building relationships, without which the most advanced communication technology in the world will be for naught.

The following case exemplifies JIT applications in a supply-chain partnership.

CASE IN POINT: Supply-Chain JIT at Dow Chemical Company

Cook and Rogowski describe a customer–supplier partnership that Dow Chemical Company initiated with one of its customers.[34] As part of a corporate move to adopt JIT methods throughout its operations, Dow invited the customer to participate in a pilot effort to reduce supply-chain waste.

The product Dow supplies the customer is anhydrous hydrochloric acid (AHCl). Prior to the partnership, the customer determined its requirements for AHCl by the usual process of forecasting demand and developing an MPS. By referencing BOMs and inventory status, the requirements were translated into purchase orders, which were released to Dow via EDI. Upon receipt of the order, Dow would pump the requested volume of AHCl into Dow-owned tank cars.

Shipments between the Dow plant in Texas and the customer plant in Michigan involved four railroads and three switching points to transfer tank cars from one railroad to another. Both Dow and the customer tracked the shipments. Although demand at the customer's plant averaged two tank cars a day, an average of 16 cars was held as a buffer. The value of the 14 excess tank cars of AHCl was $280,000; the value of the 14 cars themselves, $1,540,000.

Dow and the customer formed a team to find ways to reduce the uncertainty and variability in demand forecasts and shipping lead time. The team changed the customer's forecasting procedure and increased the accuracy of its BOMs and inventory status files. It improved the flow of sales order information through the customer's departments and Dow's own marketing department and increased the reporting frequency of information to adjust AHCl requirements. As a result, the 3-week forecast accuracy was increased from 50% to 70%; the 2-week accuracy, from 60% to 82%; and 1-week accuracy, from 75% to 95%.

Before the partnership, average delivery lead time was 8 days with a standard deviation of 3.1 days. Much of this time was spent at rail switching points. With help from the railroads the team was able to identify a shorter route (less miles) that required three railroads instead of four. This eliminated one switching point and shortened the average lead time to 6 days and the standard deviation to 1.4 days. Also, the team assigned tracking exclusively to Dow, which eliminated the customer expense of tracking. Dow agreed to send the customer weekly reports about tank car locations and expected arrival times.

Because of improved forecast accuracy and decreased lead time, the customer was able to reduce its inventory buffer from 16 tank cars to 6. A reduction of over $880,000 in working capital and a pretax savings of $170,000 resulted.

The team is now trying to reduce the buffer at the customer plant from six tank cars to two. Dow has improved its responsiveness and delivery reliability to the customer and has a much better understanding of the customer's markets, operations, and concerns.

GETTING STARTED: BEGIN AT HOME

Suppose a company intends to adopt supply-chain management concepts and expects its suppliers to adopt JIT/TQM techniques like those described. A word of warning: the company first had better make sure that it, itself, is already far along in having adopted the JIT/TQM philosophy and implementing JIT/TQM techniques, especially regarding things it expects from its suppliers. Not doing so makes no sense. Deliveries of defectfree materials to a company that itself has poor quality procedures will make little difference in the final product. Frequent small-batch deliveries of parts to a company that produces in large batches will only increase the buildup of incoming parts, paperwork, and material handling costs. Besides, frequent or daily deliveries make little sense if order lead times are long. Far better than daily deliveries for orders placed a month earlier are weekly deliveries for orders placed 1 week prior. Customers that are struggling with their own JIT/TQM programs will understand this; non-JIT/TQM customers won't.

Summary

The supply chain is the network of customers and suppliers wherein each provides the others (directly or indirectly) with materials, components, services, and orders. Both JIT and TQM acknowledge the importance of customer–supplier relationships to competitive advantage. Since every organization relies on suppliers, efforts to improve competitiveness must extend beyond the organization and to its suppliers.

By outsourcing, a company can often get goods and services that are higher quality and lower cost than if it tried to produce them itself. But the benefits of outsourcing depend in part on the nature of the relationship between the customer and supplier. By adopting a partnership-type relationship, both the customer and the supplier have something to gain. In a partnership, customers can expect more from suppliers in terms of better, faster, cheaper, and more agile response to their demands. The partnership may include sharing information with suppliers about plans and products, or giving suppliers more say in design decisions. In either case, the customer benefits because with more information the supplier is able to provide better service. When a company develops a partnership, it also reduces its suppliers to a relatively small number. Many companies have only one or two suppliers for each item needed; thus, the supplier in a partnership is rewarded with longer-term, higher volume business. Companies develop rigorous measures to evaluate suppliers for certification and to periodically reassess their performance. Building customer–supplier partnerships can be difficult, especially given the traditional, adversarial relationship existing between the two in many industries. Good relationships begin with both the customer and the supplier realizing they are not competing with each other but are together in competing against other customer–supplier groups.

The purchasing function, the traditional linkage between customer and supplier companies, serves an important role in supply-chain management. Formerly restricted to finding new suppliers, processing purchasing orders, and soliciting and evaluating contracts, the role of the purchasing function has been expanded to include participation in concurrent engineering teams and assessment and certification of suppliers.

Most of the JIT principles and techniques for reducing waste in factories can be applied to most places in the supply chain, including to the distribution channels linking customers and suppliers. Part of the purpose of partnerships is to spread the technology of continuous improvement and waste reduction to every tier of the chain. Concepts such as focused factories, employee involvement, setup reduction, small batches, teamwork, preventive maintenance, and Kanban offer opportunities to improve logistics and distribution performance everywhere.

For customer companies to receive JIT service they must provide suppliers with information about demand forecasts, projected orders, and current and projected production requirements. At the least, a customer must share information about anticipated future demand so its suppliers are able to adjust their capacity. In the best case, companies at all tiers of the supply chain receive demand information directly from the customer at the top of the chain. Direct transmission reduces the information time lags and distortions that occur when orders move through the supply chain, company by company, tier by tier. Direct information from the final customer allows all tiers of the supply chain to work together in a synchronized fashion to everywhere minimize lead times and reduce the costs of moving, handling, and storage.

Chapter Supplement

SUPPLIER KANBANS[35]

An **S-kanban** or **supplier kanban** serves a purpose similar to the conveyance or withdrawal kanban (C-kanban) discussed in Chapter 8: it authorizes withdrawal of containers from an outbound buffer to replenish a customer's inbound buffer, though the outbound buffer represents finished goods located at a supplier's plant. A difference between a C-kanban and an S-kanban is that, timewise, the former authorizes replenishment on an as-needed basis, while the latter authorizes replenishment at *fixed, periodic time intervals* as negotiated between customer and supplier.

Although this system relies on fixed-interval deliveries, it can accommodate some variation in demand through variation in the number of containers authorized for replenishment each delivery. Ordinarily, the number of containers needing to be filled in a given period depends on the number of containers consumed in the previous period.

FIGURE 19.12

Example of S-kanban.

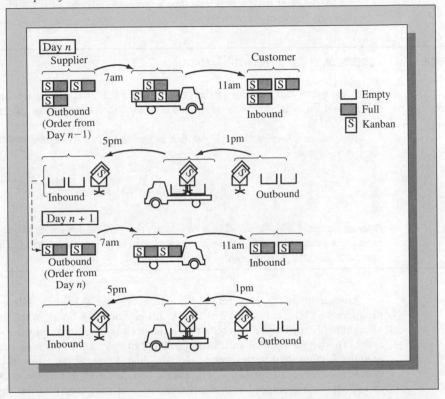

To illustrate, suppose the customer and supplier negotiate a delivery interval of 24 hours. As shown in Figure 19.12, each morning (say, at 7 AM) a truck departs the supplier plant and delivers full containers and their S-kanbans (based on the *previous day's* order) to the supplier plant (arriving at, say, 11 AM). Later that day (say 1 PM) the truck departs the customer plant with empty containers and attached S-kanbans and drops them off at the supplier (5 PM). The next day the process is repeated. The number of full containers delivered to the customer is based on the number of empty containers dropped off the day before.

If a supplier replenishes just one kind of item, there is no need for a kanban card since the containers themselves can serve as order cards. But when it replenishes more than one kind of item with the same containers, separate cards are necessary to specify the number of containers of each item to replenish.

The number of S-kanbans for each item is determined in a way similar to that of the other kinds of kanbans, namely,

$$K_\text{s} = \frac{D}{Q}(C)\left(\frac{1 + I}{N}\right),$$

where

C is the round-trip **travel CT** between the customer and the supplier, including loading and unloading time, rounded *up* to the nearest full day,

N is the number of daily conveyances (withdrawals and deliveries from/to the customer),

I is the supplier production lead time expressed in terms of the number of delivery intervals between conveyances.

Example   2:   Computation of the Number of S-Kanbans

Suppose the round trip travel time between the customer and supplier is less than one working day. The supplier requires one day to fill any order. The number of negotiated deliveries is three per day. Daily demand is 60 units and standard container size is 5 units.

During the one day required to fill each other, three deliveries occur, so $I = 3$. Rounding travel time up to the nearest full day, $C = 1$. Therefore,

$$K_s = \frac{60}{5}[1]\frac{1+3}{3} = 16 \text{ S-kanbans.}$$

At any point in time, 4 of the kanbans will be at the customer's plant (1/3 the daily requirement), while the other 12 will be en route or at the supplier's plant (the supplier is on average working on three, two-kanban batches). The 16 S-kanbans allows no safety margin, so another 2 kanbans might be added for a total of 18.

From a supplier's perspective, S-kanbans are like P-kanbans because each authorizes production to fill a container. The time to fill any order, 8 hours in the example, is the time allowed to fill any number of containers ordered (it is the rough equivalent of production lead time). Though the number varies from delivery to delivery, in the long run the average order quantity is equivalent to the average demand, and, knowing the latter, the supplier is able to compensate for small variations. The assumption, however, is that the customer is attempting to comply with a somewhat uniform schedule and that orders to the supplier will also be somewhat uniform.

Although this kind of delivery system requires a supplier to commit to regular, short-interval deliveries, it affords the supplier a degree of certainty in predicting order requirements. If the customer expects demand to change dramatically, then it must inform the supplier far enough in advance so that production lead times can be renegotiated and the number of S-kanbans readjusted.

Questions

1. In your own 10 words or less, define what constitutes the supply chain.
2. What role does the supply chain play in the competitive position of any one company?
3. To answer this question, review Chapters 1, 4, and 12: What is the role of suppliers/supplier relationships in the Toyota production system, TQM, and concurrent engineering?
4. Discuss the tradeoffs facing a manufacturer in deciding between designing and producing a product itself versus outsourcing design and production.
5. Describe briefly the philosophy of supply-chain management (SCM).

6. What is the role of supplier–customer teamwork in SCM? How is this teamwork manifested?

7. Discuss how the following aspects of customer–supplier relationships change when parties go from being adversaries to being partners: criteria for purchase decisions; responsibility for design; number of suppliers; nature of contracts; and working relationships.

8. Discuss significant differences between customer–supplier partnership agreements and traditional purchase contracts with regard to the following: time period of agreement; mutual expectations about price, quality, delivery, and ordering; and expectations about interaction between customer and supplier.

9. What is vendor-managed inventory?

10. Discuss the process of evaluating suppliers for selection and ongoing performance assessment. Besides the usual criterion of price, what should a company look for in selecting among suppliers?

11. Discuss the role of the purchasing function in managing supplier relationships.

12. Virtually all of the JIT concepts discussed throughout this book apply not just to manufacturers, but also to their suppliers and the carriers and distributors that link customers and suppliers. The section "JIT in the Supply Chain" gave examples. Give other examples of JIT applications in supply-chain management; consider in particular concepts such as focused factories and cellular manufacturing, level and mixed-model production and supply, and standard operations.

13. Give examples of how the concept of continuous improvement can be applied by teams of customers/suppliers/carriers.

Problems

1. A manufacturer negotiates with a distant supplier to deliver parts twice a day. The round-trip travel time between the manufacturer and the supplier is about 1.5 days. The supplier needs one day to fill an order. The manufacturer uses 600 units of the part daily, and the container size is 50 units.

    a. What number of S-kanbans for the part is needed?

    b. At any given time how many of the kanbans are at the customer, at the supplier, and en route between them?

    c. In general, as the round-trip customer-supplier travel time increases to three, four, or more days, so does the required number of S-kanbans. At any given time, where are these additional kanbans?

2. A supplier makes daily deliveries to three customers, similar to the case illustrated in Figure 19.7(a). Assume travel time for each leg of the route is 1 hour; loading the truck at the supplier takes 1 hour; unloading at each customer takes 1 hour. With one truck and one driver, one delivery a day to the three customers is possible in an 8-hour day. See Figure 19.13.

    a. If every customer wants two daily deliveries, how many trucks are needed? Assume one driver who switches trucks at every stop, analogous to the example in Figure 19.8. Draw a diagram like the SOR diagram described in Chapter 11 to illustrate the process. (The four stops along the route are analogous to workstations

FIGURE 19.13

Supply route for problem 2.

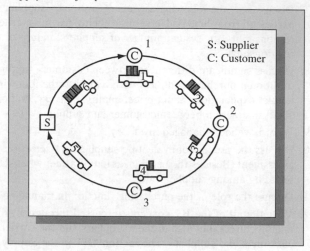

in a cell. The driver does not have to wait for trucks to be loaded or unloaded, so the load/unload times are analogous to automatic machine times.)

b. Assume two drivers; one reports each morning to the supplier, the other reports to customer 2. With six trucks, how many deliveries a day can they make to the three customers in 8 hours? Draw an SOR diagram. What happens with five trucks?

c. For problem (b) and six trucks, what is the maximum load/unload time at a customer or supplier (without affecting the number of daily deliveries)? How does reducing the load/unload time to 30 minutes affect the number of daily deliveries?

Endnotes

1. R.J. Schonberger and E.M. Knod, *Operations Management: Continuous Improvement* (5th ed.) (Burr Ridge, IL: Irwin, 1994), p. 272.

2. J.M. Juran and F.M. Gryna, *Quality Planning and Analysis* (3rd ed.) (New York: McGraw-Hill, 1993), p. 313.

3. S. Melnyk and D. Denzler, *Operations Management: A Value-Driven Approach* (Chicago: Irwin, 1996), pp. 603–5.

4. J. Womack, D. Jones, D. Roos, *The Machine that Changed the World: The Story of Lean Production* (New York: Harper Perennial, 1991), p. 58; R. Dauch, *Passion for Manufacturing* (Dearborn, MI: Society for Manufacturing Engineers, 1993), p. 94.

5. R. Markland, S. Vickery, and R. Davis, *Operations Management: Concepts in Manufacturing and Services* (St. Paul: West, 1995), p. 94.

6. S. Melnyk and D. Denzler, *Operations Management,* p. 419.

7. "Lessons from Detroit: Get Suppliers Involved Early," *Purchasing,* Oct. 19, 1995, pp. 38–42.

8. R. Schonberger, *World-Class Manufacturing: The Lessons of Simplicity Applied* (New York: The Free Press, 1986), p. 161.

9. *Ibid.*, p. 157.

10. J.D. Blocher, C.W. Lackey, V.A. Mabert, "From JIT Purchasing to Supplier Partnerships at Xerox," *Target* 9, No. 3 (May/June 1993), pp. 12–18.

11. R. Hall, *Attaining Manufacturing Excellence* (Burr Ridge, IL: Irwin, 1987), p. 233.

12. R. Dauch, *Passion for Manufacturing,* p. 100.

13. R. Hall, *Attaining Manufacturing Excellence,* p. 231.

14. Portions of this section are based on M. Abeysinghe, "Vendor Relationships of Companies with Low Bargaining Power," research report, Loyola University Chicago, February 1996.

15. L. Ettkin, F. Raiszadeh, and H. Hunt, "Just-in-Time: A Timely Opportunity for Small Manufacturers," *Industrial Management,* Jan/Feb 1990, pp. 16–18.

16. For more on supplier certification concepts and procedures *see* H.J. Steudel and P. Desruelle, *Manufacturing in the Nineties* (New York: Van Nostrand Reinhold, 1992), pp. 350–70; U. Akinc, "Selecting a Set of Vendors in a Manufacturing Environment," *Journal of Operations Management,* 11, No. 2, (June 1993), pp. 107–22; K.R. Bhote, *Strategic Supply Management: A Blueprint for Revitalizing the Manufacturer-Supplier Relationship* (New York: AMACOM, 1989); J.D. Lewis, *The Connected Corporation: How do Leading Companies Win through Customer-Supplier Alliances* (New York: The Free Press, 1995).

17. J. Juran and F.M. Gryna, *Quality Planning and Analysis,* p. 318–9.

18. Adopted from J. Juran and F.M. Gryna, *Quality Planning and Analysis,* p. 319 and S. Melnyk and D. Denzler, *Operations Management,* p. 643.

19. *Sources:* J. Juran and F.M. Gryna, *Quality Planning and Analysis,* pp. 314–21; S. Melnyk and D. Denzler, *Operations Management,* pp. 610–11.

20. S. Melnyk and D. Denzler, *Operations Management,* p. 611.

21. R. Hall, *Attaining Manufacturing Excellence,* p. 246.

22. Adapted from K. Suzaki, *The New Manufacturing Challenge* (New York, The Free Press, 1987), p. 191.

23. S. Gibson, "The Con-Way Express Cross-Dock Operation," Loyola University Chicago, research report, February, 1996.

24. W. Sandras, *Just-in-Time: Making it Happen* (Essex Junction, VT: Oliver Wight Publications, 1989), p. 175.

25. P. Ghemawat, "Wal-Mart Stores Discount Operations," *Harvard Business Review,* May 1989, pp. 1–9; R. Halverson, "Retooling Retailing via Information Technology," *Discount Store News,* May 15, 1995, pp. 73–5.

26. Adapted from K. Suzaki, *The New Manufacturing Challenge,* p. 193.

27. Adapted from R. Harmon and L. Peterson, *Reinventing the Factory,* p. 263.

28. R. Harmon and L. Peterson, *Reinventing the Factory* (New York: The Free Press, 1990), p. 263.

29. R. Schonberger, *World-Class Manufacturing,* pp. 160–1.

30. R. Hall, *Attaining Manufacturing Excellence,* p. 238.

31. Adapted from R. Harmon and L. Peterson, *Reinventing the Factory,* p. 261.

32. *Ibid.,* pp. 261–2.

33. *Ibid.,* p. 262.

34. R.L. Cook and R.A. Rogowski, "Applying JIT Principles to Continuous Process Manufacturing Supply Chains," *Production and Inventory Management Journal,* 1st Quarter, 1996, pp. 12–7.

35. Adapted from Y. Monden, *Toyota Production System* (2nd ed.) (Norcross, GA: Industrial Engineering and Management Press, 1993), pp. 287–90; *see also* H. Steudle and P. Desruelle, *Manufacturing in the Nineties,* pp. 251–54.

20 ACTIVITY-BASED COSTING

> Nothing is more terrible than activity without insight. *Thomas Carlyle*
>
> "Absorption of overhead" is one of the most obscene terms I have ever heard.
> *Peter Drucker*

Activity-based costing (ABC) is an accounting approach for estimating the costs of products and services. More specifically, it is a costing method that overcomes many of the drawbacks associated with traditional cost accounting, so organizations adopting JIT/TQM will find ABC compatible with that philosophy. This chapter describes concepts, applications, and implementation issues of ABC. Interested readers should refer to citations in the endnotes for additional information.[1]

THE IMPORTANCE OF ACCURATE COSTING

A problem with many traditional cost-accounting systems is that their reported cost figures do not necessarily reflect reality. The figures reported are derived by using simplified assumptions that make data collection and reporting easier. Although the assumptions are sometimes valid and the results are initially accurate they are not usually updated to reflect current changes. In many organizations, changes that invalidate the assumptions of the procedures go unnoticed; as a result, managers continue to rely on inaccurate results to make important decisions. Because the assumptions of the procedures are no longer valid, the decisions are not valid either.

COST ACCURACY AND PRODUCT DECISIONS

To show the effect of cost-accounting assumptions on product decision-making, consider the following example (the example is oversimplified, but a more complicated example would demonstrate the same point).

Example 1: A Short Story

A small company manufactures four products, W, X, Y, and Z. The expenses to make these products fall entirely into four categories: direct labor, direct materials, equipment, and support services. The production process requires costly equipment that the company leases. The costs of equipment leasing and support services combined constitute the company's overhead, 90% of which is leasing.

TABLE 20-1   Income Statement ($ Million)

Gross Sales	$ 7.7
Operating Expenses	8.4
Gross Margin	(0.7)
Corporate Overhead	0.5
Before-Tax Profit (Loss)	$(1.2)

TABLE 20-2   Statement of Product Profitability*

Product	W	X	Y	Z	Totals
Sales revenue	2.00	1.50	1.70	2.50	7.7
Direct labor (DL)	0.50	0.75	0.25	1.25	2.7
(Proportion total DL)	(.182)	(.272)	(.091)	(.455)	(1.00)
Materials	0.15	0.10	0.10	0.30	0.65
Overhead	0.91	1.36	0.455	2.275	5.00
Profit (Loss)	0.44	(.71)	0.895	(1.325)	(0.70)

* Overhead allocated based on % of direct labor.

The most recent income statement, shown in Table 20.1, represents the company's performance over the past few years. Table 20.2 shows the most recent statement of profitability for each of the products. The computation for the last row, profit, is

$$\text{Profit (Loss)} = \text{Sales Revenues} - \text{Direct Labor} - \text{Materials} - \text{Overhead.}$$

Because of the company's poor performance in recent years, the owner is considering drastic action, namely, dropping the unprofitable products. Some of the equipment lease agreements are about to expire, so dropping the products would result not only in reduced direct labor and materials costs, but also in substantially lower overhead costs. It appears from Table 20.2 that the worst performing products are X and Z. Given that the performance of these products has been approximately the same over the last few years, it seems clear to the owner that product Z has to go, and probably product X as well. However, products X and Z are the most labor-intensive, so dropping these products would put the most people out of work and that is something about which the owner has strong reservations.

The owner calls a staff meeting to discuss his decision. During the meeting the company accountant reviews the profitability statement and the method used to allocate overhead costs, a traditional method based on percentages from direct labor costs. According to that method, the $5 million overhead cost is allocated to each product in the following proportion:

$$\frac{\text{Direct Labor Cost for One Product}}{\text{Direct Labor Costs for All Products}}.$$

TABLE 20-3   Statement of Product Profitability*

Product	W	X	Y	Z	Totals
Sales revenue	2.00	1.50	1.70	2.50	7.70
Direct labor	0.50	0.75	0.25	1.25	2.75
Materials	0.15	0.10	0.10	0.30	0.65
Overhead	2.50	0.25	1.50	0.75	5.00
Profit (Loss)	(1.15)	0.40	(0.15)	0.20	(0.70)

* Overhead allocated based on % usage of equipment.

For example, since the direct labor cost for product W ($0.5 million) is 18.2% of the total direct labor cost ($2.75 million), then 18.2% of the total overhead cost of ($5 million), or $0.91 million, is allocated to product W.

After discussing the profitability statement, the accountant says: "We know that the large majority of our overhead costs come from equipment leasing. In allocating overhead expenses based on direct labor, we are assuming that the equipment utilization for each product is roughly proportional to the direct labor utilization. Is that assumption correct?" At that point the manufacturing manager says, "Well, no, there's no relationship there. I can tell you right now that most of the equipment is being used to make product W, and very little is being used for product X."

Upon hearing that, the accountant thinks for a moment, then states that perhaps the traditional method for allocating costs is not appropriate for these products. To determine product profitability, he explains, it is necessary to try to get the best estimate possible of all product costs. Therefore, if a cost arises from a resource shared by several products, then the amount of the cost charged to each product should be based upon the product's utilization or consumption of that resource. In this case, the resource is leased equipment and its cost, nearly $5 million, is charged to four different products. Since the utilization of the equipment differs considerably among the four products, the equitable way to distribute the $5 million would be in proportion to their relative usage of the equipment.

Suppose that based on equipment records, the manufacturing manager determines the following: 50% of all leased equipment is devoted to product W, 5% is devoted to product X, 30%, to product Y, and 15%, to product Z. If all four products use similar types of equipment (i.e., roughly the same cost to lease), then it makes sense to use these same percentages to allocate the $5 million overhead. For product W, for example, this results in that product being allocated 50% of the overhead cost, or 0.5 × $5 million = $2.5 million. This analysis for all products gives the results in Table 20.3.

This procedure gives a whole new picture, one virtually opposite that of the other method. It shows product W as the worst performer, and product X as the best. Dropping product W alone would reduce overhead by almost half (not quite half because of the small contribution to overhead for staff expenses) and eliminate most of the company's red ink. The owner decides to accept the decision supported by this analysis.

The point of the story is that carte blanche acceptance of cost figures without knowing their origins can lead to erroneous decisions. As the accountant explained, the costing procedure should apportion costs so that reported figures are as close to the real costs as possible. This is the goal of **activity-based costing,** or **ABC.**

STRATEGIC ROLE OF ACCURATE COSTING

Accurate cost measurement is a requirement for **strategic** decision making. As the above example demonstrated, decisions with long-term ramifications such as pursuing or abandoning products, or seeking new products, markets, or technologies (incremental vs. innovative improvement) stem in part from considerations of profitability. Since cost is a major element of profitability, inability to accurately determine costs is tantamount to inability to assess profitability. Believing, for example, that product W is profitable and product Z is unprofitable leads to a course of action opposite the one if the reverse is believed.

COMPARISON OF TRADITIONAL COSTING WITH ABC

The accuracy of reported costs depends on the cost-accounting system's ability to accurately trace costs to their origins. Traditional cost-accounting systems in manufacturing start by assuming that there are **natural unit cost** measures (costs per unit produced) and that total costs can be obtained by simply summing these costs over all the units. Typical measures of natural unit costs include labor cost, machine cost, and material cost. These are considered natural unit costs because they can be *directly* computed at the unit level (that is, by looking just at the cost of labor or the cost of materials to produce one unit of an item).

If, however, there are costs involved that do not occur naturally at the unit level (for example, setup costs, which occur at the production batch level, or utility costs, which occur at the department or company level), then the cost-accounting system must work *backward* from these costs to determine the **derived unit cost.**

Example   2:   Computation of Derived Unit Costs

If each unit of product L requires 30 minutes of labor time and the hourly labor rate is $20.00, then its natural unit labor cost is $10.00. Similarly if each unit utilizes $1.20 worth of materials, then its natural unit material cost is $1.20.

Assume now that making product L also requires periodic adjustment of equipment by a skilled technician to keep it within narrow tolerance requirements. The monthly salary of the technician is $4,000. To include this salary expense in the cost of the product, a **derived unit technician cost** must be computed. Assume that the technician works fulltime on adjusting equipment for product L. If 5000 units of product L are made a month, then the derived unit technician cost would be $4,000/5000 = $0.80. If there are no other costs, the total unit cost of product L is $10.00 + $1.20 + $0.80 = $12.00. If there are no other products, the monthly production cost is 5000 × $12.00 = $60,000.

For a situation like Example 2 a conventional cost-accounting system does an adequate job of accurately determining the unit cost and of estimating the production cost of all units. As the situation gets more complicated, however, the capability of the conventional cost-accounting system begins to unravel.

Suppose instead of just one product, two products, L and M, are produced. The natural unit labor cost and unit material cost for each product are determined in the same way explained in Example 2. Since these are natural unit costs, their accuracy is not in question. Assume, however, that production of both products requires time from the same skilled technician and, as a result, the unit technician cost must be derived for each. The $4000 expense of the technician must then be allocated between products L and M to obtain a unit cost for each. The traditional approach for doing so is similar to the first method described in Example 1, that is, to allocate the technician expense to each product based upon the direct labor hours required to make the product.

To show the consequences of this method on product costs, two different situations are described below. In the first, products L and M are very similar kinds of products (similar materials, processes, etc.) but are produced in different quantities; in the second, the two products are very different, but are produced in the identical quantity. In each case the importance of using an ABC approach is also described.

Example   3:   Similar Kinds of Products Produced in Different Quantities (Situation 1)

Table 20.4 shows the production data for 1 month for the two products. Although the production quantities of the products are very different, the two products utilized the same amount of the technician's time.

TABLE 20-4   Monthly Production of Products L and M

	Product		
	L	*M*	*Monthly Totals*
Monthly Volume (units)	4000	1000	5000
Direct Labor Hours/Unit	0.5	0.5	
Total Direct Labor Hours	2000	500	2500
Total (actual) Technician Time Utilized (hr)	80	80	160

The traditional method of allocating the technician expense to the products is based entirely on direct labor hours. This method starts by determining the technician cost for each direct labor hour, that is, total technician cost divided by total labor hours, or $4000/2500 = 1.60. Since product L requires 2000 direct labor hours, it allocates $2000 \times ($1.60) = 3200 of the technician cost to product L. The resulting unit technician cost for L is $3200/4000$ units $= 0.80. Similarly, the share of cost allocated to product M is $500 \times ($1.60) = 800, and the unit technician cost for product M is $800/1000 = 0.80.

The problem with this allocation method is that it assumes that technician time is **proportionate** to direct labor time. Thus, products that require more direct labor time are **assumed** to also require more technician time. However, as the last row in Table 20.4 indicates, that is not the case here. The technician actually devotes the same amount of time to 1000 product Ms as to 4000 product Ls. Now, since the two products utilize *equal* amounts of the technician's time each month, the equitable way to allocate technician expense would be to assign equal costs, $2000, to each to the two products. That is exactly what the ABC method would do. The resulting derived unit technician cost would then be $2000/4000 = $0.50 for product L and $2000/1000 = $2.00 for product M.

In general, the traditional cost-accounting method tends to *penalize* products that, other things equal, are produced in *larger quantities* since it allocates to them a larger portion of the common costs, even when they do not actually contribute to a greater share of those costs. In the same way, products that are produced in small quantities will *appear* to have the same or smaller costs than high-volume products, even if, in fact, they consume a disproportionately large share of common resources. In the above example there is only one common resource, the technician, but in the real world there are many such costs (collectively termed overhead costs), all which tend to get allocated to products in a similar way. Since overhead costs often represent a sizable sum, allocating them in the traditional way can result in gross distortion of the derived product unit costs.

Example   4:   Different Kinds of Products Produced in Similar Quantities (Situation 2)

Table 20.5 shows monthly data for two products that are produced in the same quantity. The two products, however, are very different, as shown by the amount of direct-labor time and technician time they each require.

TABLE 20-5   Monthly Production of Products L and M

	Product		
	L	*M*	*Monthly Totals*
Monthly Volume (units)	2000	2000	
Direct Labor Hours/Unit	0.5	0.75	
Total Direct Labor Hours	1000	1500	2500
Total (actual) Technician Time Utilized (hr)	120	40	160

Using the traditional method of allocation, the technician expense is computed to be $1.60 for each direct labor hour. Since product L required 1000 direct labor hours, the technician cost allocated to it is 1000 × ($1.60) = $1600; the unit technician cost is thus $1600/2000 =$0.80. Similarly, the technician cost allocated to product M is 15,000 × ($1.60) = $2400, and the unit technician cost is $2400/2000 = $1.20.

Do the unit technician costs seem fair? Look at the total actual technician time required for each product and notice that product M utilizes *one-third* the amount of technician time that product L does. Despite this, product M ends up with a unit technician cost *50%* higher than that of product L. Since the traditional cost-accounting method allocates more of the shared costs to products that require more labor, products such as M get socked with more overhead whether or not they actually contribute to a greater share of the overhead cost.

The ABC method of allocation would use the following logic: since product L utilizes 75% of the technician's time, then 75% of the total technician expense (i.e., $3000) would be allocated to product L. Likewise, the remaining 25% of the technician expense ($1000) would be allocated to product M. The unit machine cost for product L would then be $3000/2000 = $1.50, and for product M it would be $1000/2000 = $0.50.

CONCEPTS OF ABC

As the examples show, the main difference between activity-based and traditional costing is the way they handle costs that are allocated among multiple products. These costs are sometimes called **common** costs, and the result of their allocation is the derived unit costs described earlier. As explained, traditional costing methods often use direct labor as the basis for allocating common costs, even when direct labor has no bearing on the consumption of common resources by a product. Activity-based costing tries to allocate common costs to products in proportion to the resources that the products actually consume.

ACTIVITIES, COST OBJECTS, AND COST DRIVERS

The ABC method relies on three basic concepts to allocate costs: activity, cost object, and cost driver.

An **activity** is any task or responsibility that consumes resources. An activity can represent value-added work, such as assembling a product or cleaning a room, or non-value-added work, such as inspecting a product or billing a customer. It can represent a task immediately associated with a particular output (e.g., direct labor) or one shared among multiple outputs or functional areas (i.e., overhead).[2] In the previous examples, technician time was the activity. In any case, the cost of the activity is allocated to outputs to arrive at a unit cost. The goal of ABC is to allocate the cost in the most equitable manner and eliminate allocations that are arbitrary.

When multiple activities serve a common function or make up a common process, they can be clustered to form an **activity center.** For example, activities such as set-up, cleaning, and maintenance associated with one machine can be grouped into an activity center for that machine. Several activities that make up one process can be combined into a process-focused activity center. Designating a group of closely related activities as an activity center provides a coordinated way to plan and control all of them. This will be discussed in further detail later.

A **cost object** is what consumes resources and is the reason why activities exist. Cost objects are the outputs of activities and the things or places to which activity costs are allocated. The most customary cost objects are products and services, although functional departments, business units, programs, or projects might also be considered cost objects.

A **cost driver** is a measure for determining how much of a resource or activity a cost object has consumed or utilized. It determines the portion of the total cost for an activity or resource attributed to a particular cost object. The cost driver implies a cause–effect relationship between the cost object and the resource or activity: The

FIGURE 20.1

Example activities and corresponding cost objects and cost drivers.

Resource or Activity	Cost Object	Cost Driver
1. Electricity	Department	Kilowatt hours
2. Technical assistance	Product	No. hours provided
3. Ordering materials	Product	No. purchase orders
4. Account maintenance	Customer account	No. updates

amount of cost allocated from an activity to a cost object is proportionate to the amount of the activity consumed by the cost object as indicated by the cost driver.

Figure 20.1 shows some examples of these concepts. The resources and activities listed represent resources shared by multiple cost objects such as products, departments, or customer accounts. In each case the cost driver is used to determine how much of the resource or activity cost will be allocated to the cost object.

The first line in Figure 20.1 shows that the cost of electricity will be allocated to individual departments based upon each department's electrical consumption as measured by kilowatt hours. If, for example, the company's electric bill is $5,000 for 20,000 kilowatt hours and if department J used 5,000 of those hours, then the expense allocated to department J would be $(5,000/20,000)\$5,000 = \$1,250$.

The second line shows that the cost of providing technical assistance will be allocated among different products based upon the number of hours of assistance required for each product. Suppose the total monthly cost of providing technical assistance is $4000 and that 160 hours are billed. Thus, the hourly rate is $25. Suppose also that for these hours, 100 hours were charged to product L and 60 hours, to product M. Therefore, the allocation of the cost for technical assistance is $100 \times \$25 = \$2500$ for product L and $1500 for product M.

The third line shows that the cost of ordering materials will be allocated to products based on the number of purchase orders sent for each product. Suppose the ordering activity has a total monthly cost of $10,000, which originates from ordering material for products X, Y, and Z and that the following quantities of purchase orders were sent:

Product	No. Purchase Orders
X	40
Y	150
Z	10
	200

If every purchase order costs the same, then the cost per purchase order is $\$10,000/200 = \$50$. Given purchase orders as the cost driver, the allocation of purchasing costs to product X is 40 × \$50 = \$2000; in similar fashion, the allocation to product Y is \$7500; to product Z, it is \$500.

The fourth line shows that the cost of maintenance for customer accounts will be allocated to accounts using the number of transaction updates per account. In many companies every account gets charged the same maintenance cost based upon an average of the cost of all accounts. If the actual cost of maintaining accounts comes from updating account information (additions, deletions, correspondence, etc.), the average method undercharges accounts that require much updating at the expense of accounts that require little updating. A more equitable approach is to charge each account according to the number of updates it requires. Even if the company does not actually charge its customers for these costs, knowing which of the accounts cost more will be helpful for finding ways to reduce costs, alter future account-fee schedules, or redirect marketing efforts.[3] Suppose, for example, the average monthly cost of account maintenance is \$20,000, and the average number of account updates is 5,000. This leads to \$4 per update monthly, so each customer account is charged according to that rate and the number of updates it required.

Following is an example to illustrate overhead allocation in manufacturing.

Example   5:   Overhead Cost Allocation in Manufacturing

A company's \$10 million nondirect manufacturing expense (overhead) is to be allocated to three cost objects—products N, O, and P. First, define the activities that constitute the overhead cost, then for each designate a cost driver. Suppose the nondirect manufacturing expense comprises four activities: ordering components, product planning, receiving components, and inspecting products. The cost of each activity and the associated cost driver are shown in Figure 20.2(a).

Next, look at the amount of activity as (defined by the cost drivers) generated by the cost objects. This is shown in Figure 20.2(b).

Finally, allocate the cost of each activity to each cost object based on the proportionate demand the object placed on the activity according to the cost driver. Looking just at product N, for example, the product required 300 purchase orders sent, 2000 units produced, 20 shipments received, and 12000 inspections performed, so the resulting overhead allocations (in \$ millions) are as follows:

Purchasing	$(300/500) \times \$4 = \$2.4$
Planning	$(2000/8000) \times 2 = 0.5$
Receiving	$(20/100) \times 1 = 0.2$
Production Inspection	$(12000/40000) \times 3 = \underline{0.9}$
	Total \$4.0

The final allocations for all three products are shown in Figure 20.2(c).

FIGURE 20.2

Cost allocation example.

(*a*)   Activities and Associated Total Costs and Cost Drivers

Activities	Total Cost	Cost Driver
Purchasing	$4 million	No. purchase orders (P.O.)
Planning	2	No. units produced
Receiving	1	No. shipments
Production inspection	3	(No. inspections per unit) × (No. units produced)
	$ 10 million	

(*b*)   Cost Drivers (Units per Cost Object)

Cost Object	POs	Units Produced	Shipments	Inspection per Unit × Units Produced
Product N	300	2000	20	6 × 2000 = 12,000
Product O	100	2000	60	10 × 2000 = 20,000
Product P	100	4000	20	2 × 4000 = 8,000
	500	8000	100	40,000

(*c*)   Cost Allocation ($ millions)

Cost Object	Purchasing	Planning	Receiving	Production Inspection	Total
Product N	2.4	0.5	0.2	$0.9	4.0
Product O	0.8	0.5	0.6	1.5	3.4
Product P	0.8	1.0	0.2	0.6	2.6
	4.0	2.0	1.0	3.0	10.0

IDENTIFYING ACTIVITIES AND COST DRIVERS

The validity of ABC lies in using activities and cost drivers that accurately reflect the resources consumed or utilized by cost objects.[4] To keep it simple, the above examples involved only a few activities. Generally the number of activities in an ABC system would be much larger. The actual number depends on whatever is necessary to accurately trace costs and provide comprehensive information that is easy to interpret. Consider as an example the activity of purchasing. This activity might actually involve many kinds of services, and in the interest of accuracy it may be preferable to identify each service as a separate activity. Examples of these include materials purchasing, components purchasing, vendor relations, and vendor certification. Each of these activities would then have its own cost driver; for example, for the purchasing activities stated it could be the number of purchase orders for materials and components purchases, the number of vendors retained, and the number of vendors undergoing certification, respectively.

Choice of cost drivers should be based upon what logically causes the cost of an activity to increase or decrease. In Figure 20.2(*a*), for example, the cost driver for

FIGURE 20.3

Some cost drivers used in manufacturing and service industries.

Number of hours worked	Number of units processed
Number of part numbers	Number of change notices
Number of material moves	Number of processes
Number of parts received	Number of new products
Number of products	Number of employees
Number of schedule changes	Number of units scrapped
Number of vendors	Process lead time
Number of customers acquired	Number of units serviced
Number of customers serviced	Number of patients at
Number of sctups	a specified acuity level
Dollar value of payroll	Dollar value of contracts
Square footage	Number of orders

product planning is shown to be the number of units produced. Presumably, that measure was selected because the amount of planning required for a product was found a priori to be roughly proportionate to the number of units produced. It is easy to imagine other possible cost drivers for planning, including number of production batches or runs, number of product releases, number of plans, and number of planning revisions. Figure 20.3 lists a sample of cost drivers used in manufacturing and service industries.[5]

For many activities, it is easy to identify the cost driver because the relationship (and hence the measure) between the driver and the cost object is straightforward. Cost drivers such as number of hours worked or number of units processed are customary because often the cost of an activity is directly tied to the time devoted to particular cost objects. For other types of activities or resources, however, the cost drivers and cost objects are less obvious. The costs of heating, custodial work, and real estate taxes are examples where the method of apportionment is less obvious (square footage might be used to allocate these particular costs to individual departments or workcenters).

Difficulty in allocating costs also arises from the fact that some activities and resources are more or less fixed. Managers's salaries and much of the overhead on buildings and equipment remain fairly constant regardless of production output. Since these costs are not driven by any single or combination of cost objects, it is difficult to find ways to allocate them to products. Although there is no single way to handle this difficulty, the rule is to try to avoid allocations that are superficial or arbitrary.[6] One useful way to handle cost allocation is to first think of activities in terms of the following different categories:

1. **Unit** activities are performed once for each unit produced. Any activity dependent on volume of output (power consumption, equipment preventive maintenance, consumption of supplies) is usually treated as a unit-level activity.

2. **Batch** activities are performed once for each batch of units. Costs at the batch level are generated according to the number of batches processed. Examples include setting up a machine for batch processing, transporting a batch, ordering a batch, and receiving a batch.

3. **Process** activities are those that relate to an entire process. Examples include designing and setting up a new process, training workers in the process, engineering changes in the process, and team process improvement efforts. Note that these activities are *beyond* unit-level and batch-level activities in that they apply to all units and batches processed.

4. **Plant or organization** activities relate to the production of all products in all processes and serve to sustain operations throughout the entire facility or organization. Examples include accounting and administrative work, building maintenance, property taxes and insurance, and company public relations.

A typical cost object (product or service) in any organization involves effort from activities in *all* of these categories. While it is easy to find cost drivers for unit and batch activities (the cost is a direct function of units produced or time), cost drivers for process, plant, or organization activities are often less obvious. How, for example, should the expense of installing a large centralized computer be allocated among departments or products, and what are the cost drivers for such an expense? To answer such questions it is useful to further specify plant or organization activities as either service or staff activities. For example, Steimer describes a corporate law department that allocates its costs to user departments with a combination of direct and indirect cost drivers, depending on the activity.[7] Costs for labor and environmental specialists working on cases in those areas are charged directly to the departments or business units involved in the cases by using hours worked as the cost driver. Costs of staff attorneys and legal executives working on corporatewide issues are charged to all departments and business units, using as cost drivers some measure of each unit's "size" (payroll dollars, volume of revenue, etc).

It is important to point out that even with an ABC system, not all costs can be allocated in a logical, equitable manner. For some costs the allocation will remain arbitrary because it is too difficult or impossible to find appropriate cost drivers or because the amount of cost involved is not deemed worth the effort. In fact, if the allocation of the cost of an activity to cost objects ends up being arbitrary, it is better not to try to allocate the cost, at least for purposes of costing and making decisions about products, since the results will be misleading. Although an ABC system can reduce the arbitrariness of cost allocation, it cannot entirely eliminate it.

TWO-STAGE ALLOCATION PROCESS

Virtually all ABC systems allocate organizational costs to products or services using a two-stage process as shown Figure 20.4.[8]

The first stage apportions the costs of resources to individual activities or to **activity centers.** Resources include the usual ledger categories for direct costs such as labor and materials, and indirect costs such as accounting, marketing, engineering, building upkeep, taxes, and so on. An individual activity center can represent a task or responsibility (such as the activities described earlier) or they can be machines, workstations, departments, business units, processes, or some stage of a process, depending on how one wishes to apportion costs. A cost driver, referred to as a **resource cost driver,** is used to allocate the cost of the resource to an activity.

FIGURE 20.4

Two-stage cost allocation process.

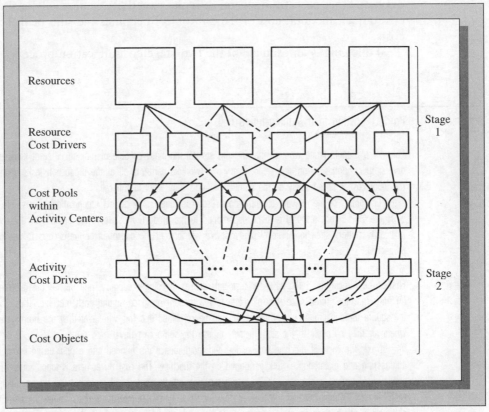

The portion of a resource cost allocated to a particular activity center is referred to as a **cost pool.** A given activity center may consist of several cost pools.

Example   6:   Allocation of Resource Costs to an Activity Center

The maintenance department performs periodic preventive maintenance (PM) on various machines. The resource here is the maintenance department; each machine is considered an activity. Since some of the cost of the maintenance department is a consequence of performing this machine PM, a portion of the departmental cost is allocated to each machine serviced. The cost driver for allocating costs can be, for example, number of instances of PM performed on a machine or number of hours devoted to PM. The resulting allocation is one cost pool for PM for each machine.

Suppose in addition to maintenance, several other resources are involved in the operation and upkeep of the machine, including engineering and custodial services. The costs of these resources should also be allocated to the machine; examples of cost drivers are hours of engineering time and square footage of space occupied by the machine, respectively. The pools for these allocated costs can be lumped together with the pool for PM to form a *machine activity center,* one for each machine.

The second stage of the allocation apportions the activity-center costs to particular products or other cost objects using another set of cost drivers, called **activity cost drivers.** Since costs from several activities or activity centers will be allocated to each cost object, the total cost of the cost object becomes the sum of these apportioned costs.

Following is an example of the two-stage cost-allocation process.[9]

Example   7:   Product Costing in a Manufacturing Cell[10]

Consider a manufacturing workcell that includes several machines capable of making different kinds of products with only simple changes in machine setup. A group of workers performs all of the production tasks in the cell. Assume the labor cost is based solely on the number of hours they work in the cell.

Categories of the relevant organizational resources (direct and indirect organizational costs) are shown at the top of Figure 20.5. Each resource is to be apportioned to the product. Most resources are allocated in two stages—first to activity centers, then to individual products. We will look at the allocation of these costs to one particular product, product Q.

First-Stage Allocation.   The costs for custodial services, building occupancy, and utilities are allocated to a cost pool for each machine's area since they all relate to the amount of space around each machine. Thus, the cost driver is the square footage around a machine. Costs can be combined like this whenever they are **homogeneous,** that is, whenever they all apply to the same activity or use the same cost driver.

Next, the costs of machine engineering and maintenance are lumped into a pool based upon the hours of engineering and maintenance work performed on the machine. The cost driver here is labor hours. This pool and the previously described pool are combined into a machine activity center that represents all nonoperating direct machine costs. In this example we assume that one machine activity center represents costs for all the machines in the cell, although in other cases an activity center could be established for each individual machine.

Costs of the next four resources in Figure 20.5—direct labor, material handling, insurance and taxes, and indirect material—are allocated to a pool that represents cellwide costs. The cost drivers for these resources are labor hours for the cell workers, material handling labor hours for deliveries to and from the cell, dollar capital cost of facilities in the cell, and number of workers in the cell, respectively. These apportioned costs might have been allocated to separate cost pools, but since here they are homogeneous (they are all consumed at rates that depend on cellwide variables), they have been lumped into a single pool that represents the costs of operating the cell. These costs contrast with the nonoperating costs covered by the machine activity center.

Next, costs for machine tooling and fixtures and product planning are allocated to a pool for the product. Both resources represent one-time costs incurred on a per-product, per-batch basis. Machine tooling and fixtures is the cost of setting up the cell for each batch of product. Similarly, product planning is the cost of scheduling and planning for each batch of product. The cost drivers are labor hours to perform the setup and to prepare plans and schedules for the product. These costs are homogeneous, so they can be lumped into a pool for the product activity center.

Second-Stage Allocation.   The costs from the machine, cell, and product activity centers are now allocated to production batches, which, when combined with the cost of direct materials, give the cost for producing a batch of product Q.

FIGURE 20.5

Cost allocation within a manufacturing cell.

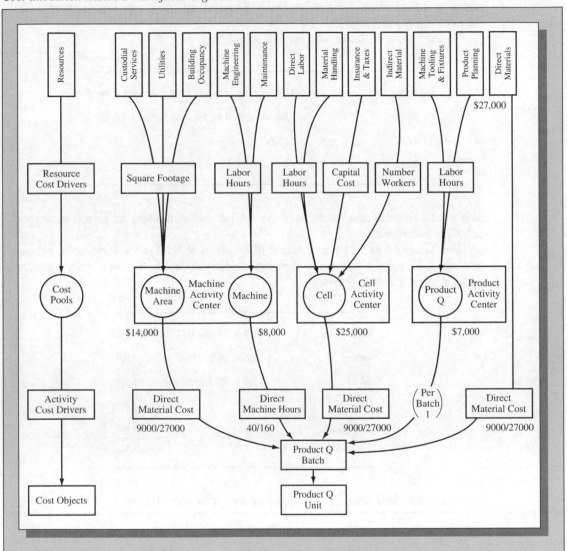

Suppose the cost drivers for allocating activity costs to each batch of product are as follows:

Cost Pool	Cost Driver
Machine areas	Direct material cost
Machines	Direct machine hours
Cell	Direct material cost

Direct material cost is used as a driver because it measures the *volume* of work for each batch that passes through the machine area and the cell as a whole. Direct machine hours is a driver because it measures hours of machine operation for a batch. There is no cost driver for the product-batch activity center since the amount in this cost pool is already a batch-based cost.

Suppose the amounts allocated to the cost pools are as follows:

Machine Areas	$14,000/wk	(sum of the costs for all machine areas in the cell)
Machines	8,000/wk	(sum of the costs for all machines in the cell)
Cell	25,000/wk	
Product Q Batch	7,000/batch	

Suppose also in an average week that the cell operates with 160 direct machine hours and processes an average of $27,000 in direct materials.

Now, consider that the cell produces a batch of 10,000 units of product Q each week and, further, that this batch involves 40 hours of machine time and direct materials costing $9,000. The allocation of activity-center costs to a batch of product Q would be as follows:

Machine Areas	$14,000 × ($9,000/$27,000)	=	$4,667
Machines	8,000 × (40 hr/160 hr)	=	2,000
Cell	25,000 × ($9,000/$27,000)	=	8,333
Product Batch	(per batch)		7,000
Direct Materials	(per batch)		9,000
			$31,000

Given that the batch size is 10,000 units, the per-unit cost for product Q comes to $3.10.

IMPLEMENTING ABC

Most discussions of ABC urge that its initial implementation be confined to a limited part of the organization, such as a single business unit, department, or workcell.[11] This allows sufficient opportunity for problems to be identified and resolved, a cost model to be developed that can be expanded to the rest of the organization, and broader implementation plans to be worked out. Following is a general procedure for implementing ABC in a business unit (department, workcell, or workcenter).

GENERAL PROCEDURE

Implementing ABC involves the following five steps:

1. Identify all significant activities performed in the unit. Observe the unit directly and talk to people who are familiar with its processes. Ask people who work there to describe what they do, and survey customers of the unit (people at the next stage of the process) about what they expect, how satisfied they are, and how they think the output of the unit could be improved. Prepare a flowchart detailing every step of the process, including material handling, storage, waiting, inspection, and so on.

2. Categorize activities as value-added or non-valued added, and scrutinize the latter to see how they can be reduced or eliminated using waste reduction tactics described throughout this book. Keeping in mind the opinions of the customers and the resource limitations of the unit, rank-order the activities according to their overall importance. Then again consider which of them might be reduced, eliminated, or outsourced.

3. Select the cost drivers. For a two-stage allocation process, it is of course necessary to identify drivers for both stages. In selecting drivers, consider the ease of obtaining data related to the driver and the degree to which the driver accurately measures consumption by the activity or product. Ease of obtaining data is very important because it determines the economic feasibility of using ABC. Ideally, drivers that employ data that already exists should be used, otherwise it is necessary to devise a method to collect the data; this requires adding new procedures, which are non-valued-added and can be costly. Of course, more important than availability and ease is that the data allow for accurate cost allocation.

4. Allocate the total budget for the business unit to the activities, one cost pool for each activity. To reduce the amount of detail and record keeping required, the activities should be aggregated so as to form relatively few activity centers. The sum of the cost pools of all the activity centers should be equivalent to the business unit's total budgeted expenses.

5. Identify the cost objects (things or places) that the activity centers serve, and use the cost drivers to trace the demand that these cost objects place on the activity centers.

6. For activities or resource costs where there are no immediate cost objects, identify a logical (or at least equitable) means for allocating the costs. Indirect costs that have no identifiable consumers (cost objects) such as corporate accounting, finance, law, taxes, real estate, and executive salaries can first be allocated to cost pools for organizational units, processes, or activities, then reallocated to specific products or services.

Though much of the data for ABC is easily obtainable from traditional cost systems, new data will have to be collected and maintained for the cost drivers. The system for collecting and maintaining ABC data can be as simple or sophisticated as the purpose dictates, however in the interest of flexibility and responsiveness, the best system might be a small, PC-based system.

This is not to suggest that ABC systems are, per se, simple or easy to implement. There are many stories of difficulties encountered by managers and accountants trying to develop ABC systems, especially in large manufacturing situations where the activities and cost drivers number in the many tens or hundreds and where data collection for many of the cost drivers does not already exist. Though ABC has been around since the 1960s, it remains a novel concept about which most organizations have much to learn.

An ABC system can be used in many ways, and the number of people who will discover them and use the system far exceeds the number who would use a conventional cost-accounting system. For this reason it is important to include the people who best understand the organization's processes and outputs (regardless of their job title) in the design and implementation of the system. In many cases, ABC methods will be instigated not by accountants but by engineers and managers. Nonetheless, because the ABC system relies on existing cost information and because the design of the system requires accounting knowledge and ability to logically relate costs to activities and cost objects, experienced cost accountants should be involved in the design of ABC systems.

LIMITATIONS OF ABC

Even with ABC systems, portions of overhead costs relating to plant/organization-level activities must still be allocated by arbitrary measures simply because no good, logical measures exists. Since plant/organization-level costs often account for the majority of overhead costs, critics argue that attempts to improve product costing by ABC will be largely fruitless. Supporters argue that that is beside the point and that improving the accuracy of *any* amount of allocated overhead is better than arbitrary cost assignment.

ABC requires considerable ongoing data collection, and unless this collection is part of existing procedures, the cost of implementing ABC might be considered too great. As a result, ABC is most frequently implemented in companies that have a fair degree of automation wherein computers routinely accumulate information about setups, inspections, machine run times, number of defects, and so on. Because of the measurement problem, nonautomated companies tend to minimize the number of activity centers. A company that relies on relatively few activity centers for product costing is called a partial ABC system.

According to Garrison and Noreen, companies most likely to benefit from ABC have some of the following characteristics:[12]

1. Products differ substantially in volume, batch size, and manufacturing complexity.
2. Products differ substantially in terms of manufacturing steps, such as inspections and setups.
3. Overhead costs are high and increasing.
4. The variety of products has increased considerably since the existing cost system was established.

5. Top management and marketing people tend to ignore the existing cost system when setting prices or making product decisions.

6. Manufacturing technology has changed since the existing cost system was established (operations have been automated, workcells and pull systems have been implemented, etc.).

CONSEQUENCES OF ABC

An ABC system can have a profound influence on organizational functioning, from the shop floor to the board room. This section reviews important ways that ABC is being applied and its consequences in terms of management practice.

PRODUCT DECISIONS

The most visible consequence of ABC is that it affords a more accurate picture of the costs of products and sources of those costs, in many cases a picture substantially different from the one provided by traditional cost-accounting systems. As illustrated before, a typical result of ABC is that small-volume products are shown to cost more than previously thought, and high-volume products, less. This is often unsettling to managers because the new information requires them to rethink strategies about product pricing, production, and marketing. Of course the method cannot be faulted for being the bearer of bad news, and how managers choose to use that news is their choice. They can alter product prices, institute cost-reduction measures, outsource production, or live with the cost. Whatever the case, ABC assures that decisions are based upon information closer to fact.

ENGINEERING DESIGN DECISIONS

Virtually all costs associated with a product—materials, number and types of parts and components, production process, product reliability and ultimate servicing requirements as well as other product features—are set during product design, and, in most cases, little about them will change throughout the remainder of the product's life. Traditionally products have been designed without regard to their **life-cycle costs** (costs associated with making the product and then supporting it afterward); however, this is starting to change as companies embrace concurrent engineering practices such as QFD and DFMA.

In the hands of design engineers and product teams, ABC has proven to be a useful design tool. Many of the product manufacturing and support costs formerly ignored by designers—costs for materials procurement, WIP, documentation, production scheduling, machine setup, machine operation, quality control, employee skills training, and product returns and warranties—are readily accessible with an ABC system. These costs can be pinpointed using **design-related cost drivers** such as the number of parts in a product, standardization of the parts, number of parts vendors, number of assembly and machining operations, number of special operations, complexity of the operations, and reliability of parts vendors, to mention a few. By considering these cost drivers, a designer can assess the long-range production cost consequences of a design.

Computer software that combines ABC and DFMA technologies enables design teams to measure the life-cycle costs of design alternatives and to choose the design that is most cost-effective. For evaluating the cost of alternative designs, the ABC system can also access the product **bill of activities (BOA),** which lists all required procurement, production, and support activities for a product and computes the cost of each activity for direct labor, materials, and supporting overhead. Rank-ordering the BOA, highest-cost activity first, reveals which activities contribute most to product cost and offer the greatest potential for cost savings. This information suggests aspects of the product that may be redesigned to reduce direct and overhead costs.

CROSS-FUNCTIONAL ORIENTATION

Making and selling a product requires the effort of many functional departments and specialties working together, although this is not obvious from a traditional cost-accounting report. Expenditures are listed by line item or function, and there is no hint as to the kinds of work performed or the cost objects affected. When it is necessary to reduce product costs, the reduction is usually directed at specific functions and line items, though it is impossible to tell a priori what precise impact that will have on the cost of the product.

Since ABC clusters all activities related to a specific cost object (product or process) into an activity center, it is easy to identify within the activity center the activities and cost pools responsible for the greatest costs. These activities are the focus of selective improvement and cost-reduction efforts. Sometimes the result is that the cost for something simple is found to be exorbitant. Take, for example, the cost of purchasing. Purchase orders can be viewed as cost objects that must be processed through numerous departments. The cost of all purchasing paperwork processed for a single purchase, when tallied, is often found to exceed (by many times) the cost of the items being purchased. By identifying the departments involved, the activities that each performs on a purchase order, and how the activities might be altered or eliminated to speed up the process, ABC helps reduce purchasing errors and costs. The following case in point illustrates another way ABC can help reduce costs.

CASE IN POINT: Engineering Changes at Petrocelli Manufacturing

An engineering change notice (ECN) is a modification to product design. Each ECN sets in motion a succession of activities, including changes to physical design documents, production procedures, materials procurement, inventory control, and product brochures. These changes involve departments such as production engineering, manufacturing, production control, procurement, and marketing. The cost of an ECN is roughly the sum of the costs of the activities contributed by all of these departments. At Petrocelli Company, the cost of ECNs had become exorbitant and a major factor in product overhead. Using an ABC system with ECNs as the cost driver, company accountants were able to identify the products with the greatest numbers of ECNs. They were also able to evaluate the effect of reducing the number of ECNs in these products on departmental and product costs.

To reduce the number of ECNs, the company adopted a policy of no longer performing customer-ordered design changes gratis. The resulting fewer ECNs reduced the workload (activity) for every department in the ECN process so much that in a few departments operating budgets were reduced with no loss in ability to handle the remaining ECNs and other tasks.

This case shows that with an ABC system, cost reduction starts with identifying the sources of costs—the cost drivers (in the above case, ECNs). The effect of reducing the cost driver is then traced back to the costs of activities and departments. The cost reduction is made selectively, and the effect on cost objects is predictable.

ROLE IN CONTINUOUS IMPROVEMENT

ABC requires that an organization define its work activities and determine their costs. This is a first step in distinguishing necessary from unnecessary activities and in determining relative priorities about improving or eliminating activities. The cost drivers used in ABC often correspond to measures commonly found in JIT/TQM organizations and mentioned elsewhere in this book, such as number of setups, length of lead time, number of defects, number of design changes, average WIP, number of suppliers, number of parts, and number of steps in a process. These measures identify activities that drive costs up but do not add value. Being able to see, for example, that one product requires three times the number of setups or inspections as another directs attention to discovering the reasons why and to finding solutions.

Perhaps it is obvious that ABC is only a tool and cannot be the driving force behind improvement, no more than it can make an organization world-class or globally competitive. No cost system can do that. H. Thomas Johnson, an authority on ABC and accounting relevance, observes that too many companies jump on the ABC bandwagon in the belief that it will lead them to world-class stature. After all, ABC is just a method to chronicle costs, and it cannot change the business worldview of managers, which is what might really be needed for the organization to become world-class. Johnson writes:[13]

> Few users of these activity-based panaceas seem to understand how activity-based tools condemn them to repeat errors of the past. (p. 26) To achieve competitive and profitable operations in a customer-driven global economy, companies must give customers what they want . . . If customers favor frequent delivery of smaller lots, or if they favor smaller-sized products, then companies must respond accordingly—*even when it initially costs more*. The long-run imperative, of course, is to find ways to reduce costs [of] producing what the customer wants in the form that the customer wants. (p. 33)

Regardless of the cost information that ABC provides, decisions about how to use that information rest with management. If, perchance, management chooses to pursue a vision of manufacturing excellence, customer satisfaction, and continuous improvement, then ABC can be a tool to service that vision.

Summary

Accurate cost information is important for making decisions about product development, promotion, productivity improvement, and waste reduction. Traditional procedures for cost accounting are based on assumptions that are invalid in many industries today, and that yield inaccurate product costs. Activity-based costing (ABC) is a procedure that overcomes the weaknesses of traditional practices and enables more-accurate allocation of organizational costs to individual activities and products.

Cost inaccuracy in traditional accounting methods stems from the allocation of overhead costs as a simple proportion of direct labor costs. As a consequence, products and services that involve high direct labor costs automatically incur a large proportion of all overhead costs. The fallacy of this method is that logically there may be no direct relationship between direct labor and the cost of supporting overhead. Just because a product involves high direct labor does not suggest that it also requires high accompanying overhead in the form of purchasing, planning, quality, legal, or other activity costs.

The ABC method seeks to determine how much overhead cost is incurred as a consequence of production. The fundamental elements in ABC are activities, cost objects, and cost drivers. An activity represents any kind of work, value-added or non-value-added. Any activity that can be directly tied to a particular output is referred to as a direct activity, such as direct labor. Any activity that is shared by multiple functional areas or outputs is called overhead. The ostensible reason that overhead activities exist is to support cost objects—the products and services of an organization. The links that connect activities to cost objects are the cost drivers. A cost driver is the measure of how much of an activity is consumed or utilized by a cost object. Cost drivers are the means by which the total cost of a product or service is tallied.

Activity-based costing influences product decisions, process cross-functional interaction, and continuous improvement efforts. Having accurate costs enables managers to make better decisions about pricing, production levels, and marketing as well as which products to pursue, promote, or abandon. By using product design cost drivers from ABC, engineers can determine the significant contributors to a product's cost throughout its expected lifetime. Design-related cost drivers overlap with DFMA principles such as number of parts, standardization of parts, number of assembly steps, and so on. Thus, information from an ABC database can also be used in DFMA to improve product quality and reduce cost. Whereas traditional accounting procedures display information only by functional area, ABC information can be clustered by cost object, making it easy to see all the activities contributing to a product and their relative costs. This provides information about functions and activities where cost reductions or improvements are necessary.

ABC also plays a role in continuous improvement. An ABC database can be used to identify the non-value-added activities and indicate which of them have disproportionately large costs. Because of its applications in product and process design, continuous improvement, and identification and elimination of waste, ABC systems are useful in JIT/TQM organizations.

Questions

1. In 10 words or less, define activity-based costing.

2. What is a derived unit cost? How does it differ from a natural unit cost?

3. What is the potential pitfall of allocating overhead costs to products using total direct labor hours as the basis?

4. Using traditional overhead cost–allocating methods, what products tend to be penalized (unfairly overcharged for costs)?

5. Explain how a company's decision to cut a product line (discontinue a product or outsource its manufacture) can cause increases in costs for the company's other product lines.

6. Define each of the following terms; give at least two examples of each: activity, activity center, cost object, cost driver.

7. Specify the difference between the following levels of activities: unit, batch, process, plant/organization.

8. For each of the following activities, give one or more cost drivers that might be used to assign costs generated by the activity to products:

   · Receiving incoming materials at the receiving department.
   · Managing parts inventories.
   · Milling all products.
   · Hiring new employees through the personnel department.
   · Designing new products and modifying existing products.
   · Servicing general-purpose equipment (by maintenance staff).
   · Issuing purchase orders.

9. Following is a list of various activities:

   · Direct-labor workers assembling a product.
   · Incoming materials for a specific product inspected by an inspection team.
   · Equipment setups performed on a regular basis.
   · Product designed by a concurrent engineering team.
   · Numerical control machines cutting and shaping materials.
   · Ongoing training provided to all workers.
   · Material-handling crew moving materials from the receiving dock to a product line.

   a. Classify each activity as either a unit-level, batch-level, process-level, or organization-level activity.
   b. For each activity, name at least one cost driver to assign costs generated by the activity to products.

10. Discuss briefly what happens in each stage in a two-stage cost allocation. Where does the concept of cost pool come in?

11. How can ABC help reduce the design, production, and other life-cycle costs of products?

12. How can ABC help reduce costs of activities such as material purchasing and engineering change orders?

Problems[14]

1. Part X is cut from a sheet of metal that costs $36.60. Six parts are cut from each sheet. It takes 20 minutes to cut one part X from the sheet, and the hourly wage rate for the operator of the cutting machine is $21.60. The machine is used for cutting other kinds of parts, although 20% of the time it is used for part X. Monthly expenses associated with the machine are $8000 for preventive and repair maintenance, $2100 for utilities, and $850 for material handling. About 96 units of part X are produced a month in batches of 12 units. The setup is performed by the machine operator and takes 15 minutes.

   a. What natural unit costs for part X can you identify from the information given?
   b. What derived unit costs can you identify?

2. Mobex Company manufactures products A and B. Data for the products follow:

Product	Direct Labor Hours per Unit	Annual Production	Total Direct Labor Hours	Direct Material Cost per Unit
A	1.8	5,000	9,000	$72
B	0.9	30,000	27,000	50
			36,000	

   Manufacturing overhead is $1,800,000. The direct labor rate is $10 per hour. The company has traditionally used direct labor hours to allocate overhead to products, but is now considering ABC and has determined its overhead costs stem from the following activities:

Activity Center	Cost Driver	Total Cost ($)	Annual Events Contributing to Cost — Total	Annual Events Contributing to Cost — Product A	Annual Events Contributing to Cost — Product B
Machine setups	No. setups	$ 360,000	150	50	100
Special processing	CPU min.	180,000	12,000	12,000	—
General factory	Direct labor hrs	1,260,000	36,000	9,000	27,000
		$1,800,000			

   a. Using the direct labor hour allocation method, compute the predetermined overhead rate per labor hour.
   b. Given (a), what is the per-unit production cost of each product?
   c. Using the ABC method, determine the overhead rate for each activity center. What amount of overhead would be applied to each product?
   d. Given (c), what is the per-unit production cost of each product?
   e. Explain the basis for the shifting of costs between the high-volume product and the low-volume product.

3. Sharry Company manufactures products in standard and deluxe models. Since introduction of the deluxe model, profits have steadily declined, despite the fact that sales for the model have been steadily increasing. For the upcoming year, Sharry

expects to sell 5,000 deluxe and 40,000 standard models. Data for the products follow:

Product	Direct Labor Hours per Unit	Direct Labor Cost per Unit	Direct Material Cost per Unit
Deluxe	1.6	$16	$150
Standard	0.8	8	112

Manufacturing overhead for the upcoming year is estimated at $2,000,0000.
a. Using the direct labor hour allocation method, compute the predetermined overhead rate per labor hour.
b. Given (a), what is the per-unit production cost of each product?
c. The company is considering ABC. It has determined that overhead costs originate from the following activities:

Activity Center	Cost Driver	Total Cost ($)	Annual Events Contributing to Cost		
			Total	Standard	Standard
Purchase orders	No. orders	$ 84,000	1,200	400	800
Scrap/rework	No. orders	216,000	900	300	600
Product testing	No. tests	450,000	15,000	4,000	11,000
Machine repair	Machine hours	1,250,000	50,000	20,000	30,000
		$2,000,000			

Using the ABC method, determine the overhead rate for each activity center. What amount of overhead would be applied to each product?
d. Given (c), what is the per-unit production cost of each product?
4. Abbie Franklyn, Senior VP of Torquell-Trans Corporation (TTC) is reviewing the figures for two of its products, Brite-day and Seamless. She is especially excited about what she sees in the income statement regarding the Seamless product:

	Total	Brite-day	Seamless
Sales	$7,250,000	$6,000,000	$1,250,000
Cost of Goods	4,500,000	3,600,000	900,000
Gross Margin	2,750,000	2,400,000	350,000
Sales Admin Expenses	2,450,000	2,300,000	150,000
Net Income	$ 300,000	$ 100,000	$ 200,000
Units Produced and Sold		30,000	5,000
Net Income per Unit		$ 3.33	$ 40.00

Abbie is convinced that the future of the company is in the Seamless line, though what puzzles her is that none of their recent competitors have tried to match that line. A Japanese firm had come out a few years earlier with a product to compete with Seamless, but dropped it after being unable to meet TCC's price, which is so low that TCC doesn't even advertise the product. Recent improvements in the plant have reduced the per-unit direct labor hours for both products, which now stand at 2 hours for Brite-day and 3 hours for Seamless. Everything seems to be in order to Abbie, except the overhead, which has increased considerably over the last few years and now stands at $1,800,000. Abbie suspects it is the productivity-improvement programs that are contributing to this increase.

a. Using direct labor hours as the basis, compute the company overhead rate per labor hour.

b. Material and labor costs are as follows:

Product	Direct Labor Cost per Unit	Direct Material Cost per Unit
Brite-day	$12	$60
Seamless	18	90

Based on (a), compute the cost to produce a unit of each product.

c. TCC'S accountant determines that the overhead is traceable to six activities:

Activity Center	Cost Driver	Total Cost	Annual Events Contributing to Cost		
			Total	Brite-day	Seamless
Machine setups	No. setups	$ 208,000	1,600	1,000	600
Quality inspection	No. inspections	360,000	9,000	4,000	5,000
Purchase orders	No. orders	90,000	1,200	840	360
Shipments	No. shipments	132,000	600	400	200
Soldering	No. solder joints	450,000	200,000	60,000	140,000
Machine repair	Machine hours	560,000	70,000	30,000	40,000
		$1,800,000			

Based on these data, do you think TCC should expand sales of the Seamless product? Explain your position. Use unit costs and the income statement to support your suggestion.

d. Why does the Seamless product sell so well, even without advertising?

e. If you were Abbie Franklyn, what strategy would you follow from here on to help the company improve profits?

f. Examine the activity costs above. Which costs might be reduced or eliminated if TCC were to adopt JIT/TQM philosophy?

Endnotes

1. Many of the concepts in this chapter are drawn from the series by R. Cooper in *Journal of Cost Management:* "Part One: What Is an Activity-Based Cost System?" Summer 1988, pp. 45–53; "Part Two: When Do I Need an Activity-Based Cost System?" Fall 1988, p. 41–8; "Part Three: How Many Cost Drivers Do You Need and How Do You Select Them?" Winter 1989, pp. 34–54; "Part Four: What Do Activity Based Cost Systems Look Like?" Spring 1989, pp. 38–49. *See also* H. Thomas Johnson, "Activity-Based Information Blueprint for World-Class Management," *Management Accounting,* June 1988, pp. 23–30; R. Cooper and R. Kaplan, "Measure Costs Right, Make the Right Decisions," *Harvard Business Review,* Sept/Oct 1988; J. Brimson, *Activity Accounting* (New York: John Wiley, 1991); and R. Hall, H.T. Johnson, and P. Turney, *Measuring Up* (Homewood, IL: Business One Irwin, 1991).

2. With the ABC method the usual direct-indirect distinction becomes largely irrelevant.

3. The author had a personal experience with this as an operations analyst at a bank. The bank always gave special treatment to the largest corporate accounts because, it believed, they were the most profitable. An investigation revealed, however, that the largest accounts had a disproportionately larger share of transactions that required additional service personnel. As a result, many of these accounts proved to be only marginally profitable and, in some cases, big money losers.

4. For a good explanation of the design process for ABC systems, *see* G. Beaujon and V. Singhal, "Understanding the Activity Costs in an Activity-Based Cost System," *Cost Accounting,* Spring 1990, pp. 51–72.

5. *See,* for example, R. McIlhattan, "Cost-Management Systems, JIT, and Quality," *Total Quality. An Executive's Guide for the 1990s* (Homewood, IL: Dow-Jones-Irwin, 1990), Chapter 13; W. Rotch, "Activity-Based Costing in Service Industries," *Cost Management,* Summer 1990, pp. 4–14.

6. See J. Brimson, *Activity Accounting,* pp. 142–3.

7. T. Steimer, "Activity-Based Cost Accounting for Total Quality," *Management Accounting,* October 1990, pp. 39–42.

8. See G. Beaujon and Singhal, "Understanding the Activity Costs in an Activity-Based Cost System."

9. This is only an example; the procedure varies with the situation and the resources, cost objects, and cost drivers used.

10. Adopted from D. Dhavale, "Activity-Based Costing in Cellular Manufacturing Systems," *Industrial Engineering,* February 1992, pp. 44–6.

11. See M. Hemli and M. Tanju, "Activity-Based Costing May Reduce Costs, Aid Planning," *Healthcare Financial Management,* November 1991, pp. 95–6; and T. Steimer, "Activity-Based Cost Accounting for Total Quality," *Management Accounting,* October 1990, pp. 39–41. The former gives an application of ABC in health care, the latter, in a staff department of a large corporation.

12. R. Garrison and E. Noreen, *Managerial Accounting* (7th ed) (Burr Ridge, IL: Irwin, 1994), pp. 204–5.

13. H.T. Johnson, "It's Time to Stop Overselling Activity-Based Concepts: Start Focusing on Total Customer Satisfaction Instead," *Management Accounting,* September 1992, pp. 26–35.

14. Problems 2, 3, and 4 adapted from R. Garrison and E. Noreen, *Managerial Accounting,* pp. 216–34.

CHAPTER 21 PERFORMANCE MEASUREMENT: MAKING BEAN COUNTING RELEVANT

There is truth in saying that what gets measured gets done since the criteria used for evaluation are the criteria people use to make decisions and do work. So, regardless of any espoused new philosophy, people revert to doing things the old way if they continue to be measured in terms of the old standards. Organizations trying to adopt the JIT/TQM philosophy of continuous improvement will therefore falter unless they adopt decision criteria and performance measures consistent with that philosophy.

This chapter discusses the role of performance measurement in business. More than just a passive means for assessing what has already happened, the act of measurement serves to motivate particular behaviors and, hence, predestine future outcomes. In modern times, accounting systems have become the primary means by which organizations track and assess performance. As discussed in the preceding chapter, many of the assumptions upon which these systems are based are no longer valid, and the systems represent an outdated worldview of business. This chapter covers the counterproductive influence of traditional systems and performance criteria on long-term organizational competitiveness. It also covers the new worldview of business, the world-class worldview, and the enlightened criteria measures that represent that worldview. Features of performance measurement systems for implementing enlightened measures are discussed as well.

CRITERIA MEASURES AND BUSINESS DECISIONS

Some years ago one of the US Big-Three automakers pilot tested ways to reduce waste by producing solely to demand and in small batches and changing layouts to reduce material handling costs. There were many positive results, including decreased inventories and greater plant flexibility. The problem was, the company's cost-accounting system, which measured results solely in terms of their effects on standardized financial criteria, showed only bad results such as increases in indirect-to-direct labor ratios, nonproductive labor time (workers not producing), and decreases in overhead absorption. Since the system had no way of accounting for the improvements, the experiment was considered a failure and was canceled.

Perhaps obvious is that one's decisions about courses of action should be based upon criteria compatible with one's objectives, and that outcomes for those actions should be assessed using the same criteria. This prominent role of criteria in decision

FIGURE 21.1

Decision-making and assessment process.

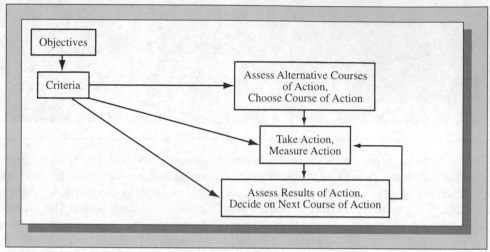

making is shown in Figure 21.1. Nonetheless, an astonishing number of organizations rely upon decision criteria and measurement systems that are incompatible with their stated objectives. Today virtually all companies utilize standard cost-accounting systems for measuring and reporting performance, but these systems, from an operations perspective, rely upon criteria that are outdated and worth little in gauging important areas of organizational performance. Worse, the criteria used give a distorted view of performance and, as in the automaker example, discourage attempts to reduce waste, continuously improve, or otherwise heighten competitiveness. Guided by traditional criteria, managers make decisions that look beneficial but in actuality are worthless or detrimental to the organization's immediate well-being and long-term viability. The following section describes the limitations of traditional measurement criteria when used in continuous improvement and waste-reduction efforts.

TRADITIONAL PERFORMANCE CRITERIA

Most criteria used today in performance-monitoring systems were developed in the early 1900s. The purpose of these criteria and systems was to provide a standardized means of reporting performance to external groups such as the Internal Revenue Service, Securities and Exchange Commission, and shareholders. Businesses maintain gross financial statistics such as net sales, cost of sales, fixed assets, liabilities, and so on, for periodic reporting in places such as the profit-and-loss statement and the balance sheet. At one time numbers like these could be relied upon to give a somewhat credible assessment of the health of a business, and could be used for making decisions that would improve competitive standing.

In a market where competition is low and brand loyalty is high, a company can increase its income by slightly raising prices or lowering the cost of sales, and such things are reflected on financial statements. Today's business world is not so simple.

Financial statements tell only part of the story, and numbers can easily be manipulated to make poor performance look good on the books. In the early 1980s, for example, Chrysler paid record-high dividends even though it teetered on the verge of bankruptcy. Decisions that optimize costs and stock prices will not guarantee that a company will thrive or even survive unless they are weighed against other, noncost criteria. Competitive advantage today translates into doing well in terms of product availability, variety, quality, and customer service, none of which are adequately addressed by simple cost-cutting measures or actions strictly geared to increasing profits.

THE PARALLAX VIEW

Traditional performance criteria often convey an image more contrived than real. The usual way for computing product cost is to add the direct cost of labor and materials to a percentage of the overhead cost. The overhead cost allocation is usually based on a percentage of the direct labor hours. Decades ago this procedure made sense because most of the cost of a product came from the direct labor involved and most of the remainder came from materials. Given the importance of direct costs, companies established standards for labor rates and materials to help control these costs. Industrial engineers developed rate standards for every operation using time-and-motion studies, and these rates became the standards by which performance was measured. Managers saw their primary goal as trying to achieve these standards. Seldom did they question the soundness of the standards themselves or the wisdom of utilizing such criteria over the long run.

Today the cost picture in manufacturing has changed dramatically. Most of the cost of a product no longer comes from direct labor, but from overhead. Direct labor contributes only a fraction to cost (about 7% to 10%), yet managers still pay plenty of attention to it because of the attached overhead cost allocation. Whenever managers need to cut costs, they look first to direct labor because savings there carry a big overhead savings bonus. Each direct labor hour saved results in an overhead cost savings on the books that is sometimes many times the labor cost savings.

Seldom, however, is the overhead actually saved. Instead it is merely *reallocated*. The traditional system must ensure that overhead costs get absorbed, if not by one department or product then by another. When one department reduces its direct labor, the overhead cost it formerly absorbed must be transferred somewhere else. The transfer results in an increase in the cost burden for other areas, making them look worse in terms of cost performance. While managers strive to improve their individual departments, products, or processes in terms of costs and rate standards, no one pays attention to the combined effects on the overall organization.

Following are traditional criteria commonly used for making decisions and measuring performance, and what is wrong with them from the perspective of continuous improvement and competitive advantage.

STANDARDS AND VARIANCES

Every kind of input and output has a normative standard to which it is compared. For example, **standard output** of 100 units/hour for an operation means that the output *should* be 100 units. The standard is considered the ideal and once determined is held fixed, perhaps indefinitely.

Variance is the difference between standard and actual performance. If the operation produces 75 units/hour and the standard is 100 units, a negative variance of the dollar equivalent of 25 units is created for the operation. The manager must find a way to make up for the variance.

Standards and variances are impediments to continuous improvement. Standards on output volume put priority on doing whatever is necessary to produce at a fixed rate, regardless of demand. They encourage producing in large batches to eliminate setups, putting easy orders first at the expense of other, possibly higher-priority orders, and maintaining high WIP buffers and backorders to keep workers busy. Standards on material prices encourage selecting vendors solely for the lowest initial price, ordering in large quantities to get discounts, and ignoring factors like vendor reliability and product quality. Standards tend to limit improvement because once the standard has been attained there is no incentive to do better.

Most standards are internally developed and some are quickly outdated; nonetheless, they are used as the normative. Although a standard might actually be quite unsatisfactory when compared to what competitors are doing, as long as the variance remains favorable, the organization is deluded into believing that it is performing as well as it has to to remain competitive.

DIRECT LABOR PRODUCTIVITY

Examples of measures of direct labor (DL) productivity are

Standard DL cost.

Standard DL time per unit output.

Earned standard DL dollars.

DL efficiency.

DL productivity.

DL utilization.

Measures like these emphasize keeping people busy at producing output, whether or not demand warrants it. They put sole importance on **quantity** at the expense of quality, customer service, and accumulation of inventory. One of the measures, **earned standard DL dollars,** converts production output into a dollar equivalent. Standard cost-accounting procedures treat earned standard dollars for inventory like revenues on a profit-and-loss statement. Thus, increasing a department's inventory is equivalent to increasing its earned revenues. It should be obvious what a measure like this does to efforts to reduce inventory.

OVERHEAD ALLOCATION AND DIRECT LABOR

Overhead costs that cannot be associated directly with particular outputs are allocated to departments and products. These costs include administrative, staff, and plant expenses for management, research, engineering, marketing, utilities, maintenance, and depreciation as well as capital expenditures for equipment and facilities. Such costs are allocated (disseminated) throughout the organization, commonly as a percentage of every direct labor hour charged. Labor hours are used because they are the most easily counted things in organizations. Roughly, the computation is

$$Total\ Labor\ Rate = Direct\ Labor\ Rate \times (1.0 + Overhead\ Rate).$$

If, for example, the direct labor rate is $30/hr and the overhead rate is 500%, then

$$Total\ Labor\ Rate = (\$30)(1.0 + 5.0) = \$180/hr.$$

Besides the problems described in Chapter 20, this method drives managers to first look at labor whenever they need to reduce costs. By reducing labor they get credited for saving not only labor (at $30/hr) but, more significantly, the attached burden ($150/hr). This overhead is reallocated elsewhere in the company. In the process of reducing labor, the ratio of overhead to direct labor costs increases throughout the organization, requiring that other areas also look for ways to cut costs. Of course they start by cutting labor, which shifts the overhead to still other areas. The organization gets caught in an ever-tightening spiral of reducing labor and increasing the ratio of overhead to direct labor costs.

The principle problem of this allocation method is the high priority it puts on reducing labor (a cost factor often of relative little cost significance) and the lack of priority it puts on reducing overhead (a factor often of major cost significance). The organization keeps reducing its skilled direct labor pool without considering the long-range effects. Only when it has little remaining direct labor to cut does the organization consider reducing overhead. Too often, however, it is then forced to reduce overhead from areas such as research, product development, and process engineering which are the company's lifeline to the future.

MACHINE UTILIZATION

Machine utilization is the proportion of available time a machine is producing output:

$$\frac{Actual\ Time\ Producing\ (\text{min/day})}{Time\ Available\ (\text{min/day})}.$$

Alternatively, utilization can be measured as the proportion of rated output at which a machine is producing:

$$\frac{Actual\ Output\ Rate\ (\text{units/min})}{Standard\ Output\ Rate\ (\text{units/min})}.$$

Criteria like these encourage maximum equipment usage. Overhead is sometimes allocated to machines in proportion to their maximum output capacity, so machines with greater capacity are expected to absorb greater overhead. To minimize the cost portion from overhead for each unit, a machine must produce at maximum output so as to spread its overhead over as many units as possible.

Although high machine utilization is not detrimental as long as it is directed toward satisfying *demand*, machine utilization for its own sake is wasteful. Every moment is spent producing; items not needed become inventory, and no time is allotted for preventive maintenance.

Machine utilization criteria also foster a proclivity toward procurement of large, fast machines. Such machines, however, are usually more costly than smaller, slower machines and, as a result, fewer machines can be purchased. In the long run, more jobs will have to be routed through each machine, which increases the complexity of job routings and the size of WIP around each machine. This in turn increases production lead times and reduces the responsiveness and flexibility of the plant as a whole.

PRODUCTION AND OPERATIONS CRITERIA

Many companies set daily, weekly, or monthly output and schedule requirements based on **internal** factors so as to yield the largest positive cost variance, the greatest number of items shipped, the smallest lead times, or whatever else will make the company look good. The criteria are largely self-serving. For example, consider lead time when computed in the following way:

$$Lead\ Time = (Time\ When\ Factory\ Ships\ the\ Product)$$
$$- (Time\ When\ Factory\ Receives\ Order).$$

This kind of measure is not particularly relevant because it centers around the factory. With a measure like this the lead time might always appear acceptably low to management while being unacceptably high to customers who, of course, use a different lead time measure, namely,

$$Lead\ Time = (Time\ When\ Customer\ Receives\ the\ Product)$$
$$- (Time\ When\ Customer\ Places\ the\ Order).$$

The point is that criteria adopted for the sake of easy achievement will not necessarily satisfy customers, beat competitors, or build strength for the future.

QUALITY REQUIREMENTS

Many organizations abide by rigorous requirements to assess product and service quality, however, like the measures described above, the criteria are developed internally and are inwardly focused. The organization does not know how customers use its products, what they like or do not like about the products, what they expect, or what the standards of excellence are for the industry. An company can fulfill 100% of its internally developed quality requirements and still go out of business for not having satisfied customers. Strict quality requirements are fundamental, but strictness must be gauged by the customer's measures.

TRADITIONAL CRITERIA MEASURES: LIMITATIONS

Most traditional performance criteria and measurement systems suffer similar limitations when it comes to continuous improvement and competitiveness. The limitations are symptomatic of a larger problem, a way of viewing the business world that is antiquated and is still perpetuated by traditional management culture and business education. The limitations fall into three categories: emphasis on financial criteria, emphasis on pieces of the system, and emphasis on the past and the present.

EMPHASIS ON FINANCIAL CRITERIA

Traditional criteria primarily assess overall performance in terms of a single perspective: financial. While financial strength is certainly necessary for organizational well-being, financial criteria alone can neither portray all realms of performance nor indicate all actions necessary to improve performance. For that matter, no single criterion tells the full story. An organization needs a wide range of measures tailored to its long-term goals so managers can determine what actions to take and assess the results of those actions. As long as emphasis remains on optimizing a few financial measures, actions necessary to achieve long-term success get pushed by the wayside.

In many organizations the emphasis is on minimizing capital expenditures and labor cost, with no consideration about the nonfinancial, long-term effects. For instance, one way of assessing a piece of equipment is to determine whether it will save enough labor or sufficiently boost output to offset its capital cost. Assessment is in terms of financial measures such as rate of return or payback period. The numbers needed to compute these measures are easy to obtain, however they often ignore serious realities that could invalidate the results. For example, the Association of Manufacturing Engineers estimates that most manufactured items spend 95% of their time in storage or transport. They spend the remaining 5% on a machine but sit idle 60% of that time. In other words, on average, $5\% \times 40\% = 2\%$ of manufacturing lead time can be attributed to machine work. Still, simple rate-of-return or payback-period analysis is used to assess the improvement contribution of a faster machine, even though the faster machine ignores 98% of the problem.

John Rydz describes a related example from the US textile industry.[1] Total lead time for fabric from when it is manufactured, through its use in making garments, to when it is purchased as an article of clothing is as much as 60 weeks—virtually all spent in various forms of storage. In recent decades most of the US textile industry has moved overseas, ostensibly to save on labor costs. Rydz argues that had the industry focused instead on reducing lead times it could have achieved comparable savings and retained many US jobs.

In general, emphasis on simple financial measures predisposes managers to look at all problems in similar ways and precludes them from looking at other possibilities. In a given situation, machine speed and labor costs might only be a small part of the problem, although traditional measures treat them as being the whole problem. If an organization chooses goals such as reducing waste or gaining competitive advantage, it must use decision criteria and performance measures compatible with those goals.

Sometimes nonfinancial criteria can be converted into dollar terms and incorporated into financial tracking and reporting systems. Canon Corporation's measure for waste-elimination profit described in Chapter 3 is an example. Other times, however, appropriate criteria cannot readily be converted into financial terms and trying to do so only diminishes their usefulness. For example, a report to employees stating that last month the customer service department received 14 complaints, 3 returns, 18 suggestions, and 9 compliments from customers is much more meaningful than one that states the department spent $15,445 responding to customer correspondence.

EMPHASIS ON PIECES OF THE SYSTEM

Traditional criteria take the reductionist approach and split organizations into pieces, treating each as if it were autonomous (the so-called **functional silos**). Standards and goals motivate employees to try to optimize the performance of their department, workcenter, or machine, without regard to the effect on the overall system. The implicit assumption is that if all subunits optimize individual performance, then the performance of the entire system is optimized. This is of course contrary to the dynamics of univeral systems behavior, that is, that optimizing subsystem performance does not optimize system performance (and can actually degrade it).[2] This nonsystems view of performance also excludes consideration of the system's environment (customers, competitors, technological advancement, and so on).

An example of this piecewise thinking is machine utilization. Each machine is treated as sovereign and has the goal of maximum utilization. In actuality, the feasibility or practicality of maximizing utilization should depend not on the machine, but on the entire process of which the machine is a part. Possibly the machine should be highly utilized, but that depends on the demand for its output and whether the machine is a bottleneck. If the machine is a bottleneck, it will be utilized more than if it were not. Even then, however, the utilization should depend on the flow of materials to the machine, which is wholly determined by the push or pull of materials from elsewhere in the process. In all cases a machine's utilization should be considered as the result of requirements imposed by the overall process, not as a goal in itself.

EMPHASIS ON THE PAST AND THE PRESENT

Traditional measurement criteria emphasize performance in recent review periods and motivate actions to achieve short-term goals. For example, a company may consider outsourcing a major portion of its production base to reduce plant operating expenses. Lower expenses make for higher profits, which result in larger dividends in the next period. But, as one study argues,[3] through outsourcing a company can also relinquish important manufacturing skills and technology, which in the long run can severely reduce its ability to keep abreast of product and process development. Meanwhile, the study states, the supplier gains the knowledge to master the technology of the product it is producing under contract. At some point the supplier might become capable of initiating its own product-development efforts, and eventually to produce and distribute the product on its own. The customer, having sold off its technology and divested itself of manufacturing capability, is forced into the paradoxical situation of relying on its (now) competitor to be its supplier. The demise of the US television manufacturing industry is a glaring example of this.

Most of the programs described in this book (e.g., TPM, setup reduction, implementation of cells and pull production) will in the short run increase costs and show few immediate benefits. However, there is a learning-curve effect, and in every new system bugs must be worked out. Similarly, efforts such as product research, new equipment procurement, worker training, modernizing facilities, and partnering with suppliers are given no credit with traditional measures, and since they all represent expenses, they actually can worsen an organization's profit-and-loss situation in the short run. By providing no stimulus for future-oriented actions and ignoring the benefits of improvement efforts, traditional measures discourage organizations from doing what is necessary to remain competitive and viable in the long run.

ACCOUNTING SYSTEMS AND WORLDVIEWS

Turney and Anderson state that the purpose of accounting is to develop "systems that reinforce the activities necessary for the success of the business. It will do this well if the systems are consistent with the worldview [of the organization], assuming that the worldview is appropriate."[4] Examining today's accounting and measuring systems we find a worldview characterized by[5]

Batch production	Design for engineering features
Maximum volume	Elimination of direct labor
Inventory buffers	Product differentiation to increase volume
Focus on individual workers	and market share
departments, machines	Accounting focus on external financial
Scrap and rework expected	reporting (watchdog)
Sales limited by production	Emphasis on profitability
Costs recovered via pricing	Long product cycle times

This view is symbolic of *yesterday*'s way of thinking about business and is largely outmoded. In contrast, the **world-class** worldview held by JIT/TQM organizations is characterized by[6]

Continuous process flow	Design for manufacturability
Employee involvement	Design for customer value
Supplier involvement	Meeting customer needs
Elimination of waste	Accounting focus on providing
Elimination of variation	information for improvement and
Visual control	facilitating change
Global competition	Emphasis on continuous improvement
Rapid change in	Short product cycle times
competitive products	
and technology	

For an organization to embrace the world-class worldview, it has to modify its existing performance measurement system to make it compatible with that view. The result is a dual system, one a version of the traditional financial system for purposes of external reporting and the other an entirely new system for purposes of internal management and decision making.

ENLIGHTENED MEASURES

Enlightened measures are ways of looking at organizational performance from a world-class worldview. Some of these measures can be used for comparing organizations in terms of world-class status, but unlike traditional measures, few are necessarily presumed to be universally applicable. Each organization must select the measures that best represent its goals. The measures should enable monitoring of all significant performance aspects of the organization, including its inputs, internal processes, final outputs, and customer satisfaction. Doing well on one or a few measures is not sufficient to allow general conclusions about the status of an organization, though doing well on many of them is a good indicator of world-class performance.

The following measures are arranged into twelve categories, the last one being a catchall. The categories are somewhat arbitrary, and many of the measures described could arguably belong to more than one category.

PRODUCTIVITY

Three enlightened measures of productivity are as follows:

Total Head Count Productivity **(HCP)**

$$= \frac{\textit{Units Produced}}{\textit{Total Number of Employees} \text{ (Direct, Indirect, Administrative)}},$$

Units per Payroll Dollar **(UPD)** $= \dfrac{\textit{Units Produced}}{\textit{Total Payroll Dollars}},$

Value-Added per Employee **(VAE)**

$$= \frac{\textit{Sales} - (\textit{Cost of Materials, Supplies, Contracted Work})}{\textit{Total Number of Employees}}.$$

The special feature of these measures is that they eliminate the usual direct-versus indirect-labor distinction that steers managers to treat direct labor and overhead costs as totally separable and to overly focus on direct labor. In world-class organizations the direct–indirect dichotomy is largely irrelevant, especially as multidisciplined workers take on jobs previously done by staff and administrators. Furthermore, the dichotomy reinforces perceptions of status differences among employees, which inhibits openness, trust, teamwork and employee involvement.

In the latter two productivity measures, economic inflation alone can increase payroll dollars and sales dollars and give the appearance that performance is changing when it is not. To offset inflation, either dollar figures must first be converted into constant dollars or some other measure must be used so that both numerator and denominator are influenced in the same way; for instance, an alternative to VAE is

Value-Added per Payroll Dollar (VAP)

$$= \frac{Sales - (Cost\ of\ Materials,\ Supplies,\ Contracted\ Work)}{Total\ Payroll\ Dollars}.$$

ASSET UTILIZATION

Asset utilization is a measure of the amount of assets necessary to generate income. Two such measures are

Return on Total Assets (ROTA)

$$= \frac{Net\ Income + [(Interest\ Expense) \times (1 - Tax\ Rate)]}{Average\ Total\ Assets},$$

Asset Turnover (AT) $= \dfrac{Net\ Sales}{Average\ Total\ Assets},$

where average total assets is the average of the assets at the beginning of the year and at the end of the year. Both measures arc derived from the total-asset figure on the balance sheet, and from the net income and interest expense figures on the income statement. Both measures eliminate the usual motivation to optimize profit on the income statement at the expense of increasing inventory on the balance sheet. Any measure can be manipulated, in the case of the above two, for example, by divesting assets (buildings, systems, and equipment) and then leasing them back. Such maneuvers make for good finance, but they diminish the assets and involve lease arrangements that can impede flexibility and long-term competitive capability. The lesson is that no matter what measures are used, others must also be used to weigh the tradeoffs.

Example   1:   Computation of Productivity and Asset Utilization

Below is partial information from the annual balance sheet and income statement for Farmower Implements Company.

Balance Sheet (partial information) ($1000s)		
	This Year	*Last Year*
Total Assets	$31,500	$29,000
Inventory	5,500	6,500
WIP Alone	1,250	1,750

Income Statement ($1000s)	
Sales	$52,000
Cost of Goods Sold	36,000 *(direct labor and manufacturing overhead, $21,000; direct materials, $15,500; change in WIP, −$500)*
Gross Margin	16,000
Operating Expense	12,860
Operating Income	3,140
Interest Expense	640
Income	2,500
Taxes (30%)	750
Net Income	$ 1,750

The company has 200 employees. This year the company sold 60,000 units and had a payroll expense of $9 million. From this information we can determine the following:

$$HCP = \frac{60,000}{200} = 300 \text{ units/employee},$$

$$UPD = \frac{60,000}{\$9,000,000} = 0.0067 \text{ units/payroll dollar},$$

$$VAE \text{ (millions)} = \frac{\$52 - 15.5}{200} = \$0.1825 \text{ valued-added/employee (\$182,500 valued-added/employee)},$$

$$VAP = \frac{\$52 - 15.5}{\$9} = \$4.06 \text{ valued-added/payroll dollar},$$

$$ROTA = \frac{\$1,750 + 640 \ (0.7)}{30,250} = 0.0727 \text{ or } 7.3\%,$$

$$AT = \frac{\$52,000}{30,250} = 1.72 \text{ times}.$$

INVENTORY

The usual categories of inventory in manufacturing are

· **Raw materials.** Materials to which the manufacturer has not yet added value.

· **WIP.** Materials to which the manufacturer has added some value but still has more to add.
· **Finished goods.** Goods ready for shipment to the customers, with no more value to be added.

The following measure can be applied to each or all of these inventory categories.

$$\textbf{\textit{Days of Inventory (DOI)}} = \frac{Quantity\ of\ Inventory}{Demand}.$$

This measure represents how many days of production or sales can be maintained solely from inventory. All things equal, the smaller the DOI, the more efficiently inventory is being used. The quantity of inventory figure is best determined from a physical count of items on hand, that is, the number of units, containers, pounds, cubic feet, etc. Demand should be estimated using the most recent daily rate at which an item is pushed or pulled through the system; specifically, demand for raw materials and WIP should be the rate at which items are consumed to make finished outputs, and the finished output rate should be the rate necessary to satisfy customer demand (no more, no less). For example, if orders for product X average 50 units per week, and each product has two part As in it, then the demand for product X would be 10 units/day, and demand for part A would be 20 units/day.

Another way to measure DOI is

$$\frac{(Average\ Inventory\ Investment) \times (Days\ per\ Year)}{Annual\ Cost\ of\ Goods\ Sold},$$

where inventory investment and cost of goods sold are obtained from the balance sheet and income statement, respectively.

A measure of inventory for WIP items is

$$\textbf{\textit{WIP Turns}} = \frac{Cost\ of\ Goods\ Sold\ in\ Period}{Average\ Inventory\ Valuation}.$$

This measure expresses how frequently inventory turns over or is used up. Generally a larger number represents more-efficient use of inventory, though actual figures vary greatly depending on the product and industry. The numerator is the cost of goods sold on the most recent income statement. The denominator is a best estimate of inventory on-hand at all stages of the process. It should be based on a frequent, periodic count, not just the on-hand amount at year end (good inventory management includes knowing how much of any item is held in stock at any given time). The inventory valuation must take into account the value of raw materials and parts plus value-added for work completed; it should never be the same as either the finished goods or raw materials valuation.

Another, simpler way to measure WIP turns is

$$\frac{Days\ per\ Period}{Days\ of\ WIP\ Inventory},$$

where the denominator is the WIP equivalent of the DOI measure described above. While six or seven WIP turns per year is a typical average, medium-size job shops are able to do 15 to 20[7] and world-class shops easily exceed 40.

These measures, too, can be abused. Unless other criteria are given equal importance, attempts to cut DOI or increase inventory turns can, in the extreme, result in shortages, longer lead times, increased costs, and reduced customer service. Almost every measure needs a countermeasure.

Example 2: Computation of Inventory Measures

Refer to the balance sheet and income statement information for Farmower Implements Company in Example 1.

$$WIP \ DOI = \frac{\$1,500 \ (365 \ days)}{\$36,000} = 15.2 \ days.$$

The average WIP inventory valuation is $1,500,000, so WIP turns can be computed by using

$$WIP \ Turns = \frac{\$36,000,000}{\$1,500,000} = 24 \ times$$

or by using the other measure,

$$\frac{365 \ days}{15.2 \ days} = 24 \ times.$$

SETUP-TIME

Setup time is the time between when the final unit of one batch (production run, contiguous job) is finished and the first acceptable unit of the next batch is finished. The concept of setup applies to innumerable activities: time necessary to changeover an assembly line; time for workers to reach minimal proficiency at doing a new job (the learning curve); time to clean an operating room and get ready for the next surgery; time to load items, transport them, then unload them; time for a manager to settle into her office, turn on the computer, check the e-mail, and do whatever else before the day's work can begin.

As argued in earlier chapters, any serious effort to reduce batch sizes and lead times or increase plant flexibility must be accompanied by efforts to reduce setup times. Setup times at bottlenecks are particularly important, although since bottleneck locations shift, priority in reducing setup times should be given to all activities that have immediate potential to constrain throughput.

Targets for setup reduction should be continuously monitored. Mather[8] suggests keeping a historical record plantwide like the following:

Setup Times (min)	1996	1998	2000
>60	84%	41%	0%
30–60	11	19	13
20–30	4	18	12
10–20	1	17	23
5–10	0	3	27
2–5	0	2	13
<2	0	0	12

Setup is but one of many factors that contribute to lead time. The best way to know if the right factors are being tapped to reduce lead time is to measure lead time directly.

LEAD-TIME

Lead time is a good measure of overall performance because it takes into account what happens throughout an organization. Despite the key role of lead time in competitiveness, most managers have little knowledge about their own company's or competitors's lead times. According to George Stalk and Tom Hout, an organization that can respond three or four times faster than its competitors will usually grow "three times faster than overall demand."[9] The only way to reduce lead time is to attack a multitude of problems such as errors or mistakes with orders, blueprints, and specs; long setup times; frequent machine breakdowns; uncoordinated schedules; undependable suppliers; delays in inspections or repairs; long transportation times; poor records; multiple handling; and large lot sizes and inventories. Longer lead times also suggest higher expenses for storage, handling, and transportation. Lead time and lead-time reduction are dominant measures at Motorola, General Electric, and Hewlett-Packard.

The **manufacturing lead time** (M) is the stacked time or sum of the individual lead times along the critical path of all sequential, required activities, including time to order and receive raw materials, time to process materials into finished outputs, and time to deliver finished outputs to the customer. Manufacturing lead time by itself is not as important as its standing compared to **customer lead time** (C), the lead time that customers expect. One way to compare the two is with the ratio

$$\textbf{\textit{Lead Time Ratio}} = \frac{M}{C}.$$

The usual case is that C is shorter than M, so the ratio is larger than 1. To reduce the discrepancy between C and M, a firm must manufacture based on forecasts or rely on inventories of finished goods. Since forecasts are always somewhat inaccurate (the farther into the future, the more so), firms tend to rely on inventory. The smaller that M (hence, M/C) can be made, the shorter the necessary forecast horizon and the less inventory needed. A contributor to M is **supplier lead time.** Suppliers should be monitored for lead time and expected to work toward ways to reduce the lead time.

If an organization can get M equal to C, then virtually everything, including purchasing activity, can be done according to customer order (MTO). At that point, the organization should replace C with a smaller value for C (to **exceed** customer expectations), then try to further decrease M. Having an M that is less than C gives a manufacturer a significant competitive edge in the marketplace.

A measure that correlates to M is the **distance traveled** by materials throughout procurement, processing, or distribution. Hal Mather, for example, describes a 2000-pound forging being moved 2.5–3 miles from the place of its receipt as a component, to the place of its shipment as a finished product—all inside one plant.[10] Cases of large, bulky items having to be moved dozens of miles in one plant are common. Distance traveled usually results more from zigzag routings than from the size of the plant.

Another measure correlated to M is number of **order changes** such as changes in sales orders, purchase orders, production orders, and shop orders. Order changes occur due to poor forecasts or mistaken estimates from customers about their needs. Order changes are correlated to M because the farther ahead an order is placed, the more unreliable it is, and the more likely it will have to be changed.

Another lead time measure is **product development time,** or the time between a new product's concept and its launch to market. All things equal, shorter development times mean better responsiveness to changes in market trends, customer tastes, technological advances, or resource restrictions. In the mid-1980s, average development time per new car for American producers was 60 months; for Europeans it was 58 months; for the Japanese, 46 months.[11] (Not only did the Japanese have a 1-year lead-time advantage, they were able to achieve it with roughly half as many workers as the Americans or Europeans.) Given equivalent priority to quality and costs, shortened product-development times can only happen by restructuring the product-development process from the usual functional, serial approach to a multifunctional, simultaneous approach like concurrent engineering.

LAYOUT

Among the general ways to assess facility layout are in terms of utilization of space and distance traveled. The following two ratios are measures of space:

Assembly Space per Product (SPP)

$$= \frac{\text{Total Square Footage of Space in Assembly Area}}{\text{Number of Units Ordinarily in Assembly Process}},$$

Storage Space Usage (SSU)

$$= \frac{\text{Square Footage of Storage Space Occupied by Materials}}{\text{Total Square Footage Available for Storage}}.$$

The first measure correlates with the cost of space. Firms with higher SPP usually also have higher plant overhead expenses (and higher production costs) than those with lower SPP. The second measure correlates with inventory; all things equal, higher SSU is the result of more materials occupying space.

Layout and space utilization also affect damage to materials. A measure of this is

Damaged Goods Rate (DGR)

$$= \frac{Number\ of\ Damaged\ Units\ Processed\ in\ a\ Time\ Period}{Total\ Number\ of\ Units\ Processed\ in\ a\ Time\ Period}.$$

All things equal, a shop that is crowded and has more inventory on the floor will result in higher DGR than one that is better organized and has less inventory.

A simple measure of **distanced traveled** is the sum of the distances between successive operations in a process. If items are moved in standard containers or batches, this can be expressed as

$$Distance\ per\ Unit\ \textbf{(DPU)} = \frac{Total\ Distance\ Between\ All\ Operations}{Units\ Per\ Container\ (or\ Batch)}.$$

All things equal, material handling costs increase with greater distance traveled. Since travel time and travel distance are related, travel time also influences production CTs and lead times.

EQUIPMENT

Enlightened measures of equipment shift emphasis from machines doing the most work to being **capable** of doing the work when work is needed and in the best way possible. These measures can be applied to individual pieces of equipment or, on average, to all equipment in the organization.

One measure, **equipment availability,** is the proportion of time a machine is available (in usable condition) for work when it is needed.

$$Equipment\ Availability = \frac{Planned\ Running\ Time\ -\ All\ Downtime}{Planned\ Running\ Time}.$$

This measure emphasizes uptime and encourages preventive maintenance. Higher equipment availability translates into less inventory needed to cover equipment break-downs.

Another measure is

Equipment Effectiveness

$$= Equipment\ Availability \times Performance\ Efficiency \times Rate\ of\ Quality$$

where availability is as explained above, and

$$Performance\ Efficiency = \frac{Number\ of\ Units\ Produced \times Design\ CT}{Actual\ Running\ Time},$$

$$Rate\ of\ Quality = \frac{Number\ of\ Good\ Units\ Produced}{Number\ of\ All\ Units\ Produced}.$$

Equipment effectiveness is a good integrative measure because it emphasizes the availability, capability, and proficiency of the equipment at any given time. Examples are given in Chapter 7.

Schonberger suggests another measure, **dollar utilization,** as an alternative to the traditional **equipment utilization** measure.[12] While equipment utilization focuses on rate of output and is typically used to justify procurement of large pieces of equipment, dollar utilization is a better measure of the advantages associated with multiple, smaller pieces. For example, compare one machine that costs $100,000 with a two smaller machines costing $20,000 each; the big machine produces at 1000 units/hour, each little machine produces at 500 units/hour. Suppose that if all jobs were routed to the big machine, the machine would be running 6 hours/day, a 75% utilization rate for an 8-hour day. The same output would be achieved by the two smaller machines running 4 hours/day, a 50% utilization rate for each. Thus,

Dollar Utilization for the Big Machine

$$= (6 \text{ hr} \times 1000 \text{ units/hr})/\$100,000 = 0.06 \text{ units/dollar invested,}$$

while

Dollar Utilization for the Small Machines

$$= (4 \text{ hr} \times 500 \text{ units/hr})/\$20,000 = 0.100 \text{ units/dollar invested.}$$

Although the hourly capacity of the two small machines together is identical to the big machine, the units-per-dollar production is greater for the small machines. A further advantage is that the small machines provide greater flexibility since jobs can be more easily scheduled through two machines than one. The results are shorter waits, shorter lead times, and less inventory.

Another equipment measure, **reliability,** is the probability that a machine or system will perform satisfactorily for a specified period of time. In addition to the measures described in Chapter 7, reliability can be measured in terms of **Failure Rate (FR),** or the number of failures that occur in a specified time:

$$FR = \frac{Number\ of\ Failures}{Number\ of\ Hours\ of\ Operating\ Time},$$

where **failure** is any change in the machine or system to an unsatisfactory condition.

A related measure is **mean time between failures (MTBF),** which is the reciprocal of FR:

$$MTBF = \frac{1}{FR}.$$

Suppose, for example, that 20 identical pieces of machinery were operated for 1000 hours. Two of the machines failed, one after 200 hours and the other after 600 hours. Of the total possible operating time of 20,000 hours for the 20 machines, the nonoperating time was 800 hours for the first failed machine and 400 hours for the second failed machine. Since the actual total operating time was only

$20{,}000 - 1{,}200 = 18{,}800$ hours, the FR is

$$FR = \frac{2}{18{,}800} = 0.000106 \text{ failures/unithour}$$

and

$$MTBF = \frac{1}{0.000106} = 9{,}434 \text{ hr.}$$

On average, a machine has 9,434 hours of satisfactory operation between mal-functions.

QUALITY

Quality can be measured in innumerable ways, the most common being scrap cost, rework cost, warranty cost, and inspection and other costs associated with quality control. All these ways share the same limitation: emphasis on cost. The problem is not that cost-focused measures are unimportant; it is that they are inadequate. Little can be learned from cost measures about the details of where quality problems lay or what must be done to improve quality or prevent problems. The biggest omission is failure to consider the customer: *what* quality means to the customer, how well products and services meet customer expectations, where the organization falls be-hind, and what should be done to meet customer needs. To maintain a strong qual-ity position, an organization needs two separate, but integrated, sets of measures: process-focused and customer-focused.

Process-Focused

Process-focused measures center on aspects of quality relevant to the organization. These measures are largely transparent to the customer. They include measures of quality of inputs (materials, components, subcontracted parts and services), processes of the organization, and final outputs. Internal product specs and design standards are measures of inputs and final outputs. Setting internal standards so that, at minimum, final outputs fulfill customer expectations and, ideally, exceed customer expectations is the purpose of customer-focused design philosophies such as QFD.

Examples of process-focused measures include

Percent of parts starting a process that do not finish.

Percent of parts that have at least one defect (world-class organizations measure this in parts per *million*).

Percent of parts that are scrapped.

Percent of parts that are reworked.

Number of errors per order shipped.

Percent of vendor-supplied parts that are defective.

Percent of processes in statistical control.

Percent of processes with C_{pk} at least 2.0 (i.e., the natural variation of the process is well within tolerance limits).

Though measures can be aggregated to give overall product and organizational averages, each unit of the organization, each product item, and each raw material should have its own quality measures and be tracked separately. This is necessary for problem areas and opportunities for improvement to be quickly identified. The quality goals established for all individual work units must be mutually compatible so that quality improvements for one unit contribute to overall quality improvement of the final product.

Customer-Focused

Ultimately, the only thing that matters with quality is what the customer thinks about the final product or service. Common customer-focused measures of quality include

Number of customer complaints.

Number of customer returns.

Percent of deliveries on-time.

Percent of deliveries that are correct.

Percent of units delivered on-time.

Customer opinions about product or service quality level regarding features that they think are important.

The last measure, potentially the most important one, is based on data gathered from surveys of what *customers* (not sales and marketing people) say is important. Even if the organization makes virtually defectfree products at a good price, customers might not be satisfied if they perceive the lead time or customer support as poor. To be competitive, a firm does not have to be first rate in everything, only those things that are important to customers. In Figure 21.2 a **snake curve** is used to show

FIGURE 21.2

Snake curve for a customer survey.

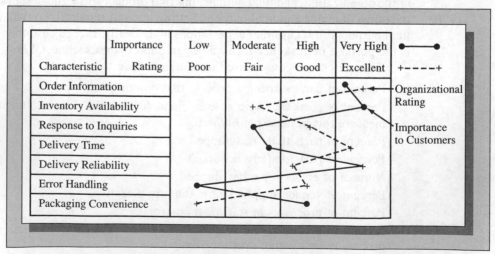

where the biggest gaps exist between the features the customer deems important and the perception the customer has of the organization's performance with regard to those features. This information suggests what quality-related actions are necessary to close the gaps, what the organization is doing right, and what does not matter to customers.

SCHEDULE

Schedule measures are used to assess adherence to production, delivery, or other schedules. Degree of compliance is called **linearity** because when calendar dates for actual deliveries are close to their corresponding scheduled delivery dates, the running plot of deliveries is a straight line (see Figure 21.3). Adherence to the schedule depends on production factors such as capacity, lead times, and interruptions, as well as validity of the schedule. The best types of schedule measures motivate improvements to comply with schedules and develop schedules that are valid.

Adherence to Schedule

A way to assess the ability of a production process to adhere to a uniform schedule is the **linearity index:**[13]

$$L = 100\% - \frac{\Sigma \mid Percent\ Deviation\ from\ Uniform\ Scheduled\ Amount \mid}{Number\ of\ Production\ Runs}.$$

The index can be computed for every product and for any time period (shift, day, or week). As an example, suppose in a 5-day period daily production is supposed to be 300 units, though one particular week it was actually 320, 305, 295, 300, and

FIGURE 21.3

Adherence to schedule.

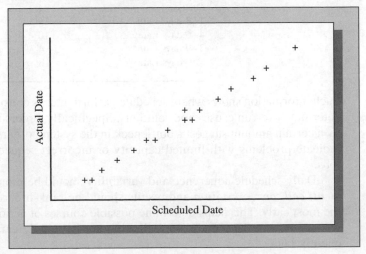

290 units. Assume one production run a day. The absolute values of the deviations are 6.67%, 1.67%, 1.67%, 0, and 3.33%, which sum to 13.34%. Thus,

$$L = 1 - \frac{13.34}{5} = 97.33\%.$$

A measure of adherence to the shipping schedule is the percent of **jobs shipped on-time** (JSOT):

$$JSOT = 1 - \frac{Number\ of\ Jobs\ Shipped\ Late\ in\ Specified\ Time\ Period}{Total\ Jobs\ Processed\ in\ Specified\ Time\ Period},$$

where "on-time" indicates that orders were shipped on or before their scheduled due dates. A limitation with this kind of measure is that it potentially encourages bad practices such as giving priority to small, easy-to-fill orders at the expense of large, difficult-to-fill (though possibly more-profitable) orders. The limitation is overcome by using measures that give equal weight to all orders, such as the percent of **units shipped on-time** (USOT):

$$USOT = 1 - \frac{Number\ of\ Units\ Shipped\ Late\ in\ Specified\ Time\ Period}{Total\ Units\ Processed\ in\ Specified\ Time\ Period}.$$

On-time schedule measures describe performance only in terms of the ability to meet a schedule; they reveal nothing about whether orders are finished early or late and by how much. To know the magnitude of scheduling adherence problems, information is needed about **variability** of schedule performance. For example,

Schedule Adherence	% Units Shipped
>6 days Early	2%
4–6 days Early	8
1–3 days Early	11
On-time	44
1–3 days Late	19
4–6 days Late	10
7–9 days Late	4
>9 days Late	2

Such information shows where schedule performance is consistent or erratic and helps determine overrun causes and solutions. Specifically, orders that are consistently late by a certain amount suggest a bottleneck in the system; orders that are highly variable indicate problems with limited capacity or incorrect sequencing and prioritizing of jobs.[14]

Daily schedule adherence and variability should be monitored for *every department, cell, or workstation* and results should be rank-ordered from the most late to the most early. This helps determine possible courses of action, such as shifting some resources from departments or cells that are habitually early to those that are frequently late.

Schedule adherence and variability should also be monitored for **suppliers** and the results should be periodically reviewed with them.

Schedule Validity

One simple way to guarantee adherence to schedule is to change the schedule; this, of course, defeats the purpose of scheduling, which is to specify what *will* happen on or by a certain date. A measure that discourages inordinate schedule changes and encourages schedule accuracy is the **number of changes to the schedule.** This measure can be applied to all kinds of schedules, including master schedules and assembly schedules. Frequent schedule changes might suggest a problem more with the way that schedules are prepared than with the way work is done to meet schedules. A schedule must fairly reflect both customer demand and the organization's capability to meet that demand. Schedule validity can be improved by better forecasting, working more closely with customers to better anticipate their future requirements, and better capacity planning and inventory management.

Many companies experience a "hockey-stick" phenomenon every period (month, quarter, or year), reflecting the struggle at the end of the period to satisfy that period's shipping goals (see Figure 21.4). They repeat this absurd pattern using expediting and overtime. To achieve level production, the percentage of total-period output produced and shipped must remain roughly the same **throughout** the period; for example 20% of the weekly orders should be filled each day, 25% of the monthly orders should be filled each week, and so on. The measure used to monitor this is called the **percent of period total produced.**

SIMPLIFICATION

The more complex or complicated something is in terms of number of parts, uniqueness of parts, or the number of steps to make it, the greater are the manufacturing cost and associated overhead. The more complex or complicated the product or process, the more difficult it is to eliminate mistakes and defects, to increase finished product

FIGURE 21.4

Hockey-stick phenomenon.

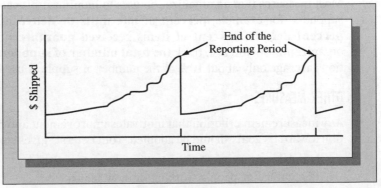

reliability, and to keep customers satisfied. For any output, if the same desired result can be achieved by simpler means (using common parts, fewer parts, and fewer operations), then simpler is better. To drive this point home, world-class organizations utilize measures that encourage simplification. To prevent abuses, they simultaneously use other measures to minimize the potential negative consequences of simplification. Following are three principle categories of simplification measures.

Total Number of Different Parts

This is a count of the raw materials or purchased parts, components, and subassemblies in a product. The higher the count is, the more complex the product, and the more wasteful the acquisition, accounting, scheduling, routing, assembly, and inspection associated with the parts. Related to this is the **number of levels in the bill of materials.** Fewer levels mean simpler MRP order systems and simpler logistics and scheduling throughout intermediate production stages.

Percent of Nonstandard Parts

The more parts in a product that are nonstandard or are unique to the product, the more types of parts the organization has to order and track. As Mather points out, however, there are possible tradeoffs here, such as a single unique part replacing several parts, thus reducing the parts count and overall product cost.[15] Often, however, standard parts are preferred because they are less expensive and have shorter lead times than unique parts.

Number of Steps and Procedures in a Process

This is the number of different steps or operations required to produce a particular output (product or service). In manufacturing this measure and the number of different parts are often correlated since fewer parts require fewer steps to assemble them. Since many steps in processes are wasteful, efforts to reduce the number of steps will direct attention to non-value-added ones that can be eliminated.

SUPPLIERS

Most measures that an organization uses to monitor itself can also be used to monitor suppliers, for example, **percent of late units or deliveries, delivery variability, percent defects, percent of items received guaranteed 100% defectfree.** The organization should also track the **total number of suppliers.** World-class organizations average only about 10% of the number of suppliers used by other organizations.

OTHER MEASURES

Any measurement criterion that motivates improvement and helps move the organization toward its goals should be adopted. Tom Peters[16] gives some interesting examples:

> Number of customer visits to the factory.
> Percentage of people working on new teams.
> Hours or dollars devoted to upgrading people's skills.

Manager's percentage of time spent out of the office and with customers and employees.

Number of awards given for interesting failures.

Speed of response to customer needs.

Number of awards given for innovative ideas.

Number of acts of organizational boundary-bashing.

R & D expenditure as a percent of sales.

Percent of payroll per employee spent on education and training.

Number of suggestions generated and implemented.

Number of ideas "swiped" from competitors or borrowed from exemplary organizations.

Some of the measures listed above are similar to those described earlier but here they apply to a particular organizational context.

ENLIGHTENED MEASURES: PRINCIPLES

In the global economy, organizations must measure performance in ways consistent with the world-class worldview. Many kinds of criteria measures fit the bill. In general, however, enlightened measures of performance (and enlightened use of traditional measures) are characterized by their focus on competitiveness, emphasis on common sense, and emphasis on long-term improvement.

COMPETITIVE FOCUS

World-class organizations succeed by anticipating, meeting, and exceeding customer expectations. They provide products and services that meet standards of quality, flexibility, innovation, lead time, and cost established by the competitive environment. Since meeting such standards is what determines a firm's ability to compete, the same standards should be the criteria an organization uses to assess its overall performance. Flexibility, for example, can be measured by the average number of jobs mastered by employees, the time to set up a machine or change over a line, or the average time to conceive, produce, and deliver a new product. A traditional measure like standard cost ordinarily does not measure competitiveness, though it *could* if it were used for comparison to competitors's costs or what customers are willing to pay. Similarly, internal due dates alone mean relatively little unless they can be used to beat the competition and exceed customer requirements. Being world-class means comparing oneself to world-class peers, competitors and otherwise. **Benchmarking,** as discussed in Chapter 4, is one way of maintaining competitive focus in performance measurement.

EMPHASIS ON CLEAR, COMMONSENSE MEASURES

Adopting enlightened measures is a move toward greater reliance on physical (as opposed to contrived) indicators of performance. Containers of inventory, setup time, number of parts, and number of defects are physical measures; standard earned dollars and hours variance are contrived measures. Contrived measures might have meaning to a manager or financial person but usually not to a person on the shop floor. Physical measures represent things that anyone can readily see, determine, and understand. They are often immediately visible and can be acted upon without calling a meeting or waiting for the next report. For example, a manager who sees inventory building up can look directly at customer orders to see whether they warrant the inventory, and, if they do not, he can take action to reduce it. Similarly, a line worker holding a defective item is able to recognize it, correct it, or stop the line, rather than ignore it for lack of knowing what to do. The concept, discussed throughout this book, is **visual management.**

Measures not of physical things, like productivity, availability, or utilization, can also be relevant and useful, but only if they tap aspects of organizational performance that make clear sense in terms of competitiveness and customer satisfaction. Any measure can be an effective motivator of behavior as long as the logic between the measure and its repercussion on competitiveness and customer satisfaction is obvious to everyone, including shop-floor level people. Lead-time ratio, machine effectiveness, and head-count productivity are examples of nonphysical measures where the logic can be readily conveyed to anyone.

Enlightened measures are not only easy to understand, they are easy to obtain and utilize. Data can usually be acquired from existing formal data collection systems or by workers and staff taking periodic counts. Computations are straightforward and can be performed and comprehended by anyone in the company because measurement is everyone's territory, not just managers's or accountants's. When everyone knows the measures and what they signify, everyone knows where the organization is headed.

Schonberger[17] gives an example of this kind of simplicity in allocating overhead. Suppose a plant makes three products, A, B, and C, with production lead times of 3 days, 9 days, and 12 days, respectively. Since the overhead consumed by a product is roughly proportionate to the lead time, product A would get 3/24 of the allocated overhead, B would get 9/24, and C would get 12/24. The scheme is simple and makes sense to workers. It also reinforces the continuous improvement ethic because it drives managers to try to reduce lead time. Since little of the lead time is devoted to value-added work, reducing lead time tends to reduce waste. If lead times for all products can be reduced, total overhead can be reduced as well.

Commonsense comprehension of a criteria measure alone does not mean the measure will be valid or appropriate, and there are many examples of traditional measures to prove it. For example, the usual way to evaluate a proposed piece of equipment is to compare its cost with the direct labor saved. The criterion is return on investment (ROI), where

$$ROI = \frac{Annualized\ Labor\ Cost\ Savings}{Capital\ Equipment\ Cost}.$$

The application of this criterion as typically used ignores certain important factors, for example, that the people being replaced (labor saved) are more flexible than a machine and can be moved around and trained to do other things. But it is difficult to quantify the cost of reduced flexibility or reduced human mind-power, which is one reason why such factors are ignored. Actually, a measure like ROI might be appropriate if *all* significant costs could be incorporated. The fault of ROI and other such measures is less with the measures themselves than with the simple-minded way they are used.

EMPHASIS ON TRENDS AND LONG-TERM IMPROVEMENT

Decisions that might improve immediate performance must always be weighed against the long-term consequences. Sole attention to traditional financial measures often leads to actions oriented toward boosting immediate economic performance while ignoring the delayed or long-term results. An organization that remains static in a world that demands continuous improvement is, comparatively, getting worse.

World-class organizations ensure their survival by investing in the future. They know that **trends** in performance are as important as existing performance and that progress is assessed in terms of steady changes upward or downward. They monitor improvement trends in productivity, quality, equipment availability, setup times, lead times, schedule adherence, and virtually every other kind of activity for which they collect data. They keep close tabs on financial and other resources committed to expanding opportunities, including expenditures for research and product development, plant maintenance, and employee skills training. To gauge improvement, they compare numbers year-to-year for organizationwide measures and more frequently for the subunits of the organization. The impact of every subunit's improvement on long-term organizational health is assessed, and units that need more improvement or that contribute the most to organizationwide competitiveness and improvement (e.g., research and employee training) get priority, even if the consequence is to reduce organizational performance on some measures in the short run.

PERFORMANCE MEASUREMENT SYSTEMS

To be competitive, a company's strategies and objectives must be tied to improvements in cost, quality, delivery, product-development innovation and lead times, and process flexibility. The company's long-term and immediate objectives should be linked to operating policies, plans, and daily decisions through a comprehensive **performance measurement system.** As Lynch and Cross[18] say, the performance measurement system should

- Link daily operations to strategic objectives.
- Balance financial with nonfinancial measures.
- Transform the organization from a rigid-vertical to responsive-horizontal decision-making system.
- Motivate workers and managers.
- Identify and eliminate waste.
- Measure what is important to customers.
- Accelerate organizational learning and acceptance of change in customer expectations.
- Translate company flexibility into specific measurements.

Notice, these points directly or indirectly overlap qualities of JIT/TQM organizations as related throughout this book. Consider the first four: strategic focus, financial and nonfinancial measures, decision making, and motivation.

STRATEGIC FOCUS

Lockamy says that the performance measurement system should "result in the firm focusing on a narrow range of pursuits, developing a consistent pattern of decision making, and embracing strategic objectives acknowledged by the entire company," as well as provide mechanisms that enable various levels and functions of the firm to focus on strategic objectives.[19]

FINANCIAL AND NONFINANCIAL MEASURES

The performance measurement system should present *a balanced scorecard* of company performance, which includes financial measures as well as the nonfinancial measures that ultimately drive financial performance. The system should provide a handful of measures that, combined, gives a complete picture of the current company status and direction. The system should help managers understand relationships among different aspects of company performance and provide information that is critical but not overwhelming. The primary interest of the performance system is less on control and more on planning and moving forward.[20]

DECISION MAKING FOCUS

Performance measurement systems should provide information appropriate to the level and functional area of the people who need it. Though the system might universally track and publicize some measures of overall business performance, mostly it should track narrower measures that people use in their daily work for decision making. The system should avoid reporting information that is overwhelming or irrelevant to people's needs.

Strategic focus, balanced-scorecard, and decision-making criteria in a performance measurement system are illustrated in the following case in point.

CASE IN POINT: Trane Corporation[21]

At the Self-Contained Systems (SCS) business unit of Trane Corporation, the largest commercial manufacturer of air-conditioners in the US, company strategic objectives emphasize product cost and quality. Material costs are considered of strategic importance because they represent 77% of the unit's manufacturing cost. The importance of quality to the business is also widely recognized and is promoted by quality improvement activities everywhere.

SCS's performance measurement systems monitor cost and quality objectives using measures that are highly visual, easy to understand, focus on daily trends, and interconnect all organizational levels and functional areas. Two kinds of performance measurement systems are used,

TABLE 21-1   Functional Area Performance Measures[22]

Function	Performance Criteria	Performance Measures	Performance Standards
Operations	Cycle counting	% Accuracy	100% accuracy
	Spoilage/scrap	Daily spoilage and scrap dollars by work team	Improving trend
	Small tools/gauges	Daily small tool and gauge account dollars by work team	Improving trend
	Housekeeping	Housekeeping grading scale	Highest grade
Supplier dev./mat'ls	Material outages	Total daily number and % due to vendor late delivery, vendor quality, BOM/inventory accuracy and material planning	No outages
	MRP exception messages	Daily ranking of no. of MRP messages by planner	No messages
	Defective material	No. of days defective materials are held in return or review area	Improving trend
	Service orders	Daily no. of service orders received	Improving trend (less service orders)
	Service order parts	Daily no. of service order parts shipped	Improving trend
	Service order processing time	No. of days to process a service order	Improving trend
Marketing	Customer hours	No. of hours spent with customers by marketing engineers	4 customer locations per month spending no. of hours necessary
	Order pace	Daily no. of incoming orders	Order forecast
	Price	Daily price of booked orders	Budgeted price
P/D Eng.	Sales order specials	No. of days to process	Improving trend
	Warranty claims	No. of days to process	5 days
Accounting	Expense vouchers	No. of days to process	Improving trend
	Invoice discounts	Frequency of using available cash discounts	100% usage
	Expense reports	No. of days to process	Improving trend
	Direct base billing outstanding	Daily dollar value of receivables	Improving trend
Human resources	Performance appraisal timeliness	% On-time performance of appraisals by management team	100% on-time

one for the functional areas and one for the total business. The purposes of the first system are to measure performance in each functional area and communicate it to other areas, monitor customer-oriented relationships between the areas, and provide information to support resource allocation decisions.

In a scheme similar to the **policy deployment** process described in Chapter 4, each functional manager must develop a business plan that

TABLE 21-2 Total Business Performance Measures[23]

Performance Criteria	Performance Measures	Performance Standards
Manufacturing performance	Units per day	5.6 Units per day
	Man hrs. paid per unit	155 hrs. per unit
	Man hrs. paid per unit per production worker (productivity ratio)	1.24
	Floor cycle	3 days
Inventory management	Turns	Finished: 20 per year
		RIP: 10 per year
		Total: 10 per year
	Inventory accuracy	98%
	% Material outage days due to late delivery, vendor quality or other reasons	No outages
	% Permanent homes for point of use inventory on plant floor (i.e., permanent locations)	100%
	Machine downtime hours due to material outages	0 hours Downtime
Shipping performance	% on-time delivery	98%
	Average days late	0 days
	Weekly promise cycle versus customer request date	Promise cycle = customer request date
	Master production schedule (MPS) changes	Weeks 1–2: <2%
		Weeks: 2–6: <5%
	Ship cycle	7 weeks
MPS performance	Weekly MPS deviations	±7%
	Monthly MPS deviations	±5%
P/D eng. performance	No. of ECN completed monthly	Improving trend (increase monthly no. completed)
	Average ECN backlog	<25
	ECN throughput rate	30 days per ECN
	% New products/options introduced in last 2 years	5% of Total sales
Business performance	Operating income dollars before interest and taxes	Financial plan
	Cash-flow before interest and taxes	Financial plan
	Order dollars (actual bookings)	Financial plan
	Sales dollars (actual billings)	Financial plan
	Operating expenses	Financial plan
	Return on sales	Financial plan
	Return on net assets	Financial plan
	Sales dollars per person	Nonproduction: $517K
		Production: $284K
	Scrap/spoilage	0.8% of Total sales
	Service expense	1.8% of Total sales
Accounting performance	Sales expense disposition	20 days
Vendor performance	% on-time delivery	95%
	% defectfree	98%
	Lead time	
	% Less than 8 wks.	85%
	% Less than 3 wks.	35%

(Continued)

Performance Criteria	Performance Measures	Performance Standards

Customer contact	Customer days:
	  Average days per month
	  Customer in Macon/SBU personnel in field
		5
		30 days per month for the combination

Personnel/safety performance	Absenteeism rate Lost time accidents	<2.0% Annually <2.5 days Annually

outlines strategies for connecting activities in the department with total-business objectives. The plan must include targets and criteria for measuring progress, and the measures used by the fuctional areas must be consistent with each other and with measures for the total business. A sampling of the measures used by the functional department is shown in Table 21.1.

The system also monitors total business performance and reports results to all departments responsible for achieving particular targets. Some of the measures for assessing total business performance are listed in Table 21.2.

To aid visual management and better enable functional areas to achieve functional and total business objectives, many of these measures are displayed at the workplace in every functional area or are made readily available to every employee.

DIRECTION AND MOTIVATION

Whatever gets measured, gets done. Thus, other purposes of the performance measurement system are to convey to everyone the vision, objectives, and direction of the organization and guide employees in working toward the same cnds. As a motivator, measures used in the system can be tied to rewards for groups, departments or business units for meeting goals or targets.

SELECTING PERFORMANCE MEASURES

Establishing a performance measurement system starts with a review of current measures and systems. The review involves[24]

- Documenting current measures.
- Confirming strategic objectives.
- Identifying success factors critical for meeting objectives.
- Identifying manufacturing process trends affecting the company.
- Determining new and revised performance measures.
- Comparing current and proposed measures.
- Assessing cultural impacts of the new measures and how to deal with them.
- Planning the approach to implement the new performance measurement system.

CASE IN POINT: Performance Measurement to Improve Manufacturing and Give Recognition[25]

Vokurka and Fliedner describe a company with seven US plants that established a new performance measurement system to (1) help drive manufacturing quality improvement and (2) give recognition to individual plants for improvement.

Ten measures were recommended by a committee of plant managers to assess each plant's performance. Each measure is expressed by an index, with 100 as the baseline for expected performance. A plant's overall performance is determined by averaging the 10 measures.

Performance awards were set according to the rules shown in Table 21.3. To insure recognition for plants with overall good performance and preclude plants with even one poor performance score, all awards have a minimum score. The award system does not drive plants to compete against each other, but rather against standards set for each of them in a given year. If multiple plants have an outstanding year, all get awards and the overall performance for the company improves significantly.

The system was well received because it was understandable by plant managers, staff, and employees. It kept management focused on improving overall plant performance rather than maximizing a few selected criteria.

Over the first 3 years of implementation some measures were changed to reflect changes in internal plant operations, customer focus, and measurement accuracy. Still, the results reported by the system were as the company had hoped: well-performing plants were given recognition, and overall company manufacturing performance improved significantly. In the first year, three plants received rewards—two president's and one merit; 2 years later, six received awards—four president's, one distinction, and one leap frog. Performance improvements for the seven plants are shown in Table 21.4.

TABLE 21-3   Performance Awards[26]

Award	Criteria
President's Award for Excellence	105 Points and no single criterion less than 95 points
Award of Distinction	105 Points and no single criterion less than 90 points
Award of Merit	100 Points and no single criterion less than 90 points
Leap Frog Award	Largest increase in points from the previous year

TABLE 21-4   Performance Accomplishments[27]

Measurement	Change
Scrap	50% Reduction
Overhead costs	20% Reduction
Period expenses	25% Reduction
Delivery	80%–93% On-time delivery
WIP turnover	60% Increase
Raw material turnover	50% Increase
Labor effectiveness	20% Improvement

The performance measurement system cannot be credited entirely or even mainly for these improvements because other improvement efforts were also underway, including a drive to reduce scrap and installation of cellular manufacturing. The authors of the report believe, however, that the performance measurement system was a significant contributor.

Once the performance measurement system is in place, the criteria measures must be periodically reviewed for relevance to current competitive requirements and business changes. The measurement system should be reassessed for its ability to connect measures at all levels and functions to company strategic objectives, motivate consistent action throughout the organization, and give a balanced financial/nonfinancial picture of performance. Similarly, each measure used in the system should be periodically reassessed for its ability to accurately reflect a particular aspect of performance, usefully serve the needs of the decision makers who use it, and motivate goal-directed behavior. Just as yesterday's measures are not representative of today's worldview, today's measures might not represent business in tomorrow's world. Different measures serve different purposes, and while one set may be necessary to move an organization to world-class status, another might be needed to keep it there.

PERFORMANCE MEASUREMENT AND COMPETITIVE MANUFACTURING MANAGEMENT

The measures that an organization chooses for gauging its performance *reflect* the organization's general management philosophy, culture, and practices. To the extent that an organization measures only what its management holds most dear, a manufacturer that actively adopts enlightened measures is more likely one that has also embraced goals, philosophy, and practices for attaining competitive advantage by producing products better, faster, and cheaper with processes that are more lean and agile than the competition. The company is certainly also customer-focused and driven to keep improving. Such is the JIT/TQM manufacturer.

Summary

Performance measures are used to decide between courses of action and assess operating status and progress toward goals. Despite the central role of measures in decision making, many organizations rely on measures that do not give a balanced picture of organizational performance or provide guidance toward strategic objectives. Problems with traditional measurement systems include overemphasis on financial criteria, a functional–reductionist viewpoint, and preoccupation with past performance and control.

Overemphasis on financial criteria such as profits and dividends discourages top management from setting strategic initiatives for improving quality and service, reducing waste, or training workers. These show up initially as costs and require years before turning into profits.

Even traditional nonfinancial measures have done little to encourage competitiveness. Typically, performance measures for one unit are divorced from those of others and from strategies and goals of the overall organization. The measures are often inward-looking and do not capture aspects of performance necessary to gain and retain customers or to build long-term competitive strength.

Given the short-term goals of many investors and the relatively short tenure of managers and executives in any one company, their interest is often on immediate performance only. This behavior is supported by traditional financial/accounting systems that report short-term variances with budgetary and internal standards and ignore many things relevant to long-term organization competitiveness.

Organizations that want to embrace the world-class worldview represented by JIT and TQM must adopt a performance measurement system compatible with that view. One key element of such a system is the use of enlightened measures, which are measures that have a competitive focus, are commonsense and easy to see and use, and look to the future. Competitive focus means knowing what is necessary to compete and succeed and then doing it. Development of enlightened measures starts with looking outside the organization to see what customers, markets, and competitors require, setting strategic objectives, and then designing measures that will guide and motivate actions consistent with strategic goals.

The commonsense, easy to see and use aspect of these measures relates to a recurring theme in this book: visual management. At the shop floor, arcane collecting and reporting systems are replaced by simple physical measures that everyone can understand and use to make decisions. Charts of measures giving a balanced scorecard are posted everywhere so even the casual observer can assess performance of a department, factory, or the overall organizational at a glance.

Enlightened measures motivate behavior that will be good for long-term improvement. Things such as research, product development, and plant and equipment acquisition and overhaul, as well at JIT/TQM programs for training, setup reduction, supplier development, concurrent engineering, and implementing pull production and cellular manufacturing systems are viewed not solely in terms of current costs, but for the opportunities and competitive advantage they afford.

Enlightened measures are a key part of a performance measurement system. The major purposes of this system are to insure behavior consistent with strategic objectives, present a balanced scorecard that gives a complete picture of the status and direction of the company in terms of both financial and nonfinancial measures, provide information for decision making appropriate to each level and functional area, and track performance trends to assess progress and spot areas needing improvement.

Questions

1. What are the drawbacks of relying solely on financial measures to assess organizational performance?
2. In what ways can measures such as cost variance, labor productivity, and machine utilization motivate behavior that increases waste?
3. Distinguish between internally (process) and externally focused performance measures. Give examples. Discuss the pros and cons of relying solely on either internally focused or externally focused measures.

4. Discuss traditional performance criteria for their ability to motivate individuals and departments to do things that enhance organizational improvement and competitiveness.

5. This chapter lists a number of enlightened measures, some already mentioned in earlier chapters. Skim through the chapters of this book and list additional performance measures mentioned there but not discussed in this chapter.

6. Discuss how enlightened measures conform to the JIT principles discussed in Chapter 3.

7. Discuss how the enlightened measures motivate customer-focused quality behavior of functional departments as described in Chapter 4.

8. Review business articles in newspapers and magazines and compile a list of the performance measures noted or implied. How do these measures compare with those discussed in this chapter?

9. The topic of visual management has been mentioned a number of times in this book. Which enlightened measures can be used for visual management?

10. Discuss the purposes of a performance measurement system.

11. How are measures of functional performance tied to measures of company performance and company strategic objectives?

12. The enlightened measures described in the chapter apply to different levels of the organization—the shop floor, functional areas, top-level management, and so on. Review the measures in this chapter and divide them into the following categories of people who would most likely use them:

> Top management.
> Functional management (define the functional area).
> Cross-functional teams (define the teams and what multiple areas they represent).
> Shop-floor workers and supervisors.

Problems

1. A manufacturer has 400,000 square feet available for storage, and in a typical month uses about 390,000 square feet of it. Also in a month it produces 350,000 units that are processed and handled in batches of 1000 units. The sum of the distances between operations in the process is 900 feet. Because the facility is crowded, an average of 2800 units monthly are damaged while in the shop. Suppose the shop switches to a cellular layout. The amount of space required for storage in all of the cells is 27,500 square feet, the total distance between operations in a cell averages 90 feet. The production of the shop is still 350,000 units a month, though items are now processed in batches of 10. The number of damaged units is now only 300 monthly.
   a. What effect did the switch to cellular manufacturing have on SSU, DPU, and DGR?
   b. Comment on the DPU for the batch and cellular processes. Why are the results not directly comparable? Suggest a way to adjust DPU to better measure the result of shifting to cellular manufacturing.

2. The information in Example 1 was for *this year*. Suppose for the same company, Farmower Implements, the information for *last year* is as follows:

Balance Sheet (partial information) ($1000s)		
	Last Year	**2 Years Ago**
Total Assets	$29,000	$28,000
Inventory	6,500	7,500
WIP Alone	1,750	1,800

Income Statement ($1000s)		
Sales	$50,000	
Cost of Goods Sold	35,000	(direct labor + manufacturing overhead $20,125; direct materials, $15,125; change in WIP, − $250)
Gross Margin	15,000	
Operating Expense	13,860	
Operating Income	2,000	
Interest Expense	550	
Income	1,450	
Taxes (30%)	435	
Net Income	$ 1,015	

Last year the company had 190 employees, a payroll expense of $8.5 million, and sold 55,000 units.

a. Determine for last year the following: WIP DOI, WIP turns, HCP, UPD, VAE, VAP, ROTA, an AT.

b. Determine the percent change in performance from last year to this year for all of the measures using the results from above and in Examples 1 and 2. Overall, has company performance improved or worsened since last year?

3. Table 21.5 gives annual performance indicators for three divisions of a large electronics corporation. Refer to this table to answer the following questions. (Before answering these questions, you might review the section "Enlightened Measures: Principles.")

a. At what organization-level audience are these measures aimed?

b. In general, what is good about the format and content of the data in the table? What kinds of general conclusions can be made about performance?

c. How might information in the table be displayed differently to highlight or clarify results?

Table 21-5   Performance Measures at Three Electronics Divisions[28]

	A	B	C
Sales, $ millions	$100	$200	$300
Production output, $ millions	$60	$100	$180
Percentage sales growth, last 5 yr. avg.	34%	41%	6%

Quality

Customer:

	A	B	C
Percentage new units returned as defective	0.110% F[a]	0.240% F	0.788% F
Quality ranking in industry by customer survey	First F	Second N[c]	Third N
Estimated mean time between failures, years	23.4 F	6.3 F	N/A[d]
Emergency service calls for instruments on first 3 years warranty, percentage	2.6% F	3.6% F	12.3% N

Internal:

	A	B	C
Final test; repair-and-retest rate, percentage	0.28% F	1.24% F	8.8% N
After-solder PCB reject rate, ppm	908 F	2493 F	3873 F
Fallout: $\dfrac{\text{(Total parts not finishing process)}}{\text{(Total parts starting process)}}$	3.1% F	7.3% F	14.3% N

Suppliers:

	A	B	C
Percentage of suppliers certified	96% F	63% F	24% F
Incoming inspection reject rate, percentage	0.04% F	0.33% F	1.23% F

Dependability

	A	B	C
On-time arrival rate	93% F	87% F	51% U[b]
On-time shipping rate	99.6% F	98% F	73% N
Delays/month for part shortages	3 U	9 F	114 U
Schedule Index (% days final production is within 10% of daily requirement)	100% N	95% F	N/A

Waste

	A	B	C
$ Value added/(Total headcount)	$214,000 F	$162,000 F	$138,000 N
$ of production/ft^2	$5182 F	$5316 F	$3205 N
Total team projects completed	48 F	37 F	26 F

Flexibility (Lead Times)

	A	B	C
Throughput time [runout calculation] ($ in WIP)/($ output rate) in days	6 N	12 F	22 F
Total inventory, days on hand	17 F	27 F	43 F
PCB lot size	1 N	1 F	8 N
Average customer lead time, work days (Backlog in units)/(Daily output in units)	43 N	55 F	62 N
Longest supplier lead time, work days	40 F	60 U	65 N
Percentage of "Hard Parts" engineering changes completed in under 4 weeks	52% F	13% F	5% U
Development time, new model, months (Concept meeting to first unit produced)	11 F	18 F	23 N

(Continued)

TABLE 21-5   Continued

	A	B	C
Innovation			
Percentage products and models new within 2 years	76% F	47% F	35% U
Percentage customers considering div. a tech ldr.	84% F	52% F	12% U
People			
Absentism, all employees, percentage unscheduled days	1.1% N	1.3% N	4.6% F
Percentage employees participating on teams:			
Production employees	59% F	26% F	15% N
All others	83% F	35% F	N/A
Number of suggestions/total headcount	1.52 F	0.12 U	0.09 N
Percentage of employees trained:			
Team leadership	100% N	87% F	34% F
Statistical process control	94% F	57% F	19% F
Personal computer tools	34% F	7% F	0% N
Financial			
Return on Investment	16% N	17% F	24% F
Debt/Equity	32%	47%	67%
Days of receivables	62 U	43 U	59 N
Average age of purchased equipment, years	2.1 F	2.9 N	3.8 F
Trend of last three annual measurements:			

[a] F = Favorable   [b] U = Unfavorable
[c] N = Not clear   [d] N/A = Not available or not found

> d. For what reasons would a corporation want to compare different divisions like this?
>
> e. Which division has superior performance to the other two? This might seem like a trick question, since no one division is superior in all measures. Look for inconsistencies in the performance measures. What are likely causes of these inconsistencies?
>
> f. What cautions should be taken in comparing and making conclusions about different organizations using measures such as the ones listed?
>
> g. How should N/A be treated? What can or might N/A indicate?
>
> h. For what kinds of decisions is the information in the table most helpful? In general, what other kinds of information are needed to get a more balanced picture of each division's current health and future outlook?
>
> i. Discuss the relevancy or irrelevancy of information in the table for making strategic decisions for each division.

Endnotes

1. J.S. Rydz, *Commonsense Manufacturing Management* (New York: Harper & Row, 1990), pp. 100–1.
2. Even at the organizational level, traditional measures are unlikely to show anything amiss because of contrivances used to measure performance. The standard cost accounting system treats

inventory in each profit center as sales. Departments earn revenues by producing output, so every department attempts to maximize output regardless of demand from customers or other departments. Earned profit for all departments collectively becomes the earned profit for the organization. It is possible for the organization to show increasing "profits" simply by having built up inventories without having shipped a single unit to customers.

3. R. Bettis, S. Bradley, G. Hamel, "Outsourcing and Industrial Decline," *Academy of Management Review* 6, No. 1 (1992), pp. 7–22.

4. P. Turney and B. Anderson, "Accounting for Continuous Improvement" *Sloan Management Review,* Winter 1989, p. 38.

5. *Ibid.,* p. 39.

6. *Ibid.,* p. 40.

7. T. Gunn, *21st Century Manufacturing* (New York: Harper-Collins, 1992), p. 201.

8. H. Mather, *Competitive Manufacturing* (Englewood Cliffs, NJ: Prentice-Hall, 1988), pp. 192–3.

9. G. Stalk and T. Hout, *Competing Against Time* (New York: The Free Press, 1990), p. 36.

10. H. Mather, *Competitive Manufacturing,* p. 199.

11. J. Womack, D. Jones, D. Roos, *The Machine That Changed the World* (New York: HarperPerrenial, 1990), p. 118.

12. R. Schonberger, *World-Class Manufacturing: The Lessons of Simplicity Applied* (New York: The Free Press, 1986), pp. 90–2.

13. R. Schonberger and E. Knod, *Operations Management* (6th ed.) (Chicago: Irwin, 1997), pp. 483–4.

14. H. Mather, *Competitive Manufacturing,* p. 196.

15. *Ibid.,* p. 203.

16. T. Peters, *Thriving on Chaos* (New York: Alfred A. Knopf, 1988), pp. 491–2.

17. R. Schonberger, *World-Class Manufacturing,* pp. 176–7.

18. R.L. Lynch and K.F. Cross, *Measure UP! Yardsticks for Continuous Improvement* (Cambridge, MA: Basil Blackwell, 1991).

19. A. Lockamy, "How to Compete in your Industry," *Production and Inventory Management,* January 1993, pp. 1–5.

20. R. Vokurka and G. Fliedner, "Measuring Operating Performance: A Specific Case Study," *Production and Inventory Management,* January 1995, pp. 38–43.

21. A. Lockamy, "How to Compete in Your Industry."

22. *Ibid.,* p. 2; reprinted with permission of APICS, the Educational Society for Resource Management, Falls Church, VA.

23. *Ibid.,* pp. 2–3.

24. P.R. Santori and A.D. Anderson, "Manufacturing Performance in the 1990s: Measuring for Excellence," *Journal of Accountancy,* November 1987, pp. 141–7.

25. R. Vokurka and G. Fliedner, "Measuring Operating Performance: A specific case study."

26. *Ibid.,* p. 41; reprinted with permission of APICS, the Educational Society for Resource Management, Falls Church, VA.

27. *Ibid.,* p. 42.

28. Reprinted with permission from R. Hall, H.T. Johnson, and P. Turney, *Measuring Up: Charting Pathways to Manufacturing Excellence* (Homewood, IL: Business-One Irwin, 1991), pp. 166–7.

MRP-BASED PRODUCTION PLANNING AND SCHEDULING

The purpose of production planning and control (PPC) is to anticipate demand for production items, to plan and schedule the necessary resources, and to execute and control production activities. Over the past few decades, many companies have implemented PPC systems based on **material requirements planning (MRP).** MRP evolved from a simple procedure for determining order quantities and schedules for parts in assembled products into a complete system for capacity planning, scheduling, and controlling shop-floor activities.

This appendix covers planning and control topics mentioned throughout the book and reviews MRP-based PPC systems, which remain the mainstay of PPC for most large- and medium-sized companies.

MRP-BASED PPC

MRP-based production is often referred to as **push-type** production because job orders at every stage of the production process are initiated according to job schedules, causing them to be pushed from one operation to the next. This is in contrast to **pull-type** production wherein jobs are initiated from downstream operations, in effect, pulling them from one operation to the next, throughout the process.

MRP systems are computer-based. They are often somewhat complex and difficult to implement, and as a result an entire computer/consulting industry has burgeoned to develop and install them. There is no shortage of advocates to extol the virtues and praise the benefits of MRP systems. In many ways the praise is justified since MRP systems do offer an improvement over earlier PPC schemes, which tended to be less comprehensive and ignored the interdependencies of planning and scheduling of components and operations in assembled products. But in other important aspects MRP has been a disappointment, and managers today are more cautious in their expectations. Just as there were many who claimed the superiority of MRP over simpler reorder-point methods only a few years ago, there are many who now claim that pull production is superior to MRP.

In truth, one system is not universally superior; pull and MRP systems both have relative advantages and disadvantages, depending on the application and production environment. The basic functions of the two systems are different. Pull production is

FIGURE A.1

Framework for an MRP-based PPC process.

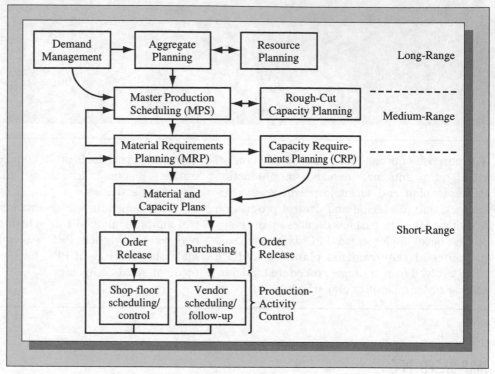

a tool for short-range work scheduling and shop-floor control. It rarely has anything to do with production planning, whereas MRP does. Even in a JIT plant that uses pull methods on the shop floor, MRP retains a rightful place as a tool for long- and medium-range planning, and, in many cases, for materials procurement.

Figure A.1 shows a general framework for the PPC process. The process is divided into long-range, medium-range, and short-range planning and shop-floor control. Notice the middle function labeled **MRP** and the many other functions to which it is linked. The centrality of the MRP function in the framework and its pervasive connections to other functions is why the process is called MRP-based PPC. We will review the functions as they appear from top to bottom in Figure A.1.

LONG-RANGE PLANNING

Long-range planning is big-picture planning. It addresses the question "What will happen to demand and how should we prepare for it?" Long-range refers to the time horizon for purposes of planning resources, which is about 1–5 years.

Long-range planning considers possible alternative levels of production necessary to meet forecasted demand. It also considers alternative strategies and tactics to achieve those levels. Those strategies and tactics are evaluated far enough in advance to allow time for modifying and acquiring the resources needed for implementation. Strategies deal with longer-range issues, such as expansion or downsizing of production capacity, and consider such factors as plant size, plant location, workforce size, new product launch, product diversification, and capital equipment expenditures. Tactics deal with shorter-range issues such as the feasibility and efficacy of meeting demand by adding work shifts or overtime, carrying inventories, or outsourcing production.

Long-range planning is a multifunctional matter. Each department has a different perspective about which strategies or tactics are appropriate. While finance people tend to be conservative and push for high utilization of existing resources, marketing and sales people want high production capacity to meet any level of sales, and operations people want to avoid scheduling changes or hiring/laying-off workers. To some extent, these perspectives are all valid and should be represented in long-range plans.

DEMAND MANAGEMENT

Demand management refers to management of all demands placed on an organization, both internal and external. External demand is customer demand. Internal demand includes service parts, intracompany requirements, and inventory stocking. Activities for managing demand include forecasting, order entry, delivery-date promising, distribution, and customer-contact activities. All potential demand must be considered for purposes of predicting resource requirements, preparing production plans, and coordinating the supply of materials and products. Demand management involves proactive activities to influence demand, such as promotional campaigns and product pricing, as well as passive activities, such as forecasting demand and responding to sales projections.

Aggregate Demand

Long-range planning is a coarse form of planning because it relies on gross measures for both product demand and production resources. Because long-range planning focuses on overall production levels, not on details, it relies on forecasts of **aggregate demand,** which is demand for product groups. A **product group** represents products that have similar routings, parts, and operating times and require similar resources. Aggregate-demand forecasts are used at this planning level because the accuracy associated with forecasts of groups is better than with forecasts of individual items.

RESOURCE PLANNING

A **resource plan** considers the amount of resources necessary to satisfy aggregate demand. A resource is measured in terms of its **capacity level,** which is its maximum output rate or time availability. In long-range planning only key resources are considered. Key resources are those that are scarce or difficult to acquire and include special workcenters, equipment, and labor skills. Bottleneck operations are considered key resources since they constrain the capacity of the entire process. Resources that are not (and will not become) bottlenecks are usually of less or no concern.

Resource planning involves checking the production capacity necessary to meet forecasted demand against the capacity of existing resources. What the organization considers available capacity depends on such factors as the number of shifts and days per week worked, the overtime policy, worker efficiency, available workforce, equipment levels, and any other factors the company considers important. A company that operates expensive equipment might value high utilization and base its maximum capacity on three shifts a day, 7 days a week. A more common plan uses 15 shifts a week as the maximum capacity and 5 or 10 shifts as normal capacity. Available capacity should be based upon what is most feasible, not what is theoretically possible. JIT/TQM companies never plan based on maximum capacity. They use a much smaller figure to allow time for unscheduled equipment breakdowns, preventive maintenance, process variability, and contingencies. Companies that plan for maximum capacity allow no time for proactive activities such as worker training or process improvement.

To estimate capacity requirements for a product group, one product is selected from the group, and its **bill of resources** (or bill of labor) is used as representative of all products. The bill of resources is a list of the resources (workcenters or machines) and the standard time required to produce a unit of the product. It includes the times for all stages of production of the product, as well as for all subassemblies and components of the product that must also be produced.

Example   1:   Estimating Capacity Requirements from the Bill of Resources

Consider product X, which has been selected as representative of product group K. Product X consists of two components, items A and B. The production process for product X involves manufacturing both components, then assembling them. Route sheets indicate the workcenters and standard times for the three items as shown in Table A.1. The

TABLE A-1   Process Routing for Product X

Item	Workcenter Assembly	Standard Run Hours/Unit
X	Assembly	0.6
A	Cutting	0.33
	Broaching	0.86
	Grinding	0.31
B	Cutting	0.45
	Milling	0.72
	Drilling	0.56
	Grinding	0.41

standard run hours per unit represent the average run time for a single unit which includes setup time, processing time, and the nominal batch size.

To derive the bill of resources for product X, sum the times given in Table A.1 by workcenter. Thus, the bill of resources, as shown below, gives the total time for each resource (workcenter) to produce one unit:

Workcenter	Standard Run Hours/Unit
Assembly	0.6
Cutting	0.78
Broaching	0.86
Drilling	0.56
Grinding	0.72

With the bill of resources, future resource requirements are estimated by converting forecasts for production volume for the product group into standard run hours. Suppose the projected production volume for product group K for a future 4-year period is as follows:

Year	2000	2001	2002	2003
Volume	12,000	13,000	13,500	14,000

For illustrative purposes, consider just one resource, the grinding workcenter. The total requirements in standard hours are computed as (production volume $\times$ 0.72). Thus, the estimated capacity requirements for the planning period are

Year	2000	2001	2002	2003
Hours	8,640	9,360	9,720	10,080

These estimates are then checked against the current hours available at the grinding workcenter. If, for example, current annual capacity is 9,500 hours, then grinding resources will have to be increased before the year 2002.

AGGREGATE PLANNING

An **aggregate production plan** is another form of long-range plan. This plan considers not only overall resource requirements, but also how resource utilization will be adjusted to meet fluctuations in demand. Given information about existing capacity (workforce and equipment levels) and about costs and policies regarding changing workforce size, using overtime, adding shifts, outsourcing, and carrying inventory, a plan is prepared indicating the nominal production output and how the output will be varied over time.

The aggregate production plan is a plan for a product group based upon the aggregate demand forecast. The time horizon of this plan begins 3–6 months in the future and extends to 12 or more months. The plan is usually divided into months and the production output is specified for each month.

The two extreme cases for setting production output are

1. Maintaining a constant-level workforce to keep the output approximately the same every month and, using inventory to absorb monthly fluctuations in demand. This approach is referred to as **level production.**

2. Varying the output as needed to match demand through a combination of changing the workforce size and using overtime, outsourcing, adding shifts, and so on. This approach is referred to as **chase production** because it varies production output to "chase" the demand level.

In establishing each month's output, the costs associated with regular and overtime payroll, hiring or laying off workers, carrying inventory, taking backorders, stocking out, subcontracting, and other options are considered. Qualitative issues such as the effect of the plan on worker morale, difficulty of hiring or training workers, and the effect of outsourcing on product quality are also considered. The resulting aggregate plan often exhibits extended periods of somewhat-level production output (and hence workforce size), punctuated by periods of increased or decreased output to accommodate brief jumps in demand and an occasional shift to a different production level.

The aggregate plan serves as a baseline and framework for more detailed medium-range plans. Aggregate planning, especially for level production, is discussed in Chapter 16.

MEDIUM-RANGE PLANNING AND SCHEDULING

Medium-range planning extends about 6 months or less into the future since this is as far as the availability of detailed production data permits. Within this time frame, the involved facilities, product groups, and processes are largely assumed as given and somewhat fixed. Production capacity changes in medium-range plans are confined to short-term measures such as overtime, subcontracting, and alternative uses of existing facilities. The planning is decidedly more detailed than long-range planning. The planning focuses on individual products, not product groups, and on weekly requirements, not monthly or yearly ones. The purpose of medium-range planning is to determine demand for each product, schedule production of the product, check the necessary resources, and schedule procurement and production of the required materials.

MASTER PRODUCTION SCHEDULING

At the center of medium-range planning is a detailed plan called the **master production schedule (MPS).** Usually an MPS must be prepared for every **end-item,** although for some kinds of items an MPS for the product family is adequate. The end-item is usually a finished product, though it may also be a major component, subassembly, or module. The latter are used when it makes more sense to plan and schedule production of major components and subassemblies than the final products into which they go. The subject of using subassemblies and modules as end-items is discussed in Chapter 16.

The MPS is typically divided into weekly **time buckets** and has a time horizon that begins with the present and ends about 3 months into the future. The MPS is used as the basis for determining order quantities and due dates for all components, parts, and materials that comprise an end-item. The MPS is derived, in part, from the aggregate production plan and should be consistent with the most immediate portion of that plan.

Unlike the aggregate plan, which is based entirely on forecasts, the MPS takes into account actual customer orders. In fact, in the most immediate time buckets in the MPS, most or all of the amounts scheduled represent actual customer orders. For time buckets farther into the future, only a portion of each amount represents actual orders while the remaining portion comes from forecasts. For time buckets the furthest out, all of the amounts scheduled might be from forecasts. In effect, as each time bucket approaches the present, progressively more of the forecasted quantity is consumed by actual customer orders.

The difference between the forecasted amount and the customer ordered amount in a time bucket is called **available to promise (ATP).** ATP tells sales people how much of an amount in the MPS has been committed to customers, and how much remains uncommitted and can be realistically promised to new customers. ATP is the difference between the MPS amount and existing customer orders.

Example 2: Available to Promise

The following table illustrates the ATP concept.

	Week				
	1	2	3	4	5
Forecast	800	600	900	300	400
Orders	700	700	300	100	0
Revised MPS	800	700	900	300	400
ATP	100	0	600	200	400

In the table, the forecast row represents the initially scheduled MPS amounts. In cases where new orders exceed the forecast, the MPS amount might be revised upward if there are enough time and production capacity to permit the increased output. In week 2, the initial MPS of 600 has been increased to 700 to accommodate orders beyond the forecast.

As a rule, salespeople should try to keep new customer orders within the ATP amount, otherwise extreme measures (overtimes, additional shifts, etc.) might be necessary to prevent the orders from being late. If incoming orders are insufficient to consume the ATP amount, the sales department might choose to reduce prices to spur sales, or the production department might choose to decrease output.

ROUGH-CUT CAPACITY PLANNING

To check the feasibility of the MPS, the workload associated with the quantity in each time bucket is compared to the capacity of available resources. When many different resources are involved, a check is made of the critical resources, specifically the rare skills, special machinery, or difficult operations that most often restrict production capacity. The purpose of this check, called **rough-cut capacity planning (RCCP)** is to ensure that scarce resources are not overloaded.

Although RCCP is only a crude estimate of capacity requirements, it is considerably more detailed than either the resource planning or aggregate planning previously described. RCCP considers the workloads imposed on certain resources as a result of the amounts scheduled in each time bucket in the MPS. Although RCCP is usually performed for individual end-items, it can also be used for product groups. The latter is a simpler and often adequate method for checking capacity requirements.

To determine the capacity requirements for a product group, an MPS for the group is developed based on the MPSs for all items in the group. Next, a typical end-item from the group is selected; its bill of resources is representative of the required resources and standard times. Then the following two steps are used to determine the capacity requirements for a resource:

1. *Prepare the load profile.* A **load profile** is a list of the standard times for each critical resource required to produce *one unit* of an end-item.

Example   3:   Preparing a Load Profile

Consider again product group K, of which product X is typical. Suppose

- The lead time allowed for assembly of any batch size of X is 1 week.
- Product X consists of two components, item A and item B. Item A has a lead time of 1 week, and item B has a lead time of 2 weeks.

To schedule production of product X and components A and B, the lead times must be considered. The procedure of starting with a due date then going backward to determine the starting date is called **backscheduling** or **time-phasing**. In the present case,

- An order for product X that is to be filled in time bucket n must be backscheduled to start a week earlier, in week $n - 1$.
- For item A to be ready for use in product X in week $n - 1$, an order for it must be backscheduled 1 week earlier, in week $n - 2$.

· For item B to be ready for use in product X in period $n - 1$, an order for it must be backscheduled 2 weeks earlier, in week $n - 3$.

Therefore, given the standard times in Table A.1, the time-phased load imposed by an order for item X in period n is as follows:

		Week			
Workcenter		$n - 3$	$n - 2$	$n - 1$	n
Assembly:	X			0.6	
Cutting:	A		0.33		
	B	0.45			
Broaching:	A		0.86		
Drilling:	B	0.56			
Grinding:	A		0.31		
	B	0.41			
Milling:	B	0.72			

The load profile for product X is the total load imposed on each resource. For example, looking at just one resource, the cutting workcenter, the load profile for product X is

	Week			
Workcenter	$n - 3$	$n - 2$	$n - 1$	n
Cutting	0.45	0.33		

2. *Prepare the resource profile.* The **resource profile** is the total amount of a resource required to produce *a specific quantity* of the end-item. To get the resource profile, multiply the load profile by the quantities in the MPS time buckets, then sum the results within each time bucket.

Example   4:   Preparing a Resource Profile

Suppose the MPS for product group K for weeks 4 through 7 is as follows:

	Units per Week			
Week	4	5	6	7
Family K units	300	400	200	500

For simplicity, consider just the cutting workcenter. Using the load profile for the cutting workcenter (Example 3), the resource requirement generated by the 500 units in week $n = 7$ is 500×0.45 (225 hours) time-phased back to week 4 $(n - 3)$ and 500×0.33 (165 hours) time-phased back to week 5 $(n - 2)$; that is,

			Hours per Week			
Week	1	2	3	4	5	6	7
Hours				225	165		

Similarly, the requirements generated by the 200 units in week 6 are 200×0.45 (90 hours) in week 3 $(n - 3)$ and 200×0.33 (66 hours) in week 4 $(n - 2)$, or

Week	1	2	3	4	5	6	7
Hours			90	66			

Requirements from the 400 units in week 5 and the 300 units in week 4 are determined in the same way. The combined requirements are

Week	1	2	3	4	5	6	7
Hours				225	165		
			90	66			
		180	132				
	135	99					

Finally, the resource profile for the cutting workcenter is obtained by summing the requirements in respective weeks as follows:

Week	1	2	3	4	5	6	7
Hours	135*	279	222	291	165		

* Plus hours already committed for production to meet the requirement for week 3 of the MPS (not shown above).

The resource profile is compared to the available capacity of the resource to determine whether the MPS or the resource capacity has to be changed. If the profile exceeds available capacity, then the MPS must be adjusted (a portion of the quantity in the overloaded time bucket must be diverted to another time bucket) or the capacity in that time bucket must be increased (overtime, etc.). If, in Example 4, the available capacity of the cutting workcenter is 240 standard hours per week, the workcenter will be overloaded in weeks 2 and 4.[1]

MATERIAL REQUIREMENTS PLANNING

Any final product or other end-item contains subassemblies or components, and these must be manufactured by the producer or procured from suppliers. Any subassembly or component that the producer manufactures itself contains parts that must also be produced or procured. Before an end-item can be assembled, all of these components and parts must be ordered far enough in advance so that they will arrive at the time they are needed.

The precise quantity and timing of orders for component parts depends on the quantity and due date of the end-item. Components are thus referred to as **dependent-demand** items because the demand for them depends on the demand for the end-item. The quantity and timing of orders for dependent-demand items are developed through the procedure of **material requirements planning (MRP)**.[2]

THE MEANING OF MRP

In practice the term MRP represents three different things. In its fundamental usage, MRP is a **procedure** for determining *how much* of and *when* dependent-demand items should be ordered to satisfy requirements for an end-item. Most companies deal with a large number of end-items, each containing a large number of components; for this reason, the MRP procedure is computerized. In its most basic form, the MRP computer system determines the required quantities of parts and components and sends out orders for them.

MRP can also represent a more complete system for PPC. This type of MRP considers both material and capacity requirements. It is called **closed-loop MRP** because it takes into account feedback about orders to be released to the shop floor. Prior to releasing production orders to departments, closed-loop MRP uses a separate capacity-planning module to check the feasibility of the orders. The workload imposed by current planned orders is added to the already scheduled workload, and the sum is checked against the available capacity. If the anticipated workload exceeds the capacity limit, a warning is issued. This is a signal that the MPS should be revised or that a way needs to be found to increase capacity. Other modules can be added to the closed-loop system for changing the lead times or revising the order schedules.

MRP can also represent **manufacturing resource planning,** or **MRP II.**[3] MRP II is closed-loop MRP combined with additional modules for planning and managing resources. With MRP II, departments such as purchasing, marketing, engineering, finance, and accounting use output from the MRP procedure to coordinate work and achieve cost savings. Marketing and sales can use information about existing and planned production requirements and order releases to determine whether a delivery date for a new order is feasible and, if not, when is the nearest feasible date. The purchasing department, given access to long-range order requirements, can make long-term agreements with suppliers. MRP II can also be used for resource and aggregate planning, as well as RCCP.

THE MRP PROCEDURE

The MRP procedure starts with the scheduled due date for an end-item, then works backward in time to determine the quantities and timing for orders of every item that goes into the end-item. The procedure determines orders for items coming from both inside and outside the plant. For items manufactured inside the plant, the MRP system issues **job orders** or **manufacturing orders;** for items procured from outside suppliers, the system issues **purchase orders.** The term "orders" used from here on refers to both of these.

INPUTS TO THE PROCEDURE

As an introduction to the MRP procedure, we start with an overview of its inputs and outputs, shown in Figure A.2. The major inputs are the MPS, the bill of materials (BOM), and the inventory status file.

Master Production Schedule

For purposes of requirements planning and order placing, the master production schedule (MPS) usually extends 20 or more weeks into the future. The actual number of weeks in the MPS depends on the **stacked lead time,** which is the time between

FIGURE A.2

Basic MRP system.

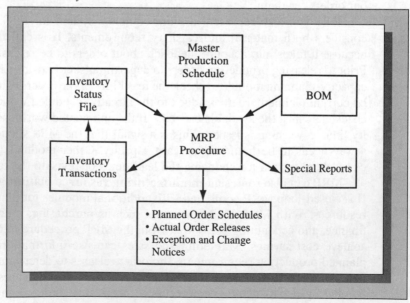

when an end-item is due and when orders for all of its components must be issued to meet the due date. Typically, the MPS uses a time horizon of approximately twice the stacked lead time.

The MRP procedure does not distinguish between feasible and infeasible schedules; it assumes that whatever is ordered *can* be produced or delivered. For that reason it is necessary to prepare an RCCP for the MPS. Even an RCCP is no guarantee of the MPS's feasibility since it is only a gross check and does not consider the impact of all end-item schedules on every department of workcenter. If the MRP software is connected to a module that does detailed capacity checking (i.e., it is a closed-loop system), the required capacity can be more accurately checked and, if necessary, the MPS can be revised and the capacity rechecked. The procedure is repeated until a feasible, "official" MPS is determined. This topic is discussed later.

The MPS is often divided into **time fences** that impose restrictions on the changes allowed to different portions of the MPS. For example, the MPS might be divided by time fences at 2, 4, and 8 weeks to specify the degree of change permitted:

- The first 2 weeks of the MPS are **frozen;** no changes are allowed within that period.
- The next 2 weeks are **firm;** only minor changes are allowed.
  The next 4 weeks are **flexible;** somewhat greater changes are allowed.
- After 8 weeks the schedule is **open** and any changes are allowed.

There are two kinds of time fences. A **demand time fence** is the scheduled point in time after which the only changes allowed in the MPS are special customer orders that require the approval of the master scheduler (person updating the MPS). This time fence is used to specify dates after which only a few important changes are allowed. The other, a **planning time fence,** represents the scheduled time at which changes to the MPS are permitted, but for which there will be trade-offs such as moving an order back so another can be moved ahead. It is the date after which changes in the MPS might adversely affect procurement schedules and resource capacity. Changes made after this time must be manually entered by the scheduler. Time fences thus reduce the need for the production system to respond to demand changes on short notice.

Product Tree Structure and BOMs

The MRP procedure starts with an end-item and determines the requirements for all parts, the **lower-level items,** of which it consists. The parts and their relationship to the end-item are specified in a **product tree structure.** Figure A.3 shows the product tree structure for end-item W. The item at each juncture is called a **parent,** and the items connected just below it are its **components.** A parent at one level becomes a component for the item at the next higher level to which it is connected. The (2) by item T in Figure A.3 indicates that two Ts are required for each item D. For illustration, Figure A.4 shows end-item W, the big gear assembly, and the parent–component relationship of all of its parts.

Product tree structure.

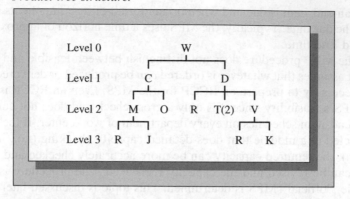

Big gear assembly: parent–component relationship.

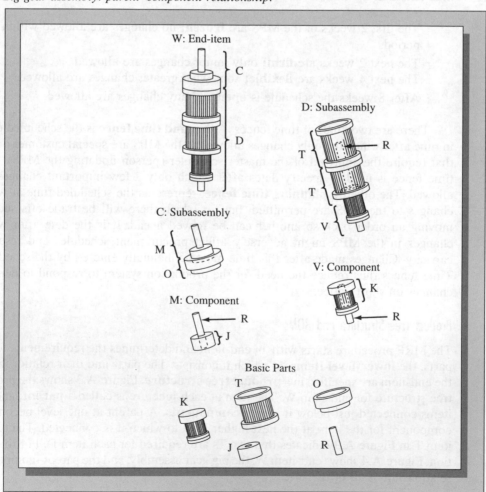

TABLE A-2   Indented BOM with OH Inventory and Lead Times

Item	OH	Lead Time (wk)
Item W (end-item): big gear assembly	30	1
Item C: drum subassembly	30	1
Item O: big drum	20	1
Item M: drum shaft	0	2
Item R: shaft	15*	1
Item J: small drum	0	1
Item D: gear subassembly	10	1
Item R: shaft	0*	1
Item T(2): big gear	30	2
Item V: gear shaft	0	1
Item R: shaft	0*	1
Item K: small gear	50	2

* Item R is allocated to item M.

Another way to represent the items in an end-item is with a BOM. Table A.2 is the **indented BOM** for end-item W. Table A.2 also shows the lead time (for production or procurement) and on-hand inventory for each item. The **lead time** is the nominal time between when an order for an item is released (sent out or initiated) and when it is received (completed). **On-hand (OH) inventory** represents the amount of the item held in stock as of a specified time period. When the same item is used in several places in the product, an allocation decision must be made for OH items. Item R is an example. In Table A.2, all OH stock has been allocated for use in item M. The BOM may indicate other information, such as the source of the item and any rules for lot-sizing orders.

Inventory Status File

A record of the current inventory status of every component is maintained in a data file. The record is broken down into weekly or daily time buckets, depending on the size of the time bucket in the MPS. The information in each time bucket includes the amount of the item required, the anticipated OH amount, and any scheduled deliveries (completions) of existing orders for the item. The MRP procedure uses the contents of the record to determine whether OH inventory plus scheduled deliveries will be sufficient to meet the requirements. If not, additional orders for the item must be issued.

The currentness of the inventory status file depends on how frequently it is updated. There are two standard approaches for updating the file. In **regeneration,** the entire file is reviewed on a regular basis (usually weekly), and the records for all components are regenerated anew, even though only a few might need changing. In **net change,** only the records that need updating are changed. The first approach reassesses the inventory status of every item and generates new orders for every item; the second reassesses only items affected by a transaction and reissues orders for them only. With MRP systems that are on-line, transactions can be entered and orders can be reissued in real time.

As a rule, companies use regeneration when demand for the end-items is stable and changes little, and they use net change when demand is erratic and changes frequently. Regeneration is more costly than net change because the records and reports for every item are redone from scratch. It also has poorer record accuracy because of the long time-lag (as much as a week) between when changes happen on the shop floor or at suppliers and when they are updated in the file. Net change has better accuracy, assuming someone is assigned the responsibility of frequent change-entry. Companies often compromise: they use net change to update records for the relatively few big changes as they occur and regeneration to handle all the other run-of-the-mill changes. As computer costs fall, many companies are using regeneration, but doing it more frequently, as often as daily.

OUTPUTS OF THE PROCEDURE

The major outputs of the MRP procedure, shown in Figure A.2, are **inventory transactions, planned order schedules,** and **actual order releases.** Most MRP systems also issue various reports and notices.

Inventory Transactions

An inventory transaction occurs whenever the MRP procedure reviews and updates a record. Transactions include updates to the gross requirements, scheduled deliveries, OH amounts, and planned order schedules.

Planned Order Schedules

The MRP procedure produces a schedule of the future orders that will be necessary to satisfy the requirements of all items in the product tree. These orders are also commonly called **planned order releases.**

Actual Order Releases

When the time bucket for a planned order reaches the present time, the order is created and sent. For a manufactured part, the order is sent to the internal department in which the part is produced. For a procured part, the order is sent to an external supplier. Once sent, the planned order becomes a **scheduled receipt,** which is an order that is confirmed and scheduled to arrive (or be completed) at a certain date. An inventory transaction converts the planned order to a scheduled receipt in the file.

Exception and Change Notices

The actual dates of delivery and amounts received sometimes differ from the dates and amounts scheduled. Some MRP systems issue notices to inform shop-floor operations and suppliers about such discrepancies. Some systems also issue notices about errors in reporting, excessive scrap rates, nonexistent part numbers in the BOM, and so on.

Special Reports

MRP systems often include provisions for generating reports to be used for planning, measuring performance, and handling exceptions. For example, future procurement and holding costs can be assessed by reviewing reports of scheduled orders and OH inventory quantities. Performance can be measured by tracking statistics of stockouts, missed deliveries, and excessive inventories. The capability to compile information and generate reports in formats useful to many departments is what distinguishes MRP II from the basic MRP procedure.

FROM GROSS REQUIREMENTS TO PLANNED ORDER RELEASE

The fundamental purpose of the MRP procedure is to determine the quantities and timing of orders. To determine how much and when to order, MRP uses as a starting point the **gross requirement,** which is the total quantity due or required of an item at a specified time.

Most MRP systems specify gross requirements for weekly or daily time buckets (only a few use continuous time). To avoid confusion about the precise timing of gross requirements, it is necessary to specify in advance whether the amount in a time bucket is an amount for the beginning or the ending of the time period. We will use the convention **beginning of week n:** whatever amount is needed *during* a week will be considered due at the beginning of that week. For example, if *during week 6* we need 75 units on Monday, 25 units on Thursday, and 20 units on Friday, then we specify that 120 units are due Monday morning of week 6.

To demonstrate the rest of the MRP procedure, we will use end-item W. The product tree structure, production illustration, and indented BOM for end-item W were shown in Figures A.3 and A.4 and Table A.2, respectively.

Suppose the gross requirement (GR) for item W for week 6 is 120 units.[4] We want to determine how many, and at what time, additional units of item W must be produced to fill this gross requirement. To determine how many, start with the GR and subtract any units on hand at the time. Referring back to Table A.2, we see there are 30 units on-hand.[5] "On-hand" here refers to stock that has been made available to fill the requirement for this item. More stock might be on-hand elsewhere, but the amount indicated "OH" is the amount that has been allocated to this particular order. These items can be applied to the gross requirement, so 90 additional units are still needed for week 6. The quantity of additional units needed is referred to as the **net requirement:**

Net Requirement = Gross Requirement − Available Stock.

A net requirement (NR), if unfilled, will result in a shortage. Thus, an order at least the size of the NR amount must be placed. Since every order has a lead time, an order must be placed in advance of the time the item will be needed. The requirement in the example is for week 6; the lead for item W is 1 week (Table A.2), so the order must be placed in week 5. Backscheduling of the NR amount to specify when to send the order is called **time-phased ordering.** A time-phased order to fill a future requirement is called a **planned order release (POR).** The table below shows the relationship among the terms GR, OH, NR, and POR:

	Week					
	1	*2*	*3*	*4*	*5*	*6*
Gross Requirement (GR)						120
On-Hand (OH)						30
Net Requirement (NR)						90
Planned Order Release (POR)					90	

Additionally, since every component has a lead time, orders for components at successively lower levels of the product tree structure must be placed further in advance of the end-item (level 0) due date as shown in Figure A.5. Notice in general that the lowest-level components are the ones ordered earliest.

The concept of stacked lead time was mentioned earlier. In Figure A.5, the stacked lead time is the cumulative time along any branch. The longest stacked lead in the figure is 5 weeks. Therefore, to fill a requirement for end-item W in any time bucket, orders for some of its component must go out 5 weeks earlier. This also indicates that the MPS time horizon for item W must be *at least* 5 weeks, the minimum time necessary to procure and assemble the components.[6]

SCHEDULED RECEIPTS

Another factor that affects the size and timing of orders is the **scheduled receipt (SR).** While GR, OH, and POR all represent future or anticipated amounts, an SR is an order that *has already been placed* and is scheduled for completion or arrival. It is an order that is currently *outstanding* and for which *arrival* is imminent.

FIGURE A.5

Lead times and order dates.

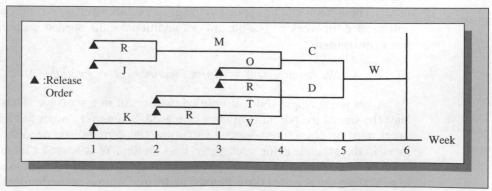

We will assume here that an SR is immutable, although often an SR *can* be changed slightly to account for changes in a GR. For example, suppose the GR for week 6 increases from 120 to 130 units due to an unanticipated increase in a customer order. Also suppose an SR of 30 units is due to arrive a week later in week 7. To help meet the increase in the GR, it might be possible to expedite all or a portion of the SR so it is completed a week earlier, in which case the SR would be moved forward to week 6. In similar fashion, an SR might be deferred to a later period to account for a decrease in demand (the MPS was not fully consumed). Whenever an SR is modified, a change notice is issued to the work area expecting the SR.

For scheduling consistency, we assume here each SR arrives at the beginning of a time bucket; that is, it is added to any OH amount to give available stock:

$$Available\ Stock = OH + SR.$$

Therefore, the net requirement is

$$NR = GR - (OH + SR).$$

Using end-item W again as an example, suppose current OH stock is 30 units but an SR of 40 units is expected next week. Derivation of the NR and POR are shown in Figure A.6.

The elements, tabular format, and procedure shown in Figure A.6 are all employed by the MRP procedure to get from a GR to a POR. From now on, such a tabular form will be referred to as an **MRP plan.** Since requirements and orders must be determined for every component of an end-item, it is necessary to develop an MRP plan like this for every component in the product tree structures.

The procedure of moving down through the product tree to develop MRP plans and determine requirements and orders for components at all levels is called **exploding the requirements.** For this purpose, the MRP procedure starts with the MPS for an end-item, then uses the product tree or BOM to explode the end-item into its component parts. Information about available stock (OH + SR) for each component is taken from the inventory status file and used to determine current GRs, NRs, and PORs that eventually are entered back into the status file. The MRP plan for each component represents information about that component in the inventory status file.

FIGURE A.6

Elements, format, and procedure in an MRP plan.

	Now	1	2	3	4	5	6
GR							120
OH	30	30	70	70	70	70	70
SR		40					
NR							50
POR						50	

GROSS REQUIREMENTS FOR LOWER-LEVEL ITEMS

The timing and quantity of GRs for the end-item (level-0 item) correspond to the MPS. However, as we move down to components at lower levels of the product tree, the timing and quantities of their GRs do not come from the MPS but from the *PORs* of their parent items.

For example, in the preceding MRP plan we determined that for item W, a POR of 50 units should go out in week 5. Referring to the product tree in Figure A.3, we see that item W is the parent of items C and D. Therefore, the GRs for items C and D will be 50 units each in week 5. The rationale is this:

> The POR of 50 units of item W in (start of) week 5 is a signal to begin producing 50 units. To do that, 50 units each of items C and D are needed. Therefore, the GRs for items C and D are 50 units in (start of) week 5.

In general, the GR for an item is derived from the PORs of its parent(s). The relationship is shown in Figure A.7.

To continue the example, given the GRs for items C and D and any OH and SR amounts, the PORs for C and D are derived. Then, given the PORs for items C and D, the GRs for the items comprising them are derived. Referring to the product tree in Figure A.3, items C and D consist of items O and M and items T and V, respectively. Since each item M contains items J and R, the POR for M gives the GR for items J and R. Similarly, the POR of item V gives the GR for items K and R.

Figure A.8 shows relationships between the PORs of all parent items and the GRs of their components. Variables (e.g., $w2$) are used to show the overall correspondence between parent PORs and component GRs.

LOW-LEVEL CODING

Whenever an item appears at more than one level in a product tree, it is treated as if it existed only at the lowest of these levels. This is the principle of **low-level coding.** For example, item R, which appears at levels 2 and 3 in Figure A.3, is, for the purpose of MRP planning, treated as if it existed only at level 3, as shown in Figure A.9. Low-level coding is used because it is more efficient for the computer system to determine GRs level-by-level than to jump back and forth between different levels.

FIGURE A.7

Relationship between the POR of the parent and the GRs of its components.

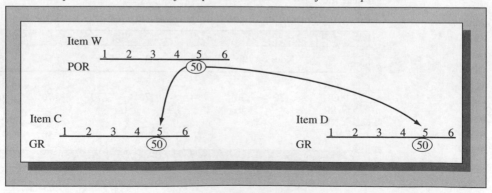

Relationship among all PORs and GRs.

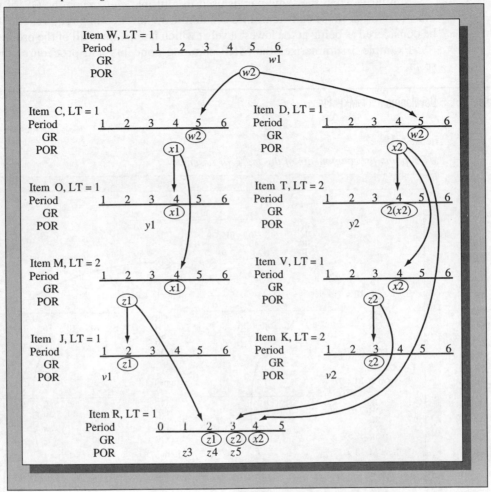

Low-level coding example.

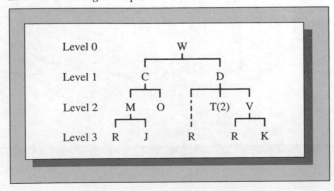

Similarly, when the same part is used in multiple *end-items,* the GR of the part must take all of those end-items into account. Low-level coding requires that the part be considered as being at the lowest level at which it appears in all of the product trees.

Example 5 summarizes the MRP planning concepts and procedures discussed so far.

Example   5:   Development of MRP Plans

Figure A.10

MRP plans for components of the big gear assembly.

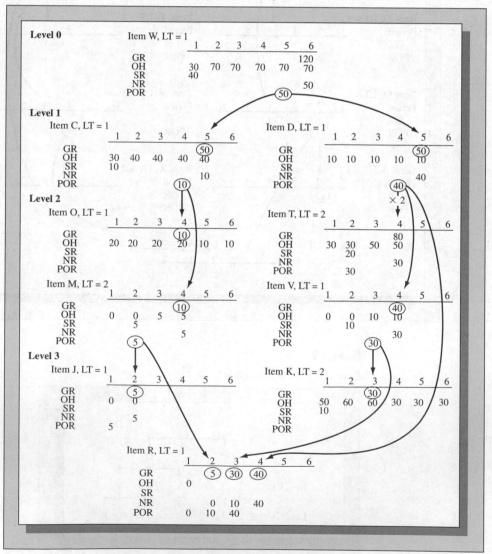

Figure A.10 shows the procedure for developing MRP plans for all components in end-item W. Assume in each plan that the week 1 OH and all SR amounts are given. Review the numbers in the figure to make sure you follow the procedure. Note that item R is located at level 3 for low-level coding and that its GR is derived from the PORs of its parents—items D, M, and V.

LOT-SIZING RULES

So far the discussion of MRP plans has assumed that the lot size of the POR quantity is the same as the time-phased NR quantity. However, the lot size of the POR quantity may be set to achieve potential economies in setup costs, order costs, or inventory holding costs. This section reviews three common methods for setting lot sizes discussed in Chapter 5 but in the context of the MRP procedure and PORs.

Lot-for-Lot (LFL)

LFL lot sizing has been the technique used in the examples so far, that is, POR quantity = time-phased NR quantity. LFL minimizes inventory holding costs because the order quantity matches the net required quantity, so (in theory) no inventory remains at the end of each period (OH = 0). But with LFL, a POR accompanies every nonzero NR, even when the NR is very small. Thus the number of orders (and production setups) is unpredictable and potentially large, which may result in large setup costs, as illustrated in Example 6.

Example   6:   LFL Lot Sizing

Assume the following situation: holding cost is $2/unit/week and is applied to units carried from week to week; setup cost is $150 and a setup is required for every POR; lead time is 1 week; starting OH is 20 units.

Table A.3 shows the MRP plan and PORs using LFL lot sizing. For cost analysis, consider only OH quantities for weeks 3 and later and PORs up through week 7 (prior to week 3, OH amount is unaffected by the lot sizing).

TABLE A-3   LFL Lot Sizing

	0	1	2	3	4	5	6	7	8
GR		10	10	30	50	20	40	20	10
OH	20	20	10	0	0	0	0	0	0
NR				30	50	20	40	20	10
POR		30	50	20	40	20	10		

The cost of the six setups is Σ (setups)$150 = (6)$150 = $900. Since inventory is zero, the holding cost is Σ (OH)$2 = 0. Thus, the total cost is $900.

Fixed Order Quantity (FOQ)

FOQ lot sizing specifies a constant amount for every order. When high setup costs make small-batch production impractical, it may be more practical to use a fixed, larger order quantity. The problem with FOQ lot sizing is that when demand (and hence GRs) is highly irregular, the fixed quantity might be too large or too small compared to the GR. Another problem with FOQ lot sizing is that, by its nature, it lumps together requirements for multiple periods, which causes lumpiness in GRs for lower-level components. How this happens and why it is a problem are discussed later.

The FOQ quantity can be set to any amount, depending on practical considerations or simple cost analysis. Example 7 uses the EOQ criteria discussed in Chapter 5.

Example   7:   FOQ Lot Sizing Using EOQ Criteria

Assume the following situation: holding cost = $2/unit/week; setup cost is $150; lead time is 1 week; starting OH is 20 units; average weekly demand, *D*, is 20 units. Therefore, the economic order quantity (EOQ) is

$$EOQ = \sqrt{\frac{2DS}{H}} = \sqrt{\frac{2(20)(\$150)}{\$2}} = 55 = FOQ \text{ amount.}$$

Assuming that every POR must be the FOQ amount of 55, Table A.4 shows the resulting MRP plan and PORs.

TABLE A-4   FOQ Lot Sizing with $Q = 55$ Units

	0	1	2	3	4	5	6	7	8
GR		10	10	30	50	20	40	20	10
OH	20	20	10	0	25	30	10	25	5
NR				30	25		30		5
POR		55	55		55		55		

Total setup cost = Σ (setup)$150 = 4($150) = $600, and total holding cost (for weeks 3+) = Σ (OH)$2 = (0 + 25 + 30 + 10 + 25 + 5)$2 = $190. Thus, total cost is $790.

Period Order Quantity (POQ)

POQ lot sizing specifies a constant interval between the time of orders. An order is placed once every *P* periods, and the quantity of each POR equals the sum of the NR quantities for the next *P* periods. When *P* = 1, POQ lot sizing is the same as LFL lot sizing.

In practice, the order frequency P is often set arbitrarily or for convenience; a systematic way to determine P is to base it upon an average order size determined from historical records or economic criteria. For example,

$$Number\ of\ Orders\ a\ Year = \frac{Demand\ per\ Year}{Average\ Order\ Size} = N$$

so,

$$P = \frac{Number\ of\ Periods\ per\ Year}{N}.$$

With POQ lot sizing, demand is satisfied regardless of variability because the POR quantity is varied to match the NRs of the immediate P future periods. Like the FOQ approach, however, POQ lumps demand for several periods together and causes lumpy GRs for lower-level components. Example 8 illustrates POQ lot sizing and its effect on costs.

Example 8: POQ Lot Sizing

Assume (from Example 7) the average order size is 55 and annual demand is (20 units/wk) (52 wk) = 10,400 units/yr. Then

$$N = \frac{1,040}{55} = 18.9, \text{ or } 19 \text{ orders/yr},$$

so,

$$P = \frac{52}{19} = 2.7, \text{ or } 3 \text{ weeks}.$$

Table A.5 shows the MRP plan with PORs 3 weeks apart. To help keep track of the numbers, an additional row for PR has been added. Each PR represents a *planned receipt*, which is the arrival of the POR placed just prior

---

TABLE A-5   POQ Lot Sizing for $P = 3$ Periods

	0	1	2	3	4	5	6	7	8
GR		10	10	30	50	20	40	20	10
OH	20	20	10	0	70	20	0	30	10
NR				100			70		
PR*				100			70		
POR			100			70			?

* Note: PR is Planned Receipt.

to it. (It is not a scheduled receipt because the POR has not actually been released yet.) The total setup cost = Σ (setup)\$150 = 3(\$150) = \$450, and the total holding cost (for weeks 3+) = Σ (OH)\$2 = (70 + 20 + 30 + 10)\$2 = \$260. Thus, the total cost is \$710.

Discussion

Despite the potential appeal of alternative lot-sizing methods, most MRP practitioners use LFL lot sizing. (In fact, most MRP computer systems can *only* do LFL lot sizing.) Not only is LFL the simplest technique, but it often results in costs no higher than other methods. It causes the most setups, but that will not be a factor if setup times can be reduced. In fact, since LFL lot sizing minimizes holding costs, if setup costs are small too, then LFL will be the least costly lot-sizing method. The benefit of FOQ, POQ, and other lot-sizing techniques is that they generate fewer PORs and are thus more cost-effective when setup and ordering costs are very high.

     Results from analyses to determine the best lot-sizing method can be deceiving because of the parent–component relationships in the product tree structure. Lot-sizing analysis tends to focus on one item at a time, although what is a good lot size for one item might be detrimental in terms of costs and schedules for the lower-level components comprising it. Lot-sizing decisions affect PORs, which in turn affect the GRs of lower-level components. Lumping PORs to achieve economies at one level results in lumps of GRs at the next lower level, and satisfying those GRs might involve PORs that are impractical or uneconomical. Besides economics, big lumps in GRs for lower-level items frustrate attempts to reduce production batch sizes and in-process inventory and to level production. One way to assess the effects of lot-sizing decisions on requirements, costs, and batch sizes throughout the product tree structure is to perform **what-if analysis** with computer simulation. A few MRP computer systems have built-in simulation models capable of performing what-if analysis.

VARIABILITY AND UNCERTAINTY IN MRP PLANNING

Like all plans, MRP plans are subject to changes originating from variability in supply and demand.[7] Delivery delays, work interruptions, and defects cause delays and shortages in SRs (supply), while changes in customer orders cause changes in GRs (demand). Safety stock, safety margin, and safety lead time are ways to deal with variability.

Safety Stock

An amount held to protect against changes in supply and demand is called **safety stock** (SS). Theoretically, MRP reduces the need for SS because it eliminates demand uncertainty for components: if the requirement for an end-item is frozen, then so are the requirements for all lower-level components. Realistically, however, some uncertainty remains because no portion of the MPS is ever completely frozen. Exceptions are permitted to allow for a slight degree of change in customer orders (being not truly frozen, the MPS is considered "slushy"). Even with attempts to hold the MPS relatively fixed, there is still the matter of uncontrollable variability in production from equipment breakdowns, bottlenecks, and material defects.

With dependent-demand items, a shortage or delay of any one component will delay the completion of the parent item and that effect will ripple *up* through the product tree, possibly delaying the end-item. Because of this ripple-up effect, some SS is usually carried for low-level components. Since changes in end-item requirements ripple *down* through the product tree, SS is also carried for the end-item to absorb changes in the MPS without requiring changes everywhere else.

A large enough SS can accommodate any increase in demand or delivery delay. However, the larger the SS, the larger the average WIP inventory, so decisions regarding the SS size must weigh the risk of shortages against the costs of holding inventory. Example A.9 illustrates this point.

Example   9:   SS with POQ

Assume the same situation as Example 8 (POQ lot sizing with $P = 3$), but with SS = 10 units. With an SS the NR is determined *after* subtracting out the SS amount. To clarify this, the row OH − SS has been included in Table A.6. Only when OH − SS = 0 is there an NR and a corresponding POR.

TABLE A-6   POQ with $P = 3$ and SS = 10

	0	1	2	3	4	5	6	7	8
GR		10	10	30	50	20	40	20	10
OH	20	20	10	90	60	10	70	30	10
OH − SS		10	0	80	50	0	60	20	0
NR			90			80			*
PR			90			80			*
POR		90			80			*	

*Note: NR, PR, and POR in these places corresponds to GR in periods 8, 9, and 10.

By comparing Table A.6 to Table A.5, the effect of the 10-unit SS is to advance orders by 1 week. Also, obviously the holding cost has been increased; whereas previously it was $260 (weeks 3–8), with the SS it is Σ OH($2) = (90 + 60 + 10 + 70 + 30 + 10)$2 = $540.

Safety stock protects not only against unexpected requirements increases but also against unexpected shortages in SR quantities. If the SR quantity is exactly the same as the NR quantity, then any reduction in the actual receipt (SR) will result in a shortage. With SS, however, the SR shortage will not be transferred to the NR unless the amount of the shortage exceeds the SS amount.

Safety Margin

Shortages result when items produced are unsuitable to fill the NR; this is called **yield loss.** The yield-loss rate is determined from rates for defects, scrap, damaged goods, and so on. Assuming an average yield-loss rate of L, every SR quantity will have $L\%$ items that cannot be applied toward the NR. To account for yield loss, the POR amount is computed as

$$POR = \frac{NR}{1.0 - L}.$$

For example, if the NR amount is 300 and $L = 2\%$, then the POR amount must be $300/(1.0 - .02) = 306$. The difference, 6 units, is the **POR safety margin.**

Table A.7 shows an example. As in Example 9, the row PR represents planned receipts (amounts scheduled to arrive if the PORs are actually released). Note that the PR quantities already account for the yield loss. For example, in week 1 although 306 units are ordered, only 300 of them are expected to be suitable for use (the PR quantity in week 2).

Shortages from yield loss can also be handled with SS. If the POR quantity is a fixed quantity (FOQ), an SS of at least the quantity $FOQ/(1 - L)$ is required. Thus, if L is 2% and FOQ is 300, the SS must be at least 6 units. If LFL lot sizing is used and the NR amount is variable, then the SS must be large enough to offset yield losses for the largest anticipated NR quantity, or $L \times NR_{MAX}$.

Since the actual yield-loss rate is usually variable, the yield-loss rate L represents an average. Thus, even POR quantities adjusted for L will sometimes fall short of the NR amount. If, for example, the yield loss is normally distributed with mean of L and if the POR has a safety margin based on L, then 50% of SRs will be short. The POR quantity must, therefore, be larger than $NR/(1 - L)$. How much larger will depend on the size of the yield-loss variability: the greater the variability, the larger the required safety margin. The same applies to SS (and safety lead time, discussed next). In any case, the necessary safety amount must exceed the amount needed to cover average losses or average delays.

TABLE A-7 $L = 2\%$, **LFL Lot Sizing, LT = 1**

		1	*2*	*3*	*4*
GR		200	500	300	100
OH	400	400	200	0	0
NR			300	300	100
PR			300	300	100
POR		306	306	102	

Safety Lead Time

To protect against delays, orders can be placed to arrive *before* they are needed. The amount of time by which an SR is planned to arrive in advance of the NR it will fill is called **safety lead time (SLT).** By planning for an order to arrive before it is needed, the risk of the order arriving late is decreased. However, orders arriving earlier than needed result in materials waiting longer before being used, which (like SS) implies greater average OH stock as Example 10 demonstrates.

Example   10:   SLT with POQ

Consider again Example 8 and assume an LT of 1 week. We will use an SLT of 1 week. In Table A.8 two additional rows, revised PR and revised POR, are included to clarify the procedure. For example, look at week 3 where OH = 0. Given $P = 3$, then NR = 100. The POR for 100 is placed 2 weeks before this (in week 1) to allow . for both the LT and the SLT. Since the expected LT is 1 week, we *expect* the order to arrive in week 2; this is the revised PR. Given that 100 is expected to arrive in week 2, the OH in week 3 will then be 100 (revised OH) and not 0 as indicated originally (OH). The PORs in Table A.8 are identical to those in Table A.5, but they arrive a week earlier. Orders that arrive earlier than needed wait in inventory. The holding cost in Table A.5 is $260 (for weeks 3+), whereas for Table A.8 it is (300)$2 = $600.

TABLE A-8   POQ Lot Sizing with $P = 3$ and SLT $= 1$

	0	1	2	3	4	5	6	7	8
GR		10	10	30	50	20	40	20	10
OH	20	20	10	0	70	20	0	30	10
NR				100			70		
PR				100			70		
Revised PR*			100			70			
POR†		100		70					
Revised OH‡	20	10	100	70	20	70	30	10	

Notes: * PR offset by 1 week for SLT.
† Revised PR offset by 1 week for usual LT.
‡ OH, accounting for revised PR.

Besides causing greater inventory, a drawback of SLT is that it tends to lose effectiveness over time. Shop workers learn which jobs are always ordered early, and eventually give those jobs lower priority than jobs they know are needed sooner. The SLT, effectively, slips back to zero.

Although SS, safety margins, and SLTs are ways to deal with uncertainty, they represent antiquated ways of thinking. Uncertainty is the result of problems with forecasting, production processes, equipment, worker skills and attitudes, supplier relationships, and so on. Safety measures like those above are crutches, ways of living with the problems. A better solution, of course, is continuous improvement—discovering the sources of the problems, fixing them, and dispensing with the crutches.

SYSTEM NERVOUSNESS AND FIRM PLANNED ORDERS

Decisions about end-items ripple down to influence all lower-level items in the product tree. The degree to which changes to the MPS or to GRs of upper-level items affect GRs and PORs of lower-level items is called system **nervousness.** A nervous system is one where small changes at higher levels induce large changes at lower levels.

One way to reduce system nervousness is to use **firm planned orders.** A firm planned order is a POR that is fixed. No matter what changes might occur to the GR and, hence, the NR, the POR remains constant; it is treated as if it were an SR. A time fence, described earlier, establishes the time period within which all planned orders are held firm. For example, if a time fence is set at 2 weeks, then no PORs during the first 2 weeks of the MRP plan can be altered. By using a time fence to freeze the requirements for an end-item, the first few weeks in the MRP plans for every item in the product tree are held firm also. As described in the section on MPS, a series of successive time fences can be established, each more restrictive than the prior one, which keeps the variability of the entire production system to a minimum.

CAPACITY REQUIREMENTS PLANNING

Capacity requirements planning (CRP) checks the short-term capacity feasibility of the MPS. The checking is done with a CRP module connected to the MRP system. CRP is similar to RCCP in that it uses the BOM, routing sequence, and standard times of operations to compute the resource loading; however, CRP is more detailed and accurate. Instead of using the MPS for product groups, CRP uses the MPS for each product or other end-item. Instead of using gross requirements to estimate capacity requirements, CRP uses the PORs generated by the MRP procedure. Because scheduled receipts and OH inventory are taken into account, the accuracy of the capacity estimate is much better than that from RCCP.

CRP PROCEDURE

CRP focuses primarily on the near-term portion of the MPS to determine whether that portion is feasible and can be frozen. The CRP module computes the total loading of every resource and compares it with the available capacity. Once the short-term portion of the MPS is frozen, GRs and PORs throughout the product tree for that portion of the MPS are finalized and PORs for the current time bucket are released.

In computing total required capacity, CRP assumes **infinite-capacity loading,** which means it accumulates in each time bucket the standard hours for all orders to be sent to a given resource, without regard to capacity limits. After the total resource loading for all orders has been computed, the CRP module considers the maximum available capacity of that resource. If overcapacity is discovered, the resource is flagged.

RESCHEDULING AND PEGGING

A limitation with most CRP modules is that while they flag an overloaded resource, they do not indicate the sources of the overload; that remains to be determined by a planner or scheduler. A simple solution might be to schedule overtime, though the resource might already be committed to overtime and have no time remaining, or the overcapacity might be so large that it cannot be met even with overtime.

One way to determine the sources of overcapacity and assess potential courses of action is by a procedure called **pegging.** Pegging links the GRs of a component to the PORs of all items upwardly linked to it in the product structure (parents and higher-level items). If an overcapacity situation is flagged, pegging can identify sources contributing to the overload. An example follows.

Example 11: Pegging for Overcapacity from Item R

Look at item R (lowest-level item) in Figure A.10 and note the POR of 40 units in week 3. Through pegging, this POR is linked directly to component D and indirectly to end-item W.

Suppose the CRP module flags department AZ, which machines item R, for overcapacity in week 3. Several PORs in addition to the one for item R contribute to the overload, but the other orders have higher priority. Suppose department AZ has been authorized to work overtime in week 3, but even with overtime there is only enough capacity to produce 20 units of item R. In other words, 20 units of the 40 original must be rescheduled.

Suppose department AZ has extra capacity in week 2 and can produce 10 of these units then. Those 10 units, if produced in week 2 (a week before required) would simply wait in stock for a week, then be released for use in week 4.

The 10 units of item R scheduled in week 2 plus the 20 units scheduled in week 3 give a total of 30 units, which is still 10 units less than the 40-unit GR for item R. Pegging shows that the GR comes from item D, which in turn is linked to end-item W. Ten units less of item R mean that 10 units less of item D can be produced in week 4, which means that 10 units less of end-item W can be produced. In other words, pegging shows that only 110 of the 120 units of item W required in week 6 can be produced. If the GR for item W represents a forecast, then the shortage will possibly have little consequence (simply notify sales of the reduced ATP). If, however, the requirement represents a firm order, then customers should be notified immediately that 10 units of the order cannot be delivered until a week later.

CRP presumes that lead times are fixed. Typically, a relatively small portion of the lead time (20–30%) is actually devoted to setting up and processing an order. Most of the lead time is for transportation between operations, inspection, or waiting before and after the operation. It is obvious that when a resource is overloaded, jobs must wait longer to be processed, so lead times will be longer. Every job order that is routed through an overloaded resource will be delayed, which will cause the SRs for those jobs and the concurrent availability of materials for use in higher-level components to also be delayed. The result is that schedules will be in error—not only the schedules for the components routed through overloaded resources, but also the schedules for all higher-level items that are upwardly linked to the components throughout the product tree.

MRP II systems that include simulation capability allow planners to assess alternative schedules. Orders are scheduled at resources, and the required load is compared to capacity limits. If the available capacity is exceeded, the simulation procedure determines which items are responsible and considers alternate ways to modify their MPSs to eliminate or reduce the overload situation. Planners can then choose the alternatives they like best. The procedure, called **finite-capacity scheduling,** is a special add-on capability that is usually not available on standard CRP modules.

Using simulation for finite-capacity scheduling has limitations too. Although it can provide good courses of action, like all simulations it is an iterative, trial-and-error approach, and the time to input and process data can be large. Even when the computer provides the alternatives, someone has to review the alternatives and make a decision. Consider that on a weekly (or shorter) basis, the simulation might have to review alternative schedules for all end-items (perhaps numbering in the hundreds) as well as alternative schedules for perhaps thousands of components, and you can understand the magnitude of the effort involved.

OTHER WAYS TO MEET CAPACITY CONSTRAINTS

When adding capacity or rescheduling are not feasible options, capacity limits can be met by reducing the production lead time. There are three ways to do this. One is to **overlap operations,** to start processing a portion of an order at a subsequent operation before all of the order has been completed at the earlier operation. This way, discussed in Chapter 5, makes use of transfer batches that are smaller than the process batch. Another way is to **split operations,** to process the order at multiple parallel operations. This assumes the facility has multiple workstations that can perform the same operation. The third way is to **split lots,** to divide the order, run part of it on an expedited basis, and run the rest of it later.

SHORT-RANGE ORDER SCHEDULING AND RELEASE

The combined PORs generated by the MRP procedure are accumulated in the **job pool.** When the time bucket for a POR reaches the present, the order is released to the shop floor as a manufacturing order or to a supplier as a purchase order.

ORDER RELEASE

The process of **order release** (or order launch) converts a POR into an SR and causes manufacturing and purchase orders to be opened. When the SR is executed (at the department, workstation, or stockroom, wherever it is received), the order is closed. Closing an order means converting an SR into OH stock. Note the progression of transactions in the inventory status file: POR becomes SR, then SR becomes OH.

A released order is an authorization for shop-floor personnel to withdraw the required materials from a storeroom or other holding area and begin production. Whether they actually begin production, however, depends on any prior work backlog. The actual conversion of SR to OH happens through a process called **picking. Picking tickets** are issued to the stockroom, each one specifying the quantity of a particular part to be removed and transferred to the workstation or department to which it has been allocated. Once the transfer has been made, the record showing the amount of physical stock for that item in the stockroom is reduced, while the record for amount OH at the workstation or department specified on the ticket is increased.

A file is maintained of all open orders (time and quantity of all SRs), and before each file is updated (net change or regeneration), it is checked for necessary corrections. For open orders still needed but at a different time or in a different quantity, orders no longer needed, or orders with delays or shortages, a **rescheduling notice** is issued to the scheduler or buyer. Whether a corresponding change is made to the status file is the scheduler's or buyer's decision. Not all files are updated because it would be too disruptive and result in the system nervousness mentioned before. The scheduler weighs the importance of the change and its influence on other schedules and orders. If an entire order is not needed at the SR date, the scheduler might choose to split the order or employ one of the other lead-time saving options mentioned.

ALLOCATED ITEMS

Another function of order release is **allocation** of OH inventory. When a component is used in multiple end-items or other parent-items, any OH inventory of the component must be allocated among the parents. Since the OH amount is to be shared, the amount made available to a parent-item at any given moment must be determined. Say, for example, that 30 units of item W are currently OH, but 10 of the units must be put aside for some purpose other than toward the GR for item W. The OH amount of item W is thus really only 20 units. What this implies is that the indicated OH amount in the MRP plan is not necessarily the total amount of an item being held in physical inventory. More of the item than the OH amount shown might exist but may have been allocated to other parent-items. This additional amount would be reflected in the OH amounts for all the other parent-items.

Before releasing a job, the MRP computer system scans all parents of a component and determines what specific portion of the component's OH amount each parent will receive. The allocation is usually based upon priority rules to reduce or avoid production delays.

Example   12: Allocation

Two PORs are about to be dispatched, one for item X and one for item Y. The product trees for the items are shown below:

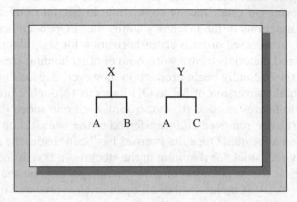

Notice that both items use component A. Suppose the OH amount of component A is sufficient to fill the NR for either item X or item Y, but not both. To which item, X or Y, should component A be allocated? To answer we need to look at the other components. Suppose that the OH amount of item B is sufficient to meet the NR for item X, but that the OH amount of item C is insufficient to meet the NR for item Y. Therefore, if component A were allocated to item X, production of item X could begin immediately (there are sufficient As and Bs). Since production of item Y must wait for delivery of additional Cs, allocation of the As to Y would be a waste. Therefore, the POR for item X should be released and so should the PORs for items A and B. Meanwhile, the POR for item Y should be held until a sufficient amount of item As and item Cs arrive.

DISCUSSION

MRP has been a source of improvement for many users, although it has been a disappointment for many others. This section reviews the benefits and limitations of closed-loop MRP and MRP II.

MRP ADVANTAGES

MRP II systems that integrate forecasting and information about product BOMs and routing sequences facilitate long-range and medium-range planning. In addition to improving both resource and capacity planning, these systems improve the coordination of information between sales and production so orders are more likely to be filled on time or as promised to customers.

Closed-loop MRP allows companies to improve predictions of capacity requirements and, as a result, to reduce overtime, delays, expediting, and shortages. With fewer delays and shortages, jobs are completed and orders are delivered closer to the scheduled due dates.

The MRP procedure, in general, reduces inventories because the supply of parts is better coordinated with demand. With MRP, most users have been able to reduce WIP inventories, although, compared to JIT standards, the inventories are still high.

MRP LIMITATIONS

The major limitations of MRP systems stem from the fact that they are centralized computerized systems and that they rely on a manual system of support that is often not up to the task.

Like any computer system, the quality of MRP system outputs is commensurate with the quality of the inputs—the old garbage-in, garbage-out problem. Information about the BOM, inventory status, and lead times must be accurate and current. Inventory status must be updated frequently to reflect current lead times, yield-loss rates, and actual OH and SR amounts. Product design changes must be incorporated into BOMs as quickly as possible. It is estimated that for valid MRP output, the BOM and master file must be at least 95% accurate, with 99% a reasonable goal.[8] Yet regardless of efforts to eliminate the garbage, MRP systems require so much information that some garbage always remains.

Consider the problem of lead-time accuracy. For order-scheduling, MRP assumes lead times are fixed, although in reality they vary depending on workload: the larger the load, the longer the lead time. To allow for lead-time variability, MRP planners use inflated lead times. As discussed before, if you plan on a lead time being longer than it actually is, you end up with some jobs finishing before they are needed and materials sitting in inventory. This contributes to the large WIP inventories often found in MRP-scheduled factories.

Successful implementation and execution of MRP is a team effort and takes the discipline and commitment of many people. Schedulers, buyers, product designers, salespeople, and shop-floor supervisors must all commit to supporting the system and meeting its requirements.[9] Amounts and times of orders must be tracked and recorded in MRP files; rescheduling notices and anything else that requires action cannot be ignored. MRP cannot work in a shop that has sloppy procedures or poor discipline, nor can it improve on those things. Good shop-floor procedures must come first. (This is not a limitation of MRP, per se, just that some companies believe they can load the MRP software and start reaping benefits. If they are unable to achieve that discipline, they fault the system. MRP and JIT/TQM are identical in the sense that they both require shop-floor discipline, as well as commitment and support from people throughout the organization.)

The primary limitation of MRP, however, is not that it requires commitment, support, and discipline, but that aspects of MRP actually serve to *discourage* those things. MRP requires *so* much effort for tracking, record-keeping, status updating, and so on, that people get frustrated since no matter what they do, the information reported by the system is always behind the times. All MRP systems are somewhat unresponsive to real-time happenings on the shop floor, which results from attempting to schedule and control *everything* on the shop floor with a system that is remote from the shop floor (physically, temporally, philosophically). It is an impossible task.

A further limitation is that MRP systems do virtually nothing to improve process or product quality. Safety measures (SS, SLT, etc.) are easily built into the MRP procedure and, as a consequence, sources of poor quality and waste are not identified and removed. Besides, with MRP people are so busy updating system inputs that they have little time to seek out and resolve problems. MRP-based scheduling and control encourages people to stick to the status quo and focus on the short-term, the antithesis of problem solving, elimination of waste, and continuous improvement.

The limitations of MRP are largely restricted to shop-floor matters and its handling of detailed scheduling, tracking, and control of every job. Of course, that is only part of what MRP systems do, the remainder being long- and medium-range planning, resource planning, capacity planning, master scheduling, and procurement planning and ordering. Generally, MRP systems do these things well. As described in Chapter 18, even companies using pull production must continue to perform these planning functions with an MRP-based or other type of system. Pull production systems can allow for very effective execution and control of work on the shop floor, but other systems are needed for resource and capacity planning and master scheduling. A company considering adopting pull production should thus hold on to its MRP II system, because it will still need it.

Questions

1. What can an MRP II PPC system do that a pull production system cannot?
2. In situations where pull production is appropriate, what can it do better than an MRP-based system?
3. Discuss the main elements of long-range planning. Whose perspective does long-range planning represent—production, finance, marketing?
4. What is the purpose of long-range resource planning? What information is needed for such planning?
5. What is an aggregate production plan? How is it different from the resource plan?
6. Describe the differences between an MPS and an aggregate plan in terms of purpose, focus, time horizon, time buckets, and so on.
7. What is available to promise? Who would use it?
8. What is the purpose of rough-cut capacity planning (RCCP)? What information is needed for RCCP? What affect does RCCP have on the MPS, and vice versa?
9. What is the difference between dependent demand and independent demand items?
10. What is the difference between MRP, closed-loop MRP, and MRP II? What does an MRP II system include that a "simple MRP" system does not?
11. Define the product tree structure and the BOM.
12. Discuss the relation between parents and components in product tree structures and BOMs.
13. Describe the contents of a typical inventory status file.
14. What is time-phased ordering? Where are lead times used? How do these lead times typically differ from the actual or required lead times on the shop floor?
15. Distinguish between regenerative and net change procedures for updating inventory files. Why use one instead of the other?
16. What is an order release? What is the difference between planned and actual order releases?

17. What is the difference between gross requirements and net requirements? What is the difference between planned order releases and scheduled receipts? When are they both the same?

18. Why in MRP processing is one level of the BOM completely processed before moving on to process the next lower level? How does the concept of low-level coding apply?

19. Among the lot-sizing rules discussed, which results in the most inventory? Which in the most number of setups?

20. What is the effect of safety stock, safety lead time, and safety margin on inventory? Discuss the effectiveness of these measures in offsetting uncertainty and process variability.

21. What is system nervousness? What problems does it create? How is it minimized?

22. Discuss the difference between capacity requirements planning (CRP) and RCCP. Why is CRP often not very accurate?

23. What is pegging? Discuss how it is used for replanning and rescheduling.

24. What happens when capacity is overplanned?

25. Discuss item allocation, what it means, and how it is done.

26. Discuss the drawbacks of MRP systems. Consider drawbacks inherent to the systems and drawbacks associated with implementing MRP systems.

27. Why would a company implementing pull production want to keep its existing MRP II system?

Problems

1. Zomby Manufacturing produces three products using three kinds of machines. The operating times per unit and setup times (in hours) are shown below.

Machine	Product L	Product M	Product N
Cutting			
Setup	0.700	0.500	
Run	0.050	0.060	
Bending			
Setup			0.800
Run			0.025
Threading			
Setup	0.500		0.550
Run	0.030		0.050
Batch size	300	250	400

Assume for a 5-month planning period the monthly forecasted demand is 1800 units of product L, 1000 units of product M, and 1200 units of product N. How many of each machine will be needed if each machine operates 40 hours/week?

2. Consider the following BOM and production data for product A.

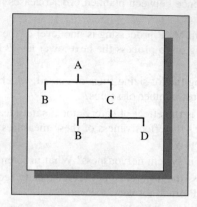

The routing (times include setup, operating efficiency, scrap, etc.) is:

Item	Workcenter	Standard Run Hours/Unit
A	Assembly	0.40
B	Cutting	0.16
	Broaching	0.45
	Grinding	0.16
C	Assembly	0.30
D	Cutting	0.45
	Milling	0.72
	Drilling	0.56
	Grinding	0.41

a. Prepare the bill of resources.

b. Monthly workcenter capacities (hours) are:

Assembly	48
Broaching	56
Cutting	48
Milling	48
Drilling	36
Grinding	48

The production plan for product A for the next 7 months is

Month	1	2	3	4	5	6	7
	50	60	55	65	65	60	60

Assuming LFL production, is this plan feasible?

3. Product A in problem 2 can be expressed in terms of the following bill of activities (lead times in weeks):

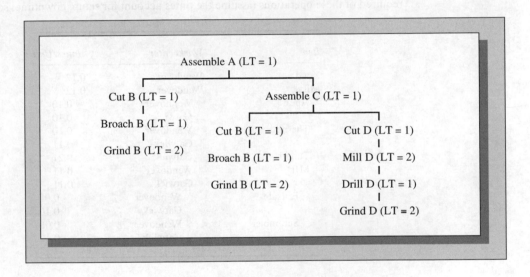

a. Use the bill of resources and the standard times from problem 2 to create the time phased load profile for product A.

b. The MPS for weeks 9 through 13 for product A is

Week	9	10	11	12	13
	15	15	18	18	16

Show the weekly resource load profile for the operations of assembly, broaching, cutting, milling, drilling, and grinding that result from this MPS.

4. A manufacturer produces two kinds of end-items called Zond and Milos. The partial indented BOMs follow:

Zond: 1 Apex component and 1 Thermal component
Milos: 1 Turgid component and 1 MJD component
    Apex component: 2 Failsafe parts
    Thermal component: 1 Scrambler part
    Turgid component: 1 Failsafe part
    MJD component: 1 Scrambler part

Two critical resources that are involved in production of the end-items, components, and parts are the Wendover and Gatwick operations. Following are the hours per unit required of these operations (assume the times account for setup, downtime, scrap, etc.):

Item	Workcenter	Hours/Unit
Zond	Wendover	0.12
Milos	Wendover	0.12
Apex	Wendover	0.10
	Gatwick	0.10
Thermal	Wendover	0.10
	Gatwick	0.11
Turgid	Gatwick	0.21
MJD	Wendover	0.11
	Gatwick	0.11
Failsafe	Wendover	0.05
	Gatwick	0.10
Scrambler	Wendover	0.06
	Gatwick	0.10

a. Draw the bill of resources for each end-item.
b. The MPS for the next 6 weeks is

	Week					
	1	*2*	*3*	*4*	*5*	*6*
Zond	120	100	140	120	160	150
Milos	110	110	100	110	140	140

The Gatwick and Wendover operations each have 120 hours/week allocated for production of Zond and Milos, including parts and components. Will they be overloaded in any weeks? If so, what do you suggest be done?

5. Consider the forecast and order information in the following table:

	Week					
	1	*2*	*3*	*4*	*5*	*6*
Forecast	600	600	600	600	700	700
Orders	700	800	500	200	200	100
MPS						
ATP						

a. Complete the MPS and ATP (available to promise) rows in the table.
b. Next, assume the order policy is Q = 1000 and complete the rows.

6. End-item A and its components have the following BOM, MPS, and OH inventory status (week 0).

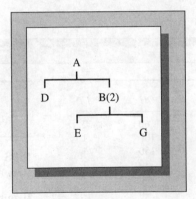

Item	OH	LT
A	90	1
B	60	1
D	50	2
E	30	1
G	80	2

MPS, Item A							
Week	1	2	3	4	5	6	7
GR		50		20		100	80

a. Create MRP plans (format of Figure A.6) for every item using LFL ordering.
b. Use all of the above information to create MRP plans for every item, but in addition

use the following lot-sizing rules and scheduled receipts:

Item	SR	Lot Sizing
A		Orders in increments of 50
B	50 in week 1	LFL
D	40 in week 2	Orders of size at least 200
E	60 in week 1	LFL
G	50 in week 1	Orders in increments of 50

7. Consider the following BOMs, MPSs, and OH inventory status (week 0).

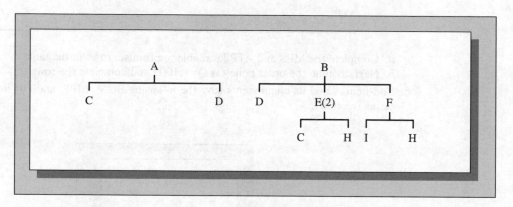

Item	OH	LT
A	60	2
B	100	1
C	150	1
D	30	1
E	80	1
F	20	2
H	160	1
I	180	1

				Week			
	1	*2*	*3*	*4*	*5*	*6*	*7*
MPS							
Item A		30	20		20		100
Item B	50		30	200		170	

a. Create MRP plans (format in Figure A.6) for every item using LFL ordering.

b. Suppose item A must be ordered in increments of 100 and item B must be ordered in increments of 200. Redo the MRP plans to determine the effect this change has on the PORs for items C and H. Discuss the result.

8. The 10-week period gross requirements for an item are as follows:

Week	1	2	3	4	5	6	7	8	9	10
GR		80	40	20		70	40	90		80

Assume that OH in week 0 is 90 units, the holding cost is \$3.00/unit/week, the setup cost is $180, and the lead time is 1 week. For the following problems, consider holding costs for weeks 3+ only.

a. Develop the MRP plan and compute the total setup and holding costs using LFL ordering.

b. Develop the plan and compute the total costs using FOQ and EOQ ordering (if NR > EOQ, set POR = NR).

c. Develop the plan and compute the total costs using FOQ and Q = 50 ordering (if NR > 50, set POR to a multiple of 50).

d. Develop the plan and compute the total costs using POQ = 2.

e. Develop the plan and compute the total costs using POQ = 2 and SS = 20.

f. Develop the plan and compute the total costs using POQ = 2 and POR safety margin of L = 3%.

g. Develop the plan and compute the total costs using POQ = 2 and SLT = 1 week.

9. Refer to Figure A.10. Suppose a GR of 10 units for item W is added to week 5.

a. What effect does this have on the GR for every other item?

b. Suppose the maximum weekly capacity of the department that produces item R is 40 units. In what week(s) will the department exceed capacity? If the department can meet requirements by shifting production of some units to earlier weeks where there is excess capacity, what effect will that have on production of other units in the product tree?

c. If the department cannot shift production to earlier weeks and is constrained to 40 units/week, what effect will that have on other units in the product tree?

10. Use the following information for parts (a) through (d): An end-item has a projected GR for the next 10 weeks of 50 units per week, a current OH amount of 150, and an LT of 1 week. The end-item has a next-level component that has a current OH amount of 100 and an LT of 2 weeks. All orders are LFL. (Treat problems (a) through (d) separately.)

a. Prepare the MRP plans for the two items.

b. Suppose time has advanced 3 weeks. How would the plans look then?

c. Suppose in week 5 the GR for the end-item is canceled. What effect does that have on the plans?

d. Assume the following costs for both items: setup costs, $700; holding costs, $10.00/unit/week. Compute the total cost for both the end-item and the component for weeks 4–10.

e. Repeat part (d) but assume the lot size for the end-item must be in multiples of 100.

11. Use the following BOM and inventory status:

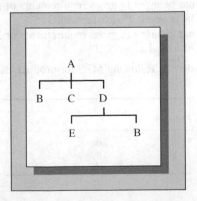

Assume LT = 1 week for every item, and only one scheduled receipt: 10 units of item C at the start of week 1. The OH amounts and the MPS for A are as shown below.

Item	OH
A	80
B	50
C	20
D	20
E	20

MPS, Item A						
Week	1	2	3	4	5	6
GR	0	100	0	20	20	50

Determine the number of A items that could be produced under conditions (a) through (d) below (treat the conditions separately).

a. All of the above information is accurate and does not change.

b. The OH amount of B is in error. Only 10 units have been allocated for use in items A and D.

c. Of 20 units of E, 10 cannot be used because of defects.

d. There is an error in the BOM. Each unit of item A actually requires two units of item D.

12. Consider the following MRP plan: $Q = 30$, LT = 1, SS = 4, and

	Now	1	2	3	4	5	6
GR		10	30	20	10	30	50
OH	20	20	10	10	20	10	10
SR			30				
NR				10		20	40
POR			30		30	60	

a. What changes in gross requirements or the initial on-hand quantity would shift the POR in week 2 back to week 3?

b. What changes in gross requirements or in scheduled receipts would shift the week 4 POR ahead to week 3?

13. Consider the following MPS for products X and Y:

Product	1	2	3	4	5	6
X	20		50	10	10	
Y	10			20	30	40

Suppose component A is used in both products X and Y. Component A has a procurement lead time of 2 weeks, an order quantity of 30, and no safety stock. At the start of week 1, $Q = 30$, $LT = 2$, $SS = 0$, and

	Now	1	2	3	4	5
GR						
OH	20					
SR		30				
NR						
POR						

a. Complete the MRP plan for component A.

b. Early in week 1 the following changes had to be made to the MRP plan:

- · An order for 30 units of component A was released.
- · An inventory count indicated that the OH amount was actually only 15.
- · The scheduled receipt that week has only 27 units.
- · The MPS for week 6 is 10 units of product X and 40 units of product Y.
- · Ten units of product X for week 3 were canceled.
- · The sales department has requested that the 20 units of product Y first requested for week 4 be advanced to week 3.

Complete the MRP plan starting in week 2. Describe what actions are necessary to accommodate the changes.

Endnotes

1. Overcapacity can sometimes be reduced by locating and diverting items from other uses. If, for example, some items A and B are in stock but are scheduled for usage in other product groups, then diverting them to group K would reduce the resource requirement for group K and possibly bring it to within available capacity. This approach, which deals with the allocation of existing stock, is covered later in the chapter.

2. The major developer of MRP was Joseph Orlicky. From early on he was also its biggest promoter, as might be inferred from the title of his book, *Material Requirements Planning: The New Way of Life in Inventory Management* (New York: McGraw-Hill, 1975).

3. The major force in turning simpler MRP into the more comprehensive (and promising) MRP II was Oliver Wight. *See.* O. Wight, *MRP II: Unblocking America's Productivity Potential* (Boston: CBI Publishing, 1981).

4. Since item W is an end-item, the gross requirement would likely come directly from the master production schedule. This example presumes that the MPS for item W for week 6 shows a total of 120 units.

5. The MRP procedure looks at the inventory status file for item W to determine the amount on-hand. This example presumes that the amount on-hand for week 6 is shown to be 30 units.

6. This is the absolute minimum for ordering purposes. For other purposes, including rough-cut capacity planning, the MPS should extend somewhat farther into the future. As a rule of thumb, the MPS should extend at least twice as far into the future as does the maximum stacked lead time in the product tree.

7. From D.C. Whybark and J.G. Williams, "Material Requirements Planning under Uncertainty," *Decision Sciences* 7, No. 4 (October 1976), pp. 595–600.

8. R. Schonberger and E. Knod, *Operations Management* (5th ed.) (Burr Ridge, IL: Irwin, 1994), p. 330.

9. J. Nicholas, "Developing Effective Teams for System Design and Implementation," *Production and Inventory Management* 21, No. 3 (1980), pp. 37–47.

INDEX